/FOURTH EDITION/

EFFECTIVE
POLICE

SUPERVISION

HARRY W. MORE / W. FRED WEGENER / LARRY S. MILLER
EAST TENNESSEE STATE UNIVERSITY

anderson publishing co.
2035 Reading Road
Cincinnati, OH 45202
800-582-7295

Effective Police Supervision, Fourth Edition

Copyright © 1990, 1996, 1999, 2003
Anderson Publishing Co.
2035 Reading Rd.
Cincinnati, OH 45202

Phone 800.582.7295 or 513.421.4142
Web Site www.andersonpublishing.com

Library of Congress Cataloging-in-Publication Data

More, Harry W.
    Effective police supervision / Harry W. More, W. Fred Wegener, Larry S. Miller. -- 4th ed.
        p. cm.
    Includes bibliographical references and index.
    ISBN 1-58360-546-0 (pbk.)

Cover design by Tin Box Studio, Inc.

EDITOR Elisabeth Roszmann Ebben
ACQUISITIONS EDITOR Michael C. Braswell

Dedication

This volume is dedicated to W. Fred Wegener, coauthor and friend, who died after a prolonged illness. His death ended a career dedicated to the continuing professionalization of law enforcement. Operationally and educationally he made significant contributions to the field through his work as a consultant, as well as through his writings. He was an exceptional teacher and strived diligently to balance theory and practice. He served as a mentor to many students in the Department of Criminology at Indiana University of Pennsylvania and had a profound influence on students entering the police field. He will be missed by many.

Contents

Foreword

Typically, a textbook reflects a certain academic level that focuses on a specific category of students, job incumbents, or other knowledge-seekers. In the unique case of *Effective Police Supervision,* many distinct objectives have been addressed simultaneously. But no matter which audience or knowledge level is targeted, this book achieves a direct hit.

I have personally used this textbook in three different capacities for more than 12 years. In all instances, the publication has served those needs exceptionally well. *Effective Police Supervision* can provide college students with an understanding of the group behaviors and organizational dynamics necessary to understand the fundamentals of police administration. Likewise, it can serve as a meaningful resource to support in-service supervisory training. Perhaps most importantly, this text is a comprehensive encyclopedia of the job skills, functional technical information, and critical insights necessary for officers studying for promotion.

Few tasks are more challenging or more contradictory than those of a law enforcement supervisor in a contemporary police agency. On the one hand, supervisors are expected to continue "business as usual"—interacting with former peers from whose ranks they have been promoted. But at the same time, they are now expected to guide, direct, and monitor these former colleagues. They are also expected to serve as the bridge between line officers and management, translating managerial goals into operational practice. In that capacity they are responsible for determining procedures to be followed, no matter how unpopular or misunderstood that policy may be.

Moreover, it is the supervisor who arrives on the scene directly after the responding officer—whether that scene is a routine police action, a disaster, a commonplace crisis, a social disorder, or worse, the unknown. Instantly, everyone looks to the person with the stripes on his or her uniform sleeve for insightful leadership. Even when the issues become tough to call or the circumstances turn a nebulous gray, *Effective Police Supervision* does not abandon the reader.

This textbook responds thoroughly to the issue of what a modern police supervisor is and exactly what that person should know and do, as well as when and how to do it. It faces up to the role conflict inevitably experienced by someone the troops must be able to trust—a leader with a foot already on the management ladder, a mentor who must oversee the performance of former peers, a critic who is expected to review reports, and an evaluator who must sign the forms that can determine the organizational future of subordinates—all under the watchful eyes of those who knew "Sarge" during those early academy days.

Effective Police Supervision describes the process of supervising others in an engaging, yet logical, manner. Few other books cover the breadth and depth of this topic as well—from conducting group discussions to jump-starting the marginal performer, providing positive feedback, developing teamwork, and recognizing legitimate grievances. As the link between operational practices and organizational mission, the sergeant is critical to the achievement of long-term goals, and this book clearly paves that path. Moreover, it brings theory to life through practical exercises, case studies, and explanations of concepts that demonstrate how to move from being "one of the troops" to a member of the management team. Whether the subject is motivation, leadership, discipline, performance appraisal, team-building, or just plain coping with the many complexities of the police organizational structure, this textbook provides the most commendable treatment in the current law enforcement literature.

As the role of the supervisor changes throughout the labor force—especially in policing—it is vital to understand what it means to empower others, be a facilitator, and lead through vision and values rather than command and control. Achieving all of that in the traditional hierarchical structure of police departments is no small accomplishment in itself.

Effective Police Supervision captures this changing role of the sergeant through state-of-the-art discussions about creating positive attitudes, utilizing the SARA process, developing sensitivity, employing referent power, and recognizing work-related stressors. Among the most important and relatively new areas of discussion are such topics as coping with organizational life, managing change, and solving problems through constructive conflict. As the nature of police recruits has changed over the years, those who supervise their work must likewise keep pace with changing expectations, motivations, and aspirations. This book clearly sends that message and achieves that mission.

These authors are to be commended for sharing their insights in a manner that provides much-needed research, guidance, and direction for those who choose to wear not only the badge, but the stripes of a recognized leader as well.

James D. Stinchcomb
Executive Assistant for Criminal Justice Kaplan College
Boca Raton, Florida
Director (retired) Miami-Dade Public Safety Regional Training Center

Preface

When a police organization is successful, it is because management is exceptional. Managerial experts acknowledge that the fulcrum of managerial effectiveness is at the level of the first-line supervisor. The best law enforcement agencies view the supervisor as an integral part of the managerial process.

In the best police departments, slowly but surely the position of sergeant has merged into management. The early assumption that the sergeant was really an extension of the line personnel has been soundly rejected. The outstanding law enforcement agency is one in which the first-line supervisor performs essential managerial activities.

When supervisors are allowed to engage in activities that are best described as knowledge-, human-, conceptual-, and affective-based, they are applying skills that can only be described as integral parts of the processes of management. While it must be acknowledged that supervisors apply the skills differently than police managers of higher rank, the fact remains that the effective police organization integrates supervisors into the management team.

Today's police supervisor must develop behavioral and social skills in order to deal effectively with a rapidly changing society. Diversity is becoming an integral term in the police lexicon and offers a new challenge for the first-line supervisor. When police executives integrate the position of supervisor into the managerial process, the organization can improve both its internal and external adaptive capabilities.

The primary aim of this book has been to help current or potential supervisors understand the differing beliefs and assumptions they hold about themselves, other officers, the organization, and society at large. The result is that the focus is on effectiveness as well as proficiency and on how a supervisor can participate in the creation of an effective organization.

Each chapter has been updated to reflect current research and knowledge in areas that supervisors must understand if they are to make a significant contribution to the law enforcement agency and function as positive supervisors. This text addresses the supervisory process in community policing, which is a unique undertaking, and the extent and degree to which this becomes a realistic part of the American policing system remains to be seen.

Effective community policing demands significant change in an organization; in particular, the operating style of each supervisor must change radically. Risk taking, originality, creativity, and problem solving must become part of the optimal operating style.

This book combines state-of-the-art behavioral theory with numerous cases that allow the reader to identify and resolve personal and organizational problems. Each chapter contains three cases, for a total of 42, that translate theory into practice. The cases serve as a base for classroom discussion and bring reality into the learning process. Additionally, they provide the reader with a means of interpreting the behavioral theory discussed in each chapter. Tables and figures augment and strengthen important elements presented in each chapter. As a means of facilitating learning, each chapter contains a summary, a list of learning objectives, discussion topics and questions, and an annotated list of material for extending their knowledge in selected areas.

The design of the text is such that it is user-friendly, pragmatic, realistic, and at the same time transcends the difficult problem that many texts in this area have of describing current behavioral theory and demonstrating how it relates to an operating agency. The primary goal of this text has been to address vital topics of interest to every manager by questioning the traditional means of supervision.

Effective Police Supervision has become a vital tool in the preparation of officers for promotion and is on the recommended reading list of numerous police departments. Users of the last edition have provided important feedback, and numerous suggestions have been incorporated into the current edition. Special recognition and thanks must be extended to Ginger and Ruth for their assistance, patience, and support during the preparation of the revision.

Harry W. More
Larry S. Miller

Supervision—
The Management Task

1

Introductory Case Study

Sergeant Roger Clark

Roger Clark has been with the Titusville Police Department for five years. The department has 329 sworn officers and 78 civilian employees. The population of the city is approximately 221,000 and is growing at a rate of nine percent a year as its manufacturing base has expanded. The community has a diverse constituency with 57 percent Caucasian, 26 percent Mexican-American, and nine percent black. The remainder are Asian and Native American. The city has attracted new businesses by creating a favorable business tax base. Major increases have occurred in telemarketing and high-tech manufacturing. Three nearby universities provide a favorable working environment and a source for trained personnel. Located in the central part of the state, the city serves as the business hub for agriculture and mining in the surrounding area.

Clark is 25 years old. He entered the department after completing two years of college with a major in criminology. He has continued to take classes at a local private university on a part-time basis, and anticipates graduating with a degree in business administration in three more years. He is an excellent student, with a grade point average of 3.5, and is in the university honors program. Clark is married to his high school sweetheart and has three children. He resides outside of the city in a rapidly growing bedroom area and is active in a local church. Clark is best described as an extrovert and a hard-charger. He approaches every assignment with enthusiasm and the desire to do whatever is needed to get the job done. In his previous assignments he got along with all of the other officers and was readily accepted as a competent officer. He was truly a "good old boy."

Clark has served in the narcotics unit for the past three years. His initial assignment after graduating from the police academy was patrol, where he worked the midnight shift in the most crime-ridden area of the city. As a beat officer, he developed numerous informants that led to the clearing of numerous crimes and the successful prosecution of drug dealers. As a consequence of developing these skills, he was transferred to the narcotics unit, where he performed exceptionally in undercover assignments. While in the narcotics unit, he took the promotional exam for sergeant and placed first on the list. Upon being promoted, he was assigned to patrol, where he supervised officers working a cluster of beats in the downtown section of the city.

Of the seven officers he supervised, only one had more than two years of field experience. Consequently, Clark found that he had to spend an inordinate amount of time backing up those he supervised and coaching them about the reality of working a beat and dealing with a wide variety of problems ranging from armed robberies to vagrancy. This consumed so much of his time that he was unable to attain assigned objectives and provide job performance feedback. There did not seem to be enough time on a shift to perform the tasks that management expected. The reality of working with officers who were willing to learn left little time for performing essential supervisory duties.

If you were Sergeant Clark, what would you do to resolve this problem? Would you deal strictly with knowledge skills to the detriment of human and conceptual skills? Would you seek help from your immediate supervisor? If so, what would you specifically ask for? Why? What precisely would you do to ensure that you perform well as a supervisor?

The changeable nature of our police agencies demands a reinvented response to the dynamics of societal and organizational transformation. Within a police organization the first-line supervisor is the pivotal managerial point. This is where the rubber meets the road. All levels of police administration must accept the challenge of making the supervisory position a primary managerial component of the agency. Crime, disorder, and the desire of members of the community to reside in neighborhoods that truly represent the best aspects of our democratic society call for a continuing and constant organizational response. This requires accepting the dynamics of continuing and constant change and developing an organizational capacity to respond to these critical social contingencies (Office of Justice Programs, 1998). The position of first-line supervisor must evolve into a position in which decisions are made and the reality of positive police work occurs. Supervisors must be given the tools needed to create a working milieu that energizes each and every member. A common denominator present in police departments that excel throughout the United States is the creation of a work environment that fosters the development of good supervisors. In exemplary agencies the first-line supervisor is not apart from, but is a viable component of, management and is directly responsible for augmenting the positive attributes of working life. Skilled employees are at a premium in every part of a police organization, and the supervisor's task is to assist employees in becoming productive members of the organization. An effectively performing supervisor makes things happen through the efforts of those supervised. Moreover, departmental and personal goals become achievable through the interaction between a motivated supervisor and subordinates. Accordingly, the community is better served and officers find themselves working in a viable organization that emphasizes the improvement of the quality of working life (Nagy, 2000). An agency committed to excellence is one that challenges each member of the organization to grow daily and contribute to the attainment of departmental objectives.

Police work is without question a complex process. Current demands and the consequences of responding to them in new and innovative ways intensify the critical role played by police. It involves the use of an enormous amount of discretion and the use of criminal and civil law to sort out a myriad of problems (Kelling, 1999). Today's police supervisor deals with problems and challenges totally unheard of several years ago.

External forces have a strong influence on every aspect of a contemporary police agency. The rapid proliferation of computer systems, telecommunications networks, and other related technologies presents concomitant widespread vulnerabilities compelling law enforcement to respond with highly trained and qualified officers (Stambaugh et al., 2000). The new millennium requires police personnel to be better prepared than ever before. Line officers and first-line supervisors of the future must be primed to deal with the diverse issues that will confront them (Woods, 1999). For example, officers are increasingly expressing a desire to become more involved in the decision-making process and the creation of operational policy. Newer officers usually have a lesser degree of commitment and set goals for themselves that in some instances transcend their commitment to the organization (Pilant, 1995; Tate, 2000). Additionally, police departments have become increasingly urban and more reflective of the ethnic composition of the community. Diversity is apparent when one realizes that three states and Washington, D.C. have seen nonwhites gain majority status. This is illustrated by the state of California, where, for the first time, white non-Hispanics make up 49.9 percent of the population (*Newsweek*, 2000). Additionally, in a seven-year period the Hispanic population has increased from 24 million to 32 million. This diversity plays an increasingly important part in both the selection of and promotion of officers (Arnold, 2000; Dale, 2000). It also involves the need for supervisors to respond to officers who retain vestiges of another culture with differing values and norms.

There are also intensifying demands for police services and an increase in the public's dissatisfaction with police services, especially with the use of deadly force (Lathrop, 2000) and more recently the use of racial profiling (Levendosky, 2000). Several years ago, a survey in one state found that 34 percent of the responding agencies had no policy regarding the progressive use of force (Cochran, 1995), but this has changed dramatically as the police have responded to public and political pressure. Today, all local law enforcement agencies with more than 100 sworn officers have a written policy pertaining to the use of deadly force (Reaves and Hart, 2000). It is anticipated that these policies will become more conditional over the years and that the search will go on to find nonlethal alternatives. Racial profiling has become the object of increasing concern, and civil rights activists have urged the collection of data on subjects stopped for traffic infractions. One study showed that blacks were five times more likely than whites to be stopped on a freeway in one state, and police policies and tactics are being reexamined and redress seems to be in order (Hall, 1999). In one southwestern community, the police department changed its training policies after an internal investigation suggested that traffic citations were issued to blacks at a rate disproportionate to their population (Barrios, 2000). Almost every state has taken at least some steps to address the problem of racial profiling, and the federal government is contemplating a study of the problem.

The selection pool of potential law enforcement officers has narrowed as more and more individuals have experimented with drugs or in the past were part of the drug culture. Screening applicants for past and current drug use has become the norm. This includes a consideration of such factors as the amount of time that has elapsed since drug use and the exact nature of the involvement. After a candidate has been hired, the police supervisor must respond to the use of drugs by officers when they are on the job. In one department approximately one-fourth of all suspensions and dismissals of police officers were for drug use (Mollen, 1994).

Ours is a *drug society*, legal and illegal, and the consequences affect not only agency personnel, but also police operations. In local law enforcement agencies with 100 or more sworn officers, a vast majority perform a special drug enforcement function (Reaves and Hart, 2000). The amount of money generated through the sale of illegal drugs has created a situation in which officers who are involved in narcotics investigations are faced with such temptation that an increasing number have become illegally involved. This involves profits so great that in one large city an officer was arrested for leading a ring of drug-dealing officers. Other officers used fellow officers as fences for stolen drugs. Still others sold drugs they stole while on duty and distributed the drugs where they lived. Recently a police officer was arrested and convicted in a major city for stealing cocaine from the police property room. Federal law enforcement is not exempt from the inimical influence of drug monies. In one incident, an FBI agent was arrested for stealing approximately 100 pounds of heroin from an evidence room. Drug enforcement, unless carefully scrutinized, can call into question the integrity of a police department. Consequently, a supervisor must be alert to signs of drug use on the part of police personnel, and under no circumstances should it be tolerated.

Many police tasks must be performed in a exceedingly violent environment where increasing numbers of officers have been injured on the job. Just slightly fewer than 60,000 line-of-duty assaults were reported in the United States during 1998. Of that number, 31 percent of the assaults resulted in injuries to officers (Federal Bureau of Investigation, 2000). Hostages are being taken more frequently, altering the way officers respond to this type of conflict. Barricaded suspects are becoming increasingly common, and many departments utilize SWAT teams to make arrests and serve search warrants. Gangs have become a major problem in many cities and are starting to emerge in rural communities (Esbensen, 2000). Drive-by shootings are increasing rapidly, and carjackings occur throughout the nation. Child and spousal abuse are far too common, and life has become cheap in the eyes of some. The homicide rate for 1998 was 6.3 per 100,000 inhabitants. This compares to 4.6 per 100,000 population in 1950. The homicide rate is of interest because it is a fairly reliable barometer of all violent crime. Even though the homicide rate has declined over the last three decades, it represents an unacceptable level of the loss of human life for a civilized society (Fox and Zawitz, 2000). One cannot discount the possibility of violence in our society, but it should not dominate an officer's perspective. Cynicism is something that should be anticipated and not allowed to spread.

A first-line manager must communicate constantly with each officer supervised by allaying rumors, interpreting policy, coaching, mentoring, or persuading when the situation dictates. A viable supervisor must work closely with every officer to ensure that they are aware of departmental policy involving personal conduct and ensuring their adherence to that policy. Ethical behavior must be the standard that governs each and every public contact. All employees must know what is expected of them, and they must be held accountable for their actions (Martin and Matthews, 2000). Continuing contact with people who have criminal inclinations makes it essential that each supervisor cultivate a working environment that acknowledges and reinforces the fact that the vast majority of the members of our society are law-abiding—not thieves or scumbags.

In other instances the failure to train officers can lead to civil liability. Like it or not, a first-line supervisor is a trainer, a mentor, a guide, and the person in the best position to identify individual weaknesses and needs. Supervisors should be watchful and strive to identify areas of weakness where training can be improved and where closer control is essential. It is a never-ending process and calls for initiative, imagination, and resourcefulness. In most instances supervisors are the first to observe training inadequacies, and top management should recognize them as a vital resource.

Our culture presents new challenges to the first-line supervisor, and it seems reasonable to assume that not only will problems increase in number, but that they will also become more diverse. This means, then, that the supervisor must respond to these critical issues as they arise and address them with a great deal of imagination and innovation as well as anticipating problems. The supervisor is at the organizational focal point between officers and other managerial levels. If the police organization is to become more effective, the first-line supervisor must play a major role in responding to change that affects the organization. Isolation must be rejected and organizational rigidity must be refuted.

If supervisors are successful in the performance of their duties, it follows that the organization will become more effective and the potential for attaining goals will be enhanced. Good supervision does not just happen; it has to be cultivated. Until recently, newly appointed supervisors were left to fend for themselves, but supervisory training courses are becoming more prevalent and are now an essential component of career development. In some states, improved performance has resulted because each newly appointed supervisor must complete a training program within a specified period after being promoted. Supervisory performance can be improved by reading supervisory periodicals, taking courses at local colleges, and networking with other supervisors (Frunzi and Savini, 1997). This is very different from the time when newly promoted individuals had to fend for themselves. "Sink or swim" used to be the cliché of the day.

In the future the new supervisor will have to work in a dynamic police organization that is continually changing and constantly creating new demands on everyone in the organization. The new supervisor will have to be more flexible and responsive to change. Figure 1.1 sets forth an array of attributes that describe a viable police organization of the future.

Figure 1.1
Attributes of a Viable and Dynamic Organization—
A Place Where Officers Want to Work

1. Locus of decision making varies but is concentrated at the lowest level of management. Empowerment is a viable managerial element, not just a passing fancy.
2. Discretion is recognized and accepted as an inevitable component of police work. It is a fundamental component of management.
3. The prospect of internal cultural conflict occurring is accepted as an inescapable characteristic of efforts to diversify the departmental workforce. In other words, conflict is managed.
4. Solidarity and isolation are viewed as organizational barriers that need to be acknowledged and overcome. Every effort is made to integrate every member into the organization.
5. Moral and constitutional values need to control every aspect of officer comportment. Honesty is viewed as an indispensable part of the managerial process.
6. Organizational rigidity impedes change and must be dealt with accordingly. Continual efforts need to be made to develop a flexible organizational system.
7. A proactive response to police problems is clearly the most acceptable standard operating procedure. Unconventional strategies should not be overlooked when confronting crises.
8. Crime fighting is viewed as only one aspect of contemporary law enforcement.

Figure 1.1, *continued*

---

9. Improving the quality of the working environment is an organizational mandate.

10. The development of guidelines and their evaluation must occur continually.

11. Acerbity of the police culture is the antithesis of modern law enforcement.

12. Acts of corruption and officer misconduct are rejected.

13. Recruitment and retention practices need to emphasize a search for quality. The numbers game has to be rejected.

14. Personnel are expected to internalize knowledge and skills throughout their career.

15. Integrity and ethical conduct must circumscribe officer behavior. Integrity must be the foundation of modern police administration.

16. Accountability applies to every level of the organization.

17. Effective officers will typically make many decisions outside the purview of supervisors.

18. Supervisors are part of the management team.

Transformation

The transformation from a line position to first-line supervisor brings numerous rewards, but it also exacts a price. These factors are set forth in Figure 1.2. However, in addition to an increase in pay, the supervisory position is marked by prestige both within and outside the department, as well as the recognition that one has attained a supervisory rank, a new title, and added responsibilities. Administratively, the supervisor usually heads a given unit or operation, is more involved in the decision-making process, and at the same time becomes a part of management. If there is any issue that causes a new supervisor difficulty, it usually is learning how to be an effective disciplinarian, especially when having to discipline a former fellow line officer. Does one maintain social relationships built up over the years, or does one discontinue this type of interaction? There is not an easy answer to these dilemmas, and each situation must govern the dictated reaction.

Further adaptation may be required as the new supervisor finds it necessary to attain objectives through the efforts of subordinates, while being held responsible for their success or failure. The transition from being responsible primarily for oneself to slowly becoming a more integral part of administration requires a greater degree of commitment to the managerial process and the success of the organization. This is an especially difficult transformation, requiring the balancing of goal attainment and the development of personnel. It is normally not acceptable to take the time-honored position that "I would rather do it myself."

Figure 1.2
Transformation from a Line Officer to a First-Line Supervisor

ADVANTAGES:
1. An increase in pay.
2. A feeling of accomplishment.
3. Enhanced reputation within and outside the department.
4. A step up in the organization.
5. A greater chance of providing input into the decision-making process.
6. An opportunity to have more control over the type of police service provided to the community.
7. An opportunity to be in charge of an operation.
8. Receiving a broader perspective of the department's overall operation.
9. Receiving additional training.
10. Different assignments.
11. Interpreting policy.
12. Prestige of rank.
13. Opportunity to influence and develop personnel.
14. Training/mentoring of personnel.
15. Becoming a part of management.
16. The obligation to be more integrative.
17. Fostering innovation.
18. Commitment to success.
19. The challenge of working constructively under stress.
20. Developing rapport with peers, managers, and subordinates.

DISADVANTAGES:
1. A greater degree of commitment to management.
2. One step removed from line operations.
3. Must function as a disciplinarian.
4. Positioned in the middle, between the line and top management.
5. Objectives must be achieved through others.
6. Accountable for work (or lack thereof) performed by subordinates.
7. Must implement policy not personally supported.
8. Difficult or impossible to return to former position if being a supervisor is undesirable.
9. At the bottom of the seniority level in shift and work assignments.
10. Must make decisions every day.
11. Increasingly vulnerable to criticism.
12. No longer just "one of the boys."
13. Must make decisions that can have an adverse impact on subordinates' careers.
14. Lesser commitment to the police union (in some instances).
15. Less freedom of action.
16. Risk-taking is part of the job.
17. The need to work through conflict.
18. Work in isolation part of the time.
19. Acting like a boss rather than a close friend.
20. The need to be effective rather than trying to be *liked*.

The transition to the position of first-line supervisor may be fraught with difficulty, depending on the individual, but most agree it presents a real challenge and demands the ability to accept and adapt to change. Historically, police executives have taken the position that prospective supervisors would intuitively know how to manage people, but this is usually not the case (Hamilton and Warman, 1997). A new supervisor may be placed in a situation that demands expertise that has not been acquired from experience or training, and if either of these conditions has not been fulfilled, the new supervisor becomes a member of the "sink or swim" school of management (Frazier and Reintzell, 1997). In some instances old ways and habits have to be overcome if one is to succeed in a new position (Pfeffer, 1994). Traditional coping mechanisms can prove to be ineffective as one begins to work in new territory. It might be that a feeling of helplessness arises, and if that happens, one should seek out counsel from other supervisors, a mentor, or other managers. Above all, new supervisors should cut themselves some slack and realize the need to learn how to cope with new challenges (Kunde, 1999). A new supervisor should realize the importance of immediately acknowledging the importance of the ecology of the organization and the fact that the department is a dynamic social system.

Officers have personal needs and objectives that the supervisor should help to fulfill while simultaneously ensuring that they do not conflict with the attainment of organizational objectives. Interaction with employees is what most first-line supervisors deal with in the workplace. The greater the supervisor's knowledge in this area, the greater the likelihood that both individual and organizational goals will be attained. Based on their experience of conflict between officers, they will be able to pick up on such situations faster and intervene sooner. Being aware of the rewards that their former supervisor could have given them will make them more sensitive to officers' needs for recognition. On the other hand, the transition will prove to be difficult if they do not accept the responsibility of correcting or disciplining officers when it is warranted (White and Chapman, 1996).

A supervisor soon becomes aware of the need to develop a range of skills if officers are to be productive and achieve the goals and objectives of the department. Good supervision is the result of the serious application of one's knowledge about human behavior to the work situation. In fact, the first priority of a supervisor is to develop the ability to obtain results through others (Salmon, 1999). This means that a supervisor must learn to value people as organizational assets.

Supervisory Skills Areas

Once an individual assumes the position of supervisor, the role changes to such an extent that there is limited comparison to the tasks performed as a patrol officer. The supervisor is a manager and must perform managerial activities. Certainly one technique of motivating employees is for a supervisor to show officers how something can be done by actually performing the activity, such as making a number of DUI (driving under the influence) arrests or conducting a number of field interviews. While such activities might accomplish an immediate objective, they represent only a small part of the activities a supervisor does to be effective.

The selection of the best worker for the position of supervisor is a common agency practice that can prove to be disastrous. The temptation to improve one's salary, enhance one's position, and achieve a rank attained by few is seldom rejected by a highly competent patrol officer. In many instances, however, this practice results in a sense of divided loyalties. A supervisor cannot forget that he or she is a part of management and no longer a line officer.

In some instances the newly appointed supervisor performs so poorly that it becomes necessary to seek employment elsewhere or be demoted. Some play the supervisory game well enough to get by, but they become marginal supervisors and, in the long run, are of limited value to the organization. Some newly appointed supervisors program themselves for failure because they impose rigid, process-oriented rules and regulations rather than striving to achieve results. Additionally, they usually refuse to admit mistakes, fail to delegate, and manage in an ad hoc manner. Generally, the inadequate supervisor feels that a laissez-faire managerial style is the best way to go. Also the feelings of inadequacy foster an approach that emphasizes "If I leave it alone, it will go away," or "Why should I bother?" or "Why not let someone else do it?" A supervisory position is not for everyone. It is a demanding job and can create an abundance of personal stress. The increase in salary and positional prestige can never compensate for the psychological discord that can occur if one is inadequately prepared, lacking in self-esteem, or just does not have the supervisory skills needed to perform effectively.

Supervisors should emphasize the development of the skills of their subordinates, rather than trying to do everything themselves. Needless to say, in many instances the supervisor could probably accomplish the task in half the time. The time-worn axiom "I would rather do it myself" must be rejected when one becomes a supervisor. As a means of maximizing effectiveness, a supervisor must work to attain objectives through the efforts of others, preferably by becoming operationally effective in one or more of the following skill areas set forth in Figure 1.3.

The skill areas are closely interrelated and overlap in their application. There is common agreement that knowledge-based skills are more important at the supervisory level than they would be to the chief of police, whereas human skills are vitally important at every managerial level. At the same time, managers at all levels must be concerned with applying some degree of conceptual and affective skills.

Figure 1.3
Supervisory Skill Areas

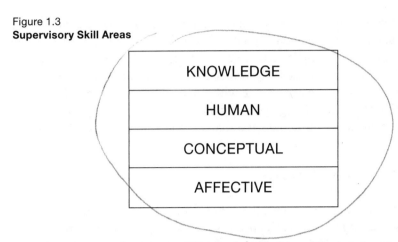

There is a continuing need for the integration of knowledge, human, and conceptual skills as modified by the emotionally based or affective characteristics that are constantly conditioning the managerial process (Imundo, 1991).

Much of the literature written about management makes a basic distinction between humanitarian and analytical supervision. The humanitarian approach deals with emotions, values, and attitudes. The organization is viewed as a social system, not simply a law enforcement enterprise staffed by individuals. It is necessary to consider both the social needs of the officers and the tasks to be performed. Figure 1.4 lists the supervisory functions.

Figure 1.4
Supervisory Functions

Knowledge	Human	Conceptual	Affective
Scheduling	Motivating	Analysis	Attitude
Evaluating	Communicating	Interpreting	Values
Organizing Work	Leading	Solving Problems	Fairness
Training	Resolving Conflict	Identification of Objectives	Equality
Directing	Integrating	Assessment	Interrelationships
Policy Implementation	Coaching	Decision Making	Integrity
			Loyalty
	Counseling		Role Model
Critically Reviews Reports	Delegating	Identifying Problems	Empathy
Provides Administrative Credibility		Prioritizing Problems	Support

Adapted from Robert L. Katz (1974). "Skills of an Effective Administrator." *Harvard Business Review,* September-October: Volume 52, No. 5, and Don L. Costley and Ralph Todd (1978). *Human Relations in Organizations.* St. Paul, MN: West.

The analytical approach views supervision problems as being conceptually based. Beyond achieving agency goals and objectives, the key is identifying problems and determining if further action is needed. The analysis, interpretation, and resolution of issues follow this. In every instance it involves the use of past and current police knowledge with a consideration of the future. Additionally, it involves identifying and using internal and external resources when necessary to ensure a comprehensive analysis and appropriate evaluation.

Knowledge-Based Skills

At the time of appointment, the supervisor is usually endowed with all kinds of knowledge-based skills because of extended duty as a patrol officer (see Figure 1.5). In most instances, promotion to the initial managerial level has been predicated on success as a patrol officer or investigator. Unfortunately, the skillful application of operational techniques can seldom ensure successful performance as a first-line supervisor. The skills are entirely different and the situation can become somewhat tenuous if during the transition period to this newly acquired position the new sergeant fails to adopt a managerial perspective. A manager can succeed only if results are obtained through the efforts of others. The supervisor must realize the necessity of training employees, because they are an organization's most valuable assets (Imundo, 1991; Albright, 1997; Leonard and More, 2000).

Figure 1.5
Supervisor's Knowledge-Based Skills

1. Provides officers with appropriate administrative and technical support.
2. Knows each officer's workload.
3. Reviews officers' reports for accuracy, thoroughness, and quality.
4. Demonstrates a real interest in seeing that officers do a good job and complete their assignments.
5. Interprets departmental policy.
6. Fairly implements departmental policies, rules, and regulations.
7. Is capable of doing all tasks an officer must perform.
8. Schedules officers according to organizational priorities.
9. Trains and develops officers.
10. Organizes work in such a way as to effectively and efficiently achieve objectives and goals.

Human Skills

At the core of successful police supervision is a consideration of human skills. Employees have to be motivated, appraised, and counseled. Standards must be established, tasks must be analyzed, and expectations must be communicated. Officers must be trained, developed, and (even though distasteful) occasionally disciplined. All those tasks are an effort to meet organizational objectives (see Figure 1.6). These activities demand the application of human skills predicated on the absolute belief that employees will work hard and diligently if incentives are such that they become highly motivated (Hawkins, 1992).

A first-line supervisor must become personally acquainted with each employee and treat each one as an individual. Every member of a team should be expected to perform the kind of work that is vital to the success of the organization (Herman, 1992). It is imperative for work to be accomplished through people; this can be done only when the supervisor is thoroughly acquainted with the capabilities and limitations of each employee. The supervisor should set high standards for those supervised, and the standards should be applied to each and every employee.

In studying supervisor/subordinate relationships, officers have an entirely different view of how they are treated by supervisors as compared to how supervisors view the needs of subordinates. Supervisors think that they clearly understand the problems that subordinates face, but subordinates think exactly the opposite. This is a gap that has to be addressed. It cannot be ignored. Such a disparity clearly reflects the importance of human skills and the need to understand the dynamics of human relationships if employees are to be successfully integrated into the organization. An emphasis on human skills addresses employee needs, including personal development, self-esteem, proficiency, and independence.

Figure 1.6
Supervisor's Human Skills

---

1. Listens and discusses problems with subordinates.
2. Deals with each officer as an individual.
3. Develops a rapport with officers.
4. Lets officers know where they stand.
5. Performs as a professional and sets the standard for employees.
6. Works with officers to increase positive attitudes and counsels them in a positive, specific manner.
7. Gives praise when appropriate.
8. Motivates employees.
9. Resolves conflict.
10. Tells employees when they have not met performance standards.
11. Coaches officers.
12. Counsels employees.

Conceptual Skills

Conceptual skills consume the least amount of the first-line supervisor's time. However, these skills are essential ingredients of the managerial process. The newly appointed supervisor, whether assigned to patrol or investigations, must integrate personal activities into the total organizational plan so that agency goals can be attained. This can be accomplished when the supervisor is thoroughly aware of the department's mission, vision, and organizational culture.

The relationship of patrol to other specialized units (such as support services or investigation) can be tenuous; therefore, it is absolutely necessary for the first-line supervisor to be capable of understanding the complexities of the interrelationship of specialized units to the total organization (see Figure 1.7). A supervisor must respond to organizational conflict with seasoned judgment and visionary thinking.

To conceptualize is to form new ideas or concepts. The first-line supervisor is in the best position to identify and resolve conflict between specialized police units by employing conceptualization techniques and using mediation skills (Umbreit and Coates, 2000). Key ambient factors of conceptualization involve identifying, prioritizing, and solving problems. The supervisor also must develop and implement solutions by evaluating new tasks and reevaluating old assignments in an effort to meet specific organizational goals (Loen, 1994). It is readily evident that knowledge-based skills are more important to the first-line supervisor than to the chief executive or the staff, but conversely, conceptual skills dominate the skills needed to be an effective top cop.

Knowledge and human skills dominate the day-to-day duties performed by a first-line supervisor. At times knowledge skills might dominate the functioning process, and in other instances it will be human skills. Each of these areas helps to define working relationships within a variety of settings. At times task accomplishment is seen as paramount and informality is encouraged as emphasis is placed on problem solving. The organization and the chain of command are utilized to facilitate communications and direct activities to the task at hand. In this instance, achievement dominates, and such factors as position power, rank, and status become subordinate.

Sometimes knowledge skills dominate the working environment, and at other times human skills prevail. A healthy relationship between the two is needed, and it demands a supervisory response that acknowledges the need for the application of both types of skills. At times it can foster a supervisory approach that is truly participative and the essence of sharing responsibilities. It is the opposite of the "we/they" style of supervision that utilizes "top down" management. In other words, it can be a one-way street. The key to this approach is to tell officers not only *what* to do, but also *how* to do it. The other side of the coin gives serious consideration to the personal needs of officers. Employees are seen as a viable and vital part of the operational equation. There is a total awareness of the need for people skills if tasks are to be accomplished. When human skills falter, it is apparent that supervisors are not using those supervised to accomplish tasks. It has been estimated that a major proportion of a supervisor's time is spent dealing with human skills.

In some instances respect is earned by a supervisor because of his or her knowledge skills, which can have nothing to do with one's actual position or title. If a line officer is more competent and knowledgeable than his or her supervisor, it can lead to disenchantment and a lessening of organizational support. If an officer always has to turn to someone other than his or her immediate supervisor for such assistance as the amplification of a technical skill or policy interpretation, the supervisor will be viewed as working beyond his or her capacity. The same thing can occur if a supervisor does not keep abreast of technological changes or state-of-the-art equipment. Additionally, if a situation occurs where a supervisor has to perform line functions in an emergency and the performance is marginal or inadequate, the speed with which this occurrence spreads, via the grapevine, throughout the organization clearly demonstrates the viability of the informal organization. When ambiguity prevails it can affect operations negatively.

Figure 1.7
Supervisor's Conceptual Skills

1. Demonstrates the ability to analyze data.
2. Works to eliminate errors.
3. Develops and shares information.
4. Identifies emerging problems and works to resolve them.
5. Utilizes all sources in an effort to deal with the positive interpretation of information.
6. Identifies objectives.
7. Assesses performance.
8. Conceptualizes the technical and human aspects of the work environment.
9. Makes decisions.
10. Enhances and improves proficiency.

Affective Skills

The fourth set of managerial characteristics are emotion-based. They interact with and modify all the other characteristics (see Figure 1.8). The supervisor (by actions) modifies the attitudes, emotions, and values of employees. At the same time, the interaction modifies the supervisor's personal view of the managerial process and his or her own self-concept (Handy, 1993).

Figure 1.8
Supervisor's Affective Skills

---

1. Integrates organizational and community value systems.
2. Creates an environment based on a belief in equality and the opportunity for all to succeed.
3. Deals fairly with subordinates.
4. Values employees and their potential contribution to the organization.
5. Knows personal strengths as well as limitations.
6. Accepts responsibility.
7. Develops relationships based on equal treatment.
8. Demonstrates the quality of integrity.
9. Performs as a role model.
10. Demonstrates loyalty to the organization and subordinates.

The emotion-based skills of the supervisor have to be utilized to the maximum. The first-line supervisor has to accept responsibility for errors and should never allow subordinates to be criticized for a mistake outside their control.

It does not take an alert supervisor long to realize he or she is not knowledgeable in every area, and that he or she has weaknesses as well as strengths. Weaknesses can be numerous, including a lack of sensitivity, emotional immaturity, a lack of drive, or the clashing of personalities. Effective supervisors apply numerous skills and perform several functions. An important duty is to perform with fairness and equity. If an organizational value based on fairness and equity is to be communicated, it has to be on a continuous basis, demonstrated to each and every employee by ensuring that everyone is treated as an equal, with absolute fairness. In most situations, subordinates believe that supervisors are more concerned with mistakes than anything else. Subordinates feel that their supervisor seldom responds to what is done correctly because of an excessive emphasis on factors other than even-handedness and fairness.

Case Study

Sergeant Bryan Martin

Bryan Martin had always wanted to be a police officer. He had an older brother and an uncle who were police officers, and he joined a police-oriented Explorer Scout unit. As a scout he went on numerous ride-alongs with officers and became personally acquainted with many officers. He was also active in the local police athletic program. As soon as he graduated from high school, he enrolled in the local community college and majored in criminal justice. He enrolled in a police academy at age 20 and completed the basic course prior to taking the police examination for the city of Sand Creek. He passed the examination with flying colors, attaining the second highest score on the test. The department hired him and he entered the field training program. After completion of in-service training and six months' supervision by a field training officer (FTO), he was assigned to a beat.

Bryan Martin was an exceptional patrol officer. He had the innate capacity to deal with every situation with which he was confronted without hesitation or reservation. He was street-smart and conscious of everything that occurred on his beat. Every merchant knew him by his first name, and he enjoyed developing neighborhood contacts. He enjoyed the independence of working his own beat and took it as a personal affront when crimes occurred on his beat. He knew the hot spots on his beat and concentrated on residences and places of business that required an exceptional amount of his attention. When needed, he called on other specialized police officers to assist him with problems such as vice, narcotics, and abandoned vehicles. On other occasions he called on the services of probation officers, parole agents, or mental health experts to deal with special situations.

After five years, Martin was eligible to take the test for sergeant, and in preparation for the test he joined a study group to better prepare himself. He had no difficulty with passing the assessment center and the written part of the test. He did very well on the test and was third on the promotion list. After a total of six years of service, he was promoted and assigned to supervise a sector with seven beats. The majority of the officers in his sector had limited police service, and he had difficulty in accepting the fact that five of the officers he was supervising constantly called for assistance and seemed to be unable to operate independently.

Martin had the knowledge skills necessary to perform his supervisory duties, but he was at a loss to understand why officers had to be closely supervised, and he knew that he had to work on developing his human skills. He had a tendency to accept less than perfection from those he supervised.

Being aware of his deficiency in human skills, Martin felt that he had several options. He could go to his immediate supervisor and ask for guidance. Would you do this? Why or why not? He could take a supervision course at the local community college. Would you do this? Why or why not? He could ask those he supervised for suggestions about how he could improve his performance. Would you do this? Why or why not?

Obviously this demonstrates the difference in line officers' and supervisors' perception of fair treatment. Further indication of this difference in how the supervisory process is viewed is evident in that the vast majority of supervisors believe that subordinates feel comfortable when they are discussing work situations. Again, exactly the opposite is true. Subordinates, in general, are uncomfortable when dealing with a supervisor. Thus, there is a barrier possibly precluding the successful communication of organizational values and their integration into the organizational value structure.

If employees perceive that managers refuse to acknowledge weaknesses and are always looking for a scapegoat, then the supervisors' affective skills will be muted and achievement of organizational goals can be jeopardized. One can apply knowledge-based human relations and cognitive skills, but the affective variable serves as a modifier and allows a manager to become aware of personal limitations as well as strengths. This activity allows the supervisor to recognize and accept responsibility for making necessary decisions and to be able to acknowledge the needs of peers and employees (Stone, 1989). The supervision of line employees is readily acknowledged as complicated and (in the view of many) demands the selection of supervisory techniques that transcend traditional responses (Woods, 1999).

Self-Appraisal

The initial and highly significant dilemma in becoming a truly competent supervisor is sorting through all the different supervisory techniques to select the approaches compatible with one's own temperament and personality. It is necessary to ask such questions as: *What is an acceptable level of conflict between employees? Can personal needs be made compatible with organizational needs? What managerial style will officers find most acceptable? How does one become an effective disciplinarian? Should one go by the book when enforcing rules and regulations? Can officer discretion be accepted as an integral part of the job?*

It is vital, for several reasons, for supervisors to have a clear idea of what they are doing and what is expected of them. First, it allows them to operate as professionals, and above potential conflict. Second, they are less likely, in the hectic day-to-day operation, to delude themselves into believing there is only one potential solution to every problem and that all officers can be treated the same.

Each officer is a distinct human being with varying skills, abilities, and personality, and is entitled to be treated as an individual. By accepting their subordinates as individuals and dealing with them on that basis, supervisors can reduce the potential for making errors and arrive at decisions suitable for both the individual and the organization (Raterman, 1992).

The pivotal factor is to understand the real attitudes toward line officers and their capacity to work. Are they viewed as having the potential to become producers, or are they regarded as drones? The real issue, then, becomes crystal clear: the way employees are treated by their supervisor is strongly influenced by the way the supervisor views the officers. Most assuredly, the best supervisors adopt a managerial style that acknowledges individual differences, and they work diligently to tailor the style to the situation and the individual.

If the supervisor is better at conceptualizing than motivating, it becomes readily apparent that his or her approach to a supervisory problem will be entirely different than when the individual excels at motivating.

The two skill areas can be combined by emphasizing conceptual skills, carefully setting forth a plan to resolve a problem and then utilizing motivational skills to implement the program. For example, a plan can be devised to focus on improving the working relationship between the line officers and other agencies dealing with the homeless in an effort to improve quality of life. Working with citizens and business owners, one patrol division created a program to identify the problems of vandalism, panhandling, loitering, thefts, and general deterioration of property. These problems were tracked, and maximum use was made of emergency shelters for homeless people as well as action plans that included counseling, casework review, housing placement, and job training. Line officers were instrumental in referring the homeless to the comprehensive treatment program (Klein, 2000).

If the supervisor's anxiety threshold is high, it may be more comfortable to resolve a problem with a knowledge skill base rather than a human skill approach. In other words, one can view an issue as a simple rule or regulation violation, or it can be approached as a conflict-resolution problem with a goal of maximizing human relations skills. In application it can become an integration of the two approaches, but it actually is a matter of fitting the style to the situation.

No supervisory philosophy works all the time. It is important to use a flexible approach. Accomplished supervisors combine different approaches. It is what John Naisbitt identified as *network management* in his landmark book *Megatrends* (Naisbitt, 1982).

Managerial networking at the supervisory level is concerned with the integration of each officer into the organization. Efforts are directed toward true communication and the sharing of ideas, information, and resources. It is the focus on decision making that improves work life and productivity. Networks exist to foster self-help, exchange information, and share resources. Focus is on the problem, and networking enhances the ability of each individual to respond to the problem. In fact, the individual is the most important element of the network. The value of networking is rooted in informality, equality, and true acceptance. It is the fait accompli of effective supervision.

Management Expectations of the Supervisor

Supervisors serve as a communications link between the line and higher management. They are responsible for turning the concepts and visions of those in higher positions into the "nuts and bolts" reality of police work. Sergeants must translate the intentions of management into actuality (Wiechmann, 1995). Management expects results (not excuses), so it is the responsibility of the first-line supervisor to respond to this challenge. The key is for the supervisor to work diligently at developing the skills that cause employees to become energized and to emphasize effective task completion. Vocational duties must be subordinate to getting work done through employees. One expert suggests asking the question, "What kind of employee would I like to have working for me?" The response to that question provides the first-line supervisor with a standard by which to work and live (Broadwell, 1998). It is a process that ensures success, because it reinforces and focuses supervisory efforts.

Positive Attitude

Everyone likes to be around people who are positive. Such an outlook can be contagious and will have a strong influence on working relationships. Think of how much better it is to be involved with people who obviously enjoy work and the challenges it presents.

When a new general order or policy is promulgated, the best way to react to it is positively. Responses should be based on a precise evaluation of ways that will ensure the policy is workable. Everyone, especially the supervisor, must refrain from finding reasons why it will not work (Dobbs and Field, 1993).

Supervisors should train themselves to think about the positive side of an idea or suggestion rather than the negative aspects. When addressing a problem, there is no room for tentativeness. Problems should be addressed directly, without circumspection. It is not a question of being unrealistic, but of looking for ways something can be done rather than focusing on why something will not work. When a supervisor focuses on achievement rather than failure, confidence becomes an integral component of success. It is fundamental to human nature that the boss will respond to recommendations by suggesting "This is what it will take to make this work" rather than "This is why that cannot be done" (Broadwell, 1998). Viewing things in a positive frame of reference focuses energies where they are needed to enhance successfully policy implementation. One can present negatives but should not dwell on them. Stressing the positive is a contagious supervisory process that works. Without question, enthusiasm is an intrinsic state of being. It is natural for one to be positive, creative, and challenged by the work being performed (Carlson, 1998).

The boss's ideas may still be questioned, but at the proper time and place. This simply means the idea should be carefully evaluated and constructively criticized, but not rejected simply because it has "never been done that way before." Individuals who think positively are results-oriented—a characteristic that management actively seeks. The supervisor must view each obstacle as an opportunity and a challenge. It is like looking at a half-filled glass of water and trying to determine whether it is half full or half empty. It is obvious that the positive thinker views the glass as half full.

Positive thinking is a way of dealing with obstacles in a constructive manner. It actually is a way of viewing life. The nature of circumstances, places, events, and attitudes toward people can always be affirmative if one wants to view them as such. Because desirable attitudes can be cultivated, the new supervisor should strive to identify means of finding workable solutions to conflict, starting with developing a positive attitude toward employees (Moody, 1994). A supervisor expresses positive thinking by noticeable enthusiasm, expressive body language, eye contact, and clarity of speech.

Loyalty

The organization anticipates specific behavioral outcomes from first-line supervisors, and one of these outcomes is loyalty. It is of extreme importance and in no way can it be discounted (Frunzi and Savini, 1997). It should be an integral part of the police culture. Loyalty is the cornerstone of character. It is an indispensable characteristic of a positive working relationship between different levels of management. Middle and top management want to feel that rules, regulations, policies, and decisions coming down through channels are supported by first-line supervisors. The supervisor should realize that policies set at one or two levels above them will in many instances lose some of their significance. In fact, their actual need for existence might be questioned by line personnel. A policy may be viewed as unreasonable when it is not fully explained. The first-line supervisor is seldom in a position to know all the facts and rationales for a new policy. The view from the top or middle of the organization is very seldom duplicated at the supervisory level. Only so much information can be sent down through channels. Most managers do not have the time to explain in-depth the rationale for each policy. Normally, managers are making decisions based upon more factual material, possibly unavailable at the operational level.

If information is needed before a new policy can be explained to subordinates, the supervisor must ask for clarifying information. When one accepts the position of supervisor, he or she accepts the obligation of being part of the team, not apart from it. This is not an easy task to accomplish, but it must be done if the supervisor is to be successful.

Supervisors translate and implement policy and procedures within the organization. The supportive supervisors should ask themselves, "How can this policy be implemented in the shortest period of time with assurance of actual compliance?" The important factor in this situation is to find the solution that is best for the department. In addition, middle and top managers dislike being referred to as the *they* who take those unreasonable stands and demand nonachievable performance. Managers at higher levels have a need for personal loyalty from supervisors, and this should be reciprocated. Loyalty works both ways. First-line supervisors want to feel they have the support and backing of their immediate supervisor.

Integrity

Management must convey to every member of the department the ethical standards that govern each and every action taken when performing law enforcement duties. Without question, it is essential to convey a tradition of excellence, professionalism, and commitment to the protection of the constitutional rights of everyone (Hiester, 1996). The equal administration of justice is the cornerstone of the integrity required of every member of a police department. People cannot be left to speculate about the values of the organization. Clear and explicit signals must be given both within and outside the organization that integrity cannot be compromised.

Management must expect every supervisor to be a role model when it comes to integrity both on and off the job. A commitment to integrity cannot be just an abstract value; it must be reflected in the day-to-day conduct of every supervisor. It can never be compromised. Every word and deed must reflect an adherence to a standard that is clearly above reproach. A supervisor is in a position to shape the attitudes and conduct of line officers by setting an example of personal conduct that exemplifies adherence to a strong code of ethics (see the code of ethics in Chapter 11).

Setting an example is a leadership task that must be provided by the first-line supervisor. Integrity can never be compromised, and every action must reflect a commitment to a principle of ethical policing (Himelfarb, 1995). A supervisor must realize that once one's reputation is tarnished, it is nearly impossible to recover. The competent supervisor will never be placed in a position that allows for the questioning of personal integrity (Garner, 1996). The significance of integrity at the supervisory level cannot be questioned. It is the administrative level where values can be reinforced and aberrant behavior controlled (Mollen, 1994). An excellent example of the importance of integrity to an organization is the mission statement utilized by the Baltimore Police Department, which expresses in no uncertain terms that the department must maintain the highest level of integrity in all of its actions.

Performance

Managers expect (and have the right to demand) the thorough completion of tasks on time. Supervisors should do everything asked of them. If an assignment cannot be completed on time, the next manager up the line needs to be consulted with an explanation. Perhaps more time is needed or help is required in understanding the problem or completing the task.

There are very few managers who will not accept a request for help if assistance is necessary in completing an assigned project. Asking for help is not an admission of incompetence; it is an acknowledgment that the manager has an expertise as yet unacquired by subordinates. Every manager expects personnel to be on time and to take appropriate coffee or meal breaks. Supervisors should set the standard not only for their officers, but also for everyone else in the department.

First-line supervisors have to accept being at the fulcrum between management and line operations. If problems occur, first-line supervisors are usually the first to know. Supervisors also have a responsibility to identify problems and respond to subordinate complaints; thus, they can serve as part of an early warning system. They are privy to the interaction between officers, they know what is being said on the radio, they read messages on mobile terminals, and they observe officers on a continuing basis. They know when things are going wrong and can act accordingly (McCarthy, 2000).

Functioning as the go-between is a supervisory responsibility. No one else can effectively accomplish the tasks of interpreting rules, regulations, policies, and translating organizational demands for attainment of agency goals. It is also essential that the supervisor be involved in the continual review of rules to ensure that they are practical (Solar, 2001).

Responding to Management

Because management is continually in need of information, supervisors must submit a wide range of requested reports in order to adequately reflect the tasks being accomplished by subordinates. Reports must be completed on time and must be comprehensive. There is nothing worse, in the view of most managers, than a poorly prepared or late report. The nature of police work is such that most supervisors are assessed primarily on the basis of reports submitted. While supervisors might have continuing contact with their immediate manager, other management superiors might use the written work submitted by a supervisor only as a means of evaluation. In fact, in many medium- or large-sized agencies, supervisors have little or no contact with the "brass." Therefore, it behooves them to do everything possible to ensure completeness and accuracy of all reports. Special care should be taken whenever a report is to be submitted to other city departments, the prosecuting attorney's office, or other law enforcement agencies so that these reports reflect favorably on the department. Figure 1.9 reflects what managers want from first-line supervisors.

Figure 1.9
What Management Wants from First-Line Supervisors

1. Meet with management as needed in order to resolve specific problems or concerns.
2. Communicate subordinates' concerns, desires, and suggestions to management.
3. Give testimony at disciplinary hearings.
4. Respond in writing to various management requests.
5. Prepare and submit budget requests.
6. Complete assigned investigations.
7. Prepare written employee evaluations.
8. Comply with procedures and policy.
9. Transmit the organizational value system to the members.
10. Take action contributing to organizational improvement.
11. Demonstrate commitment to integrity.
12. Create a positive work environment.

If there is any doubt as to when a report is due, supervisors should ask their immediate superior for clarification. If the manager wants reports done in a certain way, compliance with the requirement is essential. In order to work well with a next-level manager, an effort should be made to determine what is expected. This requires a great deal of judgment on the part of the supervisor. In general, routine matters are handled at the operational level, and other matters of consequence should be referred to the next managerial level (Garner, 1995).

Supervisors must refrain from stereotyping the manager and learn to look upon the person as a unique individual. This is especially important when it comes to determining the type of report the immediate supervisor wants in particular situations. Some managers are listeners and prefer, whenever possible, to have certain reports given orally. Others react best to written reports, allowing them time to assess and evaluate the information presented. The preference of one method over the other depends on the nature of the problem or the type of information being reported. With this in mind, supervisors should determine their managers' strengths and weaknesses, as well as their work habits and needs, before responding accordingly.

When establishing and maintaining a good working relationship with the boss, never modify a report to make it appear more favorable than it should. If something is wrong, say so. Be frank, open, and honest in all reports. To do less is to court disaster. Law enforcement is a process of responding to and resolving conflict. Naturally, mistakes will be made, and in some instances supervisory judgment, or that of subordinates, may not be what it should be. A boss is human also. Most bosses are dedicated and have a definite sense of responsibility toward their work and challenge not only themselves but also all personnel (Dobbs and Field, 1993). A supervisor should work with, not against, a boss. If it is a controversial situation, be sure to provide information that leaves the individual in a position to resolve the situation. Prior field experience will (in all probability) tell supervisors when management will be forced to respond to higher authorities or the press.

Most departments have a policy requiring a written report to be submitted when anything unusual occurs. It is at this time that the supervisor can extend a helping hand to management by submitting a detailed report, taking into consideration every possible question that might arise from the incident. The methodical application of this technique in a nonmanipulative fashion produces a supervisor who accepts what may be a management problem as a personal one. When this has been accomplished, management will start to see its supervisors not only as valuable resources, but also as helpful colleagues and trustworthy professionals who are part of the management team (Couper, 1993).

Subordinate Expectations of the Supervisor

If every subordinate worked to maximum capacity, if errors were never made, if all goals were achieved on time, and if organizations were perfect, there would not be a need for first-line supervisors. Obviously this is not the case. Law enforcement agencies are composed of human beings who deal with human problems in an imperfect environment. It logically follows that supervisors will continue to be an integral part of the managerial process in the years ahead.

Supervisors have to deal with numerous demands from a variety of sources, both within and outside the department. One that can be the most demanding is the subordinate. In fact, if there were no line personnel to be supervised, the position of supervisor would, in all probability, never have come into existence. Hence, the question has to be asked, "What should subordinates expect from a supervisor?"

The answer is not simple because of the human equation involved. Supervisors and subordinates are all different. While they are all members of the human race, they are still distinct and unique as individuals with varying needs. The primary reason for the existence of the supervisory position is the need for work to be effectively accomplished. If goals are not achieved, then there seems to be little reason for the continued existence of the organization.

The important consideration is to maximize the talents of each subordinate. What could be worse than a supervisor ignoring the skills possessed by subordinates? A supervisor certainly must utilize every skill and every bit of knowledge a subordinate possesses. This is not a simple task. It is one that demands continual appraisal and reappraisal of each employee's capabilities. Those abilities must then be directed toward the accomplishment of tasks essential to the attainment of organizational goals.

Subordinates have needs that, organizationally, must be met and satisfied (Broadwell, 1998). From an optimistic point of view, all those needs can be handled within the working environment, but usually this is not possible. If needs are met by the job, then the job is readily identified as an excellent source of motivation. If needs are not being met by the job, then the question arises as to why the job is responding inadequately to employee needs.

Under no circumstance does this mean the supervisor has to accept a person's actions or inactions as an excuse for poor performance. Failure to perform at acceptable levels must always be addressed and resolved in favor of the organization. Generally speaking, it can be assumed that 85 percent of employees will respond to positive efforts by the supervisor. This is the group with whom the supervisor should expend extra time and energy. Unfortunately, the remaining 15 percent of the subordinates (who, for whatever reason, are poor employees) will generally consume most of the supervisor's time. Eventually, that time will be nonproductive (except that employees who should never have been employed will be eliminated, or employees will receive aid to such an extent that they will become productive employees).

It is important for a supervisor to realize that people, times, and places have changed. Things are not the way they used to be. The authoritarian management approach should have been dispensed with long ago, but is still in limited use and is definitely not as viable a managerial approach as it once was. The old assumptions about employees' lack of desire and inability to work no longer apply. As a group, officers cannot be classified as lazy, indifferent, or indolent. In fact, the constituency to be supervised is generally willing and capable of working (see Figure 1.10), but for different reasons and with different expectations than their predecessors.

A large problem facing police organizations today is that many officers do not feel they are a part of the organization. Officers want job satisfaction, and this can be provided only by allowing officers to achieve individual needs while organizational needs are satisfied.

When the working environment limits the opportunity for satisfying personal goals, officers can become alienated from the organization. When an officer rejects the work situation, it can result in a lowering of work standards, general apathy, and a lessening of interest in the job.

Discontent with the job has traditionally resulted in absenteeism, tardiness, stoicism, and low-quality work. Now, however, officers have expressed this discontent by becoming more active in unions, engaging in work slowdowns, using alcohol and drugs to a greater extent, filtering information for personal reasons, and finally, leaving the police field in increasing numbers (Scarano and Jones, 2000).

Figure 1.10
Officer Behavior

The Past Century	The New Millennium
passive	involved
dependent	independent
subordinate	equal
lack of trust	mutual trust
ordered	self-directed
autocracy	democratic workplace
closed communication	open communication
acceptance	commitment
conventionality	spontaneity
conforming	nonconforming
rules dominate	goal attainment dominates
quantity	quality
personal goals ignored	personal goals attained
value neutral	value oriented
don't rock the boat	risk taker
acceptance of external direction	internalized response
pessimistic	optimistic
indifference	empathy

Many younger officers have rising expectations and are not willing to accept the demands of a traditionally managed police organization. The bureaucratic model of management is the antithesis of everything they want from an organization. The rational aspects of work are rejected for those that are more people-oriented. In the past, officers sought job and financial security and the job took precedence over outside interests. Today, however, officers express a need for:

- responsibility
- recognition
- fulfilling and consequential work
- the opportunity to excel
- involvement in decision making
- attainment of individual goals
- opportunity to use their skills and expertise
- vision
- self-management
- the acquisition of new skills

Those changing attitudes toward work suggest that younger officers want a well-rounded lifestyle. They will work and give their best efforts for a certain number of hours if they have a positive work environment. The successful police organization of the future will integrate the individual into the organization, and individual as well as organizational goals will be attained.

It is apparent that the composition of most law enforcement agencies will change dramatically (if it has not occurred already). Affirmative action mandates have changed hiring practices, and *diversity* is the buzzword of the day. In the years ahead, more minorities and women will enter the law enforcement ranks, in part because of demographics. Additionally, continuing affirmative action programs serve to correct any imbalance between the proportion of ethnic minorities, those of unique sexual orientations, different religious affiliations, and women in a community, as compared to the proportion of sworn officers. In sum, the goal is to create police departments that are more representative of the community at large (CALEA, 1999). These new employees and their white male counterparts will become a new breed of individuals with a different attitude toward work and a changing personal needs structure.

Participation

A new set of values has entered the organizational setting, and it strikes right at the heart of the supervisor-subordinate relationship. In the past, employees have been *acted upon* rather than *reacted to*. Except for a few instances, police employees have been passive rather than reactive. Today, things are different. Most police officers want a part of the action. Progressive police organizations open the decision-making process to employees. This is not to say that every employee is involved in every policy decision, but participation is allowed at all levels where employees are in a position to have firsthand information and are given an opportunity to study problems that come to the attention of the organization.

The idea of worker participation and involvement requires a redefinition of work and working relationships. It requires a fundamental change in one's view of employees and what they can contribute to the department. It demands that the supervisor work toward the creation of an environment that gives officers an opportunity for involvement and growth.

Supervisors must learn that creating a real partnership means that power must be shared, not hoarded. As the old authoritarian leadership style is discarded, it must be replaced by insight into, and a deeper understanding of, human needs and expectations. Participative management will not become operational overnight. In fact, it will undoubtedly be resisted by some in the years ahead, and in a few instances never adopted. However, as individuals change, organizations must change. As everyone knows, change can be pleasant or painful. Without a doubt, supervisors from the old school will be the recipients of high levels of stress as their work experience, training, and education are opposed to the demands of modern leadership.

The transformation of relationships between working employees and supervisors does not require an overhaul of human nature. Quite the contrary. It requires the elimination of distorted and outdated opinions of how human nature is viewed (Dessler, 1993). When supervising the new breed, the task is that of facilitator, not power broker. The real by-product of participative supervision is the creation of a working environment in which the officers *want* to work. It is absolutely necessary for the supervisor to project an air of caring for people and strive to do everything possible to make the department a pleasant place to work. This is accomplished by being constantly available for help or guidance, accepting and solving problems as they occur, making decisions based on knowledge, and exhibiting a genuine desire to empower employees to accomplish assigned tasks (Dessler, 1993). An organization achieves a standard of excellence when a participative environment that is created by the first-line supervisor causes employees to excel and attain organizational goals.

Conflict Resolution

When first-line supervisors were asked to identify the most important functions they performed, it was found that the vast majority had to do with conflict resolution (see Figure 1.11). Subordinates constantly turn to supervisors as conflict resolvers.

Figure 1.11
Functions Performed by Supervisors When Relating to Subordinates

1. Provide feedback to subordinates regarding job performance.
2. Conduct investigations of incidents in which subordinates are involved (shootings or accidents).
3. Conduct investigations of observed or reported subordinate conduct that may have vicarious liability involved.
4. Train and develop subordinates.
5. Personally conduct investigations of alleged subordinate misconduct.
6. Resolve citizen/officer conflicts.
7. Respond to subordinates' inquiries (policy, law, alternative courses of action, etc.).
8. Conduct internal investigations in accordance with rules prescribed in the Officer's Bill of Rights.
9. Counsel subordinates with personal and job-related problems.
10. Serve as an archetype of professionalism in all relationships with subordinates.
11. Ameliorate conflict between subordinates.
12. Coach subordinates.

Conflict cannot be ignored, but must be accepted as a certain consequence of human interaction. Subordinates expect, and in fact demand, that supervisors deal with and resolve conflict. Conflict is inevitable in police work. Line personnel are confronted with conflict daily, and the first-line supervisor is not exempt from the realities of conflict.

Conflict must be resolved both internally and externally. Citizens file complaints that must be investigated. Conflict even occurs between officers and likewise has to be met and resolved. Conflicts in this area range from a failure to respond rapidly when providing backup to taking too much time for a meal break. In some situations, gripes about another employee can fester to such a point that the accomplishment of tasks is impeded. The supervisor must listen to such complaints and work toward their reduction or elimination.

The first-line supervisor must learn to distinguish between real employee complaints and petty bickering. A certain amount of griping can actually be beneficial, but if it becomes excessive, it can be inimical to personal relationships and organizational well-being. Additionally, when officers engage in activities creating a vicarious liability, they must be investigated.

Subordinates can become involved in shootings or accidents, and the supervisor becomes a key factor in the investigation of such incidents. This is especially true when a firearm is discharged and someone is injured or killed. In agencies not having an internal affairs unit, the first-line supervisor is generally held responsible for conducting such an investigation.

Supervisors are the lead investigators in efforts to resolve conflicts as described above. It has been estimated that 73 percent of a supervisor's time is spent in resolving conflict. The supervisor's position is, without a doubt, primarily one of conflict identification and resolution.

Peer Expectations of the Supervisor

Successful accomplishment of tasks and goal attainment requires cooperation and coordination between supervisors. Supervision is a joint effort by numerous individuals and not the sole priority of any one first-line supervisor. Functions performed by one have a direct impact on every other supervisor in the department.

Getting along with and supporting fellow supervisors creates a more pleasant place to work. Occasionally someone will allow the desire to get ahead (or a strong drive to compete) to get in the way of positive working relationships. Other supervisors may view their duties and responsibilities differently. If the differences are to be resolved, supervisors must make an effort to understand and get along with each other (Albright, 1997).

Supervisors have to recognize that peers have objectives to be met and commitments to be honored. They have problems that have to be dealt with and they may know best how to solve those problems. The first-line supervisor should always consider how his or her actions affect the duties of others.

If it is possible to make a helping decision rather than one that hinders, it should be done. If it appears that a decision will result in conflict for another supervisor, an attempt should be made to resolve the problem by direct communication. Fellow supervisors should talk over the differences and make a sincere effort to find a solution beneficial to both (Weiss, 1988).

Reciprocal, positive relationships between peers are those where experiences are shared. At the end of a shift, situations that occurred can jointly be discussed along with views on how they were resolved. Ideas and opinions should be thrown out on the table for discussion (and even debate) when needed.

When the occasion demands, supervisors must meet with other supervisors to resolve problems, share information, and coordinate work activities. This might be especially pertinent when there is an ongoing investigation that cannot be completed on one shift.

A good supervisor does not wait for someone else to take action when a problem requiring consultation with peers occurs. The offer to help should be extended and, if necessary, a meeting should be set up to discuss and resolve the problem. There are many instances in which an end-of-shift briefing does not allow adequate time for dealing with the problem at hand.

This is best illustrated by the conflict arising when a new policy is implemented. Policies are open to interpretation, and when one supervisor stringently enforces a new grooming policy and another ignores it, there will be an immediate reaction from line personnel. Such a situation is best handled by reviewing the policy in a conference setting and allowing adequate time for discussion in order to resolve differences in interpretation.

Positive relationships with peers can take many avenues, but those that have proven to be successful focus on the work to be accomplished rather than the personalities of those involved. It is not necessary to like someone in order to work with him or her. Personal feelings should be set aside, and the need to get the job done should dominate peer relationships.

The ability to get along with people is the hallmark of the professional. It is a sign of maturity. Going out of your way to share credit and to praise people when the situation dictates is vital. Everything possible should be done to develop positive working relationships, and this usually involves communication. Peers need to explain actions, share information, let others know what is going on, send a memo, and make it a personal policy to maximize communication. In other words, take the extra step.

It should be expected that peer criticism will occur on occasion. Despite ultimate personal efforts, someone will find fault or be critical of the manner in which something is being done. Employees must try to not only accept criticism, but also to learn from it.

Summary

Attaining the rank of sergeant in a police department is an accomplishment that is achieved by few who enter law enforcement. In fact, the majority of officers will enter and leave law enforcement as a line officer or specialist. Such an achievement has its blessings and at the same time exacts its toll. It is nice to have an increase in pay and the added prestige that goes with the stripes, but not everyone enjoys enforcing policies or disciplining other officers.

Police work is a complex process, and demands on first-line supervisors are such that they must respond creatively and positively. Today's supervisors must deal with problems and challenges totally unheard of several years ago. Rapidly changing police organizations require supervisors to operate in a viable and dynamic organization. Discretion is a vital component of law enforcement and accountability is essential.

A first-line supervisor is part of management. Consequently, work has to be accomplished through the efforts of others. At the same time, a first-line supervisor must engage in the specific application of skills making up the management process: knowledge-based, conceptual, human, and affective.

Knowledge and human skills dominate the day-to-day duties performed by a first-line supervisor. At times knowledge skills might dominate the functioning process, and in other instances it will be human skills. Each of these areas serves to define working relationships within a variety of settings. A supervisor must distinguish between the importance of knowledge and human skills and apply the skills appropriate to the situation.

The supervisor's success depends on the qualities and qualifications brought to the managerial process and the methods used in resolving conflict. There is no one best way to supervise. Management is an art, not a science.

Management's expectations of the supervisor will vary from agency to agency but usually include such variables as a positive attitude, an acceptable level of performance, loyalty to the department, and responding to requests from management. Additionally, supervisors should conduct themselves in such a manner that their personal and professional integrity can never be questioned.

Subordinate expectations of management range from the need for feedback to assistance in interpreting policy or analyzing court decisions. The new breed of officers wants to be involved. These officers want a say in the decision-making process, especially when the decision affects line performance. This idea of worker participation requires a redefinition of work and working relationships. First-line supervisors must learn that real participation means power must be shared.

A supervisor's peer expectations include joint resolution of problems, sharing information, and coordinating work activities. Successfully accomplishing tasks and attaining goals requires cooperation and coordination between first-line supervisors. If there is a key to supervisory achievement, it is being a part of the management team and attaining goals through the efforts of others.

Case Study

Sergeant Roberta Miles

Sergeant Roberta Miles has been with the Rio Vista Police Department for seven years. She came to the department on a lateral transfer after serving three years in a neighboring agency. The department serves an urban community and has 269 sworn officers and 44 civilian employees. About 59 percent of the department personnel are assigned to field operations and respond to calls for service. Other departmental personnel are assigned to specialized units, including victim assistance, hate crimes, traffic regulation, narcotics, and community services.

Sergeant Miles is married and has one child. Her husband is the owner of a nursery in the community, and both of them are active in community affairs. She has a master's degree from a local university, where she majored in public administration. She was the first female to be employed by the department. Currently there are 12 female sworn officers. She was a patrol supervisor for four years and is currently assigned to the departmental planning unit. When the department initially hired her, she was generally rejected by some of the old-timers, and it took several years as a patrol supervisor before she was accepted as being well-qualified and competent. Those she supervised viewed her as fair and impartial, and she became well-liked by those she supervised. Additionally, she attained acceptance from fellow supervisors and members of management.

As a member of the planning unit, she was given the task of implementing a proposed policy regarding outside employment. The recommended policy states:

1.0. POLICY—
1.1. It is the policy of this department to require prior authorization by the chief of police before engaging in outside employment.
1.2. Examples of occupations that employees are prohibited from engaging in outside employment are:
    A. Bartenders
    B. Taxi drivers
    C. Card room operators or dealers
    D. Private investigators
    E. Polygraph examiners employed by defense attorneys
        in criminal matters

Sergeant Miles presented the new policy to managers and reviewed the application processes at roll call sessions. There was some resistance to the proposed policy, because the department had never had a written policy regarding outside employment.

If you were Sergeant Miles, how would you deal with resistance to the new policy? What information would you need prior to meeting with management and line personnel? Would it be appropriate to use conceptual skills in this situation? Would human skills be of value? Why or why not?

Key Concepts

affective skills	officer behavior
analytical approach	participation
conceptual skills	peer expectations of the supervisor
conflict resolution	performance
dynamic organization	positive attitude
human skills	responding to management
integrity	self-appraisal
knowledge-based skills	subordinate expectations of the supervisor
loyalty	supervisory skill areas
management expectations of	transition
the supervisor	

Discussion Topics and Questions

1. Discuss the difficulty that some officers have after being promoted to the position of first-line supervisor.

2. Distinguish between conceptual and affective skills.

3. How important are human skills to a supervisor?

4. Discuss the importance of conceptual skills that should be used by a supervisor.

5. How can a supervisor use network management when dealing with line officers?

6. Describe a common interpretation of knowledge-based skills and how a supervisor could apply them.

7. Discuss what management wants from first-line supervisors.

8. How can one create a truly participative organizational setting?

9. Discuss the importance of ethical standards.

10. What can supervisors do to maximize communication among themselves?

11. Why is integrity an important characteristic of a supervisor?

12. What needs do younger officers express compared to those expressed by those hired several decades ago?

13. Discuss the attributes of a viable police organization.

For Further Reading

Frunzi, George L., and Patrick E. Savini (1997). *Supervision: The Art of Management,* Fourth Edition. Upper Saddle River, NJ: Prentice Hall.

> The authors take the position that supervisors are in an integral and unique position in the organizational management team. Supervisors are viewed as being surrounded by problems and graced with opportunity. The supervisor's world is one of action and results, not hypothetical talk or theory. Supervisors must work on a daily basis with managers above them and officers below them in the organization. They link officers to the organization—a responsibility not experienced by other managerial levels. Presents an excellent discussion of the importance of technical and human relations skills.

Hamilton, Douglas, and Barbara Warman (1997). "First-Line Supervision: Preparing Officers to Face the Transition to Command." *The Police Chief,* Vol. LXIV, No. 11.

> Concerned with the difficult transition from line officer to supervisor, the Louisville Division of Police developed a program to train a prospective sergeant to become a competent and confident first-line supervisor before being promoted and faced with the challenges of a supervisory role. The training program consists of three phases. Phase One is a 120-hour curriculum that addresses topics ranging from discipline to time management. The last two phases consist of eight to ten weeks of supervised practical application in two separate patrol districts and the traffic unit. This program has received wide acceptance within the department.

Salmon, William A. (1999). *The New Supervisor's Survival Manual.* New York, NY: AMACOM.

> Presents an excellent discussion of the challenge of being a supervisor. This text identifies the cornerstones of effective supervision such as motivation, communications, delegating, decision making, problem solving, coaching, and conducting an effective meeting. The author takes the position that a supervisor is a manager. Of special interest is the chapter describing the process by which a supervisor can understand what is expected of a supervisor. Another excellent section is the discussion of how one might evaluate and manage his or her performance as a supervisor. Describes the competencies that a supervisor needs in order to perform effectively.

Solar, Patrick J. (2001). "The Organizational Context of Effective Policing." *The Police Chief,* Vol. LXVIII, No. 2.

> Suggests that police managers can maintain an adequate level of accountability and control in the absence of rigid rules and procedures by reinforcing organizational beliefs and policies through relentless ongoing training. The author takes the position that as a police organization moves away from a traditional bureaucratic model, officers become more effective operationally. Recommends that rules and procedures be written in such a way as to allow for discretionary application. Additionally, the author suggests that managers strive to develop a cooperative relationship between managers and line officers.

References

Albright, Mary (1997). *101 Biggest Mistakes Managers Make and How to Avoid Them.* Englewood Cliffs, NJ: Prentice-Hall.

Arnold, Jon (2000). "Strategic Planning for Career Development." *The Police Chief,* Vol. LXVII, No. 4.

Barrios, Joseph (2000). "Arrests of Blacks Unequal, So Police Training Will Alter." *Arizona Daily Star,* November 10:B1, B2.

Broadwell, Martin W. (1998). *The New Supervisor,* Fifth Edition. Reading, MA: Addison-Wesley Publishing Co.

Carlson, Richard (1998). *Don't Sweat the Small Stuff at Work.* New York, NY: Hyperion.

Cochran, Jay (1995). "Virginia Chiefs' Use-of-Force Survey." *The Police Chief,* Vol. LXII, No. 1.

Commission on Accreditation for Law Enforcement Agencies, Inc. (1999). *Standards for Law Enforcement Agencies,* Fourth Edition. Fairfax, VA: Commission on Accreditation for Law Enforcement Agencies, Inc.

Costley, Dan L., and Ralph Todd (1978). *Human Relations in Organizations.* St. Paul, MN: West Publishing.

Couper, David (1993). "Leadership for Change: A National Agenda." *The Police Chief,* Vol. LX, No. 12.

Dale, Nancy (2000). Survival Strategies for the Next Decade." *Law and Order,* Vol. 48, No. 10.

Dessler, Gary (1993). *Winning Commitment: How to Build and Keep a Competitive Workforce.* New York, NY: R.R. Donnelley & Sons Co.

Dobbs, Carl and Mark W. Field (1993). "Rational Risk: Leadership Success or Failure?" *The Police Chief,* Vol. LX, No. 12.

Esbensen, Finn-Aage (2000). *Preventing Adolescent Gang Involvement.* Washington, DC: Office of Justice Programs.

Federal Bureau of Investigation (2000). *Law Enforcement Officers Killed and Assaulted— 1998.* Washington, DC: FBI National Press Office.

Fox, James Alan, and Marianne W. Zawitz (2000). "Homicide Trends in the United States: 1998 Update." *Crime Data Brief.* Washington, DC: Bureau of Justice Statistics.

Frazier, Thomas C., and John F. Reintzell (1997). "Training Sergeants: Today's Leaders, Tomorrow's Executives." *The Police Chief,* Vol. LXIV, No. 11.

Frunzi, George L., and Patrick E. Savini (1997). *Supervision: The Art of Management.* Upper Saddle River, NJ: Prentice-Hall, Inc.

Garner, Gerald W. (1996). "Are Your People Ready for Promotion?" *Law and Order,* Vol. 45, No. 5.

———— (1995). *Common Sense Police Supervision: A How-To Manual for the First-Line Supervisor,* Second Edition. Springfield, IL: Charles C Thomas.

Hall, Steven J. (1999). "Racial Profiling—A Challenge for American Policing." *Law and Order,* Vol. 47, No. 11.

Hamilton, Douglas and Barbara Warman (1997). "First-Line Supervision: Preparing Officers to Face the Transition to Command." *The Police Chief,* Vol. LXIV, No. 11.

Handy, Charles B. (1993). *Understanding Organizations.* New York, NY: Oxford University Press.

Hawkins, Jeff (1992). "Officer Motivation." *Law and Order,* Vol. 40, No. 10.

Herman, Roger E. (1992). *Keeping Good People: Strategies for Solving the Dilemma of the Decade.* New York, NY: McGraw-Hill.

Hiester, Dave (1996). "Guardians of the Constitution." *Law and Order,* Vol. 44, No. 5.

Himelfarb, Frum (1995). "Rediscovering Ethics." *The Police Chief,* Vol. LXII, No. 2.

Imundo, Louis V. (1991). *The Effective Supervisors Handbook,* Second Edition. New York, NY: AMACOM.

Katz, Robert L. (1974). "Skills of an Effective Adminstrator." *Harvard Business Review,* September-October: Vol. 52, No. 5.

Kelling, George L. (1999). *"Broken Windows" and Police Discretion.* Washington, DC: Office of Justice Programs.

Klein, Sid (2000). "Dealing With Homeless and Improving Quality of Life." *The Police Chief,* Vol. LXVII, No. 5.

Kunde, Diana (1999). "How to Make a High-Risk Jump." *San Jose Mercury News,* August 10:13C, 14C.

Lathrop, Sam W. (2000). "Reviewing Use of Force—A Systematic Approach." *FBI Law Enforcement Bulletin,* Vol. 69, No. 10.

Leonard, V.A., and Harry W. More (2000). *Police Organization and Management,* Ninth Edition. New York, NY: Foundation Press.

Levendosky, Charles (2000). "No Greater Hate Crime than Profiling." *Arizona Daily Star,* October 16:B7.

Loen, Raymond O. (1994). *Superior Supervision: The 10% Solution.* New York, NY: Lexington Books.

Martin, John A. and Kurt Matthews (2000). "Measuring an Agency's Performance." *Law and Order,* Vol. 48, No. 10.

McCarthy, Robert (2000). "Steps Chiefs Can Take to Prevent Unethical Behavior." *The Police Chief,* Vol. LXVII, No. 10.

Mollen, Milton (1994). *Commission Report.* Commission to Investigate Allegations of Police Corruption and the Anti-Corruption Procedures of the Police Department. New York, NY: City of New York.

Moody, Bobby D. (1994). "Is This Any Way to Run a Police Department?" *The Police Chief,* Vol. LXI, No. 1.

Nagy, Richard A. (2000). "Improving the Quality of Life." *The Police Chief,* Vol. LXVII, No. 4.

Naisbitt, John (1982). *Megatrends: Ten New Directions Transforming Our Lives.* New York, NY: Warner Books.

Newsweek (2000). "America 2000: A Map of the Mix." *Newsweek,* September 18.

Office of Justice Programs (1998). *The Challenge of Crime in a Free Society: Looking Back, Looking Forward.* Washington, DC. National Institute of Justice.

Pilant, Lois (1995). "Spotlight on Selecting Officers." *The Police Chief,* Vol. LXII, No. 12.

Pfeffer, Jeffrey (1994). *Competitive Advantage through People: Unleashing the Power of the Work Force.* New York, NY: Macmillan.

Raterman, Max (1992). "Contingency Management for Line Level Supervisors." *Law and Order,* Vol. 40, No. 5.

Reaves, Brian A., and Timothy C. Hart (2000). *Law Enforcement Management and Administrative Statistics, 1999: Data for Individual State and Local Agencies with 100 or More Officers.* Washington, DC: Bureau of Justice Statistics.

Salmon, William A. (1999). *The New Supervisor's Survival Manual.* New York, NY: AMACOM.

Scarano, Steve, and Thomas Jones (2000). "Following by Example." *Law and Order,* Vol. 48, No. 10.

Solar, Patrick J. (2001). "The Organizational Context of Effective Policing." *The Police Chief,* Vol. LXVIII, No. 2.

Stambaugh, Hollis, David Beaupre, David J. Icove, Richard Baker, and Wayne Cassaday (2000). *State and Local Law Enforcement Needs to Combat Electronic Crime.* Washington, DC: National Institute of Justice.

Stone, Florence M. (1989). *The AMA Handbook of Supervisory Management.* New York, NY: AMACOM.

Tate, Hugh (2000). "The Recruitment Dilemma: Quick Fixes, Warm Bodies and the Eternal Search for Quality." *Law and Order,* Vol. 48, No. 5.

Umbreit, Mark S., and Robert B. Coates (2000). *Multicultural Implications of Restorative Justice: Potential Pitfalls and Dangers.* Washington, DC: Office for Victims of Crime Resource Center.

Weiss, W.H. (1988). *Supervisor's Standard Reference Handbook,* Second Edition. Englewood Cliffs, NJ: Prentice-Hall.

White, Ken W., and Elwood N. Chapman (1996). *Organizational Communication: An Introductory to Communications and Human Relations Strategies.* Upper Saddle River, NJ: Prentice-Hall.

Wiechmann, Arthur D. (1995)."A Supervisory Perspective on Community Policing." *Community Policing Exchange.* Washington, DC: Community Policing Consortium.

Woods, DeVere D. (1999). "Supervising Officers in the Community Policing Age." *Sheriff Times,* PH VII, No. 1, Issue 10.

Community
Policing—

2

Serving the Neighborhoods

Introductory Case Study

Sergeant William Horton

William Horton was promoted to sergeant after serving in the patrol division for six years and training for two years. An assessment center was part of the promotional process, and he fared poorly on this part of the examination but placed first on the written portion of the test.

He was ranked ninth on the promotion list and was promoted one week prior to the expiration of the list. His advancement came at the time a new police chief was hired, and she had a mandate from the city council to implement community-oriented policing. The former chief had retired after 12 years at the helm of the department and was not a supporter of community policing. The new chief had previously worked in a department that had been in the vanguard of community policing. The city had a population of 173,000. The city has 424 sworn personnel and 200 support personnel. The city has a high concentration of biomedical, high-technology, and software firms. It is located in the middle of the state and is the commercial center for the area.

Sergeant Horton is 37 years of age and lives on the south side of the city. He has been married for six years and he has two daughters, ages four and two. The family is active in their church. Horton completed two years of college prior to entering the force. Since then he has returned to school sporadically and has finished an additional 33 units of upper division work. The demands placed on him by his job and family leave limited time to attend college classes. He is majoring in social science, and his goal is to finish his degree within three and one-half years.

Sergeant Horton was assigned to a team to work on the creation of a community policing unit to be composed of 33 officers and assign them to specified areas of the city where it was anticipated that members of the community would be most receptive to the concept. Four areas were selected and eight officers were assigned to each area. Sergeant Horton was in charge of a sector assigned to work in an area with numerous apartment houses and small commercial establishments. Beats were created using grid lines recognized by the department's computer, and a serious effort was made to create beats within the boundaries of existing neighborhood associations.

Officers working with Sergeant Horton attended a regional community policing academy. The sector has a wide variety of crimes ranging from graffiti to armed robbery. Auto theft is a major problem, and in some of the apartments drugs are sold openly.

If you were Sergeant Horton, what would be the first thing you would do when you got together with your team? Why? What information would you want from the department? What would you do to create a viable working arrangement with the neighborhood association?

Community policing has been extolled as the panacea for all of the problems faced by law enforcement. It arrived with fanfare—supported by many national police organizations—and to a degree has taken the nation by storm. With the financial backing of the federal government, it has been embraced by most police administrators and politicians. It has become the byword of policing, the elixir we have been waiting for, the dynamic phrase of the last 20 years. It continues to grab headlines. It gained momentum as police and community leaders searched for a means of providing better police services as the fear of crime was quite high during the early 1990s.

Extolled by former President Bill Clinton, community policing became political patronage of the highest order as it supplemented municipal, county, and state budgets. Over a six-year period, starting in 1994, approximately $9 billion was awarded, in part, through three-year grants to law enforcement agencies in order to hire police officers to engage in community policing activities. Additionally, part of the funding went to the hiring of civilians and improving technology. The almighty dollar proved to be a strong incentive.

On May 12, 1999, the White House announced that the goal of funding 100,000 officers had been met. In reality, the best estimate is that by 2003, this funding will have raised the level of policing on the street by the equivalent of 62,700 to 83,900 full-time officers (*Law Enforcement News*, 2000). Political rhetoric has prevailed throughout the funding of the Community-Oriented Policing Services program (Cameron, 2000).

Efforts at grantsmanship to locally define versions of community policing have resulted in inconsistent and highly variable programs throughout the United States. As a means of obtaining funds, departments had to rewrite their mission and value statements. Some departments described programs as community policing because it was the thing to do and it brought professional recognition. Fifty-five percent of eligible law enforcement agencies requested and received at least one federal grant.

The Community Policing Consortium has extolled its virtues, and special training has prepared participants to implement problem-solving programs. It has reached the point where it is almost a game of one-upmanship as police leaders describe their community policing programs. Reformers have been adamant in their ardor for community policing and essentially absolutist in pushing the new doctrine into the forefront. This was done without any consideration of skepticism in its epistemological assumptions.

Unfortunately, there is a lack of consensus in defining community policing. It has turned out to be an imprecise term because programs have been tailored to local needs and resources (*Law Enforcement News*, 2000). Some view it as the need to emphasize a traffic program, gun tip program, working with the elderly, a gang control program, citizens on patrol, citizen police academy, or business survey projects. Other programs include cooperative truancy programs, foot and bicycle patrols, citizen surveys, and bringing probation officers into problem-solving situations. Any of these programs can be part of a community policing effort, but this is true only if it is the result of the direct participation and support of the community (Bucqueroux, 1995). Problem-solving partnerships in many instances were found to be something in name only, or simply standard temporary working arrangements. Partnerships involving short-term crackdowns are not in the spirit of problem solving, nor are partnerships with citizens and businesses in which their involvement is limited to merely being involved.

Other departments have created special units (West, 1997) similar to those created when community relations and team policing were in vogue. Numerous municipal police departments have full-time community policing officers, and about three-fourths of local departments operated one or more community substations. In larger local departments, nearly every new recruit received training in community policing even though they may not become a community policing specialist (Reaves and Hart, 2000). In the past, the community relations unit was a status symbol. It was an indicator that the agency was responding to the needs of the community and was perceived as part of the vanguard of professional law enforcement. One can only wonder if community policing in some cities is a hollow effort to keep up with what is a momentous shift in policing. Others view it as the ideological underpinning of the agency, suggesting that it provides the reason for the existence of the department. Philosophically it can be a significant change in the provision of police services (Heidingsfield, 1997). At the least it is semantical gamesmanship, and at the most it requires radical change, in which personnel work with the community in determining the delivery system for police services (Trojanowicz, Kappeler, and Gaines, 2001; Taylor, 1992; Bobinsky, 1994; Reaves and Hart, 2000).

Community policing is not a quick fix. To be successful it requires a long-term commitment. It should not be sold as a panacea, and there must be realistic expectations about its potential to improve the quality of life in neighborhoods (Bureau of Justice Assistance, 1994b). Surveys indicate that roughly two out of three police agencies in major jurisdictions report that they have adopted some form of community policing. However, other research shows that three out of four police agencies that claim to be engaged in community policing do not allow the community a voice in identifying, prioritizing, and solving problems (Bucqueroux, 1995). At this time, community policing officers are in approximately three-fourths of departments that have more than 100 sworn officers, but only 18 officers are assigned full-time to community policing duties. Thus, the remainder of line personnel continue to perform traditional police services. Only time will tell whether community policing will become more dominant within police circles (Parks et al., 1999).

If community policing is to become a reality, it has to be done by something other than executive fiat. Some of the factors that reinforce the possibility for successful implementation of a community policing program are set forth in Figure 2.1. There are many rocks in the roadway when an organization makes an effort to implement any new program, and this is especially true of community policing. When implemented, it can threaten the traditionalist, who will do everything to thwart the development of a program that dilutes his or her power and authority.

Figure 2.1
How to Ensure That Community Policing Will Have a Reasonable Chance to Succeed

1. Sharing power with line personnel.
2. Endorsing and maximizing officer discretion.
3. Enhancing and advocating community input.
4. Involving all levels in planning.
5. Creating flexible policies that maximize independent decision making.
6. Including every management level in all aspects of community policing.
7. Rewarding nontraditional duties, such as problem solving, application of evaluation techniques, and the creation and development of community groups.
8. Allowing all participants to act outside of the chain of command without fear of reprisal.
9. Creating organizational versatility.
10. Confronting efforts to undermine the program.
11. Measuring qualitative and quantitative effects.
12. Developing an atmosphere that fosters two-way communication.
13. Accepting mistakes as part of the learning process.
14. Fostering a positive working environment.
15. Absolutely supporting the philosophy of community policing.

Adapted from V.A. Leonard and Harry W. More (2000). *Police Organization and Management,* Ninth Edition, New York: Foundation Press. Reprinted with permission.

At this point it is appropriate to suggest a working definition of community policing in Figure 2.2. The definition has not been set in concrete and is deliberately general so that agencies can modify it to their operations. Key elements of this generic definition include: (1) the development of a dynamic relationship with community residents, (2) consideration of the most urgent needs of the community, (3) use of community resources, and (4) application of the problem-solving process.

If this definition is to have true meaning, it has to serve as a philosophical base for the officers involved. Each officer must accept the fact that the department needs assistance in order to maximize the public safety effort. Community policing is a mindset wherein the department believes that the public is a vital component of the operation and the public supports and understands the mission, values, and role of the police department (Heidingsfield, 1997). Community policing provides officers with an opportunity to move closer to the community. It is a procedure by which the police organize members of the community, coordinate activities, and communicate with every concerned individual and organization.

Figure 2.2
Definition of Community Policing

Community policing consists of two complementary core components, *community partnership* and *problem solving*. To develop community partnership, police must develop positive relationships with the community, must involve the community in the quest for better crime control and prevention, and must pool their resources with those of the community to address the most urgent concerns of community members. Problem solving is the process through which the specific concerns of communities are identified and through which the most appropriate remedies to abate these problems are found.

Source: Bureau of Justice Assistance (1994b). *Understanding Community Policing—A Framework for Action.* Washington, DC: Office of Justice Programs.

Community policing, if it is to be successful, demands radical change over time if there is to be a significant alteration in the way the organization attains goals. If change is to occur, it has to be leader-centered and engendered (Community Policing Consortium, 2000). The historical nature of police work, with its quasi-military orientation, mandates the need for change to emanate from top management (Moselle, 1997). It is a transitional process in which the chief executive officer removes barriers that impede change, fostering the development of a culture in which actions contrary to traditional working methods are stimulated (Cunningham, 1994; Oliver, 1998). In community policing, top management must articulate the values of community policing and communicate them to every level and every person in the organization (Overman, 1994; Rush, 1992). The police become an integral part of the community culture, and members of the community help to define future priorities and distribute resources. It is democracy in action. Active participation is required of everyone who has an interest in the welfare of the community (Bureau of Justice Assistance, 1994c). It differs substantially from traditional models of policing and places considerable power and authority at the lowest level of the organization. Line officers and supervisors are the recipients of this significant shift of power and authority.

Empowerment

The characteristics of officers and supervisors operating in a community policing program cover a broad range of traits, including integrity, risk taking, originality, creativity, individuality, and problem solving. Every aspect of the organization must foster the development of these skills in its officers. The operational atmosphere must be such that traditional ways are challenged and new and innovative approaches are the rule rather than the exception. This is the only way the organization can respond to the need to promote public safety and enhance the quality of life in neighborhoods. Responding to changing crime problems requires flexibility and critical reasoning not only from the police organization, but also from each officer (Bureau of Justice Assistance, 1994a; Bureau of Justice Assistance, 2001).

Empowerment of line personnel and first-line supervisors is an essential ingredient of community policing. If it is missing, it is not really community policing even though it might involve some degree of citizen participation. It allows personnel to arrive at decisions based on delegated power and authority (Thompson, 1995). Empowerment is the conscious decision of senior management to create a cultural shift that allows officers to assume the power of self-direction. (Ramirez, 1999). It is the placing of authority and responsibility at the lowest levels of the organization. With supervisory support and the backing of top management, there is an absolute necessity to empower line officers so that initiative can be exercised when operating within the philosophy of community policing (Parks et al., 1999). It is a question of giving community policing officers the operational freedom needed to accomplish their assigned tasks. Achieving this is not for the faint of heart. Authority and power, normally the prerogative of the supervisor, must be relinquished, and line officers must be trained and assisted in the acquisition and application of new powers.

The exercise of judgment by the first-line supervisor calls for the development of superior skills when working to identify community resources that can be used to deal with a problem or assist an officer in developing a solution for a problem. Accessing other community resources is an added dimension of supervision and calls for a different capacity than that found under more traditional approaches to policing. It is a skill that a supervisor should acquire. Instead of making decisions, the supervisor coaches, supports, mediates, and helps officers in identifying, planning, analyzing, and solving community problems. Using such a process, supervisors foster a working environment that increases officer discretion (Cunningham, 1994). The goal is to get line personnel to function independently. This makes for a fluid and dynamic procedure in which there is an ongoing process of adjustment and readjustment between officers and the supervisor. As this process evolves, each line officer becomes more independent and more aware of what information the supervisor needs to make proper decisions regarding such things as the allocation of resources. As officers gain experience, they can become responsible decision makers. Supervisors should support this evolutionary process, which fosters the acquisition of abilities and skills that officers need to work effectively.

Community policing envisions the empowerment of officers (Bennett, 1995). It is a process in which officers are given the opportunity to take independent action to solve problems, work with members of the community, and strive to improve the social ecology of the neighborhoods. Of critical importance is the necessity for officers to become sensitive to the needs of members of the community. Empowerment is the opposite of a supervisor encouraging officers to "Just do what I tell you," "Stay out of trouble," or "Don't bother" their sergeant. Challenged with problems that do not respond to routine solutions, officers can be empowered by sergeants to search for imaginative solutions to problems rather than responding in rote fashion (Kelling, Wasserman, and Williams, 1988).

Trust is the sum and substance of leadership in an empowered organization. Officers become managers of their own destiny, and it is acknowledged that line officers have the capacity and ability to make operational decisions (Reiter, 1999). Additionally, the supervisor functions as a mentor, motivator, and facilitator. Obviously, all of this calls for a significant change in attitudes and methods of supervision. Constant and close supervision and the restriction of discretion are no longer the parameters of effective police supervision. The discretionary power of officers operating under the concept of community policing increases as they strive to achieve long-term problem reduction (Travis, 1996). The community police officer does not just take reports and pass on information so others in the chain of command can make decisions. Instead, the officer becomes a decision maker, solves the problem if possible, or at least participates in decisions leading to problem resolution (Meese, 1993).

When empowerment occurs, community policing flourishes. Significant decision making becomes the responsibility of line personnel and first-line supervisors rather than the sole property of police bureaucrats. Freedom is the essence. Unduly burdensome regulations, the hallmark of many police agencies, must be rejected if community policing is to have a chance of succeeding (De Paris, 1998). Superimposing community policing on a traditional organization is fraught with difficulty and presupposed failure. With the eradication of red tape and the elimination of delays, those who are really familiar with community problems have the power of real input based on their knowledge of the local environment (Cunningham, 1994). Under community policing, the first-line supervisor in some instances is confronted with the dilemma that not every officer wants to become involved to the extent required in order to function effectively in this collaborative approach to policing. Empowerment is rejected by some officers because with it comes the assumption of additional responsibility and the concomitant risk. The added accountability and the demands of becoming innovative can be unsettling to some. Other officers will embrace the concept of empowerment and find it rewarding even though it might involve the need to take risks.

Supervisors should work with reluctant employees in an effort to balance the interests of the organization and the officer. Every effort must be made to adequately retrain employees and help them to develop needed skills so they can feel comfortable with the demands of the newly acquired delegation of power. In some instances, it is a process of changing the culture and the structure of the organization. All of this takes time. Intensive training can turn a skeptic into a proponent. The goal is to create a working environment in which empowerment becomes a win-win-win proposition (Cunningham, 1994).

Quality Supervision

The need to work smarter becomes a reality when police departments are confronted with the implementation of a community policing program (Swope, 2000). The first-line supervisor takes center stage with the introduction of community policing into a department. Expectations are varied and include those set forth in Chapter 1. To these we must add the expectations of members of the public as they join forces with the police in an effort to recognize and resolve community problems. Above all, first-line supervisors must work at understanding the needs and perceptions of the public. This demands a constant interaction with members of the public to determine which services need enhancement and whether there is a need for new services (Wycoff and Skogan, 1993).

Figure 2.3 lists several activities a supervisor must engage in when working within the parameters of community policing. Some of these are discussed below. Quality supervision envisions shared decision making, teamwork, creativity, and innovation. It involves absolute commitment to the philosophy of community policing. The supervisor must personify the attributes of a facilitator, coach, role model, communicator, and coordinator if community policing is to succeed. Beyond this, every action that a supervisor performs must be taken within the context of complete honesty and integrity (Scarano and Jones, 2000).

Quality supervision occurs when first-line supervisors decipher management's intentions and translate them into reality. Under community policing, getting officers involved in this new approach is an exceptional challenge and takes skills not needed under more traditional approaches to managing people (Albright, 1997). This supervisory process demands that the sergeant receive the training needed to adequately evaluate each officer's needs, goals, abilities, and motivation level. Having accomplished this, the supervisor can delegate responsibility and authority accordingly. If the supervisor is to accomplish his or her job, higher management must give that individual a great deal of authority and autonomy. This will allow the sergeant to exercise necessary discretion when determining the degree to which officers should be involved in the decision-making process and the extent to which they are held responsible for their actions (Wiechmann, 1995).

Figure 2.3
Responsibilities of a First-Line Supervisor in Community Policing

1. Ensure the retention of beat integrity when solving problems.
2. Monitor the creation of beat profiles to ensure that they have identified critical problems.
3. Work with officers and community residents to create a system for the allocation and use of resources.
4. Work with officers and community members to develop, implement, and manage problem-solving systems.
5. Collaborate with other agencies to work together in solving community problems.
6. Depersonalize failure and judge events—not people.
7. Motivate personnel to serve as catalysts when dealing with and solving community problems.
8. Function as a process facilitator by providing officers with support and guidance, act as a liaison, and run interference when needed.
9. Encourage officers to take risks when solving problems.
10. Foster inventiveness when solving problems.
11. Represent the unit within the department.
12. Oversee the assessment of results.
13. Work with citizens to assess the results of their efforts.
14. Resolve and mediate conflict.
15. Create a working culture that emphasizes service.

Process Facilitation

The supervisor must convey the importance of community policing—especially in convincing police officers that community engagement and problem solving are *real* police work (Bureau of Justice Assistance, 1994a). If community policing is to succeed, the supervisor must genuinely support organizational changes. In some instances the change might include organizational structure, and at the very least it will include new service policies and procedures. It is essential to articulate and reinforce the philosophy of community policing. Supervisors must become knowledgeable about the duties expected of them. Initially, a supervisor might be unfamiliar with the working implications of the new service style. He or she must therefore make an effort to perform the role as expected (Wycoff and Oettmeier, 1994). In this respect, the goal is for the supervisor to become comfortable in the new role. As the supervisor loses power to subordinates, an effort must be made to assume more managerial responsibility. A first-line supervisor is a manager, and operationally, it is essential that the focus be shifted from the traditional role of being "in charge" to the role of facilitator (Wiechmann, 1995). The operational motto is facilitate-facilitate-facilitate.

As a supervisor becomes more skillful in functioning as a process facilitator, he or she will find that considerable time is spent in educating, informing, and assisting officers in understanding, prioritizing, and resolving issues (Jensen, Tegeler, and Quinn, 1994). A supervisor should accept the reality that some officers may resist the change to community policing. This must be expected, and the sergeant should work with these employees throughout the transition. Supervisors should keep in mind that community policing is a systematic view and that what might seem to be resistance might just be part of the process of adaptation. Radical change raises many questions, and a supervisor should be patient and deal with each and every objection as they arise. Officers who do not understand or who object to aspects of a proposed change can become obstructionists if they do not see how they fit into a new program and what will be required of them. A partnership with the officers must be entered into by allowing them to help identify needs and objectives (Anderson, 1999). The supervisor has to work hard at communicating, advising, responding to, and supporting officers who are having difficulty adjusting to the new policing style (Haught, 1998). Finally, as a process facilitator, a supervisor must communicate openly, become a team member, and encourage officers to participate actively in problem solving. In community policing, beat officers are viewed as a positive resource and every effort is made to tap into their skills. A supervisor should identify officers who have the knowledge, desire, and ability to carry out viable programs using the resources inside and outside the department (Arnold, 1998).

Case Study

Sergeant Roberta Gomez

Sergeant Roberta Gomez has been with the police department for eight years. She was initially assigned to patrol, where she stayed for five years. She later became a school resource officer. She has two uncles who are in law enforcement, and since she was in middle school she had wanted to become a police officer. In high school she participated actively in the local police department's ride-along program. Being fluent in Spanish, she receives a five percent pay increment for her fluency in this second language and serves as an interpreter as needed. She majored in law enforcement at the local community college and took the entry examination for the local police department as soon as she was eligible. She scored high enough to be selected for a new recruit class. She passed the background investigation without difficulty, as well as the psychiatric examination. She was so enthusiastic about police work and so dedicated that other officers readily accepted her. She has an outgoing personality, enjoys a good joke, and mixes well with other officers as well as with members of the community.

As soon as she was eligible, Gomez took the sergeant's test. After successfully passing the test, she was assigned as a team leader working out of a storefront as part of the initial promotion group. The team had two officers working each shift and support personnel consisting of two investigators, a school resource officer, a traffic officer, and a receptionist. Additionally, there is a representative of the city's Community Resources Division. Gang activity, graffiti, and vandalism plague the area served by the storefront. In the numerous middle-aged residential complexes, most residents do not know their neighbors. One complex had two carport fires, and residents blamed the homeless people living in the carports. Many of the residents fear gangs and drug dealers, and there is a definite lack of cohesiveness in the area.

As a start, Sergeant Gomez wants to create a working environment that maximizes officer initiative. In her own experience she has found that she has been most effective when she is given enough latitude to make decisions. She has always asked for help when needed, but she has found that the freedom from close supervision has allowed her to react more favorably to different incidents and events. All six of the officers working varying shifts were unknown to her, and as she started to create a foundation, she felt that it was imperative to become acquainted with each of them and begin to evaluate the problems confronting those working in the storefront.

If you were Sergeant Gomez, what would be the first thing you would do? Why? How would you go about creating a positive working environment? How would you integrate the activities of the support personnel into the team effort? How would you use the expertise of the representative of the Community Resources Division? What is the first problem you would address? Why? What information would you collect?

Building Partnerships within the Police Department

The vital responsibility of building partnerships has several dimensions, including serving as a conduit—relaying information up the chain of command, explaining problems, and finding the means for resolving them. Additionally, efforts to build partnerships within the department, as a task, provides the supervisor with an opportunity to explain how community policing works cooperatively with other units, as well as requesting assets needed to resolve problems. This includes resources such as traffic officers, detectives, patrol officers, juvenile investigators, or a narcotics unit. It also involves relaying information to other unit supervisors about criminal activities that would be of interest to them, mediating conflict between units, and integrating unit activities with others. This activity involves not only sharing information, but also a form of salesmanship in which the supervisor tries to secure the commitment of resources to implement effective problem-solving strategies (McElroy, Cosgrove, and Sadd, 1993). These efforts are needed to encourage a spirit of cooperation throughout the ranks and to foster the commitment of every officer to the community policing process (Stipak, Immer, and Clavadetscher, 1994).

Of special importance is the working relationship between patrol officers and detectives. Under community policing it is necessary to reduce the isolation between the two units. To accomplish this, some departments (45% of larger police departments) have assigned detectives to cases based on geographic areas/beats (Reaves and Goldberg, 1999). This clearly fosters and supports a working environment that allows for greater cooperation between the two entities. Officers can use neighborhood-based information for follow-up investigation, including the arrest of offenders (Meese, 1993). Information that was not available before will become available because of the continuing and constant contact between community police officers and members of the community. A supervisor should strive to draw upon the experience of successful officers and detectives and use their proven expertise when initiating programs that involve cooperative efforts (Safir, 1997). The supervisor should ensure that detectives give feedback to the officers when information results in the successful conclusion of an investigation. This reinforces the relationship between the two groups and motivates officers to continue to provide information. When one looks at all sizes of local police departments, as of 1999, there were 91,072 full-time sworn personnel designated as community policing officers (Hickman and Reaves, 2001). For example, in Birmingham 25 officers have been appointed as community policing specialists. This means that the preponderance of the officers serve as generalists who concentrate heavily on 911 calls. It is in this area where the supervisor can work at coordinating activities and advising other supervisors about what is being done and relaying information between the two entities (Parks et al., 1999). When possible, generalist officers can support the problem-solving activities of specialists. It is possible to describe the relationship between specialized units of a police agency and the officers responsible for community policing by means of a medical model (Meese, 1993):

[T]he patrol officer in a specific neighborhood or beat area is like a general practitioner physician who has the principal interface with the individual citizen. Surrounding and supporting the police general practitioner is a series of specialists—detectives, juvenile investigators, narcotics officers, headquarters staff officers, and others—who are available for consultation or referral.

It is this medical model that the first-line supervisor should foster and cultivate. The line officer remains the key to community policing, and all other units should support problem-solving efforts. Institutionalization of this model is essential to success, and it can flourish with unified responses to underlying factors that characterize true problem-oriented policing.

Collaboration

The basic doctrine of community policing is to work with other government and community-based organizations in order to develop a wide variety of resources needed to resolve identifiable community problems (Correia, 2000). Employing external resources may range from making a referral to another agency to actually asking another agency to participate in a cooperative effort. Figure 2.4 lists several potential public and private resources. Identifying available and pertinent resources is a major phase in the development of a positive problem-solving program. If a department is fortunate enough, it will have a resource manual listing agencies, contact persons, and brief synopses of the services offered by the agencies (Bureau of Justice Assistance, 1993a). First-line supervisors should begin by contacting government and private agencies to collect information and develop responses to problems. Or, if required, ask a commanding officer to make official contact. This allows supervisors to screen and identify viable agencies and reduces the number of individuals who are contacting other agencies. In fact, in some communities, agencies encourage contact by appointed individuals.

Liaison and follow-up activities are essential if collaboration is to be effective. This is true both for units within the police organization and for other city departments. Monitoring follow-up requests is mandatory, and if the problems are not addressed within a reasonable time, the first-line supervisor should stimulate the needed response and provide feedback to line officers on accomplishments or progress made toward addressing crime and disorder problems (Community Policing Consortium, 2000). This function is critical to community policing because it proves that something can happen when citizens complain. It also directly affects the credibility of the line officer as well as that of the police department (Meese, 1993). Other city agencies have been especially effective at removing abandoned vehicles, enforcing parking regulations, enforcing building codes, and demolishing vacant buildings. They can also control vendors and eliminate hazardous conditions on private property. One police department obtained the permission of owners of abandoned buildings (by working with the department of building and safety) to enter each building and evict trespassers prior to the demolition of the buildings. In another instance, a city housing department actively helped apartment owners obtain loans to rehabilitate property, thus improving the quality of housing and setting a new standard for the community. The landlord training program emphasizes cooperation among property owners, tenants, and law enforcement agencies to help neighborhoods fight drug-related crime. The landlord program involves a commitment to substantive problem solving and to building and sustaining effective community partnerships (Bureau of Justice Assistance, 2000). Other examples include the Albuquerque Police Department, which set up an interagency team to enforce city codes against delinquent properties (Lesce, 1995). In California the civil eviction process has been used to evict drug dealers and gang members (Bessinger, 1997).

Figure 2.4
Potential Collaborative Agencies and Organizations

Agencies Serving the Elderly	Neighborhood Associations
Big Brothers/Big Sisters	Parent/Teacher Associations
Boards of Education	Parole Agencies
Boys & Girls Clubs	Police Departments
Businesses	Public Defender's Office
Chambers of Commerce	Probation Office
City or County Councils	Property Management Associations
Civic Clubs	Prosecutor's Office
Community Centers	Probation Office
Correctional Facilities	Public Libraries
Counseling Services	School Officials
Credit Reporting Agencies	Social Clubs
Federal Agencies	Social Services
Fraternal Organizations	Sheriff's Departments
Health Services	State Police
Homeowners' Associations	Taxpayer Groups
Housing Authorities	Teachers
Judicial System	Tenants' Groups
Legal Services	Transit Companies
Local United Way	Veterans' Groups
Local Utility Companies	Victim Services Agencies
Mayor or County Executives	YMCA/YWCA
Mediation Centers	Youth Groups
Merchants' Associations	Women's/Men's Clubs

Source: National Crime Prevention Council (1994). *National Service and Public Safety: Partnerships for Safer Communities*. Washington, DC: National Crime Prevention Council. Reprinted with permission. Bureau of Justice Assistance (1994c). *Working as Partners with Community Groups, Community Partnerships*. Washington, DC: Office of Justice Programs.

Supervisors can reinforce collaborative problem solving by monitoring officers' efforts. Members of other agencies can be contacted to determine how well subordinates have performed in a collaborative effort. If the supervisor finds the officer has functioned poorly, the officer should be assisted and given guidance to resolve the problem (Bureau of Justice Assistance, 1994c). If the feedback is positive, this information should be relayed to the officers involved.

Working in partnership with community members and organizations is an effective and productive way to address neighborhood problems and needs (Aragon and Adams, 1997). A partnership involves law enforcement agencies working with various groups based on equality. This means breaking new ground and developing skills in collaboration. For some, the community represents naysayers, police bashers, busybodies, vigilantes, or police wannabes. If community policing is to work, these cliches must be rejected and members of the community must be allowed to become involved in the problem identification procedure (Graves, 2000). Potential partners come from groups who are directly affected by a problem, those who must deal with the problem, and those who would benefit if the problem did not exist. This can mean a wide range of groups ranging from service organizations to tenants' groups, and parent-teacher associations. A partnership is not something that happens automatically. It can take time and sometimes a great deal of effort to overcome the opposition of those who are skeptical and certainly those who are hostile. Possibly the only way to overcome this is a combination of time, example, and word-of-mouth (Bureau of Justice Assistance, 1994c).

Community policing partnership requires residents who are active at the community level to select problems and develop and implement strategies. But partnerships also require that the community have a say at the jurisdictional level where the conditions of the partnership are set. A feeling of community can be generated by allowing the citizens of an area to actually define what constitutes their neighborhood (Mittleman, 2000). Without give-and-take when establishing the guidelines of collaboration, partnerships will reflect the needs and concerns of police departments rather than those of the neighborhood partners. Figure 2.5 is a Community Enhancement Request Form that an officer may use to request specific services from city agencies to handle conditions that may result in crime or community decay.

The police should be working very consciously in partnership with those who are affected by the problems and who are working or will work with their neighbors to solve them. In one study it was found that nearly all agencies met with various community groups during the year. The largest percentages met with school groups (76%), followed by neighborhood associations (52%), business groups (50%), senior citizen groups (45%), and domestic violence groups (41%) (Hickman and Reaves, 2001). There are two reasons for focusing on those who are organized. First, a collective community is more likely to be sustained and successful in solving problems than

Figure 2.5
Los Angeles Police Department Community Enhancement Request Form

City Police Department
COMMUNITY ENHANCEMENT REQUEST

❑ Citizen Request   Date & Time Rec'd/Obs'd
❑ Business Request
❑ Officer Initiated

PERSON REPORTING SECTION
(Leave Blank When Officer-Initiated)

Last Name, First, Middle

Residence Address   Zip

Business Address   Zip

Residence Phone No.   Business Phone No.
(   )   (   )

Location of Activity/Problem   RD   Area

Completing Officer   Serial No.

TYPE OF REQUEST FOR SERVICE

Department of Building and Safety:
❑ Abandoned/junked vehicle on private property
❑ Unkempt conditions on private property
❑ Hazardous conditions on private property
❑ Vacant buildings/houses
❑ Vendors on private property/parking lots
❑ Other (Explain in information section below)
Department of Transportation:
❑ Abandoned vehicles on street
❑ Parking enforcement
❑ Other (Explain in information section below)
Department of Public Works (Street Maintenance):
❑ Street repair
❑ Sidewalk repair
❑ Tree trimming
❑ Vacant lot cleanup
❑ Street lighting
❑ Graffiti
❑ Other (Explain in information section below)
Department of Public Works (Sanitation):
❑ Trash collection (street/sidewalk/parkway)
❑ Other (Explain in information section below)
Police Department (Confidential):
❑ Gang Activity
❑ Drinking in public
❑ Other (Explain in information section below)
Other City Department

_____

Additional Information_____
_____
_____

SUPERVISOR/OFFICER MAKING REQUEST

Name   Serial   Date

CITY DEPARTMENT NOTIFIED

Department   Time

Employee   Ph. Ext.

FOLLOW-UP INFORMATION

Date   City Employee   Ph. Ext.

Findings:_____
_____
_____
_____
_____
_____

If the complaint was initiated by a citizen,
was the original PR contacted?
          ❑ Yes   ❑ No

Was the PR satisfied with the response to the
complaint?
          ❑ Yes   ❑ No

Comments of PR (optional):_____
_____
_____
_____
_____
_____

Source: Los Angeles Police Department (2001). *Community Enhancement Request Form*. Los Angeles, CA: Los Angeles Police Department. Reprinted with permission.

individual efforts. Second, an organized effort is more likely to continue after the problem is solved. The emphasis on working with residents who are organized does not mean that law enforcement agencies should stop responding to individual calls or refuse to work with people. It means that for community policing to be an effective crime-fighting strategy, there must be an emphasis on partners who can help produce long-term crime reduction. It means that where these partnerships do not exist or are weak, there must be an investment in creating or strengthening them. Partnerships are clearly something other than name only, or simply routine, temporary working arrangements. True community partnerships, involving sharing power and decision making, are rare at this time, found in only a few of the flagship departments. Other jurisdictions have begun to lay foundations for true partnerships, and the trust needed for power sharing and joint decision making should emerge.

Problem Solving

A key characteristic of the modern approach to policing is a positive orientation to problem solving. It involves more than responding to 911 calls. It is a matter of viewing incidents from a community perspective to resolve the problem—not just *handling* an incident.

Problem-oriented policing shifts police efforts from a reactive to a proactive response to crime, in which officers work with residents to prevent crime (Police Executive Research Forum, 1996).

Citizens, police departments, and other agencies work together to identify problems and apply appropriate problem-solving strategies (Rabkin, 1995). This approach emerged in the late 1970s and was initially described by Herman Goldstein. It was his position that the police should be concerned with the problems that were of concern to residents of a community (Goldstein, 1990). The central thesis of problem-oriented policing is that underlying incidents that police respond to are more general problems that, in order to be resolved, require a different type of response than do the incidents that are indicative of the problems. Problem solving requires analysis of the incidents by people knowledgeable about the context in which they are occurring, followed by creative brainstorming about, and experimentation with, possible responses (Wycoff and Skogan, 1993). While problem-oriented policing theoretically can be conducted in the absence of community-oriented policing, it is an excellent method of achieving the goals of community-oriented policing. This is why the model that is proposed in this chapter combines both—Community-Oriented Policing and Problem Solving (COPPS).

This process is a proactive philosophy that promotes the concept that incidents consuming patrol and investigative time can best be dealt with more effectively when consideration is given to underlying problems. It also assumes that the expertise and creativity of line officers are reliable sources when developing solutions to problems. Finally, if problem solving in the community is to be successful, the police must work with the public to ensure that they are addressing the real needs of citizens.

Detectives and line officers are those who can use the problem-solving approach. It allows them to continuously identify, analyze, and respond to the underlying causes prompting citizens to request police services. It is not a one-shot project or program, but a comprehensive process for identifying, addressing, and resolving problems. It is a strategy consisting of four stages, called **SARA** (Spelman and Eck, 1987; Wolfer, Baker, and Zezza, 1999):

> **SCANNING**—Identifying the problem;
> **ANALYSIS**—Learning the problem's causes, scope, and effects;
> **RESPONSE**—Acting to alleviate the problem; and
> **ASSESSMENT**—Determining whether the response worked.

In a recent study, it was determined that 55 percent of agencies surveyed who had more than 100 officers actively encouraged patrol officers to engage in SARA-type problem solving, and 65 percent formed problem-solving partnerships through contracts/written agreements, with community groups, local agencies, or others (Reaves and Goldberg 1999).

Once a problem is identified, actions can be taken to collect information about the problem. This in turn leads to a detailed analysis of the information. The final stage shows whether the actions had the desired effect on the problems.

Scanning

Instead of relying on legal terms such as robbery, burglary, or petty theft to guide a response, officers analyze specific offenses in a broader context and address them as problems. These problems are then dealt with according to their impact on the neighborhood or on the community. For example, a police incident such as auto theft might be a part of a "chop" operation (cutting up an automobile into salable or usable parts). A series of house burglaries might in reality be a school truancy problem.

Scanning initiates the problem-solving process. In a truly problem-oriented police department, every member scans for problems and brings the problem to the attention of a supervisor. With everyone involved, one cannot assume that it is someone else's responsibility. In other words, passing the buck becomes somewhat limited. Some officers are better than others at identifying problems; some accept the new process as a challenge, and others find it is extra work, to be avoided at all costs. Other officers are reluctant to identify problems because they might be stuck with working on the problem (Eck and Spelman, 1987). Over time, objections such as those mentioned above can be overcome as officers become more accustomed to the problem-solving process. The objectives of the scanning process include:

- Looking for problems.

- Initial identification of possible problems.

- Initial analysis to determine if the problem exists and whether a detailed analysis is needed.

- Prioritizing of problems and assignment of personnel.

Agency personnel have numerous sources that can be used to identify problems, but in many instances officers will initially rely on their own experience to identify problems. Most officers are cautious about announcing the identification of a problem until they truly feel that a problem actually exists. This usually means that problems have been rejected before bringing the problem to the attention of others. In addition, crime prevention surveys can provide information on criminal behavior, such as the exact times and kinds of offenses committed, the offender's methods of operation, the targets of attack, crime generators, and "hot spot" locations. Follow-up crime surveys can identify some of the causes of crime and aid in the elimination of crime opportunities (Wolfer, Baker, and Zezza, 1999). Environmental surveys can also be used effectively by assessing as systematically and objectively as possible the overall physical environment of an area. The physical environment comprises the buildings, parks, streets, transportation facilities, and overall landscaping of an area, as well as the functions and conditions of these entities. With this data, an officer can focus on determining how the physical environment affects the social environment. In other words, an officer might want to find out how features of the physical environment contribute to crime and disorder by facilitating offenders and inhibiting nonoffenders.

Analysis

After identifying the problem, the officers assigned should collect information from every source related to the problem. This includes private as well as public sources. For example, it can include information from neighborhood associations and neighborhood watch groups. Other sources include elected officials or the news media, as well as information from other law enforcement or government agencies. Officers can use a checklist to ensure that all the needed information is collected. The three areas of concern include:

- actors involved in the problem, including victims and offenders;

- specific incidents, including the sequence of events;

- physical contact involved in the incidents; and

- responses by the community and institutional entities.

Figure 2.6
Checklist for Problem Analysis

ACTORS		
	Victim's Lifestyle	Security measures taken
		Victimization history
		This victimization
	Offenders	Identity and physical description
		Lifestyle, education, employment history, medical history
		Criminal history
	Third parties	Personal data
		Connection to victimization
		Nature of involvement
		Expectations for police action
INCIDENTS		
	Sequence of events	Target of act
		Type of tools used by offenders
		Events preceding act
		Event itself
		Events following criminal act
	Physical contact	Chronology
		Location
		Access control
		Surveillance
	Social context	Likelihood and probable actions of witnesses
		Attitude of residents toward neighborhood
RESPONSES		
	Community	Neighborhood affected by problem
		City as a whole
		People outside the city
		Groups
	Institutional	Criminal justice agencies
		Other public agencies
		Mass media
		Business sector

Adapted from William Spelman and John E. Eck (1987). *Problem-Oriented Policing.* Washington, DC: National Institute of Justice.

All the information gathered serves as a foundation for developing a thorough understanding of what is finally determined to be the real problem. This serves as a base for identifying causes and developing options for resolution. The checklist reminds officers of areas and topics open to consideration.

Implicit in the list are potential sources of information that might not have been covered under the *scanning* part of the assessment process. During *analysis*, emphasis is given to external information sources, such as consulting with citizens, business leaders, community associations, and other community groups. Another source in the analysis stage is the environmental survey that, along with other information, can lead to an understanding of conditions contributing to a problem. By measuring the physical environment of a drug-ridden area, for example, a survey may illustrate a connection between low lighting and overgrown bushes and the inability of local residents to keep watch over the area (Bureau of Justice Administration, 1993b).

One of the best sources developed in recent years is the Community Policing Consortium, which can be accessed at <www.communitypolicing.org>. This allows the officer to determine what is being done in other agencies by going to the consortium home page and clicking on *Resources*. Additionally, a review of problem-solving strategies and success stories can be found by clicking on *Publications*. One of the most helpful documents is the *Information Access Guide*, which is updated quarterly and lists contact information for individuals and organizations that have contributed to the numerous publications of the consortium.

When using the checklist, officers will not normally collect information from all of the sources listed, but only from those directly related to the problem they are dealing with. Another qualifier is the time the officer has available to search for an appropriate response to the problem under consideration (Eck and Spelman, 1987). There is a tendency for officers to identify the response to the problem before completing the analysis. If and when this occurs, options might be eliminated from consideration.

Response

This stage requires initiative by the officer as different solutions are identified and the best solution is selected and implemented. Involving outside agencies with resources and expertise seldom available within the police agency increases the number of potential solutions to a problem. This stage involves working with individuals, businesses, and private agencies. It also requires the officer to work with public agencies such as the probation department, health department, public works, and social services. All of these sources are important because other agencies and entities can come up with responses that fall outside of the normal expertise of law enforcement agencies. Combined resources can prove to be the most effective response to the problem being studied. Officers striving to find a solution to a problem should have a free rein for discovering the answer. In one city, the only restriction was that the solution had to be legally, financially, administratively, and politically possible (Spelman and Eck, 1987). It should also be pointed out that an environmental survey could guide responses to crime problems. A survey may shed light on activities within an open-air market where drugs are sold by drawing attention to the market's street design. In this instance, the response could be to work with city planners on redesigning the street to change traffic flow and accessibility (Bureau of Justice Assistance, 1993a).

Solutions to problems can be organized into five potential responses. The most desirable, but sometimes not attainable, is to totally eradicate a problem. This generally occurs when the problem is relatively small, has occurred recently, and affects a limited number of people. This could be as simple as congestion caused by the removal of a stop sign or having too few trash receptacles in a recently renovated neighborhood park.

In the second group of solutions, action taken by the police and members of the community can materially reduce a problem. These are generally found to be neighborhood crimes and disorder problems. Such a solution usually involves persistent problems. The fact that they have been around for some time is evidence that they are unlikely to be eliminated. Examples include such problems as robbery, burglary, vandalism, drug dealing, and prostitution.

The third group of solutions can most often be applied to problems where it is almost impossible to reduce the number of incidents they create but where it is possible to alter the characteristics of these incidents. These may be problems created by behavior that has unintended harmful affects. For example, officers may look for ways to reduce killings and injuries resulting from gambling among residents—the gambling is not stopped or reduced, but some of the resulting harm is reduced.

Group three solutions can be used in combination with other types of solutions. For example, group three solutions may be used to deal with commercial robberies or rapes by showing potential victims how to act to minimize the chances of being killed or injured during an incident.

Figure 2.7
Possible Solutions to Problems

1. Total problem elimination.
2. Material reduction of the problem.
3. Reduction of the harm caused by the problem.
4. Dealing with the problem with the best possible solution.
5. Removal of the problem from police consideration.

Group four solutions are generally applied to problems that are jurisdiction-wide and involve larger social concerns. For these problems, improving the way in which difficulties are handled may be the best solution in the short run. Over a much longer period, the solution, combined with other social changes, may reduce the problem. Examples include such problems as runaway juveniles, drug addiction and abuse, drunk driving, and elder abuse.

Finally, group five solutions are likely to be applied to problems that have been created by specific businesses or groups as a by-product of their ways of operating. Examples might include stores that arrest shoplifters but consistently fail to prosecute (Eck and Spelman, 1987). As a result, the problem is no longer of concern to the police.

When a solution becomes apparent, implementation should occur immediately or incrementally, depending on the circumstances. Some problems are solved immediately, because they are minor in nature or involve only a few people. Other solutions might involve broad social issues that require a complex response.

Assessment

Assessment is the final stage and involves measuring how well the program performed. Was it effective? The agency and the community work together to answer these questions. The initial analysis may have been flawed, or the wrong response may have been selected. The process of assessment can provide an officer with the information needed to determine success. For some situations, assessment is quite simple and the results are obvious. In other situations, it is complex and may involve the collection of a great deal of data. Surveys are becoming increasingly common, and among the possible objectives a police department might have are the following (Weisel, 1999):

- Evaluation of victimization—differences between reported offenses and actual victimization by individual characteristics such as race, gender, age, and income.

- Comparison of local victimization rates with those of other jurisdictions.

- Measures of citizen willingness to report crime.

- Indicators of citizen fearfulness.

- Analysis of crime and disorder problems.

- Measures of police performance—survey can measure citizen knowledge and attitudes; satisfaction reflects how well the police are doing their job from the citizens' perspective.

- Measures of public information efforts.

- Comparison of a jurisdiction's community policing efforts—and impact on victimization—with those of other jurisdictions.

Community surveys can be designed to provide the police with reliable feedback from citizens about police performance. The Office of Community Oriented Policing Services (COPS) and the Bureau of Justice Statistics (BJS) have developed a software package that includes a standardized community survey that can be administered by telephone. The entire question-naire can be obtained at no cost and addresses the following basic but crit-ical issues:

- Why are we doing a survey, and what do we want to know?

- What kind of resources and commitment do we have for this effort?

- Who should be surveyed and how?

- How many people should be surveyed?

- What do we do with the responses to the survey?

The software package includes a survey guide and a technical manual. It provides an overview of key issues involved in conducting survey research. It includes some basic "do's and don'ts" for conducting surveys that can withstand close scrutiny. To provide feedback about the community, a contractor conducts an annual citizen satisfaction survey to assess service delivery. The questionnaire can be obtained at <www.scottsdaleaz.gov>. This telephone sur-vey queries approximately 400 citizens through a random-digit dialing approach (Weisel, 1999).

Surveys can be used for a variety of purposes. For example, they are use-ful in gathering data on specific problems in target neighborhoods or among special populations. In Newport News, Virginia, a survey of residents in an apartment complex revealed concerns about the maintenance and physical structure of the complex. In Maryland, Baltimore County officers routine-ly use surveys to diagnose community problems confronted by special problem-solving units. In Los Angeles, a survey instrument was used to measure the effectiveness of a Model Neighborhood Program (Kerstein, 2001). In other communities, surveys have been used to help define com-munity concerns about drug problems. Special populations—the elderly, schoolchildren, women, minority groups, and others—can also be surveyed to learn their special concerns. When evaluating a problem-solving program, multiple surveys can prove to be most effective. For example, before-and-after surveys can be used to determine changes in citizen's fear of crime as a result of police intervention. Problem-solving units of the Baltimore County Police Department routinely use this technique to gauge their effec-tiveness (Bureau of Justice Assistance, 1993b).

Another area in which surveys are useful is recording and analyzing the environmental characteristics of a problem area. They help an officer ana-lyze the nature of a problem by identifying what factors contribute to crime and pointing to incivilities in the problem area. Used before and after implementing a problem-solving effort, environmental surveys enable the officer to measure the effectiveness of the effort (Bureau of Justice Assis-tance, 1993a). During a 12-month period, nearly one-half of the departments studied (with 100 or more sworn personnel) surveyed citizens regarding their satisfaction with police services (51%) and their perceptions of crime prob-lems (45%) (Reaves and Hart, 2000).

The values of community policing are different from those practiced under the traditional response to crime. Expressed organizational values can serve as the basis for citizens understanding the police function in a democracy. The problem-solving process can be used to reinforce the values of the police department and the community, and has proven to be an effective tool for law enforcement. Community policing involves giving officers greater control over their working conditions. This requires a new style of supervision. The authoritarian supervision style is unacceptable. No longer is it permissible to give an order and expect an officer to respond with absolute obedience.

Supervising Community Police Officers

There are many intrinsic rewards for officers who work in a problem-solving police department. An officer has greater control over the work performed, in addition to increased responsibility and a higher degree of autonomy. The most significant feature is the increased involvement of line officers in the decision-making process. All of these lead to improved job satisfaction (Bureau of Justice Assistance, 1993a). A community supervisor's typical day is set forth in Figure 2.8, which lists tasks performed. Supervisors can provide expertise needed to identify and solve neighborhood problems or provide assistance to residents (McElroy, Cosgrove, and Sadd, 1993). A supervisor can also help officers to manage their available time so they might adequately handle problems. Some agencies authorize first-line supervisors to schedule flex time, permitting officers to amend their work hours as necessary and balance demands between calls for service and problem solving. Some departments allow officers to consult with other officers and a supervisor to work cooperatively by changing days off or changing schedules to help in addressing a problem (Wycoff and Skogan, 1993).

Computer software is available that materially helps a supervisor by forecasting officer and vehicle needs by beat and neighborhood, generating alternative officer schedules that optimize services, and redesigning beats to optimally balance workloads and communities. Additionally, this software can automatically detect and rank problems by geographical area and tie them to demographics, crime reports, patterns, and known offenders (Analysis Central Systems, 1994).

Supervisors will normally meet with officers at daily briefings to discuss scheduling, personnel problems, problem-solving techniques, resources, and other matters of mutual interest. Sergeants should spend most of their time working with officers in the neighborhoods. This allows them to become familiar not only with the neighborhoods, but also with the problems facing the officers, so help can be provided as needed.

Successful community policing requires the supervisor to relay information up the chain of command about problem-solving efforts as well as requests for resources. It is also an excellent time to reinforce the importance of community policing by indicating its contributions to the attainment of departmental goals.

Figure 2.8
A Community Supervisor's Typical Day

In addition to responding to calls for service where backup is needed, a typical day might include:

1. Along with the beat officer, meeting with a tenants' group about vandalism in the complex.
2. Preparing the weekly work schedule.
3. Meeting with the health department about a sanitation problem in one of the neighborhoods.
4. Briefing command personnel on needed resources to deal with community problems.
5. Preparing a performance evaluation for one of the officers.
6. Upon request, working with an officer in analyzing school truancy and acquiring census data regarding a neighborhood juvenile vandalism problem.
7. Reviewing officer-initiated contacts with one of the members of the team.
8. Personal time (meals, coffee breaks).

Managing Failure

The first-line supervisor must manage in a casual manner. Community policing is new ground, and problem solving is a new technique. It is not uncommon for mistakes to precede innovative results. In the struggle to resolve problems, officers will make mistakes and proposed solutions will fail. When risks are taken and innovative solutions are sought, the margin for error increases dramatically as officers proceed through the learning curve. Managing and controlling failure can result in positive results. Supervisors have to develop an attitude of tolerance and accept honest failure (Wycoff and Skogan, 1993). Management of the total department begins with the attitude that positive failures can become the power that propels the organization toward the attainment of goals.

Looking for a "fall guy" must be rejected out of hand. When failure occurs, the supervisor should work with the officer and document the reasons for failure. Circulation of this information to all interested parties is an essential part of the learning process. This critique process will undoubtedly identify training needs or other errors subject to correction. The supervisor should arrange for additional training or provide feedback in order to reduce future errors. A teamwork philosophy should replace power-oriented supervision and emphasize an atmosphere of risk taking, creativity, and the acceptance of errors in decision making. When managing failure, you must engage in a course of depersonalizing the failure and judging the actual event rather than the involved individual. When this is done, failure can be turned into a positive occurrence. Failure should lead to growth, not recriminations or discipline. It should be a learning process by which a search can begin for identifying the reasons for failure, sharing that information with others, and searching for a solution that benefits the department and the community.

Summary

Community policing is fast becoming a means of operation for many police departments. Former President Bill Clinton championed it, and it became political patronage of the highest order. The Community Policing Consortium has extolled its virtues. Some 55 percent of eligible law enforcement agencies requested and received at least one federal grant under the program. It is a philosophy of policing in which officers work closely with citizens to identify and deal with neighborhood problems. The police actually become a part of the community culture in order to promote public safety and enhance the quality of life in neighborhoods. Only time will tell if community policing becomes more dominant in police circles.

Management can reinforce the prospects of community policing having a reasonable chance to succeed by considering a wide range of factors, including sharing power and accepting mistakes as part of the learning process.

Every aspect of the law enforcement organization must foster the development of skills that support the empowerment of officers performing community-policing duties. Empowerment of line personnel and first-line supervisors is an essential ingredient of community policing. It permeates the entire organization and is the conscious decision of the chief executive officer to allow others to assume decision-making power. The first-line supervisor must function as a mentor, motivator, and facilitator. Achieving this task is not easy. Power and authority must be relinquished. When such empowerment occurs, community policing flourishes.

The supervisor should articulate the philosophy of community policing through every action. This involves communicating openly, becoming a team member, and encouraging officers to solve community problems. The supervisor must genuinely support this new philosophy.

All supervisors must become familiar with a wide variety of resources that can help in the process of problem solving. First-line supervisors should initiate direct contact with government and private agencies to ask for a cooperative effort. The process of collaboration clearly enhances the potential for success.

In community policing, officers have greater control over decision making, a higher degree of autonomy, and additional responsibility. Supervisors can help officers by managing their available time to allow them to handle problems and meeting with officers frequently to discuss scheduling, personnel problems, available resources, and problem-solving techniques. Above all, supervisors must work at understanding the needs and perceptions of the public. Quality supervision occurs when first-line supervisors decipher management's intentions and translate them into reality. The supervisor has to shift gears from being in charge to being a facilitator.

It is essential that supervisors accept the vital responsibility of building partnerships within the police department. This includes serving as a conduit—relaying information up the chain of command, explaining problems, and finding ways to resolve them. Additionally, supervisors should reinforce the collaborative problem-solving process by monitoring the effort of officers.

A key element of community policing is the emphasis on problem solving—a comprehensive process for identifying, addressing, and resolving problems. It is a strategy consisting of four parts (SARA): scanning, analysis, response, and assessment. It is a unique approach to dealing with community problems, because it draws on the experience of actual working personnel, other agencies, and members of the public (as individuals or collectively). The response to problems is found in five groups of solutions that range from total elimination of the problem to removing the problem from police consideration.

In recent years, agencies have become adept at conducting various types of surveys, ranging from environmental to gathering data on specific problems. Other areas where surveys can prove to be viable include measuring citizen fearfulness, analysis of crime and disorder problems, and citizen willingness to report crimes. Consideration should be given to using community surveys prepared by the federal government.

Finally, supervisors must learn to manage failure and turn it into a positive learning experience. When risks are taken and creativity is used, failures should be expected. Failure management is a process of depersonalizing failure and judging the event rather than the individual.

Case Study

Sergeant Jeremy Braum

Sergeant Jeremy Braum is a seven-year veteran of the Trinity Police Department. The law enforcement agency serves a city with a diverse population of 242,000 consisting of 53 percent white, six percent black, and 29 percent Mexican-American, with the remainder being Asian and Native American. Until about 10 years ago, the number of Mexican-Americans in the community was limited, but in recent years the size of this ethnic group has increased dramatically as they have come to the community to work in meatpacking sheds. Many of the newcomers have limited English skills, and they have taxed the health, school, and welfare systems. Policing in the areas dominated by Mexicans has proven to be difficult because of the language barrier, but during the last two years the department has made a serious effort to recruit bilingual officers.

The city is the rail transportation center for the region. An interstate highway bisects it and there is a regional airport. Additionally, the city is the shopping center for the area, and there are numerous recreational activities that attract visitors. The city also has a university with an enrollment of 13,500 that holds numerous cultural events throughout the year.

The police department has 372 sworn officers and 152 civilian employees. The major units are field operations, administration, and investigations. The crime rate is about that of similar-sized cities, and during the last four years the violent crime rate has dropped 11 percent and property crimes have decreased by nine percent. The primary drop in the crime rate occurred in the middle- and upper-class sections of the city, while there has been a small increase of crime in the less affluent sections of the city.

The department has decided to initiate a community policing pilot program in an area that has 83,199 residents and 12 beats. The officers have completed a community policing training program, and they have all volunteered to participate in the pilot program. Sergeant Braum recently completed a problem-solving course taught at a regional police academy. He has been assigned to the pilot program to work with the beat officers in identifying patterns and using the SARA model. It has been anticipated that an emphasis will be placed on the examination of geographical, cultural, and economic aspects of hot-spot locations, along with the relationship between the victim and the offender.

If you were Sergeant Braum, what goals would you establish for the program? Why? Who would you involve in problem identification? What type of data would you collect from the department? What type of data would you collect from other city departments and community sources? How would you measure program success?

Key Concepts

actors	partnerships
analysis	problem solving
assessment	process facilitation
collaboration	quality supervision
community enhancement	response
community policing success	risk taking
empowerment	scanning
environmental surveys	sequence of events
incidents	social context
institutional	supervisory techniques
managing failure	third parties
offenders	victims

Discussion Topics and Questions

1. Discuss how one can ensure that community policing will be successful.

2. Why is empowerment important to community policing?

3. What is distinctive about quality supervision?

4. Discuss how process facilitation works.

5. Identify six responsibilities of a first-line supervisor in community policing.

6. How does a supervisor build partnerships with detectives in a police department?

7. Why is collaboration important?

8. Discuss how a supervisor manages failure.

9. How should a supervisor implement problem solving?

10. List five municipal agencies that can be called upon to help solve community problems.

11. List the four stages of SARA.

12. Discuss the use of environmental surveys in problem solving.

For Further Reading

Mittleman, Pete (2000). "Community Policing: Building Community Trust Thinking Outside of the Box." *The Police Chief*, Vol. LXVII, No. 3.

Describes the changes made in the department when community policing was implemented, including a consideration of decentralization and the provision of personalized police services. The organizational hierarchy was flattened and first-line supervisors were empowered to create a team respond to community problems. The author reviews the implementation of the community policing program, including problem-oriented policing. Consideration is given to the importance of accountability as a cornerstone of community policing. Stress is placed on the need to involve the whole department in the community policing effort.

Parks, Roger B., Stephen D. Mastrofski, Christina Dejong, and M. Kevin Gray (1999). "How Officers Spend Their Time with the Community." *Justice Quarterly*, Vol. 16, No. 3.

Using data from field observations of working line officers in two cities, similarities and differences were identified between the performance of generalist line officers and community policing specialists. The two cities studied were Indianapolis, Indiana, and St. Petersburg, Florida. The study found that community policing specialists spent less time in encounters with citizens and more time on problem solving and personal activities. The authors present data on the types of encounters and the assignment of the officers, including a consideration of citizen roles in encounters, including *problem citizens*.

Swope, Ross E. (2000). "Measuring Success." *The Police Chief,* Vol. LXVII, No. 3.

> Describes how to use program evaluation as a means of showing which plans, tactics, and initiatives have been successful. A description is provided of how a first-line supervisor addresses the concerns of residents about an open-air drug market at a specific intersection. Lists the goals of a recommended intervention, including a consideration of such things as the reduction of loitering on the corner and the reduction of fear among residents. Describes empirical indicators that can be used to measure success and reviews data sources.

Trojanowicz, Robert, Victor E. Kappeler, and Larry K. Gaines (2001). *Community Policing: A Contemporary Perspective*, Third Edition. Cincinnati, OH: Anderson.

> This book contains sections ranging from theory and definition of community policing to the actual duties of the officer, and how to evaluate officers. The discussion of theory is especially useful if one is to understand the concepts underlying community policing. Of special interest is the section on supervision, which includes a wide range of topics such as: internal functions, sources of resistance, external relationships, and measurable activities performed by a first-line supervisor. The section on sources of resistance will prove useful when a supervisor is involved in the implementation of community policing. The authors review the past and future of community policing and have included numerous problem-solving cases.

References

Albright, Mary (1997). *101 Biggest Mistakes Managers Make and How to Avoid Them.* Englewood Cliffs, NJ: Prentice-Hall.

Analysis Central Systems (1994). "Community Policing Software." *The Police Chief,* Vol. LXI, No. 10.

Anderson, Michael (1999). Building Relationships with Young People Is Real Police Work." *Community Policing Exchange*, Phase VI, No. 24.

Aragon, Randall, and Richard E. Adams (1997). "Community-Oriented Policing—Success Insurance Strategies." *FBI Law Enforcement Bulletin,* Vol. 66, No. 12.

Arnold, Henry C. (1998). "Tasking a Team Approach to Community Policing." *Community Policing Exchange*. Washington, DC: Community Policing Consortium.

Bennett, Charles W., Jr. (1995). "Followership: An Essential Component of Community Policing." *The Police Chief*, Vol. LXIL, No. 9.

Bessinger, Drew (1997). "Using the Civil Eviction Process—Ridding Rental Properties of Criminals." *Law and Order,* Vol. 45, No. 9.

Bobinsky, Robert (1994). "Reflections on Community-Oriented Policing." *FBI Law Enforcement Bulletin*, Vol. 63, No. 3.

Bucqueroux, Bonnie (1995). "Community Policing Is Alive and Well." *Community Policing Exchange*. Washington, DC: Community Policing Consortium.

Bureau of Justice Assistance (1993a). *Problem-Oriented Drug Enforcement: A Community-Based Approach for Effective Policing.* Washington, DC: U.S. Department of Justice.

_____ (1993b). *A Police Guide to Surveying Citizens and Their Environment.* Washington, DC: U.S. Department of Justice.

_____ (1994a). *Neighborhood-Oriented Policing in Rural Communities: A Program Planning Guide.* Washington, DC: U.S. Department of Justice.

_____ (1994b). *Understanding Community Policing: A Framework for Action.* Washington, DC: U.S. Department of Justice.

_____ (1994c). *Working as Partners with Community Groups: Community Partnerships.* Washington, DC: Office of Justice Programs.

_____ (2000). *Keeping Illegal Activity Out of Rental Property: A Police Guide for Establishing Landlord Training Programs.* Washington, DC: U.S. Department of Justice.

_____ (2001). *The Role of Local Government in Community Safety.* Washington, DC: U.S. Department of Justice.

Cameron, Bruce (2000). "COPS A Political Football—Research Shows Promoted Figures Are Fabrications." *Law and Order*, Vol. 48, No. 10.

Community Policing Consortium (2000). *About Community Policing.* Washington, DC: Community Policing Consortium.

Correia, Mark E. (2000). *Citizen Involvement—How Community Factors Affect Progressive Policing.* Washington, DC: Police Executive Research Forum.

Cunningham, Scott A. (1994). "The Empowering Leader and Organizational Change." *The Police Chief,* Vol. LXI, No.8.

De Paris, Richard J. (1998). "Organizational Leadership and Change Management—Removing Systems Barriers to Community Policing and Problem Solving." *The Police Chief*, Vol. LXV, No. 12.

Eck, John C., and William Spelman (1987). *Problem Solving: Problem-Oriented Policing in Newport News.* Washington, DC: U.S. Department of Justice and Police Executive Research Forum.

Goldstein, Herman (1990). *Problem-Oriented Policing.* New York: McGraw-Hill.

Graves, Michele (2000). "Giving Citizens a Voice in Policing Policy." *Community Policing Exchange*, Phase VII, No. 32.

Haught, Lunell (1998). "Meaning, Resistance, and Sabotage—Elements of a Police Culture." *Community Policing Exchange,* Phase 5, No. 20.

Heidingsfield, Michael J. (1997). "Community Policing: Chief's Definition." *Law and Order,* Vol. 45, No. 10.

Hickman, Mathew J., and Brian A. Reaves (2001). *Community Policing in Local Police Departments, 1997-1999.* Washington, DC: Office of Justice Programs.

Jensen, Pete, Bill Tegeler, and Susan Quinn (1994). " Facilitator Skill-Building in Managing POP." *The Police Chief*, Vol. LXI, No. 7.

Kelling, George L., Robert Wasserman, and Hubert Williams (1988). *Police Accountability and Community Policing.* Washington, DC: U.S. Department of Justice.

Kerstein, Alan (2001). "Model Neighborhood Program Offers Effective Complement to Community Policing Efforts." *The Police Chief*, Vol. LXVIII, No. 2.

Law Enforcement News (2000). "2000—The Year in Review." Vol. XXVI, No. 6.

Lesce, Tony (1995). "Code Enforcement Teams—Inter-agency Inspections Target Abandoned Buildings." *Law and Order*, Vol. 43, No. 9.

Leonard, V.A., and Harry W. More (2000). *Police Organization and Management*, Ninth Edition. New York, NY: Foundation Press.

McElroy, Jerome E., Colleen A. Cosgrove, and Susan Sadd (1993). *Community Policing: The CPOP in New York.* Newbury Park, CA: Sage Publications.

Meese, Edwin III (1993). *Community Policing and the Police Officer.* Washington, DC: Office of Justice Programs.

Mittleman, Pete (2000). "Community Policing: Building Community Trust Thinking Outside of the Box." *The Police Chief,* Vol. LXVII, No. 3.

Moselle, T.R. (1997). "Community Policing—Is It Police Work?" *Journal of California Law Enforcement*, Vol. 31, No. 1.

National Crime Prevention Council (1994). *National Service and Public Safety: Partnerships for Safer Communities.* Washington, DC: U.S. Department of Justice.

Oliver, Willard M. (1998). *Community-Oriented Policing: A Systematic Approach to Policing.* Upper Saddle River, NJ: Prentice-Hall.

Overman, Richard (1994). "The Case for Community Policing." *The Police Chief,* Vol. LXI, No. 3.

Parks, Roger B., Stephen D. Mastrofski, Christina DeJong, and M. Kevin Gray (1999). "How Officers Spend Their Time with the Community." *Justice Quarterly,* Vol. 16, No. 3.

Police Executive Research Forum (1996). *Themes and Variations in Community Policing.* Washington DC: Police Executive Research Forum.

Rabkin, Norman J. (1955). *Community Policing: Information on the "COPS on the Beat" Grant Program.* Washington, DC: U.S. Government Printing Office.

Ramirez, Stephen M. (1999). "Self-Directed Work Teams." *FBI Law Enforcement Bulletin,* Vol. 68, No. 8.

Reaves, Brian A., and Andrew L. Goldberg (1999). *Law Enforcement Management and Administrative Statistics, 1997: Data for Individual State and Local Agencies with 100 or More Officers.* Washington, DC: Office of Justice Programs.

Reaves, Brian A., and Timothy C. Hart (2000). *Law Enforcement Management and Administrative Statistics, 1999: Data for Individual State and Local Agencies with 100 or More Officers.* Washington DC: Office of Justice Programs.

Reiter, Michael S. (1999). "Empowerment Policing." *FBI Law Enforcement Bulletin,* Vol. 68, No. 2.

Rush, George E. (1992). "Community Policing: Overcoming the Obstacles." *The Police Chief,* Vol. LIX, No. 10.

Safir, Howard (1997) "Goal-Oriented Community Policing: The NYPD Approach." *The Police Chief,* Vol. LXIV, No. 12.

Scarano, Steve, and Thomas Jones (2000). "Following by Example." *Law and Order,* Vol. 48, No.10.

Spelman, William, and John E. Eck (1987). "Problem Oriented Policing." *Research in Brief.* Washington, DC: National Institute of Justice.

Stipak, Brian, Susan Immer, and Maria Clavadetscher (1994). "Are You Really Doing Community Policing?" *The Police Chief*, Vol. LXI, No. 10.

Swope, Ross E. (2000). "Measuring Success." *The Police Chief,* Vol. LXVII, No. 3.

Taylor, M. (1992). "Constraints to Community-Oriented Policing." *Police Journal,* Vol. 15, No. 2.

Thompson, Brad Lee (1995). *The New Manager's Handbook.* Burr Ridge, IL: Irwin Professional Publishing.

Travis, Jeremy (1996). "Law Enforcement in a Time of Community Policing." *Research Preview.* Washington, DC: National Institute of Justice.

Trojanowicz, Robert, Victor E. Kappeler, and Larry R. Gaines (2001). *Community Policing: A Contemporary Perspective,* Third Edition. Cincinnati, OH: Anderson.

Weisel, Deborah (1999). *Conducting Community Surveys—A Practical Guide for Law Enforcement Agencies.* Washington, DC: Bureau of Justice Statistics and Office of Community-Oriented Policing Services.

West, Marty L. (1997). "Gaining Employee Support for Community Policing." *Law and Order*, Vol. 45, No.4.

Wiechmann, Arthur D. (1995). "A Supervisory Perspective on Community Policing," *Community Policing Exchange.* Washington, DC: Community Policing Consortium.

Wolfer, Loreen, Thomas E. Baker, and Ralph Zezza (1999). "Problem-Solving Policing—Eliminating Hot Spots." *FBI Enforcement Bulletin*, Vol. 68, No. 11.

Wycoff, Mary Ann, and Timothy N. Oettmeier (1994). *Evaluating Patrol Officer Performance under Community Policing: The Houston Experience.* Washington, DC: U.S. Department of Justice.

Wycoff, Mary Ann, and Wesley K. Skogan (1993). *Community Policing in Madison: Quality from the Inside Out.* Washington, DC: U.S. Department of Justice.

Interpersonal Communication—

Striving for Effectiveness

3

fact, this is the third time this problem has been brought to the attention of Sergeant Pyle. When advised of the situation, the officers under his supervision have not really said a lot, but they have voiced the opinion that traffic and auto theft are the responsibility of the traffic unit. Each of the officers thinks that their attention should be directed toward controlling violent offenses and major property crimes.

Up to this point, Sergeant Pyle has advised the officers of command interest and left the resolution of the problem up to the officers. In the past this approach has worked, but in this instance all of the officers strongly believe that if they expend energy on auto thefts, it will detract from their providing citizens with the protection they need. Additionally, there is a strong belief that members of the traffic unit think they are elitists and above normal patrol duties and have always expressed the idea that they can solve the problem without the assistance of line officers. The conflict is real, and the patrol officers see little reason to support those assigned to traffic. This is a long-standing problem that has been ignored by every level of management.

Obviously Sergeant Pyle has been thrust into the middle and told to resolve the problem that rests primarily with those he is supervising. In an effort to resolve the problem, he has considered a number of different approaches, from the possibility of issuing a direct order to a presentation to the officers armed with a plethora of data delineating the problem and how to approach its resolution. Normally it would seem that such a problem could be resolved with ease, but in this case each of the employees has become overwhelmed by their dislike of the members of the traffic unit.

How would you, as Sergeant Pyle, proceed? Would you discuss the problem with the watch commander? Why? What would you do to ensure that communications are not just one-way between you and those supervised? Is it a problem of not providing adequate information or decoding? Why? Are psychological barriers involved? What could be done to improve two-way communication?

Excellent supervisors have a remarkable characteristic that distinguishes them in that they have the ability to communicate effectively. It can be said, without question, that it has proven to be the key to success. Communication is the foundation of interpersonal relations. When ideas and thoughts are communicated successfully, it fosters a positive working environment. In law enforcement agencies, the first-line supervisor engages in a number of activities, the first of which includes the interpretation of the organization's culture, managerial values, mission, goals, objectives, and operational policies into day-to-day decisions and operational activities (Southerland, 1992). In addition, a supervisor uses communication to train, develop, and motivate each officer in an effort to improve performance and provide for an improved quality of life within the community. Finally, the supervisor plans, organizes work, gives directions, issues orders, and monitors employee performance, all in an effort to improve the effectiveness of the organization.

There is an unequivocal organizational need for supervisors who understand the intricate nature of the communication process and vigorously foster a working atmosphere that encourages open communication (Gaines, Southerland, and Angell, 1991).

The Importance of Communication Skills

As the tasks performed within law enforcement agencies have become more complex and demanding, the need for good communication skills has become increasingly important. It is difficult to imagine a professional law enforcement agency without advanced communications, computer-aided dispatch, cellular telephones, and laptop computers for the analysis of data and the preparation of reports. In fact, law enforcement has readily adopted hardware, but there is a clear-cut need for improved interpersonal and organizational communication.

Interpersonal communication exists at every level of any organization, but is most prevailing at the operational level, where, of necessity, there is a continual interaction between supervisors and line personnel. When there is good communication, it is a result of effective supervision. Communication is an integral part of our everyday life, and it is difficult to imagine an organization not fostering and encouraging strong communication skills. Communication is the lifeblood of an organization. It is the process that ties the whole organization together. When a mishap occurs, the immediate reaction is to blame it on an inability to communicate effectively.

A breakdown in communication is an inevitable consequence of our inability to properly interpret what is said. It is easier to blame failures on poor or inadequate communication than to deal with the problem directly. It is like treating the symptom rather than the disease. When one becomes a first-line supervisor, it does not automatically confer the ability to be an effective communicator. It takes considerable time to develop good communication skills, but they can be learned.

If communication is to be effective, it must be nurtured by all levels of management, from the top down. As previously stated, first-line supervisors are managers, and they are an integral part of the management team. They are in constant contact with operational personnel. Without question, their position is the linchpin of the organization and the most strategic position in any law enforcement agency.

Supervisors spend a large part of their working hours engaged in tasks that can be identified as communicating. Experience shows that first-line supervisors in municipal law enforcement agencies spend approximately 55 percent of their communication time performing tasks related to subordinates, 26 percent related to superiors, 15 percent related to the public, and four percent relating to other supervisors. These percentages are set forth in Figure 3.1.

Figure 3.1
Supervisor's Communication Tasks by Level

Level	Percentage
Subordinates	55
Superiors	26
Citizens	15
Other Supervisors	4
	100

Additional support that delineates the importance of communication for supervisors is reflected in a task analysis study of the first-line supervisor's position. In considering 53 specific tasks, 51 percent involved communication. These tasks, rated in terms of their importance, are summarized in Figure 3.2 and include a wide range of activities.

Figure 3.2
Specific Communication Tasks Performed by Supervisors

1. Providing feedback to subordinates regarding job performance.
2. Responding to subordinates' inquiries.
3. Meeting with and providing direction to subordinates regarding particular incidents or investigations.
4. Meeting with and resolving disputes among subordinates.
5. Meeting with managers to resolve specific problems or concerns.
6. Resolving citizen/officer conflicts.

It can readily be seen that the first-line supervisor spends the preponderance of time communicating in various ways with subordinates. Officers need information and guidance in operational activities. In addition, when conflict occurs between subordinates, it is the supervisor who must resolve the dispute in the interest of operational effectiveness. It is essential that the supervisor listen to every side of an issue and be sensitive to the needs of all individuals involved in a conflict (California POST, 1996). These activities can dominate the supervisory workload, and it is still necessary to meet with supervisory personnel as needed, as well as to interact with citizens to resolve the inevitable conflict that occurs between officers and citizens.

It is amazing, when one stops to think of it, that so much of a human's waking time is spent communicating. This is noticed especially in the work environment, and law enforcement is no exception. The first-line supervisor must understand the importance of verbal and nonverbal communication, the art of listening, and information processing. The interaction between sergeants and subordinates succeeds or fails as a direct result of their ability or inability to communicate.

Effective communication means *getting the meaning across*. In many instances, this can prove to be a difficult barrier to overcome. When analyzing why one supervisor is a better communicator than another, one characteristic stands out: an awareness of the need to communicate well. Successful communicators are not concerned about personal self-esteem. When communication falters, they do not look for someone to blame; they work to resolve the problem. If they know they have done a poor job of explaining something, good communicators will admit that they have erred and start over. It boils down to wanting to communicate well.

A good communicator avoids meaningless or imprecise words. Today, much of our communication is impaired by wordiness. It is often assumed, erroneously, that a lot of words will clarify a situation and the problem will be resolved. The poor communicator fails to realize that, more often than not, words can confuse, confound, or mislead. Supervisors who have the reputation of being good communicators are known as individuals who have something to say. When it is necessary to communicate, they respond accordingly, whether it is on a one-on-one basis or in a group. A good communicator is a respected and valuable member of the law enforcement community.

The Communication Process

Defining communications might seem to be an easy and straightforward task, but it has confounded experts for years. In fact, one study reviewed managerial literature and found 94 different definitions of the word *communication*. This demonstrates the complexity of the actual communication process. Communication can be defined as a process by which information is exchanged between individuals through a common system of symbols, signs, or behavior. If communication is to be effective, however, there must be more than just the exchange of information.

The sender of a message must make a sincere effort to affect the behavior of the recipient. Effective person-to-person communication involves more than just sending a message—it has to be decoded so that it can be interpreted and a true understanding occurs between the sender and the recipient.

On the surface the process seems quite simple, but a careful analysis of the components indicates a number of places where the message can become misconstrued, garbled, or even ignored. It is somewhat similar to talking with someone from another country who has a limited knowledge of English.

The recipient of the message may nod his or her head, look one straight in the eye, and seemingly absorb every word and respond to every nuance. However, if one asks the listener even the most simple question, it is readily apparent that while the message was transmitted, it was definitely not decoded. Keep in mind that the same thing can also occur between two individuals who are fluent in the same language (see Figure 3.3).

The communication process is exceedingly complex, especially when one takes into consideration the fact that both the sender and the recipient of a message are affected by attitudes, skills, knowledge, opinions, and other forces existing before, during, and after the message is transmitted.

Figure 3.3
Simplistic Communication Process

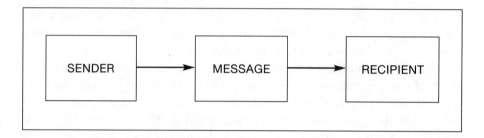

Interpersonal communication requires two or more people. Participants in a conversation send messages by verbal as well as nonverbal channels. The characteristics of senders and recipients can substantially influence the communication process, which is continually changing. For example, the sender may want to change the opinion, perception, or behavior of the recipient and will send a message in an effort to accomplish a specific goal. A problem can occur when the goals of the two individuals involved are in conflict. When this happens, there is a strong possibility of distortion and misunderstandings. When goals are compatible, there is a greater possibility that a message will be interpreted accurately.

The sender of a message determines the relevancy of each and every message. This is generally known as *gatekeeping*, inasmuch as the sender determines the importance and relevance of information. The sender, therefore, exercises complete control over the flow of information. This is especially apparent when supervisors, by virtue of their position in a police organization, operate as the primary communication point between upper management and line personnel. Operational autonomy, with the primary guidance coming from departmental policy, places the first-line supervisor in the position of controlling the amount and nature of information entering the information system. Decisions are constantly made about the need for passing information into the system. At the same time, the supervisor is in a position to control the amount of information subordinates will receive.

This is pertinent when the supervisor presides at the roll-call session preceding each shift. It can be a learning experience for the officers, or it can be conducted in a perfunctory manner with a limited exchange of information. Many first-line supervisors believe that proper communication has occurred when they have simply told a shift of officers what to do. It is difficult to believe that anyone who has been in an organization for a year or more has not heard either, "I told you what the new policy was" or "Why didn't you tell me?" It seems the message transmission could be accomplished without difficulty, but it is soon obvious that encoding the message can, and will, in all probability, become complex.

Communication is an exchange of information involving two or more parties and all must participate. It is a process modified or constrained by such features as those listed below:

- Insufficient information will seldom produce a preferred result.

- The recipient of the message determines the accuracy of the communication through decoding.

- The recipient of the message, as a result of attitudes, experiences, and motivations, determines whether the message is decoded in the way intended by the sender.

Each person involved in a communication situation both encodes and decodes messages simultaneously. It is a continuous process, and as information is received, it is decoded. From the standpoint of the first-line supervisor, answers should be sought to the following types of questions:

- What is the actual communication to be encoded?

- Is there data supporting the message's proposition?

- Does the message imply anything?

- Can the message be misinterpreted?

- What type of response will result from the message?

- Will the message yield results?

Each supervisor should make a conscious effort to deal with the practical problems readily identifiable from the above questions. With practice, a supervisor can soon develop messages that are clear, meaningful, and will obtain results (see Figure 3.4).

Another element of the communication process is the channel through which the message travels from the sender to the recipient. The term *channel* usually refers to one or more of the human senses. This involves both verbal and nonverbal aspects of communication, although the first-line supervisor usually deals with oral communication.

Failure to acknowledge the importance of nonverbal communication and its impact on the recipient will often cause problems. This was especially apparent in one agency when top management instituted a new policy prohibiting officers from carrying second weapons. When the new policy was discussed at roll call, one of the senior sergeants made light of the new policy, leading everyone in attendance to believe that the policy would never be enforced and that officers could continue the practice of carrying second weapons.

Figure 3.4
Realistic Communication Process

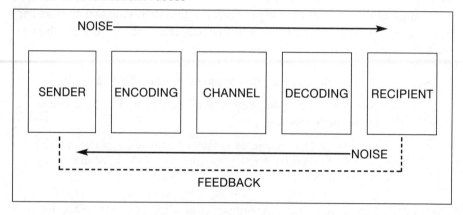

After an unfortunate shooting incident in which an officer used a second weapon, an internal investigation concluded the shooting was justified and conformed with the departmental use of deadly force policy. Nevertheless, the officer was suspended for two weeks for carrying a second weapon. The investigation also recommended a two-week suspension for the sergeant, who had failed to explain and support departmental policy. The chief of police, after an appropriate hearing, demoted the sergeant.

The distorted message sent by the sergeant in this situation proved disastrous for the officer as well as for the supervisor. The content of the sergeant's presentation to the officers was clear and concise, but the context in which it was delivered proved to be the most persuasive part of the message. The context of any message cannot be ignored, because it can be more meaningful than content.

Once the message has been sent, it is up to the receiver to decode the message and attach significant meaning. There are six aspects to consider at this point (Naval Education and Training Program, 1984):

- What the sender **MEANT** to say
- What was **IN FACT** said
- What the receiver **HEARD**
- What the receiver **THINKS** he or she heard
- What the receiver **SAID**
- What the sender **THINKS** the receiver said

These six modifiers of the communication process are involved in every message, and the receiver reacts based on personal experiences, viewpoints, knowledge, and frame of reference. It is apparent that a failure in communication can occur at many points. With feedback, the cycle becomes a viable two-way process. Based on its type, feedback can vary greatly. It can be as simple as a nod of the head or as complex as a multiple-page report. For example, the receiver could respond with a request for clarification: "As I understand it, you want me to notify every liquor store on my beat about the two armed robbers. Is that correct?" Such a technique can leave no doubt as to what was meant by the sender and whether the message was understood.

Noise is the last feature of the communication process. It is anything that reduces the accuracy of a communication. An awareness of how noise affects communication will allow one to take steps to reduce it, thereby improving the accuracy of each communication. Noise can be present at any point in the communication process, but the greatest problem area is with the use of language.

Some people seem to have the ability to explain things clearly and with a great deal of simplicity. At the same time, others never seem to be able to find the correct expressive words, and even a simple thought becomes entangled with complicated details. In a police department, written and verbal skills play an important part in one's success. Those who develop these skills are easily identified. Articulate individuals are generally at ease when discussing issues, seem to influence others easily, and get their way more often than not.

Individuals should assess their own verbal capacity and evaluate their ability to organize information and present it clearly to others. Some ideas one might want to consider are set forth in Figure 3.5.

Figure 3.5
Techniques for Assessing One's Verbal Capacity

1. Start all discussions at a level where there is an absolute certainty of mutual understanding.
2. If the topic is new, lay a foundation by providing information to bring the recipient up to the same level of understanding.
3. Carefully screen all information and provide only essential information.
4. When making a presentation, move from generalities to specifics.
5. Never assume that the recipients are as knowledgeable about a subject as the presenter is.
6. The greater the complexity of the data being presented, the greater the need to present the information step-by-step in a logical manner.
7. Summarize the salient features of the presentation before accepting questions.
8. Videotape lectures and review them with a sincere intent to improve the method of presentation.

Adapted from Karl Albrecht (1979). *Stress and the Manager: Making It Work for You.* Englewood Cliffs, NJ: Prentice-Hall, Inc.

The factors listed above delineate how to improve communication and how a supervisor can (by following these general guidelines) more effectively convey thoughts, ideas, and decisions when engaged in the managerial activities of controlling and directing.

First-line supervisors in law enforcement agencies are task-oriented: results are what count. Line officers work within operating procedures (with limited supervision), so they have considerable decision-making discretion. In fact, the application of discretion consumes a large part of the average officer's time, and when difficulties occur, officers consult their first-line supervisor. As pointed out earlier, supervisors spend 55 percent of their communication time with the officers they supervise.

The realistic supervisor works with subordinates in an effort to develop them to the point where they can become committed and motivated to such an extent that they are *self-supervised*. Within this context, one study showed that when ranking communication tasks, first-line supervisors listed the following items in terms of importance (see Figure 3.6).

Figure 3.6
Communications Tasks in Order of Importance

1. Provide feedback to subordinates regarding their job performance. This should include such things as identifying strengths, weaknesses, and exceptional or inadequate performance.
2. Prepare written employee performance evaluations.
3. Respond to subordinates' inquiries regarding departmental policy, legal questions, and the application of discretionary decision making.
4. Meet with and provide direction to subordinates regarding particular violations, investigative techniques, and case processing.
5. Brief subordinates on new or revised policies and procedures.
6. Communicate subordinates' concerns, desires, and suggestions to management.

Each of these items emphasizes the importance of the superior/subordinate relationship and alludes to the complexity of the communication process. A supervisor must continually be aware of the need to develop and maintain communication skills, because communication is the most important managerial tool. When demands are excessive and time is of the essence, a supervisor should emphasize feedback regarding job performance inasmuch as this provides immediate results. Other tasks can be responded to in order of importance. None can be overlooked, but some can be delayed. It is also essential that the supervisor serve as a conduit by communicating concerns, desires, and suggestions to management. If the supervisor does not perform this function, it will probably not be accomplished.

Communication Patterns

Communication is defined as the exchange of information between individuals, implying that it can be either one-way or two-way. Traditionally, one-way communication has dominated supervisory relationships with subordinates. In this situation, the sender communicates without expecting or receiving feedback from the recipient. Typical of this type of communication activity is when a sergeant tells officers what will be done and how to do it, without any feedback.

Two-way communication occurs when the recipient provides feedback to the sender. An example would be when a sergeant discusses a new policy, then asks for feedback. Another example would be the creation of a task force consisting of line officers who are assigned to develop a new grooming policy for officers and prepare a report for management.

Each of these methods has its advantages. One-way communication is preferable when:

- speed is important;

- orderliness is significant; or

- compliance is imperative.

When one-way communication is selected as the appropriate means to be used, the sender must spend a great deal of time preparing what will be said, because there is no feedback to clarify issues or correct errors. It protects the sender's authority and power, because mistakes are never acknowledged. Line officers might criticize the sergeant, but with one-way communication the potential criticism by subordinates is not allowed.

When a sergeant uses one-way communication, the assumption is that one's responsibility ends there and that it is the responsibility of the listener to receive and decode the message. It is a simple one-way street, and blame can be placed on the recipient for failure to understand the message. The sergeant can say, "I explained it to you, and there is no reason for you not to understand the message."

The problem is obvious. A message can be transmitted, but there is no actual communication unless the message is understood by the recipient. The sender is responsible for seeing that a message is understood, and this can be done only if the message is received and there is an opportunity for feedback.

This is where two-way communication becomes useful. It is apparent that when one engages in two-way communication, there is not only a message sent, but there is also feedback allowing for the modification and correction of the initial message. This is the exact opposite of the classical one-way communication process.

The drawback to two-way communication is that one must accept some risk and share power and authority. The sender's position may be subject to scrutiny by subordinates, and an awareness that the sender is not completely knowledgeable in the subject area may develop. Two-way communication requires less planning because of the built-in opportunity for feedback and the subsequent correction of errors or the clarification of issues. For this to work, it is imperative for the sender to listen and understand the feedback provided by the receiver; otherwise there is just the façade of two-way communication.

The success of two-way communication depends upon mutual understanding as an integral part of the communication process. The desire is to communicate, not to find fault or place blame. If there is a lack of understanding, everyone works to correct errors and clarify issues.

It is apparent from the above discussion that the advantages of two-way communication include: (Naval Education and Training Program, 1984)

- improved accuracy;

- sharing authority and responsibility;

- greater understanding;

- acknowledgement of the importance of communicating; and

- recognition of subordinates' need to know what is expected of them.

Barriers to Communication

An officer never reacts to a message in isolation. There is always a reaction to the relationship of the actual situation, the content of the message, and the recipient. An officer must feel free to discuss issues with superiors. Unfortunately, this is not always the case. If an officer is concerned about a negative reaction from a superior, then the officer is less likely to bring up the issue for discussion.

Barriers to communication are numerous, but generally include concern about one's knowledge of a subject, the probability of being looked upon with displeasure, jeopardizing one's status, environmental influences, personal expectations, and semantics.

Some officers will assume that asking for clarification on any issue will make them appear unknowledgeable. There is a concern that one might be viewed as less than a *real* officer who is aware and streetwise. Survival in the organization suggests that under no circumstances should officers leave themselves in a position in which their ability is called into question, especially if it might jeopardize favorable consideration when assignments are handed out.

Subordinates are reticent to discuss personal goals and aspirations if there is any question in their mind that the supervisor might not be receptive. They often feel that expressing concerns about the job or the need to learn something new can be taken as a sign of weakness and used against them. With inadequate two-way communication, actions taken by a supervisor are viewed as detrimental, and the subordinates will, in all probability, grudgingly accept and implement them with a complete lack of enthusiasm. These actions may even be sabotaged (Bradford and Cohen, 1984).

Physical barriers in any given situation may block or lead to garbled transmission of messages. These barriers might be the result of a poor radio transmission, a poorly written note, or even the incorrect use of the Ten Code. It can even be something like noise created by machinery or other elements of the environment that make hearing difficult. Whatever the barrier, it should be identified. Steps should then be taken to ensure that blocks or distortions to effective communication are eliminated.

Psychological barriers include an individual's beliefs, judgments, values, needs, life experiences, education, training, and goals. Also, the emotional state (hostility, apprehension, assurance) of either the sender or the recipient can impede communication. Neither can one forget personal attitudes of stereotyping, biases, and prejudice (Salmon, 1998). These all combine to form a frame of reference for both the sender and the recipient of any message. Inasmuch as everyone has distinctive combinations of the above characteristics, it should be apparent that everyone has the potential to see and hear the same situation from different perspectives (Overton and Black, 1994).

An additional barrier can be physiological in nature. Fatigue is especially important in law enforcement. Rotating shifts, working shifts out of sync with the normal workday, or sitting in court after a regular shift can negatively affect one's attention span, decision-making capacity, and ability to communicate (Vita, 2000).

Another barrier to effective communication is semantics. Some words are easily misunderstood or subject to misinterpretation (Salmon, 1998). There are many words that have multiple meanings, and these can vary with each situation. For example, to take a person into custody can have a number of meanings ranging from an actual arrest to protective custody. Effective communication can take place only when the actual symbolic meaning of words is shared. Telling a subordinate to "hit the bricks and get with it" communicates little or perhaps nothing. Is it a meaningless instruction, or does it mean there is a need to be more productive in terms of issuing more citations or conducting more field interviews? How will it affect the behavior of each officer? Figure 3.7 lists the major barriers to communication.

Figure 3.7
Barriers That Impede Effective Communication

1. Fear of being viewed as having limited knowledge about a subject
2. Fear of being looked down on
3. Concern about jeopardizing one's status
4. Physical influences
5. Psychological factors
6. Physiological obstacles
7. Semantics

Another semantics problem occurs when a supervisor uses jargon or esoteric language known as *argot*. When dealing with subordinates, a supervisor will sometimes assume that everyone is familiar with legal terms. Consequently, the process of communication may become clouded, if not completely distorted. At other times, jargon of the trade may be used to impress someone or to exclude them from a discussion.

A word is an incomplete representation of reality. It is a symbol that can be manipulated without regard to what is factual. Language can be used to distort facts and used according to the whim of the sender.

Words will often have strong symbolic significance, so using them as labels should be done with a great deal of caution. For example, using such terms as *punks, pukes,* or *dirtbags* should be avoided, because such labeling can give officers the impression that these uniquely identified individuals can be treated differently and not accorded their complete constitutional rights.

Case Study

Sergeant Tom French

Tom French has been with the police department for six years and was just promoted to sergeant. The city had just annexed an unincorporated area of 39 square miles, and six other officers were promoted at the same time to assume duties in the new area. In his new assignment in the uniformed division, he was scheduled to supervise six beats and work out of a newly opened storefront station. The last one and one-half years he worked as an auto theft investigator. In the auto theft unit, Sergeant French spent a great deal of time working undercover and excelled in this assignment. He also became very knowledgeable about chop-shop operations. The majority of his time in this assignment was spent on working cases with a citywide implication. Vehicles stolen by juveniles were taken to junkyards, where they were stripped and the parts transported to several neighboring communities. The profits were so high in such an operation that as soon as one operation was closed down, another would crop up.

Sergeant French inherited officers who had been supervised by a sergeant who just retired and had the reputation of being a taskmaster and concerned primarily with minutiae. The previous sergeant never allowed officers to make a significant decision, and he went by the book. French's predecessor never allowed officers to turn in a report with spelling errors or improper grammar. His management style could best be described as controlling. The former sergeant's day was made when he could reject an officer's report because of improper English. Everyone knew he had just been waiting out his time until his retirement date arrived.

French soon realized the extent of the work ahead of him as he assumed the new position. It was apparent that the officers viewed him as an unknown quantity. They were ignoring enforcement of narcotics laws. All of the officers he was scheduled to supervise were veterans with at least five years of street experience, and everyone had worked for his predecessor for the last three years. After reviewing the officers' personnel jackets and daily reports over the last three months, French felt that they were certainly capable of writing error-free reports but that the reports were shallow and missed many opportunities of setting forth leads that could be used in follow-up investigations.

French's first step was to speak with the members of the team and advise them of the performance standards that he intended to require. He strongly expressed the need for open and two-way communications. He passed out a schedule listing the date and time he would meet each officer to discuss the problems confronting them on their beat, how he might assist them, and how they might go about achieving an absolute certainty of mutual understanding. He asked the members of the team to think about his comments and told them to be prepared to discuss the issues involved in order to ensure that each of them performed as effectively as possible. He told them he was not concerned with what they had done before but with what their performance would be from that day forward.

When talking about the situation with one of the officers who had gone through the academy with him regarding the situation, it became apparent that the other officers were threatened by the comments and not looking forward to the meeting. Some of them were even fearful that the new sergeant might request their transfer to another shift or team. In fact, there is a rumor going around that all the officers are to be transferred. Assignment to the new area is looked on as a coveted assignment, and all the officers believe they have performed effectively and are entitled to remain in their present position. There is an obvious communication barrier to be overcome if Sergeant French is to function successfully as a supervisor. Prior to this, communication has been limited to one-way with an emphasis on total control, but two-way communication seems to be needed in the new policing environment.

Up to this point, did Sergeant French approach the problem in the best way? Why or why not? What would you do to improve communication between Sergeant French and the beat officers? How might Sergeant French develop an atmosphere of trust? What is the crux of this communication problem? Is it the sharing of authority or the lack of awareness of subordinate expectations? Explain.

Overcoming Communication Barriers

Many officers have had supervisors who have said, "Come into the office and let's talk it over." Or they have had a memo placed in their mailbox—*See me*. Messages like these can evoke all types of reactions, ranging from an open and honest discussion to the subordinate not expressing thoughts and feelings at all (see Figure 3.8).

Figure 3.8

Techniques for Overcoming Communication Barriers

1. Create a supportive relationship. Show a genuine concern for each officer and their welfare (personal and professional).
2. Develop an awareness of each subordinate's needs. Learn everything you can about the officer, especially his or her expectations.
3. Maximize the use of feedback. Clarify essential information and tell each officer about his or her job performance—strengths and weaknesses.
4. Continually use face-to-face communication. Strive to meet with each officer as often as possible in order to enhance the communication process. Personalize each contact and avoid written communications as much as possible.
5. Strive to be acutely aware of semantical differences. If there is any doubt, define terms. Always be as explicit as the situation and topic allow.
6. Use direct and simple language. Move from generalities to specifics, and screen all information that is passed on.
7. Repeat communication when needed. Use the time-honored process of telling officers what you intend to tell them, then tell them, and then summarize what you have told them.
8. Develop an atmosphere of mutual trust. This can be done by demonstrating a real interest in each officer, accepting their input, respecting their judgment, drawing upon their strengths, and assisting them in overcoming their weaknesses. Get them involved in the decision-making process.

Some officers will withdraw and turn the discussion into a one-way communication process in which the sergeant does all the talking, or the officers will say things they believe the sergeant wants to hear. In either case, feedback does not occur, so the sergeant is limited in accurately appraising or evaluating the situation (Naval Education and Training Program, 1984).

A supervisor can obtain sound feedback only when there is reason for officers to dispel fears and concerns impeding or impairing valid two-way communication. Due to the position of power, a superior must deal with the fears or misgivings of subordinates and work diligently to dispel them. This must be accomplished not only by words, but also by actions.

A supportive relationship, if it is also to be a viable and positive working relationship, is one in which the subordinate is allowed to influence the supervisor. The foundation for real two-way communication occurs when the subordinates accept a supervisor as someone who assists and supports, rather than someone who forces, demands, or orders. It cannot be a relationship in which communication is limited to such one-way positioning as "Do it now" or "I said 'do it' and that's the way it's going to be."

Subordinate involvement in a real working relationship in which there is true commitment requires some degree of power sharing. If subordinates have little or no power, or if they cannot disagree or vigorously support an opposing position, there clearly is not a viable supportive relationship. An effective relationship can occur only when there is a genuine acceptance of one another, a concern for the needs of others, and a feeling of absolute trust and mutual respect (Bradford and Cohen, 1984).

Supervisors' lives would be very simple if they did not have to work diligently to listen to subordinates' ideas and thoughts, strive to share power, create a base for compromise and conciliation, and give feedback that leads to solving interpersonal problems. Supervision is hard work. Positive supervision maximizes the use of human resources—it does not waste them. A supervisory style that not only allows for individual differences, but views them as valuable assets contributing to the success of the organization, must be adopted.

A supervisor can take many steps to ensure that individual differences do not negatively affect superior/subordinate relationships. Many times success is a combination of what the supervisor does and the way he or she does it. When a supervisor views each officer as a potential member of the team, there is the beginning of a positive working relationship. A supervisor must focus on bringing each officer into a working relationship, avoid making negative personality judgments, and stress strengths rather than weaknesses.

It is best to focus on resolving problems rather than employing criticism for the sake of criticism. Emphasis should be placed on reaching out to each employee to better understand his or her situation. The goal is to build a working relationship that allows for a continual exchange of opinions and information. Stressing tasks performed by subordinates, rather than their personalities, can enhance this process. Effective leadership involves viewing personnel in a positive light.

Employees have a right to know where supervisors are coming from. A supervisor will be judged by the nature and quality of communications. If a supervisor treats every officer as fairly as possible and does not show favoritism, these actions will support the creation of a positive working relationship. A supervisor will probably feel more comfortable with some officers than with others, but it will be incumbent upon the supervisor to perform in such a way that individuals are not singled out for preferential treatment. Fairness is the leadership attribute to be followed.

A supervisor should also vary officers' assignments so their performance can be improved and boredom reduced. In a police department, the third watch is normally less active, so the supervisor should distribute assignments to enhance working conditions and demonstrate equitable treatment.

Whenever possible, the supervisor should recommend additional training. Most employees like to be placed in a learning environment to give them additional skills. It will also make the officer more valuable to the organization. It is equally imperative for supervisors to keep abreast of changes in order to improve subordinate training.

If one of the officers does an excellent job, a direct compliment should be given as soon as possible. In addition, the supervisor should send a note to higher management levels, pointing out the significance of the contribution to the organization and make sure the officer receives a copy of the note. It carries more weight when the recognition of a job well done is made a part of the subordinate's personnel file. A sincere word of appreciation for excellent work can go a long way in building a supportive working relationship with subordinates.

Successful supervisors give serious consideration to creating a working environment in which there is mutual respect and trust between themselves and subordinates. It is not a matter of blindly trusting every officer and having faith that the task to be accomplished will be completed, because there will always be a time and place where an officer will fail to follow instructions or complete a task as required by departmental policy. A supervisor must be willing to accept a certain degree of risk, because the positive results will generally exceed the errors or mistakes that inevitably occur.

Trust and respect are prerequisites to any working relationship. These qualities must come before there can be candid and open communication (DeVito, 1992). Every officer must have the right to openly approach and resolve all interpersonal and task problems as they occur. They should be allowed to express true feelings and expect that they will be heard by the supervisor. Officers should always be able to anticipate an impartial and fair consideration of the issues (Naval Education and Training Program, 1984).

A good supervisor's actions let every officer know that he or she is being treated fairly and equitably. Every action taken must convey that supervisors always keep their word, are concerned about employee welfare, and are willing to work with their officers to resolve problems. In a working relationship in which trust and mutual respect are part and parcel of everyday activities, officers will have no need to be guarded or suspicious of each other or their supervisor, and energies can be directed to task achievement (Bradford and Cohen, 1984).

If there is but one supervisory principle a sergeant should follow, it is to practice good communication techniques. This is an essential aspect of any leadership style and must be instituted at every opportunity, even to the point of overcommunicating. Officers are more secure when they know what is going on and have the feeling of being in control.

In many situations it is necessary to communicate by memorandum, but whenever possible, face-to-face communication is strongly recommended. Feedback can be immediate and more accurate, resulting in the reduction of conflict. Most people are more accustomed to expressing themselves with a greater degree of freedom when talking as opposed to writing. The spoken word, in contrast to the written word, reinforces supportive relationships and helps to create an atmosphere of mutual trust and confidence.

Feedback

In any working relationship, it is essential for a sergeant to develop skills and techniques to provide officers with feedback regarding their performance. This can range from praising someone's work to telling an officer what he or she has done wrong.

The utility of feedback is limited unless it is viewed as a process intended to help the receiver understand the communication. The best communication is that which is supportive and offers the recipient of the message a feeling of personal worth and comfort. When a message is delivered, it should be in such a way that it is not perceived as negative (White and Chapman, 1996). When time allows, it is up to the supervisor to take the time to analyze the message. This can be done by asking the question, "Will what I am going to say really help the officer, or will it confuse the issue?" Self-examination is clearly needed so that emotions, feelings, and values will not interfere with the transmission of the message. Careful consideration should be given to how to approach an officer with feedback, keeping in mind that part of the role of a supervisor is to be a trainer. Feedback influences behavior because it allows subordinates to become knowledgeable about their performance. As such, it can prove to be a motivational factor, generating an interest in and enthusiasm for the accomplishment of tasks and contributing to the attainment of organizational goals. Additionally, feedback can be viewed as a means of increasing the frequency of desirable behavior (Dickson, Saunders, and Stringer, 1993).

Feedback that acknowledges subordinates' importance can build a foundation of trust between the supervisor and officers. However, if one resorts to an extremely critical assessment of every subordinate activity, engaging in only one-way communication, or constantly pulling rank, feedback will soon be nonexistent, because the foundation of trust will have been eroded (see Figure 3.6).

Another feature of feedback is that it should be *specific*. Specific and detailed discussion of the issue under consideration is needed. For example, if a supervisor thinks that one of the officers should respond more quickly when providing backup for another officer during traffic stops, it is best to recall definite instances when the officer was late in responding to the scene. It is entirely possible that a valid reason for the delay (of which others were not aware) will be given. At the same time, recalling the date, time, and place of the officer's tardiness helps to focus on the problem and not on personality. Feedback should be provided as soon as possible after the occurrence, while it is still fresh in everyone's mind.

In the situation above, the aspect of validity was pointed out. It should be emphasized that it is important to be sure of one's facts before providing feedback. It can be embarrassing, if not harmful, to a working relationship with a subordinate if the facts of a situation have not been verified before bringing up an issue.

When feedback is provided, it should be descriptive and nonjudgmental. Most people find it difficult to accept negative feedback concerning their performance; therefore, when an incident is described (putting it into a context of time and place), there is a greater possibility of dialogue occurring rather than one-way communication.

Figure 3.9
Positive Feedback Techniques

1. Develop a personal relationship based on trust. Officers can see through phoniness but will readily accept an open and positive working environment.
2. Treat each officer equitably and fairly. Never show favoritism.
3. Be specific. Generalities must be avoided. In other words, tell it like it is.
4. Select an appropriate time, place, and approach to provide feedback. Individualize constructive criticism and announce positive accomplishments to everyone.
5. Keep the discussion issue-oriented. Stay with the issue under consideration and avoid digression.
6. Base your reaction on fact, not personality. It is fundamental that in a feedback situation personality is a non-issue.
7. Limit feedback to that perceived to be absolutely essential. Excessive feedback can prove to be deleterious.
8. Contribute to knowledge. Specify the results of performance that can enhance future accomplishments.
9. Be motivational. Feedback can generate an interest in, and enthusiasm for, goal attainment and improved work performance.
10. Provide reinforcement. Officers readily respond to positive feedback that acknowledges appropriate behavior and accomplishment. It is a feedback characteristic that feeds upon itself by maximizing and reinforcing acceptable officer behavior.
11. Summarize your discussion and look for indicators of agreement that indicate your message has been received and understood. This is a key element of feedback and should be used in every instance.

A great deal of a supervisor's time is spent evaluating the conduct and actions of subordinates. Therefore, a good part of feedback is either instructive or corrective. This places an extra burden on the supervisor to ensure that when feedback is given, the officer is in a position to accept it. If the officer is mentally or emotionally unable to receive the transmission, then there is little gained in giving negative feedback at that time. This does not mean that negative feedback is inappropriate, but that there is a time and place for everything. Many things occur in police work that may temporarily leave an officer angry, confused, distraught, or defensive. These feelings can be the result of a situation involving an abused child, an injury at an accident, or an abusive drunk. Any of these or similar situations could call for a delay in providing negative feedback (Naval Education and Training Program, 1984).

Feedback should be selective and limited to the issue at hand. It should never be a situation in which every past omission or commission is brought to light and the supervisor "dumps" on the officer. At best, constructive criticism is difficult to accept, so it is essential to give it at an appropriate time and place. The ultimate goal is an improvement in performance.

The Art of Listening

Good supervisors generally practice a skill that is very difficult to learn: the art of listening. It is a primary qualification for the position of first-line supervisor (Johnson, 1996). Books are written on the subject, but few people have read them. The value of developing the ability to listen should never be underestimated. If there is one pet peeve in interpersonal relationships, it is that one party does not listen. This is why some of the most successful supervisors are also the best listeners.

Becoming a good listener requires work; there is no single path to success. Merely hearing what someone has said does not mean the real message has been properly received. Listening is an active process that requires one's intellectual capacities of comprehension and evaluation.

A good listener makes a sincere effort to understand the message. It might involve taking notes to ensure accuracy, asking the speaker to repeat him or herself, asking for clarification, or restating what the person said. Whatever the method or technique, the focus is on the message, ensuring that correct information has been received.

The first tenet of the art of listening is to pay attention to the speaker. As simple as this seems, the precept is often violated. When an officer wants to talk with his or her supervisor, the officer should be made to feel that no one else will be allowed to interfere with the discussion. Giving someone undivided attention can be accomplished only by shutting out all extraneous matters. An easy way to do this is to look directly at the person with whom you are conversing. Another is to avoid formulating a response until you have listened to the complete explanation from the individual to whom you are listening (Johnson, 1996). In other words, be alert to what is being said and how it is being delivered. How often has a supervisor tried to tell something to another person and it was obvious that the other person was not listening? In other instances, the supervisor may not listen to a subordinate.

Listening is as much a persuasive art as speaking, but it must be developed. A successful listener should strive to keep an open mind and be fully cognizant of his or her own biases and preconceptions (Nierenberg, 1986). An emotional block cannot be allowed to impede communication. If the officer being dealt with is someone who is personally disliked or has certain annoying mannerisms, the effect can be minimized by analyzing the reasons for the negative emotional block. A good supervisor does not allow personal feelings to prevent communication, but addresses the situation intellectually so that the officer's ideas can be heard and understood (Naval Education and Training Program, 1984).

One way to respond intellectually rather than emotionally is to concentrate on the conversation and look for value and meaning in what is being said. Listen and wait. Take time to understand what is being said, and then evaluate the content of the message. Use the time to listen for what the officer might really be trying to say. Another useful technique is to try to listen for what is *not* being said. Are pertinent points being avoided or glossed over (Salmon, 1998)? Look for implications or inferences that tell what the person really wants to say. A good listener waits until the sender completes a message before responding. This suspends judgment, reduces errors in interpretation, and allows the listener to concentrate on the entire message rather than jumping to a conclusion. A supervisor can work to improve listening effectiveness by following the recommendations listed in Figure 3.10 (U.S. Department of Health and Human Services, 1981).

Figure 3.10
Techniques That Can Be Used to Improve Listening Effectiveness

1. Give undivided attention to the speaker
   a. Maintain eye contact
   b. Show attentiveness through body language
   c. Nod approval when it is appropriate
   d. Be expressive when appropriate
   e. Make use of conversation enablers
2. Attempt to listen unemotionally
   a. Do not respond to emotion-laden words
   b. Withhold judgment
   c. Be patient
   d. Do not interrupt
3. Adjust to the sender's message
   a. Reflect on the content
   b. Search for the meaning the sender does not express
   c. Review and weigh what has been heard
   d. Minimize distractions
   e. Minimize or eliminate criticism
   f. Ask questions
   g. Repeat major points of the message

Greater accuracy in communication can be gained if one works diligently at developing good listening habits. Probably the first and most important action to be taken is to stop talking. One cannot listen if one is talking (Verderber, 1996).

The art of listening requires one to expend considerable energy in order to understand and use the information transmitted by others. The opportunities to listen when functioning as a supervisor are considerable, and it is one of the best ways to receive information from subordinates. Good listeners can easily expand their knowledge of a subject about which they know little. It is the responsibility of an effective supervisor to develop good listening skills to the highest level possible (Verderber, 1996).

Nonverbal Communication

Communication involves more than sending, receiving, and assessing a message. It is a complex process that extends beyond the actual message to a consideration of nonverbal aspects of communication. Feelings and emotions are important aspects of any message. Some experts have observed that it is more important to be competent in nonverbal communication than in actual verbal skills. There are three components of a message that contribute to the communication process. In terms of impact, only seven percent can be accredited to the actual words, 38 percent to the way it was said, and 55 percent to nonverbal facets of communication (Mehrabian, 1981).

This means the stance, the gestures used, the facial expression, and other nonverbal aspects of communication all have a serious impact on the communication process. Body language (*kinesics*) is the study of nonverbal communication and concerns itself with understanding nonverbal signals. It has been suggested that body language actually reveals one's innermost thoughts and feelings (Mann, 2000). Body language needs to be accepted as an important element of the communication process if one is to be an effective supervisor (Genua, 1992). It must be remembered that many important messages that are nonverbal transpire as part of the communication process (Leathers, 1992).

One expert pointed out that a person's state of mind can be acted out with nonverbal body language: an eyebrow can be lifted to convey disbelief; a nose rubbed to indicate puzzlement; folded arms indicate refusal or, in some instances, self-protection; a shrug of a shoulder might indicate indifference; a wink may convey intimacy; a tap of the finger or a foot may reflect impatience (Fast, 1991).

Body language extends beyond these items by including a wide range of indicators such as posture, facial expression, body movement, positioning, eye contact, and body tension. All these contribute to the communication process. Be aware of the image you project, and realize that body language cues can be picked up. Keep in mind that any single nonverbal cue might not be especially significant, but when taken in conjunction with others, it might have a great deal of significance. For example, stroking the chin accompanied by a relaxed smile will probably indicate that the listener's mind has been made up about the issue under discussion. One must develop an awareness of the fact that the body might not be conveying the message intended (Warfield, 2001).

An individual sends messages not only through language and words, but also through tone of voice, pitch, and inflection. This form of communication is called *paralanguage*. Similar to body language, it is another means by which one can express emotion. Active emotions, such as anger and fear, tend to be expressed by a fast rate of speech, loud volume, high pitch, and "blaring" tone. On the other hand, passive emotions, such as sadness, are communicated by a slower rate of speech, lower volume, lower pitch, and a more resolute quality (Pritchett, 1993).

Nonverbal communication is primarily used to convey emotions, desires, and preferences. Generally, nonverbal cues reinforce or contradict the feelings that are communicated verbally. Feelings can be expressed through various types of nonverbal behavior, including facial expressions—in particular eye contact, posture, and gestures (Dimitrius and Mazzarella, 1998).

Eye contact can be used effectively in controlling communication. It can be used to solicit or to actually suppress the transmission of a message. It can be used to support communication or to reinforce feedback. A supervisor can convey to a subordinate, through appropriate eye contact, a specific interest in him or her and the problem. Eye contact reinforces talking with a subordinate because the person is given undivided attention. The failure to maintain sufficient eye contact can display aloofness, indirectness, a lack of confidence, or anxiety. The face is the primary communicator of emotions. One expert believes that there are 250,000 different facial expressions. Nonverbal messages, such as the following, can be conveyed by easily recognizable facial expressions:

- Interest in the individual or topic
- Acceptance
- Concern
- An expression of anger
- Disapproval of one's conduct or the action taken
- Boredom with the problem or the topic

Once aware of the importance of facial expressions, the supervisor can use cues that support and reinforce communication, thereby reducing the probability that the recipient will misinterpret the sender's message.

Even one's posture serves as a cue to the communication process. When conversing with a subordinate, the supervisor can convey the importance of the topic and a definite interest in the matter simply by leaning forward. Other positive body language indicators are: nodding, maintaining eye contact, and smiling (Dimitrius and Mazzarella, 1998). One should avoid slouching and always assume an erect but relaxed position (Verderber, 1996). The supervisor's posture can be used to reinforce other nonverbal cues and reduce the potential for contradiction between an individual's verbal and nonverbal communication.

Gestures are the voluntary movement of a part of the body to explain, emphasize, or reinforce the verbal component of a message. It is an important part of what has been called the *silent language.* One expert has identified 5,000 distinct hand gestures that have verbal equivalents (Axtell, 1991). For the most part, gestures are made with the hands and arms to clarify a point or to indicate a transition point in the conversation. Because there is less awareness of the gestures used, in contrast to eye contact or facial expressions, it is essential to become familiar with these gestures. A supervisor must use good timing in the use of gestures, realizing that they must be coordinated with the verbal message. Care also must be taken to control gestures that might possibly detract from the message being transmitted. For instance, stroking the chin, folding the arms, or rubbing the nose can either reinforce or detract from the message. A simple technique for determining the extent and nature of gestures is to videotape a five-minute presentation and then review it, identifying specific gestures and determining their relationship to specific verbal points.

One should immediately be able to determine whether a conflicting message is being sent. When this is done, it can confuse others. The nonverbal message communicates emotion, so it is essential to accurately reflect the intent of your message. Supervisors can ask themselves such questions as: "Does my body language support and reinforce my verbal message?" "Are conflicting messages being sent?" "Do my actions convey a genuine and sincere interest in my subordinates?" It is important to respond to these questions and do everything possible to ensure that effective communication occurs.

Communicating with Non-English-Speaking Individuals

The communication process becomes increasingly complex and difficult when an officer deals with witnesses, victims, or individuals seeking help who do not speak English. Traditionally, this problem was dealt with by obtaining the assistance of a neighbor, friend, or relative of the individual being interviewed, who could act as translator. Many officers have used the talents of younger individuals as interpreters because, in contrast to older family members, they are often bilingual.

In some departments, officers who are bilingual serve as translators when the occasion arises. In fact, it is becoming increasingly common for police departments to hire bilingual officers, and in some instances they are paid a bonus for the additional skill. Many departments across the nation make use of the AT&T interpreter service that offers interpreters for 144 languages and can locate speakers of many less common languages, given extra time. Laminated cards that list the languages for which interpreters are available are issued to each officer. One national commission recommended that a department under review complete a language needs assessment of the areas served and develop a plan to meet those needs. As part of the assessment it was recommended that the department take into account the number of persons arrested and the number of victims and witnesses in each area who speak little or no English (United States Commission on Civil Rights, 1999). In another police department with approximately 1,000 sworn officers, the federal court ordered the department to give hiring preference to candidates who were fluent in Spanish. Thus, the availability of Spanish-speaking officers increased dramatically.

In many areas, community colleges have responded positively to police department needs and have developed special foreign language courses for officers. Typical of this is a three-unit class titled *Spanish for Law Enforcement Personnel* (Allread, 1999).

Another innovative approach, which illustrates what can be done to obtain expert assistance when language is a barrier, is the arrangement made by one department in which foreign language instructors at a government agency are available as interpreters. Their expertise ranges from Arabic to Swahili.

In the event that a first-line supervisor encounters a foreign language barrier and an interpreter is not available within the department, consideration should be given to identifying interpreters who are employees of other city or county agencies. For example, in one library system, individuals who spoke 20 different languages were identified, and a memorandum of understanding was agreed upon in order for officers to use their expertise. The opportunities for such arrangements are extensive, and departments should not overlook the language expertise to be found in high schools, colleges, or business establishments.

Intercultural Communication

Police departments are beginning to train officers in diversity as our nation becomes more multicultural (Palmiotto, 1997). The heterogeneity of our country, in many areas, has become such that communications between police officers and immigrants has become increasingly difficult. Immigrants have concentrated in selected cities and in selected areas of citizens. The ethnicity of neighborhoods has changed rapidly with the influx of varying nationalities, including Cubans, Puerto Ricans, Vietnamese, Cambodians, Mexicans, Koreans, Chinese, and Russians. As international travel has increased, tourists from other nations frequent many cities in the United States, further complicating the communication process (Hoecklin, 1995).

The communication process, while different for each culture, is comprised of essentially three components—language, culture, and ethnicity (Pritchett, 1993).

Consequently, it has become increasingly important for supervisors, as well as officers, to have an understanding of intercultural communications etiquette (Brislin, 1994) and methods of communicating with people of other nations. A rudimentary knowledge of cultural variations and values can help a supervisor deal with the culturally diverse public. One should learn the pronunciation of certain names so as not to offend. Some Spanish-speaking cultures use double surnames, the Chinese place the family name first, and Filipinos place the given name first, followed by the family name. People of Russian and Ukrainian extraction construct their names in a manner similar to that of English names. Their middle name, however, is a patronymic (a derivation of the father's given name) and the surname is the family name (Kenney and More, 1994).

Some cultures will tell you what you want to hear, rather than what is the truth. Nonverbal behavior is culturally specific. Different cultures have differing norms for both verbal and nonverbal behavior. The uniqueness of different cultures is that they each have different *rules* for speaking and listening. Some cultures converse with a great deal of emotion, while others use extensive hand gestures. In some Asian cultures, eye contact is considered disrespectful, while Americans prefer eye contact. Space is another nonverbal cultural feature. Supervisors need to understand and respect the importance of *proxemics*, or personal and social space. Arabs, Southern Mediterraneans, and Latin Americans stand close when they converse and touch while conversing—in sharp contrast to Americans, who generally reject someone who violates their personal space (Berryman-Fink and Fink, 1996). In contact cultures, physical closeness, occasional touching, and frequent gesturing are important and desired components of the communication process (Pritchett, 1993). A supervisor must be willing to become knowledgeable about intercultural communications. Above all, there should be an open-minded and flexible response to the demands of an increasingly diverse society.

Communicating with Hearing-Impaired Individuals

In the United States it is estimated that 21 million people have some degree of hearing impairment, and a large number of these individuals are completely deaf. This can be a serious problem for law enforcement officers when they are faced with someone whose communication is limited because of such an affliction. Supervisors who take the time to learn sign language can become a valuable departmental resource and assist other officers. Hearing-impaired individuals can usually be identified by careful and sensitive observation (see Figure 3.11).

Figure 3.11
Recognizing Hearing-Impaired Individuals

1. The person appears alert but fails to respond to any sounds, such as surrounding noises or spoken language.
2. The person points to the ears or to the ears and mouth with an index finger.
3. The person moves his or her lips without making any sound.
4. The person speaks in a flat, harsh, or unintelligible monotone.
5. The person gestures in a manner that suggests a desire to write something.
6. A person moving fingers and hands in repetitive patterns could be using sign language, hoping to be understood.
7. Repeating a sequence of body movements or gestures may be an attempt to communicate an unspoken thought or idea.
8. The individual appears unusually alert and follows every move with his or her eyes.

Source: U.S. Department of Health and Human Services (1981). *Emergency Medical Services (EMS) and the Hearing Impaired.* Rockville, MD: USGPO, and Office for Civil Rights (2001). *Communicating with Hearing-Impaired Individuals.* Washington, DC: U.S. Department of Health and Human Services.

Some deaf persons express themselves orally or they may combine the use of speech with signing. The latter technique is described as a form of manual communication, in which the individual uses movements of the body, hands, and face to convey messages. It is estimated there are at least 500,000 deaf people who communicate by using American Sign Language or International Sign Language as their primary method of communication (Proctor, 1997).

Lipreading (speech-reading) is another technique used by the hearing impaired. This is the process of recognizing spoken words by watching the speaker's facial expressions, lip movements, and/or body language. A deaf person must have a number of skills, including good visual acuity, knowledge of the language, and the ability to distinguish between words that look similar when they are spoken. Unfortunately, the speaker who has a beard or moustache or speaks with an accent can complicate the task of effectively reading someone's lips. When communicating with a deaf person, the supervisor should take into consideration the items listed in Figure 3.12.

Figure 3.12
Considerations When Communicating with Hearing-Impaired Individuals

1. Family members and friends may not be effective or reliable as inter-preters. They may lack objectivity and may misinterpret pertinent information. Such individuals should not be relied upon to provide sign language interpretation except in limited circumstances.

2. Lipreading is often slow and requires a high degree of concentration. Keep in mind that lipreading (or speech-reading) presumes that the hearing-impaired person speaks English. Lipreading does not facilitate two-way communication.

3. Writing notes and finger spelling are both ineffective methods of com-munications for the majority of deaf persons. These methods are very slow, and many people are unfamiliar with law enforcement jargon. Additionally, these methods presume that deaf persons are function-ally literate in English.

4. The judgment of the hearing-impaired person should be given primary consideration when determining the preferred form of communication. This is best accomplished by asking the person whether auxiliary aids and services are necessary to ensure effective communication.

5. Qualified sign language interpreters who have received specialized for-mal education and experience can ensure effective communications.

6. Persons who are deaf and who communicate in sign language cannot communicate when they are handcuffed. Handcuffs on booked deaf individuals should be removed if the removal does not result in a direct threat to the health and safety of any person in the jail (Nation-al Association of the Deaf Law Center, 2000a).

Interpreters

Interpreters facilitate communication between hearing and deaf indi-viduals. The length, importance, or complexity of the communication will help determine whether an interpreter is necessary for effective communi-cation. In a simple encounter, such as checking a driver's license, a notepad and pencil normally will be sufficient. During interrogations and arrests, a sign language interpreter will often be necessary to effectively communicate with an individual who uses sign language (U.S. Department of Justice, 1996). Operationally, there are two types of interpreters. The first is a sign language interpreter, who listens to the speaking person and informs the deaf person of the content of the message by using sign language. The second is an oral interpreter, who repeats another's words without using voice. The words are mouthed and the deaf person speech-reads the interpreter.

"State and local law enforcement agencies have a federal mandate to ensure adequate and appropriate communication with deaf and hard-of-hearing individuals. Without effective communication serious violations of constitutional and civil rights can occur" (National Association of the Deaf Law Center, 2000a). This mandate is found in two federal laws protecting the rights of individuals with disabilities (National Association of the Deaf Law Center, 2001). An important settlement agreement between the United States, two complainants, and the City of Houston, Texas, was the result of police officers, jail officials, and court officials not effectively communicating with hearing-impaired persons. The city agreed that individuals with disabilities, including but not limited to crime victims, witnesses to crimes, and people under arrest, are entitled to effective communications (U.S. Department of Justice, 1998).

Additionally, U.S. Department of Justice regulation 28 C.F.R. Part 42 (July 26, 1992) requires law enforcement agencies to ensure that hearing-impaired individuals can be communicated with effectively. They are also encouraged to use qualified interpreters who are registered with a local or state chapter of the Registry of Interpreters of the Deaf (RID), founded in 1964. This organization has the responsibility of certifying individuals as qualified interpreters and more recently has worked with the National Association of the Deaf on a new testing procedure that will take several more years until it is a reality (www.rid.org).

Interpreters should be present when a hearing-impaired individual is informed of his or her rights, when he or she is being questioned, and when a statement is taken. When a hearing-impaired individual is arrested, he or she should be provided with a printed form of the *Miranda* warning (which includes offering an interpreter to the arrestee without cost), and the form should point out that the interrogation will be delayed until an interpreter is present. This requirement is set forth in 45 Fed. Reg. 37630 (June 3, 1980).

Summary

A supervisor interacting with a subordinate elicits some kind of response or triggers an emotion. If supervisors are successful, the desired impression is created and conveyed. At other times, the officer responds to behavior in a way that the supervisor did not anticipate. One's interpersonal effectiveness depends on the ability to communicate a point clearly and influence another person in a desired manner.

Police supervisors spend the majority of their working hours communicating. In fact, one task analysis study showed they were involved in communication activities more than half the time they were at work. While some communicating is represented by written reports, the majority is interpersonal.

The communication process is highly complex and modified by the following variables: what the sender intended to say, what was actually said, what the receiver heard, what the receiver thinks he or she heard, what the receiver said, and what the sender thinks the receiver said.

While one-way communication has its uses, two-way communication should dominate the supervisor/subordinate relationship. Its advantages far outweigh its disadvantages. It improves accuracy, provides for shared authority, produces greater understanding, and acknowledges the importance of the communication process.

Barriers to communication are numerous, but those found to be of greatest concern include anxiety about one's knowledge of a subject, the probability of being looked upon with displeasure, jeopardizing one's status, environmental influences, personal expectations, and semantics. Such barriers to communication can be overcome if the first-line supervisor follows the leadership mandate of always communicating, even to the point of overcommunicating. The problems resolved by this method clearly outnumber the problems that can be created. Today's officers want to know what is going on. They want to feel that they are in control of their lives and are part of the system.

Feedback is one of the sergeant's most important communication tools. It should be offered in a specific way, conveyed fairly, selective in nature, and based on fact (not personality). Its ultimate goal is to improve performance.

Some of the most successful supervisors are also the best listeners. The opportunities to listen when functioning as a supervisor are considerable, and it is one of the best ways to receive information from subordinates. It is the responsibility of the supervisor to develop, to the highest degree possible, the skill of being a good listener.

Nonverbal aspects of communication constitute a major proportion of the communication process. This means that posture, gestures, facial expressions, and other nonverbal expressions have a serious impact on the communication process. This is especially true when intercultural communication complicates the process.

The ability to communicate is a prerequisite for success as a first-line supervisor, because virtually everything a supervisor does depends on effective communication. Task accomplishment depends on clear and precise communication.

Case Study

Sergeant Ted Oxford

Sergeant Ted Oxford has been with the department for nine years and a sergeant for three years. He spent last year as an instructor in a regional police academy. He has just returned to the patrol division and is currently on the swing shift as a first-line supervisor. As the senior supervisor on the shift, he serves as a watch commander when the lieutenant has days off or is on vacation. The town has a population of 38,000 and is a regional commerce and industry center. Additionally, the town houses the main campus of a state university that has a student body of 16,500. The department has 69 sworn officers, 11 dispatchers, 15 civilian employees, and a police reserve unit of 22. During the last few years a number of immigrants from Central America have moved to the community to work in the meat processing businesses. Many of these individuals have limited English skills.

Sergeant Oxford successfully completed his probationary period as a supervisor, and his performance ratings were excellent. Since then he has always received an excellent annual performance rating. He is scheduled to take the lieutenant's examination at the end of the year.

He supervises two officers who are increasingly negative about the minorities who have moved to the community. The officers say that they cannot communicate with the minorities and that it is impossible to help someone when you cannot understand them. Both officers have been on the force for seven years, and both of them have taken a promotional examination with negative results.

No matter what topic is discussed in the locker room or at coffee breaks, the two officers change the subject and point out the impossibility of working with minorities who cannot speak English. Their frustration is such that they seem unable to discuss any other issue. Either one or the other of the officers constantly interrupt others in order to present their view. Fellow officers can hardly complete a sentence before they are interrupted, and it is usually done in a way that suggests that the other person has no idea what he or she is talking about.

The two officers show a complete lack of respect for anyone who disagrees with them, and they openly argue with those whose opinions differ. The other officers find their abrasive nature and refusal to listen to the opinions of others totally unacceptable. Both officers ignore the fact that the department is working to solve the problem by identifying translators or subscribing to a translator service.

As a supervisor, you are fully aware of the importance of having good communication. You realize that the negativism of the two officers is hurting morale. It is your desire to work with the two officers so they might learn to listen to and accept other opinions as well as improving their conduct and general attitude. What would be your initial step in this situation? Why? Would you seek outside help? Why or why not? How would you work with the two officers to alert them to their disruptive behavior? Would diversity training be of help? Why?

Key Concepts

art of listening
communicating with non-English-
   speaking individuals
communication patterns
communication process
decoding
encoding
feedback
hearing impairment
importance of communications
intercultural communications
interpreters

lip-reading
nonverbal communication
one-way communication
overcoming communication barriers
paralanguage
proxemics
physical barriers
psychological barriers
realistic communication process
semantics
simplistic communication process
two-way communication

Discussion Topics and Questions

1. What are the psychological barriers to communication?

2. What are the components of the realistic communication process?

3. When should a supervisor resort to one-way communication?

4. Discuss the value of two-way communication.

5. Why is it important to be to be knowledgeable about nonverbal communication?

6. Discuss the importance of semantics to the communication process.

7. Discuss the value of intercultural communications.

8. How should one utilize an interpreter?

9. Identify the characteristics of feedback.

10. Discuss the role of the Registry of Interpreters of the Deaf (RID).

11. How can one recognize hearing-impaired individuals?

For Further Reading

Berryman-Fink, Cynthia, and Charles B. Fink (1996). *The Manager's Desk Reference,* Second Edition. New York, NY: AMACOM.

    This business-oriented text will prove to be very valuable to law enforcement personnel. The text discusses ways in which individuals, experienced and inexperienced, can improve intercultural communication, and addresses areas of cultural difference. Consideration is given to how one might develop intercultural communication competence and become aware of variations in cultural traditions. Recommends that cultural awareness training be instituted as a means of bridging the gap between cultures.

Dimitrius, Jo-Ellan, and Mark Mazzarella (1998). *Reading People—How to Understand People and Predict Their Behavior—Anytime, Anyplace.* New York, NY: Random House.

Of special interest is the discussion of communications in terms of do's and don'ts of good listening. Reviews a number of points ranging from "don't interrupt" to not violating another's space. Consideration is also given to the need to be aware of your body language. Special attention is given to the do's and don'ts of good questions, such as the open-ended question and the leading question.

Salmon, William A. (1998). *The New Supervisor's Survival Manual.* New York, NY: AMACOM.

Discusses the need to overcome some of the common barriers to effective communications. Reviews such barriers as interruptions and distractions, as well as one's emotional state. Includes an excellent discussion of techniques that can be used when requesting and receiving information and opinions from others. Reviews the importance of reputation, credibility, and intention of a communicator.

U.S. Department of Justice (1998). *Settlement Agreement between the United States of America, Rashad Gordon, Michael Edwards, and The City of Houston, Texas.* Washington, DC: Department of Justice.

Describes in detail the agreement to create an ADA Coordinator and lists what should be done so that individuals with disabilities, including but not limited to crime victims, witnesses to crimes, and people under arrest can be communicated with effectively. Includes such things as specific procedures for requesting an interpreter, educating personnel, and establishing grievance procedures. Additionally, there is a copy of the police department's General Order 500-13.

References

Albrecht, Karl (1979). *Stress and the Manager: Making it Work for You.* Englewood Cliffs, NJ: Prentice-Hall, Inc.

Allread, Walter (1999). "Language Skills Important." *Law and Order,* Vol. 47, No. 1.

Axtell, Roger E. (1991). *Gestures—The Do's and Taboos of Body Language Around the World.* New York, NY: John Wiley and Sons, Inc.

Berryman-Fink, Cynthia, and Charles B. Fink (1996). *The Manager's Desk Reference*, Second Edition. New York, NY: AMACOM.

Bradford, David L., and Allan R. Cohen (1984). *Managing for Excellence: The Guide to Developing High Performance in Contemporary Organizations.* New York, NY: John Wiley and Sons.

Brislin, Richard W. (1994). *Intercultural Communications Training: An Introduction.* Thousand Oaks, CA: Sage Publications.

Commission on Peace Officer Standards and Training (1996). *Supervisory Development and Guide.* Sacramento, CA: California POST.

DeVito, Joseph A. (1992). *The Interpersonal Communications Book*. New York, NY: Harper-Collins Publishers, Inc.

Dickson, David, Christine Saunders, and Maurice Stringer (1993). *Rewarding People: The Skill of Responding Positively*. New York, NY: Routledge.

Dimitrius, Jo-Ellan, and Mark Mazzarella (1998). *Reading People: How to Understand People and Predict Their Behavior—Anytime, Anyplace*. New York, NY: Random House.

Fast, Julius (1991). *Making Body Language Work in the Workplace*. New York, NY: Viking.

Gaines, Larry K., Mittie D. Southerland, and John E. Angell (1991). *Police Administration*. New York, NY: McGraw-Hill Book Company.

Genua, Robert L. (1992). *Managing Your Mouth*. New York, NY: AMACOM.

Hoecklin, Lisa A. (1995). *Managing Cultural Differences: Strategies for Competitive Advantage*. Reading, MA: Addison-Wesley.

Johnson, Robert R. (1996). "Listening—When Management Values Input, Morale Improves." *Law and Order*, Vol. 44, No. 2.

Kenney, John P., and Harry W. More (1994). *Principles of Investigation*, Second Edition. St. Paul, MN: West Publishing.

Leathers, Dale G. (1992). *Successful Nonverbal Communication: Principles and Application*. New York, NY: Macmillan Publishing Co.

Mann, S. (2000). "Body Talk: The Non-Verbal Language That Reveals Our Innermost Thoughts and Feelings." *Professional Manager*, Vol. 9, No. 6.

Mehrabian, Albert (1981). *Silent Messages: Implicit Communications of Emotions and Attitudes*. Belmont, CA: Wadsworth Publishing.

National Association of the Deaf Law Center (2000a). *Legal Rights: The Guide for Deaf and Hard of Hearing People*, Fifth Edition. Washington, DC: Gallaudet University.

————— (2000b). *NAD Position Statement on Communication Access by Law Enforcement Personnel with Deaf and Hard of Hearing Individuals*. Silver Spring, MD: National Association of the Deaf.

————— (2001). *Police and Law Enforcement Agency Responsibilities to Deaf Individuals*. Silver Spring, MD: National Association of the Deaf.

Naval Education and Training Program (1984). *Human Behavior*. Washington, DC: U.S. Government Printing Office.

Nierenberg, Gerald I. (1986). *Fundamentals of Negotiation*. New York, NY: Nierenberg and Zeif Publishers.

Office for Civil Rights (2001). *Communicating with Hearing-Impaired Individuals*. Washington, DC: U.S. Department of Health and Human Services.

Overton, W.C., and J.J. Black (1994). "Language as a Weapon." *The Police Chief*, Vol. LXI, No. 8.

Palmiotto, Michael J. (1997). *Policing: Concepts, Strategies, and Current Issues*. Durham, NC: Carolina Academic Press.

Pritchett, Garry L. (1993). "Interpersonal Communication—Improving Law Enforcement's Image." *FBI Law Enforcement Bulletin*, Vol. 62, No. 7.

Proctor, Claude O. (1997). *NTC's Multilingual Dictionary of American Sign Language.* Lincoln, IL: National Textbook.

Salmon, William A. (1998). *The New Supervisor's Survival Manual.* New York: AMACOM.

Southerland, Mittie D. (1992). "Organizational Communication." In Larry T. Hoover (ed.), *Police Management: Issues and Perspectives.* Washington, DC: Police Executive Research Forum.

U.S. Commission on Civil Rights (1999). *Racial and Ethnic Tensions in American Communities: Poverty, Inequality and Discrimination.* Volume 5: The Los Angeles Report. Washington, DC: U.S. Commission on Civil Rights.

U.S. Department of Health and Human Services (1981). *Emergency Medical Services and the Hearing Impaired.* Rockville, MD: U.S. Department of Health and Human Services.

U.S. Department of Justice (June 3, 1980) 45 Fed. Reg. 37630.

_____ (July 26, 1992) 28 C.F.R. Part 42.

_____ (1996). *Commonly Asked Questions about the Americans with Disabilities Act and Law Enforcement.* Washington, DC: Civil Rights Division, Disability Rights Section.

_____ (1998). *Settlement Agreement Between the United States of America, Rashad Gordon, Michael Edwards, and The City of Houston, Texas.* Washington, DC: U.S. Department of Justice.

Verderber, Rudolph F. (1996). *Communicate!* Belmont, CA: Wadsworth Publishing.

Vita, Bryan (2000). *Tired Cops: The Importance of Managing Police Fatigue.* Washington, DC: U.S. Police Executive Research Forum.

Warfield, Anne (2001). "Do You Speak Body Language?" *Training and Development*, Vol. 55, No. 4.

White, Ken W., and Elwood N. Chapman (1996). *Organizational Communications: An Introduction to Communications and Human Relations Strategies.* Upper Saddle River, NJ: Simon and Schuster Custom Publishing.

Motivation—

A Prerequisite for Success

4

Introductory Case Study

Sergeant Charles Pollard

Charles Pollard successfully completed a regional police academy and placed ninth in a class of 41. He was initially assigned to the night shift, where he worked under the supervision of an experienced officer for three months. After that, he worked by himself in the downtown area of the village. Pollard is 26 years old and previously worked as a truck driver for four years. He is not married and lives in an apartment complex in an adjacent community. He has recently completed all of the academic requirements for an associate's degree in criminal justice. Currently he has no plans to continue his higher education.

The village of Emperor has 19,220 residents and is a suburban community encompassing seven square miles. It is a highly desirable place to live. The community has many tree-lined streets, and homes are on large lots. There is only one major shopping center and no light industry. It has large open spaces and it is anticipated that the village will grow considerably over the next decade. Additionally, the community has an excellent school system that has proven to be attractive to new residents. A seven-member council and a strong mayor govern the community. Currently, the police department has an annual budget of $5.9 million, with 52 sworn officers and 26 civilian employees. The community has its own communications center. During the next two years it is anticipated that the department will have 105 sworn officers.

Sergeant Pollard replaced a well-liked first-line supervisor who had just retired. He has been asked to supervise a sector of the city that has four beats on the swing shift. The beat officers have an average of five years experience, and Pollard had worked on the same shift, at different times, with each of the officers. The four beat officers had taken the promotional examination and were not rated high enough to be promoted from the current list, which expires in two years. That means they will probably not be promoted off of the current list. Pollard is very concerned about how the officers will react to his management style.

If you were Sergeant Pollard, how would you approach the problem of officer motivation? How would you go about determining the basic need drives of each officer? What is the first thing you would do? Why? How would you use the hierarchy of needs?

Motives are the *why* of human behavior. A motive energizes one to take action and concerns itself with the choices one makes about goal-directed behavior. A supervisor must take a multitude of factors into consideration when trying to understand the process of motivation. Central to that understanding is the human equation (Berryman-Fink and Fink, 1996).

The preponderance of problems confronting an organization are clearly those identified as the phenomena involving human conduct. The advances in physical and biological technology have not even identified what constitutes human behavior, much less presented a solution to understanding this complex area. There is a need for a technology of behavior, but this has not evolved and we seem to know little more about human behavior today than we did a century ago. Notwithstanding, supervisors must deal constantly with both acceptable and unacceptable behavior.

The behavioral sciences trace behavior by utilizing such terms as *attitudes*, *feelings*, and *state of mind*. These concepts can be interpreted differently; consequently, problems have arisen as the field has developed. There is a continuous struggle as efforts are made to identify and measure behavior and, while a comprehensive theory of behavior has yet to be set forth, the quest goes on. In the meantime, supervisors must deal with the behavior of subordinates and use all the knowledge at their disposal to motivate each employee so that organizational goals can be achieved (Burg, 1991).

Successful supervisors know that in order to motivate employees a great deal of effort must be expended. Motivation is not just something to be turned off and on at one's leisure. It is a full-time demanding process and can be all-consuming. Employees will soon learn that a motivational speech at roll call asking them to "go out and make those streets safe" only serves to make the supervisor feel better. Rhetoric means little if it is not accompanied by other positive reinforcements.

Why Officers Work

Behavioral scientists generally accept the proposition that behavior does not happen spontaneously—it is caused. Human behavior can be explained to a great extent by determining basic human needs (Naval Education and Training Program, 1984). Needs are fundamental to our basic existence and they cause things to happen. Needs cause one to act in a certain way, and goal attainment can result in need satisfaction. For example, before acquiring the rank of sergeant, an officer's behavior was directed toward successfully passing examinations allowing for goal attainment.

It seems the more humankind is studied, the more we realize the complexity of human behavior. In the past it was believed that reason was capable of solving all problems. Aristotle believed that reason held sway over all human capacities (Nirenberg, 1986). Our current knowledge goes well beyond this. Our intricacy demands that a systematic procedure be followed in attempting to understand the internal and external factors that motivate individuals to act the way they do. In general, behavior will follow a pattern showing that:

- A need will mobilize the energy to reach an acceptable goal.

- As the need increases in intensity, goal attainment is emphasized by the individual.

- As the need increases, behavior will follow, hopefully allowing for the attainment of goals.

From the above, the characteristics of human behavior become more apparent. A need arises and one's perception mobilizes the energy needed for reaching a goal. If the goal is not attained, the person tries again, mobilizing additional energy. Additional attention is paid to excluding factors that do not foster goal attainment. The motivation cycle is a vehicle that aids in understanding human behavior. This cycle will allow you to gain an appreciation of the interacting forces and the resulting motivated behavior. Figure 4.1 depicts motivation as a continuous process consisting of three specific steps. Step 1 occurs when an individual experiences a need caused by external or internal forces and those forces are mobilized. In Step 2, a responding behavior transpires, energy increases in intensity, and satisfaction occurs. Step 3 results in goal attainment. The completion of one cycle is not necessarily the end of the process. It can repeat itself or another need can arise.

Figure 4.1
Motivation Cycle

Step 1.   NEED

Step 2.   RESPONDING BEHAVIOR   }   =   SATISFACTION

Step 3.   GOAL

Adapted from Associates of the Office of Military Leadership, USMA (eds.), *A Study of Organizational Leadership* (1976). Harrisburg, PA: Stackpole Books, 1976 and The Society for Applied Anthropology. Reprinted with permission.

An individual's motivation to act depends on two factors: the strength of the need and believing a certain action will lead to need satisfaction. For example, a patrol officer thought of becoming a sergeant and developed the desire to strive for the rank. The intensity of this person's motivation and the satisfaction of the need depend upon the perception of the real value of the goal. If his or her desire to become a sergeant is more than a transient wish and he or she wants the extra pay, the status, involvement in the decision-making process, and the power that goes with position, the individual's motivation will undoubtedly be high (Brown, 1992).

This simple example fulfills the requirement of motivation inasmuch as the need was strong and the individual pursued a course to satisfy that need. A manager has a responsibility to motivate employees. In fact, most agencies have a written directive stating that supervisory personnel are accountable for the performance of employees under their immediate supervision (CALEA, 1999). Supervisors must create conditions that maximize the productivity of the officers. Their efforts must be coordinated to achieve departmental goals. A first-line supervisor will soon acknowledge every officer as a unique individual and each individual, is generally stimulated by different needs.

Officers can be motivated by one need today and tomorrow the need may reappear or a new need may become evident. In other words, as the situation changes, the individual's wants and desires can change. It is clear that subjective and objective features affect job satisfaction (Fincham and Rhodes, 1995). Officers can be motivated by fear, values, beliefs, interests, habits, culture, peer influence, love, moral standards, or other factors. It is evident that some of these factors are internal to the officer, while others are external. The combination of external and internal factors determines what motivates an officer to act in a certain way in a certain situation.

Motivational experts point out that the whole person is hired, not just a part. This means motivating the totality of a person's drives. Motivation is as complex as human behavior. So a supervisor should keep an open mind about motivating individuals and not fall victim to the desire to find the panacea to the motivational problem (White, 2001).

At one time in the police service, the primary motivational force was based on power. If the order was to jump, the required response was "How high?" A supervisor might have the power, but the work environment is different and the employees, for the most part, will respond better to different motivational factors. It is a supervisor's responsibility to develop officers' needs and, when appropriate, make organizational needs overcome personal needs.

Effort must be directed toward attaining organizational goals through the work of individuals and groups. In order to accomplish this immense task, a supervisor should strive to create an atmosphere in the organizational working life in which most officers become self-motivated (Leonard and More, 2000).

The police supervisor who ignores the ecology of the organization will seldom be successful. A motivated employee is the product of interaction with the organization and the attitudes generated. Thus the key to motivation is not just the individual, but the department. There should be an organizational norm of supervisory activities that stimulate the development and growth of every officer. Above all, this calls for a supervisor to demonstrate consistency in the performance of supervisory duties. Extremes of supervisory style, such as tough or lax supervision, should be avoided (Dees, 1992).

The whole individual must be motivated. If an officer can be placed in a well-structured organization with identifiable goals, where the culture is such that one can readily identify with it, where tasks are challenging and accomplished individuals are rewarded, then the organization is really motivating its employees.

Historically, a number of police agencies have exhibited characteristics definitely incompatible with the above description. These agencies personify the *authoritarian mandate* leadership style reminiscent of the time when a manager gave an order and the only acceptable reply was "When, where, and how much?" Fortunately, this type of supervision is a thing of the past in most agencies (Charrier, 2000).

In our society, work is fundamental and a natural aspect of one's daily life. In fact, work performs an exceedingly strong role in the economic, social, and psychological aspects of one's life. Work is defined as effort directed to accomplish something. This definition is compatible with the concept of goals being attained through the efforts of individuals and groups.

Often an individual's sense of identity is obtained from work, as evidenced by most people describing themselves as a member of a department or agency. While this means most people identify work as having great importance in their lives, it has to be acknowledged that there are some individuals who view work as a necessary evil.

Work provides officers with a sense of accomplishment as well as something with which to identify. Police work especially challenges one's skill and ingenuity. For many employees, the attainment of work-related goals has proven to be as important as material rewards. Most officers usually find police work challenging and demanding. In fact, everything else can become subordinate to work. Police work provides a sense of belonging, a sharing of duties, and a unique social bond.

A legitimate supervisory role is to create a work environment resulting in officer satisfaction. Two types of feelings come into play when one considers work. The first is global and describes an officer's expressed feelings about the total job. The second is facet and reveals an officer's feelings about one specific job element (Fincham and Rhodes, 1995). An example would be where an officer feels all promotions are based on "juice" (connections) and the support of a "rabbi" (mentor). Even with this as a dissatisfier, the officer expresses a positive global view of the job and believes that other job factors, such as importance of the work, feeling of accomplishing something, compensation, supervision, and equipment are factors supporting a *good* working environment. In fact, a healthy place to work has five characteristics (see Figure 4.2).

Figure 4.2
Phrases That Describe a Good Workplace

1. A friendly place to work.
2. There isn't much politicking around here.
3. You get a fair shake.
4. More than a job.
5. It's just like family.

Source: Robert Levering (1988). *A Great Place to Work.* New York, NY: Random House.

Within a good workplace the relationship between each employee and the organization is one of trust. When trust is present, officers get real satisfaction from the job. When managers and supervisors view the employees as an important organizational component, it results in real participation and increased productivity. Pride is another component of a good workplace relationship. The organization instills pride in each employee; in return, each employee feels pride in what they do. Officers enjoy working in an organization described as one in which trust is present and pride dominates the style of work. Thus, the workplace becomes a place where relationships are friendly, politicking is not present, and each employee is challenged to grow personally and professionally (Levering, 1988).

Motivation

If there is one word that seems to be overworked in the managerial lexicon, it is motivation. We apparently have an insatiable appetite for keeping up with the latest motivational techniques. It has reached the point where some businesses use motivational seminars extensively as a means of boosting morale. Some have even used the fire walk technique, in which participants walk across 12 feet of glowing embers. The response of one participant was "It was a great feeling to do something that I did not think could be done, and after doing it I felt that I could accomplish anything" (Roman, 1986). Whether this type of training produces a more productive employee cannot be answered at this time, but it does illustrate the extent to which some agencies will go in an effort to motivate employees.

Why is motivation so elusive? Why have we heard so much about it? Why is it accepted as a means of achieving goals or increasing productivity? Is it something magical? A basic assumption of this chapter is that managerial skills to stimulate and motivate employees can be learned. They are skills that are not tenuous, but real, and demonstrate (without a doubt) that motivation can be managed.

Motives for each member of the department are highly individualistic. Every person has their own motivational hierarchy based on needs, rewards, and values. Another important aspect of motivation is that it is not unvarying. Motivating factors can change over time. What causes someone to respond today might not be true tomorrow or the day after that (Haasen, 1997). Motives are not static, but dynamic. Consequently, while a supervisor can observe behavior, the motive for that behavior can only be inferred. Motives are generally considered to be insentient, and for the most part one is unaware of what motivates their behavior. Optimally, the best one can do is to work at changing behavior by using a variety of motivational techniques (Berryman-Fink and Fink, 1996).

Motivation is a mental process that produces an attitude resulting in an action leading to a result. Why do officers respond to a motivational factor? The primary reason is they derive a benefit from the result. Each person interprets and defines the reward differently. For one person it might be one thing and for another the reward may be something entirely different.

The key to motivation is not only the individual, but also the organization. In practice, nearly every organization has its own approach to motivation, which is usually a difference of style, taste, or emphasis rather than one of substance (Gellerman, 1992). When an individual is placed in a department where the goals and values are easily identifiable, where there is room for growth, where one is allowed to be creative and accept a challenge and where the officer feels secure and appreciated, as well as properly rewarded, then one finds an agency where the conditions are maximized for positive motivation. Police departments, however, have their own norms, and there are clearly those in which motivation plays a very important part and those in which it does not.

Where the dull are leading the dull, all the management experts in the world could not possibly improve the performance of employees. When a healthy culture evolves, it includes values, beliefs, and behaviors built on a sound organizational base that develops and fosters the creation of truly committed and highly motivated employees. When the major motivational influence in the workforce is one's internal drive to achieve, supported by and developed by the organization, then morale is high and this in turn enhances performance (Aragon, 1993). When that occurs, the organization can be described as performing successfully. In its simplest explanation, employees need to be empowered, involved, and true participants in the decision-making process. Every supervisor must work with employees in developing their abilities, skills, and knowledge, and every employee needs the technical knowledge and skill to perform assigned tasks. The supervisor must also provide conceptual skill training. This is an ongoing process of developing employees who can relate their own performance to the mission and value structure of the organization. Each employee has an understanding of the organization's relationship to the community and how change in one part can affect the rest of the organization (Grant, 1990).

In order to become an excellent supervisor, a person must develop a plan that identifies obligations to both the officers being supervised and the immediate superiors. Some of the more specific responsibilities are listed below:

Figure 4.3
Techniques Supervisors Can Use to Motivate Officers

1. Decide what each officer should be doing.
2. Specify a time for the completion of assigned tasks.
3. Maximize the use of everyone's skills.
4. Provide for a democratic workplace.
5. Demand high performance of everyone supervised, including yourself.
6. Turn the workplace into a learning environment through appropriate coaching.
7. Monitor your performance and that of supervised officers.
8. Correct a situation immediately when something goes wrong.
9. Create a work environment where officers can grow and work toward self-fulfillment.
10. Give prompt and explicit feedback.
11. Listen to officers' ideas and opinions.
12. Recognize achievements and successes.
13. Establish a supervisory style that precludes micromanagement.
14. When appropriate, allow officers to assume new responsibilities and duties.
15. Make sure that every officer knows what is expected of him or her.
16. Solicit officer participation in the decision-making process.
17. Constantly work at improving the communication process.

In reviewing these techniques note that they are all part of what can be identified as an achievement-motivation program. The bottom line is that everybody works with greater intensity when there is something in it for him or her. A significant element of this process is that it demonstrates a caring supervisor who is concerned about those being supervised. Motivation is a complicated process and a number of theories are discussed below. Each theory is a foundation for supervisory techniques that can be used in work situations. Each theory is highly individualistic, and no single theory applies to all situations. Taken as a totality, the varying motivational theories can provide you with a different way to look at behavior. The theories should be used by supervisors when working with line personnel (Thompson, 1995).

Needs-Based Motivation

Probably the most widespread motivational theory in use is that developed by Abraham H. Maslow. He postulated that people's needs were exceedingly complex and were arranged in a hierarchy. His studies were based on a positive concept of mental health, and his research cohorts were the very best individuals he could identify (Globe, 1970). These individuals were described as being self-actualized (S-A) and constituted less than one percent of the population. The self-actualized individual's personality was found to be more harmonious, and his or her perceptions were less distorted by fears, desires, hopes, false optimism, or pessimism (Maslow, 1970).

Interestingly enough, Maslow's superior individual was found to be 60 years of age or older, and the most universal characteristic was the ability to see life clearly. The self-actualized person was creative, risk-prone, and possessed a low threshold for self-conflict. Additionally, the S-A individual possessed a healthy attitude toward work, finding it enjoyable to the point of actually being play. The ultimate key for a supervisor is to help employees actualize—in other words, let them become all they can be (Dessler, 1993).

Based on the S-A personality, Maslow created a theory of motivation showing that human beings are motivated by a number of basic needs that are clearly identifiable as species-wide, unchanged, and instinctual. This theory identified five need categories: physiological, security, social, esteem, and self-actualization (see Figure 4.4).

Figure 4.4
Hierarchy of Needs

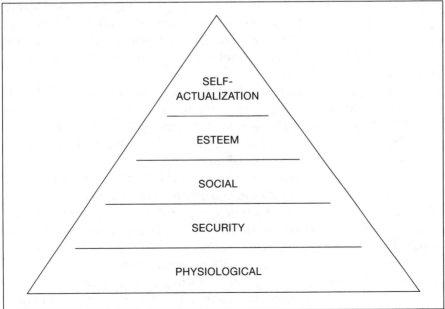

Source: *Motivation and Personality,* Second Edition by Abraham H. Maslow. Reprinted by permission of Pearson Education, Inc., Upper Saddle River, NJ.

Physiological Needs

The strongest and most fundamental needs are physiological needs. These life-sustaining needs include food, shelter, sex, air, water, and sleep. Maslow showed that throughout life the human being constantly desires something. Man is a *wanting* animal, and complete satisfaction is achieved for only a short time. As soon as one desire is satisfied, another takes its place. Imagine what it would be like to really be hungry, to the point of almost feeling starved. This could not only cause physical discomfort, but could also lead to impairment or illness. It can readily be seen that such a state of need will be dominant. In most areas of the United States, police officers' salaries place them beyond the point of minimum subsistence, so their basic physiological needs are generally fulfilled.

From a supervisory perspective, it becomes necessary to understand the degree to which officers are motivated by physiological needs. If these needs are not fulfilled, it becomes apparent that the work they are involved in has no meaning to them. When management concentrates on physiological needs as a means of motivating officers, they have made the assumption that people work foremost for financial rewards. Emphasis is placed on wage increases, better working conditions, longer breaks, and improved fringe benefits as a means of motivating officers.

Security Needs

Security needs emerge once a person's basic needs are fulfilled. The dominant security needs are primarily the need for reasonable order and stability and freedom from being anxious and insecure. Some officers have entered the police service because government agencies provide a secure and stable job. With security as a dominant need, officers will want stability and predictability above all else.

The managerial response should stress rules and regulations. Emphasis should be placed on traditional union demands such as pay and fringe benefits (Ranchlin, 1993). In addition, management that meets security needs would limit efforts to encourage individual initiative, complex problem-solving situations, or any type of risk taking.

Security-minded officers want everything in black and white. The known is stressed over the unknown. Some officers never get beyond the level of satisfying security needs. Change is rejected and every aspect of their working life has to be geared to absolute safety. This creates difficulties for some officers who want things to be stable and predictable, as when courts change the time-honored practices revolving around procedures such as advising suspects of their rights on search-and-seizure techniques.

When a supervisor seeks security above all, it is obvious that everything is played close to the vest. Rules and procedures dominate, and absolute adherence to time schedules is demanded. Such a supervisor is organized to the point of rigidity. One's boss is not only omnipotent, but also omniscient. Everything possible is done to please and placate individuals who are higher in the chain of command. The supervisor fixated with security needs ignores the needs of subordinate officers, uses manipulation when necessary, and the need to develop feelings of growth is rejected. Officers are viewed as having no need to control their own lives and the key to success is close supervision.

It would seem realistic to examine one's own security needs. How far should you go to cover up personal mistakes? Would you cover up mistakes made by your superiors? Would you do anything just to get promoted? Do you always agree with the boss just because that person is the boss? Whatever the answers, one should know more about oneself after answering these questions.

Social Needs

This level is a clear departure from the two basic needs discussed above. With the fulfillment of the physiological and security needs, the social needs emerge. Maslow pointed out that human beings will hunger for affiliation with others, for a place in a group, and they will attempt to achieve this goal with a great deal of intensity (Globe, 1970).

When this need is not fulfilled by the organization, the officer can respond by an excessive use of sick leave and inadequate productivity. It can lead to loneliness, boredom, and a poor self-image—affecting mental health. Most individuals want to be accepted by peers and supervisors. In fact, everyone has a strong tendency to identify with groups, and some people will modify their behavior to meet the group's criteria for membership.

When a supervisor becomes aware that social needs are motivating officers, then every effort should be made to promote social interaction. This can be difficult to do in a patrol unit that utilizes one-person patrol vehicles, but the supervisor can provide backup units whenever possible. In addition, the supervisor can act in a very supportive manner whenever possible. A physical conditioning room, parties, or organized sports events can all provide a means for meeting social needs.

The socially motivated supervisor emphasizes officers' needs and usually will ignore organizational needs. If options are available, the decision is always made on the side of the employee. Everything is done to ensure that the supervisor is part of the group. The approval of everyone is sought: subordinates, peers, and bosses. Supervisors must accomplish tasks through the efforts of others; thus, a good supervisor must help by supporting the efforts of those who are working to achieve departmental objectives.

What about your own social needs? When you become a supervisor can you change roles and lead? How strong is your need to be socially accepted? When you are promoted, can you accept being a part of management? These are not easy questions to answer, and they demand real soul-searching to determine where you stand in relation to your needs.

Esteem Needs

Maslow described two categories of esteem needs. The first was self-esteem, including such factors as the need for independence, freedom, confidence, and achievement. The second area was identified as respect from others and includes the concepts of recognition, prestige, acceptance, status, and reputation (Globe, 1970).

Officers who do not feel their esteem needs are being fulfilled through the job can become discouraged (if not disgruntled) employees. Officers want to be recognized for their accomplishments. This has been done in part by such things as commendations, medals, and longevity stripes. In some agencies the rank of corporal is awarded for achievement, or an unusual act of bravery is rewarded by promoting the individual.

The above-mentioned external indicators of status can fulfill an officer's esteem needs, leading to feelings of worthiness, adequacy, and self-confidence. Supervisors who recognize the importance of esteem needs do everything possible to ensure that officers demonstrate self-confidence and have few self-doubts, and a positive self-image.

The supervisor whose primary drive is esteem will, in all probability, be a successful manager. Such an individual will expend a great deal of energy in order to achieve recognition. In the final analysis, the supervisor should take the time and expend the effort to convey to every officer that he or she is an important person, doing important work in an important place (Hawkins, 1992).

Self-Actualization Needs

Maslow points out that when most of the esteem needs are fulfilled, then what man can be, he must be. This is the stage of self-actualization, which is characterized by the need to develop feelings of growth and maturity, become increasingly competent, and gain a mastery over situations. At this level the individual reaches the point where all talents and potential are put to use. Motivation is totally internalized and external stimulation is unnecessary. Efforts of an S-A individual focus on applying creative and constructive skills to work situations, and such individuals are never bothered by feelings of futility, alienation, or bitterness.

Supervisors who manage S-A officers should do everything possible to make work meaningful. Participation should be maximized so that officers can use their unique skills. Special assignments should be made when possible in order to capitalize on an officer's talents. When task forces are organized to deal with unique police problems, the S-A officer should be assigned. The self-actualized individual has a need to demonstrate the ability to assume responsibility and involvement at the highest possible level.

Maslow did not view the hierarchy of needs as a series of levels that are totally independent of one another. In fact, the categories overlap and are not entirely precise. He suggests that it is the unsatisfied needs that influence behavior. Once a need is satisfied, it has limited effect on motivation. Maslow estimated the average person is 85 percent satisfied in physiological needs, 70 percent satisfied in safety needs, 50 percent in social needs, 40 percent in esteem needs, and 10 percent in self-actualization needs. Since the initial research, Maslow developed a new list of needs identified as growth needs (social, self-esteem, and self-actualization) as compared to basic needs (physiological and safety). He believed the higher needs use the basic needs as a foundation. The higher or growth needs are set forth in the following figure.

Figure 4.5
Higher or Growth Needs

1.	Wholeness	8.	Beauty
2.	Perfection	9.	Goodness
3.	Completion	10.	Uniqueness
4.	Justice	11.	Effortlessness
5.	Aliveness	12.	Playfulness
6.	Richness	13.	Truth
7.	Simplicity	14.	Self-sufficiency

Source: Frank G. Globe (1970). *The Third Force.* New York: Pocket Books.

Maslow pointed out that the growth needs are interrelated, and when defining one value it is necessary to use the others. These values cannot be separated, and all values reflect the highest need category (see Figure 4.6). Maslow cautioned that we should not make the mistake of thinking that good working conditions will automatically transform all employees into growing, self-actualized individuals.

Figure 4.6
Behaviors When Needs Are Not Fulfilled

Need	Behavior
1. Physiological	Discomfort, distress, possible impairment, uneasiness, or illness.
2. Security	Stress, trepidation, timidity, consternation, or fear.
3. Social	Feelings of being alone, distant, forsaken, sad, or unloved.
4. Self-Esteem	Precarious, lack of a firm belief in one's own power, or a lack of conviction.
5. Self-Actualization	Alienated, astringent, restrained, exploited, or a feeling of uselessness.

Source: Abraham H. Maslow (1962). *Toward a Psychology of Being.* New York: Van Nostrand. Reprinted by permission of John Wiley & Sons, Inc.

Motivation-Hygiene Theory

The hierarchy of needs motivational theory has numerous supporters, but the motivation-hygiene theory, while somewhat more controversial, has received increasing attention. Frederick Herzberg and his colleagues developed this theory, based on semistructured interviews with 200 accountants and engineers. Job satisfaction and its relationship were examined, and the central question of the investigation was "What do people want from their job?"

In this landmark study, the researchers found 155 studies addressing this vital question. They found that different results were achieved when the research design was concerned with the elements making employees happy with their jobs, as opposed to studies stressing factors leading to job dissatisfaction. In the Herzberg study, workers who were found to be happiest with their jobs identified factors relating to the performance of tasks, work events reflecting successful performance, and factors identified as growth.

The other aspect of the two-factor study related to feelings of unhappiness, and they were found to be totally unrelated to the actual accomplishment of work. These factors, identified as hygiene because they acted in a manner similar to medical hygiene, include supervision, interpersonal relations, physical working conditions, salary, company policies, administrative practices, benefits, and job security. Figure 4.7 sets forth this theory.

Figure 4.7
Motivation-Hygiene Theory

Motivators	Hygiene
Achievement	Interpersonal Relations
Advancement	Policies and Administration
Recognition	Salary and Benefits
Responsibility	Security
Work Itself	Working Conditions

Source: Frederick Herzberg, Bernard Mausner, and Barbara Snyderman (1969). *Motivation to Work*, Second Edition. Copyright © Frederick Herzberg, School of Business, University of Utah. Reprinted with permission.

Case Study

Senior Patrol Officer Jim Hilldebrand

Officer Jim Hilldebrand has been an officer with the Crescentvale Police Department for six years. The city has a population of 114,000 and is a suburban community in a metropolitan area. It is primarily a bedroom community. It has two major shopping centers and considerable light industry. Additionally, it has a very good school system and a branch of a community college. The city government operates under a city manager. The mayor has limited power and mainly performs a ceremonial function. The chief of police has been an officer for 12 years and has spent his whole career in Crescentvale.

Officer Hilldebrand has spent his entire career in uniformed services and most recently, at his request, has been assigned to the day shift. He was eligible to take a promotional examination after four years of service but did not avail himself of the opportunity. During his years of service he has always received average performance ratings. He demonstrates an uncanny ability to determine acceptable behavior and performs no better. He is seen but not heard and accepts all suggestions from superiors without discussion. When responding to "officer needs assistance" calls, he is never first or last to arrive at the scene. He never makes any waves and limits his contacts within the department to official business. He never socializes with other officers and values his privacy. He is just there.

A moderate contributor but never an innovator, his nonwork activities are unknown other that the fact that he is married and has two children. His total focus is on his family. It seems that Hilldebrand is typical of many younger officers whose primary focus is on things other than the job.

If you were Officer Hilldebrand's supervisor, what would you do to make him a more responsive and productive officer? Would the motivation-hygiene theory be useful in such a situation? Why or why not? Are there basic needs that could prove to be motivational? Why?

Motivational factors are readily identifiable because they either relate to work itself or they revolve around such things as advancement, responsibility, or recognition. The hygiene factors are either determined by the organization or occur as a result of a memorandum of understanding negotiated by a police union. They are generally restricted to working conditions and policies, in contrast to the motivational factors that stimulate the individual. It is easy to see an immediate parallel between Maslow's concepts of self-actualization and esteem needs. What the employee wants is either growth or recognition (Bergland, 1993).

The factors that address the needs of employees that result in job satisfaction tend to satisfy an officer's needs over an extended period, in contrast to hygiene factors that are more short-lived. A unique characteristic of Herzberg's theory is that motivators can result in a positive feeling toward work, while at the same time, some individuals respond negatively.

Both the motivators and the hygiene factors meet employee needs, but it is primarily the motivators that result in job satisfaction. The workers studied by Herzberg and his collaborators found, for example, that achievement was present in more than 40 percent of what were identified as satisfying situations, and in less than 10 percent of dissatisfying situations. In terms of recognition, more than 30 percent of the situations were satisfying and less than 20 percent were dissatisfying.

Herzberg viewed satisfiers and dissatisfiers as separate and distinct entities. One can be satisfied and dissatisfied simultaneously. This means hygiene factors cannot increase job satisfaction, but only affect the amount of job dissatisfaction.

There are definite differences between the theories of Maslow and Herzberg, as well as similarities noted by the fact that both theories identify motivational factors, and in some aspects the theories overlap. Herzberg creates a category not discussed by Maslow, and he identified these hygiene factors (nonmotivators) as generally reflective of the components of a bureaucratic police organization. The Maslow theory differs because it views human beings as social individuals who can be viewed as multidimensional and suggests that individuals have the capacity to prioritize needs hierarchically.

Theory X—Theory Y

One of the best-known motivational theories was developed by Douglas McGregor. It is a straightforward theory based on the belief that managers conduct themselves according to the assumptions, generalizations, and hypotheses they have about human behavior (McGregor, 1960). Employees' attitudes and behavior are viewed by McGregor as being in response to management's perspective of their own job and their basic mindset about human behavior.

The traditional view of direction and control, identified as Theory X, is set forth in Figure 4.8.

Figure 4.8
Theory X

> 1. The average employee really dislikes work and will do whatever is necessary to avoid it.
> 2. If employees dislike work, then in order to direct activities toward the accomplishment of organizational objectives, most employees will have to be coerced, controlled, directed, or threatened with punishment.
> 3. Security is important to the average employee. This type of individual has little ambition and would rather be told what to do.

Source: Douglas McGregor (1960). *The Human Side of Enterprise.* New York, NY: McGraw-Hill. Reprinted with permission of The McGraw-Hill Companies.

This view of human behavior is still somewhat prevalent in the policing field and is reminiscent of autocratic leadership. What are the consequences of such assumptions about human behavior? What roles are supervisors and officers forced to take? Human behavior is very complex, and it seems appropriate to suggest that Theory X can explain the behavior of a few employees, but certainly not the majority.

Closely paralleling Theory X is another motivational theory called "carrot and stick." Both theories seem viable when meeting an employee's basic needs at the physiological and safety levels. The job itself, working conditions, and fringe benefits can be very strong control features when officers are struggling to just get by, but when basic need levels are reasonably satisfied and officers become motivated by higher needs, the theories leave a lot to be desired.

If managers view employees as a necessary evil, they actually view themselves as the chosen ones possessing special abilities. They view the majority of individuals as having limited abilities. Thus, employees are viewed as fundamentally lazy, preferring to have decisions made for them and readily accepting (and actually wanting) forceful leadership. Employees will continually take advantage of the work situation and have no concept of the factors constituting a fair day's work. If supervisors hold to Theory X, it will be reflected in every contact with those supervised.

Theory X places a strong emphasis on control and direction (Von der Embse, 1987). Procedures are devised for providing officers with close supervision (determining whether the task has been accomplished) and the creation of a means for providing rewards and punishments.

With the increasing emphasis on the professionalization of law enforcement and an improved standard of living, the fundamental needs (physiological and safety) have become less of a managerial issue. Thus, control becomes fundamentally inadequate as a means of motivating employees when they have developed a social, esteem, or self-actualization need (Handy, 1993).

This means a supervisor should consider a new generalization about the management of human resources, namely the assumptions outlined by Theory Y, which are set forth in Figure 4.9.

Figure 4.9
Theory Y

1. The majority of employees will respond as positively to work as they do to play or rest.
2. Control and direction are not the only techniques used to achieve departmental goals. When truly committed to an objective, employees will exercise self-control and self-direction.
3. Commitment to departmental objectives is a function of the rewards associated with the attainment of objectives.
4. Avoidance of responsibility, an emphasis on security, and limited drive are, for the most part, consequences of experience, not fundamental characteristics of human nature.
5. The ability to exercise a high degree of imagination, ingenuity, and creativity, when striving to solve an organizational problem, is a widely distributed talent among the population.
6. With industrial life conditions as they are, the intellectual potential of the average employee is only partially utilized.

Source: Douglas McGregor (1960). *The Human Side of Enterprise*. New York, NY: McGraw-Hill. Reprinted by permission of The McGraw-Hill Companies.

A careful analysis of the factors clearly suggests that management should respond to the employees with an enlightened strategy. The managerial perspective will have to be creative, discover new organizational principles, and develop new means of directing employees. It should be acknowledged that while the perfect organization might not be attainable, there is certainly room for improvement.

McGregor pointed out that the complete integration of individual and organizational goals was not realistic. The ultimate goal for which we strive should be a degree of integration whereby workers can attain their own goals by directing their efforts toward the success of the organization. Workers must be encouraged to develop to their highest capacity by acquiring knowledge and skills to make the organization successful.

Interestingly enough, when a supervisor accepts Theory Y, it does not imply the abdication of his or her responsibilities or what has become known as *soft* management. This idea stems from traditional control procedures emphasizing authority above all (Vail, 1993). Theory Y assumes employees will exercise self-direction and self-control if they are committed to departmental objectives. If commitment is slight or nonexistent, then self-direction and self-control will be slight or nonexistent. External influences will have to be exerted in order to achieve goals. If the commitment is great, then external influences should be minimal, or better yet, nonexistent.

An appropriate application of Theory Y reduces the need for external control and relies on other managerial techniques for successfully reaching organizational goals. Generally, authority will prove to be an inappropriate technique for obtaining departmental goals, but authority is something that has to be used when an organization cannot get a genuine commitment to departmental objectives. Theory Y assumes that authority is not appropriate for all situations.

It can readily be seen that when a supervisor applies the concepts predicated by Theory Y, each employee is viewed as a real asset. Officers have a definite capacity for growth and development. Employees can be highly creative and willing to accept responsibility. It is the supervisor's job to create a working environment in which the potential of every officer can be tapped. Employees are usually not indolent, stupid, irresponsible, or hostile. The supervisor accepts that there will always be a few such officers, but they are the exception, not the rule.

Such an orientation requires the supervisor to be primarily concerned with the quality of interpersonal relationships. One's effort is directed toward developing an organizational atmosphere that fosters a commitment to departmental goals. Each employee is given an opportunity to become self-directing, innovative, and growth-oriented.

There are contrasting sets of attitudes when one compares Theory X and Theory Y. What, then, is the answer? What theory should a supervisor follow? Not surprisingly, neither theory can be applied in every situation. A supervisor probably functions at some point between the two extremes. When an officer is on probation and new to the job, a Theory X approach may be more appropriate until the officer is capable of functioning alone. During a narcotics raid is not the proper time for officers to question what is being done or take it upon themselves to deviate from the prescribed procedures. Safety is imperative and officers must follow orders.

On the other hand, as an officer grows and develops, control can be reduced and the officer can be given a greater opportunity for self-direction and self-control. The assumptions a supervisor makes about what theory to use depends on a detailed evaluation of each officer's abilities and qualifications. The more knowledgeable and competent officers can be extended a great deal of freedom in their work environment. When these conditions are not met, the supervisor must emphasize control and dependent subordinate behavior.

Expectancy Theory

Predicting behavior in organizations has always challenged behaviorists. A model predictor holding promise is one developed by Victor H. Vroom. This model is predicated on the concept that it is the internal state as well as external forces impinging on individuals that will cause them to act in a specific manner. In the final analysis, a worker will be motivated to put forth the necessary effort when it will result in the attainment of desired goals.

There are four basic assumptions about human behavior that serve as the foundation of the expectancy theory. They demonstrate the complexity of not only human behavior, but also of motivation. The first assumption is that behavior is not determined exclusively by the individual. It is a product of the vitality of an individual and the environment, and within this context, each individual will develop a preference for available objectives. When the preference is high, the acceptance will be greater. On the other hand, the employee will avoid undesirable consequences. If an individual values promotion over everything else, behavior will be adjusted in order to meet that need.

Second, employees have expectancies about outcomes. Or to put it another way, each person anticipates what will occur. If the results are not compatible with efforts, then the activity is ignored or avoided. Expectations vary from individual to individual. What one police officer feels is important might be unimportant to another officer. Some individuals feel that job security is important above all else, while others want to perform demanding and challenging tasks.

One aspect of expectancy is called effort-performance (E-P), which refers to an individual's motivation to choose a specific performance objective and the relationship of effort to that objective. The factors affecting an individual's expectancy perception include such things as self-esteem, previous experience in similar situations, one's capability, and the style of supervision. This list is not meant to be comprehensive, but it does illustrate the range of such factors. It is believed that each individual seeks to increase self-esteem by searching for psychological success. One experiences psychological success when:

- A personal challenging goal is set

- Methods of achieving that goal are set

- The goal is relevant to one's self-concept (Handy, 1993)

When an officer experiences psychological success, he or she feels more competent. The more competent one feels, the more apt that person is to take risks in perceived areas of importance. On the other hand, when one is not psychologically successful, it can lead to the lowering of personal goals as the person strives to protect his or her self-concept (Handy, 1993). While the importance of self-esteem is evident, the whole process should be approached with some degree of caution, especially if there are other influencing factors such as limited manpower or inadequate equipment. All the desire in the world cannot achieve the impossible.

Another aspect of expectancy is performance-outcome (P-O), which deals with an officer's anticipation of performing at a specified level and the outcome of those efforts. This can best be illustrated by a situation in which an officer may feel that a superior effort will result in different outcomes.

Such efforts can undoubtedly result in unintended consequences. While a merit increase might be forthcoming, it might also foster resentment from peers and cause difficulties at home because of excessive absence from the family. It is clear, then, that any single outcome might be positive in some ways and negative in others.

Needless to say, one way of analyzing motivation is to view the consequences resulting from expectancies and valences. Then motivation can be viewed as:

$$\text{Motivation} = \text{E (Expectancy} \times \text{Valence)}$$

Valence is defined as the strength of an individual's desire for a particular outcome. Synonyms for valence include drive, incentive, or desire. Valences range from -1.0 to 1.0, and when the valence is in the negative range, the officer does not want to reach or attain the objective. When the valence is positive, the outcome is highly desirable. When the valence is zero, the officer is indifferent to the outcome (Luthans, 1994). It is important to realize that what really matters is the employee's perception of what will occur.

Supervisors seem to continually underrate the factors necessary for motivating employees. They forget it is the *officer's perception* that matters most—not the supervisor's perception. The expectancy motivational model combines the previously discussed need theory with the concept of perceived outcomes. Officers are motivated, for example, by satisfying their esteem needs—such as receiving a promotion or obtaining a preferred assignment to a special unit (such as a SWAT team). They can be motivated by the successful completion of the probationary period because of the security it will provide. The interplay occurring between officers who are involved in team policing can fulfill the need for socialization.

Another study revealed that when studying three levels of employees (low, middle, and upper) there was hardly any difference between the levels when they rated the importance of needs (security, social, esteem, autonomy, and self-actualization). The real difference came when the three levels rated the degree to which needs were satisfied. Lower-level employees were much less satisfied with the number of higher-order needs being met on the job (Hawkins, 1981). The most successful supervisors will concentrate on helping officers to clarify their needs and on becoming aware of how officers perceive those needs. Once this is accomplished, the expectancies of outcomes can be dealt with through such techniques as training, delegation, and acknowledgment of a job well done or the granting of greater autonomy.

Sensitivity Theory

Two researchers have suggested that sensitivity theory can be used to identify individual differences reflecting basic motivational needs. Furthermore, they suggest that fundamental motives are the keys that in time will actually predict human behavior. This theory is a genetics-behavior-cognitive model of axiomatic motivation. It is the position of the two psychologists that human behavior can be separated into two categories based on the purposes of the behavior:

Means: This is indicated when someone performs an act for a useful purpose.

End: This occurs when an individual performs a behavior for no evident reason other than its own purpose.

When *means* are important to an officer, it might be indicated by the quest of a college degree solely to make one eligible to receive a monthly increase in salary for educational attainment. Another example is an officer who works additional shifts and enhances his or her income in order to purchase a sailboat. In both instances the money provides for goal attainment. The *means* allows one to attain a desired goal that has been identified and is believed to be reachable. At the same time, the goal is one that is personally beneficial and one for which an individual has no difficulty becoming motivated because of the reward that can be received at the end of the process.

This process differs from that involving the pursuit of an *end*. What is important is the nature of the involvement. In contrast, when someone walks or hikes for the sake of enjoyment or when an individual exercises for pleasure the *end* is what is important. It does not really matter what has to be done as long as the anticipated result occurs. What occurs in this instance might serve a useful purpose, but it is something that was never intended.

Researchers postulate that human desire stems from 16 basic desires (see Figure 4.11). They range from abstracts, such as honor, or social contact, to bodily wants like eating or romance, and also to more intellectual ambient factors such as idealism and order. Of special interest to the work situation are such fundamental motives as power and independence.

Reflections of the fact that man is a social animal are such motives as social contact and social prestige. All of us are concerned with the 16 basic desires, but the intensity and the priority that one gives to them vary from individual to individual. If a supervisor finds that an officer focuses more on motives such as family, it presents an entirely different supervisory problem than an officer who is more concerned with order. When compared to other motivational theories, the list is extensive and encompasses a great deal of variance. It clearly demonstrates the complexity of human behavior. This theory goes well beyond those that stress the avoidance of pain and the maximization of pleasure (Reiss, 2000).

Figure 4.11
Fundamental Motives—16 Basic Desires

1. Social contact is the desire for social interaction.
2. Honor is the desire to behave morally.
3. Idealism is the desire for social justice.
4. Curiosity is the desire to learn.
5. Independence is the desire for self-reliance.
6. Order is the desire to organize.
7. Saving is the desire to collect.
8. Physical exercise is the desire for muscle movement.
9. Romance is the desire for sex and beauty.
10. Power is the desire for influence.
11. Acceptance is the desire for approval.
12. Eating is the desire for food.
13. Family is the desire to raise one's children.
14. Vengeance is the desire to get even with those who offend.
15. Status is the desire for self-importance.
16. Tranquility is the desire to be free of anxiety, fear, and pain.

Source:From *Who Am I?* by Steven Reiss, copyright © 2000 by Steven Reiss. Used by permission of Jeremy P. Tarcher, a division of Penguin Putnam, Inc.

How to Motivate

The theories discussed above have their place, and supervisors have been successful in varying degrees in applying these theories to the work environment. If there is a drawback in this application, it is that they are somewhat subjective. This is readily apparent when one closely examines the theories and such related terms as *needs, satisfaction, psychological success, self-concept*, and *expectancies*.

In analyzing the behavior of officers, it is necessary to study what will happen if a certain action is taken. It is important to determine what the *officer* believes the consequence of the act will be—not what the supervisor thinks. A supervisor utilizing the concept of behavior modification shapes behavior based on the belief that when an activity results in a positive consequence, the activity is apt to be repeated. If the activity results in a negative consequence, the activity tends not to be repeated (Williams, DuBrin, and Sisk, 1985).

Within the framework of behavior modification, the supervisor works to influence officer behavior in such a way that organizational objectives and goals are attained (Laird, Laird, and Fruehling, 1989). The advantage of this approach is that the supervisor does not need to become aware of such things as officer needs or motives, but can limit efforts to altering the behavior by manipulating some aspect of the reward system.

If, in the judgment of the officers, the consequences are important, then behavior can be viewed as being based on the following two principles:

- When behavior results in a positive consequence, officers will sustain that behavior.

- Officers will suspend or curtail a specific behavior when the result is negative.

On the surface, behavior modification seems to be quite simple, but in application it becomes somewhat complex. Karen Brethower, who expanded the theory to the job situation, suggests:

- When a specific behavior is desired, but another behavior results and there is a positive event, then the second behavior dominates.

- When officer behavior results in a positive outcome in one situation, but negative consequences occur in another situation, the positive behavior dominates.

- When the job does not require a specific type of behavior, or is of no consequence, such behavior will eventually cease.

- When the consequence of a certain behavior is far removed (in time) from the behavior, there will be a lesser impact on the behavior of the officer (Williams, DuBrin, and Sisk, 1985).

By utilizing the two principles and the four corollaries discussed above, a supervisor can respond to the tasks performed by officers and engage in reinforcing activities including praise, a commendation, special assignment or additional training. Officers usually have a good understanding of what management expects from them (in terms of job performance), so they act accordingly.

If behavior is to be modified, consequences must occur immediately after a behavior occurs, not days or months afterward. To delay responding leads either to officer indifference or refusal to engage in such activities. Positive behavior must always be rewarded, not ignored. Ignored negative behavior will, in all probability, either harm the supervisor or the department.

In other words, when reinforcement is used to modify behavior, it must be done continuously and consistently. Any given task performed by a police officer can be performed as management desires or in an unacceptable way. Supervisors actually want officers to perform their duties with reasonable dispatch and effectiveness. If reinforcement is to work, it must be response-contingent. Any response to officer activity should be clearly and definitely related to performance, or the effort to reinforce will be blunted or even meaningless.

Positive reinforcement works because there is a greater probability that desirable behavior will occur. It is direct, simple, clear, and practical. Above all, it is not encumbered by negative side effects. If there is a problem with managing with a reinforcement focus, it is that our society in general deals with most negative performance by punishment or criticism. If a supervisor has been reared in a family where punishment dominated, and schools as well as the job reinforce this negative approach, it becomes apparent that when this individual becomes a manager, his or her first instinct is to deal with all undesirable behavior by punishing.

Punishment is viewed by some as the quickest and most effective way of obtaining compliance, but in reality it is seldom long-lasting and, when used exclusively, is generally ineffective. Another problem is that unpredictable punishment can easily lead to more negative consequences, such as reinforcing the schism between the department and a police union.

Initially, punishment will eliminate or reduce undesirable behavior, but managing fear, coercion, or threats as a means of getting work done serves only to alienate officers from managers and from the department itself. Punishment is usually based on power, and the individual's task is to conform or punishment will occur (Handy, 1993). In many instances, officers actually feel they are not extended the common courtesy of being treated as a human being, let alone an individual. As one expert pointed out, some supervisors, wanting to improve the performance of officers they are supervising, are so effective at punishing that they actually reinforce alienation. Viewed realistically, the officer who is treated with contempt and disdain by an immediate supervisor can be expected to react negatively (Nirenberg, 1986).

At some point, some employees will have to be punished, but punishment should be as a last resort, not a supervisory style. Certainly punishment will provide a lessening of undesirable behavior, but once the punishment is eliminated from the supervisory process, the employee can resume unacceptable behavior. A punishing style of leadership requires the supervisor to operate continuously from a negative managerial style and always be alert to correct unacceptable officer behavior. It actually means the supervisor must watch employees so closely that in many instances the officers are forced to react defensively and production is reduced, not increased.

Punishment as a managerial style can, and most often will, lead to a negative emotional reaction in which an officer can react with anger, become hostile, act out aggressively, or withdraw. Any or all of these reactions can create a working environment in which it becomes uncomfortable to work, the personal satisfaction of doing a good job becomes unimportant, and the atmosphere is devoid of positive motivational factors.

In police work, an additional consequence of a punishing atmosphere can be one in which the officers respond by becoming totally inflexible in their enforcement of the law and officer discretion becomes nonexistent. In this instance the public loses, and in the long run the department loses. As one officer pointed out, "If they want conformity that's what they are going to get—absolute conformity. Go by the book and toe the line, because that's the only way to keep out of trouble."

A supervisor using reinforcement techniques is attempting to actually shape behavior. If the process is to be successful, it is necessary to use reinforcement thoughtfully and systematically. Initially, a supervisor must recognize that changing behavior is more difficult than sustaining and supporting the change once it has been put in place. This means the supervisor should apply the greatest amount of reinforcement during the early stages, and the frequency of reinforcement should be greater during this period. If the initial employee efforts go unnoticed or are ignored by the supervisor, those efforts, in all probability, will not be sustained.

It is also important for a supervisor to respond to behavior after the fact, not before. If reinforcement is used before the desired behavior, it will not shape behavior. Reinforcement must be tied to a specific act by the employee and should occur immediately after the specific activity. This is one reason the annual or semiannual performance reviews generally prove ineffective in changing job behavior. Short-term behavior changes may occur as a result of a performance review, but the change in behavior seldom lasts more than two or three months. Lasting changes in behavior can be accomplished only by immediately responding to an act, not waiting until the next review, which might be one year away. A supervisor should reinforce every performance improvement, no matter how slight. When the desired behavior becomes an established pattern, reinforcement can then be used periodically or randomly.

When instituting a behavior modification program, a supervisor should consider the following:

- Positive reinforcement will result in improved performance.

- In most instances, punishment will have numerous harmful side effects. Punishment should be used as a last resort.

- Officer response to behavior changes should be immediate in most instances.

- All employees need to know what is expected of them.

- Positive reinforcement should be consistent and unbroken.

- Reinforcement should be tied to positive behavior.

- Feedback is essential. Officers need to know that what they are doing is right or wrong.

- If officers perform poorly because of lack of knowledge, they should be trained (Williams, DuBrin, and Sisk, 1985).

Reinforcement will modify behavior. It is a technique whereby officers can be motivated to work harder and with a great degree of effectiveness. This can result in an improvement in organizational pride and loyalty and in a working environment that stimulates officers to achieve their potential (Spitzer, 1995).

Summary

If there is any clear-cut task with which first-line supervisors must deal, it is motivating officers or civilians under their immediate supervision. Employees must be motivated so that departmental objectives can be met. The motivation of employees is a demanding and time-consuming task and one in which a supervisor must engage at all times. A good supervisor develops a plan to identify obligations to both the officers being supervised and the managers in the hierarchy. Such a plan includes introducing democracy in the workplace and creating an environment that allows officers to grow and work together.

Behavioral scientists generally accept the proposition that behavior does not happen spontaneously—it is caused. Human behavior can be explained to a great extent by determining basic needs. A supervisor should keep an open mind as to what motivates individuals and not fall victim to the desire to find the panacea to the motivational problem.

Of primary importance to a supervisor is striving to create a quality of working life where most officers become self-motivated. This is done by viewing motivation as not only eclectic but synergistic. An effective supervisor must identify obligation to both the officers being supervised and their immediate supervisor. The supervisor should have an in-depth knowledge of motivational theories, such as Needs-based, Motivation-Hygiene, Theory X—Theory Y, Sensitivity, and Expectancy. This knowledge must be applied judiciously.

Abraham H. Maslow postulated that people's needs were exceedingly complex and arranged in a hierarchy. His studies were based on a positive concept of mental health, and his research cohorts were the very best individuals he could identify. The ultimate key for a supervisor is to help employees self-actualize—in other words, let them become all they can be. These people were identified as being self-actualized (S-A). This theory identified five need categories: physiological, security, social, esteem, and self-actualization.

Frederick Herzberg and his colleagues were responsible for the creation of the motivation-hygiene theory. In this study, the motivators were found to be: achievement, advancement, recognition, responsibility, and work itself. The hygiene factors include policies, security, and working conditions.

Theory X, as developed by Douglas McGregor, views employees as a necessary evil and, in an effort to maximize their output, stresses control and direction. Under Theory Y, officers are viewed as assets and emphasis is placed on interpersonal relationships. The goal is to have employees become self-directed, self-controlled, and committed to departmental objectives. Under this concept, the supervisor is primarily concerned with the quality of interpersonal relationships.

The behavioral model developed by Victor H. Vroom is predicated on the concept that it is the internal state as well as external forces that impinge on individuals that will enable them to act in a specific way. Important to this theory is that behavior is not determined exclusively by the individual. Officers have expectations about outcomes and will adjust accordingly. Supervisors often underestimate the factors necessary for motivating employees. They forget that it is the *officer's* perception that counts—not the supervisor's perception.

Sensitivity theory suggests that when one determines differences in motivational needs, one has identified the key to predicting human behavior. The theory divides human motivations into two categories: means and ends. The theory postulates that human desires stem from 16 basic desires that range from power to tranquility.

The key to motivation is the integration of the individual into the organization. Each organization approaches motivation differently, in terms of style and emphasis rather than actual substance. As the one who constantly deals with operational personnel, the sergeant becomes a key figure in the motivational process.

The sergeant who strives for excellence must develop a program in which reinforcement will modify behavior. The goal is to create a department in which goals are easily identifiable, where there is room for growth, and where officers feel secure and appreciated, as well as properly rewarded.

Case Study

Officer Sandra Wong

Officer Sandra Wong is a third-generation Chinese-American who has lived her entire life in a major city. She has an elementary education degree and taught the fifth grade for three years prior to taking the examination for patrol officer. She found teaching to be an uneventful occupation and felt she could help the community more by becoming a police officer. Her grandfather had been a police commander in Taiwan, and she had always had a special interest in law enforcement.

She speaks fluent Mandarin and Cantonese and has some knowledge of French. After successfully passing the entry examination, she was selected and entered the police academy along with 45 other candidates. She graduated third in her class and was selected by her fellow recruits as the outstanding graduate. After completing the academy, she was assigned to a precinct that had a large Asian population. She had a field training officer (FTO) who rated her outstanding at completion of the program and introduced her to many of the "movers and shakers" in the Chinese community.

In the field she was assigned to the swing shift and a beat where the majority of the residents were Chinese. She was constantly called on as a translator on surrounding beats, which she found distracting. It seemed to her that it was causing her to neglect her beat, and precluded her from responding to the needs of businesses and residents on her beat. Within six months of receiving her beat assignment, she found that she was serving as a translator 67 percent of the time.

Her supervising sergeant acknowledged her performance as excellent, and her fellow officers readily accepted her, especially when it came to the assistance she provided as a translator. Based on performance as a translator, she received an increase in her salary of five percent. She appealed to her supervisor to be relieved of translator duties so that she could concentrate on the demands of her beat. From a departmental position, translators were in short supply, and removing her from the translator category was frowned upon.

If you were Officer Wong's supervisor, how would you balance the demands of the department and the desires of the employee? Is there a motivational theory that would be fundamental to your decision-making process? Does Officer Wong exhibit a basic need? If so, what is it? What does that mean to the motivational cycle?

Key Concepts

achievement-motivation program
behavior modification
dissatisfiers
ends
esteem needs
expectancy motivational model
expectancy theory
facet feelings
global feelings
human behavior
hygiene
job satisfaction
means

motivation cycle
motivators
physiological needs
positive reinforcement
psychological success
satisfiers
security needs
self-actualized needs
sensitivity
social needs
Theory X–Theory Y
valence

Discussion Topics and Questions

1. What difficulty does one encounter when defining motivation?

2. List seven things that a supervisor should include in an achievement-motivation program.

3. Discuss security needs as identified by Abraham Maslow.

4. Identify the two major aspects of expectancy theory. Which one precedes the other?

5. What are the key characteristics of Theory Y?

6. Why is it important for line personnel to achieve self-actualization on the job?

7. How can officers be motivated to perform more effectively?

8. Distinguish between satisfiers and dissatisfiers.

9. What factors should be considered when instituting a behavior modification program?

10. Should the social needs of officers be important to a supervisor?

11. Write a short essay describing sensitivity theory.

12. List six fundamental motives.

13. Discuss Herzberg's motivational theory.

For Further Reading

Haasen, Adolph (1997). *A Better Place to Work: How a New Understanding of Motivation Leads to Higher Productivity.* New York, NY: American Management Association.

> Presents an analysis of the changing concepts of motivation. Emphasizes the shift from extrinsic determinants to intrinsic motivation. Discusses the importance of emotional choice and perception. Describes the need to ensure that factors are present to ensure that intrinsic motivation creates a situation in which people enjoy working. Recommends that people need control of their work, an opportunity to learn and master new skills, and to be part of a team.

Chandler, Steve (1996). *100 Ways to Motivate Yourself.* Franklin Lakes, NJ: Career Press.

> This text describes the necessity of clearly visualizing a goal as the first step to succeed in life, but this can only be accomplished if an individual takes action. The author presents 100 ways of thinking that lead directly to self-motivation. It is a book of useful ideas that range from the need to create a vision to the necessity of developing a purpose in life.

White, John L. (2001). "The Work Itself as a Motivator." *FBI Enforcement Bulletin,* Vol. 70 No. 2.

> This article has a unique approach to the concept of motivation. A motivational video was created depicting officers engaged in various activities as a means of showing people at work in the organization and to recognize the importance of the work being performed. The belief was that the video served as a personal motivator and dramatized the individual's role in the organization as officers worked to attain organizational goals. A

distinction is made between motivation and leadership. Of particular interest is the proposition that motivation is a set of psychological processes that energize voluntary behavior. The video also served as a strong visual presentation demonstrating the professionalism of the officers.

Reiss, Steven (2000). *Who Am I? The 16 Basic Desires That Motivate Our Actions and Define Our Personalities.* New York, NY: Jeremy P. Tarcher/Putnam.

This psychologist postulates that we can satisfy our desires at work in two different ways. First, we can use our relationships with people at work—such as bosses, subordinates, or coworkers—to satisfy our desires. Second, we can use the work itself to satisfy our desires. Additionally, the author points out that individuals with a high need for power like the supervisory role because it fulfills a basic need, but tend to dislike the role of subordinate and may even find it stressful. The author provides a simple questionnaire that can be used to literally graft one's personality.

References

Aragon, Randall (1993). "Positive Organizational Culture." *FBI Law Enforcement Bulletin,* Vol. 62, No. 12.

Associates of the Office of Military Leadership, USMA (eds.) (1976). *A Study of Organizational Leadership.* Harrisburg, PA: Stackpole Books.

Bergland, Sheila (1993). "Employment Empowerment." *FBI Law Enforcement Bulletin,* Vol. 62, No. 12.

Berryman-Fink, Cynthia, and Charles B. Fink (1996). *The Manager's Desk Reference.* New York, NY: AMACOM.

Brown, Michael F. (1992). "The Sergeant's Role in a Modern Law Enforcement Agency." *The Police Chief,* Vol. LIX, No. 5.

Burg, Mike (1991). "Goal Setting for First Line Supervisors." *Law and Order,* Vol. 43, No. 5.

Chandler, Steve (1996). *100 Ways to Motivate Yourself.* Franklin Lakes, NJ: Career Press.

Charrier, Kim (2000). "Marketing Strategies for Attracting and Retaining Generation X Police Officers." *The Police Chief,* Vol. LXII, No. 12.

CALEA (1999). *Standards for Law Enforcement Agencies*, Fourth Edition. Fairfax, VA: Commission on Accreditation for Law Enforcement Agencies, Inc.

Dees, Timothy (1992). "Identifying and Solving Morale Problems." *Law and Order,* Vol. 40, No. 9.

Dessler, Gary (1993). *Winning Commitment: How to Build and Keep a Competitive Workforce.* New York, NY: R.R. Donnelley & Sons.

Fincham, Robin, and Peter S. Rhodes (1995). *The Individual, Work, and Organization Behavior: Studies for Business and Management.* London: Oxford University Press.

Gellerman, Saul W. (1992). *Motivation in the Real World: The Art of Getting Extra Effort from Everyone—Including Yourself.* New York, NY: Dutton.

Globe, Frank G. (1970). *The Third Force.* New York, NY: Pocket Books.

Grant, Philip C. (1990). *The Effort-Net Return Model of Employee Motivation: Principles, Propositions, and Prescriptions.* Westport, CT: Greenwood Press.

Haasen, Adolph (1997). *A Better Place to Work: How a New Understanding, of Motivation Leads to Higher Productivity.* New York, NY: American Management Association.

Handy, Charles (1993). *Understanding Organizations.* New York, NY: Oxford University Press.

Hawkins, Brian L. (1981). *Managerial Communication.* Santa Monica, CA: Goodyear Publishing.

Hawkins, Jeff (1992). "Officer Motivation." *Law and Order,* Vol. 40, No. 10.

Herzberg, Frederick, Bernard Mausner, and Barbara Snyderman (1959). *The Motivation to Work*, Second Edition. New York, NY: John Wiley and Sons.

Laird, Donald A., Eleanor C. Laird, and Rosemary T. Fruehling (1989). *Psychology: Human Relations and Work Adjustment*, Seventh Edition. New York, NY: McGraw-Hill Book Company.

Leonard, V.A. and Harry W. More (2000). *Police Organization and Management*, Ninth Edition New York, NY: Foundation Press.

Levering, Robert A. (1988). *A Great Place to Work.* New York, NY: Random House.

Luthans, Fred (1994). *Organizational Behavior.* New York, NY: McGraw-Hill.

Maslow, Abraham H. (1962). *Toward a Psychology of Being.* New York, NY: Van Nostrand.

Maslow, Abraham H. (1970). *Motivation and Personality*, Second Edition. New York, NY: Harper and Row.

Naval Education and Training Program (1984). *Human Behavior.* Washington, DC: U.S. Government Printing Office.

McGregor, Douglas (1960). *The Human Side of Enterprise.* New York, NY: McGraw-Hill.

Nirenberg, John (1986). "Motivation as if People Matter." *Supervisory Management*, Vol. 26, No. 3.

Ranchlin, Harvey (1993). "A National Review of Wages and Benefits." *Law and Order,* Vol. 41, No. 11.

Reiss, Steven (2000). *Who Am I? The 16 Basic Desires That Motivate Our Actions and Define Our Personalities.* New York, NY: Jeremy P. Tarcher/Putnam.

Roman, Mark B. (1986). "Beyond the Carrot and the Stick." *Success,* Vol. 33, No. 8.

Spitzer, Dean R. (1995). *Supermotivation: A Blueprint for Energizing Your Organization from Top to Bottom.* New York, NY: AMACOM.

Thompson, Brad Lee (1995). *The New Manager's Handbook.* New York, NY: Richard D. Irwin, Inc.

Vail, Chris (1993). "Supervision Requires 'More' in Policing." *Law and Order,* Vol. 41, No. 5.

Von der Embse, Thomas J. (1987). *Supervision: Managerial Skills for a New Era.* New York, NY: Macmillan Publishing Co.

White, John L. (2001). "The Work Itself as a Motivator." *FBI Enforcement Bulletin*, Vol. 70, No. 2.

Williams, J. Clifton, Andrew J. DuBrin, and Henry L. Sisk (1985). *Management and Organization*, Fifth Edition. Cincinnati, OH: South-Western Publishing.

Leadership—

The Integrative Variable

5

Introductory Case Study

Sergeant Ken Pike

Sergeant Ken Pike is assigned to the midnight shift in a high-crime district that has a mixture of apartment houses, light industry, and businesses. Calls for service are exceptionally high, especially during the hours from midnight to 4:00 A.M. Most of the calls are divided between those demanding an immediate response and those that, by policy, should be responded to within eight minutes. During this period, less critical calls are stacked, pending the availability of officers. The department has 174 sworn officers and 101 civilian employees. The annual budget is $17 million, and the department has its own communications center, having opted not to consolidate such operations with the county. The department has three major operational entities: uniformed, investigative, and administrative. Specialization has occurred to such an extent that the uniformed division is generally undermanned.

The city has a population of 124,000 and is racially and culturally diverse. The community provides a variety of recreational opportunities, and its school system is rated as excellent. The city is governed by a city council consisting of seven members, all of whom are currently members of the same political party. The position of mayor is rotated among council members. Located on the fringe of a major metropolitan area, residents have ready access to major shopping and entertainment facilities. Within a two-hour drive one can find numerous ski resorts and other snow-related recreational facilities.

Sergeant Pike has been in the department for 12 years and a sergeant for the last five years. In fact, in terms of seniority he has been in the department longer than the majority of members. During the last five years the city has grown by 40 percent. The newer residents are primarily immigrants from Central and South America. Many of them are political refugees.

> Morale on the midnight shift is somewhat low as officers feel that all they are doing is taking calls and dictating reports. Relief is not in sight, because although the city council has approved the hiring of additional personnel, their availability for assignment is more than a year away.
>
> *If you were Sergeant Pike, how would you deal with the morale problem? What would you do to influence officer behavior toward the achievement of organizational goals? Would a participative leadership style be of value in this situation? Why or why not?*

A well-managed police department is easily distinguishable because of its positive leadership. It is the catalyst that proves to be synergistic in nature. It gets things done. It is enervative and maximizes efforts to provide the services needed to improve the quality of community life and fulfill the conditions of the police mission. A marginal or inept organization can be transformed into a successful one through effective leadership. It gives life and reinforces an organization in its efforts to achieve agency goals and objectives. While it is an intangible quality, it must be present if officers are to be galvanized into positive action.

When leadership is truly inspirational, it can be extremely contagious and result in officers achieving high levels of quality production. Without a doubt, leadership is the essential ingredient of a positive organization (Alsabrook et al., 2001). If a person has ever worked for a *good* leader, it has undoubtedly proven to be an exhilarating experience. A true leader is one who is optimistic and confronts adversity with persistence and consistency. Above all, a leader acts boldly (Baker, 2000). Additionally, a leader networks with others; works at creating open, candid, trusting relationships; and uses moral and ethical values when confronting difficult issues (Porter et al., 2000). To really excel as a leader, one must be able to convert past experiences into positive input, as well as possess the capacity to visualize a desired future (Waitley, 1995). If one has hopes of becoming a supervisor or is currently at that level, it would behoove him or her to accept the challenge to work diligently at becoming a truly positive leader (Cox and Hoover, 1992; Eisenberg, 2001).

One thing a person does not want to be is an incompetent boss. Horror stories abound in the police field about supervisors who are ignorant, dictatorial, egomaniacal, domineering, manipulative, power-happy, or simply unfit. Whatever the label attached, such supervisors can destroy or severely impede the effectiveness of line officers. In fact, officers can (and do) become the victims of exploitative leadership styles, and such a working environment has led to the resignation of many competent officers or the creation of a situation in which officers conform to meet their supervisors' low expectations and become minimally effective. Few officers work effectively when constantly under abusive stress. An incompetent supervisor can soon dampen enthusiasm and constrict even those who are highly motivated. Figure 5.1 depicts the terms that describe styles of police supervision used in the past and the style of supervision of the future.

Figure 5.1
Changing Leadership Attributes

The Past	The Future
admonish	counsel
closed	open
command	coach
control	empowerment
coordinate	facilitate
decision maker	shared decisions
decree	influence
dictate	enjoin
mandate	guide
passive	creative
pessimistic	optimistic
punish mistakes	error allowance
punish	exonerate
reactive	proactive
rigid	flexible
status quo	visionary
supporter of cohesiveness	acceptance of cultural conflict

The key question then, is: "Why is one supervisor competent and another incompetent?" This is an ageless question that still confounds the best of police thought.

Taking on a leadership position rather than being a follower involves a shift in the way people view themselves and the way they operate. A newly promoted supervisor generally has the experience of moving from being a highly proficient employee to one who is less sure of him or herself. Operational skills are still important, but other skills must now be applied in order to be an effective supervisor. Reliance on knowledge, methods, and techniques that dominated work in a line position and allowed performance of specific operational tasks must now be shifted to a greater consideration of human and conceptual skills, which are set forth in Figure 5.2.

Figure 5.2
Supervisory Skills

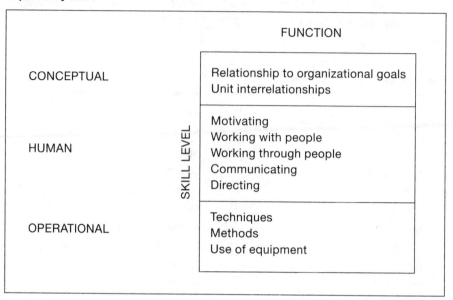

Varying demands on a person in a supervisory position call for a different mix of supervisory skills. Instructing others on how to conduct a lineup or a field sobriety test will call for operational skills. Human skills may dominate in a situation in which a supervisor combines directing with motivation in an effort to control the behavior of one or more officers.

Finally, while it does not occur as often as operational or human situations calling for the application of differing skills, the supervisor will be required to handle situations involving the application of conceptual skills. The most common situation probably occurs where there is conflict between the goals of individual officers and the primary objective of the department. One's knowledge of the overall organization and awareness of how the unit fits into this organization will allow the supervisor to work toward the enhancement of organizational life and increased efficiency (Dobbs and Field, 1993).

When one analyzes the first-line supervisory position in law enforcement, it is apparent that human skills dominate. An effective supervisor must develop the ability to understand why people behave as they do and work toward developing an effective means of changing, directing, and controlling behavior (Nanus, 1992).

First-line supervisors in police agencies exceed the number of managers in all other administrative positions. In a nationwide survey, 111 police departments indicated that the median percentage of personnel in the rank of sergeant was 9.67, while there were only 6.23 percent of sworn personnel in the combined ranks of lieutenant, captain, and major (Police Foundation, 1981). In a Florida study, it was found that in 33 municipal agencies, the percentage of personnel working in administrative positions ranged from two to 13 percent (Reaves and Smith, 1995). Managerial positions vary from agency to agency. In Tucson, Arizona, out of 532 sworn positions in field services, there are 85 sergeants (City of Tucson, 2000). This means the organizational pyramid, as it becomes constricted, offers a limited number of opportunities for promotions. Hence, when a first-line supervisor envisions rising higher in the organization, the characteristics that will set him or her apart from contemporaries will be leadership skills.

It is a stimulating experience when one meets or works for someone who exhibits genuine leadership skills. There is an increasing awareness of the importance of leadership. When leadership is missing or ineffectual, the organization is generally ineffective. Problems develop that are seldom resolved, and chaos is likely to occur. When there is positive leadership, operational tasks are completed and objectives are attained. Above all else, the effective leader is responsible for the attainment of clearly specified tasks (Cox and Hoover, 1992).

Being a leader is a demanding role and forces a supervisor to make decisions, apply discipline, or control behavior—which arouses feelings as well as responses. Whether or not leadership is effective involves a complex interrelationship of leaders, followers, and circumstances.

Studies on leadership are numerous, extending over a considerable period of time, and cover every phase of leadership. In fact, there are so many studies it is difficult to assimilate them. It can easily be suggested that the more one studies leadership, the more it can be seen as an inexact science (Fetherolf, 1994).

In recent years, Total Quality Management (TQM) has emphasized the critical roles that leaders should assume in order to deal with the organizational environment and with the continuing and constantly changing demands of the community. This has resulted in the identification of four critical tasks that skilled leaders need to carry out in a high-performance organization (Harrison, 1996; Lawler, 1986):

- building trust and openness;
- presentation of a vision and communicating it;
- allowing decisions to be made at the appropriate level; and
- empowering others.

These are demanding tasks, and a supervisor should accept this challenge. Decisions must be based on facts rather than on gut reaction. Rather than doing things the same old way, breakthrough thinking is advocated. Instead of a quick fix, stress is placed on long-term, continuous improvement (Saylor, 1992; Simonsen and Arnold, 1993). Innovation and creativity will become increasingly common, and assuming risks becomes acceptable (Engelson, 1999). All of these factors focus on creating a high-quality organizational culture in which finger-pointing and censure are replaced with problem-solving efforts, and creative efforts are endorsed and supported (Johnson, 1993). It is a question of staking out a claim on the future (Bentz, 1995).

A good definition of leadership proves to be elusive. For purposes of this chapter, the most comprehensive definition is used. Leadership is defined as the process of influencing group activities toward the achievement of goals. There are a number of implications to this definition, and it must be recognized as a process of influencing that can include such activities as telling, selling, ordering, coaching, joining, or consulting. At the same time, influencing others must be directed toward the achievement of some objective or goal—otherwise it can be an exercise in futility. Whatever the objective, whether it is an arrest or assisting a lost child, the first-line supervisor is responsible for ensuring the attainment of the objective.

Another aspect of the definition is that the first-line supervisor is no longer primarily a doer, but a coordinator of others' activities. Group members respond to and willingly accept direction from someone who has a leadership style that emphasizes the coordination of subordinates. This means a supervisor should comply with the "50-percent" rule. At a minimum, supervisors should spend half of their time managing others, rather than being just another employee (Von der Embse, 1987).

Finally, the definition demonstrates that the leader operates from a position of power based on the authority delegated to the supervisor. The position has numerous power sources, including reward, coercive, legitimate, referent, and expert (French and Raven, 1959). These sources are listed in Figure 5.3.

Figure 5.3
Supervisory Power Sources

POSITIONAL	Legitimate Coercive Reward
PERSONAL	Expert Referent

Source: J. French and B. Raven (1959). "The Bases of Social Power." In D. Cartwright (ed.), *Studies in Social Power.* Ann Arbor, MI: Institute for Social Research. Reprinted by permission.

Power

Within a police agency, power plays a very important role. In fact, the national accreditation program specifically calls for directives addressing the position of supervisor. First, it is recommended that there be one written directive setting forth the need for supervisory personnel to be held accountable for the performance of employees under their immediate supervision. Another directive should point out that in order to permit effective supervision, direction, and control, employees should promptly obey any lawful order of a superior Finally, a directive should address the necessity of having each officer be accountable to only one supervisor at any given time. (CALEA, 1999). Figure 5.4 is an example of a policy statement suggesting partial authority for a first-line supervisor. Policies such as this should be reviewed annually to ensure compatibility with agency goal attainment (Carpenter, 2000).

Figure 5.4
Authority

Compliance with Lawful Orders

The department is an organization with a clearly defined hierarchy of authority. This is necessary because unquestioned obedience of a superior's lawful command is essential for the safe and prompt performance of law enforcement operations. The most desirable means of obtaining compliance are recognition and reward of proper performance and the positive encouragement of a willingness to serve. However, negative discipline may be necessary where there is a willful disregard of lawful orders, commands, or directives.

Source: Harry W. More and O.R. Shipley (1987). *The Police Policy Manual—Personnel.* Courtesy of Charles C Thomas, Publisher, Springfield, IL.

Beyond formally derived power, the first-line supervisor can extend power by using a number of techniques when dealing with others. Figure 5.5 lists tools a supervisor can use to expand power (Covey, 1991). Persuasion is such a technique. It is imperative that the supervisor share his or her reasons and justifications when exerting influence over others. At the same time, the supervisor should genuinely demonstrate an interest in each officer's ideas and position. Officers should be told *why* as well as *what* needs to be done.

Patience is another technique to be emphasized when relating to subordinates. Consideration must be given to the shortcomings and weaknesses of each employee, and these must be balanced against an immediate desire to attain objectives. Short-term impediments, and in some instances actual opposition, must be dealt with, placed in proper perspective, and balanced with a realistic commitment to the achievement of objectives and goals.

Another technique is to be *enlightened*. Supervisors seldom have the best answer to every problem or situation. One should accept and value the insights, discernment, and seasoning of those being supervised.

The technique of openness serves as a vehicle for communicating with subordinates. Officers should be accepted not only for who they are now, but also for what they can become as growth occurs. A supervisor's perspective should be based on accurately acquired information about each officer, including an awareness of goals, values, desires, and intentions. In some instances, actual behavior can become secondary as the supervisor strives to increase power.

Figure 5.5
Ten Power Tools

1. Persuasion
2. Patience
3. Gentleness
4. Teachableness
5. Acceptance
6. Kindness
7. Openness
8. Compassionate confrontation
9. Consistency
10. Integrity

Source: Steven R. Covey (1991). *Principle-Centered Leadership*. New York, NY: Summit Books. Reprinted with the permission of the Covey Leadership Center, Provo, UT.

Consistency is another technique a supervisor should follow in order to increase power. This means doing what is expected of you so subordinates will always know where you are coming from and never have to feel like they are being manipulated. A leadership style reflecting consistency will then become a manifestation of one's true character, reflecting values and personal code.

Finally, integrity is a technique resulting in the extension of power. Officers know when they are working for someone who is honest and who demonstrates a real concern for others. A supervisor should constantly strive for control that can only be interpreted as fair, impartial, and non-manipulative (Covey, 1991).

Legitimate

The reference above to written directives provides a clear-cut example of what is known as legitimate power. The directives spell out not only the responsibility of the supervisor for subordinate performance, but also the requirement that subordinates comply with lawful orders. This power is essential for the safe and prompt performance of law enforcement operation. Officers are well aware of the first-line supervisor's status in the organization and the support of other managerial positions. At the same time, the officers are fully aware that the incumbent of a supervisory position has the formal right to exercise influence.

Expert

If the sergeant has had previous experience in either patrol or investigation and is currently supervising in that area, then there is a vast reservoir of special knowledge and expertise (expert power) to be called upon when supervising officers. Subordinates will respond to supervisors who possess this greater amount of knowledge, knowing that it ensures the successful completion of tasks. Expertise in law enforcement is coveted, and officers continually strive to improve their operational skills. A knowledgeable supervisor who demonstrates the ability to implement, analyze, evaluate and control situations, and resolve problems is readily accepted.

Expert power is extremely narrow in scope. If it is to be a continuing source of influence, it is imperative for the possessor to stay abreast of new developments, because one's expertise can rapidly become diluted in many areas. An example of this is in criminal law, where court decisions can alter criminal procedures in one term of the U.S. Supreme Court.

Referent

An additional source of influence a supervisor can call upon is referent power. It is the only aspect of a potential power base that is not directly attributable to the position the supervisor holds. It is a type of power that is associated with the leader's personality. Some would identify it as charisma. Whatever the description of this quality, it is something that makes the supervisor likable, and subordinates respond by imitating the style of the leader or struggling to accomplish tasks in order to receive the leader's approbation.

An additional source of referent power for a supervisor is a good reputation—especially when it is based on effective police work. This power is evident when subordinates refer to a supervisor as a "cop's cop" and respond accordingly. Acts of heroism and bravery or outstanding performance accompanied by departmental citations go a long way in establishing a base of referent power.

Coercive

Coercive power is based on fear and on the ability of the supervisor to administer some type of punishment. A first-line supervisor in law enforcement has coercive power, but usually much less than other managerial positions. This type of power is subject to review, depending on the nature and type of disciplinary action taken. As noted in Chapter 6, it can be construed as totally negative and may not result in the desired behavior. Supervisors have power that should be used with care, ensuring adequate employee performance (Hudson, 1994).

In some instances, coercive power can be applied without taking formal disciplinary action, such as giving an officer an undesirable work assignment or enacting a closer supervisory pattern. Reports written by officers can be reviewed with an emphasis on minutiae and returned to the officer for correction. These actions, as well as numerous others, are extensions of the formal coercive power that circumscribes the relationship between a superior and a subordinate. It is also an example of how a supervisor can extend personal power beyond that which is assigned to the position.

Reward

Reward power is somewhat limited in law enforcement, because promotions are usually based on service regulations; thus, the supervisor's role in the process is limited. It might also refer to annual raises (until an officer is at the top step) or cost-of-living raises, which are usually automatic.

Officers are more likely to respond to reward power when the authority of the supervisor affects operational working conditions. Officers will comply when the supervisor has the authority to give out preferential work assignments, influence the assignment of officers to special training programs, or support such actions as transfer requests. Compliance results in a reward, and the officers respond accordingly.

To be useful to a supervisor, power should be viewed positively. It is something to cultivate, not ignore. Power is the base that legitimizes the supervisor's position. When the five power sources are analyzed, it is obvious that each has limitations, but they must be developed and used if a supervisor is to maintain an effective relationship with subordinates. There are, of course, other ways to view power, and Gene N. Landrum believes that there are developmental stages of power, including physical, financial, knowledge, titular, charismatic and, finally, willpower. Of special interest is willpower, which is internally generated by one's mind and value system. It is of special importance because it makes each person unique and is foundational in nature (Landrum, 1997).

Theories of Leadership

Theories of leadership are as numerous as the number of individuals who have investigated the topic. The approaches to this important topic can be grouped into three categories: (1) trait theories, (2) behavioral theories, and (3) contingency theories.

Trait

The trait theory of leadership identifies distinguishing qualities or characteristics a person possesses when functioning as an effective leader. It has been widely accepted because it is appealing, simple, and straightforward (Daresh, 1989). Clearly, the abilities, skills, and personality traits found in successful leaders are not present in poorly functioning leaders.

The number of traits manifested by successful leaders varies considerably—from a few to as many as 56. It is quite improbable that any one individual could possess every trait identified. A list of traits typically includes:

- Courage
- Initiative
- Decisiveness
- Intelligence
- Determination

- Optimism
- Energy
- Self-assurance
- Enthusiasm
- Sociability

The possession of specific traits creates an impossible ideal. There are numerous examples of supervisors who do not exhibit these qualities but have proven to be highly successful (Handy, 1993). Notwithstanding the criticisms of the trait approach, it is still accepted by many managers. As an example of this approach, one agency has identified the following traits as qualities required of a good supervisor (New York Police Department, n.d.):

- Cooperative
- Courteous
- Energetic
- Fair
- Open-minded

- Prompt
- Reliable
- Resourceful
- Tolerant

Numerous problems become apparent if one attempts to use traits as a means of identifying potential leaders. In many instances it is difficult to determine whether the leadership position results in the development of the traits or if the individual had the traits before becoming a leader (Johns, 1995). Also, trait theory studies do not weigh the relative importance of each characteristic. In other words, if being tolerant is believed to be an essential trait of a good police supervisor, one must determine how much tolerance is needed before an individual can become a good supervisor.

Finally, the trait approach does not acknowledge the complex interaction between the actions of the leader and the situation. It is clear that the situation modifies the interaction between the supervisor and the follower. In many instances, the environment modifies the leadership process. This is especially evident during police emergencies.

From the discussion of the supervisor's role in Chapter 1, it is apparent that supervisors deal with three types of skills: knowledge, human, and conceptual. All are conditioned and reconditioned by the uniqueness of each situation. Acknowledging the limitations of studies of the trait approach to leadership qualities, one researcher has identified five groups of traits associated with leadership effectiveness. After analyzing thousands of articles and books, Ralph Stogdill found a relationship between leadership capacity, achievement, responsibility, participation, and status (Stogdill and Shartle, 1974). See Figure 5.6 for an explanation of each of these variables.

Figure 5.6
Leadership Traits

	Leadership Traits
CAPACITY	Intelligence Mental alertness Verbal ability Originality Judgment
ACHIEVEMENT	Knowing how to work in a group Ability to present ideas Attainment of good school grades Successful in athletics
RESPONSIBILITY	Dependability Willingness to assume responsibility Initiative Persistence Self-confidence Desire to excel
PARTICIPATION	High activity level Sociability Cooperation Adaptability
STATUS	Social position Economic position Popularity
SITUATIONAL	Mental level Status Skills Needs and interests of followers Objectives to be achieved

Source: Ralph M. Stogdill (1981). *Stogdill's Handbook of Leadership—A Survey of Theory and Research, Revised and Expanded Edition by Bernard M. Bass.* New York: The Free Press. Reprinted with permission of The Free Press, a Division of Simon & Schuster.

These leadership traits clearly illustrate the importance of groups and the need for the leader to become involved in the group. It is also supportive of our definition of leadership, which is the process of influencing group activities toward the achievement of goals (Couper, 1994).

Behavioral

A great deal of research has focused on the actual behavior of leaders rather than on the trait model. Under the direction of Carroll Shartle, the studies at Ohio State University rejected the concept of leadership behavior occurring on a single continuum and, after having subordinates describe the behavior of superiors, concluded there were two basic types of leadership behavior (Johns, 1995).

The two factors are identified as *initiating structure* and *consideration*. The concept of initiating structure is defined as "the leader's behavior in delineating the relationship between himself and members of the work group and in endeavoring to establish well-defined patterns of organization, channels of communication and methods or procedures." Consideration is defined as "behavior indicative of friendship, mutual trust, respect and warmth in the relationship between the leader and all members" (Johns, 1995).

The Ohio State University leadership studies resulted in a model of four quadrants plotted on two separated axes that identify the two principal aspects of leadership behavior defined in the preceding paragraph (see Figure 5.7).

Figure 5.7
Leadership Behavior

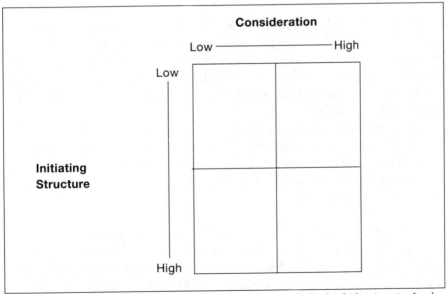

Source: Ralph M. Stogdill and Carroll Shartle (1955). *Methods in the Study of Administrative Leadership*. Research Monograph No. 80. Columbus, OH: The Ohio State University.

Studies at Ohio State University noted that leadership styles vary considerably from individual to individual. Some leaders are characterized as task-oriented and rigidly structure subordinate activities. On the other hand, there are leaders who demonstrate (through their behavior) the capacity to build and maintain good personal relationships. Finally, other individuals exhibit leadership behavior that is a mixture of consideration and initiating structure.

A supervisor who feels comfortable emphasizing consideration as a leadership approach is more likely to use two-way communication (see Chapter 3), show respect for officers' ideas, and work best when there is a feeling of mutual trust. This style is especially applicable when officers are well trained and the goals and methods of performing tasks are clear-cut and unambiguous (Johns, 1995). Such a leader continually demonstrates a concern for the needs of each officer when there is a high degree of consideration. When there is a low degree of consideration, the supervisor is more impersonal and shows less concern for the needs of those supervised.

When a supervisor emphasizes initiating structure, objectives are attained by carefully structuring a subordinate's role. Activities are carefully planned and communicated. Deadlines are established, and giving instructions dominates the interpersonal relationship between the sergeant and the officers. Tasks are scheduled, and rules and regulations are adhered to in an effort to ensure a high standard of performance. In fact, the task proves to be more important than the needs of the officers.

If there is a limitation to the Ohio State University studies, it is that they ignore the influence of the situation and concentrate on the relationship between the leader and the follower.

Contingency

Proponents of the contingency model of leadership hold that the leader's style (if it is to be effective) must match the demands of the specific situation. The situation causes the leader to use qualities that ensure success. The situationist makes the assumption that the leader will emerge from the situation. This approach broadens the scope of leadership beyond the trait or behavioral approaches.

In landmark research, Fred Fiedler and his associates developed the first contingency model of leadership. This theory postulated three factors of major importance and identified them as: (1) the leader's position power, (2) the structure of the task, and (3) the interpersonal relationship between the leader and members.

Position Power. This term is defined as the degree to which the position itself confers upon the leader the capacity to motivate officers to accept and comply with directions. Position power can be measured. Fiedler and his associates (1976) developed an 18-item checklist that incorporates various indices of power, such as:

- Leader has official rank and status.

- Leader is knowledgeable in terms of the position and work of subordinates.

- Leader can recommend punishments and rewards.

- Leader's knowledge allows for a decision about how a task is to be done.

The value of position power for a supervisor is readily apparent. The rank and status provide the leader with the tools to get the officers to perform their tasks. While the sergeant does not have the position power that can be attributed to lieutenants or those of higher rank, the power is enhanced because the first-line supervisor has more frequent and intense contact with line personnel.

Task Structure. Task structure is the extent to which a task is routine and structured as compared to an ambiguous and poorly defined task. When tasks are carefully defined, it is much easier for a supervisor to control operational duties and officers can be held responsible for their actions or inactions. In many law enforcement agencies, standard operating procedures abound and policy manuals can take up a substantial part of a bookshelf.

Routine police tasks are usually highly structured and circumscribed by numerous legal requirements. Consequently, there is little or no reason for an officer to question the right of a supervisor to give instructions supported by departmental policy. Fiedler states that the structured task is enforceable, while the unstructured, ambiguous task is difficult or impossible to enforce.

Personal Relationships. When the relationship between subordinates and a leader can be described as a good working relationship, the leader is in a favorable position to influence behavior (Johns, 1995). This is due to the trust that has developed between them.

In most instances the newly appointed supervisor, because of position power, is acceptable to a certain degree, and his or her conduct is seldom questioned unless it is clearly inept. The interpersonal relationship developing between a leader and followers depends in part upon the personality of the leader. Of the three factors, personality has been found to be the most important in terms of the leader's capacity to influence a group of officers.

When a sergeant is totally acceptable from the officer's viewpoint, loyalty is inspired, compliance is generated from the interpersonal relationship, giving rank and position power a limited meaning. When a supervisor and the officers get along reluctantly, to the point where friction is readily apparent, compliance may be obtained, but in many instances it is obtained with reservation. When there is such a strained relationship, it can cause a lessening of the leader's influence.

When the followers reject the first-line supervisor and strife prevails, it comes down to basic survival from the leader's point of view. Considerable effort must be expended if even a margin of productivity is to be achieved. Control becomes the essential means to ensure attainment of goals, and ordering officers to do something usually gets immediate results.

Fiedler points out quite candidly that it is much easier to work with followers who are loyal and devoted than with those who are tolerant or antagonistic. The life of a leader supervising the latter group will prove to be most difficult.

If effective leadership is to prevail, it is necessary for the leader's guidance style to be congruent with the demands of the specific situation. Fiedler identified two basic styles of leadership. One style is task-oriented, and the leader's satisfaction is generated by effective task accomplishment. The second leadership style is predicated on the desire to achieve personal acceptance and is identified as relationship-oriented. By themselves, neither of these styles can be described as effective; they depend on the situation as modified by the three dimensions discussed above. When there is mutual trust and respect and the task is highly structured, the supervisor has high position power and the situation can then be considered favorable. However, if the leader is not respected and has limited support, the position power is weak and the task will be unstructured and vague, creating an unfavorable situation.

The effectiveness of a leadership style is highly variable. In all probability you will find that in one situation it might be most effective to be task-oriented, while in another it might be effective if a relationship-oriented style is used. In other words, no one style is consistently successful all the time.

For the newly appointed supervisor whose influence is (in all probability) limited, the task-oriented leadership style will be most effective. When situations are moderately favorable in terms of influence, the best leadership style has been found to be relationship-oriented. If a supervisor is a failure, it is probably due to an inability to adapt to the situation. A supervisor's position demands considerable flexibility when compared to a line officer's position. As pointed out in Chapter 1, a line officer's position is dominated by the need to achieve tasks, while the first-line supervisor's position requires a response to situations in which human relations becomes more important. The situation changes when it becomes necessary to accomplish objectives through the efforts of others.

There are times in a police organization when both relationship-oriented and task-oriented supervisors have been found to function effectively under certain conditions but are less than effective under other circumstances. If a supervisor fails to function effectively, it is usually not a question of intelligence or innate ability, but the development of a different situation where the leadership style proves to be inappropriate.

In some situations the supervisor can change the leadership style by using positive features of the hierarchical organization and structuring the tasks more carefully. This will result in greater compliance with departmental policy. In addition, the supervisor can make more decisions, initiate a closer review process of certain calls for service, or let the officers know where they stand when faced with certain situations. For example, the supervisor can provide backup in certain types of situations, review all felony arrests, or care-fully scrutinize reports submitted by the line officers.

A first-line supervisor may find in some situations that the work envi-ronment is tense, and the interpersonal relationships are less than ade-quate. It would seem that task-oriented leadership has contributed to this sit-uation. The supervisor should then implement a relationship-oriented leadership style. Emphasis can be placed on reducing close supervision activ-ities (allowing line officers more discretion in specific situations), involv-ing subordinates in the decision-making process, or, in general, doing what-ever is necessary to create a relaxed working environment.

The question then might be: "How does one measure one's leadership style?" Fiedler's contingency model uses an instrument called *The Least Pre-ferred Coworker (LPC) Scale*, which is presented in Figure 5.8. When com-pleting the scale, an individual is required to think of all the people with whom he or she has worked and then think of the person with whom he or she can work least well. When completing the instrument, this person is iden-tified on the scale by placing an "X" in the appropriate place. The scale con-sists of 18 pairs of words, diametrically opposed, and the score obtained by adding the responses becomes a measure of one's leadership style.

When the total score is 64 or above, it indicates that the leader is rela-tionship-motivated and has the tendency to be most concerned with main-taining good interpersonal relations, sometimes even to the point at which the job to be done received limited attention.

If the score is 57 or below, it is an indication that the leader will place primary emphasis on the performance of the task. This leader tends to be a no-nonsense individual who works best when going by the book. If the sit-uation is at all ambiguous, this type of leader will generate rules and regu-lations to control the situation.

When the score is between 58 and 63, the individuals completing the scale will have to determine for themselves which classification they favor (Fiedler, Chemers, and Maher, 1976; Klenke, 1996). Whether a first-line supervisor is task-motivated or relationship-motivated, it is necessary to con-sider three different kinds of leadership situations:

- The high-control situation provides the leader with a work environment in which there is all of the control and influence needed to direct the activities of others.

- In the moderate-control situation, the leader is presented with mixed signals in which interpersonal relations are less than adequate but the task is structured and position power is high. On the other hand, the situation might be such that the relationships are good, position power is low, and the task is unstructured.

- In a low-control situation, the leader is not supported by the group, caus-ing control and influence to be low. At the same time, influence is not provided by either the task or position power (Fiedler, Chemers, and Maher, 1976).

The interaction of the leadership style, extent of control, and the situational dimension result in a position in which the relationship-motivated leader is most effective in a moderate-control situation and the task-motivated leader is most effective in high- or low-control conditions.

Figure 5.8
Least Preferred Coworker (LPC) Scale

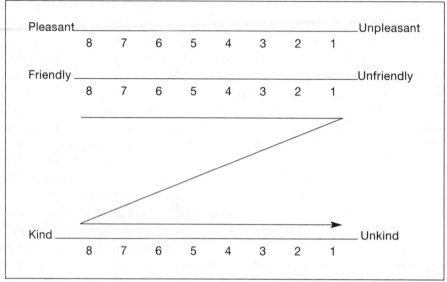

Source: Fred E. Fiedler, Martin M. Chemers, and Linda Maher (© 1976). *Improving Leadership Effectiveness: The Leader Match Concept.* New York, NY: John Wiley & Sons, Inc. Reprinted by permission of John Wiley & Sons, Inc. (Note: The actual scale has 18 variables.)

Leadership Continuum

The success of a first-line supervisor depends on numerous factors. The relationship between a supervisor and subordinates is best described as existing along a leadership continuum. Some researchers have identified two basic types of leadership and identified them as autocratic and democratic. Another researcher's list expands on this and lists five styles: authoritarian, democratic, laissez-faire, bureaucratic, and charismatic.

Other experts have stressed sharing power in the decision-making process and described seven types of leadership behavior in which the style is increasingly subordinate-centered. Whatever the number of leadership styles, it seems apparent that supervisors do not consistently use any single leadership style. Seldom is any style found in its pure form, because the supervisor's behavior varies depending on the situation.

Most supervisors—in fact, most individuals—are not capable of being infinitely flexible in applying leadership styles, but they can employ styles that are consistent with their personality. Leadership is highly personal and projects one's innermost beliefs and feelings. For the purposes of this discussion, it is best to describe three types of leadership behavior that can be used when a supervisor wants to influence the behavior of line officers: directive, consultative, and participative.

Directive

Many supervisors feel most comfortable when exerting directive leadership behavior. In many instances the supervisor who practices this style of leadership was previously supervised by someone who relied on a directive leadership style. Other terms used to describe a directive style include *autocratic* and *dictatorial*, indicating the variability of behavior and also that leadership styles are best represented on a continuum.

While some suggest that directive leadership is on the decline, this is certainly not the case in many law enforcement agencies. In fact, the work environments of some police departments are such that it is very difficult for a supervisor to use any leadership style other than directive.

The directive supervisor exhibits little concern for officers and allows little or no involvement in the decision-making process. The supervisor makes the decision and ensures it is implemented. If the situation dictates, this type of leader will listen to questions, but never for the purpose of altering the decision. Control dominates the situation, and "Do as I say" is the prevailing philosophy.

A first-line supervisor, by virtue of position power, is firmly entrenched in a position of unquestioned authority and will wield the power necessary to accomplish assigned tasks. To show weakness to subordinates is to give them an opportunity to undermine one's authority, so this is never done.

Knowledge of the task to be performed is used to support position power and status. Whenever possible, assignments to special details and tasks can bolster a positive response to authority. The description of Theory X, as set forth in Chapter 4, holds that a directive supervisor perceives line officers as being lazy and untrustworthy. Consequently, officers should be told what to do, and their conduct and activities should be monitored closely.

A directive leadership style emphasizes a combination of elements, such as structuring the tasks in such a way as to easily control officers. A supervisor who uses this style uses the authority inherent in the position as the basis for subordinate obedience. If deviation from the desired behavior occurs, then the supervisor controls the subordinates by assigning blame. Control is maintained by relying on rules and regulations as a means of ensuring compliance.

Close attention is paid to adhering to schedules. Progress reports are required to be on time; late or inadequate reports constitute reasons for immediate discipline. Failure to comply with standard operating procedures results in closer supervision and will likely result in disciplinary action.

Directive leadership, because it is authoritarian, relies on position power to reduce or suppress conflict. Authority should never be questioned, and absolute obedience is required. The supervisor makes decisions, and input is never allowed. The primary concern is to get the job done, and ignoring social interaction unless it enhances goal attainment. What this means is that personal needs are subordinate to departmental needs.

This type of task-oriented behavior for the supervisor certainly lets the officers know what is expected of them. It also ensures the use of uniform procedures and eliminates or substantially reduces officer discretion. The advantages and disadvantages set forth in Figure 5.9 make it apparent that the directive style of leadership has drawbacks. The style of leadership used by a supervisor must vary with the individual and the situation.

Figure 5.9
Directive Leadership

Advantages	<ul><li>Focuses on goal attainment</li><li>Subordinates know what has to be done</li><li>Decisions are made quickly</li><li>Decisions are not challenged</li><li>Logical extension of position power</li><li>Maximizes control of subordinates</li><li>Enhances compliance with departmental rules and regulations</li></ul>
Disadvantages	<ul><li>Isolates the supervisor</li><li>Negative feelings can be generated</li><li>Minimal compliance</li><li>Stressful for the supervisor</li><li>Can be punitive and seldom rewarding</li><li>May result in a lowering of morale</li><li>Stifles creativity</li><li>Limits two-way communication</li></ul>

Consultative

If everyone in a police organization worked at his or her maximum capacity, there would probably be limited need for a supervisor. However, such is not the case. Problems must be resolved and conflict must be reduced, thus the need for supervisors. The second style of leadership is consultative. It represents an additional description of leadership behavior. In recent years it has become an increasingly popular approach to supervision.

It is, in reality, a leadership position adopted by a supervisor as a compromise position when it has become apparent that line officers have values and attitudes different from those held by older police officers. The supervisor decides that officers can no longer live in the past. It is then necessary to acknowledge the need for changes in working conditions and proceed to make these changes.

The supervisor cannot completely abandon the directive style of leadership, however, because it is the type that higher managers expect to see in operation. However, the supervisor may believe that another style of leadership will prove to be more productive while improving officer working conditions.

The consultative supervisor shows concern for officers and their needs as well as organizational needs. Subordinates are allowed to participate in the decision-making process and are accepted as part of the team. It is, thus, an acknowledgment that officers have something to offer and that they are knowledgeable and capable.

The consultative style of leadership works best when decisions that have to be made deal with relatively simple tasks or issues. When issues are complex or there is not enough time to permit discussion and analysis, the supervisor should make the decision. This is especially true if the decision involves an emergency situation and directive leadership would be the most appropriate response.

If the decision involves the personal or work life of an officer, then input should be sought so that a mutually acceptable decision can be made. Input from subordinates should also be sought when a decision involves the behavior of one officer that affects other officers.

A supervisor should provide for officer input when it is felt that the process will result in a better decision. In addition, officers should be involved in the decision-making process when it is clear that group commitment and effort will be needed to implement a program or introduce a process. This will generally reduce resistance.

When there are two or more appropriate solutions for the same problem, the decision can generally be left to subordinates. In this way, an arbitrary decision is avoided and compliance is ensured. In addition, ideas and suggestions are sought on a regular basis and on occasion are accepted and implemented (see Figure 5.10). A consultative leadership style is a significant departure from the directive style, but is not fully participative.

Figure 5.10
Consultative

Advantages	• Involves subordinates in the decision-making process • Shows concern for the welfare of subordinates • Reduces stressful situations • Utilizes subordinate ideas • Improves the quality of decisions
Disadvantages	• Leaves personnel in the middle and they never know what to expect • Limited effectiveness in solving problems • One never knows what impact a suggestion will have

Case Study

Sergeant Claudia Faxton

The City of Red Woods has a population of 36,500 and is a wealthy suburban community. For as long as anyone can remember, the police department has had a service orientation. The department has an extensive crime prevention program, including Operation Identification, Block Parents, and Neighborhood Watch. Members of the community pride themselves in the safety of the community. Beats are carefully designed in order to equalize workloads. Each patrol officer is responsible for all crimes or reports arising on the assigned beats. Each officer is responsible for case investigation and final disposition in all crimes, ranging from major felonies to misdemeanors. When necessary, officers can ask for assistance from the department's one criminal investigator or from a supervisor. Uncleared cases represent a direct charge against the efficiency of the officer and become a matter of evaluative records. The independence of each officer is the hallmark of the department, and positions in the department are highly sought-after.

Claudia Faxton has been with the department for eight years and recently completed the promotional examination to sergeant. When the results of the promotional examination were announced, she was number one on the list. Within a month she was promoted and assigned to the third watch (12:00 midnight to 8:00 A.M.). Sergeant Faxton is 32, married, and resides in a neighboring community. She has a bachelor's degree in psychology and previously completed training as a field training officer (FTO). As soon as she was promoted, she was assigned to a supervisory training program offered by a local community college. She graduated with the second highest score in the class and had no difficulty in completing all of the course requirements. As soon as she completed the course, she reported for duty on the third watch.

Sergeant Faxton supervises three officers and functions as the watch commander. Each of the officers that she supervises also took the promotional test, but she scored higher than all of them. The officers had a minimum of eight years service, and their most recent performance evaluations were above average. Sergeant Faxton is replacing a retiring supervisor whose management style was laissez-faire and whose last two years were spent preparing for retirement. The governing rule was not to rock the boat.

If you were Sergeant Faxton, what would you tell each of the officers? What leadership style would you anticipate using? Why? What would you do to improve the performance of the officers that you are supervising? Why? Would you consider using a participative management style? Why?

Participative

A participative leadership style only can be used when the supervisor has a genuine belief in and respect for subordinates. It is in sharp contrast to the Theory X view of worker and leadership behavior described as directive. The supervisor consults with subordinates and involves them in the decision-making process. Attitudes, values, and officers' feelings are viewed as important and are taken into consideration.

Group involvement is sought and power is shared. Every effort is made to create a work environment in which two-way communication is stressed, ideas are accepted, and creativity is fostered. Officers are encouraged to develop to their highest potential, and every effort is made to get officers to accept responsibility as well as handle delegated authority. The informal organization is accepted as an integral element of the formal organization, and each officer is encouraged to think critically.

A change from directive to participative leadership style can prove to be very difficult. It is usually because of an initial misunderstanding as to what participative supervision is or is not. It does not mean that officers have veto power over the decision-making process. Employees do have meaningful input, but in every instance the supervisor or someone higher makes the final decision. At the same time, the supervisor is always held responsible for the accomplishment of objectives.

Participative leadership is not permissiveness in which leadership skills are not exercised, but exists when the recommendations of subordinates influence the decision-making process (see Figure 5.11). A truly participative leader strives to create a work environment in which controls are minimized and officers develop to their highest potential. The goal is to have employees actively managing themselves (Carr, 1994).

Figure 5.11
Participative

Advantages	• Totally acknowledges subordinates' skills and abilities • Improves working relationships • Employees are motivated • Better decisions • Committed employees • Improved communication
Disadvantages	• Slows down the decision-making process • Takes a long time to evolve • Raises officer expectations • Time-consuming

Participative leadership integrates each officer into the work unit. A work environment in which officers can achieve and master the tasks they have to perform is created. Traditions are continuously challenged and, if circumstances warrant, modifications are introduced. When planning has to be accomplished, and circumstances permit, knowledgeable officers are consulted.

A participative manager never performs the task alone when it can be accomplished through the efforts of others. Subordinate creativity in problem solving is encouraged, and traditional control techniques are rejected (Scholtes, 1998). Motivating officers consumes a great deal of the supervisory working week, and emphasis is placed on recognition of good work. When appropriate, officers are given additional authority and responsibility. When officers do good work, it is praised, and when praise alone will not suffice, commendations are forwarded through channels.

A participative management style works best when the department has a positive orientation toward its human resources and subordinates have some discretion in performing assigned tasks. When tasks to be achieved are less structured and officers given a considerable degree of freedom to perform, they are more apt to successfully accomplish the task and will do it with a greater degree of satisfaction.

A truly people-oriented supervisor functions best when serious efforts are expended to foster a work environment in which officers are viewed as an organizational asset. The atmosphere is such that people enjoy coming to work. It is a friendly and supportive ambience where officers are listened to and are involved in the decision-making process. Problem solving is encouraged, and communication is open and aboveboard. Additionally, officers are recognized for their achievement and rewarded accordingly. Teamwork is the operational mode, and supervisors are supportive. It is a good place to work.

Figure 5.12
Tasks for People-Oriented Supervision

1. Treat every subordinate with respect. Do not use language that offends or demeans officers.
2. When changes occur, tell everyone of the change prior to its implementation.
3. Consult, throughout the organization, with everyone who needs to know.
4. Involve officers in the decision-making process.
5. When actions are taken, explain the reasons for those actions.
6. Create a pleasant work environment. Always be civilized and tactful.
7. Resolve differences through mediation as quickly as possible.
8. Allow authority and responsibility to be placed at the operational level.
9. Provide supervision that is supportive and friendly.
10. Hold to a high performance standard as an integral component of a participative leadership style.
11. Encourage creative problem solving and allow for failure.
12. Allow officers to gain self-identity and an opportunity to self-actualize.

Leadership Mistakes

Functioning as a supervisor can prove to be very difficult. Often a supervisor will feel suspended somewhere between line officers and upper management. It is a difficult position to be in and one that occurs more often than one would like it to. It is imperative for a supervisor to accept being part of management, and the only way things are going to be accomplished with any degree of effectiveness is to see that assigned tasks are performed by line personnel. It is the officers who are doing the work, and it is a supervisor's job to work for and with them.

This means making certain that operational personnel are properly trained and equipped to perform their job. Supervisors work for both management and subordinates. Their task is not only to tell employees what to do, but also to coach them when the situation dictates, consult when necessary, and join with the employees to attain objectives. Do not make the mistake of trying to change human nature. Accept each employee as a unique individual. Certainly supervisors can use power to ensure compliance, but in the long run that may prove to be detrimental. Accept individual differences, and work to develop employees by improving the contributions they make to the organization. One should assist officers by really trying to understand them. Determine their needs and work to improve their self-image. Furthermore, one should realize that supervision is not a popularity contest. Making difficult decisions can ruffle the feathers of some, and being unpopular at times goes with the territory (Townsend, 1998).

Most people find it very difficult to reprimand their subordinates for poor performance. Without question it is a most difficult task. Nearly all supervisors hope that it would never have to be done. Additionally, supervisors are reluctant to admonish an officer because of the impact on everyone supervised—not just the errant individual. The keys to instituting the process with the least amount of difficulty are to:

- discuss the problem with the subordinate without letting emotions enter the exchange;

- discuss the facts, not the personality of the one being admonished;

- have the subordinate repeat what you have said so that there is a clear understanding of the issues;

- allow the subordinate adequate time to respond; and

- allow an officer to save face by indicating how the dispute might be resolved (McDevitt, 1999).

Supervisors who criticize employees in public make a serious mistake. The true mark of a competent supervisor is a strong sensitivity toward the feelings of others. When it is necessary to criticize someone, do it privately and in a sensitive manner. While it might be an unpleasant process, there are times when there is no other alternative.

Many problems facing a supervisor will stem from letting the acquisition of power become more important than the actual attainment of objectives and goals. Officers will make mistakes or errors, and by virtue of position power, you can criticize, discipline, or even become involved in the dismissal of an employee (Mendofik, 1994). Excessive or improper use of power is unacceptable. It might prove useful initially, but over time such abuse could lead to the downfall of a first-line supervisor.

Newer supervisors sometimes have trouble with subordinates and will do a task themselves rather than spending the time necessary to coach employees in the proper technique. This is a clear-cut failure to manage. As repeatedly stated throughout this text, as a supervisor you must accomplish goals through the efforts of others. The supervisor should ask him or herself such questions as: "Is too much expected?" or "Are requirements stated clearly?" or "Are the officers properly trained to accomplish the task?"

A supervisor should never show favoritism to a subordinate. One will soon find out that employees have a built-in sense of what is right and wrong and will strongly object when preferential treatment is extended to a few and denied to others. When rewards can be extended (such as assignments), they should be based on merit, not likes or dislikes. It is essential for a supervisor to be perceived as fair. A good supervisor is one who accepts the challenge of leadership with all of its problems and rewards (Cox and Hoover, 1992).

Summary

When a police department is well managed, it is always found to have outstanding leadership. Effective leadership can transform a marginal organization into a successful one. Inspired leadership is contagious and will lead to officers achieving high levels of productivity.

Like other managerial personnel, a first-line supervisor is concerned with the application of skills described as operational, human, and conceptual. In the application of these three skill areas it is readily apparent that human skills dominate the activities performed by a supervisor.

In this text, leadership is defined as the process of influencing group activities toward the achievement of organizational goals. Of particular interest concerning this definition is that the first-line supervisor is no longer a doer but a coordinator of the activities of other employees.

Supervisory power sources vary and include *positional* and *personal*. Under the positional variable one will find sources including *legitimate, coercive*, and *reward*. Personal sources of power include *expert* and *referent*. If a supervisor is to function effectively, it is essential that these five sources of power be cultivated and utilized.

Fundamental theories of leadership abound, falling into the following categories: trait theories, behavioral theories, and contingency theories. Ralph Stogdill identified five groups of traits associated with leadership effectiveness: *capacity, achievement, responsibility, participation*, and *status*.

Some researchers have focused on the actual behavior of leaders rather than on traits. The Ohio State University studies concluded that there were two basic types of leadership behavior: *initiating structure* and *consideration*. If there is a weakness to this approach, it is that it ignores the influence of the situation and concentrates on the relationship between the leader and the follower. On the other hand, the contingency model of leadership holds that the leader's style must match the demands of the specific situation.

Leadership is best viewed as existing along a continuum that depicts the relationship between a supervisor and subordinates. While the experts do not agree as to the number of leadership styles to be included on such a continuum, some researchers have identified two basic types of leadership: *autocratic* and *democratic*. Others have identified five types: *authoritarian, democratic, laissez-faire, bureaucratic*, and *charismatic*. It would seem a minimum of at least the following three must be included: *directive, consultative*, and *participative*. Leadership styles, when being implemented, are modified by the situation, and over time a first-line supervisor will use all the styles.

Truly people-oriented supervisors function best when serious efforts are expended to foster a work environment in which officers are viewed as organizational assets. The atmosphere is such that people enjoy coming to work. It is a friendly and supportive atmosphere in which officers are listened to and involved in the decision-making process.

Most supervisors find it very difficult to reprimand their subordinates for poor performance. Making difficult decisions can ruffle the feathers of some, and being unpopular at times goes with the territory. Supervisors can discipline officers by eliminating emotions from the process, discussing facts, and maximizing two-way communication. Additionally, it is important to allow the officer being reprimanded to save face.

Supervisors are obligated to accept their status as part of management and are no longer strictly operational. At the same time, if a supervisor is to be effective, it is necessary to work for (and through) subordinates. When dealing with subordinates, accept them as unique individuals and work to improve their self-image.

Case Study

Officer Roger Vanguard

The City of Rapidville Police Department serves an urban community and has 279 sworn officers and 48 civilian employees. Fifty-six percent of the personnel are uniformed, whose regularly assigned duties include responding to calls for service and incident-driven patrol. During the swing and midnight shifts 23 percent of the beats are patrolled by two officers and the remainder by one officer. The department has numerous specialized units, including hate crimes, domestic violence, vice control, environmental crimes, and inspectional services. Additionally, the department has a state-of-the-art communications system.

The city has an elected city council of five members and a city manager. The city manager is new to the community and was selected by the city council without a dissenting vote. The chief of police has been in office for five years after being selected by a nationwide selection process. The chief has a master's degree in public administration and has attended numerous executive training programs.

Roger Vanguard has been an officer with the department for three years. Prior to joining the department, he served two years in the Peace Corps. He has a degree in sociology and is currently enrolled part-time in a graduate public administration program. He takes two courses each semester and will be eligible to take the sergeant's examination in one more year. He is currently on the swing shift, working with a team of five officers. The sergeant in charge of the team uses a directive leadership approach. He is firmly entrenched in his position and wields authority so that no one questions any order or decision. Additionally, the sergeant structures each situation in such a way that officers are easily controlled.

If you were Officer Vanguard, what would you do in this situation? If you decided to discuss the matter with the supervising sergeant, what would you say? Why? Would you consider going to the lieutenant? Why or why not? Would you ask to be transferred to another team? Why?

Key Concepts

attributes
authority
coercive power
conceptual skills
consideration
consultative
contingency
directive
expert power
extending power
high control
human skills
initiating structure
leadership continuum
leadership traits

least preferred coworker
legitimate power
low control
moderate control
operational skills
participative
personal relationships
policy
position power
referent power
relationship-oriented leadership
reward power
task-oriented leadership
task structure

Discussion Topics and Questions

1. Traditionally, why has power played such an important part in most police departments?

2. How can a supervisor extend power?

3. Why is the trait theory of leadership receiving less attention today?

4. Identify the limitations inherent in emphasizing consideration as a leadership approach.

5. Describe how the situation can affect leadership style.

6. Discuss the disadvantages of a directive leadership style.

7. What are the limitations of the consultative leadership style?

8. List three mistakes a leader can make when working with officers.

9. Discuss how a leader can truly be people-oriented.

10. What are the advantages of using a participative leadership style?

11. What is it important to remember when reprimanding employees?

12. Why is it important to develop a policy manual?

For Further Reading

Alsabrook, Carl L., Giant Abutalebi Aryani, and Terry D. Garrett (2001). "Five Principles of Leadership." *Law and Order,* Vol. 49, No. 5.

> The authors suggest cultivating people within the organization. Consideration is given to inspiring people with a vision and providing them with continuous education and training. A key recommendation is to align the vision, mission, and strategies with policies and procedures. Another recommendation is to lead by example. Additionally, the authors believe it is important to recognize employee efforts and the need to create a work environment conducive to success.

Department of the Army (1999). *Army Leadership—Be, Know, Do.* Field Manual No. 22-100. Washington, DC: Department of the Army.

> Emphasizes the importance of direct leadership skills, including conceptual, interpersonal, technical, and tactical. Of special interest is the discussion of character, which points out that it helps one determine what is right and motivates you to do it regardless of the circumstances or the consequences. Additionally, there is a discussion of what a leader must do by developing the right values, attributes, and skills. Suggests that excellence is achieved by influencing, operating, and improving.

Eisenberg, Terry (2001). "Identifying Future Police Leaders: Assessment Centers as Predictors of Career Progression." *The Police Chief,* Vol. LXVIII, No 2.

> The author surveyed seven full-service municipal police agencies in order to evaluate assessment centers for first-line supervisory positions at the rank of corporal or sergeant. In the vast majority (76 percent) it was found that a candidate's first assessment center performance, when competing for a promotion to supervisory ranks, was positively related to his or her future career progression. The better the performance in the assessment center, the more likely the officer would be promoted not only to a supervisory rank, but later to a higher rank.

Shafer, Kent H. (1997). "High-Performance Policing for the 21st Century." *The Police Chief,* Vol. LXIV, No. 11.

> Describes the need for police agencies to become high-performance organizations by emulating successful businesses. Includes a discussion of the importance of people skills, the necessity of simplifying the structure of the organization, and the need for developing higher-level skills. Emphasizes the importance of developing leaders for every level in the organization. Discusses the importance of having a vision of where the agency is going, as well as having a mission statement that mandates accountability.

References

Alsabrook, Carl L., Giant Abutalebi Aryani, and Terry D. Garrett (2001). "Five Principles of Leadership." *Law and Order*, Vol. 49, No. 5.

Baker, Thomas E. (2000). "Leadership Issues in Rural America." *Law and Order,* Vol. 48, No. 12.

Bentz, David E. (1995). "Leadership with an Eye on the Future." *The Police Chief,* Vol. LXII, No. 2.

Carpenter, Michael (2000). "Put It in Writing—The Police Policy Manual." *FBI Law Enforcement Bulletin*, Vol. 69, No. 10.

Carr, Clay (1994). "Empowered Organizations, Empowered Leaders." *Training and Development*, Vol. 48, No. 3.

City of Tucson (2000). *Adopted Budget Operating Detail—Fiscal Year 2000-2001*, Volume II. Tucson, AZ: City of Tucson.

CALEA (1999). *Standards for Law Enforcement Agencies*, Fourth Edition. Fairfax, VA: Commission on Accreditation for Law Enforcement Agencies, Inc.

Couper, David (1994). "Seven Seeds for Policing." *FBI Law Enforcement Bulletin*, Vol. 63, No. 3.

Covey, Stephen R. (1991). *Principle-Centered Leadership*. New York, NY: Summit Books.

Cox, Danny, and John Hoover (1992). *Leadership When the Heat's On*. New York, NY: McGraw-Hill.

Daresh, John C. (1989). *Supervision as a Practical Process*. White Plains, NY: Longman.

Department of the Army (1999). *Army Leadership—Be, Know, Do*. Field Manual No. 22-100. Washington, DC: Department of the Army.

Dobbs, Carl, and Mark W. Field (1993). "Rational Risk: Leadership Success or Failure?" *The Police Chief*, Vol. XLII, No. 12.

Engelson, Wade (1999). "Leadership Challenges in the Information Age." *The Police Chief*, Vol. LXVI, No. 3.

Eisenberg, Terry (2001). "Identifying Future Police Leaders: Assessment Centers as Predictors of Career Progression." *The Police Chief*, Vol. LXVIII, No. 2.

Fetherolf, Louis H. (1994). "Leadership: An Inside-Out Proposition." *The Police Chief*, Vol. XLIII, No. 1.

Fiedler, Fred E., Martin M. Chemers, and Linda Maher (1976). *Improving Leadership Effectiveness: The Leader Match Concept*. New York, NY: John Wiley & Sons.

French, J., and B. Raven (1959). "The Bases of Social Power." In D. Cartwright (ed.), *Studies in Social Power*. Ann Arbor, MI: Institute for Social Research.

Handy, Charles (1993). *Understanding Organizations*. Oxford: Oxford University Press.

Harrison, Stephen J. (1996). "Quality Policing and the Challenges for Leadership." *The Police Chief*, Vol. LXIII, No. 1.

Hudson, David (1994). "The Power Gap and Police Performance Failure." *The Police Chief*, Vol. LXI, No. 6.

Johns, Gary (1995). *Organizational Behavior: Understanding and Managing Life at Work*. Glenview, IL: Addison-Wesley Educational Publishers.

Johnson, Richard S. (1993). *TQM: Management Processes for Quality Operations*. Milwaukee, WI: Quality Press.

Klenke, Karin (1996). *Women and Leadership—A Contextual Perspective*. New York, NY: Springer Publishing.

Landrum, Gene N. (1997). *Profile of Power and Success: Fourteen Geniuses Who Broke the Rules*. New York, NY: Prometheus Books.

Lawler, Edward E., III (1986). *High-Involvement Management.* San Francisco, CA: Jossey-Bass.

McDevitt, Daniel S. (1999). "Common Sense Leadership." *Law and Order,* Vol. 47, No.8.

Mendofik, Paul J. (1994). "Reflections on Leadership." *FBI Law Enforcement Bulletin,* Vol. 63, No. 8.

More, Harry W. and O.R. Shipley (1987). *The Police Policy Manual—Personnel.* Springfield, IL: Charles C Thomas.

Nanus, Burt (1992). *Visionary Leadership: Creating a Compelling Sense of Direction for Your Organization.* San Francisco, CA: Jossey-Bass.

New York Police Department (n.d.). *Police Academy Bulletin.* New York: City of New York.

Police Foundation (1981). *Survey of Police Operational Administrative Practices—1981.* Washington, DC: Police Executive Research Forum.

Porter, Constance, Susan Neal, and Ann Medina (2000). "Leadership Development at the Executive Level." *The Police Chief,* Vol. LXVII, No. 10.

Reaves, Brian A., and Pheny Z. Smith (1995). *Law Enforcement Management and Administrative Statistics, 1993: Data for Individual State and Local Agencies with 100 or More Officers.* Washington, DC: Bureau of Justice Statistics.

Saylor, James H. (1992). *TQM Field Manual.* New York, NY: McGraw-Hill, Inc.

Scholtes, Peter R. (1998). *The Leaders's Handbook—Making Things Happen, Getting Things Done.* New York, NY: McGraw-Hill.

Simonsen, Clifford E., and Douglas Arnold (1993). "TQM: Is It Right for Law Enforcement?" *The Police Chief,* Vol. LIX, No. 12.

Stogdill, Ralph M. (1981). *Stodill's Handbook of Leadership—A Survey of Theory and Research, Revised and Expanded Edition by Bernard M. Bass.* New York, NY: The Free Press.

Stodgill, Ralph M., and Carroll Shartle (1955). *Methods in the Study of Adminstrativev Leadership.* Research Monograph No. 80. Columbus, OH: The Ohio State University.

Townsend, Josephine C. (1998). "Mentors—The Art of Leadership." *Law and Order,* Vol. 46, No.5.

Von der Embse, Thomas J. (1987). *Supervision: Managerial Skills for a New Era.* New York, NY: Macmillan.

Waitley, Denis (1995). *Empires of the Mind: Lessons to Lead and Succeed in a Knowledge-based World.* New York, NY: William Morrow.

Discipline—

An Essential Element of Police Supervision

6

Introductory Case Study

PSO Jane Roberts

Public Safety Officer Jane Roberts has just fulfilled her six-month probationary period with the department. She had high evaluations from you, her sergeant, and from her field training officer, Andrew Tibbetts. You had some doubts when she was first hired about placing her with FTO Tibbetts. After all, Roberts was an attractive single woman who had just graduated from college. Tibbetts, although married with three children, is considered to be a "ladies man" according to the officers under your supervision. Tibbetts is also affectionately known as "Adonis" by other officers because of his extreme neatness and concern for his physical appearance. However, Jane Roberts had a no-nonsense demeanor about her and seemed to have a good head on her shoulders. She was a bit cocky and seemed a bit too sure of herself, which was one reason you decided to assign her to Tibbetts for field training during her probationary period. But that has been completed, and Roberts is on her own as a regular member of the shift.

A couple of months have passed since Roberts completed her probationary period, and she seems to be doing fine performance-wise. She still seems a bit cocky and overly confident, but you believe she will get over those traits eventually. You have noticed that she and Tibbetts seem to be together more than is usual for the officers on your shift. They eat together, back each other up on calls and, it is rumored, see each other at the end of their shift. It concerns you somewhat, although you have always made it a point to stay out of the personal lives of officers under your supervision, unless it affects their job performance. In this case, Tibbetts and Roberts have been doing a good job, and you see no reason to interfere with anything that may be considered personal between them.

One afternoon at the end of your shift you notice Tibbetts and Roberts having a heated argument in the police parking garage. When you intervene to find out what is wrong, both turn away from you and leave without saying a word. Probably a lover's spat, you think to yourself. The next morning, after roll call, Roberts asks to speak to you alone. You escort her to the supervisor's office and ask her to sit down. Roberts begins to explain what the argument was about in the parking garage.

"Sergeant, I wanted you to know first. I'm pregnant. The baby belongs to Tibbetts. He won't leave his wife and won't have anything to do with me now."

"Oh, Jane, I'm sorry to hear about that. But you know our policy about pregnancy. You'll have to take a leave of absence and—"

"Damn your policies," Roberts interrupts. "This happened because of you. It's your fault. You put me with that ladies' hound for over six months. You knew what kind of man he was and how vulnerable I was. You didn't supervise us at all, just turned us loose. And to top it off, I got pregnant on duty. I talked with a lawyer friend of mine last night, and she said I could claim worker's compensation since my condition occurred on duty, right under your nose."

Roberts seems to be amused at the astonished look on your face. You don't know what to say or how to react to her statements. You just sit there, with your mouth open.

Who is at fault in this case? What recourse do you have at this point? What mistakes were made from the beginning, and how can future situations like this be prevented? Do you think Roberts has a worker's compensation claim?

The Nature of Discipline

The **goal of discipline** is to produce desirable behavior. This function can be accomplished by encouraging appropriate behavior and punishing inappropriate or unacceptable behavior.

Discipline, as an operational concept, is closely related to the other managerial aspects of first-line supervision in paramilitary-type police organizations. It should not be viewed as a derogatory term or dirty word. In fact, discipline is regarded as the essential element in work that ensures overall productivity and an orderly environment. Unfortunately, it is the word *discipline,* in and of itself, that causes the problem. It has a number of different (at times conflicting) meanings and must be used carefully in order to avoid confusion.

The term *discipline* is most often used to describe an adversarial process resulting in the application of various kinds of negative sanctions or punishments. It may also refer to the state of affairs within a given organization that produces order, a shared sense of purpose, and common goal-oriented behavior. In this particular context, discipline is considered positive and means teaching, instruction, training, and remediation. Its purpose is to facilitate collective action, the internalization of self-control based on the norms and values of the work force, predictable behavior, and organizational efficiency. From this perspective, maintaining discipline is a management function that involves conditioning subordinates in order to promote: (1) obedience; (2) internal self-control; (3) acceptance of punishments designed to curb individual deviance or professional misconduct.

Discipline in the Ranks

Human resources provide the linchpin for delivery of all public safety services in a given community. Police work is, in itself, a labor-intensive government activity in which personnel costs consume the lion's share of the budget. Attempting to maximize the efficiency, effectiveness, and productivity of the police department, while holding the line on spending, is clearly a management function. It is the first-line supervisor, normally a sergeant, who has direct responsibility for accomplishing the organization's mission, goals, and objectives through the collaborative efforts of immediate subordinates. Consequently, each first-line supervisor must develop the skills necessary to influence the behavior of others, coordinate their activities, and lead or direct employees in such a way as to gain their respect, confidence, trust, and positive cooperation. Supervision, based on this model, is viewed as an art rather than a science.

As first-line supervisors charged with getting police work done through others, sergeants play two distinct, yet related, roles when it comes to the on-the-job behavior of their subordinates. Sergeants are expected to nurture professionalism in the employee, yet on the other hand they are responsible for initiating disciplinary measures when formal action is required to deal with individual deviance. The trick is to find the appropriate balance between employee self-regulation and organizational control (Covey, 1992).

Like all other first-line supervisors, police sergeants find themselves sandwiched between upper management and operational personnel. While their authority is often ambiguous, sergeants are generally expected to use existing human resources in an effort to translate official department policy into both efficient and effective action on the street. In order to fulfill this awesome responsibility and to play a meaningful role in police personnel administration, sergeants use positive as well as negative discipline. No matter which form they choose, the objective is always the same. Sergeants try to encourage safe, reasonable, and predictable conduct in the workplace so as to create an environment in which competent, well-trained police officers "protect and serve" the community while satisfying their personal needs and achieving their professional goals. Needless to say, police sergeants play a pivotal leadership role in the administration of criminal justice. In the long run, it is the first-line supervisors who (based on their ability, training, and human relations skills) will determine the success or failure of the police department in achieving its mission, goals, and objectives. According to Dwight Eisenhower, "Leadership is the art of getting others to do something you want done because they want to do it!"

Positive Discipline

The words "disciple" and "discipline" have the same root meaning: *to teach or mold*. **Positive discipline** involves a systematic approach that is designed to instruct or guide employees in such a way that they become loyal, dedicated, responsible, and productive members of the organization (Sherman and Lucia, 1992). From a practical point of view, discipline is considered positive or "good" when all police employees share a common sense of purpose, practice self-discipline, and voluntarily follow the policies, procedures, rules, and regulations established to promote order and to facilitate work within the department. Positive discipline is used to prevent deviation from group-shared expectations or to deal with difficult employees without resorting to punishments or other kinds of negative sanctions. This particular orientation to discipline (built on an esprit de corps) is not unique to police organizations and is based on the fundamental assumption that police personnel are no different than other employees. Police officers who have mastered their craft, who know what is expected of them as professionals, and who understand the rationale behind those expectations, are much more likely to identify with the department in terms of its mission, goals, and objectives and to invest their time, energy, effort, and expertise in work-related activities. According to the legendary O.W. Wilson (sometimes referred to as the father of modern police administration), positive discipline manifests itself in the officer's willingness to conform and participate in self-restraint, based on professional dedication or a personal commitment to the ethos of the police department (Fyfe, Greene, and Walsh, 1997).

The most positive form of discipline is the self-discipline that is built on the human tendency to do what needs to be done, to do what is right in a given situation, and to voluntarily comply with the reasonable standards of performance and conduct that apply to all members of the workforce. Mature employees know that following instructions and obeying rules is part of the game. Responsible and cooperative behavior at work is a tacitly accepted condition of employment in virtually all organizations.

Every first-line supervisor should strive to create an environment in which self-discipline is rewarded and external or imposed discipline is held to an absolute minimum. In modern police work, the sergeant plays a crucial role in the employee development process. It is the sergeant's job to promote professional growth and to foster a sense of self-worth in each subordinate. The success or failure of this effort will depend, in the long run, on the supervisor's technical knowledge and human skills. All first-line supervisors in healthy police organizations are multidimensional players who act as technical advisors, role models, teachers, counselors, leaders and, when all else fails, disciplinarians. They learn to accentuate the positive and to cultivate each employee's sense of competence, craftsmanship, and pride through constructive interpersonal relationships built on a bedrock of empathy and mutual respect. Effective supervision and good supervisors help keep subordinates interested in their job and satisfied with working conditions (see Figure 6.1).

Figure 6.1
Basic Supervisory Roles

1. Planner	7. Role model
2. Technical advisor	8. Leader
3. Problem solver	9. Coach
4. Teacher	10. Facilitator
5. Motivator	11. Disciplinarian
6. Counselor	

Even though money and other material rewards are powerful incentives, recognition (based on sincere assessment of an employee's personal worth) can have an even more dramatic impact on job-related behavior. It costs little or nothing, and yet, as with money, almost everyone responds to it in one way or another. It is amazing how hard police officers will work when the psychological payoff is feeling appreciated and important. While she may have overstated the case somewhat, Mary Kay Ash, the woman who turned an idea into a $600 million-a-year cosmetics business, believed that there are two things people want more than sex or money. They covet both recognition and praise from those in a position to judge their on-the-job performance and exert a positive influence on their career (LeBoeuf, 1985).

Good supervisors are enthusiastic team players who have the skills necessary to influence their subordinates in a positive way. They help create an environment in which police personnel buy into and make a willing contribution to the organization. According to the legendary Dale Carnegie (1992), there are nine ways in which a sergeant can change a person's attitude without giving offense or arousing resentment:

1. Begin with praise and honest appreciation.

2. Call attention to the other person's mistakes indirectly.

3. Discuss personal mistakes before criticizing others.

4. Ask thoughtful questions instead of giving direct orders.

5. Always try to let the other person save face.

6. Praise, whenever possible, even the slightest improvement.

7. Give the other person a fine reputation to live up to.

8. Use encouragement and make faults seem easy to correct.

9. Make the person happy about doing what has been suggested.

Effective supervisors have learned to criticize *the work* done by an employee rather than the employee him or herself. They know what Michael LeBoeuf has called "The Greatest Management Principle": The things that get rewarded get done. Recognition and praise are rewards.

Police departments use commendations, citations, certificates, and plaques as physical indicators of a job well done. These psychological rewards are among the most powerful motivators at the disposal of the first-line supervisor. They are the key ingredient in morale and serve as the cornerstone of esprit de corps. According to the Commission on Accreditation for Law Enforcement Agencies Standard 26.1.2, "A written directive establishes procedures and criteria for recognizing and rewarding employees for good performance" (CALEA, 2001).

Camaraderie, unity of purpose, technical expertise, and effective supervision create natural parameters for accepted and expected behavior in a given organization. Once internalized and continuously reinforced with positive sanctions or rewards, these parameters form the basis for self-control. Self-control is an important trait of police professionalism. Once employees know their job and accept the standards by which their on-the-job performance will be judged, they gain a great deal of self-confidence and personal security. They feel more comfortable exercising discretion and accept the fact that there are limits beyond which they must not go. If a subordinate crosses over one of these boundaries, it must be understood that some type of legitimate disciplinary action will follow.

Total Quality Management (TQM) is a technique designed to assist in developing a positive performance-oriented culture as well as employee commitment within the work environment. TQM empowers employees, through meaningful participation, to become partners in making the organization work more efficiently and effectively by removing the barriers that inhibit commitment, creativity, and high-quality service. First-line supervisors must become facilitators who elicit from their people their maximum effort to contribute ideas, creativity, innovative thinking, attention to detail, and analyses of process, products, and services in the workplace (Whisenand and Rush, 1993).

From a practical point of view, all police officers must be treated as adults if that is the behavior expected in return. Supervisors can almost guarantee improvement in employee performance through use of the **PRICE protocol**. PRICE is the acronym for *pinpoint, record, involve, coach,* and *evaluate* (Blanchard, 1989).

1. **Pinpoint**. Supervisors must continually scan the work environment in order to pinpoint performance problems that merit attention.

2. **Record**. Supervisors should record (and quantify) the current performance level of those who are having problems.

3. **Involve**. Supervisors must involve the employee or employees in determining the best way to deal with the problem, the coaching strategies to be used, how the supervisor will be monitoring progress, and the rewards or punishments to be associated with success or failure of the corrective process.

4. **Coach**. Supervisors should implement the agreed-upon coaching strategy by observing performance and providing timely advice, continuous encouragement, positive reinforcement, and retraining (if and when it is necessary).

5. **Evaluate**. Supervisors must evaluate and provide feedback on a continuous basis in order to determine whether the goals of the PRICE protocol have been achieved.

If employee performance does not reach the mutually agreed-upon level, the supervisor needs to determine the cause. There may be a need to redefine goals. On the other hand, there may be a need for further assistance (Aragon, 1993). Additional time or training might be required. Police officers who "cannot" or "will not" perform at an acceptable level should be disciplined, and—if necessary—separated from the police service.

The Commission on Accreditation for Law Enforcement Agencies includes in its standards a section detailing the necessity for establishing a directive for a disciplinary system (Standard 26.1.4, CALEA, 2001). The disciplinary system is to include:

1. Procedures and criteria for using training as a function of discipline.

2. Procedures and criteria for using counseling as a function of discipline.

3. Procedures and criteria for taking punitive actions in the interest of discipline.

Negative Discipline

In ideal circumstances, employees are expected to be willing and capable of assuming responsibility for the quantity and quality of their productive output. Under these conditions, the employee's ego satisfaction, pride in achievement, professional competence, and job security become very powerful motivators and are key ingredients in a work-based reward system built on self-discipline. Unfortunately, this Utopian view of on-the-job behavior is overly simplistic and, in many ways, a figment of the management theorist's imagination. As valuable as it is, self-discipline is insufficient, in itself, to regulate behavior in complex criminal justice organizations. Consequently, the police sergeant must be prepared, when circumstances warrant, to supplement employee self-discipline with external, and at times negative, imposed discipline.

Discipline that is based on the use of punishment rather than rewards is referred to as **negative discipline**. When used in this context, it is synonymous with the phrase "disciplinary action" and is imposed by those in authority when all positive approaches have failed to produce conformity with specific performance standards or behavioral expectations. Disciplinary action is adversarial in nature and is inherently punitive. It is designed to regulate work-related behavior and to safeguard the integrity of the organization. Negative discipline in the form of disciplinary action is considered a legitimate and necessary behavior-control mechanism in virtually all paramilitary-type police departments.

First-line supervisors in bureaucratic police organizations spend a great deal of time and energy trying to cope with marginal employees. A marginal employee is not a deviant per se. Some individuals (for a variety of idiosyncratic or cultural reasons) simply do not measure up to reasonable expectations. These employees do the minimum amount of work to get by. They lack or have lost interest in their job and have adapted their behavior to, and are comfortable with, their present level of incompetence. Many marginal employees freely admit that they are just "putting in time."

Sergeants are expected to deal with employee problems, motivate marginal employees, and increase the employee's productivity through effective supervision. Unfortunately, a sergeant may or may not have the diagnostic or human skills needed to accomplish this objective.

In large police departments, first-line supervisors may have access and be authorized to refer marginal employees to an employee assistance program designed to deal with mental health problems, alcoholism, drug addiction, stress, domestic difficulties, and so on. In smaller departments, the sergeant serves as the employee assistance program. Problem-solving and counseling come with the stripes. As a result, sergeants are expected to have a wide range of knowledge and a knapsack full of human relations skills.

When all else fails, sergeants are forced to rely on the imposition of negative discipline to deal with both deviant and marginal police personnel. This tends to overload the system and is not cost-effective. Discipline and morale begin to suffer when most of the sergeant's time is spent on a few deviant or marginal employees. From a practical point of view, formal disciplinary action should be the last resort in human resources management.

While it is clear that the vast majority of all American police personnel exercise a considerable degree of self-discipline, there are always a few (up to 15 percent) who will, for one reason or another, continue to violate departmental policies, procedures, rules, and regulations, even though they are aware of the potential consequences of their deviant behavior. They simply cannot or will not toe the line and accept responsibility for disciplining themselves. At this point, the sergeant is obligated to initiate appropriate disciplinary action. Under these conditions, negative discipline becomes a necessary, albeit time-consuming, aspect of effective supervision.

Sergeants as Disciplinarians

Due to their position in the department hierarchy and the legitimate authority vested in their rank, sergeants play a much more important and direct role in the disciplinary process than almost any other police manager. For all practical purposes, they are the departmental disciplinarians—with the power to discipline nearly every line officer engaged in the delivery of police services. Many of their subordinates are inexperienced, inadequately trained, or in need of some corrective remediation. When all else fails, it is the sergeant's responsibility to:

1. Identify the weaknesses, deficiencies, failures, or overt behavior of subordinates that indicate the need for corrective action.

2. Analyze all relevant factors to determine the appropriate action to be taken.

3. Initiate and in many cases carry out the disciplinary action.

4. Document the case (in terms of "cause," "analysis," "action," and the "appropriateness of the discipline") for subsequent review by superiors (see Figure 6.2).

Figure 6.2
The Sergeant's Role as Disciplinarian

1. Recognize disciplinary problems as they arise.
2. Gather pertinent data concerning the situation.
3. Analyze factors relevant to the problem.
4. Determine appropriate disciplinary measures.
5. Initiate disciplinary action.
6. Discipline subordinates when authorized.
7. Document the case for subsequent review.

Sergeants, as responsible first-line supervisors, have a professional duty to act reasonably, decisively, and promptly in resolving disciplinary problems. They are expected to act in the best interests of the employee, the department, the law enforcement profession, and the community at large. Needless to say, all disciplinary actions should be "constructive" rather than "destructive," in the sense that they are administered in a firm, fair, and impartial manner. **Constructive discipline** is built on a foundation of sensitivity and good judgment. Its goal is the correction or remediation of deviant behavior as it occurs, as well as improvement in the overall behavior of the employee and other members of the police department in the future (Hilgert and Haimann, 1991).

Fair and Equitable Discipline

Disciplinary action in complex criminal justice organizations should not be an idiosyncratic or random exercise of power by those in authority. As noted earlier, it must be viewed as an essential part of a goal-oriented process designed to control the disruptive behavior of individual employees, while ensuring the overall efficiency, effectiveness, and productivity of the workforce. Employees who cannot measure up to reasonable performance standards, or who refuse to toe the line in terms of their on-the-job behavior, are legitimate targets of formal disciplinary action. They should be penalized in such a way that they learn to achieve acceptable performance standards and exhibit appropriate behavior. Employees who do not respond or who are incapable of making a substantive change become a liability to the department and must be removed from their job for the good of the service.

Fair and equitable disciplinary procedures are necessary to protect the integrity of the service and provide an adequate frame of reference for all police personnel. Police officers (like all other employees) have emotional job-related security needs that must be considered by management. As the first-line supervisor, it is the sergeant who has the primary responsibility for satisfying a subordinate's:

1. need to be treated as an individual with intrinsic value and the capacity to make a contribution to the organization;

2. need to know exactly what management expects in terms of work performance and on-the-job conduct;

3. need for regular feedback from management concerning job performance (including praise as well as censure);

4. need to be treated fairly and impartially by those in management; and

5. need to be judged by management based on facts and standards rather than on personal opinion or assumptions.

The failure to recognize and deal with employee needs in these very critical areas often leads to job dissatisfaction, interpersonal conflict, poor performance, disciplinary problems, and high employee turnover (Robbins, 1989). It represents a sergeant's dereliction of duty and the abdication of responsibility by management.

All seasoned first-line supervisors know that rationality is a prerequisite for effective disciplinary action in law enforcement. Good disciplinary systems do not materialize out of thin air; they are, in fact, very carefully crafted by management (Plunkett, 1992) and generally exhibit the following characteristics:

1. Proper assignment of personnel to jobs within the organization based on their interest, skill, utility, and specialized training.

2. Necessary and reasonable job-related policies, procedures, rules, and regulations formulated to govern behavior in the workplace, meet employee needs, and accomplish the department's mission, goals, and specified objectives.

3. Effective communication of information regarding expected performance and acceptable behavior to all employees along with an explanation of the probable consequences of noncompliance.

4. Continuous review, evaluation, and appraisal of all personnel to assess strengths, detect weaknesses, and identify disciplinary problems that may require immediate attention.

5. Consistent, fair, and equitable enforcement of all policies, procedures, rules, and regulations within the organization.

6. Mutually acceptable, institutionalized disciplinary procedures based on a "due process" model that is in harmony with applicable civil service regulations and negotiated collective bargaining agreements.

7. A formal appeals procedure designed to ensure the fairness of all disciplinary actions and to serve as a check and balance on the imposition of punitive sanctions.

While no manager really likes the idea of being the disciplinarian, using disciplinary action is an unavoidable part of each first-line supervisor's job. No matter how alert or skillful the particular supervisor is, the imposition of discipline (in one form or another) is inevitable in virtually all work situations. Consequently, supervisors must face the fact that in all likelihood, they will be called on to take disciplinary action against a subordinate. The imposition of punishment is normal and to be expected, though hopefully an infrequent aspect of the first-line supervisor's role in complex criminal justice organizations.

Inconsistency and favoritism in disciplining subordinates will have an adverse, potentially destructive effect on employee morale and productivity (Guthrie, 1996). The effective sergeant understands departmental policies, procedures, rules, and regulations; trains and guides immediate subordinates; and is both fair and impartial when dispensing discipline. From a pragmatic point of view, a sergeant's actions must be legal, reasonable, consistent, and timely. Employees react strongly and frequently challenge management prerogatives in court when they believe they have been treated unfairly due to the arbitrary denial of some "due process" right. As the first-line supervisor, it is the sergeant who is the central character in the drama to preserve management's authority to discipline errant, disruptive, or deviant subordinates.

The Use and Abuse of Discipline

Although punishment might produce some negative effects (such as resentment, interpersonal conflict, and lower morale), it must sometimes be used simply because there is no practical alternative. Some of the adverse reactions to punishment will be tempered, however, if it is carried out in an intelligent, fair, and predictable manner, and if the employee targeted for disciplinary action understands that it was necessary due to poor performance or misconduct, not because of someone else's behavior (Iannone, 1994).

Lack of trust is another factor that must be taken into consideration. Police officers learn to fear, lose respect for, and distrust supervisors who become entrenched in company politics, make decisions too quickly or irrationally, and invoke disciplinary measures for the slightest infractions. Mature officers want their sergeants to be equitable and to act in good faith when disciplining. When their first-line supervisors fail to live up to these expectations, the dissonance created makes matters even worse.

Each sergeant's approach to the use of discipline indicates the sergeant's view of the administrative power inherent in the rank. If the sergeant has an authoritarian personality, misunderstands the nature of the job, or lacks rudimentary leadership skills, the potential for abuse of the disciplinary apparatus is great. There is a solution for this problem, however. All newly promoted first-line police supervisors should be required to successfully complete a supervisory/management training program designed to familiarize them with their new administrative duties, their role as a supervisor, and their authority vis-à-vis the formal disciplinary system. Sergeants, like their subordinates, need to know what is expected of them.

The imposition of disciplinary action within an organization has two distinct, yet interactive, objectives: (1) to reform the individual offender and (2) to deter others who may be influenced by what has happened. From this perspective, all imposed discipline has value in terms of correcting errant, disruptive, or deviant behavior as well as for its future effect on the individuals involved as offenders or observers. In light of these objectives, each sergeant must determine which penalties are available, feasible, and appropriate for use in a particular set of circumstances. While evaluating the alternatives, both the short-term and long-term effect that punishment is likely to have must be estimated. It is then up to the sergeant, in conjunction with superior officers, to select the most effective form of punishment. All other things being equal, the punishment should be adequate based on the offense. Excessive punishment is counterproductive and becomes a stressor in labor-management relations.

On the other side of the coin, first-line supervisors, as human beings, must avoid the pitfalls of subjectivity and continuously guard against making discipline-related decisions based on emotion. Based on the "people orientation" in contemporary applied management theory (Peters and Waterman, 1982), it is safe to say that there is no place for anger, revenge, or retribution in the disciplinary process. It is illegal for supervisors to harass employees through the capricious exercise of power or to intentionally humiliate those who have been targeted for disciplinary action. Finally, there is absolutely no justification for the behavior of supervisors who displace aggression by scapegoating their employees. The proper goal of imposed discipline is to make the future more satisfactory, not to vent emotions or to fulfill some abstract sense of justice (see Figure 6.3).

Figure 6.3
Objectives of Disciplinary Action

MOTIVE/GOAL	LIKELY EFFECT

Legitimate
  Reform
  Deterrence
	
	Improved performance or conduct
	Prevent similar violations by others

Unacceptable
  Revenge
  Capriciousness
  Displaced Aggression
  Humiliation
  Retribution
	
	Anger, provocation to more violations
	Fear, loss of respect, distrust
	Uncertainty, confusion, resentment
	Anxiety, personal conflict, hatred
	Frustration, accusations of legalism

Adapted from Aaron Q. Sartain and Alton W. Baker (1978). *The Supervisor and the Job*. New York, NY: McGraw-Hill Book Company.

Administering effective discipline is one of the most demanding aspects of any first-line supervisor's job. It is both complex and time-consuming. The accused employee is presumed innocent until proven guilty, and in establishing that guilt (as a justification for using disciplinary action in the workplace), the burden of proof is almost always on those involved in direct supervisory management (Steinmetz and Todd, 1992). Many courts have now ruled that an employer violates an implied contract if a subordinate is disciplined without sufficient and just cause.

In the public sector, *just cause* refers to a cause of action that is legally adequate to sustain a decision to inflict negative sanctions. At this point, "sufficient and just cause" clauses have been incorporated into virtually all civil service regulations and grievance procedures mandated by negotiated collective bargaining agreements. The imposition of disciplinary action without just cause is viewed by most Americans as an unconscionable and unacceptable abuse of authority. This type of unprofessional conduct undermines the individual supervisor's effectiveness and subjects management itself to ridicule, charges of unfair labor practices, political repercussions, and civil lawsuits. The misuse of power destroys the sergeant's credibility and diminishes legitimate authority over subordinates.

While most supervisory personnel do an adequate job, police work has its share of poor first-line supervisors. There are sergeants who are merely putting in time and trying to survive. They take disciplinary action against coworkers only when they are backed into a corner, and do not want to make waves or rock the boat unless their own career is on the line. Other sergeants are simply inept. They do not have the sensitivity, judgment, knowledge, training, or human skills needed to deal effectively with recalcitrant employees. These men and women are shackled by their own inadequacy. Malfeasance, misfeasance, and nonfeasance interact synergistically to produce a dual impact: police professionalism is diminished, and public safety is jeopardized. In the long run, it is American society that suffers the consequences of poor first-line supervision in law enforcement.

Saying that **firm, fair, equitable, and lawful disciplinary action** is an essential ingredient in effective supervision is one thing; achieving it in a complex criminal justice organization is another matter altogether. Guthrie (1996) has proposed an automated system to apply disciplinary action fairly. A computerized database of complaints, officer characteristics, and disciplinary actions over a five-year period was developed by the internal affairs unit of the Fresno, California, Police Department. The automated system allowed supervisors to review histories, department-wide complaint characteristics, and disciplinary actions taken for categorized employee misconduct. The system helped supervisors to achieve more consistent and equitable disciplinary decision making.

Keys to Effective Discipline

In order to make disciplinary action more effective, it should be proactive as well as reactive in that police sergeants must be prepared, based on their education, training, and job-related supervisory experience, to detect and correct discipline problems before they become malignant and spread throughout the organization. Good supervisors know the keys to effective discipline (Preston and Zimmerer, 1983) and apply them as conscientiously as possible:

1.   **Don't Be a Discipline Ostrich**. First-line supervisors should not slip into a pattern of overlooking discipline problems. In fact, they have a duty to take immediate and appropriate action to correct the situation. Failure to act promptly and decisively tends to perpetuate the problem and sets the stage for more debilitating interpersonal conflict. In addi-

tion, other employees will begin to question the sergeant's ability and fairness if they see that disciplinary action is put off or avoided altogether. Under these circumstances, subordinates will assume that most, if not all, of the department's policies, procedures, rules, and regulations are worthless. Violations may become the rule rather than the exception. This *anomie* or "normlessness" is inherently destructive.

2. **Become a "Caesar's Wife."** All of the sergeant's behavior must be above reproach. There can be absolutely no doubt in the subordinate's mind about the sergeant's loyalty to the organization or willingness to comply with departmental policies, procedures, rules, and regulations. Employees cannot be expected to practice self-control if their immediate supervisors are poor role models who fail to set an example worthy of emulation. Sergeants lead others by example. Seeing supervisory personnel bend or break the rules promotes disruptive and deviant behavior by others in the workforce.

3. **Practice the "Hot Stove" Rule.** According to this basic concept, discipline (like touching a hot stove) should be immediate, based on known rules, consistent, and impersonal. While the abstract principle of "the hot stove" is easy to remember, it is much more difficult to translate into practice in complex criminal justice organizations. Under less-than-ideal conditions, effective discipline is largely a matter of chance.

4. **Never Lose Control.** First-line supervisors must remain calm and in control as they deal with various types of disciplinary problems. They are expected not to show emotion, fly off the handle, or touch their subordinates. Unless the sergeant's authority is challenged publicly, employees should be disciplined in private and with dignity (Whittenberg, 1995). An open display of anger or power is normally counterproductive. It leads to resentment, game playing, and lower morale. The supervisor's failure to exercise self-control and behave in a consistent and mature manner will result in a loss of respect (for the person and the rank) and the further erosion of authority.

5. **Be Instructive.** Good first-line supervisors are also teachers and counselors (Mahoney, 1986). Whenever disciplinary action becomes necessary, the errant, disruptive, or deviant employee should be told why the discipline is being imposed and how it can be avoided in the future. As supervisory managers, sergeants function as culture carriers. They clarify and explain policies, procedures, rules, and regulations to their subordinates. When it comes to disciplinary action, the sergeant is obligated to advise subordinates of the "due process" options available to them should they choose to challenge the propriety of the disciplinary process or the punishment. Sergeants should never hide anything from the employee. Deception will come back to haunt the supervisor. Sergeants should be open and honest with their subordinates and impose the discipline in an intelligent, reasonable, and mature manner.

6. **Be Firm but Fair.** The first-line supervisor must always be firm but fair in administering disciplinary action. If the police sergeant wants subordinates to feel that discipline is both firm and fair, the sergeant must be open, honest, reasonable, and direct. Attitude is the key. Effective supervisors never joke about discipline; they take their responsibility as disciplinarians very seriously. They know that discipline administered in a firm, fair, consistent, and impartial manner helps correct performance problems; deters errant, disruptive, or deviant behavior by others; and generates respect for both the supervisor and the authority inherent in the rank. On the other hand, ambiguity and inconsistency will destroy the sergeant's credibility and overall effectiveness as a disciplinarian.

7. **Stay Out of the Employee's Private Life.** All other things being equal, a subordinate's private life is just that—private. Unless the employee's personal beliefs or off-the-job behavior have a direct bearing on job performance, they should not be factored into the disciplinary process (Marmo, 1986). As first-line supervisors who are charged with delegating authority, sergeants are responsible for the work being done under their personal direction. It is imperative to avoid making assessments based on irrelevant data. Personal value judgments often lead to interpersonal conflict and covert as well as overt discrimination. The scope of provisions dealing with "conduct unbecoming an officer" has been narrowed considerably by the courts in a series of recent decisions. This is hazardous uncharted territory.

8. **State Rules/Regulations in a Positive Manner.** Effective sergeants avoid negativism and treat department policies, procedures, rules, and regulations as being positive control mechanisms designed to promote order and facilitate work related to the organization's mission, goals, and objectives.

9. **Don't Be a Disciplinary Magician.** A good supervisor avoids becoming the type of person who makes rules as he or she goes along, in an effort to trap subordinates. The key to success as a disciplinarian is to ensure that all employees know and fully understand the department's policies, procedures, rules, and regulations. The best advice is to be upfront with all employees; don't spring new rules or variations of the old rules on them after the fact. Effective supervisors give every employee an ample opportunity to comply with performance standards and behavioral expectations.

10. **Be Precise.** As first-line supervisors and departmental disciplinarians, sergeants must (based on the civil liability inherent in their position) comply with labor laws, collective bargaining agreements, and civil service regulations. Because their actions are subject to both administrative and judicial review, sergeants must be precise in assessing job performance and taking formal disciplinary action. They must not

deviate from prescribed procedures and should very carefully document all of their actions. Lack of precision lessens the sergeant's credibility, weakens the case, and increases the likelihood that there will be subsequent litigation of the issue or issues under civil law.

While there is really no way to avoid the use of negative discipline in complex criminal justice organizations, it can be made more effective and much less stressful if supervisory personnel use these keys to unlock the productive potential of their immediate subordinates. Once again, the sergeant is in the catbird seat and, in the long run, will determine the effectiveness of the discipline and the overall credibility of the disciplinary system.

First-line supervisors must realize that any disciplinary action they take with a subordinate will result in a negative response from the subordinate. Whittenberg (1995) indicates that employees facing disciplinary action go through five stages: denial, anger, bargaining, depression, and acceptance. In order to provide dignity to the subordinate being disciplined, the supervisor must allow him or her to progress through these stages. The supervisor should give the employee the opportunity to vent feelings, display anger, and show some disrespectful emotion without taking the reaction personally. If the supervisor has followed the keys to effective discipline, the subordinate will rapidly go through the five stages and accept the disciplinary action without an adverse effect on the employee/supervisor relationship. In fact, it should strengthen the relationship.

The Hot Stove Revisited

Taking appropriate disciplinary action creates a dilemma for first-line supervisors. Police sergeants walk a tightrope between two seemingly incongruent roles. As noted earlier, they are expected to be "teachers," "helpers," and "leaders" who nurture their subordinates; on the other hand, they are the "disciplinarians" who punish them for their errant, disruptive, or deviant behavior. The trick is to balance these roles in such a way as to avoid creating interpersonal conflict or generating deep-seated resentment.

Douglas McGregor, a noted management theorist, provides us with a very useful analogy concerning disciplinary tasks and earned punishment. He called his idea the **Hot Stove concept**, comparing an organization's disciplinary system to a hot stove and the burn victim to an employee who has earned punishment (Plunkett, 1992). When you touch a hot stove, the discipline is immediate, predictable, consistent, and totally impersonal.

McGregor's Hot Stove analogy is used to illustrate the essential elements of a functional disciplinary policy. It points out that when you burn your hand as a result of your own stupidity, you become angry with yourself. While you might be mad at the stove, the anger cannot last long, because you should have known the consequences of your act. According to the Hot Stove rule, you learn your lesson quickly and effectively because:

1. The burn is IMMEDIATE, with no question as to cause and effect. The sooner the disciplinary action is taken, the more automatic it will be and the more closely it will be associated with the errant, disruptive, or deviant behavior. While speed is an essential ingredient in effective discipline, undue haste should be avoided because it could lead to carelessness and the imposition of unwarranted punishments.

2. You had ADVANCE WARNING and knew (because the stove was red hot) exactly what would happen if you touched it. Unexpected discipline is almost always considered unfair and usually creates a great deal of resentment. Consequently, employees must be given a clear warning that a particular offense or type of behavior will result in disciplinary action, coupled with a definite warning as to the nature and extent of the discipline to be invoked.

3. The discipline is CONSISTENT, because everyone who touches the hot stove is burned. Consistency means that each and every time there is an infraction, appropriate disciplinary action is taken. This helps to set internal as well as external limits in terms of what subordinates may or may not do. Consistency also means that the punishment inflicted should be no more or no less than expected for a particular offense. On the other hand, inconsistent disciplinary action leads to uncertainty and confusion. It destroys the integrity of the disciplinary process and erodes the sergeant's legitimate authority. Inconsistency produces anxiety, insecurity, interpersonal conflict, resentment, and poor morale.

4. The discipline is IMPERSONAL in that victims are burned for touching the red hot stove regardless of their identity. They are on the receiving end of discipline not because they are "bad," but because of their errant, disruptive, or deviant behavior. This helps to remove the personal "You are always out to get me" element of disciplinary action, because the discipline is directed against an act or unacceptable behavior, not the individual. When discipline is automatic and impersonal, it reduces resentment and clears the way for subordinates to assume responsibility for their own performance or job-related conduct.

In addition to their other supervisory responsibilities, sergeants add the human element to McGregor's Hot Stove concept. They tend the stove to make sure it operates efficiently and effectively. Under ideal circumstances, the hot stove not only serves as a deterrent against whom it is applied, but also serves as a form of conditioning or training that will orient other police employees to the types of performance or on-the-job behavior the organization cannot and will not accept. Telling employees what is expected of them and explaining the negative consequences they may face is an absolute prerequisite for effective discipline in law enforcement (see Figure 6.4).

Figure 6.4
Discipline and the Hot Stove Analogy in Law Enforcement

1. Delineation of what is unacceptable

2. Reasonable negative sanctions

3. Advance warning of consequences

4. Certainty of punishment

5. Immediate disciplinary action

6. Consistent application of negative sanctions

7. Impersonal and goal-oriented discipline

8. Adequate due process

9. Appellate review of all disciplinary action

Inflicting punishment is a painful experience for both the employee and the first-line supervisor. In order to reduce the unpleasantness and stress associated with the use of discipline, sergeants should incorporate the Hot Stove concept into their management repertoire. The Hot Stove replaces subjectivity with a philosophy of firm, fair, and impartial discipline that is designed to correct and deter the errant, disruptive, or deviant behavior of subordinates (Plunkett, 1992).

Various states, such as Illinois (Local Government Uniform Peace Officer's Disciplinary Act; 50 ILCS 725), have adopted **peace officer bill of rights** laws that superimpose additional constraints on the disciplinary process. These laws often mandate the warnings to be given and procedures to be followed when certain types of disciplinary actions are anticipated. Supervisors need to know and comply with what is required if they are to prevail when it comes to the imposition of discipline (Redlich, 1994).

Another right afforded police officers involved in disciplinary proceedings is known as *Garrity* **protection**, under the doctrines set forth in *Garrity v. New Jersey* (385 U.S. 493, 1967). The *Garrity* protection applies whenever an employee is required to answer questions in an internal investigation. Under *Garrity*, the employer cannot use information provided by the employee in a criminal procedure against the employee. For *Garrity* to apply, the employee must believe that the statements he or she provides are compelled under threat of substantial disciplinary action or dismissal from his or her job (McGuinness, 1999).

Case Study

Officer Hugh Davis

Officer Hugh Davis has been a productive member of the force for near-ly 15 years. He twice turned down promotion offers to take the sergeant's exam because he felt "too inexperienced to supervise others" as he put it. You are Davis's supervisory sergeant. The two of you graduated from the police academy together and worked side-by-side in many situations, good and bad. You have been to Davis's home for dinner on numerous occasions and consider him one of your best friends. He is also a good police officer and has been cited numerous times for bravery and superior service. He even received the local TV news channel Officer of the Year award for saving two people in a burning building three years ago. However, the past 15 months have been devastating for Hugh Davis.

Davis's 14-year-old son fell out of a deer stand while hunting and broke his back in several places. The doctors have indicated that he will never walk again. Davis blames himself because he was with his son when the accident occurred. He has become despondent and is quick to anger these days. You have tried to encourage him to seek counseling and take time off, but he refused, stating that he "needed to work."

You are very concerned over Davis's quick temper. On several occasions you have had to call him down and write him up over verbal abuses and excessive force in arrest situations, especially in domestic calls. You made careful notations regarding his temper in his evaluations, and he has even indicated to you that he needs to work on his quick anger and that he will seek counseling. However, he never pursued any counseling that you are aware of. You are concerned about Davis's temper for another reason. Last year, one of the officers in your department was captured on videotape beating up a suspect. The news media came down hard on the department, and the officer was fired and brought up on criminal charges. The police chief made it known that any use of excessive force would not be tolerated by the department.

Today, you are informed that a suspect Hugh Davis arrested two days ago has filed charges of police brutality against him. Internal Affairs wants to see you and your written evaluations of Davis for the past two years.

What would you say to Internal Affairs? Do you think Davis has a chance of keeping his job? What could have you done to prevent this from happening in the first place?

Firm but Fair Disciplinary Action

Sergeants are the keystone around which the police discipline system is built and, as such, exert a tremendous influence on the disciplinary process. Consequently, they are expected to be "firm but fair" when inflicting negative sanctions on their subordinates. "Fairness" means being able to say that the punishment was warranted, justified, and appropriate in terms of its goal. In order to be fair, the first-line supervisor must be sure that all employees in the workforce are familiar with and understand the reasoning behind the department's policies, procedures, rules, and regulations. If a subordinate's performance or job-related conduct is errant, disruptive, or deviant, that person must be investigated. The sergeant should conduct an objective inquiry into the situation and must never, under any circumstances, exceed his or her legitimate authority when punishing subordinates.

According to Steinmetz and Todd (1986), one way to ensure basic fairness is to ask certain questions concerning the need for discipline or negative sanctions in a particular situation. These questions might include the following:

1. **Is the disciplinary action based on violation of a known policy, procedure, rule, or regulation?** The bottom line is determining whether there has been a "statutory violation." In other words, is the policy, procedure, rule, or regulation clearly spelled out in an employee handbook? Has it been posted as a general order? Or is it otherwise known to all employees within the police department? Have employees received a copy? Is the material easily understood? Is the policy, procedure, rule, or regulation reasonable in terms of promoting efficiency and effectiveness within a safe and orderly environment? Is it legal in that it complies with labor laws, collective bargaining agreements, and civil service regulations? Are you sure, as the responsible first-line supervisor, that there are no extenuating circumstances that may have contributed to a misunderstanding or belief that a policy, procedure, rule, or regulation does not apply to the situation? If all of these questions can be answered in the affirmative, the sergeant is justified in taking action against the subordinate.

2. **What has happened to others who have knowingly violated this policy, procedure, rule, or regulation?** This question is designed to help sergeants explore and understand the nature, significance, and appropriate disciplinary response to errant, disruptive, or deviant behavior in the workplace. Assuming the employee knowingly violated a departmental policy, procedure, rule, or regulation, the next logical step is to determine the seriousness of the problem and chart a course of action to correct or deter it in the future. The sergeant must determine whether other employees have been disciplined under similar circumstances and ascertain the kind of disciplinary action that was taken. In order to make the punishment fit the offender as well as the crime, the sergeant should study the subordinate's background relative

to the particular offense or unacceptable conduct. The worse the record in relation to others, the more severe the disciplinary action should be. Progressively severe discipline is often required because habitual offenders tend to develop a chronic attitudinal problem in which they do not care whether departmental policies, procedures, rules, and regulations are followed.

3. **What is the subordinate's record concerning this specific policy, procedure, rule, or regulation?** The sergeant must determine exactly how the employee has violated the specific policy, procedure, rule, or regulation, and whether there had been a prior warning about this type of behavior. If the subordinate had been formally warned or disciplined on previous occasions, the disciplinary action should be more severe than for those who have neither been warned nor disciplined. In theory, this employee should know the policies, procedures, rules, and regulations, and should understand the consequences of errant, disruptive, or deviant on-the-job behavior.

4. **Has the employee ever received a written "final warning" from the supervisor?** If an errant, disruptive, or deviant employee had previously been given a written final warning, the case must be treated more severely. It is the sergeant's job to ascertain whether the employee understood both the seriousness and consequences associated with the final warning before disciplinary action is taken. As a general rule, if the employee was given a final warning and still continues to violate the policy, procedure, rule, or regulation, termination should be seriously considered as the appropriate response. The health of the organization will suffer unless this type of action is taken.

5. **What caused the poor performance or unacceptable conduct?** Here again, it is the sergeant who must determine whether the errant, disruptive, or deviant behavior was intentional. Was it triggered by ignorance or by maliciousness? Was it deliberate, or was it caused by an oversight by the employee? In a rational disciplinary system, punishment is always contingent on and measured in relation to the offender's motive. Consequently, it is the sergeant's primary responsibility to assess the seriousness of the problem and to determine (as accurately as possible) why the subordinate is behaving in an errant, disruptive, or deviant manner. This information must then be factored into the disciplinary process.

6. **What evidence is there that the employee intentionally or maliciously violated a departmental policy, procedure, rule, or regulation?** As noted before, the accused employee is presumed to be innocent until proven guilty. It is the sergeant's job to identify disciplinary problems, analyze all of the relevant factors, initiate or carry out appropriate disciplinary action, ensure due process, and document the case for subsequent administrative or judicial review. The sergeant, like the prosecutor in a criminal case, builds a case designed to

demonstrate the extent, seriousness, and deliberateness of the errant, disruptive, or deviant behavior. In addition to this prosecutorial role, the sergeant is expected to discover any extenuating or mitigating circumstances that might justify lessening the punishment.

7. **Are the intended disciplinary measures appropriate for use in this particular situation?** The basic question comes down to whether the discipline to be inflicted is commensurate with the seriousness of the errant, disruptive, or deviant behavior. Is it consistent with the employee's prior record? Sergeants should base their actions (and measure the appropriateness of the discipline) on how other subordinates have been treated in similar situations and how prior service to the department has been factored (positively or negatively) into the punishment. If the officer has an extensive prior record, has been on the job a long time, and has involved others in serious discipline problems, the punishment must be severe. If, on the other hand, the officer is relatively new, has had few problems, acted as an individual, and has exhibited a cooperative attitude, the punishment should be much less severe. Progressively severe punishment is calculated to correct or deter disciplinary problems. Here again, the strategy is to use the right type and amount of punishment in a given situation to achieve the goals of the disciplinary system.

Firm but fair discipline is the ideal that each first-line supervisor should strive to achieve. Actually achieving this ideal in a complex criminal justice organization is another matter. Whether the discipline is firm and fair will depend, in the long run, on four critical factors: (1) the quality of the personnel being recruited by the department; (2) the effectiveness of the promotion system; (3) the training given to newly promoted sergeants; and (4) the support that first-line supervisors receive from their superiors.

Types of Disciplinary Action

The decision to discipline a subordinate is not an easy one and should be made with a great deal of care. Sergeants are expected to know each employee; the employee's work record; and the nature, relative seriousness, and cause or causes of the particular offense. First-line supervisors must be aware of and understand the powers listed in their job description. In order to be effective, they must be familiar with the department's personnel policies (including applicable collective bargaining agreements or civil service regulations) as well as the basic policies, procedures, rules, and regulations that govern on-the-job behavior.

Once the decision to discipline has been made, the sergeant (in consultation with superiors) must select the appropriate type of punishment. As a general rule, the different types of punishment available to the first-line supervisor are spelled out in departmental manuals, civil service regulations, or labor contracts. This specificity is designed to eliminate ambiguity, ensure fair treatment, and protect police employees from impulsive, arbitrary, and unusually harsh punishments.

Most police departments have created discipline systems based on the idea of **progressive discipline,** which provides for an increase in punishment for each subsequent offense. Certain steps have become institutionalized as part of the disciplinary process. These steps have been incorporated into the process to ensure fundamental fairness and to demonstrate to trial boards, arbitrators, and the courts that the supervisor made a good faith effort to correct the errant, disruptive, or deviant behavior through some type of remediation or rehabilitation. The normal sequence of punishment with progressively severe discipline action is as follows: informal discussion, oral warning, written reprimand, final written warning, transfer, suspension, demotion, and discharge.

1.   **Informal Discussion.** If the offense is relatively minor and the employee has not been disciplined for similar misconduct in the past, an informal, friendly discussion will often clear up the problem. During the discussion, the sergeant should determine the cause of the errant, disruptive, or deviant behavior; reaffirm the employee's responsibility for self-discipline; and make constructive suggestions for improvement. Should this approach fail to produce the desired result, the sergeant must be prepared to give the subordinate a more formal oral warning.

2.   **Oral Warning.** The oral warning is probably the most common form of punishment inflicted on employees. When subordinates fail to meet prescribed performance standards and continue to violate policies, procedures, rules, or regulations, they must be put on "notice" that their behavior is unacceptable and that repetition will result in formal disciplinary action. They need to know, in no uncertain terms, that their misconduct will not be condoned and that future violations will produce more severe punishments. The effectiveness of an oral warning will generally depend on past experience, the strength of the supervisor-subordinate relationship, and the employee's desire to conform to shared group expectations. The spirit in which the warning is given is often more important than the oral warning itself. If the oral warning fails to correct the problem or deter an employee's errant, disruptive, or deviant behavior, the sergeant must be prepared to use a formal written reprimand.

3.   **Written Reprimand.** As the term implies, the written reprimand is a formal warning issued to an errant, disruptive, or deviant employee by the immediate supervisor. For all practical purposes, it is the first official step in progressive discipline. No matter whether it is general or specific, the written reprimand is designed to spell out the problem, recommend corrective measures, and specify the probable con-

sequences of further misconduct. Written reprimands must not exaggerate the problem or make idle threats. They should be used sparingly in an effort to accentuate their importance. As a general rule, written warnings should be fairly simple and to the point. The original letter should be given to the employee with a copy placed in the personnel file. When appropriate, a copy of the reprimand should be sent to civil service or the union. The written reprimand becomes part of the case file and can be used as evidence in a subsequent arbitration or civil action. If the written reprimand fails to correct the problem or deter further misconduct, the sergeant should issue a final written warning to the employee.

4. **Final Written Warning.** Because we live and work in a litigious environment in which employees frequently challenge management's authority, the sergeant must be able to prove (based on objective evidence) that progressively more severe disciplinary action was required to correct the problem or to deter further misconduct. Keeping written records is extremely important in complex criminal justice organizations. Written records help to demonstrate that the employee was apprised of the seriousness of the situation and that notification had been given indicating that there would be a significant escalation in punishment for continued errant, disruptive, or deviant behavior. The final written warning becomes the bottom line, so to speak, and shifts all responsibility for compliance to the employee. If this strategy fails to resolve the problem, the sergeant has no alternative but to consider transferring or suspending the subordinate.

5. **Transfer.** Transferring an officer from one unit or assignment within the department to another as a form of punishment has long been used. However, transfers in and of themselves are merely punitive and generally do not correct the officer's behavior. In fact, the transferred officer may become disillusioned and become an even worse disciplinary problem. There are times when transfers for disciplinary action may be appropriate. For instance, officers who need more structured supervision might be transferred from a low supervision position to a more structured, highly supervised position. The transfer cannot be viewed solely as punitive, but must be constructive and for the good of the officer as well as the oranization. Many police agencies do not have transfers as a part of their progressive discipline policy.

6. **Suspension.** The suspension, or "disciplinary layoff" as it is called in the private sector, is the next step in progressively severe disciplinary action and is not uncommon in police work. The police officer who has not profited from informal discussions or a formal warning is suspended. Suspension may be with or without pay for a period ranging from a few days to one week, or more. Under normal circumstances, the employee loses wages and the fringe benefits based on those wages. Suspension is viewed as being severe in that it "hits the employee where it hurts most, in the pocketbook." In addition, suspensions usu-

ally become common knowledge and the focus of peer interest. While an ill-conceived suspension can aggravate the situation and might even make the employee's behavior worse, if used properly it can be one of the most effective disciplinary tools available to the supervisor. It might shock the errant, disruptive, or deviant officer back to a sense of responsibility. It shows that the department means business. If, on the other hand, there is no substantive change in the employee's work-related behavior, further disciplinary action must be taken. The suspension is merely a prelude to further disciplinary action in the form of a demotion or discharge.

7. **Demotion.** Due to the paramilitary structure of most police departments, demotion from a higher to a lower rank within the same department has persisted as an alternative form of disciplinary action. It is common in highly political situations. Many police administrators, however, are beginning to question the validity of demotion as a disciplinary measure. They contend that the negatives far outweigh the positives, and they prefer resocialization or retraining to demotion. Maintaining good morale is the issue. Demoted officers suffer the loss of income, social status, and self-esteem. They tend to become resentful, discouraged, and dissatisfied. Disgruntled personnel normally continue to challenge legitimate authority and sow the seeds of discontent. When all else fails, the errant, disruptive, or deviant employee must be terminated or discharged for the good of the police service.

8. **Discharge.** Discharging an employee is, without doubt, the most drastic form of disciplinary action and, as such, must be reserved for only the most serious offenses. In today's legalistic environment, the employee must be given every opportunity to change his or her behavior and conform to departmental policies, procedures, rules, and regulations. While it is possible under unusual circumstances, very few police officers are discharged without warning. Discharge is a costly, albeit necessary, type of discipline in some cases. The employee loses his or her income, seniority and, in some cases, even employability. The department, on the other hand, loses an experienced and potentially valuable human resource. It also forfeits all that has been invested in that particular employee's professional development. In addition, there are costs associated with recruiting, screening, training, and orienting a replacement. Because discharge is viewed by many as a form of industrial capital punishment, it often leads to lengthy, costly arbitrations or civil court cases. This does not mean that supervisors should not recommend that management discharge an employee in appropriate situations. There are times when the department must take a stand and notify all personnel that there are certain behaviors that simply cannot or will not be tolerated. Used sparingly and in a judicious manner, discharge is the ultimate disciplinary tool.

No matter what type of disciplinary action sergeants opt to use, they must be careful to observe all labor laws, collective bargaining agreements, and civil service regulations. In addition, the sergeant must pay close attention to procedural due process. Failure in either area will destroy the first-line supervisor's credibility and substantially undermine authority. Of primary importance is the first-line supervisor carefully documenting any and all discussions with the subordinate regarding behavior and discipline issues.

Modern management theory has rejected the imposition of negative sanctions for the sake of inflicting punishment. It views disciplinary action as being an essential ingredient in a goal-oriented intervention strategy that is designed to correct problems and deter future misconduct. Progressive discipline (see Figure 6.5) is based on the notion that the punishment should fit the crime and that progressively more severe punishment will trigger a "hedonistic calculation." The repetitively recalcitrant offender assesses the pleasure derived from the errant, disruptive, or deviant behavior vis-à-vis the pain caused by the escalating punishments. All other things being equal, when the perceived pain outweighs the pleasure, there will be a substantive change in the employee's behavior. Progressive discipline is not a cure-all; it is a tool.

Figure 6.5
Steps of Progressive Discipline

1. Informal discussion
2. Oral warning
3. Written reprimand
4. Final written warning
5. Transfer
6. Suspension
7. Demotion
8. Discharge

Progressive discipline may not work with indifferent, irrational, or socially maladjusted subordinates. When it becomes necessary to discharge an employee, progressive discipline is used. While the decision to fire an employee is the prerogative of management, it is almost always based on direct input from the first-line supervisor. Again, this awesome responsibility is part of the job and rests squarely on the sergeant's shoulders.

Making the Disciplinary Action Stick

In what some managers consider to be the "good old days," employers hired their employees at will and could discipline or fire them for any reason or for no reason at all. Employees had no right to their jobs. Consequently, they had no legal standing to sue their superiors for arbitrary or capricious disciplinary action. Needless to say, things have changed dramatically. Labor laws, collective bargaining agreements, and civil service regulations are now in place to protect workers in the public sector. In addition, the courts have begun to recognize that employees have (at least to some extent) a **property right** in their jobs (Swanson et al., 1993; Schofield, 1997). A property right or interest is an aggregate of rights that are guaranteed and protected by government. When an employee is hired by a public agency and the rules require discipline or termination only "for cause," the employee is said to have a property interest—an expectation of continued employment. Property interest for police officers generally takes effect after the initial probationary period. This swing in legal philosophy has ushered in a new era of judicial activism. Gone forever are the days when sergeants could talk tough, act on impulse, and inflict punishments on subordinates without careful administrative or judicial review.

Even with these constraints, however, it is still possible to use disciplinary action as a tool to promote efficiency, effectiveness, and productivity within the workplace. Police officers, in particular, are held to a higher standard of conduct than private employees (*Merrifield v. Illinois State Police Merit Board*, 691 N.E. 2d 199, 1997). It is the sergeant (as the responsible first-line supervisor) who plays the pivotal role and, in large measure, determines whether the police department will face unfair labor practice charges, costly arbitrations, lengthy litigation, and more union activism. According to many labor relations specialists, reasonable disciplinary action can be made to stick if it is fair and if first-line supervisors learn to avoid the following mistakes:

1. **No Clear-Cut Misconduct or Violation.** Under normal circumstances, disciplinary action is considered to be a legitimate option only when it can be tied to a specific offense.

2. **Inadequate Warning.** Trial boards, civil service hearing officers, arbitrators, and the courts have held that police personnel are entitled to both direct and sufficient warning that their poor performance or misconduct will not be tolerated.

3. **Absence of Positive Evidence.** The absence of positive evidence to support the charge against the employee jeopardizes the case, subjects the sergeant's motives to question, and destroys confidence in the department's disciplinary system.

4.   **Acting on Prejudice.** Real or imagined favoritism or discrimination has a debilitating effect on discipline, undermines legitimate authority, and creates poor morale.

5.   **Inadequate Records.** The value of written records of warnings and reprimands cannot be overestimated, because they are documentary evidence of the action taken to correct personnel problems and to deter further misconduct. It is recommended that the first-line supervisor keep a log or notebook documenting any and all discussions with subordinates regarding behavior and discipline. Such documentation should include not only the nature of the discussion, but the time, date, place, and any results observed from the discussions.

6.   **Excessive Punishment.** Most civil service hearing officers, arbitrators, and judges subscribe to the concept of progressive discipline and look unfavorably on punishment that is too severe, especially for first-time offenders.

7.   **Violation of Procedural Due Process.** A lack of concern for just cause and procedural due process taints the disciplinary action and pits the employee against the employer in a struggle for power (Bittel and Newstrom, 1990).

In order to make any disciplinary policy or procedure work effectively and remain within the legal guidelines, management and supervision must ensure that employees:

1.   Know the expected standards of behavior.

2.   Know what sanctions will be imposed if the standard is violated.

It is the responsibility of police managers and supervisors to communicate to each officer under their command or supervision these expected standards of behavior. Such communication may be in the form of training; through observation of desired behaviors (role models); and seeing disciplinary action applied to others. Above all, supervisors should carefully document all forms of communication regarding acceptable and unacceptable behavior with subordinates in the event an inquiry needs to be made later. Poorly prepared, carelessly investigated, and inadequately documented cases reflect negatively not only on the first-line supervisor who conducted the inquiry, but also on the police department that based disciplinary action on it. Consequently, the errant, disruptive, or deviant employee who should have been severely disciplined or even discharged for the good of the service often wins the case on appeal. More often than not, that employee returns to the job an embittered, marginal performer who attempts to contaminate others at every opportunity. Not only does the employee's morale suffer, but the morale of all those who work with that employee suffers as well. From a very practical point of view, greater harm may result when the undeserving subordinate is returned to duty because the disciplinary action was not sustained than if that particular employee had never been disciplined at all. It is the sergeant's responsibility to take appropriate disciplinary action and to make sure that it sticks.

Constructive Discharge

Many police officers facing severe disciplinary action may elect to resign from their position voluntarily rather than risk formal discharge. Typically, this is seen as a benefit to the employee, who would rather resign than face formal charges and termination. It is also a benefit for the organization in that formal charges do not have to be made and the matter can be closed. However, **constructive discharge** is a claim or legal finding that an employee who purportedly voluntarily resigned from a position should be treated as though the employee was actually discharged or fired by the employer. In other words, if the employee feels compelled to resign under threat of management pursuing termination, the resignation is actually a constructive discharge. Constructive discharge is much more beneficial to the employer than to the employee, because time and money are saved by forcing the employee to resign. An employee who voluntarily resigns has little legal recourse against his or her employer. However, there are two situations in which an employee who resigned may obtain legal remedy against the employer. These issues are:

1. Was the employer attempting to avoid the legal protections due the employee?

2. Did the employer make the working situation intolerable for the employee?

In order for the employee to prevail in a legal case against the employer, the court must find that a reasonable person faced with similar unfair conditions would leave rather than continue to suffer such condition or treatment.

Results of Absent Discipline

The lack of self-control and the absence of meaningful disciplinary action in police organizations are antithetical to the common good. When they are compounded by benign neglect or deliberate indifference on the part of police supervisors and managers, they lower the quality of service provided by a given department and undermine the integrity of the entire profession.

We have argued that disciplinary action must be prompt, certain, reasonable, and fair if it is to deter misbehavior and help purge undesirables from police work. The absence of effective (positive as well as negative) discipline is the harbinger of systematic failure.

In a series of well-researched and very disturbing articles, the *Washington Post* (Flaherty and Harriston, 1994) chronicled such a failure in a large police department located in the mid-Atlantic region of the United States. The department hired nearly 1,500 new police officers in a two-year period (1989-1990). For unfathomable reasons, the department was not effective in screening, selecting, appointing, training, and evaluating many of these new officers. On-the-job supervision was lax and in many cases nonexistent. According to the *Washington Post*, inaction on the part of police supervisors and managers tacitly allowed incompetence, misconduct, and corruption to flourish.

While it is impossible to quantify incompetence or to assess the impact of minor misconduct as well as unreported misconduct, there is one chilling statistic in the *Washington Post* series that should give every professional police officer cause for concern. Since 1991, 256 of the police officers who were suspended or fired have had the adverse disciplinary actions overturned by the courts or labor arbitrators solely because the department took too long to initiate formal disciplinary action. The lack of prompt disciplinary action has permitted incompetents, malcontents, and criminals to remain on the public payroll in critically important positions.

The *Washington Post* series underscores the importance of self-control and formal discipline. Poor supervision and the lack of effective disciplinary mechanisms allow "loose cannons" who are in positions of power to abuse that power.

Personal and Vicarious Liability

Failure to sustain a disciplinary action against an employee puts the supervisor at risk for a subsequent civil suit. The suit may involve abuse of authority, discrimination, or defamation of character. Employers and supervisors also incur civil liability if they deprive a subordinate of a guaranteed due process right. As a general rule, police officers can go to either state or federal courts to seek monetary damages or injunctive relief against an employer or supervisor at any stage of the disciplinary process if it is determined that they may have been denied procedural due process.

Public employees have always been liable for their own negligent or wrongful acts. They are liable, in most situations, for compensatory as well as punitive damages. Until quite recently, however, public entities (units of state, county, and local government) were considered immune from civil liability resulting from the negligent or wrongful acts of their employees. Once again, things have changed rather drastically. While the individual employee is still liable, the courts, based on case law and recently enacted statutes, have held that public agencies are often liable for compensatory damages when the wrongful acts or omissions occur while employees are acting within the scope of their employment. Based on the fact that government is perceived as having "deep pockets" and a virtually inexhaustible source of revenue, **vicarious liability** suits have become commonplace. If the litigant can show by a preponderance of evidence that the police department failed to train, supervise, or discipline errant, disruptive, or deviant employees properly, the department may be held liable. It will pay for the misconduct of its personnel when that misconduct (violation of policies, procedures, rules, or regulations) causes injury to others. Recent monetary judgments have been enormous. Some local governments have been forced into bankruptcy. It is in the police department's best interest, then, to promote only competent employees to the rank of sergeant and to strengthen the internal disciplinary system (Iannone, 1994).

Summary

As noted earlier in this chapter, discipline is the essential element in productive work that produces an orderly environment, cooperative goal-oriented behavior, and esprit de corps. There are two types of discipline: internal (positive) and external (negative). Internal discipline is the self-discipline learned from significant others and acquired through the socialization process. While self-discipline is tucked away in the subconscious mind, it controls behavior and produces willing conformity to various group-shared expectations. External, or negative discipline, on the other hand, is imposed from the outside on the errant, disruptive, or deviant employee by someone in a position of authority. Negative discipline (in the form of disciplinary action or punishment) is a tool used by supervisors to correct existing personnel problems or to prevent these problems from occurring again in the future. As a general rule, the amount of external discipline required by an employee will vary inversely with the degree of self-discipline exercised by the individual.

Effective disciplinary action is always based on just cause, is appropriate in terms of the offense and the needs of the offender, and becomes progressively more severe if the subordinate fails to change his or her behavior. According to the Hot Stove concept, punishments must be immediate, with advance warning, consistent, and impersonal. Punishments must also be reasonable, lawful, and must fit the offense. In order to be effective disciplinarians, sergeants must be firm, impartial, and fair to their employees. Anything less distorts the process and undermines the entire discipline system.

There is probably no area in supervisor-subordinate relationships that creates more of a challenge than the administration of discipline. In this context, discipline means strict and regular training for obedience and efficiency; a system of planning, orderly control, and appropriate conduct; and the use of rewards and progressively more severe punishments. Discipline must be insisted upon and sustained before there can be any continuous and cooperative effort to accomplish the organization's mission, goals, or objectives. On the other hand, the growing emphasis on employee rights and freedom in the workplace runs counter to the prerogatives of management in the area of behavior control. The challenge is clear. It is up to the first-line supervisor—the sergeant—to maintain control while encouraging self-discipline, and to take appropriate disciplinary action in such a way as not to threaten but to enhance the employee's self-esteem, sense of worth, and job-related productivity. The goal is total quality management.

Capricious and excessive discipline has provided much of the impetus for the unionization of police personnel. It has also led to the enactment of peace officer bill of rights laws. The labor relations movement and its impact on the American law enforcement establishment is explored in Chapter 12.

Case Study

Officer David Repass

You are a police sergeant in a fairly large city of about 150,000. You have 12 officers under your supervision in a patrol unit. One of your officers is David Repass, a 25-year veteran of the force. David is one of those officers who does only what he has to do to get by and nothing more. He is dependable in getting to work, diligent, and does adequate work but nothing superior. He receives the same "good" on evaluations each year but has never tried to better himself in the department. He usually stays by himself and rarely socializes with the other officers. He is not married and has no children, only a dog that you have never seen except for the strands of dog hair on his blue uniform.

One day, while eating lunch at one of your favorite hangouts, the manager comes up to you.

"Bill, I've been meaning to mention something to you but didn't know how to go about it."

"Go ahead, Charlie, you know you can tell me anything. After all, I've been eating here for the last 10 years," you say, grinning.

"Well, it's about one of the officers on your shift. That Repass guy. Well, he's a real moocher if you know what I mean," Charlie says with a serious look on his face.

"He comes in here maybe four or five times a week to eat and never pays. Sometimes he just comes in and orders something to go, and he never pays or tips or anything. Now, you know, I don't mind giving out a free lunch or dinner to our boys in blue, but he's gettin' a little out of hand. It's startin' to cost me."

What Charlie says doesn't surprise you. You have heard rumors from the other officers that Repass has been mooching free food and other things, like movie tickets and such, but you never had any official complaints about it, so you never said anything. After all, you have eaten for free many times at restaurants and know of other officers on your shift that do the same. And although it is against department regulations, it is something officers have been doing for years. However, most of the officers do not take advantage of the situation and usually leave very good tips when they receive free meals. It's not graft or gratuities—many restaurant owners enjoy giving public servants a free meal once in a while. In this case, it's different. Charlie is concerned enough about it to mention it to you, and if you don't do something about it, the situation may get reported officially to the brass. The brass may be getting free meals too, but they don't like it reported in newspapers or to city council.

What should or would you do as the supervisory sergeant in this case? Are there any times that violation of department rules and regulations can go uncorrected? What are the usual consequences of such actions? If you were to discipline Officer Repass, would it be fair because other officers as well as yourself have received free meals in the past?

Key Concepts

constructive discharge
constructive discipline
disciplinary action
disciplinary action made to stick
firm, fair, equitable, and lawful disciplinary action
first-line supervisors as disciplinarians
Garrity protection
goal of discipline
"Hot Stove" concept

negative discipline
objectives of the discipline system
peace officer bill of rights
positive discipline
PRICE protocol
progressive discipline
property right
total quality management (TQM)
types of discipline
vicarious liability

Discussion Topics and Questions

1. Compare and contrast the concept of positive discipline with that of disciplinary action.

2. Explore the PRICE protocol and show its relationship to the concept of total quality management (TQM).

3. Explain the sergeant's role as a disciplinarian within the police hierarchy.

4. What are the two basic objectives of any disciplinary system?

5. What is the "Hot Stove" concept, and how has it been adapted to law enforcement?

6. In order to be fair, what factors should a sergeant take into consideration before recommending or imposing disciplinary action on a subordinate?

7. Trace the steps involved in progressive disciplinary action.

8. Identify and discuss the various types of disciplinary actions that are commonly used as corrective mechanisms in American police departments.

9. Why has it become increasingly difficult to enforce disciplinary action in police agencies covered by civil service, collective bargaining agreements, or peace officer bill of rights laws?

For Further Reading

Bennett, Wayne W., and Kären M. Hess (2001). *Management and Supervision in Law Enforcement*, Third Edition. St. Paul, MN: West Publishing Company.

> Comprehensive exploration of discipline and related processes as applied to the complexities of supervision and self-control in modern police work. The authors present specific guidelines for administering negative discipline in a constructive rather than a destructive manner.

Fulmer, Robert M. (1988). *The New Management*, Fourth Edition. New York, NY: Macmillan Publishing Co.

> Analysis of management's role in controlling on-the-job behavior and using disciplinary action, where appropriate, to enhance efficiency, effectiveness, and productivity. This is a general management text emphasizing basic principles that apply to the use of discipline in police work.

International Association of Chiefs of Police (1985). *Police Supervision: A Manual for Police Supervisors*. Gaithersburg, MD: International Association of Chiefs of Police.

Walsh, William F., and Edwin J. Donovan (1990). *The Supervision of Police Personnel: A Performance-Based Approach*. Dubuque, IA: Kendall/Hunt Publishing Company.

> Practical guide to discipline and the use of disciplinary action to help police personnel accomplish the organization's mission, goals, and objectives. It offers a no-nonsense, performance-based approach to discipline within the context of administrative due process.

References

Aragon, Randall (1993). "Positive Organizational Culture: A Practical Approach." *FBI Law Enforcement Bulletin*, Vol. 62, No. 12.

Bittel, Lester R., and John W. Newstrom (1990). *What Every Supervisor Should Know*, Sixth Edition. New York, NY: McGraw-Hill Book Company.

Blanchard, K. (1989). "A PRICE That Makes Sense." *Today's Office*, September, p. 18.

CALEA (2001). *Standards for Law Enforcement Agencies*, Fourth Edition. Fairfax, VA: Commission on Accreditation for Law Enforcement Agencies, Inc.

Carnegie, Dale (1992). *The Dale Carnegie Course* (syllabus). New York, NY: Dale Carnegie and Associates.

Covey, Stephen R. (1992). *Principle-Centered Leadership*. New York, NY: Simon and Schuster.

Flaherty, Mary P., and Keith Harriston (1994). "Law and Disorder: The District's Troubled Police." *The Washington Post*, Aug. 28-31: Section A.

Fyfe, James J., Jack R. Greene, William F. Walsh, O.W. Wilson, and Roy McLaren (1997). *Police Administration*, Fifth Edition. New York, NY: McGraw-Hill Book Company.

Guthrie, Martin (1996). "Using Automation to Apply Discipline Fairly." *FBI Law Enforcement Bulletin*, Vol. 65, No. 5.

Hilgert, Raymond L. and Theo Haimann (1991). *Supervision: Concepts and Practices of Management*, Fifth Edition. Cincinnati, OH: South-Western Publishing Company.

Iannone, Nathan F. (1994). *Supervision of Police Personnel*, Fifth Edition. Englewood Cliffs, NJ: Prentice-Hall, Inc.

LeBoeuf, Michael (1985). *GMP: The Greatest Management Principle in the World*. New York, NY: Barkley Books.

Mahoney, Thomas (1986). "Problem Employee or Problem Supervision?" *Journal of California Law Enforcement*, Vol. 20, No. 1.

Marmo, Michael (1986). "Off-Duty Behavior by Police: Arbitration Determines if On-The-Job Discipline is Appropriate." *Journal of Police Science and Administration*, Vol. 14, No. 2.

McGuinness, James M. (1999). "Point of Law." *Police*, Vol. 23, No. 9.

Peters, Thomas J. and Robert H. Waterman, Jr. (1982). *In Search of Excellence: Lessons from America's Best-Run Companies*. New York, NY: Warner Books, Inc.

Plunkett, Richard W. (1992). *Supervision: The Direction of People at Work*, Sixth Edition. Boston, MA: Allyn and Bacon, Inc.

Preston, Paul, and Thomas W. Zimmerer (1983). *Management for Supervisors*, Second Edition. Englewood Cliffs, NJ: Prentice-Hall, Inc.

Redlich, James W. (1994). "Disciplinary Interrogations: Which Warnings Apply? And When?" *The Police Chief*, Vol. LXI, No. 6.

Robbins, Stephen P. (1989). *Organizational Behavior*, Fourth Edition. Englewood Cliffs, NJ: Prentice-Hall, Inc.

Sartain, Aaron Q. and Alton W. Baker (1978). *The Supervisor and the Job*, Third Edition. New York, NY: McGraw-Hill Book Company.

Schofield, David (1997). "Constitutional Issues in Employee Discipline." *Police Law Journal*, 5:119-127 (May).

Sherman, Mark, and Al Lucia (1992). "Positive Discipline and Labor Arbitration." *Arbitration Journal*, Vol. 47, No. 2.

Steinmetz, Lawrence L., and H. Ralph Todd, Jr. (1986). *First-Line Management: Approaching Supervision Effectively*, Fourth Edition. Plano, TX: Business Publications, Inc.

———— (1992). *Supervision: First-Line Management*, Fifth Edition. Boston, MA: Richard D. Irwin, Inc.

Swanson, Charles R., Leonard Territo, and Robert W. Taylor (1993). *Police Administration*, Third Edition. New York, NY: Macmillan Publishing Co.

Whisenand, Paul M., and George E. Rush (1993). *Supervising Police Personnel*, Second Edition. Englewood Cliffs, NJ: Prentice-Hall, Inc.

Whittenberg, Paul (1995). "Discipline with Dignity: A Positive Approach for Managers." *Federal Probation*, Vol. 59, No. 3.

Performance Appraisal—

The Key to Police Personnel Development

7

Introductory Case Study

Sergeant Wayne DePriest

Sergeant DePriest is a regional patrol supervisor for the state highway patrol in the second patrol district of the state. Sergeant DePriest has eight troopers under his supervision. There are six sergeants, two lieutenants, and one captain in the second patrol district. For nearly 20 years, the state highway patrol has had one type of performance appraisal for all troopers in the state. It was a brief BARS-type form, but emphasized quantity such as number of citations issued, number of traffic accidents worked, number of DUI arrests, and so on. In other words, it was a pretty simple procedure to annually fill out for each trooper. And with few exceptions, all the troopers received basically the same evaluation every year. In fact, the troopers would agree among themselves how many citations they would average writing each month and work together so that productivity among themselves was fairly equal. The evaluation process was nothing more than a mechanism to help terminate or relocate troopers who were considered to be "problem officers."

With the election of a new governor and a slate of new commissioners and department heads within the state, a new highway patrol commissioner was appointed last year. The new commissioner decided to revamp the old trooper evaluation form and produce one that was in keeping with the governor's promise to upgrade and professionalize the highway patrol. The new evaluation process was a paired-comparison form that pitted each trooper against another in terms of productivity. The new form simply emphasized quantity of citations issued, arrests made, accidents worked, and so on. There were few behavioral scales—with the exception of following orders, court demeanor, being late for work, and so forth. Along with the new evaluation form came merit pay increases for being selected as the best trooper. Sergeant DePriest now found himself having to select the best trooper each year from few standards and award merit pay to the "better" troopers under his supervision.

Problems immediately began to surface. First, the troopers became competitive. Because the evaluation was quantity-oriented and tied to merit pay, the more citations the troopers wrote and the more arrests they made, the better they looked on the evaluation form and the more likely they were to receive merit pay. Backstabbing also arose among the troopers. There were more citizen complaints about trooper behavior on traffic stops and the overly aggressive actions of troopers looking to make an arrest.

If you were Sergeant DePriest, how would you use the new paired-comparison evaluation? Can this type of evaluation process work in an objective, fair, and equitable way? If you had the authority to change this evaluation process, what would you do?

People Power

Police work is a unique, multibillion-dollar, labor-intensive industry built around order maintenance, law enforcement, and the provision of other essential government services. By the early twenty-first century, for example, more than 17,000 police agencies at all levels of government spent nearly 48 billion dollars to "protect and serve" their constituents. Most of these funds—80 to 90 percent—went to cover salaries and benefits for more than 850,000 full- and part-time law enforcement personnel. Municipal governments spend more than 20 percent of their total budgetary outlay on police services. The per capita expenditure for police service in cities and counties ranges anywhere from $88.18 to $528.93 per year, with a mean expenditure of $177.92 (U.S. Department of Justice, 2001). It is estimated that it now costs more than $300,000 per year to field a fully equipped and professionally trained police officer around the clock in urban high-crime areas (Hamblin, 1994).

In light of these phenomenal costs, local governments are now beginning to realize that they have a vested interest in recruiting, hiring, and retaining only the most efficient, effective, and productive personnel. Police managers are becoming sensitive to the fact that numerical strength alone does not guarantee quality service. Quality is much more likely to be determined by the intelligence, ability, skill, experience, integrity, and dedication of the police department's human resources. Consequently, police managers are forced into being much more personnel-conscious.

Many observers have come to the conclusion that personnel development may be the only truly viable solution to problems caused by an erosion of the tax base and dwindling resources in the public sector. Personnel development focuses on the employee. It is a management strategy designed to improve both the quantity and quality of each individual's output, while ensuring that employees work collaboratively (in groups) to achieve the organization's mission, goals, and objectives. Based on modern management theory, personnel development is an ongoing process that begins on the day the rookie police officer joins the police department and continues throughout his or her career.

Systematic performance appraisal is regarded as the key to employee development and is now viewed as the centerpiece of an effective police personnel system (Travis and Brann, 1997; Kramer, 1998).

Performance Appraisal

The evaluation of job performance is a managerial task that is normally delegated to first-line supervisors in healthy, work-based organizations. Formal (objective) performance appraisal has been emphasized in government and has become the standard by which we judge the legitimacy of any public sector personnel system.

Many police supervisors do not fully understand the purpose of, or need for, regular performance appraisal. They approach the evaluation of subordinates in a negative manner. Evaluation becomes an unpleasant and stressful chore that requires them to assume the awesome responsibility for honestly assessing the job-related strengths and weaknesses of their fellow police officers. Some police supervisors are simply not prepared to take on this very important role-related responsibility.

In a generic sense, there are seven common justifications used by management for requiring first-line supervisors to evaluate their personnel. They are summarized below:

1. To determine whether subordinates are doing the job they were hired to do.

2. To measure the quantity of work and quality of performance and provide rewards for those who are doing well.

3. To correct specific problems and improve the employee's overall performance.

4. To estimate employee potential and prepare that employee for promotion within the organization.

5. To assess employee attitudes and strengthen each supervisor's understanding of subordinates.

6. To let employees know exactly how they are doing, where they stand, and what they can do to improve their own on-the-job performance.

7. To provide supervisors (and management) with sufficient objective data to make and, if necessary, defend decisions concerning personnel within the agency.

In addition to these specific objectives, many management theorists contend that an objective and fair performance appraisal tends to fortify and enrich supervisor-subordinate relationships in the workplace (Swanson et al., 1993).

A great deal of time, effort, and creative thought have gone into the search for a comprehensive, multipurpose performance-appraisal process designed to give police managers objective data that can be factored into administrative decisions concerning salary increases, promotions, transfers, discipline, or personnel development. While progress is being made, no such process presently exists, and it is doubtful that one will be perfected in the near future (Travis and Brann, 1997).

Many personnel specialists, or human resources managers, as they are now called, believe that the achievement of multiple objectives is not feasible and think that a performance appraisal system should be limited to one (and only one) objective: to inform employees about the quality of their work so they can strive to improve their own performance. This is commonly referred to as "developmental" as opposed to "judgmental" performance appraisal (Steinmetz and Todd, 1992).

According to Hilgert and Leonard (2001), the purpose of a formal merit rating, performance review, or employee appraisal is to synthesize, in objective terms, the performance, experience, and capabilities of individual employees and to compare them with the requirements of a particular job. This assessment is almost always based on observable criteria, such as cooperation, dependability, productivity, quality of output, follow-through, judgment, or safety. Regular performance appraisal provides rank-and-file police officers with some assurance that they are not being overlooked and that the supervisors, managers, and various superiors within the police organization know something about them as individuals.

The key to effective performance appraisal is knowing exactly who is responsible for doing what and how it (the job) is to be done. The essential components or elements of the total job must be carefully identified and communicated to the subordinate personnel. The most important elements of performance appraisal have the following characteristics:

1. They are job-centered and focus on the specific task or tasks to be performed.

2. They are clear and simply stated.

3. They are observable as well as objective.

4. They target actual on-the-job performance.

5. They are measurable in terms of predetermined performance standards.

The second step in effective performance evaluation is applying a standard designed to specify the minimum level of acceptable performance for each particular job. This standard becomes critically important as a performance-measuring device (Jones, 1998). It clearly delineates what is expected from the police officer in terms of productivity, accuracy, completeness, timeliness, dependability, or safety. It is the first-line supervisor, normally a sergeant, who is in the best position to utilize the information concerning elements of the job, performance standards, and objective appraisal criteria to forge a meaningful composite that accurately reflects each subordinate's job performance (Iannone and Iannone, 2001). The performance profile is an invaluable source of information for management decision making.

There are literally thousands of different performance-appraisal instruments in use today. Virtually all of them incorporate elements of the job (based on a job description), some type of graduated performance measurement, and objective evaluative criteria. Needless to say, none of them is perfect.

The four universal aspects of performance appraisal are: (1) a performance goal, standard, or plan; (2) measurement of job-related performance; (3) comparison of employee performance with the goal, standard, or plan; and (4) the use of corrective action as required in a given situation (Walsh and Donovan, 1990). These represent the conceptual pillars on which the employee evaluation process is built.

The Employee Evaluation Process

While the actual mix may differ from one jurisdiction to another, there are nine basic steps in most formal employee evaluation systems. These steps have been summarized below.

1. Preparing a detailed job description and specifying minimum performance requirements. In other words, local management determines what is to be done and how well each employee is expected to do it.

2. Discussing the job, acceptable performance standards, and the formal evaluation process with the employees, and making adjustments if necessary.

3. The employee does the work. How well it is done will be influenced by personal ability, training, adaptability, time, resources, and an error factor based on chance.

4. Observing and evaluating the employee's job performance by appropriate supervisory personnel. This will be influenced by the skill of the evaluator, the frequency of the observation, the predispositions of the supervisor, and random error.

5. Evaluative data derived from objective criteria are recorded on an appraisal form designed to measure the quantity as well as the quality of an employee's work using very specific performance standards.

6. Explaining the mechanics of the particular evaluation and discussing the contents of the evaluative report with each employee.

7. Forwarding the evaluative report to the central personnel unit or the appropriate manager, where it is interpreted from an organization-wide perspective.

8. Alternative responses are considered and appropriate administrative action is taken.

9. An appeals process is made available to ensure administrative due process and to safeguard the rights of the employee.

These steps have become institutionalized in public sector personnel administration. In police work, for example, they have become an integral component of all civil service systems, collective bargaining agreements, and municipal human resources management programs. From a management perspective, performance appraisal is necessary in order to: (1) allocate resources, (2) reward competent employees, (3) provide valuable feedback to workers, and (4) maintain fair relationships and open communication (Fulmer, 1988).

Police officers, first-line supervisors, and managers play very distinct, yet interrelated roles in performance appraisal. They are assigned specific responsibilities but must work cooperatively to ensure the success of the evaluative process (see Figure 7.1). Unity of purpose is a critical variable.

While performance evaluation is always a major undertaking in complex criminal justice organizations, it is an absolutely essential component of managerial control. Job performance must be observed, compared with objective standards, and evaluated so that police supervisors and managers can implement effective strategies designed to mitigate performance problems or remove employees from the workforce who cannot or will not change their unacceptable job-related behavior.

Frequency of Evaluation

The National Advisory Commission on Criminal Justice Standards and Goals emphasized the importance of regular performance appraisal in law enforcement. According to Standard 17.1, every police agency should adopt a policy of retaining or promoting to higher ranks

> only those personnel who successfully demonstrate their ability to assume the responsibilities and perform the duties of the position to which they will be promoted or advanced. Personnel who have the potential to assume increased responsibilities should be identified and placed in a program that will lead to full development of that potential (National Advisory Commission on Criminal Justice Standards and Goals, 1973).

Figure 7.1
Roles and Responsibilities in the Evaluation Process

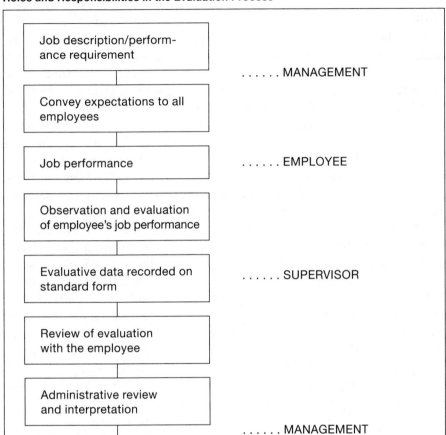

Adapted from Richard W. Holden (1994). *Modern Police Management*, Second Edition. Englewood Cliffs, NJ: Prentice-Hall, Inc.

Nearly 20 years later, the Commission on Accreditation for Law Enforcement Agencies (CALEA) reiterated the importance of regular performance evaluations. According to Standard 35.1.2, "A written directive requires a performance evaluation of each employee be conducted and documented at least annually" (CALEA, 2001). The key ingredient in this type of screening process is an accurate assessment of the employee's past performance, initiative in the area of self-development, and the person's potential for advancement within the organization. Standardized performance appraisal for both probationary and certified police personnel has become the norm in progressive police departments.

While conscientious supervisors continuously evaluate the performance of their subordinates, formal objective evaluations, such as those discussed earlier, are much less frequent. From a very practical point of view, formal evaluations should be performed on a predictable schedule. Sequencing is critical. If employees are evaluated too often, the supervisor is likely to place undue emphasis on and be swayed by normal day-to-day occurrences. If, on the other hand, they are infrequent, evaluators tend to forget critical incidents and much of the data that should be factored into the appraisal.

As a general rule and for CALEA standards, police departments evaluate their permanent personnel once a year. Due to the nature of the work and the value that is placed on proper performance of the police role, it would be a better and more reliable practice to evaluate certified police officers twice a year. This would provide management with a cumulative database upon which to make decisions concerning the individual employee.

No matter how careful a department has been in selecting its new personnel, there is a continuing need for quality control. Probably the most valuable technique for determining a rookie's suitability for police service is a trial period on the job. Police managers and seasoned first-line supervisors firmly believe (almost as an article of faith) that a probationary period is an essential element in the personnel screening process. It gives them the necessary time to judge the new employee in terms of ability and character. It also allows them to assess the recruit's capacity to cope with the demands of police work and to detect deficiencies that manifest themselves only under actual working conditions.

Probation, if it is to fulfill its role in quality control, must be predicated on a very careful, consistent, and objective evaluation of each new employee's on-the-job performance. The men and women who are truly unsuited for a career in law enforcement should be separated from police service as quickly as possible (Gaines, Southerland, and Angell, 1991). While it has been customary in many civil service systems to evaluate probationary employees once or twice before they are certified and given permanent status, most management theorists and many practitioners now recommend more frequent evaluation. CALEA Standard 35.1.3 recommends at least quarterly evaluations of all entry-level probationary employees (CALEA, 2001). Under ideal circumstances, police departments should require at least two years of probation with rookie police officers evaluated every six months. After four objective and very thorough evaluations by a competent first-line supervisor or group of supervisors, it is usually clear to supervisory personnel, management, and the employee whether the awarding of permanent status will be in the best interests of the police department. The department should be given the benefit of the doubt in all borderline cases (Leonard and More, 1993).

Objective, thorough, and frequent performance appraisals help to ensure the quality of police service. They protect the public and promote professionalism within the ranks. When used regularly and in an appropriate manner, performance reviews foster professional growth and create a genuine esprit de corps.

The Sergeant's Role

As first-line supervisors, sergeants play a leading role in the employee evaluation process. Based on their strategic position in the management structure, they are responsible for appraising the on-the-job performance of almost all line personnel. For all practical purposes, they provide quality assurance within the police establishment. The assessment of human resources "goes with the turf."

As noted before, many sergeants do not fully understand or appreciate their unique role in the evaluative process. They perceive it as a difficult and distasteful part of their job. Consequently, they attempt to insulate themselves from the stress associated with performance appraisal. If they cannot avoid it altogether, they approach it as perfunctory and adopt a blasé attitude. This is very unfortunate, because apathy is normally a precursor to deterioration in police service.

Due to insecurity, immaturity, poor training, or the inability to cope with criticism, many sergeants fear the thought of judging their subordinates and use all sorts of excuses to avoid it. They claim that it takes too much time away from their other duties, strains personal relationships, is ignored by management, and is almost always perceived by fellow employees as an unwarranted intrusion in their professional lives. These rationalizations are unacceptable. Sergeants must be prepared to accept responsibility for meaningful performance appraisal.

Accepting sergeants' stripes means more than merely an increase in pay. It represents an advancement in rank that thrusts the newly promoted noncommissioned officer into a different, very demanding role within the organization. Sergeants are expected to assume the risks inherent in the evaluative function. They must honestly assess how well each employee is doing the job and articulate, in meaningful terms, what they think about that person's overall performance as a police officer. Once again, personnel evaluation goes with the territory.

Not everyone has the inclination or the talent to be a good evaluator. In fact, whether or not a particular first-line supervisor becomes a competent evaluator will, in the long run, depend on that person's:

1. Ability to be firm, fair, and impartial when dealing with others

2. Orientation to and understanding of the personnel evaluation process

3. Self-confidence in making judgments about the strengths and weaknesses of other people

4. Human relations and communication skills

5. Capacity to empathize with subordinates

6. Knowledge of the assigned tasks performed by the employee

7. Training as an evaluator

8. Experience with performance appraisal

9. Ego strength when it comes to dealing with disagreement or criticism expressed by significant others within the police organization

Being a good evaluator requires natural talent, knowledge, and the acquisition of special skills. Personnel evaluation is one of the most difficult aspects of a very complex job.

Human factors alone cannot guarantee the success of a particular performance appraisal program. Institutional support is absolutely essential. First-line supervisors exhibit enthusiasm for and derive satisfaction from their role as evaluators when they are given adequate management support. Genuine support does not come from professional rhetoric; it comes from action.

To do their job effectively, sergeants need to have clear-cut authority based on department policies, procedures, rules, and regulations in order to perform a meaningful evaluation of subordinates. They must also believe that their assessment will be accepted and respected by their superiors as a professional judgment concerning the competence of the employee. Unless police sergeants are given time, training, and access to adequate institutional resources, performance appraisal becomes a sham. It is nothing more than window dressing. Ritualistic performance evaluations that lack relevance are an unwelcome burden that helps to destroy the supervisor's morale and undermines the credibility of management (see Figure 7.2).

Figure 7.2
Institutional Support for Performance Appraisal

1. Role—A job description outlining the sergeant's role in performance appraisal.

2. Authority—Formal department policy granting first-line supervisors authority to evaluate immediate subordinates.

3. Procedure—Mutually acceptable procedures specified in department manuals, civil service regulations, or collective bargaining agreements.

4. Relevance—A clear-cut statement about how the evaluative data will be factored into administrative decisions concerning personnel.

5. Resources—Supervisor training and career development opportunities.

6. Utility—Evaluative data factored into the actual decision-making process.

7. Stature—Sergeants accepted as members of the management team who make valuable contributions to the department through their quality control and personnel development functions.

First-line supervisors in healthy, work-based organizations take their job very seriously. Top-notch sergeants evaluate their employees frequently. They accept performance appraisal as a challenge and are willing to take the risks associated with it, because it gives them an opportunity to provide both form and substance to the department's human resources. They help weed out incompetent personnel, identify employees who need assistance, and provide positive reinforcement for good workers. Police sergeants are in a key position to influence the efficiency, effectiveness, and productivity of the individual employee, as well as the police department as a whole.

While performance evaluation protocols differ in design, they have three common objectives:

1. To assess each employee's contribution to the organization

2. To provide employees with valuable feedback concerning their on-the-job performance

3. To develop a mutually acceptable plan for correcting performance-related problems

The evaluation process itself consists of: (1) assessment, (2) evaluation interview, and (3) remediation. The sergeant is a central figure in the evaluation process.

Methods of Appraisal

There is no consensus about the best way to approach performance appraisal in complex criminal justice organizations. In fact, there are several competing schools of thought. Some of the most important are outlined below.

Graphic Rating Scale. The graphic rating scale is probably the most frequently used performance assessment device. Each characteristic or trait that is to be evaluated is represented by a line (or scale) on which the evaluator indicates the degree (usually 0 to 100) to which it is believed the person possesses that particular trait or characteristic. Scales represent a graphic continuum that ranges from one extreme (negative) to another (positive). A space for rater comments is found on most graphic rating scales. This gives a supervisor the opportunity to support a rating with facts (see Figures 7.3, 7.4, 7.5).

There are a number of advantages associated with a graphic rating scale:

1. It is fairly simple to design and construct.

2. It is easy for supervisors to use.

3. Interpretation is not particularly difficult.

4. Employees can be compared based on a composite score.

There are disadvantages as well. Rigidity, rater error, and intentional manipulation can skew results. They undermine the credibility of the evaluation process and strain interpersonal relations within the organization.

Figure 7.3
Performance Evaluation Report

INSTRUCTIONS
FOR USE OF THE PERFORMANCE EVALUATION REPORT FORM

GENERAL:

1. Using preliminary draft sheet and pencil, complete Section A first, then other appropriate sections. The rater should review the draft report with his own supervisor. Markings and comments should then be typed or inked in on the final form. Either the rater or reviewer (or both) should then review the rating with the employee in a private interview. All signatures shall be in ink. Changes and corrections shall be initialed by the employee.

2. If space for comments is inadequate, dated and signed attachments may be made (either typewritten or in ink).

3. Due dates shall be observed, and are particularly important for final probationary reports. Filing dates for these are flexible, and both the first and the final reports may be filed any time between the receipt and the printed due date.

4. All probationers (either entrance level or promotional) shall be evaluated at the end of each month of probationary service. Probationers may be separated at any time such action is deemed necessary by the Township Manager, through use of either a scheduled or an unscheduled performance evaluation report.

5. All permanent employees and entrance level probationers in their second year shall be evaluated annually as of the printed due date.

6. The "Guide to Performance Evaluation" should be consulted for suggestions, definitions, interpretations and further instructions.

7. The main purposes of this form are to inform the employee of his performance, to improve performance when possible, and to sustain superior performance.

SECTION A: Check one column for each factor. Column (5) may be checked when a factor is not considered applicable to a particular job. Additional spaces have been provided to write in any additional factors. Each check mark in Columns 1 and 2 requires specific explanation in Section E. In the absence of specific standards for a factor, use your own opinion as to what constitutes standard performance. Standard does not mean average; in fact, standard performance can often be higher than average performance.

Exceeds Standards: Total performance is well above standards for the position. This evaluation should be reflected by marks for critical factors in Section A, and superior or excellent performance should be noted in Section B. Only a few employees would normally qualify for this rating.

Effective—Meets Standards: Consistently competent performance meeting or exceeding standards in all critical factors for the position. If margin is narrow and standards barely met, explain in Section E. Most employees would be rated in this category.

Some Improvement Needed: Total performance occasionally or periodically falls short of normal standards. Specific deficiencies should be noted in Section E. This evaluation indicates the supervisor's belief that the employee can and will make the necessary improvements.

Not Satisfactory: Performance clearly inadequate in one or more critical factors as explained or documented in Section E. Employee has demonstrated inability or unwillingness to improve or to meet standards. Performance not acceptable for position held.

SECTION B: Must be used to describe outstanding qualities or performances when check marks are placed in Column 4. Use this section to record other progress or improvements in performance resulting from employee's efforts to reach previously set goals.

SECTION C: Record agreed-upon or prescribed performance goals for the next evaluation period.

SECTION D: Use for describing standard performance.

SECTION E: Give specific reasons for check marks in Columns 1 and 2. Record here any other specific reasons why the employee should not be recommended for permanent status, or—if the employee is already permanent—any specific reasons for required improvement.

SIGNATURES: Both the rater and the employee shall sign the report. The employee's signature indicates that the conference has been held and that he has had an opportunity to read the report. If he refuses to sign for any reason, explain that his signature does not necessarily imply or indicate agreement with the report, and that space is provided for him to state any disagreement. Further refusal to sign shall be recorded in the report after which it shall be forwarded.

ROUTING: Keep the preliminary draft at the division level until the next rating period and then discard. Route the permanent copy through channels to the Township Manager's Office.

Figure 7.3, *continued*

PERFORMANCE EVALUATION REPORT

EMPLOYEE NAME	(Last)	(First)	(Initial)	EVALUATION NO.	DEPARTMENT	DIVISION

POSITION TITLE	EMPLOYEE STATUS	ASSIGNMENT	**DUE DATE:**

SECTION	1	2	3	4	FACTOR CHECK LIST	5
	NOT SATISFACTORY	SOME IMPROVEMENT NEEDED	MEETS STANDARDS	EXCEEDS STANDARDS	Immediate Supervisor Must Check Each Factor in the Appropriate Column	DOES NOT APPLY

SECTION B — Record job STRENGTHS, superior performance incidents, progress achieved, or checks in Col. 4.

					1. Observance of Work Hours	
					2. Attendance	
					3. Grooming & Dress	
					4. Compliance with Rules	
					5. Safety Practices	
					6. Public Contacts	
					7. Employee Contacts	
					8. Knowledge of Work	
					9. Work Judgments	
					10. Planning and Organizing	
					11. Job Skill Level	
					12. Quality of Work	
					13. Volume of Acceptable Work	
					14. Meeting Deadlines	
					15. Accepts Responsibility	
					16. Accepts Direction	
					17. Accepts Change	
					18. Effectiveness Under Stress	
					19. Appearance of Work Station	
					20. Operation & Care of Equipment	
					21. Work Coordination	
					22. Initiative	
					23. [Additional Factors]	
					24.	
					25.	
					26.	
					27.	
					28.	
					29.	

SECTION C — Record specific GOALS or IMPROVEMENT PROGRAMS to be undertaken during next evaluation period.

SECTION D Describe STANDARD performance.

SECTION E — Record specific work performance of DEFICIENCIES or job behavior requiring improvement or correction. (Explain checks in Col. 1 and 2.)

OVERALL RATING

Not Satis.	Needs Imp.	Meets Std.	Exceeds Std.

FOR EMPLOYEES who SUPERVISE OTHERS

					30. Planning & Organizing	
					31. Scheduling & Coordinating	
					32. Training & Instructing	
					33. Effectiveness	
					34. Evaluating Subordinates	
					35. Judgments & Decisions	
					36. Leadership	
					37. Operational Economy	
					38. Supervisory Control	
					39. [Additional Factors]	
					40.	
					41.	

☐ I DO

RATER: I certify this report representing my best judgment. ☐ I DO NOT recommend this employee be granted permanent status. (For final probationary reports only).

(RATER'S SIGNATURE)　(TITLE)　(DATE)

REVIEWER: (IF NONE, SO INDICATE)

(REVIEWER'S SIGNATURE)　(TITLE)　(DATE)

EMPLOYEE: I certify that this report has been shown to me and/or discussed with me. I understand my signature does not necessarily indicate agreement. ☐ I wish to discuss this report with the reviewer.

Comment:

CHECKS IN CODE 1 AND 2 MUST BE EXPLAINED IN SECTION E

(EMPLOYEE'S SIGNATURE)　(DATE)

–SEE INSTRUCTIONS ON REVERSE SIDE–

Figure 7.4

Performance Evaluation Report

PERFORMANCE EVALUATION REPORT		NON-SUPERVISORY

NAME	CLASS TITLE	DIVISION

PERIOD COVERED BY EVALUATION REPORT FROM: TO:	ASSIGNMENT

RATING INSTRUCTIONS:

1. Check each item box.
   - ◆ STRONG   ✓ STANDARD
   - – WEAK   N NOT OBSERVED
2. Rate each factor by circling the appropriate number.
3. Multiply the circled number by the weight for each factor and write the results in the "score" column.
4. Add the "score" column and record the sum.

Use spaces below for comments. Ratings other than competent should be substantiated in writing. Use reverse side for additional space.

PERFORMANCE FACTORS	1 = UNSATISFACTORY	2 = IMPROVEMENT NEEDED	3 = COMPETENT	4 = HIGH COMPETENT	5 = OUTSTANDING	WEIGHT	SCORE (RATING x WEIGHT)
QUANTITY ☐ AMOUNT OF WORK PERFORMED ☐ COMPLETION OF WORK ON SCHEDULE	1	2	3	4	5	25	
QUALITY ☐ ACCURACY ☐ NEATNESS ☐ THOROUGHNESS ☐ ORAL EXPRESSION ☐ WRITTEN EXPRESSION	1	2	3	4	5	25	
WORK HABITS ☐ PUNCTUALITY ☐ ATTENDANCE ☐ COMPLIANCE WITH ORDERS ☐ INTEREST ☐ INITIATIVE ☐ RESOURCEFULNESS ☐ AGGRESSIVENESS	1	2	3	4	5	15	
PERSONAL TRAITS ☐ EMOTIONAL STABILITY ☐ MATURITY ☐ ATTITUDE ☐ COMPATIBILITY WITH OTHERS ☐ PERSONAL APPEARANCE ☐ COMMAND PRESENCE ☐ LOYALTY	1	2	3	4	5	15	
ADAPTABILITY ☐ PERFORMANCE IN NEW SITUATIONS ☐ PERFORMANCE UNDER STRESS ☐ PERFORMANCE WITH MINIMUM INSTRUCTIONS ☐ ABILITY TO LEARN	1	2	3	4	5	10	
JOB KNOWLEDGE ☐ TECHNIQUES ☐ PROCEDURES ☐ SKILLS	1	2	3	4	5	10	
						100	
						SUM	SUM

1. Examples of work well done; Superior performance:
   _____
   _____
   _____
   _____
   _____
   _____

2. Performance deficiencies; Suggestions for improvement or continuing development:
   _____
   _____
   _____
   _____
   _____
   _____

3. General comments (e.g., over-all performance, progress since last report, plans, goals; any other remarks):
   _____
   _____
   _____
   _____
   _____
   _____
   _____
   _____

This report represents my best judgment of the employee's performance based on my observations and knowledge.

RATING
SUPERVISOR _____ DATE _____

I have read and approved this report.

DIVISION
COMMANDER _____ DATE _____

This report has been discussed with me.

EMPLOYEE'S
SIGNATURE _____ DATE _____

F 2021-54

Figure 7.5

Performance Evaluation Report

PERFORMANCE APPRAISAL REPORT FOR POLICE OFFICER

EMPLOYEE _____ DATE OF EVALUATION _____

JOB TITLE _____ FROM _____ TO _____

DEPARTMENT _____ PURPOSE OF EVALUATION: Probationary _____ Annual _____ Special_____

Performance Measures and Evaluation

	ALWAYS DOES IT	USUALLY DOES IT	SELDOM DOES IT	NOT APPLICABLE	COMMENTS
1. EMERGENCY CALLS FOR SERVICE					
a. Responds quickly but safely when dispatched within established "Code 3" procedures					
b. Exercises reasonable caution in response to emergency calls for service					
c. Gains effective and prompt control of the situation and properly utilizes necessary supporting resources					
d. Exhibits calm, tactful, deliberate, organized and poised demeanor when handling emergency situations					
2. GENERAL ASSISTANCE CALLS					
a. Responds within a reasonable time and safely when dispatched in conformance with established procedures					
b. Minimizes "out of service" time and completes the assignment within an acceptable time period					
c. Exhibits concern and interest in the call even when routine and maintains a highly professional manner					
3. COMMUNITY AND HUMAN RELATIONS					
a. Projects a positive image to individuals and groups as a professional, competent and helpful police officer					
b. Communicates effectively and openly with all types of individuals and groups					
c. Relates well to people even in stressful situations					
d. Exhibits sincere interest in, and concern for, the problems and viewpoints of others					
e. Takes proper care of equipment and vehicles and pride in their appearance					
f. Maintains effective working relationships with co-workers and supervisors					
4. CASE INVESTIGATION					
a. Uses productive techniques in case investigations Recognizes and carefully collects and preserves all evidence					
b. Prepares clear, concise, accurate and logical reports for department and court use					
c. Exhibits a professional and poised demeanor in court and functions well as an objective witness					
d. Maintains acceptable clearance and complaint issuance level					
e. Works cooperatively and constructively with other organizations and resources					
5. ARREST PROCEDURES					
a. Protects the safety of himself/herself and others in the apprehension process					
b. Utilizes only reasonable and legal levels of force and restraint in accordance with department policy in arrest situations					
c. Makes "quality" arrests which are compatible with departmental or team goals					
d. Respects the civil rights of persons placed in custody					
6. TRAFFIC CONTROL					
a. Maintains acceptable enforcement levels and relates activities to the location, time and causes of serious accidents					
b. Gains effective and prompt control at an accident scene and properly utilizes necessary supporting resources					
c. Minimizes citizen friction and complaints in traffic law enforcement					
d. Maintains an acceptable record of judicial support of citations issued					
7. CRIME PREVENTION					
a. Keeps abreast of crime problems, hazards, and prevention priorities in assigned patrol sector					
b. Maintains acceptable and productive levels of field activity, including "on-view" stops and arrests, which can actually impact crime levels					
c. Exercises initiative in finding and developing resources in the community to help in crime prevention					
d. Makes citizens aware of their crime prevention responsibilities and assists them in reducing hazards					

The accuracy of a particular scale (in assessing an employee's performance) is almost always contingent on the selection of identifiable and measurable on-the-job traits, the design of the rating instrument, and the competence of the person doing the rating. The rater's knowledge, training, and inclination to take a risk are critical variables that actually may determine the success or failure of the performance evaluation process. Unless sergeants take responsibility for performance appraisal and play their role as first-line supervisors very skillfully, performance evaluation will become just another element in mutual admiration that perpetuates mediocrity. Sergeants should not forget that excellence is the by-product of selectivity and that they are in a position to mold the department's human resources into a more efficient, effective, and productive workforce.

Critical Incident Method. The critical incident method involves identifying, classifying, and recording significant employee behaviors. A critical incident can be favorable or unfavorable, but both must be recorded accurately. The events chosen by the supervisor for analysis must be concrete indicators of effective or ineffective on-the-job performance. The three basic steps in the critical incident approach to performance appraisal are:

1. Gather and record accurate information about critical incidents involving employees.

2. Abstract the information into a manageable number of categories describing significant job behaviors.

3. Provide the evaluator with a list of categories and a form on which to record an analysis of the employee's performance during various critical incidents.

The worksheet becomes an accurate record of actual behavior and gives management a profile of each employee in terms of that employee's performance-related strengths and weaknesses. The critical incident method has a number of distinct advantages. It deals with factual situations, zeroes in on positive and negative aspects of behavior, and is well-suited for the employee-counseling aspects of performance assessment. However, the critical incident method also has several disadvantages. It takes a great deal of time, specialized training, and management oversight to do it correctly.

The critical incident approach to performance evaluation is much more subjective when compared to the use of graphic rating scales. It requires a great deal of interpretive skill and introspection on the part of the evaluator. The sergeant must know how the critical incident should have been handled as well as have the expertise to judge the performance of subordinates in relation to that standard. This requires professional competence and confidence in the supervisor's ability to evaluate the on-the-job performance of working police officers. Critical incidents, if evaluated objectively, help alert supervisors to problems and raise "red flags" that tell a great deal about that employee's ability to function as a police officer. These red flags often indicate the type of remediation that may be necessary to correct a performance deficit. While the critical incident method has proven effective in certain situations, it has not been widely used in police work, because it is too complex. However, as the police profession matures, we will undoubtedly see more enthusiasm for and interest in the critical incident approach to performance evaluation.

Behaviorally Anchored Rating Scales. Behaviorally Anchored Rating Scales (BARS) are gaining popularity as performance-measuring devices in police work. They focus on what employees should be doing rather than on their personal traits, by relating specific performance to critical job responsibilities.

Each scale identifies specific on-the-job activities to be evaluated. There are sample statements describing (in behavioral terms) what is considered unacceptable, average, and excellent performance in representative incidents. Supervisors look for and rate definite, observable, and measurable job behavior related to these categories. They choose a numerical designation that best fits the performance level of the person being evaluated (Holt, 1990).

The behaviors (tasks or activities) being evaluated are incorporated into a matrix configuration, using a continuum of performance measurement ranging from 0-10. The actual score is assigned by raters based on their professional judgment. This produces a multidimensional assessment of performance as that performance relates to critical tasks or activities.

Figure 7.6
Application of BARS to Police Work

	Performance Level	
	___ 10	—EXCELLENT
	___ 9	
BEHAVIORAL STATEMENT	___ 8	
	___ 7	
Is cognizant of the need for officer safety while	___ 6	
carrying out professional duties (give spe-	___ 5	—AVERAGE
cific example, such as a domestic violence	___ 4	
call or a traffic stop).	___ 3	
	___ 2	
	___ 1	
	___ 0	—UNACCEPTABLE

Behaviorally Anchored Rating Scales use a sufficient array of critical incidents and corresponding behaviors to determine the level of performance as displayed in a graphic rating scale format. In order to work effectively, it is essential to have a participatory environment in which behavioral statements (see Figure 7.6) are developed by consensus between police officers and managers who are thoroughly familiar with the actual behavior being evaluated.

While the BARS approach to performance evaluation is fairly complex, it elicits valuable information for input into the self-development and managerial decision-making processes. Complexity can be overcome through training of first-line supervisors and a cooperative spirit on the part of rank-and-file police officers. The effective use of BARS produces a "win-win" situation for both police managers and the rank-and-file officers, because there is no confusion as to what performance activities are being measured.

Paired Comparison. Paired comparison evaluations can be a formal process or an informal process. In the formal procedure, the supervisor is provided with a set of all possible pairs of officers and instructed to select the individual in each pair who is the "better" performer. Eventually, the process can rank the entire group from best to worst. Some of the advantages of this procedure are:

1. Does not require the use of standards

2. Officers who perform similar duties are compared against each other

3. Relatively simple and saves time

However, the formal paired comparison procedure has several disadvantages. First, it forces supervisors to make tough choices. More importantly, there is no mechanism or process to provide a reason or explanation to support the supervisor's decision. Every individual has strengths and weaknesses, and making a forced choice comparison may prevent a supervisor from making a proper assessment. If used informally, however, the advantages of paired comparisons can be adopted to use with another form of performance evaluation. In the informal process, the supervisor selects the positive characteristics and abilities among all the subordinates and creates a model officer that can be compared with each individual officer. In this way, each individual officer is evaluated on duties and activities they specifically perform.

Management by Objectives. Management by Objectives (MBO) is viewed as a complete management and control system. It is a process designed to convert goals and objectives into specific programs. MBO identifies exactly who is to do what within a given time frame, based on the allocation of existing resources. MBO is a novel approach to performance evaluation. Rather than focusing exclusively on past performance, the first-line supervisor and the employee get together to map out future goals and objectives (which are consistent with the organization's mission). They work together to develop goals and objectives, measures of achievement, and mutually acceptable time frames. The next regularly scheduled performance review, based on the concept of MBO, is held to evaluate how well the employee has done in accomplishing specified objectives. Richard Plunkett

(1992) has identified a series of distinct steps that he feels will make MBO work in just about any organizational setting. They are:

1. Setting mutually acceptable goals and objectives

2. Identifying resources and necessary actions

3. Prioritizing goals and objectives

4. Setting precise timetables

5. Evaluating the results

Clarity and specificity are essential components of MBO. While MBO produces a precise measurement of accomplishment, it requires time and a great deal of planning.

The accuracy of a performance evaluation protocol based on MBO will ultimately depend on the individual rater's judgment, knowledge, training, and ability to establish a positive, empathetic, collaborative, and goal-oriented relationship. Sergeants must have the desire, competence, and human relations skills to help working police officers formulate legitimate, realistic, and measurable job-related performance objectives. When used properly, MBO cuts through ambiguity and wishful thinking to establish concrete benchmarks with which to assess each employee's accomplishments. All successful MBO performance evaluation programs are built on a foundation of cooperation, collaboration, and trust. Whether an MBO performance evaluation protocol works in a particular police department will depend on the caliber of the supervisors who come up through the promotion process.

There are many other forms of performance appraisal that are currently being used or experimented with by police agencies. Self-evaluation, peer evaluation, group ratings, and rank-order methods have been used by several agencies with mixed results.

Regardless of the method selected, police sergeants are in a strategic position to determine the success or failure of the performance evaluation process. Through neglect or by design, they can sabotage everything. Success in achieving the goals and objectives of performance appraisal, on the other hand, depends almost entirely on their knowledge, maturity, specialized training, and human skills. Their decisions must reflect sound judgment, and their actions must be firm, yet fair.

The Human Factor

The integrity of the performance assessment process is inexorably linked to the ability and skill of those who have been promoted to the rank of sergeant. It is nurtured by experience and reinforced through continuous training.

In order to become impartial evaluators, sergeants must first accept themselves as human beings who are fallible and susceptible to influences that can bias their judgment and skew their decisions. Acceptance of oneself as flawed is the first step on the road to objectivity.

In the jargon of personnel evaluation, influences that distort perceptions and interfere with an objective assessment are known as errors. While the chance of error cannot be eliminated altogether, supervisors can be trained to recognize common errors and to devise strategies designed to mitigate their effect on performance appraisal. Police departments with a desire to make the performance assessment process work train raters to recognize and deal with these errors so that supervisors can avoid some of the common pitfalls (Iannone and Iannone, 2001). Some of the most widespread rating errors are explored below.

The Error of Leniency

The error of leniency is probably the most common error in rating police personnel. It involves the human tendency to give people the benefit of the doubt and evaluate their on-the-job performance beyond what the circumstances warrant. Police sergeants succumb to exactly the same pressures that tempt all other supervisors to be lenient with subordinates: the desire to be popular, to avoid interpersonal conflicts, to shield one's ego from criticism, and to protect those who are less talented and more vulnerable. Some sergeants believe that by giving negative performance appraisals (even to officers who deserve them) they draw undue attention to themselves and showcase their own limitations as a first-line supervisor. To many, it is an unacceptable risk. In some cases, sergeants opt to be lenient in evaluating their immediate subordinates in a calculated effort to offset the leniency of other supervisors within the police department. This is their attempt to create balance and ensure that their employees have a fair shot when it comes to advancement.

Regardless of its cause, the error of leniency (if unchecked) acts to undermine the objectivity of the performance assessment process and almost always has a debilitating effect on the organization itself. Supervisors lose their credibility, morale suffers, and employees are placed in positions for which they are unprepared. Good first-line supervisors simply do not allow personal considerations to cloud their judgment. They strive to ensure the integrity of the performance evaluation process by being impartial and fair in their evaluation of each subordinate.

The Error of Central Tendency

In a normal distribution, more people will be rated closer to the mean than to any other point on the evaluative scale. This becomes an error of central tendency only when it fails to reflect a truly objective appraisal of on-the-job performance, and forces many employees into an artificial category labeled "average." Whether supervisors lack sufficient data for valid assessments, fear there will be repercussions, or are merely lazy, central tendency is an escape. It offers them a way to avoid risks. Average evaluations are the safest and least controversial. Thus, supervisors are able to avoid justifying high and low evaluations. By taking the middle road, the sergeant avoids criticism from other supervisors and minimizes the chances of a confrontation during the evaluation interview.

Central tendency is most likely to rear its ugly head in situations in which sergeants are unfamiliar with the person or persons being evaluated, there is a lack of verifiable performance data, or there is some ambiguity in terms of policies, procedures, rules, and regulations. Labeling everyone as average does a disservice to individual employees and the police organization. It penalizes competent, achievement-oriented subordinates and rewards marginal employees. Central tendency destroys the credibility of the evaluation process and plays havoc with employee morale. Sergeants must recognize the problem created by central tendency and be ready to deal with it. This knowledge and a commitment to regular, thorough, and objective performance appraisal will help to safeguard the integrity of the evaluation process.

The Halo Effect

One of the most frequently committed errors is known as the halo effect. This means that the first-line supervisor permits just one outstanding (positive or negative) characteristic or critical incident to shape the overall rating that is given to the employee. Once the supervisor formulates a general impression that the subordinate's on-the-job performance is good or poor, all evaluative ratings are adjusted to reflect that particular judgment. In other words, the sergeant assigns similar values to all characteristics or traits irrespective of the police officer's actual on-the-job performance. In this situation, the evaluator uses selective perception to justify the initial assessment.

The halo effect is the MBO version of the self-fulfilling prophecy. The distortion caused by the halo effect is often compounded by the error of related traits and the error of overweighting (Iannone and Iannone, 2001). The error of related traits occurs when the evaluator assumes that an employee who exhibits one strength will automatically possess others. The error of overweighting (or recency) is the tendency of a supervisor to be unduly influenced by a critical incident, either good or bad, involving the evaluated near the end of the performance review period. Due to the dynamics involved, a recent critical incident can skew a performance evaluation to the point at which it becomes meaningless. Formal performance appraisals should profile the whole person. Better supervisors guard against letting isolated traits or critical incidents dominate performance analysis.

The Error of Bias

One of the most important and widespread errors involves personal bias. Many supervisors have a tendency to rate the employees they know and really like much higher than can reasonably be justified by an objective assessment of performance. Factors such as race, sex, sexual preference, color, creed, lifestyle, and physical appearance may be either intentionally or unintentionally imbued in the evaluation, based on the first-line supervisor's norms, values, prejudices, and operational stereotypes. It is human nature for supervisors to write much more favorable performance evaluations for those with whom they are compatible and to view the people they dislike as being of little or no value to the organization. It is fairly easy for supervisors to fall into the trap of overrating subordinates they helped select or currently supervise in elite or highly specialized units. There is a certain egoism involved in stating that "employees are good because they work for me" or "if they work for me, they must be good." These supervisors have forgotten a basic principle in personnel management—they are rating the person rather than on-the-job performance. This type of "personal politics" destroys the morale of truly competent employees and induces other supervisors to become more lenient when they evaluate their own personnel. Unless a police officer's social background and personality interfere with personal performance, they should not be factored into the appraisal process. While the sergeant may not like a subordinate, the evaluation must be fair and based on the analysis of objective data. First-line supervisors simply cannot allow personal biases and prejudices to cloud their judgment about the performance of an employee. Supervisors need to recognize and deal with their biases in order to keep them from subverting the performance assessment process.

The Contrast Error

This particular rating error, according to Robert Trojanowicz (1980), arises from the tendency of some first-line supervisors to judge subordinates in terms of their own expectations and aspirations. Police officers who vicariously fulfill the personal needs of the sergeant are generally rated higher than others, regardless of their actual performance on the job. They are valued by the supervisor for what they represent, not for what they accomplish or the skill required to accomplish it. This type of emotion-based evaluation is inherently subjective and self-serving. The contrast error forces the employee to guess what qualities or traits the supervisor is looking for and to curry favor (in the form of a positive appraisal) through gamesmanship or outright deception. First-line supervisors must learn to separate their own expectations and aspirations from those of the evaluation protocol. A valid and reliable performance assessment can be derived only from an analysis of what really exists rather than from what supervisors would like to see. Subjective personnel appraisals increase anxiety and threaten to undermine the credibility of the evaluation process itself.

Recency Error

Recency error occurs when too much weight is placed on the employee's behavior immediately prior to the rating evaluation. Most performance evaluations are designed to cover a specific time frame, such as one year. If the supervisor does not keep documentation on the subordinate's activities during the evaluation period, there may be a tendency to overemphasize early recalled behavior, usually the most recent. If recent performance is not indicative of the entire evaluation period, the evaluation is subverted. Generally, recency error results in a higher rating than actually deserved by the subordinate. Most subordinates are aware of evaluation dates and are most likely to improve their performance in anticipation of evaluations.

Sergeants are the human ingredient in performance appraisal. If they are knowledgeable and competent, the performance evaluation process will work. They hold the key to efficiency, effectiveness, and productivity in police work.

The Validity and Reliability of Performance Appraisal

Performance assessments are a waste of time and energy unless appropriate steps are taken to make sure they are both valid and reliable. The objective is to develop a reasonably accurate profile that reflects the competency of personnel, their individual capabilities, and their overall value to the police organization. This is an inordinately complex process that involves the use of an objective measuring instrument and the exercise of mature judgment by the first-line supervisor. Validity and reliability are critical variables in the success or failure of the performance review process.

A valid performance appraisal is an accurate measurement of traits (graphic rating scale), applied problem-solving (critical incident), or goal acquisition (management by objectives) the evaluation process purports to measure. It zeroes in on the essential elements of the job and a limited number of important job-related behaviors. The appraisal itself is an assessment of the degree to which a very specific accomplishment is related to a clearly stated performance standard. If the measuring device is sound, essentially the same results will be achieved by any rater who uses it.

The employee appraisal process is considered reliable when it measures appropriate job-related performance accurately and consistently each time it is used. A reliable performance appraisal is not biased by the idiosyncrasies (or errors) of the rater, manipulation by the person evaluated, flaws in the design of the measuring device, or the constraints of time or place. Reliability relates to the degree of confidence one has that the supervisor, with the tools available, developed a realistic profile of the subordinate's on-the-job behavior.

Due to the nature of performance appraisal in criminal justice organizations, reliability is often difficult to achieve. No evaluative protocol is perfect. Performance ratings are developed, administered, scored, and acted on by people who exhibit prejudices and who, at times, exercise poor judgment. While these problems are fairly serious, they are not insurmountable. The following actions may be needed:

1. Adoption of clear-cut policies, procedures, rules, and regulations designed to govern the performance evaluation process.

2. Selection of a relatively simple, yet valid performance appraisal instrument.

3. Training for supervisors in gathering and analyzing objective evaluative data.

4. Active participation by those being evaluated in all aspects of performance assessment.

5. A commitment by management to base appropriate personnel decisions on data derived from formal performance appraisals.

These measures will add to the reliability of the process and should help allay the anxiety of police officers who are scheduled for a performance appraisal. A relevant, reliable, and fair evaluation protocol is the keystone of a sound police personnel system.

The Evaluation Interview

Once the formal performance rating has been compiled, it (along with all recommendations for remediation) should be communicated to the employee as soon as possible. This is almost always done in what is known as an **evaluation** or **appraisal interview**. Again, the sergeant is the lead actor in this drama.

If the evaluation interview is handled well, everyone benefits. The employee is molded into a more competent police officer, the sergeant gains self-confidence in the area of personnel development, and the police agency becomes more efficient, effective, and productive. Mature human beings are able to deal with and accept criticism they view as deserved, constructive, and fair. On the other hand, if the interview is handled poorly, no one benefits. What started out as a creative way to motivate subordinates quickly degenerates into misunderstanding, distrust, resentment, and open hostility. Under these circumstances, performance appraisal becomes a demotivating factor that can jeopardize the organizational health of the entire police department.

The performance appraisal interview is a forum for positive face-to-face interaction between first-line supervisors and their subordinates. It is designed to facilitate collaborative problem solving and mutual goal setting. Both parties share responsibility for making the process work. Sergeants need to be open, honest, helpful, and supportive in dealing with employees. Police officers, on the other hand, must be willing to cooperate with and take reasonable direction from their superiors. Sincerity, empathy, and mutual respect are essential.

Statistically speaking, one-half of all employees fall below the median in terms of performance. Nonetheless, research shows that average employees estimate their own performance level at around the 75th percentile. Consequently, appraising and reporting on another person's performance (especially when there is a conflict in perception) can become one of the most emotionally charged of all management activities (Robbins, 1989).

The purpose of the appraisal interview is to explore the employee's strengths and weaknesses in light of objective evaluative data. If the performance meets or exceeds reasonable expectations, positive reinforcement should be provided. Praise or a sincere "thank you" is appropriate. Other types of rewards may also be in order. If deficiencies or performance problems are identified, however, remedial action must be agreed upon and initiated. At this point, the appraisal interview is transformed into a vehicle for collaborative problem solving and mutual goal setting. The two parties must work cooperatively to formulate a strategy for improving the employee's on-the-job performance. The ultimate value of the interview will depend on a police officer's ability to recognize the need for self-improvement and the sergeant's ability to stimulate that subordinate's desire to change.

Case Study

Sergeant Theo Thorndike

Sergeant Rudolph Holleran retired with 32 years of service with the department. Sergeant Holleran was well liked and respected among his subordinates as well as those in upper management of the police department. A newly promoted sergeant from another patrol unit has filled Sergeant Holleran's position with a squad of seven patrol officers. Sergeant Theo Thorndike is young, ambitious, and well educated, having completed a master's degree in criminal justice administration. Sergeant Thorndike has aspirations of becoming a police chief one day. He wants to be the best supervisor on the force and has vowed to be firm but fair with his subordinates. Sergeant Holleran advised Sergeant Thorndike that he was inheriting the best squad in the police department. From Sergeant Holleran's past performance appraisals of the officers, that was evident as each of the seven patrol officers had been receiving extremely high evaluations over the past several years.

After a few months on the job as supervisor, Sergeant Thorndike began to believe Sergeant Holleran had been inflating the evaluations of the officers. None of the officers seemed to live up to or perform in the manner that Sergeant Holleran had indicated on previous evaluations. Perhaps it was him and not Sergeant Holleran. Perhaps the officers were slacking off because they had a new supervisor and thought they could get away with being nonproductive. Sergeant Thorndike called each officer in for an appraisal interview and informed them that they were not living up to the evaluations they had previously received under Sergeant Holleran. Sergeant Thorndike was a firm believer in the utility of performance evaluations and wanted to use them to better the performance of his subordinates. Surprisingly, none of the seven officers under his supervision appreciated his comments. Instead, they filed formal complaints with Lieutenant Jamerson. Now, Sergeant Thorndike must address the officers' complaints to Lieutenant Jamerson.

If you were Sergeant Thorndike, what would you say to Lieutenant Jamerson? How would you convince the officers under your supervision that the performance evaluation process is supposed to be helpful to the subordinate. Do you think Sergeant Thorndike used good judgment?

A constructive performance assessment interview is designed to focus the subordinate's attention on the future rather than belaboring the past. According to management theorists like George Bohlander, Scott Snell, and Arthur Sherman (2001), first-line supervisors should:

1.   Discuss actual performance in very specific terms and express their criticism in a helpful, tactful way.

2.   Emphasize the strengths on which the employee can build, as opposed to stressing only the weaknesses to be overcome.

3.   Avoid suggestions involving only a cosmetic change in traits by promoting conformity through acceptable on-the-job behavior.

4.   Concentrate on the opportunities for both personal growth and professional development that exist within the framework of the person's present position.

5.   Limit expectations and specific plans for substantive change to a few important items that can be achieved within a reasonable period, based on the expenditure of available resources.

The performance appraisal interview is a supervisor-employee activity that involves evaluating, teaching, coaching, and counseling. Once again, this task is not nearly as simple as it might appear. In order to accomplish even these relatively modest objectives, the sergeant must be able to establish rapport, empathize, and communicate effectively with subordinates. Sergeants must also possess the leadership skills necessary to motivate their personnel. Without natural talent, specialized training, supervisory experience, and leadership ability, sergeants are bound to fail. Under these conditions, performance appraisal is nothing more than a ritualistic exercise in futility.

While there is no best way to handle the performance appraisal interview, there are a number of operational steps that can add structure to the process and help to ensure a positive outcome. These steps are discussed below.

STEP 1.   Exercise care in scheduling the formal performance appraisal interview. Choose a time and place that affords maximum privacy and is free of unwarranted interruption. Encourage meaningful interaction by allowing sufficient time for a full exploration of the evaluative data as well as the sergeant's report. Solicit input and relevant feedback from the officer. Defuse anxiety and reduce defensiveness by using techniques designed to put the officer at ease and to stimulate a dialogue about performance problems and possible solutions to those problems. The environment in which the interview takes place is a critical variable in determining the overall value of the performance appraisal.

STEP 2.   Adequate preparation is absolutely essential. Both parties (supervisor/subordinate) should be ready and willing to review documentation, compare notes, and reach a consensus concerning the employee's job-related performance. Thorough preparation and uninhibited participation are key elements in effective performance appraisal. Anything less tends to undermine the reliability of the subordinate's performance profile.

STEP 3.   Compare the police officer's accomplishments with specific objectives or targets. Use objective data derived from the appraisal instrument. Do not be vague or use generalizations. Be precise about what was expected and about how close the employee came to actually meeting the goal. Specificity is an essential element in the performance assessment process.

STEP 4.   Give adequate credit (in terms of recognition and other forms of positive reinforcement) for what the police officer has, in fact, accomplished. Do not succumb to the temptation to take for granted the things that have been done and to zero in on the employee's deficiencies or problems. Give credit where credit is due; build on the employee's strengths. Use the appraisal interview as a vehicle for growth and development, not as a forum for punishment.

STEP 5. Carefully review objectives or tasks that have not been accomplished by the subordinate during the review period. Emphasize exactly where improvement is required. Explore with the officer why on-the-job performance must be improved and just how it can be done. Encourage dialogue and develop a plan to ensure full participation. Mutual problem solving and collective goal setting represent other key elements in the performance evaluation process.

STEP 6. Do not assume that the fault is all due to the subordinate. If both parties have contributed to the performance problem, admit it. Do not overemphasize the officer's mistakes, faults, or weaknesses. Judge the police officer's performance, not his or her personality. Never compare the subordinate to an ideal-type third person. Stick to a mutual examination of concrete data and facts in an effort to determine exactly what they mean to the police officer, the sergeant, and the police department as a whole.

STEP 7. Formulate and agree on new objectives and goals to be achieved during the next evaluation period. Be very specific in terms of what and how much is to be accomplished in a particular period. Show how the new objectives and goals are directly related to what has or has not been accomplished during the current evaluation period. This sets the stage for an even more objective performance appraisal the next time around.

STEP 8. Review what you, as a first-line supervisor, can do to help the officer achieve specific objectives and goals. Identify resources that are available and explain how to access them. Play the role of teacher, coach, and counselor. Improvement in job performance is almost always a mutually dependent activity. Sharing the responsibility for personal and professional development brings about mutual respect, a shared sense of confidence, and renewed enthusiasm, as well as a commitment to the job.

STEP 9. Formulate (in conjunction with the employee) a plan to monitor remediation and reevaluate the situation as conditions change. The belief that there will be some type of follow-up is a powerful catalyst for change. It motivates police officers to improve their own on-the-job performance and places an affirmative responsibility on the sergeant to make sure that actual improvement takes place (Bittel, 1993).

The appraisal interview is critically important. From a human resource development perspective, it is the nexus between police department needs and improved employee performance. The goal of the sergeant should be to handle the interview in such a way that officers (with the exception of incompetents and malcontents) will return to their job with an enthusiastic attitude and a genuine desire to improve their own on-the-job performance.

Performance appraisals and evaluative interviews are meaningless exercises unless there is remediation and follow-up. Follow-up is the synergistic ingredient in the performance evaluation process.

Remediation

As previously noted, there are three basic elements in the formal performance evaluation process. They are (1) objective assessment, (2) appraisal interview, and (3) remediation. Remediation refers to using available resources to correct a personnel problem or remedy a deficiency. While sergeants are almost always responsible for the assessment and normally conduct the appraisal interview, their role in remediation is often less direct.

If a deficiency or performance problem is relatively minor or fairly easy to correct, the sergeant is almost always authorized to deal with it directly. Due to the rank structure used in police work, sergeants resolve most performance-related problems informally and at their level (in the organization) based on their appraisal, teaching, coaching, and counseling skills. They keep noise out of the system. As first-line supervisors, sergeants are also responsible for the maintenance/direction function. They continuously monitor each officer's job-related performance in an effort to keep it on an even keel and to make sure it is consistent with the police department's mission, goals, and objectives. Sergeants use the formal performance appraisal process to diagnose serious problems, communicate concern, plan for remediation, provide follow-up, and schedule the more difficult cases for administrative intervention. The performance review process is built on a medical model that has been adapted to police management.

In the event that there is no improvement in the police officer's on-the-job performance, or if it continues to deteriorate, the sergeant has an obligation to take further action. The sergeant may be forced into recommending remediation through retraining, increasingly severe disciplinary action, or total separation from police service.

Due to the nature of bureaucracy, more serious and persistent performance problems are handled in a much different manner. They are "kicked upstairs," so to speak, for remediation or resolution. Consequently, the sergeant's role shifts to that of a supporting actor. All major personnel decisions are made by superior officers and are based on an organization-wide perspective. The sergeant gathers information for and makes recommendations to decision makers, but no longer controls the evaluation process. Under these circumstances, the administration assumes responsibility for quality assurance within the police department.

Many of the more progressive police departments in the United States have initiated comprehensive **employee assistance programs** (EAPs) designed to help deviant, maladjusted, or marginal personnel who still may be capable of making a contribution to the organization. They also provide a variety of positive support services, such as marital counseling, stress management programs, and financial as well as preretirement planning. Specialized employee assistance programs represent an investment in the department's human resources, and a tacit recognition that first-line supervisors are not miracle workers. Sergeants are simply not equipped to handle problems related to health, stress, alcoholism, drug addiction, domestic conflict, and so forth. Sergeants can be trained (using a thorough performance evaluation) to formulate a preliminary diagnosis of the problem and to make an appropriate referral. According to CALEA Standard 35.1.15:

> A written directive establishes a personal early warning system to identify agency employees who may require agency intervention efforts. The system should indicate procedures for:
>
> a.   Provisions to initiate a review based on current patterns of collected material.
>
> b.   Agency reporting requirements of conduct and behaviors.
>
> c.   Annual evaluations of the system.
>
> d.   The role of first and second level supervision.
>
> e.   Remedial action.
>
> f.   Some type of employee assistance such as a formal employee assistance program, peer counseling, etc. (CALEA, 2001).

The EAP movement is predicated on the assumption that it is better and often much more cost-effective to salvage employees through medical, psychological, and social intervention than it is to apply negative sanctions or to separate them from the service. Therefore, sergeants play a pivotal role in the development of a police department's human resources.

Follow-Up

Follow-up by the supervisor completes the evaluation cycle, sets the stage for subsequent appraisals, and provides momentum for the performance assessment process. Sergeants are expected to check on each subordinate's progress in meeting the mutually acceptable goals established during the performance appraisal interview. This role-related task requires surveillance and continuous examination of data derived from a variety of performance measurements. In order to fulfill this responsibility, the sergeant should:

1. Recognize and reward police officers who are doing a good job.

2. Provide positive reinforcement for police officers who are making a good faith effort to change their behavior and improve their on-the-job performance.

3. Assist (through training, coaching, counseling, and other referral services) police officers who need help to improve their performance.

4. Recommend appropriate disciplinary action for individual police officers who will not change their behavior or work to improve their job-related performance.

Follow-up is a supervisory activity designed to motivate personnel and serve as a springboard to professional growth and development.

Without adequate follow-up, periodic performance appraisals become rather mundane, routine managerial tasks with little or no practical value. Police managers, sergeants, and their subordinates merely attempt to project the impression that they care about the efficiency, effectiveness, and productivity of human resources in police work. Perfunctory performance appraisal is used to disguise the discrepancy between the status quo and what could be; honest assessment motivates those in search of excellence. Appraisal should be a daily activity that is summarized periodically in a formal appraisal report and interview. All other things being equal, police officers who accept the inevitability of fair and continuous assessment will try to perform their best work at all times, not just during the formal evaluation period (see Figure 7.7).

Trends in Performance Appraisals

While Total Quality Management guru W. Edwards Deming called performance appraisals "management by fear" (Behn, 1994), they are not headed for extinction in modern police work. On the contrary, they are becoming much more help-oriented and far less punitive. Based on the realization that rank-and-file police officers are the primary source of all productive gain, the philosophy stressed throughout this chapter is that supervisors must lead their subordinates to higher levels of performance by using natural forces within the work group, as opposed to the formal authority vested in them by virtue of their position in the organization (Kennish, 1994). This is a quantum leap from the days when negative discipline reigned supreme and humane concern was the exception rather than the rule.

Two new trends that will have an impact on first-line police supervision are now emerging. The first deals with evaluating police officer performance under community-oriented policing. The second relates to subordinates evaluating their supervisor's performance. Both of these trends are by-products of the new emphasis on participatory management in modern police work.

Figure 7.7
The Sergeant's Role in Performance Appraisal

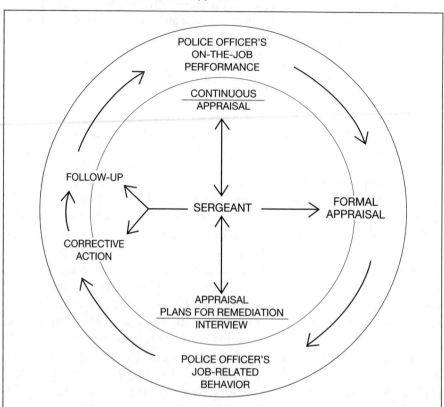

Performance Evaluation in Community-Oriented Policing

Community-oriented policing, regardless of its specific form, is essentially a program in which the police adopt organizational arrangements that focus on fear reduction and order-maintenance activities through the involvement of citizens, while using mutually acceptable problem-solving techniques (Gaines and Kappeler, 2003). It is an interactive process in which police officers and citizens work together collaboratively.

More and more municipal governments are experimenting with community-oriented policing. It is designed to elicit different kinds of resources for use in the battle against crime. First-line police supervisors are expected to achieve total quality results (TQR) with human resources in the work group, coupled with those in the community at large.

Community-oriented policing is based on the assumption that delegation of authority plus meaningful participation in decision making leads to empowerment. The empowerment of police personnel and members of the community is viewed as the bottom line in any effective law enforcement strategy (Whisenand and Rush, 2001).

Traditional performance evaluation methods are not, in and of themselves, sufficient to gauge the quality of officer performance in a community-oriented policing environment. Three other dimensions have been identified and must be integrated into the process. Performance evaluations are also used to:

1. Convey reasonable expectations to police personnel about both the content and style of their behavior, while reinforcing commitment to the department's mission, values, goals, and objectives. This serves as a vehicle for socialization.

2. Document the types of problems and situations that officers encounter in the neighborhood and approaches they take in resolving them. This provides an analysis of the types of resources and other managerial supports needed to deal with problems. It gives police officers an opportunity to have their individual efforts recognized.

3. Identify organizational factors that hinder performance enhancement or the solicitation of ideas for dealing with changing conditions. This gives the people doing the work a meaningful role in reshaping that work in order to improve departmental as well as individual performance.

The Houston Police Department embraced community-oriented policing as its new policing style in 1986. Known as **Neighborhood-Oriented Policing** (NOP), it provides managers with a philosophical foundation and conceptual framework to direct the organization in a manner that is consistent with community needs. From an operational point of view, it encourages police officers to assume responsibility for managing the delivery of essential services in the geographical areas to which they are assigned.

A task force composed of police officers and first-line supervisors spent a considerable amount of time gathering, manipulating, and collating information. A second group, consisting of police volunteers, took the information gathered by the task force and developed a new performance evaluation protocol. This process and the resulting instrumentation sought to bridge existing roles and responsibilities with emerging ones, based on the neighborhood policing philosophy.

Performance evaluations of patrol officers and their respective sergeants used six newly developed forms designed to elicit data and feedback. Each of the forms is described below:

1. **Patrol Officer's Biannual Assessment Report.** This form is used by sergeants to evaluate police officer performance based on 22 specific criteria. In addition, space is provided for written comments regarding work assignments, overall work progress, and special recognition. The criteria reflect the department's expectations concerning police officer performance when it comes to Neighborhood-Oriented Policing.

2. **Patrol Officer's Monthly Worksheet.** The form is designed as a tool to guide each officer's actions during a designated tour of duty. Police officers are given direct input into their own appraisal. This allows officers to identify the different types of projects or programs they have worked on during the evaluation period and report on progress they have made.

3. **Community Information Form.** Citizen-police officer interaction is implicit in all Neighborhood-Oriented Policing strategies. This particular form, if the officer chooses to submit it, elicits information from citizens who worked on projects with specific officers. The information requested is very specific and provides sergeants with additional insight into what the officer was trying to accomplish and how the officer is going about doing it.

4. **Calls for Service—Citizen Feedback Form.** Like almost all police departments, the most frequent source of officer-citizen interaction is the call for service. The Calls for Service—Citizen Feedback form is designed to gather information on the quality as well as the nature of the contact. Citizens are asked a few questions by sergeants. The responses are made a matter of "record" and factored into the overall evaluation. Sergeants use the form at least once a month.

5. **Investigator Questionnaire.** All police officers are expected to conduct high-quality criminal investigations. Even though the information contained in an investigative report provides a critical database for case managers, this material was seldom reviewed by the officer's immediate supervisor. The function of the investigator questionnaire is to obtain information from investigative sergeants concerning an officer's knowledge and quality of performance as these factors relate to both preliminary and follow-up investigations. The police officer determines whether to submit the form.

6. **Officer's Immediate Supervisor Assessment Form.** The officers are given an opportunity to evaluate their immediate supervisors in relation to different dimensions of supervisory work. While the feedback is fairly general in nature, the form must be completed and returned to the sergeant's superior. The information helps to identify significant trends in the relationship between the sergeant and subordinate personnel (Wycoff and Oettmeier, 1994).

Needless to say, the performance evaluation protocol described above represents a radical departure from past practices in law enforcement.

Some police departments have experimented with team evaluations and entire department evaluations using citizen surveys. These types of evaluations focus on how well the entire agency is accomplishing its mission. While many departments use crime rates, arrest rates, ratios of police-to-citizen population, and timely response to calls as measures of effectiveness and efficiency, these measures do not truly reflect the effectiveness and efficiency of the police per se. Because of the increased emphasis on community policing, it is the community who can best evaluate how well the police are doing. Therefore, reduction of the fear of crime within a community is a better measure of the police than experiencing a lower crime rate. To assess how a community feels about the police, several departments have initiated citizen and community surveys that measure fear of crime and citizen concerns with their local police. This allows for feedback and prevents the police from losing touch with the community they serve.

A.J. McKee (2001) has developed and tested a community survey that addresses how well a police department's community policing efforts measure up with the community. The evaluations survey was tested in Hattiesburg, Mississippi, and examined four scales: (1) quality of police contact, (2) perceptions of crime and disorder, (3) personal fear factor, and (4) community cohesion. Surveys such as McKee's allow smaller police departments to evaluate their community policing efforts without undue expense (see Figure 7.8).

New approaches to police work generate a need for new performance evaluation strategies. Houston's evaluation protocol is experimental and undergoing continuous revision. One thing is certain—it has changed the traditional role of the police sergeant in the performance evaluation process. It also subjects first-line supervisors to performance evaluation by their subordinates.

Evaluating the Performance of Supervisors and Managers

In a related development, management theorists are placing more emphasis on employees evaluating the performance of their own supervisors and managers. The theorists link this to the popular participatory management and worker empowerment movements sweeping the country today.

While some mainstream academic, industrial, and corporate entities see some value in having employees rate their supervisors (McGaney and Smith, 1993), the concept has been slow to develop in police work. In most police departments, performance evaluation is still considered the prerogative of management. The evolving participatory management and worker empowerment movements in law enforcement may alter the status quo, however.

Thomas Whetstone (1994) has outlined what should be evaluated in terms of beneficial supervisory traits as well as the pitfalls inherent in the evaluative process. Because much of a supervisor's or manager's work is not observed by subordinates, he argues that the appraisal of performance should focus primarily on leadership issues.

Figure 7.8
The Community Policing Evaluation Survey

Quality of Police Contact Scale:

1. How good a job do you think the police in this area are doing in helping people out after they have been victims of crime?
    Very Good (5) Good (4) Fair (3) Poor (2) Very Poor (1)

2. In general. how polite are the police in this area when dealing with people around here?
    Very Polite (5) Somewhat Polite (4) No Opinion (3) Somewhat Impolite (2) Very Impolite (1)

3. In general, how helpful are the police in this area when dealing with the people around here?
    Very Helpful (5) Somewhat Helpful (4) No Opinion (3) Not Very Helpful (2) Not At All Helpful (1)

4. In general. how fair are the police when dealing with people around here?
    Very Fair (5) Somewhat Fair (4) No Opinion (3) Somewhat Unfair (2) Very Unfair (1)

5. How good a job are the police doing in keeping order on the streets and public places?
    Very Good (5) Good (4) Fair (3) Poor (2) Very Poor (1)

Perceptions of Crime and Disorder Scale:

6. How big a problem is people breaking windows out of buildings in this area?
    Big Problem (1) Somewhat of a Problem (2) No Opinion (3) Hardly a Problem (4) No Problem (5)

7. How big a problem is people drinking in public places in this area?
    Big Problem (1) Somewhat of a Problem (2) No Opinion (3) Hardly a Problem (4) No Problem (5)

8. How big a problem is people being attacked or beaten up by strangers in this area?
    Big Problem (1) Somewhat of a Problem (2) No Opinion (3) Hardly a Problem (4) No Problem (5)

9. How big a problem is people being robbed or having their money, purses, or wallets taken?
    Big Problem (1) Somewhat of a Problem (2) No Opinion (3) Hardly a Problem (4) No Problem (5)

10. How big a problem is vacant lots filled with trash and junk in this area?
    Big Problem (1) Somewhat of a Problem (2) No Opinion (3) Hardly a Problem (4) No Problem (5)

Personal Fear Scale:

11. How worried are you that someone will try to rob you or steal something from you when you are outside in this area?
    Always (4) Often (2) Sometimes (3) Rarely (4) Never (5)

12. How worried are you that someone will try to break into your home while someone is there?
    Always (4) Often (2) Sometimes (3) Rarely (4) Never (5)

13. How worried are you that someone will attack you or beat you up when you are outside in this area?
    Always (4) Often (2) Sometimes (3) Rarely (4) Never (5)

14. How worried are you that someone will try to steal or damage your car in this area?
    Always (4) Often (2) Sometimes (3) Rarely (4) Never (5)

15. How worried are you that someone will try to break into your house while no one is there?
    Always (4) Often (2) Sometimes (3) Rarely (4) Never (5)

Community Cohesion Scale:

16. If I were sick, I could count on my neighbors to shop for me at the supermarket, go to the drug store, etc.
    Strongly Disagree (1) Disagree (2) No Opinion (3) Agree (4) Strongly Agree (5)

17. When I am away from home, I can count on some of my neighbors to keep their eyes open for possible trouble.
    Strongly Disagree (1) Disagree (2) No Opinion (3) Agree (4) Strongly Agree (5)

18. If I had to borrow $25 for an emergency. I could turn to my neighbors.
    Strongly Disagree (1) Disagree (2) No Opinion (3) Agree (4) Strongly Agree (5)

19. The people in this area work together to solve problems.
    Strongly Disagree (1) Disagree (2) No Opinion (3) Agree (4) Strongly Agree (5)

20. I know several people in this area well enough to ask a favor.
    Strongly Disagree (1) Disagree (2) No Opinion (3) Agree (4) Strongly Agree (5)

Adapted from A.J. McKee (2001). "The Community Policing Evaluation Survey: Reliability, Validity, and Structure." *American Journal of Criminal Justice* 25:2, pp. 199-209.

In order to provide superiors with meaningful feedback, police officers should have sufficient training to perform the evaluation. In Whetstone's opinion, the officers should use a standard forced-choice instrument designed to provide structure and guide the rater in evaluating the attributes that the police department feels are most important.

While there are several commercially available upward-feedback rating forms on the market, Whetstone believes that departments may be ahead in the game by creating their own. In doing so, they can target the traits that are most important to them (see Figure 7.9).

The notion of supervisor evaluations sounds good, although some police officers are reluctant to support this concept for fear of some type of retaliation by those who receive negative appraisals. This fear, coupled with the "errors" discussed earlier in this chapter, could have an adverse effect on the objectivity of the evaluation and create morale problems. The success or failure of the upward-feedback program depends on management's commitment to the concept, as well as the safeguards built into the implementation process.

Whetstone argues that the police officers doing the evaluation should sign the rating form. This gives top management the opportunity, when necessary, to check with the evaluator on specific incidents used as the basis for the evaluation. He also recommends that the completed rating forms be turned in to a neutral evaluation proctor. In one pilot program, it was found that officer confidence, candor, and security increased when they were allowed to have meaningful input in the proctor selection process. Individual evaluations are held in total confidentiality, with the contents integrated in such a way as to produce a composite profile.

Upward-feedback programs are designed to promote more positive interaction between employees, provide top management with a new source of information about individual on-the-job performance by all police personnel, and aid in the career development of those who are involved in the process. Armed with knowledge (concerning their strengths and weaknesses), supervisors and administrators are in a position to adjust their leadership style to benefit subordinates, the police department, and themselves. The ultimate goal is self-improvement.

Even though bureaucratic inertia is well entrenched in police work, changes are in the air. The emerging emphasis on meaningful employee participation, total quality management, total quality results, community-oriented policing, and empowerment makes it a truly exciting time to be in law enforcement.

Summary

The success of any organization in accomplishing its mission, goals, and objectives depends in large measure on the quality of its personnel. This is particularly true when it comes to law enforcement. Police work is labor-intensive and is propelled by people power. According to human resources managers, personnel are the arms, legs, and mind of the police service.

Personnel development is a contemporary management strategy designed to produce a more efficient, effective, and productive workforce through proper use of available human resources. A comprehensive and objective performance evaluation process is the keystone in personnel development. Police sergeants play a central role in all aspects of performance evaluation and personnel development.

The performance evaluation process consists of an objective assessment, the appraisal interview, and remediation. Some type of follow-up completes the evaluation cycle and reactivates the entire process. Performance appraisal is an ongoing activity that works best when it is used on a daily basis. A valid, reliable, objective, and error-free performance assessment provides management with a database for effective decision making. Evaluation protocols, using graphic rating scales, critical incidents, goal acquisition, and behaviorally anchored rating techniques objectify the evaluation process and help the evaluator to focus on truly significant performance, as opposed to the subordinate's personality.

A work-centered performance evaluation process allows all of the participants (managers, supervisors, and employees) to formulate mutually acceptable goals, set realistic performance standards, and determine what remediation (in terms of training, coaching, counseling, and developmental experiences) the employee will need to reach those objectives. The evaluation process also helps to establish a plan designed to foster the police officer's personal growth and professional development.

Case Study

Sergeant Gina Thompson

Sergeant Gina Thompson is a 12-year veteran of the police department. She was promoted to sergeant six years ago and had been assigned to CID. She requested a change of assignment primarily because she missed patrol duty. She enjoyed investigations but found it a little boring and less challenging than patrol work. At least that is what she told her superiors. The fact of the matter was she simply liked the excitement of patrol better than investigations. While a detective, she did not have any supervisory duties. Now that she is back in uniform, she has a platoon of officers that she will have to supervise and evaluate on an annual basis.

Sergeant Thompson was assigned to Baker 3, a patrol zone in a low-income area of the city. It was made up of predominantly low-income government housing units. Two years ago, the department initiated a community policing program in Baker 3. Sergeant Thompson was instructed to increase the community policing efforts there. Because Sergeant Thompson was unfamiliar with supervisory duties, she had to familiarize herself with the performance evaluation process that she would now have to use with her platoon. The evaluation process was a graphic rating scale form that had been in use for as long as she could remember. It was the same form she had been evaluated on when she was a patrol officer.

Sergeant Thompson is concerned that the officers under her supervision will not score well on the old form. However, the officers have been very productive within the community and effective in bringing about a number of community changes that will ultimately benefit the police. The community has a different feel about it. Citizens are helping the police in their efforts rather than shying away from things they consider to be "police matters." The officers themselves seem to be enjoying their new relationship and partnership with the community, but the evaluation form does not measure these types of positive changes. In fact, the officers in Baker 3 may look worse, because the crime rate has increased in the area. The increased crime rate is the result of more arrests and citizens coming forward with information on criminal activity—a true measure that the community is beginning to trust and have faith in the police.

If you were Sergeant Thompson, how would you conduct the performance evaluations? What changes could you make that would reflect the true performance of these officers? What other types of evaluations might be a better measure of individual as well as group performance?

There are some exciting developments on the horizon. One is finding an effective performance evaluation protocol adaptable to the total quality management aspects of community-oriented policing (Cordner and Williams, 1999). We are also more likely to see increased emphasis on police officers evaluating the performance of supervisors and administrators.

The effectiveness of the performance evaluation process will be determined to a large degree by the talent, training, and human relations skills of men and women promoted to the rank of sergeant. As first-line supervisors, they set the tone, as well as manage and safeguard the integrity of the evaluative process. They maintain the quality of the workforce and determine the success or failure of the organization.

Key Concepts

appraisal interview

community-oriented policing

cycle of evaluation

employee assistance program (EAP)

errors

evaluating supervisor performance

evaluation interview

evaluative methods

follow-up

frequency of evaluation

goals and objectives

institutional support

Neighborhood-Oriented Policing (NOP)

objectivity, validity, reliability

objective assessment

participation and empowerment

performance appraisal

performance evaluation

performance measures

personnel and productivity

personnel development

remediation

roles and responsibilities

sources of error

supervisor's leading role

Discussion Topics and Questions

1. Why is performance appraisal now being emphasized by leading police management theorists?

2. What are some of the justifications for use of performance appraisals in police agencies?

3. Identify the components of the performance evaluation process. Why does the sergeant play such a critical role in performance appraisal?

4. Which of the evaluative methods described in the text do you favor? Why do you like this particular method as compared to the others?

5. To the best of your knowledge, what type of error influences you the most? What can you do to neutralize its influence?

6. How would you explain the difference between validity and reliability?

7. How would you, as a first-line supervisor, structure and conduct the evaluative interview to ensure that it will accomplish its purpose or purposes?

8. Why is follow-up such a critical element in the performance evaluation process?

9. What institutional resources are required to ensure that performance appraisals are done properly?

10. Should employees be given the opportunity to evaluate the performance of supervisors and other administrators? What basic principles did you consider in arriving at your conclusion?

11. What steps should be taken by top management to ensure that performance evaluation does not degenerate into "management by fear"?

For Further Reading

Bennett, Wayne W., and Kären M. Hess (2001). *Management and Supervision in Law Enforcement,* Third Edition. St. Paul, MN: West Publishing Company.

Contains a comprehensive chapter dealing with police performance appraisals as well as excellent advice on how to make sure they withstand legal scrutiny if challenged in court.

Brodeur, Jean-Paul (1998). *How to Recognize Good Policing: Problems and Issues*. Thousand Oaks, CA: Sage Publications.

Discusses evaluation of community policing efforts and offers direction for formulating evaluation methods for individual police performance as well as evaluating the efforts of the entire police agency.

Kappeler, Victor E. (2001). *Critical Issues in Police Civil Liability*, Third Edition. Prospect Heights, IL: Waveland Press, Inc.

Discusses civil liability based on administrative negligence or deliberate indifference. Demonstrates the consequences of management's failure to properly monitor performance and effectively supervise police personnel.

Roberg, Roy R., and Jack Kuykendall (1990). *Police Organization and Management*. Pacific Grove, CA: Brooks/Cole Publishing Company.

Explores performance appraisal in terms of evaluation categories, standards and measurements, and evaluation problems (errors). Performance appraisal is viewed, in a sense, as a component of the career enhancement process.

References

Behn, Robert D. (1994). "Motivating without Rewards: A Challenge to Public Managers." *Governing*, Vol. 7, No. 8.

Bittel, Lester R. (1993). *What Every Supervisor Should Know*, Seventh Edition. New York, NY: McGraw-Hill Book Company.

Bohlander, George W., Scott A. Snell, and Arthur W. Sherman, Jr. (2001). *Managing Human Resources*, Twelfth Edition. Cincinnati, OH: South-Western Publishing Company.

CALEA (2001). *Standards for Law Enforcement Agencies*, Fourth Edition. Fairfax, VA: Commission on Accreditation for Law Enforcement Agencies, Inc.

Cordner, Gary W., and Gerald Williams (1999). "Community Policing and Police Agency Accreditation." In Larry K. Gaines and Gary W. Cordner (eds.), *Policing Perspectives: An Anthology*. Los Angeles, CA: Roxbury Publishing Co.

Fulmer, Robert M. (1988). *The New Management*, Fourth Edition. New York, NY: Macmillan Publishing Co.

Gaines, Larry K., and Victor E. Kappeler (2003). *Policing in America*, Fourth Edition. Cincinnati, OH: Anderson Publishing Co.

Gaines, Larry K., Mittie D. Southerland, and John E. Angell (1991). *Police Administration*. New York, NY: McGraw-Hill Book Company.

Hamblin, Ken (1994). "Why the Surprise at Crime Bill's Catch-22?" *Denver Post*, Oct. 23: 3F.

Hilgert, Raymond L., and E. Leonard (2001). *Supervision: Concepts and Practices of Management*, Eighth Edition. Cincinnati, OH: South-Western Publishing Company.

Holt, David H. (1990). *Management: Principles and Practices*, Second Edition. Englewood Cliffs, NJ: Prentice-Hall, Inc.

Iannone, Nathan F., and Marvin Iannone (2001). *Supervision of Police Personnel*, Sixth Edition. Englewood Cliffs, NJ: Prentice-Hall, Inc.

Jones, Tony L. (1998). "Developing Performance Standards." *Law & Order*, Vol. 40, No. 7.

Kennish, John W. (1994). "Managing: Motivating with a Positive, Participatory Policy." *Security Management*, Vol. 38, No. 8.

Kramer, Michael (1998). "Designing an Individual Performance Evaluation System: A Values-Based Process." *FBI Law Enforcement Bulletin*, Vol. 67, No. 3.

Leonard, V.A. and Harry W. More (1993). *Police Organization and Management*, Eighth Edition. Westbury, NY: The Foundation Press, Inc.

McGaney, Robert, and Scott Smith (1993). "When Workers Rate the Boss." *Training*, Vol. 3, No. 1, March.

McKee, A.J. (2001). "The Community Policing Evaluation Survey: Reliabilty, Validity and Structure." *American Journal of Criminal Justice*, Vol. 25, No. 2.

National Advisory Commission on Criminal Justice Standards and Goals (1973). *The Police*. Washington, DC: U.S. Government Printing Office.

Plunkett, Richard W. (1992). *Supervision: The Direction of People at Work*, Sixth Edition. Boston, MA: Allyn and Bacon, Inc.

Robbins, Stephen P. (1989). *Organizational Behavior*, Fourth Edition. Englewood Cliffs, NJ: Prentice-Hall, Inc.

Steinmetz, Lawrence L., and H. Ralph Todd, Jr. (1992). *Supervision: First-Line Management*, Fifth Edition. Boston, MA: Richard D. Irwin, Inc.

Swanson, Charles R., Leonard Territo, and Robert W. Taylor (1993). *Police Administration*, Third Edition. New York, NY: Macmillan Publishing Co.

Travis, Jeremy, and John Brann (1997). "Measuring What Matters: Developing Measures of What the Police Do." *National Institute of Justice Research in Action*. Washington, DC: U.S. Department of Justice.

Trojanowicz, Robert G. (1980). *The Environment of the First-Line Police Supervisor*. Englewood Cliffs, NJ: Prentice-Hall, Inc.

U.S. Department of Justice (2001). *Sourcebook of Criminal Justice Statistics*. Washington, DC: Bureau of Justice Statistics.

Walsh, William F., and Edwin J. Donovan (1990). *The Supervision of Police Personnel: A Performance-Based Approach*. Dubuque, IA: Kendall/Hunt Publishing Company.

Whetstone, Thomas S. (1994). "Subordinates Evaluate Supervisory and Administrative Performance." *The Police Chief*, Vol. LXI, No. 6.

Whisenand, Paul M., and George E. Rush (2001). *Supervising Police Personnel*, Fourth Edition. Englewood Cliffs, NJ: Prentice-Hall, Inc.

Wycoff, Mary Ann, and Timothy N. Oettmeier (1994). *Evaluating Patrol Officer Performance Under Community Policing: The Houston Experience*. Washington, DC: National Institute of Justice.

Team Building—

Maximizing the Group Process　　8

Introductory Case Study

Sergeant Debra McDonald

Debra McDonald has been with the department for seven years. She was assigned to patrol immediately after graduation from the academy. There she served under a field training officer (FTO) who assisted her considerably in adapting to the reality of street policing. After four years she was promoted to sergeant and assigned to the jail, which was a normal assignment for newly promoted sergeants. Three years later she was transferred back to the uniformed division. Sergeant McDonald accepted her jail assignment in stride, but she was really looking forward to returning to a field position. She was assigned to the midnight shift in a moderately high-crime area, and her sector has an exceptionally high number of calls for service. Departmental goals for the current fiscal year were:

1. Respond to life-threatening incidents within five minutes (90 percent of the incidents).

2. Respond to emergency calls within 10 minutes (90 percent of the incidents).

3. Respond to calls requiring a police presence within 30 minutes (90 percent of the incidents).

During the first half of the year, the team to which she had been assigned had the poorest response time when compared to other sector teams. This was especially true for responses to emergency situations and calls requiring a police presence. Regarding the response time to life-threatening situations, team officers had the best response time in the department (93 percent of the incidents). Some team members felt that responding to life-threatening situations was *real* police work and other

---

duties were clearly secondary. Sergeant McDonald had requested data from a crime prevention specialist and had information regarding the performance of the nine members of her team for the last six months.

Members of the team had an average of three years of patrol service, with two members having more than five years' service. Departmental policy was such that officers remained on the midnight shift until openings were available on either of the other two shifts. Overall officers assigned to this late shift had been on the shift for six years and under normal circumstances could anticipate assignment to the swing shift after nine years of police service unless they received an assignment to a specialized unit.

Sergeant McDonald spent the first month in her new assignment becoming acquainted with each of the nine team members. The majority of the officers accepted her as a new supervisor but seemed to take a position of waiting to see how things would work out. She briefly discussed the problem with the response time to each of the specified categories, and in general the officers felt that they were complying with departmental policy. Several officers expressed the belief that they could probably improve, but thought that it was essential for all members of the team to work together. The team was viewed as a coalition rather than a team. Several officers expressed the belief that they could accomplish more by working independently.

If you were Sergeant McDonald, what would you do next? Why? If you decide to hold a team meeting, what items would you have for an agenda? Would you include members other than those on the team? Why or why not? How would you go about getting the officers to work as a team?

Exceptional management on the part of first-line supervisors is the catalyst that creates an effective team. This is especially true because the first-line supervisor is at the focal point of translating departmental goals into reality. Group dynamics are an actuality in a police organization. They will not go away and must be dealt with if the organization is to function effectively. When dealing with human behavior as a supervisor in a police organization, it is of foremost importance to acquire an understanding and working knowledge of group dynamics. Generally speaking, everyone has been involved with different groups, such as the family, church, school, clubs, or the military. Some of these groups are highly structured, and others are informal and loosely organized. Some have had a substantial impact on the individual, while others have had a limited influence.

An effective supervisor is one who has taken the time to become aware of group processes. It is impossible to ignore groups in a law enforcement agency. They are a meaningful and indispensable component of the organization. The interrelationships between groups within an organization can be exceedingly complex and can influence effectiveness.

A group consists of two or more people who interact with and influence each other for a common purpose. Two factors are important to the definition of a group: (1) interaction and (2) influence. The interaction of group members can be either extensive or limited. It can be based on a close interrelationship between two or more officers, or it can be distant to the point where there is no face-to-face contact. Even if there is some degree of contact between members, it might turn out that body language will prove to be the most important variable in the group process.

The second component of our definition is influence, and its impact may range from limited to extensive. Such factors as position power, rank, experience, reputation, or expertise generate influence. Individuals seldom exhibit behavior not influenced by the group to which they belong. For many, individual success depends on one's ability to get along within the group.

The Individual

Socialization into the police agency is the means by which rookies are transformed from civilian status to productive members of an operating agency. It is the means by which the new employee is indoctrinated into (and acquires the values and norms of) the organization. The police culture, or in the case of some police organizations, a subculture, sets the norms that guide the behavior of police officers. They are the truths that officers feel in their bones—the touchstones that rule their attitudes and behavior (Gaffigan and McDonald, 1997). Furthermore, the police, for the most part, subscribe to specific values that set them apart from the public at large (Kappeler, Sluder, and Alpert, 1994).

For the majority of officers, the police occupation is not only demanding, but also requires a positive identification with the police task and fellow police officers. This can occur even to the point where there is a degree of paranoia and the job becomes one of "them or us." The police view themselves as the thin blue line against the world.

The job itself socializes the officer because it is highly circumscribed by law. The law underpins the vast majority of action taken by officers. It serves as a foundation for interpreting citizen conduct and justifying police actions. The law is the focal point for police actions, and there is a powerful normative pull through the socialization process (Herbert, 1998). If that is not enough, there are always policies, rules, and regulations tending to influence beliefs, attitudes, values, and actual behavior. Additionally, the organizational structure designates a formal reporting relationship between groups and individuals and facilitates communications (Johnson, 1994).

The new candidate for a police position interacts with the police social system from the point of initial contact when applying for a position through the socialization occurring throughout one's career. In the traditional organization the new employee is expected to adjust to the organization—under no circumstances is the organization allowed to adjust to the individual. This reinforces the customs and traditions of each department. The police have a distinctive job-related vocabulary. Officers are expected to remain unruffled and composed in highly stressful situations. Violations of the folkways can result in negative reaction by other members of the department.

The officer adapts to the police value system, and this is the only acceptable conduct allowed. In other words, this obedience is the price that must be paid in order to become a member of the organization. The agency will generally require officers to acquire norms, values, and specific behaviors that emerge from their inculcation into the organization. Officers within some agencies have been found to have a number of strong beliefs, which are set forth in the following figure. Each of these items can have a significant impact on the group process.

Figure 8.1
Significant Beliefs of the Police Culture

1. The real crime fighters are the police.
2. Only a police officer can understand the reality of police work.
3. The most important value is loyalty.
4. The war against crime can only be won by bending the rules.
5. The least desirable job is working in patrol.

Source: *Beyond 911: A New Era for Policing* by Malcolm K. Sparrow, Mark H. Harrison, and David M. Kennedy. Copyright © 1990 by Basic Books, Inc. Reprinted by permission of Basic Books, a member of Perseus Books, L.L.C.

A significant mindset of the police culture is that the police are the true crime fighters in our society and that members of the public do not support the police effort. In fact, most members of the public are viewed as being antagonistic. Additionally, many line officers express the belief that a police officer is the only one who can understand and appreciate the reality of working the street. In general, even police management is viewed as being divorced from the actuality of what is really going on when interpreting and applying the law to genuine situations. This is viewed as being especially true when police managers have been removed from operations for more than four years. Many line officers value discretion and believe they are in the best position to interpret the law and should be allowed to bend the rules in their view of what should be done to protect society. Finally, except for a few departments, specialized assignments such as investigations are highly sought after, and many officers think that patrol is the least desirable assignment.

The police academy is a significant point in the new officer's career socialization process, because this is where identity with the occupation is emphasized (Bahn, 1984). In the academy, conformity is emphasized throughout the process, and new officers are molded in such a way as to become the visible expression of the ideal cop. It is somewhat of a cookie-cutter mentality in which the candidate is expected to dress appropriately, accept authority, never criticize the agency, and become a member of the team. Expression of individuality is rejected. There is usually one best way to do things—the way it is taught at the academy. Historically, police academy training was adopted from the military model that emphasized loyalty, discipline, and conformity. In recent years, some agencies have shifted to a more academic model of training, blending it with the traditional paramilitary training (Weinblatt, 1999).

On completion of the academy, the officer may be coached by a field training officer (FTO) or at least by a senior officer (Molden, 1998). Field training officers can either support organizational value systems or pass on their own cultural norms. This can bring into play the old adage "Forget everything you learned in the academy, this is the real world" (Johnson, 1993). Thus the socialization process continues and the norms of the agency are emphasized. At the same time, the peer value system comes into play. This, in some instances, is where new police officers are told, "Now that you are in the real world, this is how we actually do things rather than the way you were taught in the academy." Identification with the department, rather than with the community, serves to isolate the officer and reinforce police solidarity.

In recent years there seems to have been less organizational effectiveness in promoting and reinforcing a strong and viable police identity. Several reasons have been suggested to explain why the current recruits are not adjusting to the agency as they have in the past. First, it is seldom possible for every member to go along with all the group norms (Cohen et al., 1992). Next, the average recruit today is older and, in many instances, has more work experience and education. Third, the standards for entry into the field have been modified by affirmative action, so the ethnic mix of some departments has changed drastically. Finally, the recruitment of women is altering a previously male-dominated occupation. Each factor contributes in varying degrees to the impact of the individual's socialization process and to the perceived weakening of the police identity.

Even though there is an indication that the identity of the individual to the department is not as strong as in the past, it is still an important factor because it is a means of building commitment and creating a feeling of loyalty to the department. Esprit de corps and high morale are by-products of the socialization process. Thus, the more committed the individual becomes to the agency, the sooner the possibility that he or she will become a full-fledged member of the organization.

The Individual and the Group

In the day-to-day work environment, the police officer will often work alone. However, police departments are becoming increasingly aware of the benefits to be obtained from the use of groups of officers formed to operate in a team, a task force, a quality control circle, or certain aspects of community policing. Healthy groups can satisfy officer needs in many ways, including association, friendship, recognition, and self-esteem.

A police department is a social organization, and by creating groups, a sense of belonging can develop, there is an attachment to the agency, and officers have a sense of stability. An individual can find that the group becomes a social anchor. Groups are not automatically more effective than individuals when performing certain tasks. Everyone is aware of the cliché "too many cooks can spoil the broth." Thus, there are some situations in which the group approach to problem solving is best, and other instances in which an individual effort will prove most effective. Certainly most of us are more comfortable working with friends and associates. In a group, some of the members become leaders and others become followers. These roles can change as expertise becomes operational and new situations occur. Groups can generate motivational energy that becomes synergistic in nature. As officers become involved in team efforts that result in positive experiences, self-esteem is reinforced (Haasen, 1997).

Some police tasks are accomplished most effectively by a joint response to the situation. Barricaded individuals, an armed robbery in progress, or house-to-house searches for a lost child are examples. It would be difficult to accomplish such tasks in any way other than a coordinated group effort.

In this approach to management, it is the primary responsibility of a supervisor to achieve results through people. It is impossible for a good supervisor to perform all tasks without the assistance of others. Thus, interaction with others to obtain positive results is imperative. In this context the human being is important, and the supervisor can have a positive influence on the individual and their work effectiveness as a part of a group. A positive leader excels in obtaining active individual involvement, bringing commitment to achieving both unit and departmental goals.

As the law enforcement function has become increasingly complex, the supervisor soon discovers a lack of knowledge in some areas; therefore, every decision may not be correct. Interaction with other units, such as tactical, traffic, or the investigative division, requires the supervisor to depend on their information and knowledge if goals are to be attained. Interaction is essential (especially if the decision affects more than one unit of the organization), and both individual and group knowledge must be tapped if the best decision is to be made.

Unquestionably, some individuals have difficulty adapting to groups due to personality, the specific situation, or even variables unknown to the supervisor. Officers within a group perform a number of social roles. The exact role will vary from group to group, depending on the tasks being performed, the nature of the group, and the situation confronting the group. The most common social roles are set forth in Figure 8.2.

Figure 8.2
Social Roles within a Group

1.	Leader
2.	Follower
3.	Expert
4.	Enforcer
5.	Facilitator
6.	Devil's advocate
7.	Scapegoat

Source: *Behavioral Police Management* by Harry W. More and W. Fred Wegener. Copyright © 1992. Reprinted by permission of Pearson Education, Inc., Upper Saddle River, NJ.

Not all of these roles will be played out in every group, but they recur enough to be of special interest to every supervisor. The facilitator can be especially useful in promoting compromise and consensus-building. On the other hand, the devil's advocate will question every suggestion or management decision and, if left to run amok, will destroy the effectiveness of the group. The supervisor should work diligently to ensure that the failure of the group does not reflect on any particular member of the group, resulting in scapegoating. The expert should be allowed to bring his or her relevant skills to the decision-making process of the group. Finally, the enforcer can stabilize a group by seeing that group norms and values are understood. This typology allows the supervisor to analyze the dynamics of a group.

Nevertheless, a reduction in conflict between the individual and the organization must always be the goal. When considering the relationship between the individual and the group, the supervisor should consider the following (Cartwright and Lippitt, 1957):

- Groups, both formal and informal, will always exist within an organization.

- Groups can become power centers that will have an important impact on the agency.

- Groups can be both destructive and supportive.

- An understanding of group dynamics will enhance the achievement of goals.

The individual is an essential part of the group. The more knowledge a supervisor accumulates about each member of the group, the greater the opportunity for effective work with the group. A supervisor should review personnel files and interview other supervisors and officers who have worked with potential candidates for a group effort. Emphasis should be placed on finding individuals who can contribute to the achievement of team goals. Additionally, consideration should be given to finding people who have a positive attitude and will mesh well with the rest of the team. The supervisor should also look for good communicators and those willing to share responsibilities (Eng and Hummel, 1997). Time spent in the selection process will yield an abundance of rewards.

Role and Function of the Group

If a supervisor is to understand how an organization actually operates, it is essential to develop an acute awareness of how a group functions. This is especially critical for the first-line supervisor position. While a great deal of a sergeant's time is spent with individual officers, it must be kept in mind that those officers belong to one or more groups. When a supervisor understands the interaction between individuals and groups, it will (in all probability) lead to more effective problem solving (Gray, 1984). When considering organizational behavior, groups can usually be described as either formal or informal.

Formal Groups

Formal work groups are those created and supported by the organization for the express purpose of fulfilling specific organizational needs or performing special tasks. These groups can be either temporary or permanent, depending on the needs of the organization. A shift of officers under the supervision of a sergeant is an excellent example of a command group or team. Another example is a group created to function as a sting operation for purchasing stolen property. This undercover operation culminates with the arrest and prosecution of the accused.

The assignment of officers to a special traffic detail—conducting a sobriety checkpoint in an effort to identify impaired drivers—is another example of a work group set up by the organization and then dissolved after its task has been accomplished (NHTSA, 2001).

Another type of formal work group that is becoming increasingly common in law enforcement is the *task force*. It is usually a temporary group formed to achieve a specific objective or perform a specific task. In recent years police departments have set up special task forces to apprehend fugitives. In some instances, task forces have involved the coordinated efforts of more than one agency (Buhler, 1999).

Narcotics task forces are being used increasingly in joint efforts, normally within a county, and usually are formed on a permanent basis. It has been estimated that there are more than 1,000 multijurisdictional antidrug task forces in the United States. Temporary task forces have been used to deal with a wide range of problems, including the development of policies or the creation of rules and regulations. In one instance, a task force consisting of nine members from various units and levels of the organization was chaired by a lieutenant with the purpose of determining when an officer should or should not wear a hat while in uniform.

Informal Groups

Formal work groups are quite obvious to any new employee, but it can take some time before one can identify informal groups. In many instances, these groups have never been sanctioned by the formal organization. It is also interesting to note that informal groups cut across organizational lines—rank is usually not important when forming an informal group. For example, an informal group can be composed of individuals who have a common interest, such as pistol shooting, who get together for the pure enjoyment of the sport. The department does not sanction this group.

Informal groups form quite naturally and according to personal preferences. Officers will establish a variety of personal relationships as they search for a means of fulfilling their needs. Informal groups evolve as a result of the inability of the formal organization to meet all social or departmental officer requirements. Such groups can work to support or not to support the formal organization.

Workers become members of informal groups for various reasons, such as to improve working conditions or to obtain equipment to enhance job performance. In one department, a group of officers worked together in an effort to set up a shift rotation system rather than the current seniority-based system. Some might argue, then, that the majority of police unions evolved from informal groups.

Informal groups have also often proven to be the most supportive of the formal organization. This is particularly noticeable when officers assist each other in performing tasks that are supposed to be performed by another officer, or when they have shown there is a better way of doing something. One observer pointed out that in many instances, if it were not for such activities, the organization would undoubtedly perform less effectively.

Another informal group can be based solely upon social needs for friendship and interaction with others. Such a relationship can effectively support task accomplishment, reduce absenteeism, and elevate job satisfaction. On the other hand, the social interaction between members of a group can occur to such an extent that it distracts them from getting work done. One of the most common examples is the coffee or smoke break, suddenly extending from a 15-minute break to 20 minutes and then 30 minutes. In other instances, officers congregate at certain eating establishments for coffee or meal breaks and there are so many police vehicles in the parking lot that it almost looks like a police substation.

There are some informal groups that control the rate of production. This seems to occur most often in such areas as the number of field interrogations performed by an officer or the number of traffic citations issued. Take note of those who work too hard or whose production clearly exceeds the norm for a shift of officers constantly interacting. There is nothing wrong with competition, but one should never do anything to make another officer look bad. The group will bring pressure on anyone who does not abide by the accepted code of behavior. Punishment of nonconforming officers usually takes the form of excluding them from after-hours social events (Cohen et al., 1992).

Informal groups can evolve into *cliques*—something a supervisor should be aware of. Cliques can easily lead to misunderstandings and hostility (Gastil, 1993). Cliques generally fall into one of three categories: vertical, horizontal, or random.

Vertical Cliques. This type of clique generally occurs in one unit of the police department, such as patrol or investigation. The relationship is generally between the first-line supervisor and subordinate officers.

The supervisor in this type of clique does everything possible to assist and protect underlings. When it is necessary to demand something from an officer, the request is temporized as much as possible. When errors are made, they are disregarded or everything possible is done to minimize the problem. The goal is to humanize the organization and reduce friction between the department and the officers.

This clique is not a one-way street. The officers also look out for the welfare of the first-line supervisor. If there is a threatening situation, the supervisor is made aware of the incident immediately. For example, when a manager of higher rank appears unannounced, the word is instantly relayed back to the supervisor. Officers also apprise the sergeant of all situations that might cause trouble or generate waves, such as any type of occurrence to which the press will respond.

Horizontal Cliques. This type of clique cuts across departmental lines and will normally include a number of first-line supervisors. This clique will function either defensively or offensively depending on the situation and the nature of the threat. If the threat is imminent, the clique will take an aggressive posture, but such groups prefer to work defensively because of the bureaucratic nature of most police departments. The horizontal clique functions effectively under most circumstances because of the experience its members have acquired from working within the bureaucracy.

This clique functions most effectively when it is dealing with problems perceived as weakening someone's authority or creating some type of change that is viewed as inimical to its members' welfare. New policies that erode operational authority are always suspect. This might include instituting new review procedures when making felony arrests and reducing the first-line supervisor's power. The expansion of controls from above is considered fair game in terms of the type of issue with which this clique should be concerned.

The horizontal clique generally assumes a defensive posture and functions only when the situation dictates that it must respond to ensure the status quo. It is generally more powerful than the vertical clique and can be used effectively by a first-line supervisor when the issue is of general interest. This is especially true when it involves such issues as a reduction in authority, an expansion of review procedures, a significant reorganization, or a reduction in force.

Random Cliques. This type of clique bears no similarity to the other two types of cliques. Rank, role, and unit assignments have no bearing in terms of its membership. Officers become members primarily to exchange information. There is no effort by its members to strive for a change in working conditions, just a basic desire to associate with other members of the department.

In most departments, members of this clique are not active members of either horizontal or vertical cliques. The random clique proves to be important to the first-line supervisor because it is usually the primary source of rumors. It can be used to pass on information or as an information source. It serves a highly important function by intensifying social relationships within the department. The officers who get together at the end of the shift for a beer or a meal are an excellent illustration of a random clique.

Group Development Process

As a newly organized group evolves, it passes through six stages: orientation, conflict and challenge, cohesion, delusion, disillusion, and acceptance (Jewell and Reitz, 1981). In some instances the process can be rather fast, but in other situations the evolution from stage one to stage six might never occur. It all depends on a number of variables, including difficulty of the task, the maturity of the group, and the time and resources allocated to the group (see Figure 8.3).

The initial stage, *orientation*, can be most crucial to the group's success. Thus, the supervisor should do everything possible to properly prepare for the first meeting to ensure that as many members as possible are aware of the ground rules. Questions such as "Who is the head of the group?" "What procedures are to be followed?" and "Why does this group exist?" need to be answered in order to clarify ground rules. New members of a group want to know what is going on and what is expected of them.

Figure 8.3
Group Development Stages

Number	Stage
1	Orientation
2	Conflict and challenge
3	Cohesion
4	Delusion
5	Disillusion
6	Acceptance

Source: Linda N. Jewell and H. Joseph Reitz (1981). *Group Effectiveness in Organizations.* Glenview, IL: Scott Foresman. Reprinted with permission of H. Joseph Reitz.

The *conflict and challenge* stage may occur almost immediately and is a result of the ambiguity arising in any group. It is normal to anticipate that the leader of the group will be challenged as procedures for conducting meetings are agreed upon, as potential decisions are discussed, and as resource allocation is considered. A supervisor should work diligently at handling conflict in a constructive manner (Eng and Hummel, 1997). Conflict should not be swept under the table or ignored. Handling conflict takes time, and effort spent at this point can be highly beneficial.

Stage three is *cohesion* and occurs when each member of the group has received enough information to accept group objectives and leadership as legitimate. If the problem to be considered and resolved by a group is controversial, or if the group is highly polarized, cohesion might never occur. But if a great deal of care is taken when the composition of the group is decided, the potential for reaching stage three will be enhanced. Creating a working relationship in which employees feel their values can enhance cohesiveness resulting in organizational alignment (Kouzes and Posner, 1993).

Stage four, *delusion*, is the point at which uncertainty enters the picture. Members of the group become aware of the fact that everything is not moving smoothly and that in fact the group has numerous interpersonal problems. In some instances, members will go along with the group even though they disagree with the way things are being handled. Others will take the position that it is of no use to fight it, because they cannot change anything anyway.

Stage five, *disillusion*, concerns a process by which members of the group fully accept that they are on a treadmill and are going nowhere. There is a polarization between members who want to confront issues and others who resist the process. It is at this point that strong leadership must exert itself—issues should be clarified and differences resolved. The supervisor should do everything possible to see that this stage is passed through with the least amount of disruption and divisive turmoil.

The last stage is *acceptance*. It is the point at which a newly organized group interacts positively as it strives to achieve its assigned goals. If the supervisor remains positive throughout the developmental process, the group will arrive at this stage more quickly and with less trauma. The supervisor should focus on the benefits of working as a group, such as how much more can be achieved through a team effort and the fact that every member can benefit from the expertise of other team members. A supervisor who is positively focused can generate the enthusiasm needed to ensure team success.

Group Norms

As a group evolves from the interaction of its members, group norms come into play. Norms are the techniques members of a group develop as a way of controlling the behavior of others. As members interact, initial norms are developed that specify the way members should conduct themselves. Members of a group soon learn the difference between acceptable and unacceptable behavior.

A supervisor constantly responds to group norms and must deal with the conduct they generate. Undeniably, norms exert a strong influence over an individual's conduct. If officers are to perform effectively, they must have some common areas of agreement on which to base their attitudes, values, and perceptions. In the absence of norms, the guidance necessary for success is nonexistent.

Norms are unwritten, but in many instances are more influential than organizational rules and regulations. Norms strongly influence conduct because they are backed by the power of the group in terms of some type of sanction when the situation calls for it. They not only set forth the type of acceptable behavior, but also include the group's value judgment as to what is permissible and whether something is right or wrong.

Norms come into existence because of social interaction of the members of the group. In most instances, norms are not established by any formal process, nor are they consciously decided. Norms provide continuity in the work environment—the predictability of behavior that leads to a feeling of well-being, and the carrying out of routine procedures without disruption. A realistic evaluation of the importance of the group should lead to awareness by the supervisor of each member's importance and the fact that groups have a definite impact on the behavior of each and every member.

Law Enforcement Norms

The identification of the norms in any particular agency proves to be difficult because certain departments will have some of the operational norms listed below, while other departments will have all these norms as well as others not identified here.

Figure 8.4
Law Enforcement Norms

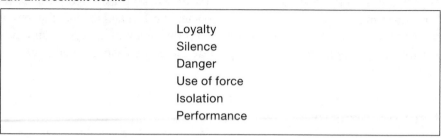

Loyalty
Silence
Danger
Use of force
Isolation
Performance

Loyalty. Most police departments have a quasi-military structure, and the chain of command mentality is strongly entrenched (Johnson, 1994). Consequently, police departments exact a strong degree of loyalty from all members, including non-sworn personnel. Extensive rules and regulations serve to reinforce this norm, and specific sanctions apply to those who deviate from the expected behavior. Loyalty is demanded in terms of every action and reaction. Nonconformists are ostracized both formally and informally. Under most circumstances, loyalty applies to the police at large and is not restricted to the department to which an individual belongs. In other words, loyalty is to the profession first. This is apparent in instances in which the investigation of a fellow officer is mishandled in order to shield that officer and prevent untimely publicity. This occurred in Tucson, Arizona, during the investigation of a DUI (driving under the influence) case in which a captain was involved in a one-vehicle accident. As a result of the mishandling of the case, an assistant chief and a sergeant were demoted and three other officers were suspended. The chief took the position that the officers handled the investigation without regard to their training and experience (Burchell and Sandal, 1998). This is clearly a case of misplaced loyalty to a fellow officer.

In Oakland, California, a small group of officers known as the "Riders" enforced the law by planting evidence and beating suspects. All four of the officers involved were fired. One is currently a fugitive, and the other three have been charged with 34 felonies and misdemeanors. Prosecutors have thrown out more than 60 cases handled by the "Riders." Rookie officers were pressured to sign reports indicating criminal activities they never witnessed. One of the "Riders" stated:

> "F— probable cause and everything you learned in the academy." "If you're a coward, I'll terminate you." If you're a snitch, I'll beat you myself and if you're a criminal, I'll put you in handcuffs, and put you in the back of the car and put you in jail myself" (Read, 2001).

Silence. The socialization process within a police department makes it abundantly clear that the Code of Silence is operational at all times and under no circumstances will officers discuss police procedures with outsiders or tell them how they cope with the demands of the occupation. While department policy may control conduct, the norm of secrecy coupled with that of loyalty dictates that one officer will never inform on another officer. This is true even though it might involve brutality by an officer. The secrecy norm even extends to all police incidents, and one officer *never* turns in another for sloppy work, sleeping on the job, delaying response to a call for service, or failing to perform his or her duties.

When the code of silence is operational, it forces officers to cover up crimes committed by other officers—even when the crime is an act they strongly disapprove of. In addition, officers will feel the need to falsify records and perjure themselves when the code is defended from the investigation of wrongdoing.

What is also troubling about the code of silence is its pervasiveness when it comes to corruption. There are grave consequences for violating the code. Officers who report misconduct can be ostracized and harassed. They can become targets of complaints and even physical threats. Additionally, they can be left alone on the street in a time of crisis. A former New York City police officer testified:

Question: Were you ever afraid that one of your fellow officers might turn you in?
Answer: Never.

Question: Why not?
Answer: Because it was the Blue Wall of Silence. Cops don't tell on cops. And if they tell on them, just say if a cop decided to tell on me, his career's ruined. He's going to be labeled as a rat. So if he's got fifteen more years to go on the job, he's going to be miserable, because it follows you wherever you go. And chances are if it comes down to it, they're going to let him get hurt (Mollen, 1994).

This same conduct has been reported in the Los Angeles Police Department, where a former LAPD whistleblower pointed out:

When an officer finally gets fed up and comes forward to speak the truth, that will mark the end of his or her police career. The police profession will not tolerate it and civil authorities will close their eyes when the retaliatory machine comes down on the officer (Chemerinsky et al., 2000).

Danger. From the first day at the academy through the termination of supervision by a field training officer (FTO), the dangers of police work are continually emphasized. This is done in order to combat complacency, but to such an extent that many officers perceive almost every situation as potentially dangerous. Officers can make numerous vehicle stops without incident, and the next stop might result in a violent confrontation. Danger is reinforced by the social interaction between officers, and it can reach the point where officers view the majority of the public with some degree of suspicion. This suspicion tends to strengthen the kinship felt between police officers. Policing occurs in a dangerous work environment. During the 17-year period from 1976 to 1998, an average of 79 police officers were murdered each year in the line of duty. To put it another way, one out of 11,000 officers was murdered (Brown and Langan, 2001). The number of local, state, and federal officers killed in 1998 was 61 (Federal Bureau of Investigation, 1998). Sixteen officers were slain in arrest situations, and the same number were slain while responding to disturbance calls. Most disturbing of all was the fact that 10 officers were murdered in ambush situations. Furthermore, 78 officers were accidentally killed during the same year. The majority of the latter group were killed in automobile, motorcycle, and aircraft accidents (Federal Bureau of Investigation, 2001). A statistic that is of concern to many is that since 1980, 42 percent of officer deaths could have been prevented if the officers had been wearing body armor (Knight and Brierley, 1998).

Additionally, 59,545 officers were assaulted during 1998, and 26.6 percent of those officers were injured. Law enforcement is a dangerous occupation, and even an arrest for an apparently minor infraction can result in a felonious assault against a police officer. All members of law enforcement agencies, especially supervisors, should prepare those they supervise to be aware of the risks and guide them in actively responding to the risk in order to ensure their safety (Pinizzotto, Davis, and Miller, 1998).

Use of Force. The only government agent that routinely has the authority to use physical force against citizens is the police. Although there has been a significant reduction in violent crimes during the last decade, we are still a violent society and unfortunately police officers take lives. It has been estimated that the police killed 600 suspects, wounded approximately 1,200, and fired on 3,600 (Geller, 1992). From 1976 to 1998, 8,578 felons were justifiably killed by police in the United States (Brown and Langan, 2001). Most use of deadly force occurs at night, in public locations within high-crime areas of large cities. These incidents often involve on-duty, uniformed officers firing at suspects in the crime-prone age range of 17 to 30 (More, 1998).

During a five-year period in Atlanta, there were 267 total shots-fired incidents. Fifty-four civilians were shot, with 28 killed. During the same five-year period in Houston there were 314 shooting incidents, with 94 citizens injured and 54 killed. Houston is much larger than Atlanta, but the size of the city is only one variable that is considered when attempting to analyze the use of deadly force. Other variables, such as the nature and extent of crime in each city and policy governing the use of force, must also be considered (Geller, 1992).

In Los Angeles, California, 700 shooting incidents were reviewed, resulting in one-half of the officers being retrained and one-quarter being punished by reprimand, suspension, or dismissal. The remainder (one-quarter) of shooting incidents warranted no action (*Los Angeles Times*, 1994). With these statistics in mind, it is essential that the first-line supervisor be on the alert for subordinates engaging in activities that might result in the nonessential use of force. As incidents are reviewed by shooting boards, supervisors should pass that information on to officers in order to minimize the number of shooting errors.

The overall concern with officer safety is a major characteristic of some police departments and determines how officers respond to specific calls in which danger can be anticipated. This is especially true when a community has areas that are perceived as antipolice. In these parts of the community, the antennas go up immediately and safety becomes paramount. Officers become more cautious, more observant, and are more apt to wait for backup. Safety governs every move, with the goal of preserving the well-being and life of responding officers. Additionally, responding officers are especially concerned with obtaining all the information they can about the location and possible occupants so that they can make the best possible decision on how to approach and enter a dwelling or business. Of special concern is whether the subjects in question are armed or whether they have a police record. Other important information includes the frequency of response to a specific location and previous action taken by responding officers. All of these actions are taken to ensure officer and citizen safety (Herbert, 1998).

Isolation. Law enforcement, as an occupation, leads to isolation from the community. Many view the police as a necessary evil. When you need them, they are never there, and when you commit a traffic infraction or violate a minor ordinance, they are always there. Officers soon conclude that their work usually is not appreciated and that the public they are supposed to protect is uncaring. This leads officers to turn inward for recognition and support. In time, many officers limit their socialization to other officers and their families. The more they are rejected by members of the community, the more they turn to their job and the police social system. Isolation reinforces clannishness and occupational solidarity. Additionally, the shifts that many officers work preclude them from interacting with non-police personnel, and much of their social life revolves around other officers and their families.

Insularity erects protective barriers between the police and the public and creates an "us versus them" mentality. Far too many officers see the public as a source of trouble rather than as the people they are sworn to serve. This mentality starts when impressionable recruits and rookies are led by veteran officers to believe that the ordinary citizen fails to appreciate the police and that their safety depends solely on their fellow officers. Consequently, officers learn early that they must protect themselves from the public (Mollen, 1994). In the Los Angeles Police Department, it has been reported that there is a siege mentality that justifies excluding those who are not a part of the department from evaluating or criticizing it (Chemerinsky et al., 2000).

Performance. The police are no different from other working groups in the sense that they have working norms that officers accept. In most instances it is not a question of restricting productivity, because the dispatcher usually dictates the workload. In large cities the demand is such that calls for service of a nonemergency nature are stacked until an officer can respond. Within this context, officers can control the number of cases they handle by being exceedingly meticulous when completing reports. Officers know what other officers are doing, so norms affecting performance come into existence. At other times, officers on the midnight shift will find the work flow very slow; thus, patrol can become exceedingly monotonous. In this situation, officers will take long meal breaks, numerous coffee breaks, sleep if the opportunity presents itself, or leave their beat to socialize with other officers. In other instances, officers will violate department policy and congregate at certain eating establishments. One officer will advise another as to what is acceptable and what is not acceptable in terms of personal and work performance. The more cohesive the group, the greater the possibility that productivity will be controlled by establishing tolerance levels (Cohen et al., 1992).

Group Performance

A supervisor's attitude toward the group and its ability to perform is critical to its success and the attainment of departmental objectives. If working with a group is viewed as forcing one to conform and is a process by which one loses identity or is never allowed to excel, then it is a group doomed to failure.

There is no doubt that problems must be faced and dealt with before a group can become effective, but it should be accepted as a challenge. This is best accomplished by cultivating a positive attitude toward groups. They should be viewed as a tool for bringing collective judgment together for the purpose of solving problems.

Exceptional performance can occur when the group uses its resources effectively and each officer is motivated to achieve. Groups have the potential for greater productivity for several reasons, including allowing officers to specialize and use their own unique skills.

Groups serve as a vehicle for enhancing personal relationships, because social needs are more easily satisfied. Furthermore, as a group develops and becomes more close-knit, members of the group will obtain status. As they become more productive, recognition will be received from the group.

Cohesiveness can be important to the group and is the result of the officer's desire to be a member of the group and the degree of commitment felt by group members. If individuals satisfy their needs in a group, the group becomes something the officers seek out so they can become members. A group generating a high degree of cohesiveness finds that its members are more loyal, readily identify with the group, accept group decisions, and are more apt to conform to group norms. Group cohesiveness becomes evident when everyone is aware of his or her team spirit. If a positive outcome is generated by cohesiveness, it is the development of a workplace that officers find more friendly and pleasant.

When a group performs successfully by attaining its objectives, it becomes more cohesive. When there is a degree of positive participation and a great deal of communication, coupled with acquiescence to norms, the group will be more successful. For many reasons, cohesiveness is a positive factor for a supervisor to cultivate, but this is only true when the group's goals are compatible with organizational objectives. For example, if a group of officers violates the rights of defendants as a means of achieving an agreed-upon arrest standard, then cohesiveness can create a problem for a supervisor rather than serving as a factor that integrates and energizes a group.

Cohesive groups can also become a concern for first-line supervisors because they have more power than any one officer. A group of managers in a medium-sized police department successfully destroyed the effectiveness of a team policing program by resisting it in every way they could, because they felt their power and authority was threatened.

Notwithstanding the negative aspects of cohesiveness, the positive aspects are such that the supervisor should work diligently to create a work environment that fosters cohesiveness. The more cohesive the group is, the more likely it is to be highly productive.

Building a Winning Team

When analyzing the behavior of effective supervisors who have demonstrated the capacity to change a random collection of officers into a productive work unit, it is obvious that they perceive their role as being one in which they wear many different hats. This includes being a coach, facilitator, developer, and team builder (Garfield, 1986). It also includes an acceptance that the aggregated energies and inventiveness of a team are far greater than those of the individual. A positively focused supervisor works to develop a team that is best characterized as a cohesive entity. When cohesion occurs, the team members will value their participation in the group and will defend the group's purpose. Members will work to see that goals are attained. As cohesiveness increases, members will work to maintain open channels of communication and position and status becomes secondary to the group process (Watts, 1993).

Effective team building involves more than learning a few interpersonal skills. Team building is a complex process that does not just happen—it takes a great deal of leadership and team effort. Real teamwork becomes a reality when responsibilities and decision making are shared. Members of a team have to learn how to work together, and that is not easily accomplished (Plas, 1996). Team members need direction, not explicit orders; they need to be coached, not ignored; they need to be trained, not left to fend for themselves.

Above all, they need to be led, not supervised to the point of distraction (Leonard and More, 2000).

Effective group leaders generally exhibit a number of readily identifiable behaviors (Hellriegel, Slocum, and Woodman, 1983). These behaviors can result in the development of a winning team. One characteristic they have in common is goal attainment. This is the ability to focus on attaining results.

Figure 8.5
Five Characteristics That Make a Group Leader Effective

1.	Focuses constantly on the goal as a means of achieving group effectiveness.
2.	Actively participates in the group, but does not dominate or thwart individual input.
3.	Observes the activities of the group. Serves as a coach and as a facilitator.
4.	Assumes responsibility for interrelating with groups and units and reporting results to group members.
5.	Supports group members in assuming leadership roles as the need arises. In fact, does everything to foster each member's growth.

In addition, effective group leaders serve in a liaison capacity with other units, facilitate the participation of every member of the group, and actively participate in the group as needed.

There are a number of characteristics of successful teams that have been found in all types of organizations, and these features must be present if the team is to be operationally effective (Neck, 1999; Larson and LaFasto, 1992).

Absence of the easily identifiable characteristics can result in less-than-adequate performance. Above all, team members must have shared values. It creates the foundation on which a team leader can achieve the other characteristics of a successful team. Shared values are based on trust and confidence in the team. A group of officers begins the process of becoming a team when members value cooperation, commitment, competence, and positive collaboration. These are genuine, definitive values. Team members are committed when varying opinions are readily accepted even when members obviously disagree. Another key element of teamwork is the willingness to take risks. Teams that are resoundingly effective have a crystal-clear understanding of team goals with an underlying belief that the goals are worthwhile, achievable, and genuinely elevating. Values, goals, and commitment might never occur without principled leadership. Member effectiveness has been shown to improve dramatically when the work environment makes them feel like they belong and that they are making a significant contribution (Ray and Bronstein, 1995). The ethical and professional standards of the first-line supervisor should be of the highest order, and every action should be above reproach. Finally, and most critical, is positive and constructive feedback. Effective feedback is best described as a process that is direct, usable, and timely (Larson and La Fasto, 1992; Carr, 1992).

An operationally effective group can easily be identified, because authority emanates from knowledge rather than rank or position. The degree of participation is focused and based on enhanced knowledge and the skill of team members resulting in the creation of a positive work environment. An observer of such a group can see that members are staunch supporters of the team and are committed to obtaining results. Members trust each other and genuinely believe they are on a winning team. The energy of the group is synergistic, and group members are given an opportunity to achieve and grow. Their opinions are respected and contributions are acknowledged. Accolades are given to those who contribute to the unity of the group and to those who facilitate goal attainment (Leonard and More, 2000).

Numerous factors influence the effectiveness of the group, including the size of the group, its norms and goals, and the environment in which the group operates. In every instance, strong leadership can overcome limitations imposed by any of these factors. The goal of a supervisor should be to create a climate in which the officers supervised develop to the point at which they truly function as a team. Team building does not just occur—it is the result of hard work and a consideration of the behavior of both the members of the group and the leader.

Figure 8.6
Four Cs of Team Membership

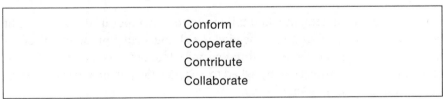

Conform
Cooperate
Contribute
Collaborate

Source: Ken W. White and Elwood N. Chapman (1996). *Organizational Communications—An Introduction to Communications and Human Relations.* Upper Saddle River, NJ: Prentice-Hall.

It is the task of a supervisor to develop a truly winning team in which each officer accepts and promotes the four Cs of team membership. The first consideration is the willingness to conform to each team decision. Each and every team member must pull his or her weight, and the supervisor must ensure conformity and bring recalcitrant members into line. At the extreme, this could mean replacement of a team member.

The second consideration is a willingness to cooperate with other team members and setting the interests of the team above individual interest. In the beginning, this can be difficult for officers who have been used to working alone. Team members have to contribute skills to problem solving and not hold back for personal or selfish reasons. Additionally, there must be a willingness to collaborate with another member on a creative idea, regardless of who receives more recognition for success. It is best if supervisors praise not only the accomplishments of the team, but also those of individual team members.

When officers fulfill the criteria of the four Cs, tasks will be accomplished with enthusiasm, self-discipline, and minimum supervision. This leads to the attainment of objectives that could not be achieved by the efforts of individuals working separately.

Effective Relationships

When supervising a group, it is best to develop a personal relationship with that group. At first it may seem like a waste of time, but some members of the group do not view the supervisor the way supervisors view themselves. In fact, one might be surprised to find that some view the supervisor as highly competent, while others view the supervisor as mediocre. There may be others who either dislike or even despise a supervisor. Some may view the same supervisor as warm and understanding, and others may see him as cold and indifferent. Whatever the actual situation, the supervisor should determine an exact personal status of each of the team members and use this information in the work relationship.

A supervisor can do this by approaching those with whom there is a close relationship and asking for their opinion. This should give some idea as to the supervisor's standing with members of the group. Then the supervisor should sit down and talk with each member of the group, in the most relaxed environment possible.

The opening statement when talking with a member of the team might be something like, "Your help is needed in solving a team problem." The initial reaction might not be everything anticipated, but it is an opening, and then numerous questions can be asked to enhance the personal working relationship with team members.

Figure 8.7
Questions for Determining Effective Group Relationships

1. How can the performance of the team be improved?
2. Is there adequate sharing of information?
3. Are team goals clear?
4. Is everyone allowed to participate in the decision-making process?
5. Does everyone feel like a member of the team?
6. Does the team use all possible skills?
7. Are meetings informative?
8. Can meetings be more productive? How?
9. Is planning adequate?
10. Is everyone on the team treated with respect?
11. Does the team have adequate resources to accomplish its task?

It is important to ask questions that deal with problems rather than with personalities. Solutions are needed, or, at the very least, the identification of problem areas. Once the concerns of other members of the team are determined, the supervisor should review his or her own opinion regarding the matter in an attempt to resolve a problem. This can be difficult, but it must be done, and every effort should be made to really understand everyone on the team.

Personal judgments about other officers should never be allowed to interfere with team efforts. As a supervisor it is imperative to make every effort to see that team members agree to working together (Rogers, 1986). A great deal of time and effort can be expended on resolving problems between members, but such efforts can be better spent on goal attainment. Intergroup conflict can be devastating. It is best dealt with by a supervisor who is thoroughly knowledgeable about the needs of each team member and who works to meet their needs and reduce conflict with organizational needs.

Developing positive personal relationships takes time; it cannot be accomplished overnight. It can also be frustrating—one might never reach the stage needed to have a well-coordinated team. But it is a goal worth striving for, and the rewards will usually outweigh the disappointments. Every effort should be made to develop a team that is self-managed (Straub, 1998).

Size of the Team

The larger the team, the more difficult it is to create a positive work environment leading to esprit de corps and a cohesive working unit (Gray, 1984). The smaller the size of the unit, the greater the potential for interaction between group members. Also, group norms are more easily developed in a small group and have a greater impact on group activities.

There is no magic number where a group changes from small to large, but it seems to be in the area of 10 members. This is particularly evident in patrol, where officers usually function independently. In a selection of departments from a nationwide survey, it was found that the number of officers supervised by a sergeant ranged from 4.5 to 16.6, and the average team consisted of slightly more than eight members (Police Foundation, 1981).

The same study reflected that when departments had tactical units, the number of officers supervised by a sergeant ranged from 4.5 to 10.6, and the average team had slightly more than seven members. In the same study of 61 departments, it was found that a sergeant supervised 22 percent of the tactical units. The majority of departments serving cities with populations of less than 75,000 fell into this group (Police Foundation, 1981). In another study, it was found that 76 percent of larger departments assigned full-time officers to multiagency drug enforcement task forces (Reaves and Goldberg, 1999).

Group identity and team spirit are a reflection of the size of a team; consequently, it is recommended that teams be kept under 10 members whenever possible as a means of fostering cohesiveness within the group.

Interaction

One of the most difficult tasks for a supervisor to do when assigned to patrol is to arrange for officer interaction. In many departments this is limited to roll call and can become a one-way communication process unless the sergeant makes a sincere effort to create an atmosphere that fosters interaction.

When new policies are discussed, ample time should be allowed for determining their impact on operations or the conduct of employees. This necessitates follow-up by the sergeant on a one-on-one basis when officers are supervised in the field. If the policy proves to be ambiguous or subject to varying interpretations, it should be discussed not only at the next roll call, but also (if there is a need) at a special team meeting.

If adequate time cannot be found during working hours, the supervisor should hold meetings outside the job. This technique should be used sparingly and only when the situation dictates. The scheduling of officers' time should be such that there is adequate time for group interaction (Gray, 1984).

Case Study

Corporal Juan (John) Cabalar

The community of Waterville has a population of 92,000. It is in a major metropolitan area contiguous to a major high-tech city. It has a mixed population, consisting of 28 percent Asian, four percent black, and 32 percent Hispanic, with the remainder being white. It has two major shopping areas and an automobile assembly plant. Its crime rate has dropped considerably, along with most other communities throughout the nation, but the city is still plagued by numerous convenience store armed robberies and crimes of opportunity. Many perpetrators use the freeway system to enter the city, commit a crime, and then depart with the intent of spending limited time at the crime scene. Patrol units have directed special attention to businesses that crime prevention specialists have identified as potential targets.

John Cabalar had served as a corporal for three years and is currently in the patrol unit of the Central Station. In addition, he is a member of the departmental SWAT team. On regular workdays, he responds to 911 emergency calls overlapping several sectors and backs up other officers as needed. This flexible assignment allowed him to respond to SWAT calls as needed. He has been a police officer for nine years. Last year he took the promotional examination for sergeant and was promoted after scoring high enough to place fifth on the promotional list. He has spent his career in patrol and finds it to be the most challenging and enjoyable type of police work.

As a newly promoted sergeant, Cabalar has been assigned to the special shift in charge of a task force of eight officers who are to work exclusively on reducing convenience store robberies and crimes of opportunity. The task force will operate from 6:00 P.M. to 2:00 A.M., which is the period when most of the incidents have occurred during the previous six months.

If you were Sergeant Cabalar, what data would you want from the crime prevention specialist? How would you coordinate your efforts with patrol units? What would be your agenda for the initial team meeting? Why?

Controversy and Conflict

Controversy within a group is inevitable and should be handled openly. When a disagreement occurs, it should be discussed with all members of the team in a forthright manner. Keep in mind that disagreements are a normal consequence of the interaction between team members. Above all, discuss issues, not personalities. This allows team members to deal with facts and reduces the nature and degree of emotional response.

A supervisor should endeavor to treat every team member's opinion respectfully. Favoritism toward any particular member's opinions over those of others should never be shown. In other words, a supervisor should be as impartial and fair as possible.

One should work diligently to spot potential problems and personality clashes before they occur by being aware of everything happening and by dealing with undercurrents. A good way to do this is to constantly interact with every team member and, above all, *listen.* There is a lot more to be learned this way than can ever be learned from communication that can easily become one-way rather than two-way (Rogers, 1986).

If conflict has occurred, or is possible, deal with it immediately. Conflict can lead to the creation of factions within a team as well as misunderstanding, a reduction in cooperation, and destruction of team morale. A supervisor should identify and attempt to eliminate conflict before it occurs. The best strategy is to encourage controversy and discourage discord.

It is helpful to deal with problems that result from a lack of cooperation on the part of team members by approaching each situation with a sincere effort of problem resolution. One's attitude is important, and a supervisor should take the position that resolution is possible. Team members can prove to be difficult to deal with when they have a difficult personality, have power that other members do not have, or are obstinate and refuse to yield on any point. There is no easy solution for these situations—they can prove to be highly frustrating and formidable, but they are challenges that must be dealt with frequently as team members interact with each other. The goal is to create an environment that fosters trust. Listen to the ideas of others and strive to find common ground that leads to resolution. As a supervisor, you must sincerely believe that resolution is inevitable and develop an ongoing learning process in which team members are accepted and respected for their viewpoint even when it is in conflict with team goals. Being open, fair, and sincere is difficult but essential if resolution is to occur (Levine, 1998).

Figure 8.8
A Supervisor Needs to Develop an Attitude of Resolution

1. Accept team members as they are—not how you would like them to be.

2. Strive to learn where each member of the team is coming from and what his or her needs are.

3. Emphasize cooperation and the necessity of coordination rather than conflict.

4. Be responsive and accept the fact that team members can and will have other positions.

5. With an understanding of differing views and positions, consideration can be given to formulating a resolution strategy that minimizes differences.

6. Emphasize the cost of inimical conflict that impedes team goal attainment.

7. Present a solution that stresses how the team can gain from implementing the proposal. When possible, illustrate how the change will positively affect each team member.

8. Involve the team members in a discussion of the proposal, making a sincere effort to get them to buy into the resolution process.

9. When an impasse occurs, consider obtaining the assistance of a knowledgeable manager to intercede, which hopefully will result in a positive impact on those resisting the proposed solution.

10. Keep at it. It is amazing how often things will fall into place when one is persistent without being offensive.

11. Constantly evaluate the process to ensure that you can see all sides of a problem.

Source: Reprinted with permission of the publisher. From *Getting to Resolution—Turning Conflict into Collaboration*, copyright © 1998 by Stewart Levine, Berrett-Koehler Publishers, Inc., San Francisco, CA. All rights reserved. 1-800-929-2929.

Team Goals

A first-line supervisor should set forth a sense of direction for the group. There should be no doubt concerning where they are going and how they will achieve objectives. Priorities must be established, and there should be no room for misinterpretation. Each member of the group should know what is expected of them specifically and what their responsibilities will be. Every goal should be truly meaningful (Cox and Hoover, 1992), and every member should have a specific assignment with a designated deadline for accomplishment of assigned tasks (Eng and Hummel, 1997).

Whenever possible, one should stress what has to be accomplished in measurable terms. Objectives should be achievable. If there are risks involved, or if it is questionable that goals can be achieved, this must be communicated and allowances should be specified. An example would be the setting forth of a group objective, as follows:

Objective: Increase the percent of stolen property recovered during the next calendar year by 15 percent.

Means: Use selected members of the investigative division to:

- Conduct surveillance of known fences, pawn shops, flea markets, and garage sales.

- Conduct extensive interviews of all suspected offenders arrested by surveillance teams.

- Use reserve personnel to compile comprehensive lists of stolen property, emphasizing readily identifiable items.

- Use reserve officers to provide follow-up on all thefts, emphasizing accurate property descriptions.

Measures: Increase of recovered stolen property during 90-day period as compared to previous time periods.

The supervisor can facilitate goal attainment by ensuring that all necessary information is shared. There is no room for secretiveness or hidden agendas. When there is openness and issues are discussed candidly, the framework is laid for the development of a cohesive group. When everyone knows what is going on and they are privy to all the information needed to do their work, it reinforces team spirit (Tarkenton, 1986).

Group Problem Solving

In recent years, the police field has turned to the group as one process to be used effectively in solving problems. The group is commonly known as a task force and is distinguished from other groups because it is usually temporary in nature and focuses its attention on one subject or problem. The task force has been especially useful in dealing with problems affecting the entire department, such as a policy for the use of roadblocks, or the selection of a new handgun.

It is widely accepted that groups can be highly productive when it is necessary to generate many ideas, recall information accurately, or evaluate uncertain situations (Hellriegel, Slocum, and Woodman, 1983). The role of the supervisor is to maximize the advantages inherent in group decision making so that the best possible decision is reached.

Another advantage of a team is the greater likelihood of the final solution being implemented because of the involvement of a cross section of the department (Bellman, 1992). The involvement of individuals in the task force from various units throughout the department enhances the awareness of how others function. This leads to better coordination as the members work to achieve organizational goals (see Figure 8.9).

Figure 8.9
Advantages of a Team Effort

1. Improved decision making
2. Greater acceptance of the decision
3. Improved coordination
3. Broader perspective on problems
4. Shared power
5. Greater access to information
6. Increased job satisfaction
7. Sense of self-fulfillment for members
8. Greater unity of purpose
9. Intrinsic legitimacy in the process
10. Improved communications by member involvement
11. Collaborative problem solving

Team efforts can serve as vehicles for training employees as they learn how to work with others and arrive at a decision based on consensus. This process contrasts sharply with many police situations in which the officer makes a decision, usually independent of immediate supervision. The officer is expected to command the situation. Such group interaction forces its members to think of broader issues and their implication to the whole agency. Finally, the team force serves as a vehicle for power sharing. Members have the opportunity to express their opinion and become a part of the decision-making process. Just the establishment of the team reduces the power of the individual who has authorized it.

There are, of course, problems that may occur when a team is created. A supervisor should review these carefully and try to avoid them. An individual can come to a team assignment with a complaint and defend this position at all costs, never giving the slightest consideration to alternative solutions. Such an individual can serve as a disrupting influence, so the supervisor must demonstrate strong leadership skills by structuring the meetings in such a way that all sides of an issue are discussed.

Another situation that works to a supervisor's disadvantage occurs when one individual exerts an exceptional amount of influence on the team, to the point at which the total decision-making process is impaired or disrupted. In some instances, individuals who have a higher rank, or have a great deal of expertise in an area under consideration, influence the process excessively (Davidson, 1986).

From time to time, a team will have a member who dominates every meeting. This domination usually does not stem from rank, expertise, or bias, but from the personality of the individual. It can be due to the individual's charisma, but is more likely to be based upon exceptional interpersonal skills. One technique that is useful to a supervisor who must deal with such an individual is to encourage others to express their opinions by directing specific questions to them and asking other members to summarize issues and positions. If techniques such as this do not work, it will be necessary for the supervisor to meet privately with the disruptive member and firmly establish ground rules for subsequent meetings.

When a team makes a recommendation, it is based on the judgment of the group. Consequently, members usually take the position that they are not individually responsible for the final decision. There is little a supervisor can do about this particular disadvantage but accept it as an inherent disadvantage (see Figure 8.10).

Figure 8.10
Disadvantages of a Team Effort

1. Bias of members may be intensified.
2. Excessive influence of individuals with rank or expertise.
3. Domination by a member of the group.
4. Responsibility may be diffused.
5. Cost in terms of time and money.
6. Pressure to conform.
7. Decision-making process limited by groupthink.
8. Interpersonal gamesmanship may dominate the proceedings.
9. "Win at all costs" may interfere with the team process.

Finally, it is necessary to consider the cost of including officers in the decision-making process. In one law enforcement agency, the cost per hour for a patrol officer, including all benefits, is $35. Just stop and think how quickly that can add up with a task force of nine officers plus the sergeant in charge of the task force, whose cost is $50 per hour. The cost, then, for each hour of meeting will be $365. A team taking 10 hours to reach a decision will cost $3,650. If the meetings are held during working hours, it is a loss of 100 man-hours of work that could have been devoted to other police tasks.

Undoubtedly, teams can contribute to the effective management of an agency, but each time they are established consideration should be given to the expenses involved. The benefits should outweigh the costs.

Conducting Meetings

An important function with which a supervisor must immediately become acquainted is conducting effective meetings. Meetings are viewed by many as an exercise in futility and a total waste of time. Clearly, some meetings are unproductive and costly in terms of time and money. A supervisor should prepare for a meeting by setting aside adequate time to conduct the research needed to become familiar with the topic to be discussed. *Preparation is the key to success.* If you anticipate spending eight minutes for the initial team orientation, it can, in all probability, take several hours of preparation. This ensures that you have an introduction that gets everyone's attention. This should be followed up with the identification of key components of your proposal. Every point that you stress should be easily understandable. Above all, you should strive to obtain team member commitment to the program you are describing. This can be accomplished by providing several reasons for each of the components of the program. By following such a highly organized and structured procedure, one conveys the capacity of being orderly, logical, and clear (Repp, 2001).

Supervisors can learn skills to utilize a team effort in such a way that problems can be resolved and solutions can be recommended. It is a team leader's function to perform as a facilitator. Every effort should be made to bring out the best in people and create a working environment that maximizes problem solving (Tarkenton, 1986). A key to meetings is to make them productive. To maximize effectiveness and clarity, meetings should start on time and be limited in duration. There is little reason to hold a meeting any longer than 45 minutes. Meetings that go longer tend to be bogged down in trivia. When short meetings are held, there is a tendency for people to arrive on time, be better prepared, and to follow the agenda (Kriegel and Brandt, 1996).

A supervisor should start out on the right foot by clearly establishing ground rules at the first meeting. Information should be set forth as to how often meetings will be held. Subsequently, the nature of the problem should be identified and the authority set forth. It is also best to state the various subjects not included within the authority of the task force, such as grievances or personnel matters. If the group is merely to present a recommendation (rather than make a final decision), the facts should be presented so that misunderstandings about the reasons for forming the task force are eliminated.

After these issues have been clarified, it is necessary to outline specific rules to use in governing each session. The group should participate in this process by agreeing on such basic issues as (1) meetings will begin and end on time; (2) members will not be interrupted when they are presenting their views; (3) ideas will not be criticized; (4) agendas will be prepared and given to each member before the meeting; (5) members will be treated as equals regardless of rank or seniority; (6) discussion time will be limited to that set on the agenda; and (7) the focus will be on issues, not personalities.

The extensiveness of these ground rules depends upon the composition of the group and the nature of the problem to be solved (Tarkenton, 1986; Stone, 1995). Some groups have proven to function effectively with a minimum of rules, and other groups need an extensive list of rules to govern their activities.

It cannot be emphasized too strongly that the rules are decided by the group, not imposed by the leader. Consensus is important and greatly facilitates the decision-making process inasmuch as members have a greater commitment to rules when they have been involved in their development. While experts vary in their judgment about how to conduct the meeting, it would seem at the very least that a leader should consider the points set forth in Figure 8.11 (Watson, 1992).

Figure 8.11
Conducting a Successful Meeting

1. State the problem in a straightforward manner without any indication of a solution.
2. Provide all necessary data and information pertinent to the problem under consideration.
3. Encourage the presentation of all ideas.
4. Listen and learn from others' beliefs and ideas.
5. Never ask leading questions.
6. Never make specific recommendations, including a solution to the problem.
7. Ask questions to stimulate discussion.
8. Summarize and clarify.
9. Set the time and date for the next meeting.
10. Close each meeting on a positive note.
11. Refrain from criticizing individuals.
12. Strive to not monopolize the discussion.
13. Function as a facilitator, not a dictator.

One of the most difficult problems for a meeting leader is to deal fairly and justly with every member. The leader must control those attempting to dominate meetings (especially those who talk just for the sake of talking) and whose wordiness exceeds their knowledge. One way to do this is to set a time limit for each presentation or set up a rotation system for presentations.

A definite barrier to effective group communication can easily occur if members will not enter into the discussion because they are unwilling to oppose the opinion of someone of a higher rank, or if they are uncertain whether their judgment will be accepted. The reason for noncommunication is unimportant; however, the situation must be controlled, preferably by structuring every meeting to ensure maximum participation by everyone. When a group member seems reluctant to state opinions, specific questions can be asked to stimulate their participation. In other instances, in order to get the meeting started, you might want to ask one of the more vocal members of the team to share their ideas or experiences (Stone, 1995).

Those who might attempt to dominate the meeting can be scheduled as the last participants. The same might be done for those who have rank or seniority. It is essential for the overall group work environment to be positive and straightforward so that members feel free to express ideas even though they might conflict with the opinions of others (Gray, 1984). Some supervisors are very adept at dealing with disruptive behavior. Some have been successful at doing nothing and letting other team members take care of the problem. Another way to deal with disruptive behavior is for the supervisor to discuss the problem with an offender either before or after the meeting and spell out exactly what he or she expects from particpants. Behavior that is sarcastic, cynical, or exceptionally competitive is not acceptable and must be confronted. As distasteful as it may be, face-to-face feedback may be the only alternative (Salmon, 1998).

Groupthink

Irving Janis coined the term *groupthink* and it has received a great deal of attention for more than a quarter of a century. Like many theoretical concepts, it has its supporters and its detractors (Turner and Pratkanis, 1998). Groupthink is a potentially inhibiting factor that the group leader must consider if the group is to accomplish assigned tasks and achieve organizational goals. It is a deliberating style that can be used by members when consensus is more important than arriving at the best solution. Generally, discussion is limited to reviewing a limited number of alternatives, while the consequences of the decision are ignored. In other words, do not let reality get in the way, because the process is more important than results, and alternative solutions just get in the way, so they are ignored (Moorhead, Neck, and West, 1998). Another groupthink characteristic is the extensive amount of time spent justifying the decision. It can be an endless process, and it is seldom that the leader can justify the expenditure of such resources. When a group becomes increasingly isolated from the department, groupthink is more likely to occur. In addition, the group begins to feel that it has solutions to every problem and input from external sources only gets in the way.

Groupthink can be handled effectively by selecting someone in the group to be the devil's advocate—to seriously question the solution. The position of critical evaluator should be rotated within the membership. Asking the group to identify and review the weaknesses of the solution one-by-one might be helpful. Finally, the leader can bring in experts to present their position.

With imagination and resourcefulness, a group leader can maximize the positive aspects of group decision making and negate the objectionable. Groups can make excellent decisions, so the leader should strive for consensus, as this provides a basis of support for a decision and helps to ensure its implementation (Robbins and Finley, 1995).

Summary

Groups are an important part of a law enforcement agency. They can either help or hinder the functions of the department. A group has been defined as "two or more people who interact with and influence each other for a common purpose." The terms *interaction* and *influence* are essential elements of the definition.

A new officer interacts with the police social system from the time the initial application is filed until retirement. The department expects each officer to acquire the norms, values, and behavior compatible with organizational goals and policy. There are a number of beliefs that are found to exist in the police culture. These range from loyalty to the need to bend the rules in order to enforce the law.

Within a police department, both formal and informal groups will always exist. They can become power centers within the organization. Groups can be either destructive or supportive, but if properly managed, they will contribute to the achievement of departmental goals.

Formal work groups are created for the specific purpose of performing special tasks. Task forces have become increasingly common in police circles. They are usually temporary and are created to perform a single task, such as developing a plan for a departmental reorganization or investigating a case involving a serial murderer. One department created a task force to determine when officers should wear their uniform hats.

Informal groups are formed because of the natural human desire of most officers to interact with each other. They can either support or detract from the attainment of organizational goals and can evolve into vertical, horizontal, or random cliques. They can be based solely on social needs for friendship and interaction with others.

A newly organized group will normally pass through the following six stages: orientation, conflict and challenge, cohesion, delusion, disillusion, and acceptance. The speed with which a group passes through these stages depends on a number of variables, including the difficulty of the task, the maturity of the members of the group, and the time and resources allocated to them.

Norms are unwritten, but in many instances are more influential than organizational rules and regulations. Norms peculiar to law enforcement include loyalty, secrecy, danger, isolation, and performance. These norms and their intensity will vary from agency to agency and may even be nonexistent in some departments.

Cohesiveness is a very desirable trait that can be cultivated, so a supervisor should work diligently to create a work environment that fosters its development. The more cohesive the group, the more likely it is to be highly productive. A group that generates a high degree of cohesiveness finds that its members are more loyal, readily identified with the group, easily accept group decisions, and more likely to conform to group norms.

In building a winning team, a supervisor should assume the role of coach, facilitator, developer, and team builder. Tasks to be performed by a supervisor include developing effective relationships, limiting the size of the team to less than 11 members, creating time for positive interaction with each member, constructively handling controversy and conflict, and carefully identifying team goals.

Group problem solving in law enforcement has been facilitated by the development of temporary team efforts to resolve special issues or problems. The advantages of a team effort definitely outweigh the disadvantages in contributing to effective management. Recommendations of teams are more likely to be accepted because of the involvement of numerous individuals. Additionally, an attitude of resolution is important to a supervisor, and consideration should be given to dealing with difficult personalities and readily accepting the need to try different approaches to problems. A truly effective supervisor promotes the four Cs of team membership: conform, cooperate, contribute, and collaborate.

A supervisor can develop skills in order to improve the quality of decisions made in team meetings. With imagination and ingenuity, a group leader can maximize the positive aspects of group decision making while negating the undesirable. Adequate preparation is essential. A supervisor should strive to be viewed as logical, organized, and clear-thinking. Key points must be emphasized during an orientation, and reasons for supporting the proposed program must be given. Consideration should be given to a wide range of activities such as establishing clear-cut rules, creating an agenda, and closing the meeting on a positive note.

Furthermore, the group leader should consider *groupthink* as a potentially inhibiting factor and try to ameliorate its impact on the group process.

Case Study

Sergeant William Ackers

In the City of Carsonville, Sergeant William Ackers has recently been reassigned to patrol after serving the last four years in the departmental training division. He has been a police officer for 11 years, and prior to that he served four years in the army, where he had been a military police officer and attained the rank of sergeant. He is currently a member of a reserve unit. During his active duty, he completed a degree in business management. He is single and resides in an apartment that he shares with another officer.

The police department has 352 sworn officers and 91 civilian employees. There are three major divisions: line operations, administration, and investigations. Specialized units include community policing, youth services, and technical services. The city operates under a city manager, who appoints the chief of police to a five-year contact. During the last five years, the Part I crimes have decreased an average of six percent annually. The only exception to the reduced crime rate is in the area of auto theft, which has increased substantially, and only 10 percent of the thefts have been cleared by arrests. The public has been up in arms for months because of the rise in auto thefts. Many citizens believe that no section of the city is safe and if they park a vehicle, they will return to find it gone. It is believed that many of the stolen vehicles are taken out of state to chop shops.

Sergeant Ackers supervises a team of nine officers, who are responsible for policing an area where many of the auto thefts have occurred. All first-line supervisors have been asked to address the auto theft problem.

If you were Sergeant Ackers, what would be the first thing you would do to address this problem? Why? What preparation would you make prior to meeting with the team? What information would you need from the records unit of the department? What would you do to coordinate your activities with other supervisors?

Key Concepts

building a winning team	importance of the individual
cliques	informal groups
conducting meetings	interaction
collaborate	isolation
conform	law enforcement norms
contribute	loyalty
controversy and conflict	performance
cooperate	police culture
deadly force	preparation
effective relationships	random cliques
formal groups	resolution
group development process	role of the group
group development stages	silence
group norms	size of the team
group performance	stages of group development
group problem solving	task force
groupthink	team building
horizontal cliques	team goals
individual	team meetings
individual and the group	vertical cliques

Discussion Topics and Questions

1. How is the individual important in the decision-making process?

2. Why should a supervisor be concerned about dealing with group performance?

3. Contrast vertical, horizontal, and random cliques.

4. Identify the differences between formal and informal groups.

5. What should a supervisor do in order to work effectively with an informal group?

6. How should a supervisor deal with controversy and conflict?

7. What are the six stages of the group development process?

8. Discuss the importance of law enforcement norms.

9. How should a supervisor conduct a team meeting?

10. What is *groupthink*? Why is it important?

11. What are the advantages of a team effort?

12. How does one build a winning team?

13. Discuss the four Cs of team membership.

14. What should a supervisor consider when conducting a meeting?

15. Discuss the importance of the significant beliefs of the police culture.

16. How might a supervisor develop an attitude of resolution?

For Further Reading

Field, Mark W. (1995). "The Abilene Paradox—Dealing with the Difficulty of Reaching a Group Decision." *Law and Order,* Vol. 43, No. 3.

> Discusses the phenomenon called the Abilene Paradox, which comes into operation when organizations or groups of people take actions contrary to the desires of any of their members and end up defeating the very purpose they hope to achieve. The author attributes this phenomenon to mismanaged agreement and sets forth six steps for defeating the Abilene Paradox. Attention is also given to the reality of peer pressure, and the fear of separation from the group.

Levine, Stewart (1998). *Getting to Resolution—Turning Conflict into Collaboration.* San Francisco, CA: Berrett-Koehler Publisher, Inc.

> The author recommends that one should develop an attitude of resolution, because it immediately places one in a position of leadership. One's attitude about conflict is reviewed in terms of developing listening and learning skills. Presents nine behaviors that are helpful when involved in resolution, ranging from respect everyone to humor and tranquility. Reviews the necessity of maintaining a commitment to resolution when dealing with conflict situations.

Repp, Bill (2001). "Seeking Positive Exposure is Vital to Getting Ahead." *Arizona Daily Star,* April 19:D2.

> Reviews the importance of adequate preparation before making a presentation in front of a group. Recommends spending eight minutes in preparation for every minute of presentation. This management expert also points out that some topics might require extensive preparation. It is recommended that during a presentation key points that call for commitment and understanding should be stressed. Every idea should be supported by two or more reasons that emphasize the logic of the presentation, and every effort should be made to seek agreement/understanding. Additionally, it is recommended that when your idea conflicts with other positions, it is essential to accept confrontation and negativity as part of the human equation.

Salmon, William A. (1998). *The New Supervisor's Survival Manual.* New York, NY: AMACOM.

> This author has an excellent chapter on conducting meetings. Most helpful is a discussion of the reasons that group meetings fail. Reviews such topics as conflicting objectives, bad timing, and inappropriate meeting format. Also, he points out that too much time can be spent ventilating, complaining, or finger pointing. Additionally, he lists 10 questions that can one can ask to ensure that maximum benefits can be obtained from a collective effort.

References

Bahn, Charles (1984). "Police Socialization in the Eighties: Strains in the Forging of an Occupational Identity." *Journal of Police Science and Administration,* Vol. 12, No. 4.

Bellman, Geoffery M. (1992). *Getting Things Done When You Are Not in Charge.* San Francisco, CA: Berrett-Koehler Publishers.

Brown, Jodi M., and Patrick A. Langan (2001). *Policing and Homicide, 1976-1998: Justifiable Homicide by the Police, Police Officers Murdered by Felons.* Washington, DC: Bureau of Justice Programs.

Buhler, Milan L. (1999). "The Fugitive Task Force—An Alternative Organizational Model." *FBI Law Enforcement Bulletin,* Vol. 68, No. 4.

Burchell, Joe, and Inger Sandal (1998). "Ass't. Chief, Sergeant Demoted." *Arizona Daily Star,* Vol. 157, No. 133, April 23:1A, 16A.

Carr, Clay (1992). *Teamwork: Lessons From America's Top Companies on Putting Teampower to Work.* Englewood Cliffs, NJ: Prentice-Hall.

Cartwright, D., and R. Lippitt (1957). "Group Dynamics and the Individual." *International Journal of Psychotherapy,* Vol. 7, No. 1.

Chemerinsky, Erwin, Paul Hoffman, Laurie Levenson, R. Samuel Paz, Connie Rice, and Carol Sobel (2000). "An Independent Analysis of the Los Angeles Police Department's Board of Inquiry Report of the Rampart Scandal." Los Angeles, CA: University of Southern California.

Cohen, Allan R., Stephen L. Fink, Herman Gadon, Robin D. Willits, and Natasha Josefowitz (1992). *Effective Behavior in Organizations,* Fifth Edition. Homewood, IL: Richard D. Irwin, Inc.

Cox, Danny, and John Hoover (1992). *Leadership When the Heat's On.* New York, NY: McGraw-Hill.

Davidson, Jeffrey P. (1986). *Checklist Management.* New York, NY: Practicum Press.

Eng, Sherri, and Jim Hummel (1997). "Building a Better Team." *San Jose Mercury News,* July 23:10G, 12G.

Federal Bureau of Investigation (1998). *Law Enforcement Officers Killed and Assaulted, 1963 to 1997.* Washington, DC: U.S. Government Printing Office.

——— (2001). *Law Enforcement Officers Killed and Assaulted, 1998.* Washington, DC: FBI National Press Office.

Gaffigan, Stephen J., and Phyllis P. McDonald (1997). *Police Integrity—Public Service with Honor.* Washington, DC: Office of Community Oriented Policing Services, and National Institute of Justice.

Garfield, Charles (1986). *Peak Performers.* New York, NY: William Morrow and Company.

Gastil, John (1993). *Democracy in Small Groups: Participation, Decision Making and Communications.* Philadelphia, PA: New Society Publishers.

Geller, William A. (1992). *Deadly Force: What We Know—A Practitioner's Desk Reference on Police-Involved Shooting.* Washington, DC: Police Executive Research Forum.

Gray, Jerry L. (1984). *Supervision.* Belmont, CA: Kent Publishing.

Haasen, Adolph (1997). *A Better Place to Work: How a New Understanding of Motivation Leads to Higher Productivity.* New York, NY: AMACOM.

Hellriegel, Don, John W. Slocum, Jr., and Richard W. Woodman (1983). *Organizational Behavior,* Third Edition. St. Paul, MN: West Publishing.

Herbert, Steve (1998). "Police Subculture Reconsidered." *Criminology,* Vol. 36, No. 2.

Jewell, Linda N., and H. Joseph Reitz (1981). *Group Effectiveness in Organizations.* Glenview, IL: Scott Foresman.

Johnson, Robert A. (1993). "Culture, Mission, and Goal Attainment." *FBI Law Enforcement Bulletin,* Vol. 62, No. 1.

_____ (1994). "Police Organizational Design and Structure." *FBI Law Enforcement Bulletin*, Vol. 63, No. 6.

Kappeler, Victor E., Richard D. Sluder, and Geoffrey P. Alpert (1994). *Forces of Deviance—Understanding the Dark Side of Policing.* Prospect Heights, IL: Waveland Press, Inc.

Knight, Anna, and William Brierley (1998). " In the Line of Duty—1998 Survivors' Club Update." *The Police Chief,* Vol. LXV, No. 5.

Kouzes, James M., and Barry Z. Posner (1993). *Credibility: How Leaders Gain and Lose It, Why People Demand It.* San Francisco, CA: Jossey-Bass.

Kriegel, Robert, and David Brandt (1996). *Sacred Cows Make the Best Burgers—Paradigm-Busting Strategies for Developing Change-Ready People and Organizations.* New York, NY: Warner Books.

Larson, Carl E., and M.J. LaFasto (1992). *Teamwork: What Must Go Right, What Can Go Wrong.* Newbury Park, CA: Sage Publications.

Leonard, V.A., and Harry W. More (2000). *Police Organization and Management,* Ninth Edition. New York, NY: Foundation Press.

Levine, Stewart (1998). *Getting to Resolution Turning Conflict into Collaboration.* San Francisco, CA: Berrett-Koehler Publishers, Inc.

Los Angeles Times (1994). "Police Reports Show Frequent Misuse of Guns by Officers." August 15:3B.

Molden, Jack (1998)."The Care and Feeding of the FTO Program." *Law and Order,* Vol. 46, No. 5.

Mollen, Milton (1994). *Commission Report: Commission to Investigate Allegations of Police Corruption and the Anti-Corruption Procedures of the Police Department.* New York: City of New York.

Moorhead, Gregory, Christopher P. Neck, and Mindy S. West (1998). "The Tendency Toward Defective Decisionmaking within Self-Managed Teams: The Prevalance of Groupthink for the 21st Century." *Behavior and Human Decision Processes*, Vol. 73, Nos. 2/3, February/March.

More, Harry W. (1998). *Special Topics in Policing.* Cincinnati, OH: Anderson Publishing Co.

NHTSA (2001). *Sobriety Checkpoint State Case Law Summary.* Washington, DC: NHTSA. <www.Nhtsa.dot.gov>.

Neck, Christopher (1999). *Leadership, Self-Actualization.* Upper Saddle River, NJ, Prentice Hall.

Pinizzotto, Anthony J., Edward F. Davis, and Charles E. Miller (1998). "In the Line of Fire: Learning from Assaults on Law Enforcement Officers." *FBI Law Enforcement Bulletin,* Vol. 67, No. 2.

Plas, Jeanne M. (1996). *Person-Centered Leadership: An American Approach to Participatory Management.* Thousand Oaks, CA: Sage Publications.

Police Foundation (1981). *Survey of Police Operational Administrative Practices—1981.* Washington, DC: Police Executive Research Forum.

Ray, Darrel, and Howard Bronstein (1995). *Teaming Up: Making the Transition to a Self-Directed, Team-Based Organization.* New York, NY: McGraw-Hill.

Read, Dan (2001). "Accused Cops Get Hearing Today—Story of Riders Corruption Unfolds." *San Jose Mercury News,* May 21:1B, 5B.

Reaves, Brian A., and Andrew L. Goldberg (1999). *Law Enforcement Management and Administrative Statistics, 1997: Data for Individual State and Local Agencies with 100 or More Officers.* Washington, DC: Bureau of Justice Statistics.

Repp, Bill (2001). "Seeking Positive Exposure is Vital to Getting Ahead." *Arizona Daily Star,* April 19:D2.

Robbins, Harvey and Michael Finley (1995). *Why Teams Don't Work: What Went Wrong and How to Make it Right.* Princeton, NJ: Peterson's/Pacesetter Books.

Rogers, Henry C. (1986). *The One-Hat Solution.* New York, NY: St. Martin's Press.

Salmon, William A. (1998). *The New Supervisor's Survival Manual.* New York, NY: AMACOM.

Sparrow, Malcolm K., Mark H. Harrison, and David M. Kennedy (1990). *Beyond 911: A New Era for Police.* New York, NY: Basic Books.

Stone, Florence M. (1995). *The Highly Valued Manager: Developing the Core Competencies Your Organization Demands.* New York, NY: AMACOM.

Straub, Joseph T. (1998). *The Agile Manager's Guide to Building and Leading Teams.* Bristol, VT: Velocity Business Publications.

Tarkenton, Fran (1986). *How to Motivate People.* New York, NY: Harper and Row.

Turner, Marlene E., and Anthony R. Pratkanis (1998). "Twenty-Five Years of Groupthink Theory and Research: Lessons from the Evaluation of a Theory." *Organizational Behavior and Human Decision Processes,* Vol. 73, Nos. 2/3, February/March.

Watson, Jane (1992). *The Minute Taker's Handbook.* North Vancouver, BC: International Self-Counsel Press.

Watts, George W. (1993). *Power Vision: How to Unlock the Six Dimensions of Executive Potential.* New York, NY: Richard D. Irwin.

Weinblatt, Richard B. (1999). "The Paramilitary vs. Academic Training." *Law and Order,* Vol. 47, No. 12.

White, Ken W., and Elwood N. Chapman (1996). *Organizational Communication—An Introduction to Communication and Human Relations Strategies.* Upper Saddle River, NJ: Prentice-Hall.

Change—

Coping with Organizational Life 9

Introductory Case Study

Sergeant Frank Hernandez

Frank Hernandez has been a sergeant in the Foxview Police Department for three years and in the patrol division for eight years. The community has a population of approximately 108,000, with 118 sworn officers and 47 civilian employees. The community is a suburb of a major metropolitan area with many professionals who commute to research parks in other cities. The community is fortunate to have a crime rate that has come down for a number of years. Currently its biggest problems are juvenile delinquency, sporadic vandalism, a very high truancy rate, and an increasing graffiti problem. There has also been an influx of street people who have proven to be aggressive panhandlers.

Until now his entire career has been spent on the midnight shift in the patrol division. Recently, Hernandez was transferred to the swing shift, which is the shift he has always wanted to work. The uniformed division is viewed by its members as the outstanding unit in the department. Officers get along well together and over the years have been credited with performing at an acceptable level. The normal policy is to assign new officers to patrol on the midnight shift, then to the swing shift, and finally to the day shift. In some instances, officers have to wait for an extended period to obtain a desirable transfer. All of these transfers are based on seniority. Officers view the swing shift as the most desirable assignment, because each of the teams have worked together for several years and function as cohesive entities.

A recently released study by the human resources unit of the department recommends that seniority be eliminated as the criteria for shift selection and that it be replaced by performance evaluations. The recommended policy has been submitted to the chief of police for review. In the locker room and at meal breaks, the new recommendation is discussed repeatedly. The policy is viewed by some as threatening working relationships that have developed over the years and is perceived as something that is not needed. Some of the officers are talking about the possibility of asking the union to oppose the implementation of such a policy. Sergeant Hernandez has not taken a position on the new policy and has refrained from voicing his personal opinion to management or to the line officers. As a supervisor, he knows that he is a part of management and could become responsible for implementing new policy. On the other hand, he believes the new policy will in all probability have a negative impact on the patrol division.

If you were Sergeant Hernandez, would you decide not to express your opinion about the proposed policy? Why? Would you discuss this dilemma with your lieutenant? Why? What would you tell the officers under your supervision while you are going through this decision-making process? Would you consider organizing opposition to the recommended policy? Why or why not?

We live in a dynamic social system in which change is kaleidoscopic in nature. Change affects every aspect of our lives, and the police environment is no exception. Our bodies of knowledge, social trends, officer expectations, more active participation by citizens, and demographics have had a resounding impact on police agencies (Community Policing Consortium, 1998). At the same time, all of these trends have had a significant impact on organizational life within police departments. It is impossible to ignore change. It is a process that can be simple or convoluted, unhurried or rapid, but it must be confronted and dealt with (Leonard, 1997). Furthermore, it is both exciting and challenging for those involved in the change process on a daily basis (Kriegel and Brandt, 1996). It is a reality of the work environment in which policing is done. One does not have to work long in a department to realize that very little is static. The dynamics of the situation exemplify anything but the status quo. At the same time, there is a significant difference between superficial and profound change. Change may be simple window dressing, a political expediency, or it may dramatically alter the working relationships within the organization.

While change might make one uncomfortable, it is certain to occur and must be accepted as part of the price one pays to work in a law enforcement bureaucracy. In fact, it is vital to the growth of a law enforcement agency. As a bureaucratic institution, the police usually respond to change rather than initiate it. In fact, change in law enforcement agencies has never been viewed as a positive event. The dislike for significant change in law enforcement is endemic, and the typical authoritarian managerial style has stifled efforts at innovation and creativity. Police innovation has always had to confront resistance from within. If an organization is to change, there must be a change in the behavior of department members. Officers join an organization with certain expectations, and when those are confirmed, they have an investment in the organization with the expectation that things will continue to function in the same way. Relationships and commitments are made that provide a sense of stability and continuity. When crucial changes are announced, it can create a range of responses from uncertainty to out-and-out opposition (Moore and Stephens, 1991). Sustained organizational change will not occur unless the police organization acknowledges the potential impact of change, confronts the reality of organizing the department in such as way as to respond to community needs, and develops new departmental norms (DeParis, 1997).

It is necessary to realize that while the police have seldom fostered change, they certainly react to it. Change must not only be met and accepted, but also anticipated whenever possible, and finally it must be managed (Farias and Johnson, 2000; Garfield, 1986). In fact, police managers should always anticipate the potential for continuing and constant resistance to the change process. This is especially true at the operational level (Zhao, 1996). Police planners can disclose the need to change, but the process seldom affects them. It is more normal for them to function as change agents. At the same time, high-level police managers are somewhat distant from the reality of operational change. They foster change, yet are only affected indirectly. It is the first-line supervisor who must deal with the reality of change on a day-to-day basis.

A careful observer of the functions performed by a line supervisor will immediately acknowledge that practically everything pertinent to everyday police operations is concerned with implementing change. This can range from breaking in a new officer to implementing a new procedure. For example, it was not too many years ago that a bag of white powder found at an intersection was just kicked over to the gutter. Now it is treated as a hazardous materials spill and the intersection is closed, pending the arrival of experts and identification of the unknown substance. At one time, high-speed police pursuits of dangerous suspects were standard policy, but currently many departments are rethinking and standardizing pursuit policy because of the danger to the general public (Sweeney, 1997). It also has to be acknowledged that *real* organizational change is effectuated by first-line supervisors, not middle or upper management (Charrier, 2000).

The ability to deal with change requires the application of numerous skills discussed throughout this text, including interpersonal communication, motivation, team building, training, and leadership. For officers to change, it is necessary to challenge their long-held beliefs, and this can be done only by reconsidering and revising those beliefs. Most of us find change disconcerting. Some find it unwelcome. Those who have conducted research on organizational change suggest that approximately 10 percent of employees will actively embrace change. Eighty percent will wait to be convinced, or will wait until the change is unavoidable. The remaining 10 percent will actively resist change. For these people, change is very upsetting. In some cases, this latter group may even seek to subvert or sabotage the process.

Dissenters, in many instances, will not openly oppose changes that disturb and disrupt the way things have always been done, but will passively resist the proposed change by doing things just the way they have always done. It is usually easy for the first-line supervisor to use the 10:80:10 ratio as a frame of reference for managing change. Because of their knowledge of those they supervise, potential supporters or detractors can be identified and strategies developed to ensure the fulfilment of the intended change. By working for consensus, an organizational environment will be created in which priorities can be set, timetables can be created, and programs can be implemented. (Community Policing Consortium, 1998). When challenging the process of change, a supervisor should enable others to act and should strive to foster collaboration by promoting cooperative goals and building trust (French and Stewart, 2001).

Factors That Foster Change

Time itself implies change, and time becomes a proxy for maturation, growth, and learning. It affects not only the individual, but also the organization (Pennings, 1997). Change does not occur in a vacuum, nor is it static. Change is synergistic and cumulative, often being called for in one area because it has taken place in another. For example, in recent years, numerous county and city jails have become so overcrowded that convicted offenders have been released early because of a court order. An indirect impact has been the implementation of a new policy in some departments in which minor offenders are cited rather than booked. While a supervisor might feel that in a particular instance the accused would most likely benefit from incarceration and society would be protected, it cannot be done because of conditions that are beyond the control of any first-line supervisor or the department.

Change places many demands on supervisors and includes factors that range from changing social values to the increasing power of police unions, technological change, and a constantly changing legal system.

Social Values

Not only are organizations changing—so are people. Change is a continual process that at times can be gradual, but sometimes is rapid. Change can be supported or resisted. The more bureaucratic the department, the more it will resist change. The larger the department, the more likely that supervisors will be confronted by barriers to change.

The majority of first-line supervisors are selected from their own department—thus, they normally have a somewhat narrow view of the ways in which a task can be accomplished. The manager's view is usually predicated on a maze of rules and regulations that they have been responsible for developing and implementing. Thus, management's view can easily become one that says "This is the way that it will be done, because it has always been done this way."

In this type of department, a supervisor acquiesces and becomes deeply committed to the status quo. Strict interpretation of rules and regulations is a must. First-line supervisors generally have a value system that differs from that of line personnel. Generally, supervisors are at least five to 10 years older, and their organizational attitudes are set (Washo, 1984).

The image of a good police officer has changed because of necessity. No longer is the primary criterion for selection based on "give me someone with a lot of strength and muscle." Today's image is as diverse as the culture in many of our communities. Officers come in all shapes and sizes—they are not all six feet tall and perceived as being able to handle themselves in a barroom brawl.

Today's officer is likely to be better educated, more intelligent, more emotionally stable, and more compassionate than many of those in positions of higher authority. Rigorous selection criteria, based on an array of examinations and tests ranging from psychiatric to polygraph, result in the selection of candidates who are highly qualified. With this changing nature of the workforce, it is no longer appropriate to treat every employee the same way. Increasing diversity—age, gender, race, and ethnicity—has important implications for how a supervisor should deal with the new breed of officer. Supervisors will have to find ways to support the desire of employees to use their skills and expertise. Officers must be given a variety of tasks and must be allowed to use them in order to find their job satisfying (DeSantis and Durst, 1998).

Younger officers are more likely to be dissatisfied with departmental policies that require them to "go by the book" at all times regardless of circumstances. Many of these officers perceive absolute conformity as stifling initiative, but soon find that implementing discretion can result only in being written up by a supervisor or someone else in the chain of command.

Today's line officer is more likely to have been raised in a lenient family setting and is less likely to have spent time in the military. These two factors, coupled with less rigid schooling, have resulted in many officers never having experienced a no-nonsense leadership style that demands unquestioning obedience and absolute compliance with orders. It has been shocking and decidedly unsettling to many young officers to be treated as mere cogs in the wheel and to have their opinions ignored.

Today's line officer has needs and expectations that are not met in a police department that is extremely bureaucratic and structured along traditional paramilitary lines. The values and attitudes of line officers are different from those of earlier generations. Supervisors cannot live in the past or yearn for the "good old days" when those supervised were more pliable, willing to accept authority, and take orders without question.

Supervisors must adjust to situations that they find undesirable. When values differ greatly between supervisors and those they supervise, conflict is inevitable. Line officers have demonstrated their frustration by defying management in different ways, including marching in front of city hall to oppose working conditions.

One of the main targets of officers has been oppressive and exceedingly detailed departmental policies. These conditions often make officers feel as though they are powerless and "just a number." When treated with such indifference, they feel like nonentities. As political and social conditions affect an agency, department policies change and consistency becomes the exception rather than the rule (Leonard, 1997). Placed in this situation, the first-line supervisor again becomes the reactor to change and must serve as the mediator and implementer between line officers and top management.

Police Unions

Police unions are powerful organizations in most cities. They exercise a great deal of power not only within the department, but also within communities. They have a great deal of influence over their members and within legislative chambers. In many instances, police unions have fostered the insularity that characterizes the police culture. Union representatives have, over the years, opposed commissions that were responsible for the investigation of police corruption. In New York City during the Mollen Commission investigation, such action created a negative attitude toward the investigative process and reinforced the public's cynicism toward members of the department, as well as enhancing departmental insularity. Just after the commission began its inquiries, the Captains' Benevolent Association initiated a lawsuit to dissolve the commission (Mollen, 1994). On the other hand, there is a positive side to police unionization. When police management has proven to be capricious, incongruent, or antagonistic to agency personnel, the response nationwide has been to unionize. Unions have often been responsible for departments developing positive personnel programs. Overall, police unions have done much to increase the pride and professionalization of police officers.

Consequently, line officers have shown increasing support for labor unions. It has been estimated that 73 percent of police officers in the United States are represented by some form of association or union (More, 1998). It does not take a new officer long to realize that there is strength in numbers. A police union is viewed as a way to fight for improved working conditions, institute grievance procedures, or have a say in the management of the organization.

Police officers have willingly accepted union leadership when it has led to the opportunity to participate in decisions that affect their future, provide for some semblance of economic security, and challenge the autocratic power of police managers. *Collective bargaining*, a process by which the department and the union negotiate a formal written agreement about wages, hours, and working conditions, is legal in about one-half of the country and has become a means of clarifying management rights. Some of the primary interests of police employee organizations are to have a voice in policy making and to improve benefits, including salaries, overtime, compensation time, pensions, paid holidays, health insurance, and tuition reimbursement (Guyot, 1991).

Police unions have viewed collective bargaining as the best means of checking or stalemating the abuse of power by police managers. Unions have been successful in altering rules and regulations, and it is quite common for unions to bargain for the right to review new policies before their implementation.

Active support of police unions increases daily because officers view administration as nonsupportive and far apart from line officers. In many instances, unions battle for control of the police department and influence the appointment of a new chief of police (Bouza, 1990). There certainly are departments that do not fit this description, but enough of them exist to call into question the relationship between line officers and managers.

It does not take an officer long to learn that it is necessary to safely cover all personal actions. In many instances, bureaucratic restrictions protect the top-level supervisors to the detriment of line officers. Another issue in collective bargaining involves the first-line supervisors and whether they should be considered a part of management or labor. The answer is self-evident, because a sergeant is a manager and an integral part of the management team. Under no circumstances should a supervisor be a part of a line bargaining unit.

Police unions cannot be ignored if organizational change is to occur. Police executives should explain their rationale and concerns to union leaders so that a collaborative effort can be directed toward the implementation of the change process. Recommended changes, if not carefully thought through, can conflict with contractual issues such as staffing requirements, shift assignments, disciplinary procedures, or promotional criteria. Unions must be involved in planned organizational change and should not have to find out about something after the fact. First-line supervisors should interact with union representatives, explaining the rationale for the change and stressing the need to work together (Glensor and Peak, 1996). In one department, the police union was successful in eliminating the implementation of an early warning system designed to monitor officer behavior. In this instance, the union had not been involved in the planning and implementation of the system.

The Law

The law conditions and reconditions the functions performed by the police. "All you have to do is wait for the next session of the U.S. Supreme Court and you will have to change the way you enforce the law" is a common complaint of many officers. Other problems are the ambiguity and vagueness of the law. The language of some statutes is so unclear that the courts must interpret it, but this is usually done after the fact, not before. The officer on the street is continually faced with the problem of enforcing the law and then accepting the consequences if the decision is questioned.

Other laws are obsolete and outmoded but are still on the books. In practice, the police are expected to enforce all laws; however, many are unenforced and routinely disregarded. Occasionally, police officers are criticized because they do not enforce a law. This usually occurs with sumptuary laws involving gambling. In one case in which the police department was not enforcing the law, bingo games were being sponsored as a means of raising funds for charity by several churches and other organizations, such as the Elks Club. Before the issue receded from the front page of the newspaper, it was necessary to change the state statute on gambling to exempt bingo.

It seems that the United States has become a society inundated by laws. The policy seems to be that if there is something we do not like, then we must pass a law against it. At the focal point of this landslide of laws, one finds the members of patrol units. Undoubtedly, there are too many criminal laws. There are too many purely personal activities involving law violations that should not be within the purview of the law (i.e., social gambling in a private residence).

This is obviously true in the area of victimless crimes, where, in general, enforcement is limited, but the police must deal with it as a continuing issue when working the streets. Political pressure can alter enforcement of victimless crimes overnight as a specific crime becomes a headline and the mayor's office comes unglued. It seems strange for an officer to ignore a minor drug violation or sexual offense one day and be expected to fully enforce the violation of the law the next day. It is the ambiguity of the whole process that is of concern to the officer, because the process is unpredictable and such changes are frustrating and difficult to handle.

Positive Aspects of Change

The first-line supervisor deals with the reality of change from two perspectives. First, the sergeant is usually the person who interprets new policies and is immediately placed in the position of being the spokesperson for management. On the other hand, supervisors are concerned because the work group that deals with those new policies on a continuing basis is primarily made up of line officers. Their concerns must be dealt with if the squad of officers is to operate effectively. It surprises new officers to find out that the main person to consult for advice on these matters is the immediate supervisor, not top managers. Beyond an occasional roll-call session or a major emergency, the other officers in the department are seldom seen.

The sergeant whose supervisory style exemplifies objectivity, fairness, and concern for the welfare of subordinates will soon find that not all change is resisted. Not many organizations accept change as readily as law enforcement agencies. The police are subject to continual change from external agencies, and their greatest dissatisfaction seems to be with the failure of police managers to adapt to changing times.

The average police officer takes the position that the police department fails to provide an environment that satisfies important personnel needs. It is the quality of work life that takes priority in satisfying the need system of officers. The job is viewed as dominant and the positive feelings generated by the job lead to increased job satisfaction.

One study found that when examining the actual police job, the most important characteristic (as perceived by the employees) was the feeling that the job was important and yielded a feeling of accomplishment. Job satisfaction differs for each employee, but studies seem to confirm that essential elements include a wide range of ambient factors, such as relationships and the type of supervision. Several of these variables are listed in Figure 9.1.

Figure 9.1
Characteristics of Job Satisfaction

1.	Accomplishment	7.	Management
2.	Accountability	8.	Relationships
3.	Advancement	9.	Resources
4.	Challenge	10.	Supervision
5.	Comfort	11.	Workload
6.	Compensation		

Source: Karl L. Albrecht (1981). *Executive Tune-Up*. Englewood Cliffs, NJ: Prentice-Hall.

The supervisor must work with these variables and identify those that are important to each individual, then strive to achieve selected departmental goals by optimizing worker needs and reducing undesirable side effects.

When the variables listed above are recognized and handled with dispatch, there is less likelihood of negative reaction to change. Unfortunately, this particular negativism will always overshadow the positive aspects, because it seems that bad news is always of greater interest than good news. Officers are not, by nature, anti-change in their approach to new situations, but they can become burned out to the point where they become negative in their outlook toward life and their job. If this is allowed to happen, police management has lost its chance to tap its most important resource: its employees.

Officers are certainly adaptable to change and will accept it more readily when they are involved in the decision-making process. If officers are informed, resistance will be less when they know that changes are being made, as well as the advantages of those changes (White and Chapman, 1996). If supervisors accept this premise, they can proceed to determine reasons for resistance when it occurs and confront it objectively (Harvey, 1990).

Accepting Change

The reasons for acceding to change vary considerably and are listed in Figure 9.2:

Figure 9.2
Reasons for Accepting Change

1. Choice
2. Improvement
3. Informed
4. A need is satisfied
5. Planned

Source: From *Supervision*, 1st edition, by Jerry L. Gray. Copyright © 1984. Reprinted with permission of South-Western College Publishing, a division of Thomson Learning. Fax 800-730-2215.

An important feature of change is the prospect of *choice*. If individuals are knowledgeable about the consequences of the change, a decision to accept is more likely to occur, because it is something they want to do—not something they have been forced to accept. *Choice* implies the possibility of rejection, but providing adequate information and involving members in the decision-making process can foster a positive response to change.

Another reason for accepting change is that the event can create *improvement*. This is especially true if a change improves working conditions; it becomes immediately acceptable to most officers. For instance, after having driven a squad car for more than 100,000 miles, it is a great feeling to get behind the wheel of a new vehicle. The same concept applies to working conditions when, for example, a city adopts computer-aided dispatching, allowing the officer to respond more quickly.

When officers are to be affected by change, acquiescence is more likely to occur if they are informed (Beck and Wilson, 1997). It is reassuring to know all pertinent facts right from the start. It is disconcerting when a decision has been made that affects the way officers are required to operate.

With today's means of communicating, there is every reason for management to keep its employees fully informed. In fact, it can be suggested that in the majority of instances, too much information will be helpful rather than detrimental. When personnel are aware of all operations, it reduces anxiety.

When a fundamental need is satisfied, change becomes acceptable to those affected. If an officer has a need fulfilled by a change, there is less reason to anticipate resistance to the change. Each person has needs that the job can fulfill. This can vary from providing greater self-esteem to improved job satisfaction. It is believed that when management meets the majority of officer needs, there will be a decrease in absenteeism and turnover. In addition, it is theorized that there will be increased productivity and fewer accidents.

When change becomes necessary, it is important to *plan for* it rather than to *react to* it (Dalziel, 1988). Planned change acknowledges that officers will be affected and that any alteration of policy or procedure can have a positive or negative impact. For example, when computers are introduced into patrol cars, they affect not only the officers, but the entire department, including records, dispatching, and even deployment of personnel. When events or situations are *planned for*, acceptability is enhanced.

With the changing composition of many police departments, it is essential to plan for social changes. The introduction of women into patrol units, preferential selection of employees who are bilingual, and the promotion of officers to obtain racial balance are all programs that require careful planning. Such programs must be monitored carefully and adjusted when necessary. When fully aware of the reasons officers accept change, the first-line supervisor is in a better position to deal with the variables that support, rather than impede, change.

Resistance to Change

Resistance to change can occur because of a wide range of contingencies. It can arise from such things as confusion, denial, or even silence (Maurer, 1996). There is a great deal of speculation as to why people resist change. One author postulated that there were at least 33 reasons individuals were resistant to change, ranging from homeostasis to human mindlessness (O'Toole, 1995). A clear understanding of the reasons officers resist change will allow a supervisor the opportunity to deal with **resistance**. When a change is viewed as threatening, most employees will resist it. If the change is immaterial or of no consequence, it will probably not be resisted. If the change proves to be supportive or helpful, everyone will most likely welcome it. Resistance to change is mainly an effort to maintain the status quo (Carr, 1996). In part, resistance occurs because of the fear of the unknown. It may be felt that a new procedure may be more difficult to use than the current system. Change may require members of the organization to behave in an entirely different manner, require more effort, or require officers to learn new things. Additionally, it might be a question of whether the change is worth it. The gain may not be worth the conflict created by the change (Tosi et al., 1990).

Resistance takes many forms and can range from just ignoring something to open resistance (De Meuse and McDaris, 1994). In one police agency involved in a pay dispute, most of the officers left the state so they would not be served with a court order requiring them to return to work. In another instance, officers enforced traffic regulations to the maximum, causing a public outcry when the resulting traffic jams created havoc in the downtown area. Figure 9.3 lists some of the reasons employees resist change.

Figure 9.3
Resistance to Change

1. Economic reasons.
2. Ambiguity is created.
3. Relationships are restricted.
4. Habits are altered.
5. Discretion is restricted or eliminated.
6. Unpopular decisions.
7. Cultural reasons.

Economic Reasons

Money (in terms of salaries and fringe benefits) is a key issue for most police officers. This is especially noticed when income is below what is considered par. If the officers know the neighboring agencies have higher pay levels, they are more likely to engage in activities that are adverse to the department.

If the city moves to reduce or eliminate overtime pay, it can be a definite threat to an officer's welfare. In agencies that allow overtime to become an integral part of the payroll, an elimination or reduction will have an immediate and negative impact on the lifestyle of each officer. The same can occur when city councils reduce fringe benefits, such as dental, medical, or retirement benefits, which have become an integral part of a pay package. Recently, a California sheriff's office increased its retirement benefits from two to three percent annually. This means that an officer at age 65, after 25 years service, can retire at 75 percent of his or her salary. This, along with a significant pay raise, occurred because so many deputies were transferring laterally to obtain a living wage.

Money weighs heavily in officers' decisions to resist change. If any part of a pay package is threatened, it is difficult to imagine that it would not be met with collective resistance.

Such resistance has increasingly been expressed through associations or unions. Like other occupations, officers have found that a united response will generally produce results when compared with individual efforts to right a perceived monetary wrong.

Ambiguity

The effects of change are often unknown, so officers are more likely to oppose it when there is doubt as to the possible consequences. The greater the ambiguity, the greater the potential for resistance (Holton and Holton, 1992). Most officers soon learn that one positive value of numerous rules and regulations is the tendency to create stability and reduce uncertainty. When things are done by the book, each officer is provided with guidance, increasing the probability that the outcome is known and predictable. Change, especially when it is extensive, can disturb or disrupt established procedures and generate resistance (Ortiz, 1994).

If a specific change is looked upon as creating uncertainty (although there is no evidence to support this conclusion), it will make most officers anxious about the new change. If a proposed change is slight or viewed with indifference, officers will be more likely to accept it, especially if they perceive the change as being somewhat beneficial. Again, however, there is no evidence to support such a position. If positive management practices are to occur, ambiguity must be confronted and leadership must internalize key characteristics of the change (Dale, 2000).

Restricted Relationships

With the exception of certain shifts or areas of a community, it has become increasingly common for officers to work alone. The result is that social relationships between officers become very important. Generally, officers will go to great efforts to socialize with fellow officers by eating meals together, taking breaks at locations where other officers gather, getting together at the end of a shift, or engaging in off-duty activities together.

Most officers generally resist efforts by management to restrict or limit social interaction. Group norms determine behavior and can be the most difficult source of resistance for managers to control. Patrol officers are usually isolated from the community, so they turn to each other for support. The result is the development of a police subculture in which common occupational values come into existence. Officers readily share job coping techniques in an effort to deal with policies that affect social relationships negatively.

A change in organizational structure may be resisted if it revises or alters working relationships between officers. One such example is a department in which officers traditionally had the responsibility of coordinating certain types of investigations with neighboring beat officers when the circumstances dictated. A new policy provided that investigators would now be responsible for coordinating such investigations. An immediate and vociferous resistance scuttled what management perceived as a needed reform.

Altered Habits

Individual resistance to change can stem from something as simple as habit (Tichy and Devanna, 1990). Officers become comfortable doing something a certain way, prefer to keep things the way they are, and see no reason to change. This is especially true if the officers receive satisfaction from an established habit (Kirby, 1989).

If officers are required to learn new skills to perform their job, but it is not viewed as an improvement over the way they are currently doing it, resistance will occur. There is comfort in doing things in a familiar way. The greater the chances of change altering an established habit, the greater the possibility that it will be resisted. Change causes losses and people resist, in many instances, because of the loss, not the actual change itself (Bridges, 1991).

Restricted or Eliminated Discretion

Management will often take steps to spell out authority, responsibility, and accountability in an effort to limit the power of line officers. In most instances, predictability becomes a means to an end and discretion is viewed as a necessary evil that must be controlled under all circumstances. The bureaucracy must prevail and must never be subjected to criticism. Reporting procedures are carefully spelled out, and rules and regulations abound.

The more discretion is controlled, the greater the amount of power that is taken away from the line officer. The street cops will generally feel that excessive control limits their ability to perform effectively. Managers (especially those at the top) are perceived as bureaucrats who have lost touch with street reality and have forsaken line personnel (Chemerinsky et al., 2000). The freedom to act when confronted with uncertainty is viewed by many officers as paramount to providing the public with high-quality police services that enhance their safety.

Unpopular Decisions

All managers must, at some time, make an unpopular decision, and this is certainly true of first-line supervisors. Certain decisions seem to be of more concern than others, and it is important to know which managerial decisions might cause dissent and how to obtain compliance when it is known that a decision will be unpopular.

Just as important is the need to determine what action employees will take when an unpopular decision is first announced. One study identified the following three situations as unpopular managerial decisions: actions dealing with discipline, changes in work schedules, and changes affecting salaries (Malik and Wexley, 1986).

Compliance-gaining techniques vary depending on the situation, but the most effective technique is to give officers adequate justification for the decision. Another method of reducing resistance is to obtain input from officers before issuing what is likely to be an unpopular decision.

It should be noted that, in general, the more highly educated the officers and the greater their career longevity, the more likely they are to want some justification of, or input into, the decision-making process. It is also important to note that the majority of officers will not take overt actions when responding to unpopular decisions. The decision is either accepted without dissent because management is perceived as having the authority to make it, or the resistance increases in proportion to the unpopularity of the decision.

Cultural Reasons

The police culture is unique, deep-seated, and powerful. Through the years, a distinct social orientation has developed within police organizations. Values, attitudes, expectations, norms, and behavioral patterns are transmitted from one officer to the next, and become operational reality. Figure 9.4 lists a number of characteristics of police subculture. The typical culture of a police organization develops certain values, and long-time members believe that the way their organization approaches problems is the only way it should be done. Attitudes and values support the customary way of doing things (Cohen et al., 1992). To conceive of other ways of doing something is usually perceived as wasteful, so doing so is resisted. Organizational culture reinforces the need to do something the way it has always been done. It has worked for many years, so why change?

Figure 9.4
Attributes of the Police Subculture

1.	Shared attitudes	8.	Loyalty
2.	Conformity	9.	Solidarity
3.	Insularity	10.	Social orientation
4.	Secrecy	11.	Common values
5.	Organizational norms	12.	Code of silence
6.	Group mores	13.	Taboos
7.	Cohesiveness	14.	Protectors

The police academy transmits the attributes of the subculture. New officers are taught how to act, think, and feel as they are inculcated into the police subculture. When they hit the streets, the on-the-job experience reinforces the values of the formal organization, and the new officers are introduced to the influences of the informal organization. Officers share a common language and argot of the profession (More and Wegener, 1992). They are loyal to each other, and the realities of police work reinforce their commitment to each other.

As proud members of the thin blue line, they perceive themselves as the true protectors of society. Officers soon see the need for secrecy, and the code of silence further isolates the police from the community (Chemerinsky et al., 2000). Additionally, the isolation of the police, the loyalty ethic, and esprit de corps socialize officers into the police subculture (Mollen, 1994).

Law enforcement has traditionally demanded conformity, making the organizational culture unreceptive to change (Tichy and Devanna, 1990). Changing the culture of a police organization is not only difficult, but it is also a long-range proposition. Management must be committed to change—it cannot be mere lip service—and this can be accomplished only by a strong commitment at every level of management within the organization. Change will have a limited potential for implementation unless it is supported by first-line supervisors (Ortiz, 1994). The features present in law enforcement agencies reinforce the need for the first-line supervisor to be aware of the uniqueness of the police social system and work within that system to foster change. In view of the individuality of cultural impact, a supervisor is advised to work with each officer before engaging in group discussions. The best results are obtained when significant change is phased in over time, to allow for individual adjustment. Mandated change, catchy phrases, and buzzwords tend to hinder change rather than promote it (Mulder, 1994).

The Nature of Resistance

Resistance to change can, at times, be completely rational and have no emotional basis whatsoever. When first challenged with a proposed or actual change, officers have sometimes become immediately aware that a new procedure will create more problems than it will solve. This form of resistance should be viewed as enhancing the change process, because it results in an in-depth analysis of the problem. A first-line supervisor should carefully analyze a change to see if there might be a real basis for rational resistance. When identified as such, the resulting conflict can be used to alter the change so that line personnel as well as management can support it.

For example, officers in one agency resisted a new procedure for booking youthful offenders in juvenile hall. While it simplified the booking process for probation personnel, it doubled the time that police officers had to devote to their booking process. In this instance, the proposed procedures were altered to the satisfaction of both agencies and all personnel.

Emotional resistance to change presents the supervisor with an entirely different problem. In some instances, the problem seems to be with the first-line supervisor, who may view a proposed change as beneficial to everyone involved, while officers view it differently.

The perception of change is usually individual rather than collective, so it is essential for a supervisor to try to understand how others view the change (Gray, 1984). In one department, a change in radio procedures received negative reactions because line personnel believed that dispatchers were given too much authority. An analysis of the resulting conflict determined that the resistance was emotionally based, because officers believed it limited their control of emergencies and was the first of multiple efforts to restrict their authority. It was the position of management, however, that the proposed change would enhance officer security.

Supervisors must distinguish between rational and emotional resistance if organizational change is to be accomplished. If a supervisor makes a serious effort to distinguish between the two types of resistance, it can then be handled to the benefit of all concerned. In some instances, providing officers with more information might resolve the problem and in other situations the supervisor may need to deal directly with each officer in an effort to determine the reason for resistance.

Case Study

Sergeant Teresa Larson

The Vibrant Police Department serves a community of 89,000. It is located in a Midwestern state. The community has a considerable amount of light industry but is still dominated by several steel plants and also serves as the hub for a farming region. The city is located on a major east-west highway with easy access to two major metropolitan areas. The city population has increased, and it is anticipated that with new light industries moving to the community, the population will increase by 4,500 annually for the next nine years. The police department has 148 employees, with 115 sworn officers. The chief has just appointed Teresa Larson as a first-line supervisor. She had taken a lateral transfer examination and was number one on the list. She was formerly a corporal in a large city, where she was employed for six years. Her credentials were impeccable. Prior to becoming a police officer Sergeant Larson worked as a psychiatric nurse. She has a bachelor's degree and has completed 15 units of an academic program leading to a master's degree in public administration.

The chief has been directed to hire more women. In fact, the whole city administration has been under a great deal of pressure from local and national women's groups to appoint more women, especially to supervisory positions. The police department resisted the pressure, but eventually capitulated in order to avoid a civil rights lawsuit. Sergeant Larson will be the first woman supervisor in the department. During the past years, five women have completed the academy and are currently assigned to patrol, where they are being supervised by field training officers (FTOs). Every indication is that the women are competent officers, and resistance has lessened as they have proven themselves. There is a hard core of street officers who are quite vocal in their opposition to the use of women on patrol, although they concede that women can be very effective in such areas as crime prevention and working with juveniles. One of the most vocal opponents to women in patrol is assigned to the team Sergeant Larson will supervise.

Overall, the department seems to have been unable to keep up with the new demands being placed upon it by a changing society. The department functioned as a typical bureaucracy for many years and was run by the book, which is especially true of patrol. The department was best described as a legalistic department. In past years, officers entering the department have stayed for a few years to gain experience, then left for greener pastures. As a result of substantial pay raises during the last two years, the department has been able to retain more officers and the department has stabilized. Without question, the department is going through a transitional period, and officers have begun to accept the new managerial style.

What should Sergeant Larson do in anticipation of the resistance she will find because she is a woman? Is gender or managerial style the major issue in this case? What change factors are at work? If you were Sergeant Larson, what agenda would you develop for your initial meeting with other supervisors? Would you meet with individual officers before the initial meeting? Why?

In addition, a supervisor should keep in mind that what might be construed as line officer resistance might not actually be resistance. Adapting to a new culture is difficult, and officers might just be making an effort to determine whether a new program or policy is viable and what effect it will actually have on each of them. There should be a reasonable adjustment period during which officers can be allowed to assess proposed changes and be allowed to obtain additional information that will assist them in the transition process. It is normal for people to want to check things out and really see how changes affect their daily working life (Haught, 1998).

It is essential that first-line supervisors remain focused on the fundamental issues of any change process. Under no circumstances should they take acts of resistance personally. Overreacting to internal backlash is an unacceptable response (Dolan, 1994). Conflict should be worked through, and it is essential that all issues be discussed openly. Due to the competing demands within the organization and the competitive nature of human beings some conflict is inevitable. Fortunately, most of the potentially damaging conflict that occurs is preventable. Managed conflict can reveal and clarify problems, improve solutions, and promote growth. Conflict can be positive when it helps the first-line supervisor ameliorate or eliminate negative attitudes and feelings, correct misunderstandings, and generate the commitment for change (Tracey, 1990).

Working for Change

Resistance must be identified before it can be handled properly. Solutions to the resistance problem might be as simple as providing those in opposition with more information or, at the other extreme, involving personnel in the decision-making process. It has become increasingly common to be almost constantly involved in some type of change process. In some instances, the consequences of change are identified as having the potential for limited impact. In other situations, it can be interpreted as potentially harmful. Finally, there might be no way of determining what will happen when a change occurs.

If several changes occur at the same time, the problem of dealing with resistance can become quite complex. At this point, it becomes necessary for those who are working for change to use more than one strategy when making an effort to overcome resistance to change. If the supervisor is a part of management, there is a greater potential for being involved in the planning that precedes change. If not, the first-line supervisor will be at a definite disadvantage. Dealing with conflict occurs after the fact and limits the alternatives the supervisor can use.

Whatever the realities of the situation, there are techniques a supervisor can use when attempting to defuse situations that can develop into resistance to change. There are always forces that support the belief that no change is good change. On the other hand, change for the sake of change is of questionable value. It is somewhat like managers who feel they have to be at the forefront, always involved in implementing the latest fad, whether it works or not.

The first-line supervisor is not in a position to resolve every occurrence that creates resistance, nor will his or her use of a specific technique always be successful. In other words, there is no proven method that will successfully sell change, but some techniques have proven to be more successful than others. Some of these methods are discussed below.

Figure 9.5
Working for Change

1. Being knowledgeable
2. Involvement
3. Effective communications
4. Using the influence of informal leaders
5. Mandated change

Being Knowledgeable

Ignorance might be bliss, but it is out of place when a supervisor is working to develop a strategy for selling change. Change seldom occurs without stimulation from management, so supervisors must take the view that change must be sold. Before a person can be convinced that a change should occur, it is necessary to gather and assimilate all the available facts regarding any proposal. It takes work to become knowledgeable about a proposed change and it takes time to acquire information. This is especially pertinent when change drastically alters the current habits of officers or their social relationships.

Above all, officers must always be apprised of pending changes and given as much information as possible. To do less is to create an atmosphere of distrust in which rumors will become rampant. Rumors can negatively affect the work environment and the general process of planned change. Supervisors must work diligently to keep channels of communication open and deal directly with rumors. When rumors are not confronted with accurate and complete information, they can cause irreparable damage to the change process (White and Chapman, 1996).

Human behavior is complex, so a supervisor should develop more than one strategy for fostering desired change. The advantages and disadvantages of each alternative should be reviewed, and the strategy with the greatest promise should be selected. In one instance, a sergeant (who had the complete support of management) considered several alternatives and finally decided that the greatest resistance would come from three informal leaders within the department. Meeting with them on an individual basis to explain the change before presenting the new proposal at roll call was believed to be the best strategy to enhance its implementation.

Involvement

The potential for creating a positive environment that will be more receptive to a proposed change is enhanced by involving those who will be most affected by it. This is not to suggest that this will always succeed, but experience has shown that the advantages of this technique outweigh the disadvantages. Those involved in the change process are in a position to use facts to combat rumors and erroneous information. Another important feature is the reduction or elimination of anxiety as officers become less concerned about pending change (Gray, 1984).

Involvement reduces resistance because the unknown becomes the known. It is important that those who will be affected become knowledgeable about why a specified change is needed and be made aware of the advantages of the change. Including employees in discussions about change does this best. When the decision is made to involve personnel in the change process, it is imperative for management to totally support the implementation of such a program. Open communications and involvement of line personnel can alert managers to potential problems that might arise when the change is implemented. Lip service or the tactic of manipulation will, in short order, weaken or destroy future efforts to involve personnel in the decision-making process. In many departments, street cops have been highly successful at thwarting change that has been forced on them by management. In fact, the ingenuity of officers in opposing change has resulted in the failure of numerous programs as departments have instituted the fads of the day (Skolnick and Fyfe, 1995)

Participation is time-consuming, so the rewards should exceed the costs. This brings up the question of when, during the decision-making process, affected employees should be involved. There is no simple answer, but in general it has been found that participation can be maximized if management has done its homework efficiently and gathered all the data needed to initiate a positive participation process.

Often it will be important to spell out that participation will be limited to the specific topic under consideration. This sets limits that allow for a freer exchange of ideas and will keep the decision-making process on target. As involvement becomes a part of the leadership style, the supervisor may find that some subordinates feel most comfortable when they are not involved in the decision-making process. However, what is of utmost importance to many subordinates is being given an opportunity to be involved if they so desire and becoming knowledgeable about proposed changes. When employees are involved in deciding how to implement changes, the changes become *their* changes, and cooperation is more likely to follow (Stone, 1997).

Communication

Without communication, it is likely that a proposal to implement a new policy or any other type of change will have a limited chance of succeeding. Keeping channels of communication open will usually provide a supervisor with information to be used when working at change implementation (Farias and Johnson, 2000). In most instances, change generates an emotional response that can range from mild to extreme, depending on the extent of the impact that it will have on individuals and how much it will alter working relationships. As a means of dealing with this, the supervisor should actively listen to every officer and respond accordingly. The supervisor should encourage the free flow of information. Letting the officer tell you what he or she thinks does this best. At this point, careful listening is imperative and there is a need to demonstrate a real interest in what is being said. The supervisor should ask open-ended questions and phrase them in such a way that the officer cannot answer with a simple "yes" or "no." An actual dialogue must occur. This serves as a ventilating process and provides for the exchange of facts and the reduction of emotions (Stone, 1997).

Even overcommunication will generally prove to be beneficial, although it can create unnecessary employee anxiety. This will be especially so if the information involves a change in working conditions. While it can be argued that waiting until more information can be obtained would upset a number of employees, it is still a judgment call. The evidence seems to support the importance of as much communication as possible, as soon as possible (Gray, 1984).

When officers know that management has made every effort to maintain and foster open communication, it will reduce resistance and provide them with greater prospects of implementing change. Efforts to restrict the flow of information can only enhance resistance and reinforce the informal organization. In such a situation, the grapevine will soon prevail and rumors will abound.

As a supervisor, it is essential to make a compelling case for any proposed change. Everything possible should be done to communicate every aspect of the change to those supervised. Every technique should be used to convey information about the change, including team meetings, roll-call sessions, personal contacts, e-mail, and memorandums. The key is to address not only *what* is being done, but also *why* it is being done. As a supervisor, you should never assume that the reasons for change are obvious—*communicate, communicate, communicate* (Stone, 1997).

Using the Influence of Informal Leaders

As previously indicated, a normal by-product of groups is the development of **informal leaders**. Officers who fulfill this role can usually be easily identified. Normally, one officer in a group will be the social leader and another officer will be seen as the group leader. The more the supervisor knows about each of the informal leaders in terms of their concerns, objectives, and personal styles, the better the chances of influencing those individuals (Cohen and Bradford, 1991). Informal leaders are a vital resource in the change process. In almost all instances they should be integrated into the team or group as soon as possible so that they will be a part of the change process.

Circumstances will dictate whether a first-line supervisor should include formal leaders in the change process. When it is evident that informal leaders are influential, they should be involved; otherwise, supervisors may be totally unaware that individuals (or situations) are playing an important part in resistance to change.

Involved informal leaders who are committed to the proposed change can usually reduce employee resistance and facilitate implementation. Informal leaders can provide information to the decision-making process that might otherwise be unavailable, allowing those involved the opportunity to meet this resistance head-on.

Informal leaders have influence that should be used, not ignored. It must be kept in mind that informal leaders should never be manipulated when being integrated into the decision-making process. First-line supervisors should respect the ideas of the rank-and-file and maximize their input when working for change (Peak, 1994).

Mandated Change

It is inevitable that a supervisor will eventually meet a situation in which every effort has been made to involve officers in the change process, but they are unsuccessful. Change may occur without consultation or involvement because of inadequate time to prepare for the change. This is a fact of managerial life, and there is no easy solution for this situation.

It is imperative for a supervisor to be open and candid with everyone and carefully explain the reasons for the change. Obviously, such a straightforward approach is an effort to deal rationally with anticipated or actual resistance. Such an appeal will be ignored if resistance is based on emotion.

At this point, the supervisor must make every effort to emphasize the positive aspects of the change, explaining the way it can help each officer. Everything the supervisor does will elicit a reaction of some sort from the officers, so the sergeant (supervisor) should strive to be a reliable source of information and a steadying influence during the initial stages of a change.

It is the supervisor's responsibility to shield subordinates as much as possible from the anxiety created by change. Showing genuine concern for the officer's welfare can do this. In other words, a supervisor must have a caring attitude (Tarkenton, 1984). Officers will generally respond positively to their supervisor's efforts to stabilize a situation and show sound judgment. If officers respond even slightly to such efforts, the supervisor has begun to lay a foundation, hopefully leading to a reduction or elimination of resistance.

Summary

Change is inevitable and is becoming an increasingly important part of the police officer's working life. Change places exceptional demands on supervisors. They must deal with social values, the law, and police unions. None of the three dominates the change process. In different agencies, one of the three factors may be central to change issues, while in other departments it may be of limited impact.

The first-line supervisor is deeply involved in the change process, functioning as the primary interpreter of new policies and serving as the focal point of relationships with line personnel.

Changes take place as a result of careful planning, taking into consideration the consequences of their implementation. Reasons for accepting change include officers having a choice, improving working conditions, employees being fully informed, and needs being satisfied.

Officers will normally resist change when it involves a negative economic impact, a lack of stability, altered social relationships, a change in habits, restricted or eliminated discretion, or a fundamentally unpopular decision.

Resistance to change can be either rational or emotional. Rational resistance can be dealt with objectively, while emotional resistance requires the supervisor to expend a great deal of effort in attempting to overcome it.

When a supervisor does everything possible to gather all the facts relating to any proposed change, he or she is using the best tool available to combat resistance. The supervisor can use information to deal objectively with resistance to change. In most cases, involving officers in the change process can lessen this resistance.

Other means of overcoming resistance include developing effective communication skills and using the influence of informal leaders as vital resources in making change.

Case Study

Sergeant William "Bill" Foster

William Foster is a sergeant in the Foxville Police Department. The agency has a sworn strength of 61 officers and 24 civilian employees that serves a community of 26,000. The department has an annual budget of $6.7 million. The town is governed by a city council and has a council-manager form of government. The town is located in a major metropolitan area and is primarily residential with a shopping mall. Many of its citizens commute to jobs in a large contiguous city. Like many communities across the nation, the incidence of crime has dropped—especially those involving acts of violence. Traffic is a significant problem, as is residential burglary.

In the past, the position of supervisor was not considered part of management, and sergeants functioned as controllers of line personnel. For the last year there has been a strong effort to involve sergeants in the managerial process. As managers, they are expected to serve in a role where officers have greater discretion. A participative managerial style has been fostered, and all organizational levels have received additional training. There have been numerous rocks in the roadway, but overall the department has been successful in moving away from an authoritarian managerial style.

Sergeant William Foster has just completed a special supervisory training program on results-oriented leadership. During the last two years he has been assigned to a regional narcotics task force and has just returned to the patrol division, where he is scheduled to supervise officers working on the swing shift. During his initial supervisory assignment to patrol, he made all of the decisions and exerted close supervision over his subordinates. He was instrumental in developing the officers he supervised into a cohesive unit that worked together in solving problems. Every officer knew exactly where he or she stood and responded accordingly.

Sergeant Foster is ambivalent about the changes in the supervisory process. He had been very comfortable in the authoritarian management style. But although he sees value in the participatory leadership style, he wonders if the line officers can perform effectively under such a style. His initial weeks on patrol were anxiety-producing, and he felt somewhat uncomfortable with the new program. Through the grapevine he has become aware of the fact that some of the officers were opposed to including sergeants in the management team. In the past, with sergeants grouped together with line officers, a united front could be presented to management. Some officers felt that the change weakened their bargaining position.

If you were Sergeant Foster, what would you do first to deal with this problem? Would you consult with your supervisor? Why or why not? Would you discuss your dilemma with the officers you supervise? Why or why not? He knows that he wants to maximize participation by the supervised officers, but how can this be done? Sergeant Foster is anticipating some resistance. What resistance do you think he can anticipate, and how should he deal with it?

Key Concepts

accepting change
ambiguity is created
being knowledgeable
collective bargaining
communication
cultural reasons
discretion is restricted or eliminated
factors fostering change
habits are altered
informal leaders
involvement
job satisfaction

law
mandated change
nature of resistance
need satisfaction
police unions
positive aspects of change
relationships are restricted
resistance to change
social values
unpopular decisions
working for change

Discussion Topics and Questions

1. Why is change such an integral part of contemporary organizational life?

2. What social values are characteristic of many police departments?

3. How does the law condition and recondition the functions performed by the police?

4. What are the five reasons employees accept change?

5. What are the characteristics of job satisfaction in law enforcement?

6. How should a supervisor deal with mandated change?

7. What factors foster change?

8. Discuss the positive aspects of change.

9. Why can change create ambiguity?

10. Why is involvement important to the change process?

For Further Reading

Beck, Karen, and Carlene Wilson (1997). "Police Officers' Views on Cultivating Organizational Commitment: Implications for Police Managers." *Policing: An International Journal of Police Strategy and Management,* Vol. 20, No. 1.

> This article summarizes police supervisors' and officers' opinions as to how management might improve organizational commitment. Supervisors identified problems with the structure and processes of the organization. The study recommends that organizational commitment can be improved by programs designed to increase interaction between the ranks within the department. Stresses the need for supervisors to receive accurate information about proposed changes to organizational processes and structure.

Charrier, Kim (2000). "Marketing Strategies for Attracting and Retaining Generation X Police Officers." *The Police Chief,* Vol. LXII, No. 12.

> This article asserts the position that today's police recruits are part of a Generation X, which has its own set of values and expectations. Suggests that Generation X recruits are prepared and willing to confront authority and that they often work to live, not live to work. The author views the ideal supervisor as a performance coach who spends time developing employees' skills and asking for employees' opinions. Predicts that police management of the future will be team-oriented.

De Paris, Richard J. (1998). "Organizational Leadership and Change Management—Removing Systems Barriers to Community-Oriented Policing and Problem Solving." *The Police Chief,* Vol. LXV, No. 12.

> Discusses the need for police management to develop a highly supportive environment that changes the culture from one of risk-averse to risk-tolerant. Recommends the reduction of direct supervision and standardization of the work process. Suggests they be replaced with less restrictive forms of control with a performance model of supervision. Believes that officers should be guided by organizational vision expressed through value and mission statements, and that goals should be pursued through collaboration.

International Association of Chiefs of Police (1999). "Police Leadership for the 21st Century." *The Police Chief,* Vol. LXVI, No.3.

> A group of 25 leading law enforcement executives developed a list of forces of change for the twenty-first century. Forces that were identified include collaborative demand, management style, workforce educational level, and decision horizons. Other forces included citizen expectations, community demographics, and litigation trends. The group recommended continually evaluating change forces—both internal and external. The group believes in assuming a proactive management style and fostering participatory management, with an emphasis on empowerment, both of which are essential for high levels of morale and enthusiasm.

References

Albrecht, Karl L. (1981). *Executive Tune-Up.* Englewood Cliffs, NJ: Prentice-Hall, Inc.

Beck, Karen, and Carlene Wilson (1997). "Police Officers' Views on Cultivating Organizational Commitment: Implications for Police Managers." *Policing: An International Journal of Police Strategy and Management,* Vol. 20, No. 1.

Bouza, Anthony V. (1990). *The Police Mystique: An Insider's Look at Cops, Crime and the Criminal Justice System.* New York, NY: Plenum Press.

Bridges, William (1991). *Managing Transitions: Making the Most of Change.* Reading, MA: Addison-Wesley Publishing.

Carr, David K. (1996). *Managing the Change Process: A Field Book for Change Agents, Consultants, Team Leaders, and Reengineering Managers.* New York, NY: McGraw-Hill.

Charrier, Kim (2000). "Marketing Strategies for Attracting and Retaining Generation X Police Officers." *The Police Chief,* Vol. LXII, No. 12.

Chemerinsky, Erwin, Paul Hoffman, Laurie Levenson, R. Samuel Paz, Connie Rice, and Carol Sobel (2000). *An Independent Analysis of the Los Angeles Police Department's Board of Inquiry Report on the Rampart Scandal.* Los Angeles, CA: University of Southern California.

Cohen, Allan R. and David L. Bradford (1991). *Influence without Authority.* New York, NY: John Wiley & Sons.

Cohen, Allan R., Stephen L. Fink, Herman Gadon, Robin D. Willits, and Natashe Josefowitz (1992). *Effective Behavior in Organizations,* Fifth Edition. Homewood, IL: Richard D. Irwin.

Community Policing Consortium (1998). *Module Four: Managing Organizational Change.* Washington, DC: Community Policing Consortium.

Dale, Nancy (2000). "Turning Around an Agency—How the Fort Pierce Police Department Did It." *Law and Order,* Vol. 48, No. 11.

Dalziel, Murray (1988). *Changing Ways.* New York, NY: AMACOM.

De Meuse, Kenneth P., and Kevin K. McDaris (1994). "An Exercise in Managing Change." *Training and Development,* Vol. 48, No. 2.

DeParis, Richard, J. (1997). "Situational Leadership: Problem-Solving Leadership for Problem-Solving Policing." *The Police Chief,* Vol. LXIV, No. 10.

DeSantis, Victor S., and Samantha L. Durst (1998). "Job Satisfaction Among Local Government Employees: Lessons for Public Managers." *The Municipal Yearbook—1997.* Washington, DC: International City/County Management Association.

Dolan, Harry P. (1994). "Coping with Internal Backlash." *The Police Chief*, Vol. LXI, No. 3.

Farias, G., and H. Johnson (2000). "Organizational Development and Change Management: Setting the Record Straight." *Journal of Applied Behavioral Science,* Vol. 36, No. 3.

French, Barbara, and Jerry Stewart (2001). "Organizational Development in a Law Enforcement Environment." *FBI Law Enforcement Bulletin,* Vol. 70, No. 9,

Garfield, Charles (1986). *Peak Performers.* New York, NY: William Morrow and Company.

Glensor, Ronald D., and Ken Peak (1996). "Implementing Change: Community-Oriented Policing and Problem Solving." *FBI Law Enforcement Bulletin*, Vol. 65, No. 7.

Gray, Jerry L. (1984). *Supervision.* Belmont, CA: Wadsworth Publishing.

Guyot, Dorothy (1991). *Policing as Though People Matter.* Philadelphia, PA: Temple University Press.

Harvey, Thomas R. (1990*). Checklist for Change: A Pragmatic Approach to Creating and Controlling Change.* Boston, MA: Allyn and Bacon.

Haught, Lunell (1998). "Meaning, Resistance and Sabotage—Elements of a Police Culture." *Community Policing Exchange,* Phase V, No. 20.

Holton, Bill, and Cher Holton (1992). *The Manager's Short Course.* New York, NY: John Wiley & Sons.

International Association of Chiefs of Police (1999). "Police Leadership for the 21st Century." *The Police Chief*, Vol. LXVI, No. 3.

Kirby, Tess (1989). *The Can-Do Manager: How to Get Your Employees to Take Risks, Take Action, and Get Things Done.* New York, NY: AMACOM.

Kriegel, Robert, and David Brandt (1996). *Sacred Cows Make the Best Burgers—Paradigm-Busting Strategies for Developing Change-Ready People and Organizations.* New York, NY: Warner Books.

Leonard, Karl S. (1997). "Making Change a Positive Experience." *Law and Order*, Vol. 45, No. 5.

Malik, S.D., and Kenneth N. Wexley (1986). "Improving the Owner/Manager's Handling of Subordinates' Resistance to Unpopular Decisions." *Journal of Small Business Management*, Vol. 32, No. 4.

Maurer, Rick (1996). *Beyond the Wall of Resistance—Unconventional Strategies That Build Support for Change.* Austin, TX: Bard Books.

Mollen, Milton (1994). *Commission Report—Commission to Investigate Allegations of Police Corruption and the Anti-Corruption Procedures of the Police Department.* New York, NY: City of New York.

Moore, Mark M., and Darrel W. Stephens (1991). *Beyond Command and Control: The Strategic Management of Police Departments.* Washington, DC: Police Executive Research Forum.

More, Harry W. (1998). *Special Topics in Policing*, Second Edition, Cincinnati, OH: Anderson Publishing Co.

————, and W. Fred Wegener (1992). *Behavioral Police Management*. New York, NY: Macmillan.

Mulder, Armand E.R. (1994). "Resistance to Change—A Personal Assessment*." Law and Order,* Vol. 42, No. 2.

Ortiz, Robert L. (1994). "Police Culture: A Roadblock to Change in Law Enforcement." *The Police Chief,* Vol. LXI, No. 8.

O'Toole, James (1995). *Leading Change—Overcoming the Ideology of Comfort and the Tyranny of Custom.* San Francisco, CA: Jossey-Bass.

Peak, Ken (1994). "Police Executives as Agents of Change." *The Police Chief,* Vol. LXI, No. 4.

Pennings, Johannes M. (1997). "Innovation and Change." In Arndt Sorge and Malcolm Warner (eds.), *The IEBM Handbook of Organizational Behavior*. London: International Thomas Business Press.

Skolnick, Jerome H., and James J. Fyfe (1995). "Community-Oriented Policing Would Prevent Police Brutality." In Paul A. Winters (ed.), *At Issue: Policing the Police.* San Diego, CA: Greenhaven Press.

Stone, Florence M. (1997). *The Manager's Balancing Act*. New York, NY: AMACOM.

Sweeney, Earl M. (1997). "Vehicular Pursuits—Balancing the Risks." *The Police Chief,* Vol. LXIV, No. 7.

Tarkenton, Fran (1984). *Playing to Win*. New York, NY: Harper and Row.

Tichy, Noel M. and Mary Anne Devanna (1990). *The Transformational Leader*. New York, NY: John Wiley & Sons.

Tosi, Henry L., John R. Rizzo, and Stephen J. Carroll (1990*). Managing Organizational Behavior,* Second Edition. New York, NY: Harper and Row.

Tracey, William R. (1990). *Leadership Skills: Standout Performance for Human Resource Managers.* New York, NY: AMACOM.

Washo, Brad D. (1984). "Effecting Planned Change within a Police Department." *The Police Chief,* Vol. LIV, No. 9.

White, Ken W., and Elwood N. Chapman (1996). *Organizational Communication—An Introduction to Communication and Human Relations Strategies*. Needham Heights, MA: Simon & Schuster Custom Publishing.

Zhao, Jihong (1996*). Why Police Organizations Change: A Study of Community-Oriented Policing.* Washington, DC: Police Executive Research Forum.

Supervising the Difficult Employee—

Special Considerations

10

Introductory Case Study

Officer Pete Hammonds

Officer Pete Hammonds has been a police officer for the Willamont Police Department for nearly 12 years. He has an associate's degree in police science and a bachelor's degree in criminal justice. He was hired just after he graduated from the university under a COPS grant program as a DARE and school safety officer. After two years in the DARE and school safety program, he transferred into patrol. His evaluations have been good each year, but not outstanding. He does his job, is responsible, diligent, and has a great deal of common sense, but has never gone out of his way to receive higher evaluations or pursue a promotion.

Part of the reason for this is his family. Pete is a true family man. He has two young children and loves to spend as much time with them as he can. His wife, however, was never supportive of him being a police officer. She always felt he could better himself by going to work for her father in an accounting firm. For this reason, Pete and his wife argued constantly.

About seven months ago, Pete's wife met another man and had an affair. She ultimately divorced Pete, got custody of the children, and married her newfound love. Pete never knew about the affair and had reluctantly agreed to the divorce on the condition that he could see the children frequently. However, Pete's ex-wife and children moved 3,000 miles away, and Pete could not afford to visit or have the children visit him as often as he wished. Pete was devastated.

Over the past few months, Pete has changed his work habits. He volunteers for every detail that comes along, works as much overtime as he can, and takes moonlighting jobs in security. He has told several of the officers on his shift that he wants to get promoted and needs to work moonlighting jobs in order to pay for visits to see his children. Pete has also been more sociable with the other officers. He spends more time going to parties and to bars with other officers. He has increased the number of arrests he makes and the number of citations. In fact, he has outperformed every officer on the shift.

At first, Sergeant Guthrie thought it was a good change. After all, Pete had never fully put forth an effort in police work. Now he's outperforming every officer under his supervision. Sergeant Guthrie has begun to think that Pete doesn't sleep. When Pete is not at the police department, he's working at department stores in security or partying with "the boys." Sergeant Guthrie believes this is just a stage Pete is going through, adapting to not having his children around.

If you were Sergeant Guthrie, would you be concerned about Pete's behavior? Is Pete heading for a burnout, or will he adjust? How would you document the changes in Pete's behavior? If you were discussing Pete's next evaluation with him, what would you say?

Contemporary supervisors must set the tone, change the paradigms, and create a foundation that results in a truly supportive working environment. There is a need to change supervisory values and beliefs. They should be built on, or replaced with, new ones (Zook, 1994). This changing role presents not only a challenge to each supervisor, but also the concomitant possibility of creating apprehension and anxiety caused by the change. It demands the application of new skills and the modification of traditional guidelines and creeds. Imaginative leadership will be the key if consistent, high-quality performance is to be required of every employee. The supervisor plays a crucial role in managing a productive contemporary workplace. There is a need for a new accountability within police organizations, which strains the traditional way of dealing with employees. A transformation is necessary as organizations change, the workforce becomes increasingly diversified, and communities demand improved police services at lower costs. The first-line supervisor is the key if the new organization is to become a learning organization.

The quality of a psychological work environment should be such that employees feel at ease and new patterns of thinking are accepted. It is where officers are encouraged to improve themselves and where new ways of thinking about problem solving occur (Zook, 1994). In a positive working environment, supervisors tailor the supervisory techniques they use to fit the competence level of each employee. Some employees will need closer supervision than others. Some will respond to one motivational technique, while others respond to a different technique.

Employees should be part of the decision-making process and should be responsible for results. This makes officers accountable and allows them the freedom to "buy in" to the situation. This results in the actual implementation of accountability (Cottringer, 1994). As an officer assumes responsibility and completes operations successfully, supervisors can increase officer responsibility. All of this leads to an improved quality of life in the workplace.

In recent years, value statements have set the tone for many organizations. Typical of these is the value statement of the Alexandria, Virginia, Police Department as it relates to the members of the organization (see Figure 10.1). Values are the basis for the beliefs and actions taken by the department. The values guide the work and decisions of the department. They represent ideals and are the foundation for the policies, goals, and operations that affect employees. They are nonnegotiable and are never ignored for the sake of expediency or personal preference. Such values constantly remind supervisors and managers of the factors that contribute to a positive work environment (Samarra, 1992).

Figure 10.1
Alexandria Police Department Values

OURSELVES

We are capable, caring people who are doing important and satisfying work for the citizens of Alexandria.

Therefore:

We respect, care about, trust, and support each other.
We enjoy our work and take pride in our accomplishments.
We are disciplined and reliable.
We keep our perspective and sense of humor.
We balance our professional and personal lives.
We consult those who will be affected by our decisions.
We have a positive, "can-do" attitude.
We cultivate our best characteristics: initiative, enthusiasm, creativity, patience, competence, and judgment.

Source: Charles E. Samarra (1992). *Alexandria Police: These Are Our Values*. Alexandria, VA: Alexandria Police Department.

Employees as Individuals

Unfortunately, there are many rocks in the roadway that impede progress as change occurs. One of these is the problem employee. Dealing with problem employees occurs more often than most supervisors would like. We do not live in a perfect world, and employees are not perfect. Everyone is not equal, as is clearly evident in our society and the workplace. Some employees are more productive than others. Some are more analytical than others. Some have special skills that others do not have, such as writing, verbal, or physical skills. Others are more effective working with young people or with older people. Some officers function most effectively on undercover assignments, and others would never be selected for such a task.

Each officer is a distinct person with a personality, definite needs, and a personally unique lifestyle.

A supervisor is also an individual with experiences, needs, and drives that may or may not be similar to those he or she supervises (Harvey, 1990). This presents a real challenge, especially if the value systems conflict. The police field is in a state of flux, and diversity is increasingly common in the workplace. As the work environment has undergone change, the role of the first-line supervisor has become increasingly important. The supervisor must develop or be knowledgeable about the skills of his or her subordinates and provide a supportive climate in which the common purposes of the organization become achievable (Kouzes and Posner, 1993). This presents the supervisor with a dilemma. When an employee becomes difficult to work with, tasks are not accomplished, or work is done with indifference, a supervisor must take corrective action. In some situations, unsuitable behavior can impair the effectiveness of the officer, and in other cases, unacceptable behavior can negatively affect other organization members. Inappropriate behavior can occur at any stage of an officer's employment, ranging from newly appointed individuals to those who are nearing retirement.

Types of Employees

One expert found three types of individuals in organizations: *ascendant*, *indifferent*, and *ambivalent*. The number of employees in each group varies from agency to agency, and this grouping of employees seems to be what supervisors actually find in an organization (Leonard and More, 1993). We acknowledge that it is not easy to categorize employees because of our limited knowledge of why people behave the way they do. Human beings are very complex, and individuals can and do change, depending upon needs, aspirations, attitudes, and beliefs. With a change in departmental policies, some officers have shifted from one class to another. In other instances, officers who are either ascendant or ambivalent have "burned out" because of excessive stress. These generalized groupings can be used by the supervisor for viewing employee conduct that is similar to other employees. Also, the supervisor must deal with employees on an individual basis (Steinmetz and Todd, 1992). Figure 10.2 lists the attitudes that each of these groups has toward work.

Ascendant

There are few ascendant officers within an organization, compared to the other two groups. In fact, if a supervisor had to manage a squad of ascendants, In all likelihood, it would prove disastrous for both the supervisor and the officers. The ascendant is a workaholic, an "organizational person," or someone on the "fast track." This group of employees is work-oriented and perceives the job as being uppermost in life (More and Wegener, 1992). They are success-driven and exhibit a high energy level. They focus on their assignment as well as the needs of the department, and are self-starters. Recognition and promotion are the name of the game, and everything else is secondary. Ascendants believe in themselves and know that they can produce. They especially accept the challenge of the unknown and relish working on difficult assignments. They are loners and believe they are the only ones who accomplish tasks quickly and effectively.

Ascendants are usually intolerant of others who fail to work rapidly and effectively. They usually take the position that if something is to be done, they would rather do it themselves. Goal orientation dominates their work style, and they ardently support the values and mission of the department. Ascendants actively seek advancement and do everything possible to make themselves eligible for promotion. Whenever possible, they volunteer for special assignments, attend as many training programs as possible, and vigorously pursue advanced academic degrees. Their allegiance is usually to the profession rather than the department, and they actively pursue openings in other agencies. Others with similar views attract them, and they use information obtained from others to enhance their own position.

Supervisors usually work well with ascendants. This is because unless they become excessively exuberant, they require little supervision. Because they are achievers, supervisors turn to them when time constraints are such that immediate completion of a project is essential. This is done with the full knowledge that the task will be accomplished swiftly and correctly. Ascendants readily accept and follow departmental rules and require limited supervision. This allows supervisors to spend more time with subordinates in the other groups (Steinmetz and Todd, 1992).

Indifferent

Some police departments have more indifferents than they would like to have, but most agencies usually have to deal with few such officers. They perform their duties at what they perceive is an acceptable level, which proves to be minimal. It does not take them long to determine what is an acceptable performance level, and they never exceed that level. Yet they make sure they never do so little that discipline, reprimand, or termination might occur. Their primary motivation is to earn enough money so they can concentrate on their family or nondepartmental activities. Indifferents have a strong affiliative drive and get along with almost everyone (Steinmetz and Greenridge, 1976). The department becomes just a place of work for this type of employee. Such an individual never volunteers or seeks promotion. The desirable operating mode is maintaining existing conditions—change is definitely undesirable. If change is personally inimical, the indifferent seeks protection from the work group or the union. This type of individual strengthens informal workgroups and views peers as a primary support element. He or she will social-ize with other officers and is prone to violate departmental rules. Even though policy might prohibit officers from leaving their beat, indifferents will leave the beat and join other officers at restaurants. When the union wants cooperation from officers during negotiations, these are the officers who will respond. They will enforce the letter of the law or engage in a slow-down. Then, for some reason, they will get the "blue flu" when appropriate.

When working with this group, supervisors find that motivational efforts have a short lifespan and that close supervision is the only way to ensure com-pletion of tasks within a reasonable time. Indifferents, by their performance, require the supervisor to constantly document their activities. This is done to ensure compliance with departmental policy and their functioning at an acceptable work level. They are really "good old boys," but they can be a headache for a supervisor. These individuals just slide by, seldom make waves, and escape by daydreaming. They function at such a borderline level that discipline can occur only after an extensive paper trail. One needs to expend an exceptional amount of effort documenting an unacceptable performance level. Officers in this group have decided the pace at which they will work even if that work level is less than acceptable. Even at a slow pace, these employ-ees accomplish a considerable amount of work (Steinmetz and Todd, 1992).

Ambivalent

Most officers in a police organization are ambivalent. They are often imaginative and intelligent. They spend a considerable amount of time becoming knowledgeable about critical areas such as the use of deadly force, narcotics, and dangerous drugs. They also concentrate on such areas as surveillance, crime prevention, juvenile delinquency, and problem solv-ing. Upon mastering a technique or procedure, they search for more inter-esting work. To the ambivalent, the routine task quickly becomes boring and is usually put off. Procrastination becomes the order of the day.

If the frustration level becomes excessive, these officers will become anx-ious about their work and become less decisive. As a result, poorer decisions will be made. Resistance to new rules is quite common and becomes a typ-ical behavior pattern. Additionally, ambivalent officers will, over time, become less committed to the department. If work is dull and routine, this type of employee will become less productive. Many employees in this group do not aspire to higher ranks because of a general distrust of man-agement. In fact, many officers in this group become antagonistic toward high levels of management. If appropriate, they will actively oppose policy changes that they perceive as detrimental (Leonard and More, 1993).

A challenging assignment is what this type of individual needs if per-formance is to remain high. The supervisor must spend considerable time finding new assignments, identifying new responsibilities, and recognizing solvable problems to motivate and challenge these employees. Similar to the ascendants, ambivalents respond to praise and commendation for work done well. They readily participate in professional development programs, and supervisors can recommend them for training as a motivational technique. They covet promotions at least to the level of first-line supervisor or promotion within rank. Sergeants can use this desire to increase their involvement, improve work habits, and change behavior (Steinmetz and Todd, 1992).

Supervisory expectations are critical to subordinate performance. No matter what group an employee might fall into, it is essential for the supervisor to express and act in such a way that every employee knows the acceptable level of job performance. High expectations are an essential ingredient of positive performance. The reason for this is that research supports the motivational aspects of the Pygmalion effect. Most employees in an organization perform as they are expected to perform. If a supervisor conveys to an officer that a task will probably not be completed up to standards, there is every reason to believe that the employee will respond accordingly. If one expects poor performance, that will be the result. If one expresses high expectations, the results are more likely to be positive (Steinmetz and Todd, 1992). A supervisor should never conduct him or herself in such a way that negative expectations are part of the message received by those supervised.

Figure 10.2
Officer Attitudes Toward Work

Ascendant

High achievement orientation
Identifies with the department
Strong work orientation
Works effectively under pressure
Receptive to feedback from superiors
Readily accepts rules and regulations
Can overcome failure by hard work

Indifferent

Works at a minimal level
Resists motivational efforts
Does not seek promotion
Gravitates toward off-the-job satisfaction
Reluctant to accept change
Identifies with the work group and police union
Will not seek added responsibilities

Ambivalent

Does not like to make decisions
Seeks approval and recognition
Superior work performer if the tasks are challenging
Often creative and intelligent
Most likely to challenge departmental policies
Receptive to change
Tends to rise to a supervisory position

As a supervisor, you will have to deal with a wide range of employee behavior. Like most supervisors, you will do your best to deal with officers fairly and competently when assessing their behavior. A simple way to rate yourself is to identify the most troublesome employee supervised. It should be someone you feel a little uncomfortable with and someone to whom you have difficulty giving negative feedback. List the beliefs, attitudes, and behavior of that individual that cause you difficulty. The goal is to describe what it is about the employee that distinguishes him or her from others. Next, create a second list that describes the employee with whom you are most comfortable. List that officer's behavior, characteristics, attitudes, and beliefs (Holton and Holton, 1992).

Compare the descriptions, and you will find that if you are like most supervisors, you are much more similar to the officer with whom you are comfortable. All of us are more comfortable around people who have similar beliefs, attitudes, and behaviors (Mann, 1993). You will judge those who are different from you more severely. You might want to use this information to rate how you deal with those you supervise.

Problem Employees

Supervisors spend a considerable amount of time dealing with conflict created by officers. These officers behave in a way that is unacceptable to the organization. One study pointed out that approximately 70 percent of behavior problems involve the organization itself, the immediate supervisor, and the employee (Bennett and Hess, 2001). In many instances, the conflict affects performance negatively. When managing personnel, you must consider a minimum of three variables: the supervisor, the officer, and the officer's performance. Too often, one of these variables is no longer part of the equation.

The failure to perform effectively is conditioned by other variables. Each feature must be given careful consideration as modified by the situation. Performance problems require a supervisor to analyze the situation carefully and spend the time necessary to resolve the problem (Kottler, 1994).

Problem behavior seldom evolves from a personality conflict between a supervisor and an officer. Most often it is the result of the failure of one of the involved parties to accept tenets, behaviors, and views other than their own (Steinmetz and Todd, 1992). Whatever the cause of conflict, the supervisor must deal with conduct that is inimical to the organization. If unacceptable behavior occurs, the supervisor must respond. If ignored, it can negatively affect other employees as well as the organization itself (Mahoney, 1986; Jones, 1999; Bennett and Hess, 2001). Problem employees can usually be placed in one of the following categories: erudites, tyrants, defeatists, manipulators, or indecisives. These categories are not mutually exclusive, and they provide the supervisor with a typology that can be useful when dealing with conflict (see Figure 10.3).

Figure 10.3
Problem Employees

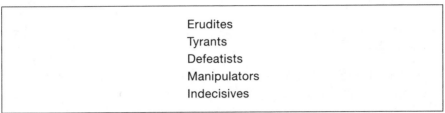

Erudites
Tyrants
Defeatists
Manipulators
Indecisives

Erudites

Erudites have an opinion on just about everything. This is especially true if they have just completed a college course or a specialized training program. Officers in this group are seldom at a loss for words and pride themselves on their command of language. The more loquacious they can be, the better they like it. They see themselves as intellectuals, learned, and in a class by themselves. Their tolerance level is somewhat low, and acceptance of others usually comes with reluctance. This is especially true when there is a difference of opinion. They respect order and work comfortably within departmental regulations. These officers use their expertise as a power base for influencing decisions.

Supervisors can deal with this type of employee by using their own expertise, especially when facing the unknown or engaging in complex problem solving. The supervisor should assimilate the knowledge of erudites in such a way that others do not take offense. The erudite should never be allowed to take over the leadership position. As a supervisor, you should acknowledge their contributions with appropriate praise.

Tyrants

Tyrants are control-oriented and do not respect others. These officers respond explosively and do everything possible to intimidate anyone who stands in their way. If someone resists their ideas, the reaction of the tyrant is immediate. Denunciations and even personal attacks are used to maintain their position. Domination of the situation is the goal, and open warfare is the game. This type of officer wants to win and will not hesitate to use coercion or create a climate of fear. They also will use threats to get their way. Their technique of choice is that of overwhelming the opposition. They follow the principle of always attacking to keep those they oppose off-balance. This behavior allows them to gain control over others.

Supervisors must deal with this type of behavior by responding at the same level. The supervisor should maintain control and rebuff aggressive behavior. It requires an authoritarian response, and the supervisor must convert a lose-lose situation to one that is win-lose. Rejection of aggressive behavior is essential, and supervisors should use every tool at their disposal. Confrontation may be necessary, and it should be done privately and as often as needed.

Defeatists

Defeatists are those who resist every new idea. Change is something of which to be skeptical, and enjoyment is only found in performing a cynical role. These officers never say anything good about anyone or anything. They are chronic "bitchers." They never have solutions, feel comfortable being disrupters, and are rigid (CareerTrack, 1995). The name of the game is that no one wins, and everyone is a loser. Defeatists complain about administrators, politicians, citizens, the Supreme Court, and prosecuting attorneys. New policies are rejected out-of-hand, and new programs are viewed as worthless.

The way to deal with this type of employee is to confront him or her about an issue by asking for specifics, not generalities. Make the employee explain his or her position. Ask penetrating questions and address the core of the issue. When rules are in dispute, review a copy of the document and discuss it in depth. Everything possible should be done to clarify the situation and deal with the specific problem. It is not the supervisor's place to try to change the personality of the defeatist.

Manipulators

There are a few officers who fall into this group. Manipulators are fundamentally unethical and have no difficulty doing anything necessary to gain an advantage. Half-truths and innuendo are acceptable and part of the arsenal used to maintain or enhance their position. Knowledge is power, and manipulators gather and impart information that will lead to an advantageous position. They enjoy dividing and conquering and, when possible, play one person against another, or officers against managers. Manipulators are masters of deceit, and they strive to create conflict and an atmosphere in which they win and others lose (Jones, 1999). Supervisors must investigate every action taken by a manipulator, then provide feedback to reduce or neutralize the impact of this type of officer. The supervisor must learn to pass judgment based on facts and objectively refute the manipulator.

Indecisives

Indecisives are impervious to praise and punishment. Officers in this group will work diligently to avoid making a decision and are experts at procrastination. Their position is to delay until tomorrow what can be done today. They hide their attitudes and beliefs. They suppress their feelings and remain as neutral as possible. This makes it very difficult for the supervisor to judge their response. One never knows whether they support or disapprove of a decision. By never expressing support or rejection of anything, they become experts at neutrality. If indecisives do not respond negatively or positively, they are protected from others who pass judgment.

Case Study

Corporal Vernon Stillwell

Corporal Vernon Stillwell is a 10-year veteran with the Ridgeview Police Department. The Ridgeview Police Department has 255 sworn officers and its own police academy. It is located about an hour away from a university that houses one of the finest traffic accident institutes in the world. Corporal Stillwell graduated from the university with a master's degree in criminal justice three years ago. He also graduated from basic training as well as several advanced classes in traffic accident reconstruction. He is a certified reconstructionist and is highly sought-after by other area police departments to help work fatal and serious traffic accidents.

Stillwell was promoted to corporal last year. The rank of corporal is basically just a promotion rank for specialized officers and is really not a supervisory position. However, Corporal Stillwell is considered to be second to Sergeant Jones in his unit. When Sergeant Jones is away, Corporal Stillwell takes over as the supervisor for the squad.

Corporal Stillwell changed once he received his master's degree and certification as a traffic accident reconstructionist. He tends to think of himself as a highly educated expert and is quick to point out to others how intelligent he is and what an asset he is to the department. He writes articles for police journals on traffic accident reconstruction and has given numerous interviews with the news media during the past several months. This has done nothing but fuel his ego even more. He is critical of policy and tries to show his expertise by making numerous suggestions to "the brass" on policy issues. He is also quick to correct his sergeant in front of the other officers. After all, Sergeant Jones has only an associate's degree and does not have nearly the intelligence or expertise that Corporal Stillwell has. Sergeant Jones is a laid-back individual and seems to take Corporal Stillwell's ego in stride. The other officers on the squad also seem to tolerate Corporal Stillwell and even make jokes about him.

Last week, Corporal Stillwell was supposed to go to a special one-day seminar on domestic violence, but opted out at the last minute due to "sickness." That same evening, Sergeant Jones saw Corporal Stillwell on the local news tesifying in a civil case involving a traffic fatality. Apparently, Corporal Stillwell had been hired by a civil attorney as an expert witness in a serious traffic accident case. While there is no policy forbidding officers from hiring themselves out as expert witnesses in civil trials, Corporal Stillwell did violate the policy on sick leave use.

If you were Sergeant Jones, what action would you take at this point? Would you use a punitive or a positive approach? How would you deal with Stillwell's ego and behavior?

Supervisors must try to determine why the indecisive is stonewalling. What is the real reason he or she refuses to make a decision? One must listen carefully, then ask specific questions directed toward clarification and illumination. Ask the indecisive officers to simplify their response, and do not allow them to use platitudes, vagueness, or a nondefinitive posture. The supervisor should respond with specificity and decisiveness to every dubious answer.

The Marginal Performer

When officers perform marginally, they become a problem for a supervisor and can consume an inordinate amount of supervisory time. A minimally performing officer does just enough to get by, with the intent of avoiding reprimand or discipline. The marginal performer knows all of the work norms and consistently performs just below the acceptable level. Report writing takes longer than expected, fewer traffic citations are issued, and field interviews may be conducted, but with reduced frequency. Coffee and meal breaks are either taken more frequently, or the time of each break is extended. In some instances, marginal performers accept the challenge of finding ways to barely get by. These officers take the position that there is no reason they should work any harder than necessary. Just getting by seems to be a badge of honor.

Some marginal performers are habitually late and absent themselves from duty as much as possible. They believe sick leave is a right, not a privilege (McNaught and Schofield, 1998). They never volunteer for any assignment and, if selected, beg off. Their general demeanor is such that they always look busy and highly involved, but this is not the case. Their complacency extends to every aspect of the job, and their primary interests are external to the department. Their overall behavior is passive, and they have a short-term perspective.

The marginal performer readily accepts a subordinate position and strives to never "rock the boat." Promotions are of little consequence. Opposition to change is part of an overall resistance format. They point out that there is nothing wrong with the way the organization is currently doing things. If the proposed change is important enough, they will vigorously oppose the change, but this is usually done through the informal structure of the department.

Beyond the problems generated by their supervisor, the police organization is seen as the real culprit. Top brass are viewed as being out of step with reality. Hiding behind their desks, marginal performers see policy makers performing in a vacuum. Blaming management for their problems is a means by which marginal employees excuse themselves from personal responsibility. They believe that if the supervisor and the "brass" are the sources of the problem, there is little they can do to correct the situation.

Marginal employees seldom have clearly defined short- or long-range goals, and if this is true, the supervisor should sit down with the employee and formally set goals. A plan should be agreed upon that will help the employee to achieve his or her goals. The supervisor should ensure that the goals are compatible with departmental mission and value statements. If there is a question of formal authority, the supervisor should review what makes up the mutual working relationship. All employees must understand their status and place within the organization. The supervisor's task is to place responsibility where it belongs. Job descriptions should be reevaluated, and the supervisor should review the tasks that are the employee's responsibility (Brown, 1992).

The supervisor should praise marginal employees when they have performed effectively and should keep in mind the need for giving feedback as soon as possible after the completion of a task or assignment. The supervisor should express confidence in the employee and voice the need for the employee to maintain acceptable performance standards and a positive attitude. The employee should be told about promotional opportunities and encouraged to attend special training programs as a means of improving his or her performance. The officer should be made aware of the importance of volunteering for new assignments. Hopefully, all of these will increase the officer's potential for promotion.

The supervisor should strive to deal with the employee on a positive level, displaying enthusiasm and a positive attitude. The employee should have every opportunity to improve performance and become a viable member of the organization. When performance exceeds recognized standards, the officer should be given better assignments. He or she should be supported for promotion and, at the very least, praised for a job well done. If the employee fails to follow performance standards, this should be documented and corrective action should be taken. See Chapter 11 for a discussion of internal discipline.

Work Stressors

Organizational stress can have an effect not only on the organization, but also on the individual. From an organizational viewpoint, supervisors can see productivity slip and morale decline. They can also see delayed task completion, increased use of sick leave, and other signs of employee discontent. Figure 10.4 lists a number of personal and organizational effects of work stressors. For the individual, stress can result in numerous problems, ranging from alcohol abuse to suicide.

The police culture and work environment have a definite impact on police officers, and this interaction can result in an acute interruption of psychological or behavioral homeostasis. These reactions or disruptions, if prolonged, are believed to lead to a variety of illnesses. The most commonly researched job stress-related illnesses are hypertension, heart disease, alcoholism, and mental illness. Additionally, unrelieved stress can cause chronic headaches and gastric ulcers. Job stress can lead to severe depression, alcohol or drug abuse, aggression, marital problems, and suicide. Other stressors that are endemic to police work include boredom, danger, shift work, lack of public support, unfavorable court decisions, unfair administrative policies, and poor supervision (More and Wegener, 1992).

Everyone is affected by stress to one degree or another; in some instances it is positive, and in others, negative. Of concern to the supervisor are the negative consequences of stress, which can affect officers' alertness, physical stamina, and their ability to work effectively (Goolkasian et al., 1985). Stress can also lead to excessive absenteeism, disability, or early retirement; thus, stress can be costly to an organization. For example, in one state, courts have ruled that heart disease is occupationally related.

Figure 10.4
Personal and Organizational Effects of Work Stress

Personal

Alcohol abuse	Anxiety
Drug abuse	Psychosomatic diseases
Emotional instability	Eating disorders
Lack of self-control	Boredom
Fatigue	Mental illness
Marital problems	Suicide
Depression	Health breakdowns
Insomnia	Irresponsibility
Insecurity	Violence
Frustration	

Organizational

Accidents	Unpreparedness
Reduced productivity	Lack of creativity
High turnover	Increased sick leave
Increased errors	Premature retirement
Absenteeism	Job dissatisfaction
Damage and waste	Poor decision making
Antagonistic group action	

Adapted from Lawrence R. Murphy and Theodore F. Schoenborn (eds.) (1987). *Stress Management in Work Settings*. Washington, DC: U.S. Government Printing Office.

Task Stressors

Task stressors are wide-ranging and include role conflict and ambiguity, control of work, use of excessive force, danger, boredom, and shift work. All of these complicate not only the officer's personal life, but also the officer's organizational life.

Danger. The possibility of an officer being seriously injured or killed when on duty is somewhat remote, but these events do occur. Unfortunately, attacks on police officers are happening with increasing frequency. When emergency calls come over the radio, the officer usually responds and energy is mobilized to deal with the contingency. In 1999, 42 officers were feloniously killed in the line of duty in the United States. The situations in which these killings occurred were: disturbance calls, arrest situations (i.e., robberies and burglaries in progress), drug-related arrests, and attempting other arrests. It also included investigating suspicious persons/circumstances, ambush situations, traffic pursuits/stops, and mentally deranged individuals. Additionally, 65 officers were accidentally killed in the line of duty—the majority in automobile accidents. During the same year, 55,026 officers were assaulted and 29.6 percent of those were injured (U.S. Department of Justice, 2001). In recent years, soft body armor has been worn by more and more police officers, and it has saved numerous lives. Over a 20-year period ending in 1992, there were 1,448 officers "saved" from assaults and accidents. Of these, the top three circumstances were traffic pursuits/stops, investigating suspicious persons, and drug-related matters (Geller and Scott, 1992).

Boredom. One major stressor that is unique to the operational role of law enforcement is boredom. Patrolling a beat in a low-crime area can be less than challenging. Time can pass very slowly during the wee hours of the morning with little to do. Dealing with the same drunk time after time presents little challenge. The same applies to those who are mentally ill or live on the street. When enforcing traffic laws, officers soon find that in a short time they have heard every excuse possible for failure to comply with the law. On the other hand, an emergency can arise in which an officer must shift gears and respond to stressful and traumatic events. Confronting an armed suspect, entering a dark building, viewing the victim of a drive-by shooting, and comforting an abused child are all emotionally traumatizing events that can take their toll (Phillips and Schwartz, 1992).

Role Conflict and Ambiguity. These two factors are significant sources of stress for law enforcement personnel and the police organization. This is especially true with the move toward community policing and the emphasis on resolving community problems. How does this new approach balance out against the more traditional crime-control role? Which is more important—responding to calls for service, or working with a neighborhood to reduce narcotics trafficking? These competing demands can result in role pressures that cause conflict. The greater the conflict, the greater the potential for the creation of negative stress.

Role ambiguity occurs when there is a lack of clarity about the way tasks should be carried out. This is especially true when managers create policies that leave line personnel hanging out to dry. This happens, for example, when a new policy is written so broadly that it makes interpretation difficult, such as a use-of-force policy in which the phrase "use force necessary and appropriate for the situation" is used. Without amplification, such a statement is open to conflicting interpretations (More and Wegener, 1992).

Ambiguity includes lack of clarity about objectives associated with the work role, expectations concerning the work role, and the scope and responsibilities of the job (Murphy and Schoenborn, 1987). Employees who experience role ambiguity and conflict often have low self-confidence, higher job-related tension, and lower job satisfaction.

Control over Work. Recent evidence suggests that the amount of work is not as critical to the health of a worker as the worker's control over the pace of work and related work processes. In departments engaging in community policing, it is anticipated that the officer will have more control over the tasks he or she has to perform. Hence, it is hoped that there will be a reduction in stressors. One study found that workers with a heavy workload and low control have an increased risk of heart disease and high blood pressure, and smoke more than employees in jobs without these characteristics.

Shift Work. An additional job demand that affects the health of workers is shift work. There is evidence that night shifts and rotating shifts can lead to gastrointestinal disorders, emotional disturbances, and an increased risk of on-the-job injury. There is a disruption of biological rhythms that results in biochemical and physiological disturbances. The shift worker becomes sleep-deprived for two reasons: (1) sleeping during the day conflicts with the biological clock, which says it is daytime, and (2) numerous interruptions occurring during a normal day (Mahowald, 1994). The average day-shift worker gets eight hours more sleep weekly than the typical night-shift worker. Cumulative sleep deprivation causes the night-shift worker to be sleepier while on the job.

In a study of scheduling shift changes, the researcher recommended that shifts be changed in a clockwise direction. It was also suggested that officers spend three weeks on each shift and limit their work time to either a four- or five-day week. When comparing officers working under the new system to officers who worked under the old system, it was determined that:

1. The frequency of poor sleep decreased fourfold.

2. There was a decline of 25 percent in incidents of falling asleep on the night shift.

3. Officers had 40 percent fewer on-duty automobile accidents per mile compared to the previous two years.

4. When officers experienced sleep deprivation, they used alcohol and sleeping pills less often (*Law Enforcement News*, 1989).

Shift work causes officers to have impaired judgment, insight, and reasoning; as a consequence, it can create supervisory problems (Mahowald, 1994). Shift work is an essential ingredient of police work, and the supervisor should strive to create a work environment that provides for optimal functioning.

Use of Excessive Force. Civilian deaths caused by police in the United States average approximately 375 per year. The number of felons killed by police in justifiable homicides in 1998 was 367 (U.S. Department of Justice, 2001). Accurate data on the actual number of justifiable and unjustifiable killings of civilians by police simply do not exist. Official reports submitted to the FBI and information collected by coroners and medical examiners on death certificates may not reflect the true nature of the deaths.

Actually, police shootings are infrequent, and only one officer in 60 has killed someone during a 15-year period (Fyfe, 1982). In a study of the Los Angeles Police Department, it was determined that a significant number of officers repeatedly misused force and persistently ignored written policies. An assistant chief of the department pointed out that the department had failed miserably to hold supervisors accountable when excessive force was used under their command (Independent Commission on the LAPD, 1991).

Officers who have been involved in use-of-excessive-force situations can have severe legal, physical, and emotional problems (Neubauer, 1999). In one study, respondents to a survey indicated that involvement in a shooting incident was the most dangerous and traumatic experience that an officer could face during a career. Post-shooting traumatic responses include a wide range of stressful reactions, and these are listed in Figure 10.5.

Figure 10.5
Post-Shooting Traumatic Responses

1.	Guilt
2.	Anxiety
3.	Fear
4.	Nightmares
5.	Flashbacks
6.	Social withdrawal
7.	Impaired memory
8.	Inability to sleep
9.	Sensory distortion
10.	Grasping for life
11.	Crying
12.	A heightened sense of danger
13.	Sorrow over depriving a person of life
14.	Family problems
15.	Alcohol abuse
16.	Fear of being fired, criminally charged, or sued

Adapted from Harold E. Russell and Allan Biegel (1990). *Understanding Human Behavior for Effective Police Work*, Third Edition. New York: Basic Books; Roger M. Solomon and James M. Horn (1986). "Post-Shooting Traumatic Reactions: A Pilot Study." In James T. Reese and Harvey A. Goldstein (eds.), *Psychological Services For Law Enforcement*. Washington, DC: Federal Bureau of Investigation; and Bill Clede (1994). "Stress Insidious or Traumatic is Treatable." *Law and Order*, Vol. 42, No. 6.

Without question, an officer involved in a shooting is seldom prepared to cope with such a traumatic event, and the same is true of the officer's family, fellow officers, and supervisors. The supervisor should ensure that an officer involved in a shooting is referred to available employee assistance programs. In one survey, it was found that 79 percent of police psychologists counseled officers charged with excessive force (Scrivner, 1994).

Personal Problems

Information can come to the attention of the supervisor that could possibly require his or her intervention. In some instances, the supervisor intervenes directly, and in other cases an officer asks for help. Of all management levels, the close contact the supervisor has with line personnel will usually result in his or her becoming aware of inadequate or deteriorating work performance before other managers. In some situations, the supervisor can function as a counselor, and in others the officer can be referred to the appropriate employee assistance program. Symptoms of stress can lead to a wide variety of maladies, and those that have been studied and found important to law enforcement officers are discussed below.

Suicide

Studies conducted from the 1930s through the 1960s concluded that police officers had a high suicide rate. These studies included officers from such diverse police departments as San Francisco, Chicago, and New York. In a Wyoming study, it was determined that the suicide rate for officers was the second highest among occupational groups studied. In Tennessee, a report published in 1975 found that police officers had the third highest suicide rate among occupational groups. In a study of Chicago police officers, it was found that 60 percent of the suicides were linked to alcoholism (Wagner and Brzeczek, 1983).

From 1950 to 1967, the suicide rate of officers in the New York City Police Department averaged 22 per 100,000 (Friedman, 1967), and in 1994 there were 29 per 100,000 annually (*Law Enforcement News*, 1994b). This contrasts with the general population rate of 12.2 per 100,000. In 1998 the suicide rate in the United States was 11.31 per 100,000 (U.S. Department of Justice, 2001).

Nationally, some 300 officers committed suicide in 1994, compared to 137 who were killed in the line of duty by weapons or other causes (Hays, 1994). In the 10 years prior to 1995, 64 New York City Police officers killed themselves, and during the same period, 20 officers were killed in the line of duty. One of the suicides in 1994 was an officer who had been implicated in the "Dirty 30" drug corruption scandal. In another instance, a 30-year-old officer killed himself after being charged with drunk driving and leaving the scene of an accident. In a study conducted in 1994, the New York City Police Foundation concluded that the fundamental reasons officers kill themselves are because of personal problems, substance abuse, and despondency. The study further stated that suicide was not from job-related stress, as many would believe (*Law Enforcement News*, 1994b). There is no single reason for the suicide of police officers, but it is happening with such frequency that supervisors should not overlook the possibility of such an occurrence.

Alcohol Abuse

Studies by the federal government point out that one in 10 adults in the United States has a drinking problem. Nationally, 64 percent of the adult population drinks alcoholic beverages (U.S. Department of Justice, 2001). In 1992, the adult population used 37.4 gallons of alcohol per capita. A 1990 study showed that of those 26 years of age and older, 5.51 percent had five or more drinks in a single day during the two weeks before the study (Statistical Abstract of the United States, 1994). Additionally, in 1989 there were 374,437 adults in alcohol treatment programs. It has also been estimated that 200,000 individuals annually die of alcohol-related diseases (Autry, 1994). One estimate puts the number of alcoholics at 10 million, including individuals from every occupation and age level. Many use alcohol as their drug of choice to reduce discomfort and provide a degree of pleasure. It has been suggested that stress may be involved in the decision to use alcohol (Violanti et al., 1985). Whatever the reason for the consumption of alcohol, it can become a serious supervisory problem.

Alcohol as a drug of choice is extolled in advertisements suggesting that it leads to happiness and enjoyment. Based on advertising, one can hardly imagine having a party without alcoholic refreshments (Campbell and Graham, 1988). Police officers in many agencies find a subculture that supports heavy drinking (Farmer, 1990). Within the police field, the practice of "hoisting a few" is common and has become known as "choir practice." When officers drink to deal with problems, it can lead to a wide range of job behaviors.

Alcoholics Anonymous (1998) has defined alcoholism as follows:

> Whether or not you are an alcoholic is not determined by where you drink, when you started drinking, how long you have been drinking . . . what, or even how much. The true test is the answer to this question: What has alcohol done to you? If it has affected your relationships; if it has influenced the way you schedule your days; if it has affected your health . . . if you are in any way preoccupied with alcohol—then the likelihood is that you have a problem.

As far back as 1955, the Chicago Police Department organized officers to help other officers with a drinking problem. Another early program was the police stress program of the Boston Police Department. It initially focused on police officers with drinking problems and, in later years, expanded to include a wide range of stress-related difficulties (Goolkasian et al., 1985). Today, it is quite common to find departments that have their own counseling program for alcoholics or refer officers to other agencies or organizations (Alpert and Dunham, 1997). Treatment has proven to be effective as indicated by a program in the Philadelphia Police Department. Officers had a 38 percent reduction in sick days and a 62 percent annual reduction in injury days (Campbell and Graham, 1988).

Divorce

The incidence of divorce has increased considerably over the years. In 1970 the divorce rate was 4.3 million in the United States, and this increased to more than 17 million by 1996 (Statistical Abstract of the United States, 2000). Whatever the divorce rate, most observers agree that police work is especially demanding on the officer's personal life. Officers can become very involved in their work and often bring their problems home. Consequently, police work tends to become a 24-hour-a-day involvement that can strain the best of relationships. Shift changes are especially difficult for family members. It seems to some police officers that they are on a constant shift merry-go-round in which they hardly get accustomed to a shift and it is time to change. It interrupts the social life of the officer and his or her spouse. In many instances, officers socialize only with other officers and their spouses.

Early research reflected a high divorce rate. In three communities, the percentage of divorced officers ranged from 17 to 33.3 percent. This was in contrast to a 1983 study, which showed a divorce rate of five percent in the Los Angeles Police Department. Training programs for spouses describing the nature and problems of police work, support groups, and counseling have all contributed to stronger police families (Alpert and Dunham, 1997).

Spousal Concerns about Danger

Spouses are also in the position of being constantly concerned about the physical well-being of officers. Our society can be violent and police work can be a violent occupation. In 1999 there were 55,026 assaults on law enforcement officers, with 29.6 percent of those involving officer injury (U.S. Department of Justice, 2001). If other officers in the department are injured or killed, the spouse reacts by becoming increasingly concerned about his or her loved one. Peer counseling, spouse support groups, and police psychologists have been especially effective in dealing with this problem.

Early Warning Systems

The early warning system has been instituted in several departments as a means of monitoring officer conduct and alerting managers to inappropriate behavior. The development of these programs is still in its infancy. There is a clear-cut impetus and need for developing a system that deals with certain traits or behavior patterns. This system usually uses information based on the behaviors of officers who have been fired for disciplinary reasons and then identifies officers who have been recognized as having similar problems.

Using computer software, the department tracks and records incidents as they occur. It is a nondisciplinary management system and "flags" officers at risk. Behavioral activities are used to establish a pattern even though a single activity may, in and of itself, prove to be of limited consequence. When combined with other activities, the early warning system may indicate a behavioral pattern that needs to be reviewed by management (Oliver, 1994; Guthrie, 1996). It allows managers to intervene before the occurrence of serious misconduct that could result in officers being arrested, fired, or sued (*Law Enforcement News*, 1994a).

Factors considered relevant vary considerably. One set of factors used to assess an officer's propensity to misuse force is listed in Figure 10.6. In Chicago, information used to identify behavior problems included such variables as race, sex, age, education, marital status, and frequency of sick days. It also includes traffic accidents and lost weapons or badges. This list of characteristics was derived from the analysis of information about 200 terminated officers (*Law Enforcement News*, 1994b). Of the police officers who were fired, a majority of the problems identified extended over a number of years. Treated as isolated incidents, they were not serious enough to warrant disciplinary action (Ehrenhalt, 1994).

Figure 10.6
Factors Used to Assess an Officer's Propensity to Misuse Force

1. Complaints
2. Discipline records
3. Commendations and evaluations
4. Assignments, including partners and supervisors
5. Rate of disorderly conduct charges filed against arrestees
6. Rate of charges against arrestees for resisting or assaulting the officer
7. Shooting incidents
8. Incidents resulting in injury

Source: William A. Geller and Michael Scott (1992). *Deadly Force: What We Know*. Washington, DC: Police Executive Research Forum.

Another list of elements, prepared by Will Oliver (1994), includes:

1. Loss of equipment

2. Vehicular accidents

3. Injured on duty reports

4. Discharge of firearms
   a. Accidental
   b. Duty-related

5. Use of excessive force reports

6. Sick leave in excess of five days

7. A pattern of taking one or two days of sick leave over a long period

8. Complaints

9. Reprimands

10. Disciplinary action

11. Pursuits

12. Resisting-arrest reports

13. Performance reports

14. Financial difficulties

15. Frequent transfers

The early warning system should be monitored by supervisors or higher-ranking management personnel. Those conducting such a review should remember that the process at this point is nondisciplinary. Database information should be analyzed in an attempt to discover the source of a problem. The goal is to intervene and prevent behavior from becoming a disciplinary problem. This is done by tailoring a response to the identified behavior. The response can include (Oliver, 1994):

1. Counseling

2. Training

3. Referral to departmental resources, such as an employee assistance program

4. Psychological examination

5. Physical examination

6. Urinalysis

The response is predicated on a discussion with the officer during which the problem or problems are identified and treatment strategies determined. The desire is to move the officer back into the departmental "mainstream." It is nondisciplinary, and the officer has the right to refuse to participate (*Law Enforcement News*, 1994a). In one department, treatment strategies are referred to the chief for approval before the implementation of corrective action. It is essential to monitor an officer's progress on a quarterly basis to see that the treatment strategies are effective (Oliver, 1994).

Employee Assistance Programs

The majority of organizations recognize that it is very costly to keep non-productive employees who have personal or behavioral problems on the staff. On the other hand, managers know that it is costly to lose well-trained, experienced officers. Consequently, agencies have created programs to provide structured assistance to employees. These programs have been a part of businesses for many years and, more recently, a part of public administration. One part of these programs, employee counseling, has been a fixture in law enforcement for a long time. In 1990 approximately 77 percent of municipal police agencies had a policy about this activity (Reaves, 1992). During the last decade, a wide range of assistance activities have been incorporated into what are called employee assistance programs (EAPs). Comprehensive programs use in-house and external specialists when providing assistance to employees. Employees are offered the same kind of assistance that is given to those who have physical illnesses (Plunkett, 1992). Today, EAPs cover a wide range of services to help employees deal with emotional, family, psychological, financial, and retirement matters. Figure 10.7 lists some of the problems addressed by employee assistance programs.

Figure 10.7
Problems That Can Be Dealt with by an Employee Assistance Program

Alcohol and drug abuse	Job stress
Anxiety	Legal problems
Career development	Marital problems
Compulsive gambling	Monetary problems
Depression	Nutrition
Disciplinary action	Police shootings
Divorce	Retirement planning
Eating disorders	Smoking
Exercise	Spouse abuse
Grief	Termination
Job burnout	Weight control

Adapted from John G. Stratton (1987), "Employee Assistance Programs-A Profitable Approach for Employees and Organizations." In Harry W. More and Peter C. Unsinger (eds.), *Police Managerial Use of Psychology and Psychologists*. Springfield, IL: Charles C Thomas; James M. Jenks and Brian L.P. Zevnik (1993), *Employee Benefits: Plain and Simple*. New York, NY: Collier Books.

Critical-Incident Stress Management

Extreme violence and trauma do not occur on a daily basis in the lives of a majority of police officers. When they do occur, they can leave numerous psychological scars. It is not just the taking of a life. It can be involvement in a shooting or assisting at a disaster such as an earthquake, tornado, or flood. Other incidents that can cause significant emotional responses include vehicle and airplane crashes. Continued exposure to violence can result in post-traumatic stress disorder (PTSD), a psychological condition that is caused by one's inability to successfully manage an emotional response triggered by severe trauma (Paradise, 1992).

The symptoms of PTSD generally include:

1. When exposed to places and situations resembling the initial traumatic event, the officer reexperiences the traumatic event. The officer can have nightmares, flashbacks, or hallucinations.

2. Continual avoidance of any thought about the traumatic event.

3. A sense of detachment from others, including family members.

4. Insomnia.

5. Spontaneous outbursts of anger.

6. Preoccupation with thoughts of death or dying.

7. Inability to concentrate (Phillips and Schwartz, 1992).

If any of the above symptoms persists for more than one month, an officer is probably suffering from PTSD. The daily pressure of police work can take a toll on officers, because they are repeatedly exposed to critical incidents. These officers will have marital problems, become chronically irritable, and may abuse alcohol or drugs. They can also suffer from depression, use excessive force, or develop ulcers (Clede, 1994). All of these can impair the officers' usefulness—not only to the agency, but to themselves.

Early intervention after a critical incident or identification of an officer who is having problems similar to those listed above can help eliminate the propensity for the development of full-blown symptoms of PTSD (Paradise, 1992). As soon as possible after a critical incident, officers should participate in a debriefing session. Typical of these programs is the one used by the Drug Enforcement Administration (DEA). This organization requires agents involved in a shooting to attend a briefing session within 48 hours. During this session, it is stressed that the officer is human, and although a reaction may not have occurred yet, it can occur. Information about PTSD is discussed. As trauma occurs, the DEA utilizes trauma teams composed of trained agents who provide nonclinical supportive intervention (Paradise, 1992).

Peer Counseling

One of the first programs in peer counseling was started by the Boston Police Department. Its first program was limited to officers with alcohol problems. Peer counselors have several years of "street experience" in order to enjoy the trust and respect of fellow officers. One's credibility rating is high when one has "been there." Peer counselors can truly empathize with fellow officers who are experiencing problems created by the unique demands of police work. Officers trust other police officers and, if non-police personnel are used, they must first demonstrate their credibility.

Officers are often reluctant to seek help or admit that they have stress-related problems with which they are not coping (Shearer, 1993). Professional psychologists have been used to train police peer counselors, serve as consultants, and function as referral sources (Stratton, 1987). Peer counselors have been highly successful in dealing with such problems as alcoholism, drug abuse, terminal illness, deaths, on-the-job injuries, and retirement. The real advantage of peer counseling is that it provides officers and their family members with an opportunity to confidentially discuss personal and professional problems (Janik, 1995). Peers are equals, readily available, and have a greater ease of interaction than professionals. Some peer counseling programs are quite well-developed, as illustrated by the Fort Worth Police Department program. It has a ratio of one peer to every 60 officers, allowing for an immediate response to critical incidents, including mass casualty situations (Greenstone et al., 1995).

Fitness-for-Duty Evaluations

When an officer's behavior calls into question his or her judgment, stability, self-control, or emotional control in performing the duties of a police officer, a fitness-for-duty evaluation (FFDE) may be appropriate (IACP, 1998). Most states require emotional and psychological stability as a requirement for entry-level police officers. However, few police agencies require routine or periodic mental evaluations after employment. If a police officer begins to experience severe depression, anxiety, problems in judgment or emotional control, the police agency may be liable for any improper or illegal actions the officer takes. According to IACP guidelines:

1. Fitness-for-duty evaluations are highly specialized activities within the police psychology discipline and should only be conducted by qualified mental health professionals.

2. An FFDE is not a substitute for supervision or modes of discipline.

3. No FFDE should be conducted without either the officer's informed consent or a reasonable alternative.

4. The client in an FFDE is the referring agency and not the officer being evaluated (IACP, 1998).

However, fitness-for-duty evaluations should not be used unless there is strong documentation from the officer's supervisor that the officer is mentally unstable and may be a hazard to him or herself, other officers, or the organization itself.

Summary

Supervisors must set the tone, change the paradigms, and create a foundation that results in a truly supportive working environment. This can be done by drawing employees into the decision-making process and making them responsible for results. In recent years, the tone of many police organizations has been set by creating departmental value statements. Values become the basis for the beliefs and actions that are taken by each officer.

Dealing with problem employees occurs more often than one would like. When an employee becomes difficult to work with, tasks are not accomplished, or work is done with indifference, a supervisor must take corrective action. In some situations, unsuitable behavior can impair the effectiveness of the officer, and in other cases, it can impair the effectiveness of other organizational members. Problem employees can usually be placed in one of the following categories: erudites, tyrants, defeatists, manipulators, or indecisives.

One expert found three types of individuals in organizations: ascendant, indifferent, and ambivalent. The number of employees in each group varies from agency to agency, but these are what supervisors actually find in an organization. These generalized categories can be used by supervisors as a way to view employee conduct.

Marginal performers are a problem for supervisors and can consume a considerable amount of supervisory time. Such employees should be given every opportunity to improve their performance. They should be praised when work performance improves. They should be monitored, and when they perform inadequately, corrective action should be taken.

The police culture and work environment have an impact on police officers, and this interaction can result in an acute interruption of psychological or behavioral homeostasis. These reactions or disruptions, if prolonged, are thought to lead to a variety of illnesses.

Specific task stressors in law enforcement are wide-ranging, and include role conflict and ambiguity. They also include the use of excessive force, danger, boredom, and shift work. All of these complicate not only the officer's personal life, but their organizational life as well.

In some situations, the supervisor can function as a counselor, and in other instances, the officer should be referred to the appropriate employee assistance program. Symptoms of stress can result in a wide variety of maladies, and those that have been studied and found important to law enforcement are suicide, alcohol abuse, spousal concerns about danger, and divorce.

The early warning system has been instituted in several departments to monitor officer conduct and alert managers to inappropriate behavior. This system uses information based on the behavior of officers who have been terminated for disciplinary reasons. Using this data, it then identifies currently employed officers who may have similar problems.

Employee assistance programs offer the same type of assistance that is given to those who have a physical illness. Comprehensive programs use in-house and external specialists when providing assistance to employees. Today, EAPs cover a wide range of services to help employees deal with emotional, psychological, family, financial, and retirement matters.

Case Study

Officer William Clark

Officer William Clark has been a patrol officer with the Davenport Police Department for four years. He is well liked by other officers and has always performed outstandingly with the department. In fact, his sergeant has recommended that he take the promotional examination for sergeant next year. Officer Clark also serves on the special operations squad (SOS), a detail that is used for hostage situations, drug busts, and other situations that require an assault team. For the last four years Officer Clark's evaluations have been exemplary. He has never taken a sick day and is always prepared and willing to take on additional duties and responsibilities.

Officer Clark is young and unmarried. During the last four years, he has had a few girlfriends, but nothing serious. He dated a girl at the court clerk's office last year, but nothing came of it. He seemed the type to be married to his job and not one to settle down. However, a couple of months ago, he met a woman at an elementary school where he had given a lecture to some children. She was a teacher's aide and ready to graduate with her degree and teaching certificate. Peggy was an extremely beautiful girl. The other officers in the department thought she was a model when they saw her with Officer Clark. Officer Clark began to date Peggy frequently, and they became somewhat of a couple. But Peggy had a job waiting for her in Williamsville, a city about four hours from Davenport. Peggy had grown up in Williamsville and had gotten a job as a teacher in one of the elementary schools there. She was looking forward to the job, but Officer Clark wasn't too excited about it.

When Peggy left for her new job, Officer Clark was depressed and despondent. He was in love, and the separation from Peggy was almost more than he could bear. Over the next few months, he travelled to Williamsville as much as possible. In fact, he would sometimes get to work late because he had driven to see her the previous evening and would just be getting back. Officer Clark's behavior on the job began to change for the worse. He started coming to work late or calling in sick and sometimes would not show up or call at all. When he did get to work, his uniform was wrinkled, he appeared as though he had not slept, was sometimes unshaven, and he was becoming forgetful. He forgot to go to traffic court last week, and the judge dismissed all of the traffic citations he had written.

Sergeant Roberts, Clark's supervisor, understood what was wrong with Clark, but things were getting out of hand. Officer Clark needs to straighten up.

If you were Sergeant Roberts, how would you "straighten up" Officer Clark? Can the problems Officer Clark is experiencing be overcome with minimal effort, or will it take more substantial action to correct his behavior?

Key Concepts

alcohol
ambivalent employees
ascendant employees
critical-incident stress management
departmental values
defeatists
divorce
early warning systems
employee assistance program (EAP)
erudites
fitness-for-duty evaluations
indecisives

indifferent employees
manipulators
marginal performers
peer counseling
post-traumatic stress disorder
problem employees
suicide
task stressors
tyrants
value statements
work stressors

Discussion Topics and Questions

1. Why is it important to create departmental values?

2. What is the difference between ascendant and indifferent employees?

3. Discuss the different types of problem employees.

4. What are some of the organizational effects of work stressors?

5. Discuss the behavior of marginal employees.

6. Why are manipulators difficult to supervise?

For Further Reading

Baker, Thomas E., and Jane D. Baker (1996). "Preventing Police Suicide." *FBI Law Enforcement Bulletin*, Vol. 65, No. 10.

> Police officers kill themselves more often than they are killed in the line of duty. This article examines reasons why police officers commit suicide and offers suggestions for supervisors of warning signs to look for and ways of dealing with the suicidal officer.

Garner, Joel, John Buchanan, Thomas Schade, and John Hepburn (1996). *Understanding the Use of Force By and Against the Police*. Washington, DC: National Institute of Justice.

> This study examined more than 1,500 adult custody arrests in Phoenix, Arizona, to determine the use of force both by and against the police. Force was used infrequently by police and less often by suspects. Suspects used force in one out of six arrests. When force was used by police, it was less severe than the force used by suspects. Weapons were used by police in 24 percent of all arrests, with flashlights being the weapon used most frequently. The single predictor of police use of force was the suspect's use of force against the police officer.

Geller, William A., and Michael S. Scott (1992). *Deadly Force: What We Know*. Washington, DC: Police Executive Research Forum.

> A definitive study of the use of force by American police. Includes an excellent chapter on shooting control strategies, encompassing policy development, enforcement, and personnel practices. Of special interest is the section that discusses the delicate balance of supporting officers while holding them to high standards of conduct.

Greenstone, James L., J. Michael Dunn, and Sharon C. Leviton (1995). "Fort Worth's Departmental Peer Counseling Program." *The Police Chief*, Vol. LXII, No. 1.

> Since its inception, the peer counseling team has grown from six counselors to 25. The authors point out that all peer counselors serve without compensation and are available 24 hours a day. All are volunteers and are carefully screened, tested, evaluated, and trained prior to appointment. Counselors provide crisis intervention services and critical-incident stress management in the form of debriefing and defusing.

Mahowald, Mark W. (1994). "Sleep Disorders and Their Effect on Law Enforcement." *The Police Chief*, Vol. LXI, No. 6.

> Sleep requirements appear to be determined by heredity rather than personality factors. The same seems to be true for one's internal clock. The author discusses shift work, pointing out the well-documented impairment of such functions as judgment, insight, and reasoning. He lists rules of thumb that can be used to deal with shift work.

Oliver, Will (1994). "The Early Warning System." *Law and Order*, Vol. 42, No. 9.

> Describes the emerging concept of an early warning system. Emphasizes that it is a nondisciplinary management system used to identify potential problem officers. It describes a computer database that tracks individual officers based on reportable behavior elements. The article describes behaviors used, ranging from the discharge of a firearm to motor vehicle damage.

References

Alcoholics Anonymous (1998). *The Grapevine*. New York, NY: Alcoholics Anonymous.

Alpert, Geoffrey P., and Roger G. Dunham (1997). *Policing Urban America*, Third Edition. Prospect Heights, IL: Waveland Press, Inc.

Autry, James A. (1994). *Life and Work*. New York, NY: William Morrow and Company, Inc.

Baker, Thomas E., and Jane D. Baker (1996). "Preventing Police Suicide." *FBI Law Enforcement Bulletin*, Vol. 65, No. 10.

Bennett, Wayne W., and Kären M. Hess (2001). *Management and Supervision in Law Enforcement*, Third Edition. St. Paul, MN: West Publishing Company.

Brown, Michael F. (1992). "The Sergeant's Role in a Modern Law Enforcement Agency." *The Police Chief*, Vol. LIX, No. 5.

Campbell, Drusilla, and Marilyn Graham (1988). *Drugs and Alcohol in the Workplace*. New York, NY: Facts on File Publications.

CareerTrack (1995). *How to Overcome Negativity in the Workplace*. Boulder, CO: CareerTrack.

Clede, Bill (1994). "Stress: Insidious or Traumatic, is Treatable." *Law and Order*, Vol. 42, No. 6.

Cottringer, William (1994). "Managing: Creating Quality Work Environments." *Security Management*, Vol. 38, No. 6.

Ehrenhalt, Alan (1994). "Cops, Computers and the Concept of Character." *Governing*, Vol. 91, No. 10.

Farmer, R. (1990). "Clinical and Managerial Implications of Stress Research on the Police." *Journal of Police Science and Administration*, Vol. 17, No. 4.

Friedman, P. (1967). "Suicide among Police." In E. Schneidman (ed.), *Essays in Self-Destruction*. New York, NY: Science.

Garner, Joel, John Buchanan, Thoams Schade, and John Hepburn (1996). *Understanding the Use of Force By and Against the Police*. Washington, DC: National Institute of Justice.

Fyfe, James J. (1982). *Readings on Use of Deadly Force*. Washington, DC: Police Foundation.

Geller, William A., and Michael S. Scott (1992). *Deadly Force: What We Know*. Washington, DC: Police Executive Research Forum.

Goldstein, Harvey A. (1986). *Psychological Services for Law Enforcement*. Washington, DC: Federal Bureau of Investigation.

Goolkasian, Gail A., Ronald W. Geddes, and William DeJong (1985). *Coping With Police Stress*. Washington, DC: National Institute of Justice.

Greenstone, James L., J. Michael Dunn, and Sharon C. Leviton (1995). "Fort Worth's Departmental Peer Counseling Program." *The Police Chief*, Vol. LXII, No. 1.

Guthrie, M. (1996). "Using Automation to Apply Discipline Fairly." *FBI Law Enforcement Bulletin*, Vol. 65, No. 5.

Harpold, Joseph A., and Samuel L. Feemster (2002). "Negative Influences on Police Stress." *FBI Law Enforcement Bulletin*, Vol. 71, No. 9.

Harvey, Thomas R. (1990). *Checklist for Change*. Boston, MA: Allyn and Bacon, Inc.

Hays, Tom (1994). "Suicide Continues to Stalk the Police Beat." *The Washington Post*, Dec. 31:A6.

Holton, Bill, and Cher Holton (1992). *The Manager's Short Course*. New York, NY: John Wiley and Sons, Inc.

IACP (1998). "Fitness-for-Duty Evaluation Guidelines." *The Police Chief*, Vol. LXV, No. 10.

Independent Commission on the Los Angeles Police Department (1991). *Report of the Independent Commission on the Los Angeles Police Department*. Los Angeles, CA: Independent Commission on the Los Angeles Police Department.

Janik, James (1995). "Who Needs Peer Support?" *The Police Chief*, Vol. LXII, No. 1.

Jenks, James M., and Brian L.P. Zevnik (1993). *Employee Benefits: Plain and Simple*. New York, NY: Collier Books.

Jones, Tony L. (1999). "Confronting the Problem Performer." *Law Enforcement Technology*, 26:10.

Kottler, Jeffrey (1994). "Beyond Blame: Resolving Conflict at Work." *Hemispheres*, (April) 4:1. Chicago, IL: Pace Communications, Inc.

Kouzes, James M., and Barry Z. Posner (1993). *Credibility: How Leaders Gain and Lose It, Why People Demand It*. San Francisco, CA: Jossey-Bass Publishers.

Law Enforcement News (1989). "Police Study in Philadelphia Finds Benefits in Revised Shifts." Oct. 15, Vol. XV, No. 300.

Law Enforcement News (1994a). "Artificial Intelligence Tackles a Very Real Problem—Police Misconduct Control." Sept. 30, Vol. XX, No. 408.

Law Enforcement News (1994b). "NYPD Officials Grope for Answers to Record-Tying Binge of Cop Suicides." Oct. 31, Vol. XX, No. 410.

Leonard, V.A., and Harry W. More (1993). *Police Organization and Management*, Eighth Edition. Westbury, NY: The Foundation Press, Inc.

Mahoney, Thomas (1986). "Problem Employee or Problem Supervision?" *Journal of California Law Enforcement*, Vol. 20, No. 1.

Mahowald, Mark W. (1994). "Sleep Disorders and Their Effect on Law Enforcement." *The Police Chief*, Vol. LXI, No. 6.

Mann, Robert (1993). *Behavioral Mismatch: How to Manage Problem Employees Whose Actions Don't Match Your Expectations*. New York, NY: AMACOM.

McNaught, Michael, and David Schofield (1998). "Managing Sick and Injured Employees." *FBI Law Enforcement Bulletin*, Vol. 67, No. 1.

More, Harry W., and W. Fred Wegener (1992). *Behavioral Police Management*. New York, NY: Macmillan Publishing Co.

Murphy, Lawrence R., and Theodore F. Schoenborn (eds.) (1987). *Stress Management in Work Settings*. Washington, DC: Department of Health and Human Services.

Neubauer, Ronald S. (1999). "Police Use of Force in America: An IACP Update." *The Police Chief*, Vo. 9, No. 2.

Oliver, Will (1994). "The Early Warning System." *Law and Order*, Vol. 42, No. 9.

Paradise, Paul R. (1992). "The DEA Trauma Team." *Law and Order*, Vol. 39, No. 6.

Phillips, Wayne, and Gene Schwartz (1992). "Post-Traumatic Stress." *Sheriff*, Vol. 44, No. 2.

Plunkett, W. Richard (1992). *Supervision: The Direction of People at Work*, Sixth Edition. Boston, MA: Allyn and Bacon, Inc.

Reaves, Brian A. (1992). *Law Enforcement Management and Administrative Statistics, 1990: Data for Individual State and Local Agencies with 100 or More Officers*. Washington, DC: Bureau of Justice Statistics.

Russell, Harold E., and Allan Biegel (1990). *Understanding Human Behavior for Effective Police Work*, Third Edition. New York, NY: Basic Books.

Samarra, Charles (1992). *Alexandria Police: These Are Our Values*. Alexandria, VA: Alexandria Police Department.

Scrivner, Ellen M. (1994). *Controlling Police Use of Excessive Force: The Role of the Police Psychologist*. Washington, DC: National Institute of Justice.

Shearer, Robert W. (1993). "Police Officer Stress: New Approaches for Handling Tension." *The Police Chief*, Vol. LX, No. 8.

Solomon, Roger M., and James M. Horn (1986). "Post-Shooting Traumatic Reactions: A Pilot Study." In James T. Reese and Harvey A. Goldstein (eds.), *Psychological Services for Law Enforcement*. Washington, DC: Federal Bureau of Investigation.

Statistical Abstract of the United States (1994). *Statistical Abstract of the United States, 114th Edition*. Lanham, MD: Bernard Press.

_____ (2000). *Statistical Abstract of the United States, 120th Edition*. Washington, DC: U.S. Census Bureau.

Steinmetz, Lawrence L., and Charles D. Greenridge (1976). "Realities That Shape Managerial Style: Participative Philosophy Won't Always Work." In Steinmetz, Lawrence L. and Charles D. Greenridge (eds.), *Participative Management: Concepts, Theory and Implementation*. Atlanta, GA: Georgia State University.

Steinmetz, Lawrence L., and H. Ralph Todd, Jr. (1992). *Supervision: First Line Management*, Fifth Edition. Homewood, IL: Richard D. Irwin, Inc.

Stratton, John G. (1987). "Employee Assistance Programs—A Profitable Approach for Employees and Organizations." In Harry W. More and Peter C. Unsinger (eds.), *Police Managerial Use of Psychology and Psychologists*. Springfield, IL: Charles C Thomas, Publisher.

U.S. Department of Justice (2001). *Sourcebook of Criminal Justice Statistics, 2001*. Washington, DC: Bureau of Justice Statistics.

Violanti, John M., James R. Marshall, and Barbara Howe (1985). "Stress, Coping, and Alcohol Use: The Police Connection." *Journal of Police Science and Administration*, Vol. 13, No. 2.

Zook, Frank B. (1994). "Deming's Ideas to Live By: Not Just Empty Buzzwords." *Pennsylvania Business Central*, Vol. 3, No. 9.

Internal Discipline—

A System of Accountability

11

Introductory Case Study

Sergeant Dave Wilcox

You are a newly promoted supervisory sergeant named David Wilcox. Your experience has been in traffic enforcement and patrol for the past five years. You have been a sergeant for three months. You have been given a supervisory assignment to a patrol unit of eight officers you have never worked with before. According to department policy, all new supervisory sergeants are assigned to new units so that old friendships will not become a problem for the new sergeant. The eight officers under your supervision have excellent performance evaluations, are dedicated to their job, and seem eager to help you adjust to your new position.

After a couple of months in your new position, you have begun to notice certain behaviors from your subordinates that make you uncomfortable. All the officers seem to take excessive liberties on their incident reports and arrest reports. Much of what the officers state officially on their reports as to what happened during incidents and arrests simply did not occur. For instance, last week you backed up one of the officers on a drunk and disorderly call. By the time you arrived, Officer Bates had already put an intoxicated man in the back of his cruiser and was ready to transport him to the jail. When you talked with the intoxicated man's wife, she indicated that Officer Bates went inside the house and dragged her husband out of the bedroom, handcuffed him, and put him in the back of the cruiser. When you asked her if she had given Bates permission to come into the house, she said "no," and that she had even told the officer to leave him alone and let him sleep it off there in the house. But, she stated, her husband had been foul-mouthed to the officer and had made the officer mad. When you asked Officer Bates about the situation, he indicated that the man was disorderly and threatening and had come outside onto the front yard to confront him. "That's when I arrested him," Officer Bates stated.

Other incidents have occurred that worry you. Many arrests involving searches for drugs and contraband, traffic stops for obscure probable cause reasons, and even voluntary confessions to burglary and larceny cases have been obtained and reported by your officers. Their reports seem very detailed and legal to the letter. But your observations of what the officers actually do and what they report do not always seem to match up. You decide to talk with your former sergeant to get some advice.

"Oh, Dave, you're talking about the magic pencil," Sergeant Weems responds.

"Magic pencil? I never heard of that one," you say in a puzzled fashion.

"Where have you been the last five years? We all do that from time to time. Your officers are simply making sure the official account is legal and will be upheld in court. In fact, most of the time it's plea-bargained anyway, and this is just another way to make sure it's pled out," Sergeant Weems explains.

"Yeah, but this time I'm having to sign off on the reports and my butt is on the line, too."

"Look, Dave, it's our job to make sure the bad guys go to jail. If we have to doctor things up a bit to make sure that gets done, then we do it. Otherwise, the bad guys get off and we look bad. I think your officers are doing a good job. Let them keep doing a good job for you. They'll make you look good, too." Sergeant Weems said.

How would you respond to Sergeant Weems? Do the ends justify the means in a democratic society? As Sergeant Wilcox, what would you do or say to your subordinates? If you forbid your officers to continue to use the "magic pencil," will this create any new problems? If so, what kinds of problems would likely develop and how would you handle them?

Police Work

Police work is an incredibly complex human enterprise. The assigned mission of the American police establishment is to serve and protect the community. While the "law enforcer" image has been made popular by the mass media, it is inaccurate and far too simplistic (Crank, 1998). According to one expert (Newman, 1986), general assignment police personnel spend no more than 10 to 15 percent of their on-duty time actually enforcing criminal law. Most of their time is spent keeping the peace and providing essential nonpolice services. In carrying out their mission, police departments are expected to:

1. protect life and property;

2. resolve interpersonal conflict and preserve the peace;

3. maintain social order;

4. prevent crime by proactive patrol and other measures;

5. repress crime through effective law enforcement;

6. create and perpetuate a sense of security;

7. identify and apprehend those who have broken the law;

8. regulate various types of noncriminal behavior;

9. recognize and deal with police/public safety hazards;

10. facilitate the movement of people and motor vehicles;

11. provide essential emergency services;

12. help individuals who cannot care for themselves; and

13. safeguard the legal and constitutional rights of citizens.

The job is complex; it lacks clear-cut boundaries and is frequently underrated, unappreciated, and unpleasant. Even though policing is a rewarding career, it is often dull, monotonous, dirty, and dangerous.

Police officers work at the critical pressure point where law, human tragedy, and society's expectations (for safety and a sense of security) come together. The police represent the fine line that separates freedom from chaos and legitimate social control from tyranny. American police officers are inundated with complexity and buffeted by change, ambiguity, stress, and radically different demands coming from various segments of the community. While they also come from the community, police officers are isolated from it in terms of their power, formal authority, occupational role, and distinct subcultural orientation. American police personnel exercise virtually unlimited discretion in low-visibility transactions with all sorts of people. They are constantly bombarded with reality as they grapple with uncontrolled passion, brutality, and the evil side of human nature. Men and women who wear the badge see crime, predatory violence, human degradation, insanity, corruption, and bizarre behavior on a daily basis. They are often confronted with grisly reminders of man's inhumanity and mortality. Mark Baker (1985) has observed that police officers are a composite of their unique experiences and a reflection of the people they police. Many police officers perceive themselves as society's "garbage men."

Due to their broad discretionary power, the inordinately complex nature of their work, and the type of clientele with whom they interact, police officers are particularly vulnerable to corruption and other forms of police deviance. Police deviance describes activities that are inconsistent with the officer's legal authority, organizational authority, or standards of ethical conduct. Corruption usually refers to the sale of legitimate authority for personal gain. Police occupational deviance includes not only corruption, but also the unlawful use of force, mistreatment of prisoners, discrimination, illegal search and seizure, perjury, planting of evidence, and other forms of misconduct that are committed under the color of police authority (Barker and Carter, 1994). For the purpose of analysis, occupational deviance can be broken down into three general categories:

1. **Nonfeasance.** Failure to take appropriate action as required by law or department policy.

2. **Misfeasance.** Performing a required and lawful task in an unacceptable, inappropriate, or unprofessional manner.

3. **Malfeasance.** Wrongdoing or illegal conduct that depends on or is related to the misuse of legitimate authority.

Police deviance is a persistent and inescapable reality that serves to spotlight incompetence and the seedy side of human nature.

Police personnel work in a complex, hazard-prone environment and, like all other human beings, are fallible. Some make errors, fail to perform assigned duties, abuse authority, misuse discretion, commit illegal acts, and engage in behavior "unbecoming an officer." Police administrators and first-line supervisors (i.e., sergeants) are responsible for policing the police.

No one can say with certainty just how much corruption, crime, and other forms of deviance exist in law enforcement, because those who participate in it often have the power and know-how to cover it up. In addition, most police departments are simply not equipped to keep score. According to many of those who study this phenomenon, the nature of police crime, corruption, and occupational deviance makes it impossible to quantify. Consequently, when we try to estimate the extent of the problem, we are forced to deal with general impressions and isolated bits of information.

Due to the nature of their job, the clientele with whom they interact, and the wide variety of temptations they face every day, police officers represent an at-risk population in terms of illegal and other forms of inappropriate behavior. They find themselves with ample opportunity to commit crimes and to benefit from the largesse of those who seek to influence them. There are police officers who sell their professional souls for power, money, sex, and drugs. They mortgage the public interest for their own personal gain. Incompetent and corrupt police officers are a plague.

Police administrators are finally beginning to acknowledge that crime, corruption, and other forms of occupational deviance may be endemic to policing and accept the idea that many types of unlawful behavior exist in all police agencies (Kappeler et al., 1994). Many now realize that corruption may be the oldest and most persistent problem in American policing (Walker, 1999). Policing the police is a paramount issue and a growing concern for all police managers.

Researchers have identified five basic problems in urban policing as institutional preconditions for police crime, corruption, and occupational deviance:

1. **Broad Discretion.** Discretion does not, in itself, make illegal police behavior inevitable, but it enables police officers to conceal their poor decisions and improper conduct. If it is used inappropriately, discretion fosters the belief that justice is a matter of personal judgment that should be auctioned to the highest bidder.

2. **Low Managerial Visibility.** Police officers, as a general rule, work on their own or with one partner. Due to the nature of police work, supervisors rarely observe line officers as they provide services, conduct investigations, make arrests, enforce criminal laws, or use discretion. Institutional controls on the use of police discretion are very weak (and almost always after the fact). Officers prefer to be left alone to do the job. Sergeants, on the other hand, often adopt the attitude that what they do not know will not hurt them.

3. **Low Public Visibility.** If police supervisors have little knowledge about the on-the-job behavior of their immediate subordinates, the public has even less knowledge. When they see the police in action, they rarely know what is going on. Low public visibility, like low managerial visibility, gives police officers the opportunity to conceal poor decisions, corruption, and criminal behavior.

4. **Peer Group Secrecy.** The person most likely to see a "blue coat" criminal or corrupt cop at work is another cop. In many, if not most, cases they do little or nothing about the illegal behavior. The socialization process in the police department may promote illegal behavior or encourage other officers to passively accept the crime and corruption of their colleagues. Loyalty, brotherhood, and an "us against them" attitude (a garrison mentality) help to protect those who have become morally bankrupt.

5. **Managerial Secrecy.** Most police supervisors come from the ranks. They have been socialized by the system and have used it to enhance their status. They are reluctant to investigate and discipline police officers for criminal behavior unless they are forced to do so. Even today, proactive strategies against police crime and corruption (accessible complaint procedure, active investigation, imposition of effective sanctions, and an ongoing effort to stop wrongdoing before it starts) are not being used in all police departments. Police administrators often want to keep the problem within the department. Police supervisors are not immune from the effects of the "garrison mentality" (Johnston, 1982; Crank, 1998).

Low visibility, coupled with a vast amount of discretion, creates an environment in which police crime, corruption, and occupational deviance can germinate and flourish. Discretion, secrecy, and lack of supervision are three important factors that lead to police deviance.

The most effective means of fighting deviance and corruption within the police department is to build a strong supervisory structure in which sergeants have both the authority and the skills needed to regulate the behavior of their subordinates. Supervisors and managers must make an up-front and proactive commitment to integrity. They must do everything they can to prevent deviance and corruption in the department. They must also be willing to do whatever it takes to separate undesirables from the police service.

While there is no doubt that individual police officers must be held accountable for unacceptable on-the-job performance or inappropriate behavior, police managers must establish realistic ethical and professional standards by which to judge their employees. The organizational response to occupational deviance should be tempered with an understanding of human nature and some appreciation for the milieu in which police work takes place.

Americans have traditionally had a love/hate relationship with the police establishment. While the police are generally acknowledged to be an essential element in the glue that holds our pluralistic society together, they are (at the same time) viewed with a great deal of suspicion. Power, authority, discretion, and the potential for abuse are indigenous to the police role. Trust in and fear of authority are deeply rooted in the American psyche and are wrapped in the persona of the individual police officer. We often cast police officers as superheroes who:

> are expected to be knights errant, fearless in the face of danger, incorruptible in the midst of corruption, cool and knowledgeable in the determination of constitutional questions over which learned judges may reflect and wrangle and divide. They are supposed to be tough on criminals but tender regarding rights of individuals, minority groups, and the innocent generally. They are asked to be incessantly courteous, kind and cheerful, and to be ready to lay down their lives at any moment if need be in the defense of law and order (Smith, 1965).

No police officer can reasonably be expected to play each and every one of these roles simultaneously. There is far too much ambiguity; there are too many contradictions. It appears that the pathway to professional police work may have been booby-trapped with good intentions.

When police officers act appropriately and in accordance with the law, they are treated with deference and respect. If, on the other hand, an officer's job-related behavior falls short of culturally prescribed or group-shared expectations, there is likely to be a collective sense of betrayal. Under these particular circumstances, even petty violations tend to elicit very strong reactions from the community. Conflicting perceptions are formed and are used to vilify the police as a group and to scapegoat individual officers for the transgressions of their peers. The misconduct of one police officer frequently casts suspicion on the entire department, and police managers soon discover that the integrity of the police force cannot be restored by simply punishing the offending officer. Such discipline is usually viewed as being merely cosmetic. A managerial commitment to continuous monitoring (for accountability) is by far superior to an occasional witch hunt. It represents a genuine good-faith reaffirmation of the community's control over the police.

Strong internal discipline and a commitment to accountability are required in order to safeguard the organizational health of the police department. The integrity of police work and those who serve as police officers can be maintained only if there is an efficient, effective, and responsive discipline system. Public confidence will be restored and strengthened if there is a proactive effort to protect all citizens from police deviance. This can be accomplished by revising inadequate policies and procedures and correcting or separating from police service the individuals who have been found guilty of serious professional misconduct.

Controlling the Police

Police officers are government officials with a special duty to serve and protect the community. They are responsible for public safety and security. The concept of responsibility encompasses such notions as professional ethics, answerability, and accountability (Gaines and Kappeler, 2003). While these are noble ideals, they often degenerate into empty rhetoric. Ethical ambiguity permits the police to operate in a vacuum. Left uncontrolled, police officers may pursue their own ends by whatever means they choose. Under these circumstances, deviance (legal, moral, and ethical) often becomes the rule rather than the exception. Police occupational deviance represents an insidious threat to the democratic process.

The National Commission on Law Observance and Enforcement (1931), the President's Commission on Law Enforcement and the Administration of Justice (1967), The National Advisory Committee on Criminal Justice Standards and Goals (1973), and the American Bar Association's Task Force on the Urban Police Function (1973) came to the conclusion that public control over the police is a national imperative. In the words of the American Bar Association:

> Since a principal function of police is the safeguarding of democratic processes, if police fail to conform their conduct to the requirements of law, they subvert the democratic process and frustrate the achievement of a principal police function. It is for this reason that high priority must be given for ensuring that the police are made fully accountable to the police administrator and to the public for their actions.

Ethics, answerability, and accountability are essential ingredients in police professionalism and have, as guiding principles, been incorporated into a new Police Code of Conduct (see Figure 11.1). It is the police manager's job to develop and implement the policies, procedures, rules, and regulations that are needed to translate ethics theory into practice. First-line supervisors, on the other hand, are the operating engineers who make sure that the internal discipline apparatus works properly.

Figure 11.1
1989 Police Code of Conduct

All law enforcement officers must be fully aware of the ethical responsibilities of their position and must strive constantly to live up to the highest possible standards of professional policing.

The International Association of Chiefs of Police believes that it is important that police officers have clear advice and counsel available to assist them in performing their duties consistent with these standards, and has adopted the following ethical mandates as guidelines to meet these ends.

Primary Responsibilities of a Police Officer

A police officer acts as an official representative of government who is required and trusted to work within the law. The officer's powers and duties are conferred by statute. The fundamental duties of a police officer include serving the community, safeguarding lives and property, protecting the innocent, keeping the peace and ensuring the rights of all to liberty, equality and justice.

Performance of the Duties of a Police Officer

A police officer shall perform all duties impartially, without favor or affection or ill-will and without regard to status, sex, race, religion, political belief or aspiration. All citizens will be treated equally with courtesy, consideration and dignity.

Officers will never allow personal feelings, animosities or friendships to influence official conduct. Laws will be enforced appropriately and courteously and, in carrying out their responsibilities, officers will strive to obtain maximum cooperation from the public. They will conduct themselves in appearance and deportment in such a manner as to inspire confidence and respect for the position of public trust they hold.

Discretion

A police officer will use responsibly the discretion vested in the position and exercise it within the law. The principle of reasonableness will guide the officer's determinations and the officer will consider all surrounding circumstances in determining whether any legal action shall be taken.

Consistent and wise use of discretion, based on professional policing competence, will do much to preserve good relationships and retain the confidence of the public. There can be difficulty in choosing between conflicting courses of action. It is important to remember that a timely word of advice rather than arrest—which may be correct in appropriate circumstances—can be a more effective means of achieving a desired end.

Use of Force

A police officer will never employ unnecessary force or violence and will use only such force in the discharge of duty as is reasonable in all circumstances.

The use of force should only be used with the greatest restraint and only after discussion, negotiation and persuasion have been found to be inappropriate or ineffective. While the use of force is occasionally unavoidable, every police officer will refrain from applying the unnecessary infliction of pain or suffering and will never engage in cruel, degrading or inhuman treatment of any person.

Confidentiality

Whatever a police officer sees, hears or learns of that is of a confidential nature, will be kept secret unless the performance of duty or legal provision requires otherwise.

Members of the public have a right to security and privacy, and information obtained about them must not be improperly divulged.

Integrity

A police officer will not engage in acts of corruption or bribery, nor will an officer condone such acts by other police officers.

The public demands that the integrity of police officers be above reproach. Police officers must, therefore, avoid any conduct that might compromise integrity and thus undercut the public confidence in a law enforcement agency. Officers will refuse to accept any gifts, presents, subscriptions, favors, gratuities or promises that could be interpreted as seeking to cause the officer to refrain from performing official responsibilities honestly and within the law. Police officers must not receive private or special advantage from their official status. Respect from the public cannot be bought; it can only be earned and cultivated.

Cooperation with Other Officers and Agencies

Police officers will cooperate with all legally authorized agencies and their representatives in the pursuit of justice.

An officer or agency may be one among many organizations that may provide law enforcement services to a jurisdiction. It is imperative that a police officer assist colleagues fully and completely with respect and consideration at all times.

Personal/Professional Capabilities

Police officers will be responsible for their own standard of professional performance and will take every reasonable opportunity to enhance and improve their level of knowledge and competence.

Through study and experience, a police officer can acquire the high level of knowledge and competence that is essential for the efficient and effective performance of duty. The acquisition of knowledge is a never-ending process of personal and professional development that should be pursued constantly.

Private Life

Police officers will behave in a manner that does not bring discredit to their agencies or themselves.

A police officer's character and conduct while off duty must always be exemplary, thus maintaining a position of respect in the community in which he or she lives and serves. The officer's personal behavior must be beyond reproach.

Occupational deviance will occur in virtually all police departments over time. Allegations of personal and professional misconduct are commonplace. In fact, they are an occupational hazard. As long as police officers are empowered to restrict the activities of people, intervene when they commit criminal acts, and engage in authoritative control over their behavior in ways that cause inconvenience or resentment, complaints can be expected. It is imperative, then, that every police department establish a fair and impartial mechanism designed to deal with these complaints. This will help ensure the integrity of the police department and the law enforcement process.

The chief executive officer of the police agency is ultimately responsible for the discipline and control of all subordinate personnel. In order to fulfill this responsibility, the chief should formulate policies, procedures, rules, and regulations that define occupational deviance and specify how complaints against police officers are to be received, processed, and adjudicated.

Policing the police is a volatile issue in contemporary American society. Good intentions are simply not enough to placate the community. Police administrators must now demonstrate, through policy statements and deeds, that they are willing to ferret out and deal decisively with all types of police misconduct (Los Angeles Police Commission, 1997). Anything less will fan the fires of social discontent and could rekindle the spark of violent civil disobedience that was so prevalent in the late 1960s and early 1970s. This phenomenon manifested itself again during the Lozano incident in Miami (1989) and throughout the Rodney King (1991) and O.J. Simpson (1995) affairs in Los Angeles.

Personnel Complaint Investigation Policy

A forthright policy that defines, prohibits, and encourages the reporting of occupational deviance is in the public interest and represents yet another step on the road to accountability. Policies of this nature serve as a guide to thinking and decision making within the police department. They reflect the purpose and philosophy of the organization and help convey that purpose and philosophy to all members. Policy creates realistic parameters that control the use of discretion in criminal justice organizations. The control of discretion is absolutely essential if the department is to:

1. Protect individual citizens from police misconduct.

2. Build community confidence in the police department.

3. Protect the integrity and reputation of the entire police force.

4. Protect the accused employee from unfounded or malicious allegations of occupational deviance.

5. Guarantee equal protection of the law and administrative due process to those accused of misbehavior.

In order to accomplish these critically important objectives, police managers must make a commitment to investigate all substantive complaints that are lodged against their personnel. In addition, they must become proactive in preventing police deviance. It is no longer sufficient to merely react to complaints initiated by those outside the organization (Leonard and More, 1993; Arnold, 1999).

Police officers must understand policies, procedures, rules, and regulations if they are to conform to them. Consequently, directives should be written clearly and concisely and distributed to those expected to obey them. According to the Commission on Accreditation for Law Enforcement Agencies (CALEA, 2001):

> Accredited agencies must have a formal written directive system. The system can be in paper or electronic form. Components of the written directive system should be suited for the specific communications needs and capabilities of the agency. Clarity and rapid access to information are essential to effective implementation of agency written directives.

The agency's written directive system should evolve from its legal authority, core values, and mission statement. All agency personnel should have a clear understanding of their individual discretionary powers in carrying out their duties in accordance with agency written policy, procedure, rules, and regulations (Standard 12). Additionally, CALEA Standard 52.1 (2001) stipulates:

> A written directive requires all complaints against the agency or its employees be investigated, and specifies:
>
> a.   the type of complaints to be investigated by line supervisors;
>
> b.   the type of complaints that require investigation by the internal affairs function; and
>
> c.   the type of complaints to be reviewed by the internal affairs function.

While the police department's personnel complaint investigation policy cannot, and indeed should not, be written to cover every possible contingency, it is a valuable administrative tool that establishes a regularized approach to defining, detecting, and dealing with various forms of police misconduct. The written policy statement must be carefully crafted to strike a synergistic balance between managerial control, community expectations, professional ethics, and the discretionary flexibility needed to perform complex police work on the streets (see Figure 11.2). Ill-conceived, hastily prepared, and overly rigid policy statements are inherently counterproductive and tend to aggravate the problems they were designed to resolve.

Figure 11.2
The Synergistic Balance

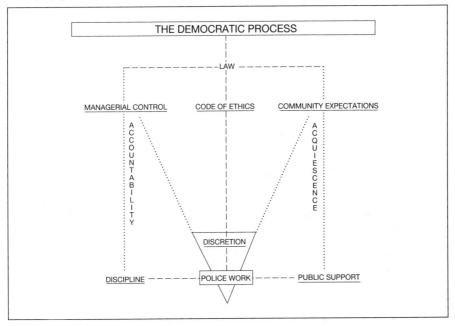

Dealing with Police Occupational Deviance

As previously noted, the chief executive officer of the police department is responsible for the discipline and control of agency personnel. In medium- to large-sized police departments, occupational deviance occurs frequently enough to justify the creation of a specialized internal affairs unit. In small departments, the chief or chief's designee (often a patrol sergeant) conducts internal investigations. Most of the municipal police agencies in the United States are small. More than 80 percent of them have fewer than 20 sworn officers (Adams, 2001). Consequently, sergeants often take center stage in dealing with occupational deviance at the local level.

The procedures (or specific guidelines for action) involved in conducting internal personnel complaint investigations will differ somewhat depending on the origin, nature, and seriousness of the allegation. If, during the normal course of supervision, the sergeant observes a minor infraction, the situation should ordinarily be discussed with the employee, an on-the-spot warning may be issued, and the incident is recorded for future reference or follow-up to determine what effect the intervention had on that individual officer. The procedures to be followed by a supervisor confronted with a serious complaint of misconduct coming from inside or outside the police department, however, will be more structured and much more formal. The seven basic steps involved in the investigation of serious personnel complaints are as follows:

1. The nature and extent of the alleged police occupational deviance must be determined.

2. An internal investigation must be conducted to ascertain the merit of the complaint and the extent to which the accused police officer is culpable if the allegation is, in fact, sustained.

3. Logical conclusions must be drawn based on the evidence that is uncovered during the investigation.

4. Alternative courses of action must be evaluated and converted into recommendations concerning an appropriate disposition of the case.

5. If corrective disciplinary measures are required, they must be administered in an impartial, firm, fair, and timely manner.

6. Precautions must be taken to ensure administrative due process and equal protection under the law for those who are accused of serious misconduct.

7. Supervisors must perform a follow-up in order to assess the positive or negative effects of any disciplinary action that has been taken.

Department-specific policies, procedures, rules, and regulations will determine the investigative protocol to be used in police misconduct cases.

Personnel Complaints

A personnel complaint is a formal accusation alleging that a particular employee is guilty of legal, moral, or professional misconduct. These complaints run the gamut from trivial to extremely serious. Trivial complaints should be filtered out immediately and disposed of through appropriate administrative action. Substantive personnel complaints, on the other hand, should be plugged in to the internal investigations process and dealt with in a very straightforward manner. If there is any doubt as to how a specific complaint should be classified in terms of its validity or seriousness, it should be targeted for a thorough internal investigation. While discretion may be the better part of valor, the zealous pursuit of integrity is a prerequisite for police professionalism.

Misconduct complaints lodged against police officers come from two sources. Internal complaints originate within the organization. They are initiated by first-line supervisors or command officers who have witnessed occupational deviance firsthand and choose to deal with it. Unfortunately, some police managers tacitly condone less than professional conduct rather than create bad publicity or risk employee hostility by aggressively pursuing cases of police misconduct. Internal personnel complaints also come from police officers who, based on their particular job in the department or their personal interaction with other employees, know or have reason to believe that another employee is guilty of misconduct. Mark Baker (1985) has noted that good cops often are more outraged by the misdeeds of their colleagues than are the general public, simply because these officers know that their reputation and character are being maligned because the "bad cops" wear the same uniform.

External complaints, on the other hand, come from outside the police department. These complaints come from lawyers, elected officials, pressure groups, relatives, and others who (for whatever reason) have chosen to focus their attention on (real or imagined) police misconduct. Most of the complaints lodged against municipal police personnel come from external sources.

Due to the nature of their job, the power they wield, and the milieu within which they work, police officers are often targeted for criticism or allegations of wrongdoing. Some of these accusations are justifiable and serve as indicators of real occupational deviance or personal misconduct, and others are not. Unless personnel complaints are obviously frivolous, they should be investigated. Sergeants must also be concerned with due process. Perceptions are not always accurate, and complainants are not always truthful. In addition, there are those (criminals, political activists, and mentally ill individuals) who are inclined to fabricate stories designed to discredit the police or the entire criminal justice system. They will do anything to achieve their own personal, political, or social goals. The end justifies the means (distortion, lies, and false accusations). Sergeants often walk a tightrope between fact and fiction. They are the guardians of integrity and represent the bulwark of professional responsibility. Receiving, investigating, and resolving personnel complaints tests the mettle of the men and women who are first-line supervisors in complex criminal justice organizations. It is the inglorious part of the job that many sergeants avoid.

Personnel complaints are a fact of life in modern police work. They are a permanent part of the occupational landscape and will not disappear just because they are cloaked in a "blue veil of secrecy" (Crank, 1998). While most personnel complaints prove to be unfounded (Alpert and Dunham, 1997), they still provide first-line supervisors and police managers with invaluable feedback. Complaints, whether they are substantiated or not, increase awareness of both actual and potential problems, help sharpen problem-solving skills, and provide yet another basis for the evaluation of the department's human resources. Consequently, every precaution must be taken to guard against artificial barriers that hinder or discourage the filing of legitimate personnel complaints. Without complaints, problems that could be resolved fester and poison the whole system. Inaction almost always makes the problem worse. Problems that are hidden or ignored are like a cancer. As the malignancy spreads, it eats away at the integrity of the police department and undermines community confidence in the police establishment. Hence, the purpose of police internal affairs is fivefold:

1. It ensures a professional image.

2. It fosters confidence and trust between the public and its police department.

3. It provides a mechanism for the public to seek redress for alleged acts of police misconduct.

4. It ensures that policies exist to provide guidelines for internal affairs investigations.

5. It ensures that members of the police agency know that a code of conduct exists and is enforced.

From a practical as well as a theoretical point of view, internal and external "whistle-blowing" should not be considered negative. In fact, it is one of the checks and balances built into the democratic process. The most effective way to prevent abuse of police power (occupational deviance) is through vigilance and the prompt use of disciplinary action when abuse is found.

Processing Personnel Complaints

Even though an overwhelming majority of the misconduct complaints filed against police personnel are proven to be unfounded, most police organization and management theorists agree that all substantive complaints (from whatever the source) should be accepted and thoroughly investigated. This type of openness is the natural enemy of arbitrariness and an ally in the battle against occupational deviance (Kappeler et al., 1994). The Commission on Accreditation for Law Enforcement Agencies Standard 52 (2000) recommends that:

1. all complaints of misconduct against department members be accepted.

2. any attempt to discourage, interfere with or delay an individual from filing a complaint be prohibited.

3. the process for filing a complaint should be professional, convenient, and prompt.

4. the complainant need not physically come to the police department to lodge a complaint.

Filing a complaint alleging police misconduct should be a quick and simple process. The public has the right to present reasonable grievances and to have them properly investigated. By ignoring negative feedback from citizens, police supervisors and managers improperly insulate themselves from those whom they are sworn to protect and serve (Kappeler et al., 1994).

Sergeants and command officers often share responsibility for receiving and processing personnel complaints in the nation's small police departments. They deal primarily with three types of complaints:

1. **Primary Complaints.** Complaints that are received directly from the alleged victim of the police misconduct.

2. **Secondary Complaints.** Complaints from persons who, while not victims themselves, complain about police misconduct on behalf of others.

3. **Anonymous Complaints.** Complaints of police occupational deviance coming from an unidentified source.

Complaints from anonymous sources must be handled with the greatest care and utmost discretion because of the impact they might have on the morale of the employees involved. No police supervisor or manager, however, can afford to discount the validity of a personnel complaint solely because it comes from an unidentified source. Each complaint must be judged on its own merits.

Nathan Iannone and Marvin Iannone (2001) have pointed out that some of the most serious and bizarre cases of police misconduct have been brought to light by anonymous information. Once it is determined that a personnel complaint is not merely frivolous, it is preferable to deal openly and honestly with it in the public arena. Openness serves as an antidote to suspicion and distrust.

In order to initiate a formal inquiry, the complaint should be summarized on a personnel incident report form (see Figure 11.3), assigned an administrative control number, and processed according to department policies, procedures, rules, and regulations. The person filing the complaint should be given a copy of the report form as a receipt. This is tangible evidence that the personnel complaint is being taken seriously and that the police department is making a sincere effort to monitor the legal, moral, and professional conduct of its employees. It is in the best interests of the police service that all incidents of serious misconduct be discovered. Unless the public is convinced that the police department is truly receptive to complaints, it will not actively participate in this critically important process.

Personnel Complaint Investigations

There are more than 17,000 law enforcement agencies in the United States. While some of them (such as Chicago, Los Angeles, and New York) are huge bureaucracies, most police departments are small and not very sophisticated in terms of their organization/management structure. Under these circumstances, specialization is usually the exception rather than the rule. As generalist administrators in small organizations, sergeants play a variety of different and, at times, unconventional roles. Consequently, it is difficult to describe with precision the part that sergeants play in personnel complaint investigations.

Sergeants are usually the most visible and often the most approachable members of the police department's management team. They interact with police officers and civilians from all walks of life on a regular basis. Because they represent the first link in the chain of command, it is likely that many, if not most, of the allegations of personal or professional misconduct will be channeled through them to their superiors. Dealing with the corrupt side of human nature (inside and outside the department) goes with the territory. Streetwise supervisors know the score. As one sergeant put it, every cop has had a bad day (a hangover, a domestic squabble, a mistake at work, or disagreement with the boss) and has taken it out on the people the officer has sworn to protect and serve. The officer may be rude, insulting, intimidating, or downright criminal in dealing with others.

Figure 11.3
Personnel Incident Report

Commendable Action [ ]   Censurable Conduct [ ]

          Personnel Investigation _____ - _____

Officer(s) _____ Rank _____

          _____

Complainant _____ Telephone: Home _____

Address_____   Office _____

Incident: Date ___/___/___   Time: _____ Hours   Unknown [ ]

          Location _____

Summary of incident: Department Complaint # (if any) _____

Witness No. 1 _____ Telephone: Home _____

Address _____   Office _____

Witness No. 2 _____ Telephone: Home _____

Address _____   Office _____

Violations(s): Section _____ Major _____ Minor _____

          Section _____ Major _____ Minor _____

          Section _____ Major _____ Minor _____

Assigned Investigating Officer _____

Date _____

According to Mark Baker (1985), many cops give in to temptation and misuse their discretionary power to gratify their own ego by tormenting a civilian, like a cat tormenting a mouse. As one cynical officer said, in any department five percent of the officers are hardworking and honest in all situations. They never do anything wrong. Five percent are always on the other side of the continuum. They have character flaws and would be ordinary criminals if they had not become police officers. The remaining 90 percent tend to go whichever way peer pressure goes. While this might be a gross overstatement, sergeants have an ethical obligation, as well as a functional obligation, to accept, investigate, and resolve all legitimate allegations of personal or professional misconduct lodged against their subordinates.

Sergeants, as first-line supervisors, are almost always given the power to receive and process personnel complaints. Based on the authority inherent in their rank, they monitor employee performance and serve as departmental disciplinarians. In minor cases involving police deviance, they bring charges, investigate, adjudicate, and (where appropriate) punish their subordinates. Summary action of this type is normally subject to administrative review, and must be consistent with departmental policy, civil service regulations, collective bargaining agreements, and the law. In large police departments, specialization rather than rank determines who will conduct the investigation of serious personnel complaints. Corruption and other forms of serious occupational deviance are usually investigated by a special internal affairs unit. Internal affairs units report directly to the chief executive officer. In smaller departments, sergeants normally work in tandem with command officers and are frequently called on to help investigate serious allegations of police misconduct.

Case Study

Sergeant Hank Patterson

Sergeant Patterson is a nine-year veteran of the Waynesville Police Department. Waynesville enjoys a large tourist industry due to the number of outlet malls, a nearby Indian reservation with casino gambling, and a federal park and forest area. Consequently, Waynesville has a substantial number of transients, and property values are quite high because it is a resort-type town. The Waynesville Police Department has 31 full-time sworn officers and a number of reserves. Sergeant Patterson is a senior shift supervisor for seven patrol officers and two criminal investigators. During nights and weekend duty, Sergeant Patterson is in charge of the entire on-duty force. During day shift, he is third in command of the department due to his senior status.

There is not much crime in Waynesville, but thefts and burglaries always seem to lead the crime statistics. In fact, the two criminal investigators spend most of their time working burglaries and larcenies. When a burglary or larceny call comes in, the department sends out a patrol officer to do a preliminary report and then calls in a detective if needed.

Two years ago, Waynesville hired a patrol officer by the name of Tim Payne. Officer Payne receives good evaluations and gets along well with other officers and the community. He is personable and well liked by nearly everyone. The criminal investigators say that Officer Payne does a great job on preliminary investigations at crime scenes. He has made the investigator's jobs easier by the detail and extra effort he puts forth during preliminary investigations. The chief has even suggested that Payne would be the next candidate for a criminal investigator position with the department.

Sergeant Patterson has some uneasiness about Officer Payne. It seems when Officer Payne works a preliminary investigation at a burglary, more items turn up missing than were first reported. When Officer Payne makes an arrest, particularly in a drunk case, money is reported missing from the wallet of the arrested party. Just the other evening, a lady complained that $700 was missing from her husband's pocket after Officer Payne had been in the house. Officer Payne had been the first officer to respond to a dead body call. An elderly man had died after suffering what appeared to be a heart attack. Officer Payne entered the house and had the wife wait in another room while he checked the body. All this occurred before the ambulance had arrived. The dead man's wife said that she was fairly certain her husband had $700 in his pocket when he had the heart attack, but it was now missing. Officer Payne and the ambulance workers claim they never went through the man's pockets.

There are just too many complaints and suspicions of theft coming to you about Officer Payne. So far, there is no evidence against Officer Payne to verify any complaints.

If you were Sergeant Patterson, how would you deal with this situation? If there was no legal evidence to indicate Officer Patterson was taking goods and money, would you, as supervisor, say anything to him about your suspicions? If so, how would you go about it? Is there any other action you could take to either obtain evidence against Patterson for termination purposes or to stop this sort of behavior from happening again?

Investigating alleged police misconduct requires a great deal of skill. In order to be effective, the investigator (a sergeant, an internal affairs officer, or a police manager) must be specifically trained for the task and given constant guidance and administrative support. Because the internal investigation process must be swift, certain, fair, and lawful, only the most competent employees should be selected and trained to conduct personnel investigations. Few of the small police departments provide any, let alone sufficient, training for those involved in personnel complaint investigations. Police managers in smaller agencies do have several options when faced with an internal affairs investigation situation. The police manager may conduct the investigation him or herself; assign the case to a supervisor; or, if the situation is serious enough, request an outside police agency to investigate. There are advantages and disadvantages for each option. Whichever option is selected, the chief executive officer of the department must ensure that a high-quality, fair, and impartial investigation will be conducted (Courtney, 1996).

Once a formal personnel complaint enters the internal investigations process, official fact-finding begins. The tools and techniques used to investigate police misconduct should not differ substantially from those used in other types of investigations. The investigator must approach each complaint objectively and should avoid drawing any conclusions concerning the merits of the case until all the evidence has been collected and analyzed.

The first step in a personnel investigation is to interview the complainant. When accusations have been raised anonymously, or by second parties, every effort should be made to contact the victim or whistle-blower directly. All other things being equal, direct evidence is the best evidence. The function of the interview is to:

1. Gather additional information concerning the personnel complaint.

2. Identify witnesses and investigative leads related to the alleged police misconduct.

3. Assess the complainant's credibility.

4. Determine the merits of the accusation.

5. Ascertain, if possible, the complainant's motive or motives for making the allegation.

The interview is a primary source of investigative data, and as such, its importance should not be underestimated.

Preparation is the key to conducting a successful investigative interview. The person assigned to conduct the internal investigation should carefully review the personnel incident report (filed by the complainant) in order to become familiar with the case and to make a preliminary determination as to the specific department policies, procedures, rules, and regulations that may have been violated by the accused. In addition, the investigator should develop a complainant profile. Based on a thorough records check, the profile should indicate whether the complainant has had previous encounters with the police, the nature of those incidents, and that individual's proclivity to file misconduct complaints against police personnel. Armed with this type of information, the internal investigator is in a position to more accurately assess the validity of the individual's complaint.

The interview itself must be handled discreetly and conducted in a skillful manner. Sergeants or other internal personnel complaint investigators should not editorialize or reveal information that could be misconstrued by the complainant. The interviewer should be careful not to:

1. Commit the police department to a particular course of action regarding the internal investigation, disposition of the complaint, or discipline to be imposed.

2. Indicate his or her personal professional opinion concerning the merit of the allegation, the culpability of the accused officer, or the officer's behavior in similar situations.

3. Prejudge the validity of the complaint or formulate subjective conclusions as to the complainant's veracity.

The interview gives direction to and provides a foundation for the internal investigation. It is, therefore, a critically important component in the personnel complaint investigation process.

Information acquired during the investigative interview should be put in writing as soon as possible. The official written account of the interview must be clear, concise, and accurate. Depending on the nature, seriousness, and complexity of the police deviance it may be advisable to have the interview transcribed or tape-recorded. This is standard operating procedure in cases involving criminality, corruption, serious misconduct, and vicarious civil liability. As a general rule, the scope of the investigative interview and the precision with which the information is recorded should be proportional to the severity of the alleged misconduct (Redlich, 1994). It should also be noted that what starts out as fact-finding might well become documentary evidence in a subsequent criminal trial. In many states, it is illegal to make false reports to law enforcement authorities (Scoville, 1999). According to the Pennsylvania Consolidated Statutes (Title 18, Chapter 49a, Section 4906):

False Reports to Law Enforcement Authorities

(a) Falsely Incriminating Another. A person who knowingly gives false information to any law enforcement officer with the intent to implicate another commits a misdemeanor of the second degree.

(b) Fictitious Reports. A person commits a misdemeanor of the third degree if he:

(1) reports to law enforcement authorities an offense or other incident within their concern, knowing that it did not occur; or

(2) pretends to furnish such authorities with information relating to an offense or incident when he knows he has no information relating to such offense or incident.

While recent court decisions have given sergeants and other internal personnel complaint investigators some leeway in dealing with police misconduct, they are still constrained by the due process provisions contained in administrative law, civil service regulations, and collective bargaining agreements. The rules governing procedural due process almost always require that police officers accused of serious misconduct be informed of their civil law and contract rights, notified as to the specific nature of the allegation, and advised when they are under investigation. Notice must be timely and in sufficient detail to permit the accused officer to prepare an adequate defense.

If the allegation of police deviance constitutes a violation of the criminal law as well as a breach of agency policies, procedures, rules, and regulations, the officer involved should (with a few exceptions arising from his or her personal role as a government official) be allowed to exercise the constitutional rights accorded to all other citizens of the United States (see Figure 11.4). Consequently, first-line supervisors and other internal personnel complaint investigators must familiarize themselves with administrative and constitutional rules governing procedural due process in criminal justice organizations. Procedural due process protects innocent police officers and ensures that those who are guilty of legal, moral, and professional misconduct are treated fairly as they are brought before the bar of justice (Rothlein and Lober, 1996).

Roger Dunham and Geoffrey Alpert (1997) argue that the use of administrative discipline should not be viewed as a substitute for, or an impediment to, criminal prosecution when serious police deviance is discovered. While justice can often be served by the administration of internal discipline, police managers must not resist or avoid criminal prosecution. The police service must not treat employees who break the law differently from other criminal offenders within the community.

Once the complainant has been interviewed and it is determined that there may be some substance to the accusation, the internal investigation should be expedited. Delays hamper the inquiry, lower employee morale, and erode public confidence in the police force. If first-line supervisors and police managers fail to put their house in order, someone from the outside (i.e., an interest group or civilian review board) will attempt to do it for them.

Some type of immediate intervention might be required in cases involving crime, corruption, or other kinds of serious misconduct. In the absence of departmental policy to the contrary, the sergeant should attempt to defuse the situation. Police officers who are temporarily unable to function due to alcohol or drug abuse should be relieved of duty and taken home by the supervisor. Appropriate disciplinary action can be taken at a later time. Officers who are suspected of corruption or serious misconduct and pose a threat to the integrity of the department should, based on the authority of a command officer who has reviewed the evidence, be suspended from duty pending a thorough internal investigation. Any officer engaged in felonious crimes involving violence, moral turpitude, or theft should be suspended from the department, arrested, and booked. The decision to arrest a police officer must be approved by the chief executive officer of the department. Immediate and radical action of this type is usually unnecessary. Most criminal complaints against police officers may be processed normally through the district attorney's office.

Figure 11.4
Statement and Rights Prior to Interrogation

Given to _____

Officer _____ Date _____ Time _____

Rank _____ Badge No. _____

Unit Of Assignment _____

The law provides that you are to be advised of the following:

1. Any admission made in the course of this hearing, interrogation, or examination may be used as evidence of misconduct or as the basis for charges seeking your suspension, removal, or discharge.

2. You have the right to counsel of your choosing to be present with you to advise you at this hearing, interrogation, or examination, and you may consult with him or her as you desire. Your counsel may be present at any stage of this interrogation.

3. You may request counsel at any time before or during this interrogation. You have a right to be given a reasonable time and opportunity to obtain counsel of your own choosing.

4. You have no right to remain silent. You are ordered to truthfully answer questions put to you. You are advised that your statements or responses constitute an official police report.

5. If you refuse to answer questions put to you, you will be ordered by a superior officer to answer the question.

6. If you persist in your refusal after the order has been given to you, you are advised that such refusal constitutes a violation of the rules and regulations of the police department and will serve as a basis for which disciplinary action will be sought.

7. You are further advised that by law, any admission made by you during the course of this hearing, interrogation, or examination cannot be used against you in a subsequent criminal proceeding.

8. The law provides that you may not be subjected to interrogation without first being informed in writing of the nature of the investigation. The nature of this investigation is as follows:

The undersigned hereby acknowledges that he/she was informed of the above at:

_____ This _____ Day of _____

Year _____, Time _____

and that he/she received a copy of this document entitled Statement and Rights Prior to Interrogation.

Signature _____

Witnesses _____

_____

_____

As a condition of employment, police officers are required to cooperate with supervisors and others within the department who are investigating them for alleged legal, moral, or professional misconduct that is directly related to the performance of their assigned duties. Administrative law and recent court decisions give internal personnel investigators a great deal of latitude in dealing with police employees suspected of serious misconduct. The failure to cooperate subjects them to further disciplinary action and possible separation from the police service.

Legislatures and courts have generally supported the right of government agencies to protect themselves (and the public) against unethical or criminal employees. In many jurisdictions, supervisors and other personnel complaint investigators have been given the authority to:

1. Access the accused officer's personnel file, performance evaluations, merit ratings, attendance records, and other relevant information.

2. Deny the accused officer's request for legal representation during the investigatory interview.

3. Obtain a verbatim transcript or tape-recording of the investigatory interview.

4. Search, with or without a warrant, areas in the workplace where there is no reasonable expectation of privacy.

5. Require the accused officer to participate in a properly constituted and representative lineup.

6. Order the accused officer to take a polygraph examination (unless such an order is specifically prohibited by a collective bargaining agreement or state law).

7. Demand that the accused officer submit to physical testing (blood, urine, breath, etc.) designed to yield tangible evidence that can be used in disciplinary hearings.

This authority must be carefully regulated and should be codified in department-specific policies, procedures, rules, and regulations. According to Nathan Iannone and Marvin Iannone (2001), the law is clear—almost any "reasonable" order to an employee is administratively enforceable. The courts have been reluctant to interfere in employer/employee relations unless the employer's directives are arbitrary, capricious, or breach procedural due process requirements in established administrative law, civil service regulations, or labor contracts.

After all the relevant evidence has been gathered and evaluated, the sergeant, internal affairs officer, or police manager must attempt to reconstruct reality in such a way as to prove or disprove the allegation. The findings should be integrated into a comprehensive investigative report (keyed to who, what, where, when, why, and how) and used to formulate a recommendation concerning the best disposition of the case (see Figure 11.5). All of the material should be forwarded to the chief executive officer of the police department for appropriate administrative action.

Figure 11.5
Personnel Incident Final Report

Final Report Censurable Conduct   Personnel Investigation ___-___

Summary of Findings

Attachments: Complainant Statement [ ], Witness Statement [ ], Officer
Statement [ ], Other [ ] (explain) _____
Recommendation: Unfounded [ ] Exonerated [ ] Not Sustained [ ]
Sustained [ ]
(State Section # charged)

Recommended Disciplinary Action (Refer to Manual Section 5-055/000)

          Investigator _____
          Division Commander _____
Final Disposition:
Concur [ ]   Do not concur [ ]
Reason _____
_____
_____
_____

Final Disposition:
_____
_____
_____
_____

Date _____ Chief of Police _____

The Adjudication of Personnel Complaints

The chief executive officer of the police department is responsible for the adjudication (or final disposition) of all internal discipline complaints. The person who conducted the investigation and prepared the investigative report, however, should have laid the foundation for the adjudication. If everything works properly, the chief executive's decisions should flow logically from the investigation, conclusions, and recommendations made by the internal complaint investigator. Steps must be taken to ensure the assumption of responsibility and to safeguard the integrity of the decision-making process. According to the National Advisory Commission on Criminal Justice Standards and Goals (1973):

> Every police agency immediately should ensure that provisions are established to allow the police chief executive ultimate authority in the adjudication of internal discipline complaints, subject only to appeal through the courts or established civil service bodies, and review by responsible legal and governmental entities (see Figure 11.6).

1. A complaint disposition should be classified as sustained, not sustained, exonerated, unfounded, or misconduct not based on the original complaint.

2. Adjudication and, if warranted, disciplinary action should be based partially on recommendations of the involved employee's immediate supervisor. The penalty should be at least a suspension up to six months or, in severe cases, removal from duty.

3. An administrative fact-finding trial board should be available to all police agencies to assist in the adjudication phase. It should be activated when necessary in the interests of the police agency, the public, or the accused employee, and should be available at the direction of the chief executive or on the request of any employee who is to be penalized in any manner that exceeds verbal or written reprimand. The chief executive of the agency should review the recommendations of the trial board and decide on the penalty.

4. The accused employee should be entitled to representation equal to that afforded the person representing the agency in the trial board proceeding.

5. Police employees should be allowed to appeal a chief executive's decision. The police agency should not provide the resources or fund the appeal.

6. The chief executive of every police agency should establish written policy on the retention of internal discipline investigation reports. Only the reports of sustained and, if appealed, investigations that are upheld should become part of the accused employee's personnel folder. All disciplinary investigations should be kept confidential.

Figure 11.6
Statement of Charges

Civil Service [ ]   Non-Civil Service [ ]

Employee _____ I.D. # _____

Position Classification _____

Personnel Investigation # _____ Dept. Complaint # _____

Date of This Statement _____

Person Making Personnel Complaint _____

Police Department Manual of Policy and Procedures—Section(s) Violated:

_____

Personnel Rule(s) Violated (if applicable):

_____

Section Description:

Synopsis of Incident:

Findings:

Disciplinary Action Taken:

_____

I have read and understand the charges filed against me and have received a
copy of said charges. I also understand that I may appeal this finding within
seven (7) calendar days from the date shown below to either the Civil Service
Commission or the Department Personnel Officer depending upon my status
as indicated on this form.

_____

Employee Signature   Date

_____

Officer Serving Charges   Date

7. Administrative adjudication of internal discipline complaints involving a violation of law should neither depend on nor curtail criminal prosecution. Regardless of the administrative adjudication, every police agency should refer all complaints that involve violation of law to the prosecuting agency for the decision to prosecute criminally. Police employees should not be treated differently from other members of the community in cases involving violations of law. The complainant, witnesses, and accused employee should be encouraged to participate in the process that leads to a final disposition, even though that decision rests squarely on the shoulders of the police chief executive.

Regarding the classification of personnel complaint dispositions, the following general categories may be used to reflect adjudicatory findings.

1. *Sustained* indicates that, based on the facts obtained, the accused committed all or part of the alleged police misconduct.

2. *Not Sustained* means that the investigation produced insufficient evidence to prove or disprove the allegation and that the matter is being resolved in favor of the employee.

3. *Exonerated* denotes that the alleged act or omission occurred, but was, in fact, legal, proper, and necessary.

4. *Unfounded* is used when the alleged police misconduct did not occur and the complaint was false.

5. *Misconduct Not Based on Original Complaint* means that while there was misconduct on the part of the police officer, it was separate and distinct from that alleged in the original complaint.

6. *Policy Failure* means that the allegation was true; the action of the agency or the officer was not inconsistent with agency policy.

In the event that someone other than the employee's immediate first-line supervisor conducted the internal personnel complaint investigation and prepared the comprehensive investigative report, the chief executive officer should contact the sergeant before making a final disposition in the case. All other things being equal, the sergeant is in the best overall position to assess the accused officer's job performance, professional conduct, and value as a human resource. The sergeant's input must be carefully evaluated in terms of its objectivity and consistency and should be considered a major factor in determining the final disposition and selecting the appropriate disciplinary action.

When an internal discipline complaint is sustained, the chief of police must select the most appropriate remedy available. Corrective measures may include reassignment, retraining, psychological counseling, or participation in a multipurpose employee assistance program. The most frequently used sanctions in serious misconduct cases, however, are separation from the police service, suspension, and loss of seniority in lieu of suspension.

If a serious personnel complaint is sustained by the evidence and the loss of time, a suspension, or a dismissal is considered an appropriate sanction, emphasis during the investigation should be placed on procedural due process. If accused officers are arbitrarily denied procedural due process, the courts will reverse on appeal and the police department may be civilly liable. Nathan Iannone and Marvin Iannone (2001) suggest that the safest way to avoid reversal and civil liability in cases involving serious legal, moral, or professional misconduct is to adhere to the minimum requirements of procedural due process as outlined by the U.S. Supreme Court in the 1972 case of *Morrissey v. Brewer:*

1. Written notice of the specific charge or charges filed against the officer.

2. Disclosure of the evidence that will be used against the officer during the disciplinary hearing.

3. The opportunity to appear in person and to present witnesses and evidence.

4. The right to confront and cross-examine adverse witnesses (unless the hearing board specifically finds good cause for not allowing the confrontation).

5. An impartial hearing before a "neutral and detached" administrative body.

6. A written statement by that body concerning the evidence it relied on and the reasons for its action.

7. Administrative and/or judicial review of adverse dispositions.

These provisions represent the concern for fairness and procedural due process in labor/management relations and should be incorporated into department policies, procedures, rules, and regulations.

Many police departments have adopted some form of trial board system. These trial boards are designed to help the police chief executive make sound decisions in internal discipline cases. They provide for a diversity of opinion and allow more direct participation in the adjudication of police misconduct cases by those who conducted the internal complaint investigation.

Under ideal circumstances, the administrative trial board should consist of five police officers from within the department. Four of the members should be appointed by the chief and one by the accused officer. Trial boards should not have any investigative authority and should handle only serious cases of police misconduct assigned to them by the chief of police or cases (regardless of their seriousness) in which accused officers specifically request a disciplinary hearing.

Trial boards are administrative proceedings in which a "neutral and detached" body hears the evidence and oral arguments and renders a decision concerning the appropriate action to be taken on a personnel complaint. Members of the trial board are expected to use rational, objective, and analytical reasoning in reaching that decision. The board is responsible for determining fact and making a recommendation to the chief executive.

Trial boards are quasi-judicial entities. Their hearings must be governed by the principle of fundamental fairness and need not comply with strict courtroom protocol. The board should, however, have a presiding officer who understands the adjudication process and is familiar with parliamentary procedure. Decisions (usually determined by majority vote) should be based on "a preponderance of evidence" and not "proof beyond a reasonable doubt." The rules of criminal procedure are simply not germane to administrative decision making. According to Larry K. Gaines and his colleagues (1991), the trial board should conclude its deliberations with a formal recommendation accompanied by a written summary of the evidence it relied on and the rationale behind its recommendation.

The recommendation of the trial board, however, is purely advisory. It is up to the police chief executive to institute proper corrective action. If the chief habitually ignores or modifies the trial board's suggestions, this noble experiment in what Mary Parker Follett (Fox and Urwick, 1977) or Stephen Covey (1992) might refer to as "participatory management" is bound to fail. Under these circumstances, the police are denied the right to police themselves and lose the key element needed to achieve professional status (Walker, 1999).

Unless it is carefully monitored and managed, the trial board apparatus can become defective and function as an impediment to good discipline. Instead of an objective "peer review" process, it may become self-serving by shifting to a cover-up modality situated in the morass of procedural due process. The Los Angeles Police Department has been criticized in this regard. Additionally, in Pittsburgh, the trial board system deteriorated to such a degree that the city had to seek state legislative relief to correct the problem. The union contract and state law that created the original system made it virtually impossible for police administrators to exercise management's right to discipline officers even in cases of serious occupational deviance.

In most police departments, only the internal personnel complaint investigations that are sustained are placed in the employee's personnel file. It is standard operating procedure in some agencies to remove investigative reports from personnel files after what is considered to be a reasonable length of time (from two to five years) if no other complaints are sustained. Keeping unproven and possibly false personnel complaints on file is a dangerous practice, because they are subject to subpoena in subsequent civil litigation against the officer or the police department. Because the introduction of this evidence could prejudice a jury, the benefit of keeping it must be weighed against the risk of incurring greater civil liability. In addition, it is inappropriate for police managers to use unsubstantiated allegations of police misconduct as a negative factor in performance evaluation or promotion considerations. Superfluous paperwork of this type should be disposed of on a regular basis.

The prompt adjudication of serious personnel complaints gives police chiefs an opportunity to make it clear, through the imposition of firm and fair disciplinary action, that they will not tolerate serious employee misconduct. In addition, when serious personnel complaints are not sustained, it allows them to go on record in support of the legal, moral, and professional conduct exhibited by the vast majority of the nation's police personnel.

The Civilian Review Movement

Many police departments have flirted with the concept of civilian control since the late 1950s. Direct review of police behavior is as popular with critics of the police as it is unpopular with police officers themselves. Most traditional civilian review boards, like those established in New York, Philadelphia, Detroit, and Kansas City, were created in response to specific police-community relations problems. They were organized so that complaints about police occupational deviance could be channeled through a formally structured committee of citizens who would examine complaints and recommend remedial action. Unfortunately, the civilian review process did not resolve problems and in many situations made the problems worse. Consequently, most of the traditional civilian review boards have been abandoned (Johnson, 1998). Because police misconduct has not disappeared and the internal investigation process does not always work as well as it should, other alternatives are now being explored (U.S. Department of Justice, 2001).

The renewed interest in civilian oversight of government activity in the mid-1980s has produced a second generation of review strategies with interests far broader than law enforcement. The "accountability" movement is based on the fact that unless government is receptive and agrees to deal with citizen complaints, there will be more than the usual amount of fear and distrust (Walker and Kreisel, 1996). The ombudsman and the independent review panel are examples of this renewed emphasis on accountability. The ombudsman, or "citizen advocate," is a government official who acts as a grievance commissioner with the authority to investigate all complaints of administrative abuse. The ombudsman has discretion in determining which cases to probe. While ombudsmen usually have no power to discipline or prosecute government employees, they usher in openness, raise issues, and marshal public sentiment. The advantage of the ombudsman approach to accountability is that it does not single out one particular agency (like the police) but covers all government agencies (Johnson et al., 1981; Walker and Kreisel, 1996).

On the other hand, some political subdivisions are establishing independent review panels to deal with citizen complaints. The panels accept complaints, conduct fact-finding inquiries, and make remedial recommendations to appropriate authorities. While some independent review panels have a great deal of authority, others are very limited in scope. The review process ensures that all public employees are to be treated in the same way regardless of their job classification. Many police officers and public employee unions oppose outside review in any form. Only time will tell whether independent review will be any more successful than the first-generation civilian review boards and which model, if any, will survive (Alpert and Dunham, 1997).

Forecasting and Dealing with Potential Disciplinary Problems

One approach to forecasting and dealing with potential disciplinary problems that is now being used in progressive police departments is known as the early warning system (EWS) (see Chapter 10). The EWS is programmed, either manually or by computer, to keep track of all personnel complaints lodged with the department, whether they are substantiated or not (Guthrie, 1996). The program tracks complaints in terms of type, seriousness, location, and other important variables. After a specified number of complaints have been filed against a particular officer, the proverbial red flag is raised and the officer's entire file is reviewed to assess potential problems (Walker, 2000). Even a number of unsubstantiated or relatively minor complaints, for example, trigger the review and interview process built into EWS.

The sole function of EWS is to alert internal affairs personnel and first-line supervisors that there may be potential disciplinary problems on the horizon. Because EWS is a diagnostic tool, it need not be cloaked in the same procedural due process as an internal investigation or a formal disciplinary action (Walker, 2000).

The interview is a critical component in the EWS process. After meeting with the officer, it may become apparent that the concerns are unfounded. The officer might be assigned to a high-crime area and has been tough on both crime and alleged criminals. Complaints against the officer may be an orchestrated attempt to have the officer transferred from the area so that the criminal element can return to its old habits.

The same interview could produce a different result, however. Internal affairs personnel or the sergeant might realize that the officer's on-the-job behavior is being adversely affected by problems at home, alcohol abuse, emotional stress, or other factors. As a result, the investigator or sergeant (based on impetus from EWS) can advise police managers that the officer is in need of help before the problem becomes too serious. Help may come in the form of coaching, counseling, professional care, or referral to the department's employee assistance program (EAP).

The Los Angeles Police Department has incorporated a number of policies in direct response to the Mark Fuhrman affair. In the context of the internal affairs investigation of Mark Fuhrman, five central issues surfaced: gender bias, racial discrimination, excessive force, code of silence, and discourtesy. In addition to addressing these issues through training and policy statements, the Los Angeles Police Department developed their version of EWS known as TEAMS (Training Evaluation and Management System). TEAMS is an incident-based computerized database that allows a review of employee histories to better identify trends and patterns of employee behavior (Los Angeles Police Commission, 1997).

An early warning system, whether manual or computerized, is diagnostic and help-oriented rather than punitive. It is part of the Total Quality Management commitment to personnel development within the police department (Alpert and Dunham, 1997).

Discipline and the Employee Assistance Movement

Many progressive police administrators now realize that formal disciplinary action that is designed primarily to punish marginal employees or to separate them from police service may be objectionable and even counterproductive. Collective bargaining agreements and civil service regulations often stress intervention and remediation rather than termination of employment. Consequently, employee assistance programs have sprung up all over the country. These programs offer a wide range of diagnostic, counseling, and other remedial services to police officers whose on-the-job performance is adversely affected by physical, psychological, or social problems. Employee assistance programs are based on the assumption that it is more humane to treat (and hopefully to resolve) an employee's problems rather than to terminate that employee. It is also considered more cost-effective to invest in existing human resources than it is to recruit, screen, hire, orient, and train new employees.

Employee assistance programs give police managers the opportunity to use intervention and remediation strategies to keep discipline problems from developing. As first-line supervisors, sergeants are expected to know their personnel well enough to spot personal problems that could have a negative impact on performance. They act as referral agents. In some cases, police officers are given a choice. Participation in the employee assistance program is strictly voluntary. At other times, it is mandatory and stipulated as a condition of continued employment.

The employee assistance program may also be incorporated into the department's disciplinary process. Under these circumstances, officers being disciplined are required (by trial board or chief of police) to participate in counseling or other forms of remedial treatment in lieu of demotion, suspension, or termination. As in the case of probation, these negative sanctions will be held in abeyance, or not imposed at all, if the officer makes an honest effort to change behavior. Employee assistance programs substitute intervention and treatment for punishment when remediation is in the best interests of the police department. Sergeants monitor the on-the-job performance of the officer during and after treatment. They must be willing to make an objective appraisal. Officers who do not respond to the treatment provided through the employee assistance program must (based on the recommendation of their supervisor) be considered for termination. This is a great responsibility.

Summary

Police work is a complex occupation with the inherent potential for personal misconduct and occupational deviance. The situation is complicated by the fact that many of the clients do not want the service and resent those who exercise control over their lives. Police work is performed in an emotion-charged environment, booby-trapped with all kinds of temptation. Officers also wield vast amounts of discretion with little or no direct supervision. We expect mere mortals to exhibit the perfection of an automaton and become angry when they fail to meet those expectations.

A personnel complaint is a formal accusation that a particular employee is guilty of some type of legal, moral, or professional misconduct. These complaints come from both internal and external sources. The complaints run the gamut from abusive language to major forms of "blue-coat" crime. Most are minor and are handled by the sergeant; others are more serious and require a much more thorough investigation. First-line supervisors, acting as the chief's designees, conduct internal investigations in many of the nation's small police departments. They are less directly involved in the disposition of serious misconduct complaints in larger police departments with internal affairs units.

The purpose of an internal investigation is to determine whether the allegation is valid and to assess the police officer's culpability in the matter. The disciplinary process itself can be broken down into four distinct phases: (1) complaint reception, (2) complaint investigation, (3) complaint adjudication, and (4) disciplinary action. Quasi-judicial trial boards are unique entities created to hear testimony, evaluate evidence, and make recommendations concerning appropriate disposition in serious misconduct cases. Emphasis is placed on neutrality, objectivity, and procedural due process.

The imposition of punishment in the form of negative sanctions is designed to produce conformity with police department policies, procedures, rules, and regulations; change the officer's future behavior; safeguard the integrity of the police establishment; and earn respect from the community. In order to accomplish these goals, internal discipline must be firm, fair, swift, timely, and consistent. Maintaining effective discipline takes time, effort, and a great deal of energy. The quality of discipline is inexorably linked to the human skills of and ethical tone set by sergeants, commanders, and police executives.

If used properly, internal discipline is a positive force that meets the needs of the department, the accused officer, and the community. Effective internal discipline systems almost always have the following characteristics:

1. They are proactive rather than being merely reactive.

2. They are firm, fair, impartial, and compassionate.

3. Emphasis is placed on equity and procedural due process.

4. They are open and easily accessible to the public.

5. The inquiry and sanctions imposed are proportional to the seriousness of the police misconduct.

6. Employees are allowed to participate in all phases.

7. They are perceived by everyone involved as a vehicle for personnel development rather than simply being a means of punitive coercion.

8. They promote professionalism and collegiality through participatory management.

9. The police chief executive sets the moral tone for the department and exercises ultimate control over all disciplinary action.

In an effort to minimize the need for formal disciplinary action in cases involving noncriminal and less serious police deviance, many departments are experimenting with early warning systems and employee assistance programs. The objective is to deal with the needs of personnel rather than to dispose of them through the disciplinary process. Investment in human resources is an essential element of Total Quality Management.

If the police are to attain and maintain professional status, they must work hard to translate the abstract concept of accountability into reality through self-discipline. It is in the public interest for the police to police themselves. Unless they do, someone else will attempt to do it. Their world will be invaded by an army of lawyers, litigants, and political activists demanding civilian review of police actions. The police hold their destiny in their own hands.

Case Study

Sergeant Juanita Cardenas

Sergeant Juanita Cardenas is a senior supervisory sergeant with the Williamsport Police Department, a CALEA-accredited police department of 277 sworn officers. Sergeant Cardenas was appointed to the Internal Affairs unit just two years ago and serves as the senior Internal Affairs investigator for the department. Her duties also involve developing policies and procedures for internal personnel complaint processing. For the past 15 years the department has used a trial board system for serious personnel complaints. The process involves a formal hearing before a board of officers and civilians who then make recommendations to the police chief for action. During this time, the chief has merely signed off on the recommendations of the trial board. It has been a good system, and even though it has only been in session a few times over the years, there have been no problems with the system.

Three months ago, Williamsport hired a new police chief to replace the retiring chief. Chief Adams came to Williamsport from a larger Midwestern city. While the Williamsport Police Department had no real problems organizationally or administratively, the city council had decided to select a new chief from outside the department. Chief Adams had excellent credentials—he is a former FBI agent, has been an assistant chief in a larger metropolitan city, and holds two master's degrees, one in public administration and the other in criminal justice. However, Chief Adams does not endorse the participatory management style. In fact, he has indicated to Sergeant Cardenas that he wants the trial board system removed and replaced with a review board with the chief as the review board chairperson. Chief Adams believes this will give him more discretionary authority to handle complaints against his officers and will allow him more control over personnel.

Sergeant Cardenas firmly believes the trial board system is the better way to handle complaints. It provides for due process and participative management. And with the civilian component, the board provides more objectivity and community support.

If you were Sergeant Cardenas, how would you convince the chief to keep the current trial board system? Are there any compromises that might be made to satisfy the chief and keep the trial board system? Are there any other outside resources available that might help convince the chief to keep the trial board system?

Key Concepts

adjudication

complaint receipt

disciplinary action

dispositions

due process

early warning system (EWS)

employee assistance programs (EAP)

executive leadership

fairness

internal discipline

occupational deviance

participation

personnel complaints

police deviance

police misconduct

proactive policy

professionalism

responsibility

supervisor's role

trial boards

Discussion Topics and Questions

1. What is the assigned mission of the American police establishment? Based on their strategic role in our society, why are they so vulnerable to personnel complaints?

2. How do corruption and other forms of legalistic police deviance differ from moral and/or professional misconduct?

3. Policies are a guide to thinking within an organization. Why is a proactive personnel complaint investigation policy in the public interest? What are the implications for police professionalism?

4. Who is ultimately responsible for leadership and control of the internal disciplinary system? How do the public, police officers, and the police department benefit from an easily accessible and open forum for the resolution of personnel complaints?

5. Most misconduct complaints are minor, not serious. Where do personnel complaints come from? What are the three basic types of external complaints that sergeants, internal affairs officers, and police managers deal with most of the time?

6. What techniques would you, as a sergeant, use to interview and investigate an employee accused of serious misconduct? What investigative tools are available to you? Why do you have more latitude in a personnel investigation than you would have in a criminal case?

7. What is the function of an administrative trial board? How are they usually structured? How do they arrive at a decision? What are their options in terms of classifying findings and recommending disciplinary action?

8. Why is procedural due process so very important when it comes to the imposition of disciplinary action? Are the due process standards spelled out in *Morrissey v. Brewer* adequate to protect personnel who are accused of occupational deviance? Where would you look to research your due process rights as a member of the police department?

9. Why is it so difficult to state with precision exactly what role sergeants play in the administration of internal discipline? Can anything be done to reduce this role conflict?

10. What is the early warning system (EWS)? How does it differ from the disciplinary process? What should its relationship be to the department's employee assistance program?

For Further Reading

Gaines, Larry K., Mittie D. Southerland, and John E. Angell (1991). *Police Administration*. New York, NY: McGraw-Hill Book Company.

> Includes an excellent chapter on operational accountability and control. Emphasis is placed on initiating and investigating complaints related to police misconduct. Outlines specific procedures applicable to the internal investigation process.

Roberg, Roy R., John Crank, and Jack Kuykendall (2000). *Police and Society*, Second Edition.. Los Angeles, CA: Roxbury Publishing Co.

> Details police behavior and discretion with special attention to occupational deviance, professional misconduct, and illegal acts or omissions. The authors also discuss a systematic theory of police corruption.

Skolnick, Jerome H., and Thomas C. Gray (1975). *Police in America*. Boston, MA: Education Associates/Little, Brown and Company.

> Classic study of police corruption and "blue-coat" crime. It sets the tone for much of the work that has followed. The book provides a comprehensive framework for the exploration of a very complex social phenomenon.

Swanson, Charles R., Leonard Territo, and Robert Taylor (1993). *Police Administration*, Third Edition. New York, NY: Macmillan Publishing Co.

> Contemporary review of the internal discipline process based on both procedural and substantive due process.

References

Adams, Thomas F. (2001). *Police Field Operations*, Fifth Edition. Englewood Cliffs, NJ: Prentice-Hall, Inc.

Alpert, Geoffrey P., and Roger G. Dunham (1997). *Policing Urban America*, Third Edition. Prospect Heights, IL: Waveland Press, Inc.

American Bar Association (1973). *Standards Related to the Urban Police Function*. Chicago, IL: American Bar Association.

Arnold, J. (1999). "Internal Affairs Investigation Guidelines." *Law & Order*, Vol. 47, No. 5. (May).

Baker, Mark (1985). *Cops: Their Lives in Their Own Words*. New York, NY: Pocket Books/Simon & Schuster, Inc.

Barker, Thomas, and David L. Carter (1994). *Police Deviance*, Third Edition. Cincinnati, OH: Anderson Publishing Co.

CALEA (2001). *Standards for Law Enforcement Agencies*. Fairfax, VA: Commission on Accreditation for Law Enforcement Agencies, Inc.

Courtney, Kevin M. (1996). "Internal Affairs in the Small Agency." *FBI Law Enforcement Bulletin*, Vol. 65, No. 9.

Covey, Stephen R. (1992). *Principle-Centered Leadership*. New York, NY: Simon & Schuster, Inc.

Crank, John P. (1998). *Understanding Police Culture*. Cincinnati, OH: Anderson Publishing Co.

Dunham, Roger G. and Geoffrey P. Alpert (1997). *Critical Issues in Policing*, Third Edition. Prospect Heights, IL: Waveland Press, Inc.

Fox, Elliott and L. Urwick (eds.) (1977). *Dynamic Administration: The Collected Papers of Mary Parker Follett*, Second Edition. New York, NY: Hippocrene Books, Inc.

Gaines, Larry K., and Victor E. Kappeler (2003). *Policing in America*, Fourth Edition. Cincinnati, OH: Anderson Publishing Co.

Gaines, Larry K., Mittie D. Southerland, and John E. Angell (1991). *Police Administration*. New York, NY: McGraw-Hill Book Company.

Guthrie, Michael (1996). "Using Automation to Apply Discipline Fairly." *FBI Law Enforcement Bulletin*, Vol. 65, No. 5.

Iannone, Nathan F., and Marvin Iannone (2001). *Supervision of Police Personnel*, Sixth Edition. Englewood Cliffs, NJ: Prentice-Hall, Inc.

Johnson, Richard R. (1998). "Citizen Complaints: What the Police Should Know." *FBI Law Enforcement Bulletin*, Vol. 67, No. 12.

Johnson, Thomas A., Gordon E. Misner, and Lee P. Brown (1981). *The Police and Society*. Englewood Cliffs, NJ: Prentice-Hall, Inc.

Johnston, Michael (1982). *Political Corruption and Public Policy in America*. Monterey, CA: Brooks-Cole Publishing Company.

Kappeler, Victor E., Richard D. Sluder, and Geoffrey P. Alpert (1994). *Forces of Deviance: Understanding the Dark Side of Policing*. Prospect Heights, IL: Waveland Press, Inc.

Leonard, V.A. and Harry W. More (1993). *Police Organization and Management*, Eighth Edition. Westbury, NY: The Foundation Press, Inc.

Los Angeles Police Commission (1997). *Mark Fuhrman Task Force: Executive Summary*. Los Angeles, CA: Los Angeles Police Department.

National Advisory Commission on Criminal Justice Standards and Goals (1973). *The Police*. Washington, DC: U.S. Government Printing Office.

Newman, Donald J. (1986). *Introduction to Criminal Justice*, Third Edition. New York, NY: Random House.

Pennsylvania Consolidated Statutes (1993). Title 18, Chapter 49a, Section 4906—False Reports to Law Enforcement Authorities.

Redlich, James W. (1994). "Disciplinary Interrogations: Which Warnings Apply? And When?" *The Police Chief*, Vol. LXI, No. 6.

Rothlein, Steve, and Ronald Lober (1996). "The Ramifications of Internal Affairs Investigations." *The Police Chief*, Vol. LXIII, No. 5.

Scoville, Daniel (1999). "Citizen Complaints Are Part of the Business." *Police*, Vol. 23, No. 11.

Smith, Ralph Lee (1965). *The Tarnished Badge*. New York, NY: Thomas Y. Crowell Company.

U.S. Department of Justice (2001). *Citizen Review of Police*. Rockville, MD: National Institute of Justice.

Walker, Samuel, and Brian W. Kreisel (1996). "Varieties of Citizen Review: The Implications of Organizational Features of Complaint Review Procedures for Accountability of the Police." *American Journal of Police*, Vol. 15, No. 3.

Walker, Samuel (1999). *The Police in America*, Third Edition. New York, NY: McGraw-Hill Book Publishers.

———— (2000). *Responding to the Problem Police Officer: A National Study of Early Warning Systems*. Rockville, MD: National Institute of Justice.

Labor Relations—

Problem Solving through Constructive Conflict 12

Introductory Case Study

Sergeant Bill Toomey

Sergeant Bill Toomey has been with the Edwardsville Police Department for more than 22 years. The Edwardsville Police Department is a medium-sized department with 312 sworn officers. The local chapter of the Fraternal Order of Police established a collective bargaining unit nearly 15 years ago. Since that time, the collective bargaining unit has worked fairly smoothly in getting a number of much-needed changes in the police department. Much of the credit goes to Sergeant Toomey, who has been the lead negotiator for the unit since its inception. In fact, most of the negotiators on the collective bargaining team have been on it since it began. When the unit began, Sergeant Toomey was the only member who was a first-line supervisor. Over the years, many of the officers on the negotiating unit have been promoted to sergeant and a couple have been promoted to lieutenant. Although the lieutenants are not now part of the negotiating team, the team has six sergeants and nine officers.

Over the past several months, many officers have filed grievances and morale has been low due to the city's financial strains. In a few months, a new collective bargaining contract will be negotiated, and there is talk among the city leaders that many benefits the police are now enjoying will be terminated with the new contract. This has created quite a stir among the union employees, and there is a call for a new slate of negotiating team members. One of the major controversies is the presence of sergeants on the negotiating team. Many of the union members claim that the sergeants are condescending to management's side, resulting in contracts that are not truly good faith agreements. They also point out that many of the negotiating team members have been promoted as a reward for helping management in these contract agreements. The FOP has petitioned the State Labor Relations Board to hold a hearing on the merits of having sergeants on the negotiating team. The FOP claims that sergeants are more policy-making managers than first-line supervisors and should be excluded from any bargaining unit.

As the senior supervisor on the collective bargaining unit, Sergeant Toomey has been asked by the FOP and the chief of police to testify at the State Labor Relations Board hearing on the matter.

If you were Sergeant Toomey, what issues would you address at the hearing? What kinds of information would you need to present at the hearing? Should sergeants and first-line supervisors be allowed to serve on bargaining teams? Why or why not? Should there be a limit on how many supervisors can serve on a collective bargaining team?

Sowing the Seeds of Unionism

European-style unionism never caught on in the United States. As a matter of fact, labor unions were banned in this country until the mid-1930s. It took the economic upheaval of the Great Depression to change public policy concerning collective bargaining. The legalization of collective bargaining ushered in a new and very different era.

The Wagner Act was signed into law by Franklin D. Roosevelt in 1935. Officially known as the National Labor Relations Act, it permitted workers in private industry to form labor unions and actually encouraged them to bargain with their employers concerning "wages, hours and working conditions." While the National Labor Relations Act is often referred to as organized labor's Magna Carta, it was never intended to cover everyone in the workforce. Government employees, for example, were specifically excluded from participation in the collective bargaining process.

After the initial surge of organizing activity in traditional blue-collar industries, union membership stabilized and then began to decline. In 1945 union membership reached an all-time high of 35.5 percent of the workforce (Foulkes and Livernash, 1989). By the late 1970s, fewer than one-fourth of the nation's workers were still unionized (Dressler, 1979). It is now estimated that only 16.1 percent of all American workers are represented by unions (*World Almanac*, 1993). The face of organized labor has changed, and the future of the labor movement is uncertain.

Public employees at all levels of government resented the fact that they were excluded from collective bargaining and rejected this prohibition as an unwarranted intrusion on their First Amendment right to freedom of association. As their influence and purchasing power lagged behind that of other workers, they became much more militant in their demands for equality under the law (Stahl, 1983). Union organizers seized on this widespread discontent. It gave them a chance to fan the fire of collectivism among government employees. Unionism was actively promoted as a viable alternative to the managerial despotism of the past. By working together, public employees and unions delivered a classic one-two punch, and the legal barriers to collective bargaining in the public sector slowly began to erode.

The Boston police strike of 1919, viewed by many unionists as one of the most important events in American police history, was the cause célèbre that gave the nation its first real exposure to labor problems in municipal government. The basic issue involved the right of the police, as public employees, to form a union and to affiliate with the American Federation of Labor. The strike shocked the national conscience and solidified political opposition to all forms of collective bargaining. The response was both swift and decisive. The Boston police had to be kept in their place irrespective of the cost. According to Jay Shafritz and his associates (2001), it was political power and not strict rationality that determined the rules of play and the winner of the game. While the unionization of public employees is now legal in most states, there is a distinct undercurrent of antiunion sentiment that can be traced directly to the Boston police strike of 1919.

In 1919 Boston police officers earned $1,400 a year and had not received a pay raise in nearly 20 years. They worked an average of 87 hours per week under deplorable conditions. The cost of living had skyrocketed (by 86 percent), and promotions were based solely on political considerations. The situation was truly grim. Morale hit an all-time low. When the police officers' demand for a $200-a-year pay raise was rejected, they voted to convert their social club into a bona fide labor union and join the American Federation of Labor. The city's police commissioner reacted immediately. He suspended the leaders of the new organization. Tension mounted. All attempts at mediation failed and a strike seemed to be inevitable. On September 9, 1919, 1,117 Boston police officers went on strike in the first publicly proclaimed "job action" against a municipal government in the United States. Only 427 policemen remained on the job (Walker, 1999).

Violence, disorder, and crime erupted as Boston reverted to a Hobbesian "state of nature." Looting was commonplace. Lawlessness and mob action became the rule rather than the exception. Declaring a state of emergency, the mayor asked the governor to help restore law and order in the city. On the third day of the strike, more than 7,000 fully armed members of the state militia took control of the city. In defending the state's action, Governor Calvin Coolidge made the famous statement that now serves as a rallying cry against unionism in the public sector saying "There is no right to strike against the public safety by anybody, anywhere, at any time." All of the strikers were fired, and antiunion sentiment spread like wildfire throughout the nation.

While the Boston police strike failed to achieve its objectives, it sent reverberations throughout the American political establishment. Maintaining control over public employees became a national obsession. State legislatures, in what amounted to a knee-jerk reaction, enacted very repressive legislation prohibiting the unionization of state and local government employees. The courts, responding to social and political pressure to maintain the status quo, consistently ruled that public employees per se had absolutely no statutory or constitutional right to organize for the purpose of collective bargaining with their employers. In most states it was illegal for any government unit to engage in collective bargaining with its employees. The gerrymandering of public employees out of the National Labor Relations Act was by no means accidental. The die was cast in Boston. Public employees were to be excluded from the collective bargaining process for the next 40 years.

Public sector labor-management relations deteriorated during World War II. Poor pay, rampant inflation, and a generalized sense of exploitation took its toll on police morale. Perceiving strength in numbers, the police flirted with unionism once again. While they had absolutely no legal standing, beginning in 1943 these unions experienced some limited success in negotiating with their employers. The informal collective bargaining process seemed to be working. Within a few years, however, these fledgling unions were crushed by even more restrictive legislation, unfavorable court decisions, firm opposition from police administrators, and the refusal of local politicians to alter the existing balance of power in any way, vis-à-vis meaningful collective bargaining with their employees. No one was willing to compromise. The battle lines were drawn.

Government employees did not give up on the idea of collective bargaining. They formed unionlike professional associations and continued to push for substantive changes in the law. These groups lobbied legislators, agitated for social change, and, on occasion, took illegal job actions to press their demands. As the number of state and local government employees mushroomed, these groups flexed their muscles and were able to exercise more clout in the political arena. Everything seemed to come together in 1959. In that year, Wisconsin became the first state in the nation to grant public employees a limited right to bargain with their employers concerning typical union items such as wages, hours, and working conditions. Wisconsin's public employees were specifically prohibited from using the strike as a tool for impasse resolution. Public employees found the door open and were prepared to seize the opportunity to solve their problems through constructive conflict.

Things have changed dramatically since 1959. More than 80 percent of the states have now adopted legislation that permits public employees to participate in the collective bargaining process. In some states, public employees (with the exception of fire and police personnel) are allowed to strike. Ohio's 1984 public bargaining law is a classic example. It gives all employees, except public safety personnel, the right to strike (after a mandatory 10-day advance notice). By 1985, 24 states had opted to provide public employees with some type of arbitration as an alternative to a strike. Figure 12.1 is an analysis of Pennsylvania's Act 111. While compulsory binding arbitration was initially intended only for those involved in critical services, there has been some movement to broaden the scope of coverage to include other types of public employees as well (Swanson et al., 1993).

Figure 12.1
Public Employee Act

In May 1968, Governor Raymond Shaffer appointed a commission to review the Pennsylvania Public Employee Act of 1947. The commission was to be known as the Heckman Commission, taking the name of its chairman, Leon E. Heckman. Governor Shaffer directed this commission to "review the whole area of public relations dealing with public employees and public employers and to make recommendations to him for the establishment of orderly, fair and workable procedures governing those relations; including legislation, if the commission deems it appropriate."

After several intensive months of review, the commission stated that the Public Employee Act of 1947 had at least three (3) major weaknesses in its basic structure.

[a]   The act does not require public employers to bargain collectively with their employees. This has led to a near breakdown in communication, where the public employer has not chosen to recognize the right of its employees to bargain collectively. This inability to bargain collectively has created more ill-will and led to more friction and strikes than any other cause.

[b]   The act forbids any and all strikes by public employees. Twenty years of experience have taught us that such a policy is unreasonable and unenforceable, particularly when coupled with ineffective or nonexistent collective bargaining. It is based upon a philosophy that one may not strike against the sovereign. However, today's sovereign is engaged not only in government, but in a great variety of other activities. The consequences of a strike by a police officer are very different from those of a gardener in a public park.

[c]   The mandatory penalties of the 1947 Act are self-defeating. Forbidding a public employer to give normal pay increases for three years to one who has struck and has been reemployed simply reduces the value of such position to that employee and drives him or her to seek other work.

The commission made the following recommendations:

[A]   The Public Employee Act of 1947 should be replaced by an entirely new law governing relationships between public employees and employer.

(1)   The commission forged a single statute for all public instrumentalities and their employees in order to ensure a uniform policy for all agencies of government.

Figure 12.1, *continued*

[B] The new law should recognize the right of all public employees, including police and fire fighters, to bargain collectively subject to enumerated safeguards.

(1) The bargaining unit should be determined in each instance by the Pennsylvania Labor Relations Board pursuant to statutory guidelines.

(2) The bargaining agent should be determined only by elections supervised by the Labor Board.

(3) Bargaining should be permitted with respect to wages, hours, and conditions of employment, appropriately qualified by a recognition of existing laws dealing with aspects of the same subject matter and by a carefully defined reservation of managerial rights.

(4) Employees should be protected from an obligation to become members of an employee organization as a condition of employment, but the right to collect dues from members of the employee organization should be recognized as a bargainable issue under appropriate safeguards.

[C] The law should require both parties to bargain in good faith through the following steps:

(1) Face-to-face collective bargaining between the parties, the final agreement to be reduced to writing and signed by representatives of all parties.

(2) The utilization of the state mediation service in the event collective bargaining is not successful without it.

(3) Fact-finding, recommendations, and publication thereof by a tribunal of three experienced arbitrators appointed by the Labor Board.

(4) In disputes involving police officers and fire fighters, if collective bargaining and mediation do not resolve the dispute, mandatory binding arbitration.

[D] Except for police officers and fire fighters, a limited right to strike should be recognized, subject to these safeguards:

(1) No strike should be permitted for any reason whatsoever until all of the collective bargaining procedures outlined above have been fully complied with.

(2) No strike should be permitted to begin or continue where health, safety, or welfare of the general public is in danger.

(3) Unlawful strikes should be subject to injunctions and violations thereof enforced by penalties that will be effective against the bargaining agent or individual employee(s) or both.

Figure 12.1, *continued*

> The Heckman Commission favored a single statute for all public instru-
> mentalities, but Pennsylvania now has two laws providing for collective bar-
> gaining for public employees. These two laws are indeed a strange contrast,
> particularly because they were passed by essentially the same legislature and
> signed by the same Governor.
>
> As a result of a constitutional change in 1967, Act 111 of June 24, 1968
> provided for collective bargaining of police officers and fire fighters of pub-
> lic jurisdiction in the Commonwealth. It designates binding arbitration for
> impasses in lieu of the right to strike. Act 111 was rushed through the legislative
> process in four days without staff work, publicity, or public hearings.
>
> It took a little more than two years to complete Public Employee Relations
> Act 195 from commission to operation. Members of the commission wrote the
> act, public hearings were held, interest and viewpoints of opposing parties were
> solicited, and the Act received widespread publicity. As passed by the gen-
> eral assembly, Act 195 permits strikes by public employees in nonsafety
> categories, such as teachers, health care providers, social services person-
> nel, and so forth. Act 195 is completely silent on the salient issue of binding
> arbitration.

While Act 111 has been modified somewhat, its basic thrust remains
unchanged. Pennsylvania labor law encourages collective bargaining between
local governments and certified employee organizations authorized to represent police personnel. Act 111 has served as the prototype for collective
bargaining statutes throughout the United States.

According to O. Glenn Stahl (1983), most state and local government
employees are now represented by labor unions. The American Federation
of State, County, and Municipal Employees (AFSCME) is one of the largest
and most powerful unions in America. AFSCME has more than 3,000 locals
and more than 1,280,000 members. It is affiliated with the American Federation of Labor and Congress of Industrial Organizations (AFL-CIO). In
addition to AFSCME, there are scores of smaller labor organizations (like
the American Federation of Teachers, Fraternal Order of Police, International
Association of Fire Fighters, Service Employees International Union) that
are engaged in collective bargaining on behalf of public employees. Independent and unaffiliated local unions have sprung up to represent the unique
interests of specialized government personnel. Teachers, firefighters, and
municipal police officers are the most heavily unionized groups in the public sector.

The public sector is a natural habitat for labor unions. They serve two
masters, by providing gains for workers and political support for legislators,
as well as government managers. Given this situation, it is conceivable that
the upper limit of public sector unionization may reach nearly 100 percent
at some time in the future (Bellante and Porter, 1992).

The dramatic rise of membership in police unions can, in large measure, be attributed to one or more of the following factors:

1. Job dissatisfaction (especially with regard to wages and working conditions).

2. The perception that other public employees are improving their situation through the collective bargaining process.

3. A deep-seated belief that the public is unsympathetic or even hostile to the personal and professional needs of police officers.

4. An influx of younger police officers who hold a far less traditional view of authority and bureaucratic regimentation.

5. A strong recruiting effort by organized labor to make up for a decline in membership caused by the shift from an industrial to a service-based economy.

Today, nearly three-fourths of all American police officers are dues-paying members of labor unions (Cole and Smith, 2001). In fact, law enforcement membership in unions is one of the fastest growing labor groups in the nation (Stone, 1998).

Many of the existing police unions evolved from social or fraternal organizations. Local police benevolent associations and the national Fraternal Order of Police are excellent examples of this phenomenon. Due to the decentralization of municipal government (with more than 17,000 separate police departments), unions were forced to focus on local issues rather than national concerns. Consequently, there is no national labor organization that can legitimately claim to represent the interests of all police personnel in the United States. Hervey Juris and Peter Feuille (1973) argue very convincingly that it is the local character of the employment relationship that helps explain why the relatively centralized national police organizations have not attracted large numbers of rank-and-file police officers as members.

While they do not represent the interests of all police officers, national labor organizations like the American Federation of State, County, and Municipal Employees (AFSCME), Fraternal Order of Police (FOP), International Brotherhood of Police Officers (IBPO), International Conference of Police Associations (ICPA), International Union of Police Associations (IUPA), and the Teamsters wield a substantial amount of political power and have the ability to influence public policy making at all levels of government. Unionism and collective bargaining have now become permanent fixtures in public sector labor relations (Stone, 1998).

Unionism and collective bargaining by police officers represent what Samuel Walker has referred to as "the hidden revolution" in contemporary police administration. According to Walker (1999), there has been a fundamental shift in the balance of power as far as management and labor are concerned. Unilateral decision making by supervisors and managers is a thing of the past. Participatory, bilateral management is a fait accompli. Collective bargaining is a vehicle for problem solving through constructive conflict (Carter and Sapp, 1993).

One of the most important issues in labor relations relates to the scope of bargaining. What should or should not be determined at the bargaining table? Management has not, for a variety of reasons, been particularly successful in limiting the scope of negotiations. An analysis of various police collective bargaining agreements shows that most of them do not have the strongest management rights clauses. This would suggest that police administrators have been less than vigorous in preserving their prerogatives. They have failed to regulate the input of organized labor in the decision-making process (Rynecki et al., 1984). Consequently, police unions have had a profound influence on such matters as:

1. Salaries, supplemental pay, and benefits

2. Hours and working conditions

3. Manpower allocation

4. Job assignments

5. Occupational safety

6. Discipline and procedural due process

7. Evaluation and promotion procedures

8. Resource allocation

9. Law enforcement policy

10. Police-community relations

11. Training and professional development

Balanced power is the key to success in collective bargaining. In some unionized departments, however, there is an unhealthy shift of administrative power from the chief executive officer to the union. This is unfortunate. An organization needs someone to take charge and provide a sense of direction. The leader must have the managerial skill and legitimate authority to keep the organization operating as a goal-oriented system of coordinated and cooperative effort. The function of the police executive is to mobilize the human and economic resources necessary to accomplish the police department's mission, goals, and objectives (Barnard, 1976).

Many first-line supervisors, managers, elected officials, and police theorists have not come to grips with unionism. They do not fully appreciate the magnitude of the hidden revolution that has taken place over the last 25 years. Many practitioners seem content to muddle their way through life and are unconcerned with the legacy they will leave to the next generation of managers. Some police theorists, on the other hand, are in a state of denial.

Some new textbooks on police management and supervision fail to mention labor relations, unions, collective bargaining, or contract administration. This ignorance and denial could transform the hidden revolution into degenerative conflict between organized labor and management.

Management Rights

Management rights refers to decisions that govern the conditions of employment over which management claims to have exclusive jurisdiction. Because almost every management right can be and has been challenged by unions, the ultimate determination will depend on the relative bargaining power of the two sides. Union concessions and cooperation have a price tag. Under these circumstances, time-honored management rights are often negotiable.

There are two basic ways to approach the management rights issue. One is the *reserved rights* concept. The other is referred to as the *designated rights* concept. They are based on different sets of assumptions. The reserved rights approach presumes that management authority is supreme in all matters except those it has expressly conceded in the collective bargaining agreement or when its authority is restricted by law. Consequently, little or nothing is said about management rights in the contract. The designated rights approach, on the other hand, is specifically intended to clarify and reinforce the rights claimed by management. A management rights clause is made part of the bargaining agreement in an effort to reduce confusion and misunderstanding. A strong management rights clause sets very clear boundaries designed to help both parties understand the ground rules for future negotiations (Bohlander, Snell, and Sherman, 2001).

The lack of attention to the issue of management rights has had a far-reaching effect on police organization and management. In a national survey of police administrators, almost 50 percent of the respondents stated that their managerial prerogatives related to improving the police service had been "lost" as a result of collective bargaining (Sapp et al., 1990).

Understanding Labor Relations

Collective bargaining is built on the assumption that a certain amount of controlled conflict is healthy. It promotes organizational growth and development. If police officers are going to benefit fully from their association with one another (in labor unions), they and their managers should be willing to differ, to push self-interests, and to accept the idea that there is inherent value in conflict. If employees and managers do not oppose each other enough, their relationships tend to become static or counterproductive. If they oppose each other too much, conflict may get out of hand and could upset even routine operations in the police department. Here again, balance is the key to success in labor relations. Mutually acceptable collective bargaining procedures and sound judgment help to ensure that differences and conflict will remain within reasonable limits. Integrity, goodwill, and procedural regularity are essential elements in an ethical collective bargaining process. While tension may be a catalyst for mutual problem solving and coordinated action, there is nothing to be gained from the intraorganizational conflict created by petty feuding, malice, or self-destructive behavior. Management prerogatives, employee rights, and organizational needs might best be viewed as a three-legged stool. If one of the legs is weakened, the stool will collapse. No matter how strong the other legs are, they cannot, in and of themselves, keep the stool in an upright position. When the stool collapses, the community is the loser. It is the community that ends up paying (in higher taxes and fewer services) when the collective bargaining process breaks down (Ewing, 1983).

As peripheral members of the management team, sergeants interact most directly with the line personnel who do the actual work of the police department. They deal with unionized employees on a daily basis. In order to do their job properly, sergeants need to have a fairly comprehensive understanding of human behavior, work, workers, unions, and the collective bargaining process. In addition, they must prepare themselves for a unique role in labor contract administration.

Selecting a Bargaining Agent

Police officers, as public employees, are not covered by the National Labor Relations Act of 1935. As was noted previously, more than 80 percent of the states have passed enabling legislation specifically authorizing collective bargaining by public employees. No two bargaining statutes are exactly the same. Some public employee bargaining laws are fairly permissive (even allowing strikes under certain circumstances), while others are more detailed, specific, and much more restrictive. In most states, the State Labor Relations Board (SLRB) administers the law and regulates the collective bargaining process. Almost all administrative and regulatory decisions made by these boards are reviewable in the courts.

An employee, a group of employees, a union, or an employer can petition the SLRB for a representation election. The purpose of the election is to determine whether the employees want to select an exclusive bargaining agent. In most cases, a petition must be supported by a show of interest on the part of a specified percentage of the workforce. The federal standard of 30 percent has been adopted in a large number of states.

Once a petition for a representation election has been accepted, it is up to the SLRB to determine (based on job descriptions) who should and should not be in the proposed bargaining unit. In determining the exact composition of the unit, the SLRB looks for a commonality of interest, based on factors such as:

1. the similarity of duties, skills, wages, and working conditions;
2. the pertinent collective bargaining history of those involved;
3. the nature and extent of union organization that is already in place;
4. the employees' wishes in the matter (when they are consistent with other factors); and
5. the appropriateness of the proposed unit in relation to the organizational structure of the department.

Unions should represent employees whose jobs are similar and who also share a common interest. Unfortunately, labor relations theory is not always translated into practice. Bargaining unit determination in law enforcement has been a mixed bag. In Pittsburgh, for example, the FOP represents all police officers up to the rank of captain. In Toledo and Detroit, the union represents only the employees at the rank of police officer. Toledo has a separate Command Officers' Association that represents sergeants, lieutenants, and captains. Civilian personnel are often represented by AFSCME. It is not uncommon for a local government to deal with three or four separate unions representing employees in the same police department.

From a practical point of view, it is far better for management personnel to be in the same bargaining unit with other managers who have similar duties, responsibilities, and interests. This is also true when it comes to sergeants. They are much more likely to support management initiatives and function as effective first-line managers if they consider themselves to be a real part of the management team (Ayres and Coble, 1987). Unfortunately, there has been little consistency in this area, and many existing bargaining unit configurations simply cannot be justified in logical terms.

Assuming there are no problems in determining the composition of the proposed bargaining unit and that no other group has been certified as the exclusive bargaining agent for the employees, the SLRB is obligated by law to conduct a representation election. If everyone agrees, the staff of the SLRB will conduct what is called a *consent election*. In the event that there is any disagreement, an election will be authorized after a formal hearing has been held and an official finding is made by the board. The time and date of the election will be set in an effort to ensure that most of the eligible employees on all shifts will have the opportunity to vote. All parties to the election are expected to adhere to the preelection campaign guidelines set by the SLRB. Both labor and management have the right to appoint a number of observers to act as poll watchers, checkers, challengers, and tabulators. Everything must be done to ensure the fairness of the election and the validity of each ballot.

If no objections are filed, or if those that are filed are rejected, the board has the legal authority to certify the results. There are two basic types of certification:

1. **Certification of Representation.** Attesting to the fact that a majority of those in the bargaining unit voted for the union.

2. **Certification of Election Results.** Attesting to the fact that the employees in the bargaining unit voted against union representation.

Certification of representation makes the union the sole bargaining agent for all members of the bargaining unit. It also gives the union authority to enter into legally binding negotiations with the state or local government (Anderson, 1975).

A certified police union is a force to be reckoned with. It is, by law, the exclusive bargaining agent for all members of the bargaining unit, whether they belong to the union or not. Management is not permitted to negotiate directly with individual police officers or other groups within the police department. There are other benefits to certification as well. For example:

1. The employer (state or local government) must bargain in good faith with a certified union and usually is required to meet and discuss items of mutual concern on a timely basis.

2. The employer (state or local government) is obligated to seek a collective bargaining agreement or contract with the certified union representing bargaining unit employees.

3. Certified unions may be authorized to file policy grievances, to strike, or (if strikes are prohibited) to seek binding arbitration in an effort to enforce the collective bargaining agreement, depending on how the public employee bargaining law is written.

4. Rival unions are not permitted to engage in striking or picketing for recognition under the collective bargaining statute if there is a certified labor organization already in place.

5. Even if the parties cannot reach a collective bargaining agreement, rival unions are normally prohibited from filing a petition for a new representation election within 12 months of the original certification election.

6. An existing contract (for a definite term of up to three years) is usually considered a bar to a new election while it is in force.

In the event that union members become dissatisfied with its performance, they can petition for "decertification" of the union as their collective bargaining agent. A petition for an election to decertify a union can be filed by another union, a group of disaffected members, or an individual member of the bargaining unit. If after review the SLRB accepts the petition, it has an obligation to conduct a fair and impartial decertification election. While decertification efforts are usually unsuccessful, the process serves as a check and balance. It helps to ensure that the union's leadership continues to be responsive to the needs of its members (Myers and Twomey, 1975).

Most state public employee bargaining laws ban certain unfair labor practices. The prohibition against unfair labor practices is designed to keep labor and management coequal for purposes of collective bargaining. According to Arthur Sloane and Fred Witney (2001), it is usually considered an unfair labor practice for management to:

1. Interfere with, restrain, or coerce employees in the exercise of their rights to organize, bargain collectively, and participate in other activities for their mutual aid or protection.

2. Dominate or interfere with the formation or administration of any labor union or contribute financial or other support to it.

3. Encourage or discourage membership in any labor union organization by discrimination with regard to hiring or tenure or conditions of employment (with the exception of a valid union-security agreement).

4. Discharge or otherwise discriminate against an employee because he or she filed unfair labor practice charges against the employer.

5. Refuse to bargain collectively and in good faith with the employees' bargaining agent.

On the other hand, it is considered to be an unfair labor practice when unions do any of the following:

1. Restrain or coerce employees in exercising their rights under the law.

2. Restrain or coerce an employer in the selection of a bargaining agent or grievance representative.

3. Cause or attempt to cause an employer to discriminate against an employee based on the person's membership or nonmembership in a labor organization.

4. Refuse to bargain collectively and in good faith with an employer if the union has been designated a bargaining agent by a majority of the employees.

There is an assumption that collective bargaining is the product of independence and strength. The strong are inclined to bargain. The weak cave in. Weakness undermines the bargaining process.

Once the ground rules have been accepted and the union is in place, collective bargaining is set to begin. The initial bargaining session is a prelude to participatory management in police work.

Collective Bargaining

Collective bargaining is the process by which a labor contract is negotiated and enforced between the employees' exclusive bargaining agent (the union) and the state or local government responsible for operation of the police department. Labor and management have a mutual obligation to meet at reasonable times and to confer in good faith with respect to wages, hours, and other terms and conditions of employment. While there is an affirmative duty to bargain, neither side is required to accept a proposal or make a concession. Most labor negotiations do, however, result in a formal written agreement that both sides can live with until the next regularly scheduled round of contract talks (Bittel and Newstrom, 1992).

The Bargaining Team

One of the first steps in the actual bargaining process is for each side (union and management) to select a competent negotiating team. This is an extremely important and, at times, difficult task. Most bargaining teams are fairly small. They normally consist of a chief negotiator, a recording secretary, and three or four members who have conducted research in areas of special interest to management or the union. The knowledge, skill, and dedication of the negotiators will determine the quality of the collective bargaining agreement and set the moral or ethical tone for all future labor relations. Selectivity is a prerequisite for success.

While there are no hard-and-fast rules concerning the composition of the union's bargaining team, there are a few general principles that should be kept in mind. The union president (or a designee) almost always serves, along with other members of the bargaining unit, as part of the core team. The chief negotiator, who is usually not a police officer, leads the team and coordinates the bargaining effort. By bringing in an outside labor relations specialist as its chief negotiator, the union strengthens its position with regard to management and gains practical advantages from that person's experience, expertise, and objectivity. The chemistry of the team usually determines the quality of the contract.

The chief of police, on the other hand, seldom, if ever, serves as an official member of the management bargaining team. The chief's designee (or designees) represents the department's interest during the negotiations. This is an attempt to separate the politics of negotiation from the science of contract administration (Fyfe et al., 1997). Other department heads (legal, personnel, finance, etc.) are often pressed into service as members of the core team. In most jurisdictions, the director of labor relations serves as chief negotiator for the state or local government. Here again, the composition of the team and the way members of the team work together become critical factors in the outcome of the negotiations.

A major problem in many jurisdictions is that either police management has no representation at the bargaining table, or its representation is inadequate to deal with the task at hand. Civilian managers normally represent the municipality. While these people may know a great deal about public administration and the budgetary process, they often know little or nothing about the needs of police managers. Consequently, they frequently bargain away management rights for concessions in the economic package. This leaves police managers who are accountable for achieving the department's mission, goals, and objectives without the necessary authority to do the job (Ayres and Coble, 1987).

Once the bargaining teams have been formed, they must try to reach a consensus on the appropriate scope of the bargaining. In other words, what issues are to be discussed? While it is in management's interest to limit the scope of collective bargaining, organized labor normally wants everything placed on the table for discussion.

Scope of the Bargaining

Most public employee bargaining laws are patterned after federal statutes and, as such, attempt to identify the subjects that are either appropriate or inappropriate for collective bargaining. There are three types of bargaining proposals that merit further attention:

1. **Mandatory Subjects.** These are subjects (such as disability pay, occupational safety, and minimum staffing requirements) that clearly fall within the category of wages, hours, and other terms and conditions of employment.

2. **Voluntary Subjects.** These are topics (such as health club memberships, volume discounts based on group purchases, and new benefits for retirees) that clearly fall outside the mandatory category but are placed on the table for voluntary consideration and agreement. The other party is not required to bargain on them or to agree to include them in the new contract.

3. **Illegal Subjects.** These are subjects (such as union shop agreements, binding arbitration, and the right to strike) that have been specifically prohibited by the public employee bargaining law.

Negotiating the first contract requires a great deal of preparation and skill. The issues related to the mandatory subjects of wages, hours, and conditions of employment become mind-boggling in complex criminal justice organizations.

While both the union and management want to negotiate a contract that gives them the greatest control over decision making, parameters must be established to give some focus to the collective bargaining process.

"Rights and responsibilities" clauses are usually built in as an integral component of the collective bargaining agreement. These clauses are specifically designed to limit the scope of bargaining and delineate areas of mutual concern.

According to the Police Executive Research Forum (1978), the goal of management is to obtain contract language that gives it maximum discretion and flexibility in running the police department. The power that management retains is ordinarily spelled out in a management rights clause. A strong management rights clause gives the police administration a great deal of control over the operation of the department. A weak management rights clause gives away too much power. The National League of Cities (Rynecki et al., 1984) has recommended that a management rights clause be inserted in all municipal collective bargaining agreements. Such a clause could be stated as follows:

> It is agreed that the department possesses all of the rights, powers, privileges, and authority it had prior to the execution of this agreement. Nothing in this agreement shall be construed to limit the department or the operation of the police enterprise, except as it may have been specifically relinquished or modified herein by an express provision of the collective bargaining agreement itself.

In simple terms, this contract language states that management retains certain rights that may not be challenged by the union, no matter how infrequently they are used (Thibault et al., 1998).

Cal Swank and James Conser (1983) argue that a strong management rights clause is probably the most important part of any contract or negotiation with an employee organization. A strong management rights clause and a mutually acceptable no-strike impasse resolution process are essential components of an effective management strategy. A good management rights clause should contain, but not be limited to, the following items:

1. Determining occupational qualifications and hiring human resources.

2. Directing the workforce through the formulation of departmental policies, procedures, rules, and regulations.

3. Establishing work schedules and regulating overtime in a manner that is most advantageous to the employer.

4. Determining the method, process, and manner used to perform police work.

5. Disciplining, suspending, demoting, and discharging police personnel for reasonable and just cause.

6. Relieving and/or laying off police officers due to a lack of work, lack of funding, or for disciplinary reasons.

7. Assigning, transferring, and promoting police officers to positions within the department.

8. Consolidating and reorganizing the operations of the police department.

9. Taking action in emergency situations to ensure proper operation of the police department.

While the enumeration of management rights may prove to be a stumbling block in negotiations, specificity is critically important. Managers need to know what is expected of them. They must be free to exercise legitimate authority.

Management rights clauses are usually negotiated in tandem with an employee responsibility clause. The first union responsibility clause in Detroit was very specific. According to the contract between the City of Detroit and the Detroit Police Officers Association (1973):

1. Recognizing the crucial role of law enforcement in the preservation of the public health, safety, and welfare of a free society, the union agrees that it will take all reasonable steps to cause the employees covered by this agreement, individually and collectively, to perform all police duties, rendering loyal and efficient service to the very best of their ability.

2. The union, therefore, agrees that there shall be no interruption of these services for any cause whatsoever by the employees it represents; nor shall they absent themselves from their work or abstain, in whole or in part, from the full, faithful, and proper performance of all the duties of their employment.

3. The union further agrees that it shall not encourage any strikes, sit-downs, stay-ins, slow-downs, stoppages of work, malingering, or any acts that interfere in any manner or to any degree with the continuity of police services.

Management rights and union responsibility become the starting point for all future negotiations.

The rights and responsibilities discussed above are fairly easy to understand. They are also subject to change. Management's right to make policy, for example, can be weakened or lost entirely as the result of negotiation, arbitration awards, court challenges, or substantive changes in the collective bargaining statute. The only inherent rights of management are those that labor does not bargain away from it (Bouza, 1990). Unions, on the other hand, have been known to abdicate their responsibility to the public when they try to win policy concessions from their employers through intimidation rather than constructive conflict. It takes a great deal of time and effort on the part of labor and management to make the collective bargaining process work the way it was designed to work.

The Bargaining Table

The basic purpose of bargaining is to reach a mutually acceptable agreement on the issues raised at the table. The first meeting is ordinarily devoted to establishing the bargaining authority of each team, determining the ground rules for the negotiations, and adopting a schedule. If the parties have not previously distributed their formal proposals, they may be distributed and clarified at this time. This gives the other side some indication as to why particular proposals are being made, how much thought has gone into them, and the amount of support they have. The first session almost always sets the tone for subsequent meetings and may eventually determine the success or failure of the collective bargaining process.

Labor contract negotiations take on the characteristics of a poker game in which each side attempts to determine the opponent's hand without revealing its own (Bohlander, Snell, and Sherman, 2001). The parties try to avoid disclosing the relative importance they attach to each proposal. They do not want to pay a higher price than is necessary to achieve the proposals that are of the greatest importance to them. Proposals can generally be divided into four basic categories:

1. **Non-negotiable.** Those the team feels it must have.

2. **Negotiable.** Those the team would like to have, but on which it is willing to compromise.

3. **Trade-off.** Those the team should submit for trading purposes.

4. **Expendable.** Those the team is willing to give up.

All proposals should be realistic. Unrealistic proposals serve only to irritate the opponent and can, if taken seriously, create an impasse. It has been noted that unrealistic bargaining proposals have an unpleasant way of becoming real issues.

In order for a bargaining issue to be resolved satisfactorily, the point at which an agreement is possible must fall within limits that both the union team and the management team are willing to concede. This is called the *zone of acceptance*. In some situations, proposals to the negotiations made by one party clearly exceed the tolerance limit of the other party. If this is the case, the solution is outside the zone of acceptance. If the party refuses to modify its demands enough (through compromises or trade-offs) to bring them within the zone of acceptance, or if the opposing party will not extend its tolerance limit (based on some other form of compensation) to accommodate those demands, an impasse will result. The key to successful collective bargaining is to ascertain the parameters of the opponent's zone of acceptance and to compromise in such a way that all proposals fall within those parameters. This requires a great deal of skill.

The proposals submitted by each side must, regardless of the importance attached to them, be dealt with at the table if there is to be a collective bargaining agreement. Once a particular issue, clause, or proposal is placed on the table, the other team is obligated to respond to it. There are four basic responses:

1. Accepted

2. Accepted with minor modification

3. Rejected

4. Rejected with counterproposal

An opponent cannot reject an issue, clause, or proposal without an explanation. This would not be considered bargaining in good faith. A reason for the rejection must be given and that reason must, in and of itself, be reasonable. Having been informed of the opposing team's position, the bargaining begins. And, as noted above, the bargaining process involves a great deal of give and take. It is designed to move the opposing teams closer to a mutually acceptable middle ground within the tolerance limits of both labor and management. From this perspective, collective bargaining is an applied art rather than an exact science.

Union Goals

The union always enters the collective bargaining process with a preset agenda. It wants to share power with the top police executive through bilateral negotiations and to have a meaningful say in the day-to-day operations of the police department. Anything less is unacceptable and would be considered a sellout by the membership. The union bargaining team's big-ticket items usually fall into seven basic categories:

1. Wages and working conditions

2. Union security measures

3. Impasse resolution techniques

4. Meet-and-discuss provisions

5. Grievance procedures

6. Procedural due process

7. Job security and seniority. Two additional bargaining categories have emerged as priority items for police officers in recent contract negotiations. One deals with issues surrounding officer safety in terms of personnel deployment, workplace security, and equipment. The other focus is on adequate insurance coverage and the maintenance of fully

paid health care benefits for officers who have been injured on or retire from the job.

Concern about wages, hours, and other terms and conditions of employment are traditional items that serve as a catalyst for unionization. A recent study indicated that 96.5 percent of the officers surveyed were primarily concerned about their compensation (Leonard and More, 1993). Union security measures, impasse resolution techniques, and "meet-and-discuss" mechanisms are specifically designed to ensure the stability of the union; whereas the grievance procedure, due process, job security, and seniority deal with the noneconomic issues that are considered most important to the membership.

Union bargaining teams place a high priority on negotiating very strong union security measures. These measures, such as dues checkoff, maintenance of membership, and compulsory participation, give unions stability and enhance their clout in dealing with management. Basic union security measures can be summarized as follows:

1. **Dues Checkoff.** Management agrees to deduct union dues directly from the pay of its employees and to deliver the funds to the union on a regularly scheduled basis.

2. **Maintenance of Membership.** Management agrees that voluntary membership in a union cannot (as a condition of continued employment) be terminated by an employee while the negotiated contract is still in force.

3. **Compulsory Participation.** Management agrees that as a condition of employment, newly hired employees will join the union (union shop) or pay a "service fee" in the form of union dues to the employee organization (agency shop).

Whether union or agency shop agreements can be negotiated as part of a labor contract depends on the state's collective bargaining statute. In many southern and western states with so-called "right-to-work" statutes on the books, most union security measures are outlawed. It is a different story in the northeastern states, however. The Pennsylvania General Assembly narrowly defeated a very comprehensive agency shop bill for public employees during its 1987 legislative session. The agency shop bill was endorsed by Governor Robert Casey in 1987 and later enacted into law as Act 84 of 1988.

There are trying times when, due to the nature of the collective bargaining process, negotiations become deadlocked and something must be done to resolve the impasse if there is to be a mutually acceptable accord. The best way to prevent police strikes (and other job actions) is to provide for some combination of methods that will diffuse conflict and help implement the impasse resolution process (Holden, 1994). The most common impasse resolution techniques used in police work today (mediation, fact-finding, final best offer arbitration, and binding arbitration) have been borrowed from private sector labor relations. Impasse resolution techniques are generally categorized as being either "nonbinding" or "binding" and may best be described in the following manner:

1. **Mediation.** Mediation is a nonbinding impasse resolution technique in which an authoritative third party attempts to help the disputants reach a mutually acceptable agreement. Mediators facilitate communication and clarify issues. Their value lies in their ability to review the dispute from an objective perspective, inject fresh ideas into the negotiations, recommend solutions, and, when appropriate, extricate the parties from difficult or untenable positions. Professional mediation services are available from various state and federal agencies. While mediation is certainly not a panacea, the evidence suggests that it has worked in more than 50 percent of the documented cases.

2. **Fact-Finding.** Fact-finding is a nonbinding impasse resolution technique in which a fact-finder or panel of fact-finders gathers, interprets, and assigns relative weight to data related to an issue in dispute. The process involves quasi-judicial hearings, compilation of an investigative report, and formulation of very specific recommendations for resolving the impasse. An old study found that 89 percent of the disputes submitted to fact-finding were resolved (Stern, 1967). More recent data suggest that a success rate of 60 to 70 percent would probably be more accurate.

3. **Final Best Offer Arbitration.** Best offer arbitration is a binding impasse resolution technique in which each side submits a "final" offer to the arbitrator chosen to decide the issue. The arbitrator has absolutely no power to compromise and must select one of the final offers submitted by the two parties. It is up to the arbitrator to choose the offer that is, on the whole, the most reasonable and fair. This plan encourages all parties to make concessions, because the arbitrator's "award" is most likely to go to the party that has moved closest to a reasonable middle-ground position.

4. **Binding Arbitration.** Binding arbitration is an impasse resolution technique in which the disputants elect (voluntary) or are required (compulsory) to submit impasses to a neutral and mutually acceptable third party who is empowered to decide the issue. The decision is legally binding and enforceable in the courts. Most collective bargaining agreements now require that certain, if not all, labor disputes be submitted to binding arbitration for resolution (Myers and Twomey, 1975). A list of qualified and experienced arbitrators is available from the American Arbitration Association.

The most popular approach to impasse resolution in police work appears to be binding arbitration. The power that makes the arbitration binding may be found in the collective bargaining agreement, state law, a local ordinance, jurisdictional policy, and court decisions (Sapp and Carter, 1991).

Whether these impasse resolution techniques work will depend, in large measure, on the importance of the issue, the intensity of the conflict, and the good-faith bargaining of the disputants. Although some elected government officials attempt to renege on arbitration awards and openly challenge the legitimacy of the arbitration process as an unlawful encroachment on their legislative or administrative power, the courts have generally upheld the use of binding arbitration in the public sector. Many state and local governments have been forced, through the judicial process, to fund expensive, as well as very unpopular, police arbitration awards.

Communication is the lifeblood of the collective bargaining process and is an absolutely essential ingredient in successful conflict management. Regularly scheduled (and contractually mandated) meet-and-discuss sessions are designed to bring union representatives and managers together in an effort to promote communication, resolve issues, and guarantee joint administration of the contract. Meet-and-discuss sessions provide a vehicle for participatory management in criminal justice organizations.

Dealing with Grievances

A grievance is a complaint arising out of the interpretation, application, or compliance with provisions of a collective bargaining agreement. Grievance procedures and due process safeguards are built into virtually every labor contract. According to the Commission on Accreditation for Law Enforcement Agencies (CALEA, 2001), Standard 25 stipulates:

Unless there is controlling construct language, a written directive establishes a grievance procedure, which includes the following:

a. Identification of matters that are grievable (scope) and the levels in the agency or government to which the grievance may be filed and/or appealed.

b. Establishment of time limitations for filing or appealing the grievance to the next level.

c. A description of the type of information to be submitted when filing a grievance.

d. Establishment of procedural steps and time limitations at each level in responding to grievances or appeals.

e. Establishment of criteria for employee representation.

A written directive identifies a position responsible for coordination of grievance procedures and for the maintenance and control of grievance records.

A written directive requires an annual analysis of grievances.

A multistep grievance process is the norm in police work. In most cases:

1. There is a specific time limit within which a grievance must be filed once the police officer becomes aware that there is, or appears to be, a violation of the contract.

2. The officer is expected to discuss the alleged grievance informally with the immediate supervisor in an effort to resolve the problem.

3. If the grievance cannot be resolved informally and the employee wishes to pursue it further, a formal grievance is filed with the appropriate command officer.

4. The command officer processes the formal grievance and holds hearings at which the employee (and the union) present oral and written statements.

5. The command officer, based on the evidence, determines the merit of the grievance and notifies the grievant of the decision.

6. If the grievance is not resolved satisfactorily at the command level, it is sent to the chief executive officer for a final in-house disposition.

7. In many states (depending on the language of the public employee bargaining statute), an unresolved grievance goes to the political executive, Civil Service Commission, State Labor Relations Board, or an arbitrator for final disposition.

If the grievant and the police union are dissatisfied with the final disposition of the grievance, they may (under most state laws) go to court for judicial review or injunctive relief. Winning the grievance is very important to both of them. A victory in each case is considered a victory for the union and for the organized labor movement as a whole.

Procedural due process is near and dear to the heart of every unionist. It has long been the rallying cry for union activism in police departments. Unions and their members want to protect themselves from the arbitrary and capricious behavior of their employers. From their perspective, a "police officers' bill of rights" and due process standards for discipline are indispensable in a good contract. Procedural due process is considered sacrosanct and nonnegotiable by virtually all rank-and-file police officers.

According to the Bureau of National Affairs (2001), more than 90 percent of all union contracts emphasize the importance of worker seniority. Police work is no exception. In some cases, seniority has (based on negotiated collective bargaining agreements) become an overriding factor in the promotion, scheduling, and assignment of personnel. In Pittsburgh, Pennsylvania, for example, police officers select their shifts, patrol zones, and partners based on the seniority principle (Contract between the City of Pittsburgh and the Fraternal Order of Police, 1992). The city can bypass a uniformed police officer for an open vehicle assignment on a particular shift only if it believes in good faith that because of incompatibility, the officer will not be effective in that assignment on that shift. Under these circumstances, it is not uncommon to find two rookie police officers patrolling high-crime areas together on a midnight shift. While seniority should be considered, it is often antithetical to merit and often unduly limits management's ability to use its human resources in an efficient, effective, and productive manner.

Impasse Resolution through Job Actions

Most police union goals are attained at the bargaining table or through very skillful political manipulation. Police unions have usually been able to deliver the goods to their members with a minimum amount of hassle. Tangling with the union is often considered to be political suicide. Consequently, most unions have been content to walk softly and carry a big stick.

When a police union is unable to obtain its goals through constructive conflict in collective bargaining and all of the normal impasse-resolution techniques have failed, it may be forced to use a coercive strategy. While union leaders tend to oppose the tactical use of job actions, they know that job actions (whether they are legal or not) are a necessary part of the bargaining process. Without job actions to back them up, police unions believe they may lack the wherewithal to pressure the employer into making necessary concessions. A job action is, and should always be, the impasse resolution of last resort.

A job action is defined as a calculated disruption in normally assigned duties. The term can be used to describe any of several different types of activities that police officers engage in to show their dissatisfaction with a particular person, event, condition, or situation. A job action can also be used in an effort to influence the deliberations of policymakers. Job actions send out a clear signal that there has been an unhealthy escalation in conflict and that the collective bargaining process has broken down.

Even though almost all states legally prohibit job actions by police personnel, the law has not proven to be an effective deterrent to poor labor relations. In 1979 alone, there were 52 police strikes throughout the United States (U.S. Department of Labor, 1981). While there were actually fewer job actions by police personnel in the 1980s and 1990s, no one should be lulled into a false sense of security. The Johnstown, Pennsylvania, police strike of 1987 is a clear demonstration that if they believe it is necessary, union members will attempt to resolve a bargaining impasse through some type of job action. Due to public safety considerations (directly related to the strike), the Pennsylvania State Police assumed jurisdiction over and provided law enforcement services for the city of more than 37,000. Prohibition of police walkouts without a viable alternative to resolve a labor-management impasse is, in reality, no prohibition at all.

Job actions short of actual strikes or other work stoppages are much more common in today's labor relations environment. In New York City, where police officers were protesting an impasse in contract negotiations, the union—the Police Benevolent Association—tacitly supported a well-orchestrated work slowdown to demonstrate its displeasure with city government. As a result, the number of traffic tickets and summonses issued by 21,000 rank-and-file police personnel declined by more than 60 percent. This resulted in $1.5 million in lost revenue that the cash-starved city could ill afford to lose. Needless to say, the conflict was resolved rather quickly and in favor of the police. The power of organized labor should not be underestimated (Swanson et al., 1993).

Case Study

Sergeant Frank Emerson

Sergeant Frank Emerson is a 16-year patrol supervisor with the Davidson City Police Department. Sergeant Emerson has been an active member of the International Brotherhood of Teamsters, which represents the Davidson City Police Department's nearly 1,600 members. Communication between the union and police management has been anything but constructive over the past several months. Numerous grievances have been filed, and there have been several work slowdowns. Morale is very low among the sworn officers.

Much of the problem has been the obvious violation of labor contract agreements by the city. The city took away several benefits the union had negotiated, including overtime pay, educational tuition payments and leave time, and even maternity leave for the female officers. The city claims they are in a serious financial crunch and that they are invoking the exigent circumstances clause on the union contract. The exigent circumstances clause stipulates that if the city undergoes a financial downturn for which there was no expectation, the city can override the union contract in the best interests of the city.

The union maintains that the financial "crunch" was negligence on the part of the city leaders. They cite the city's purchase of two golf courses and the building of a multimillion-dollar performing arts center that have resulted in the loss of several million dollars. The union indicates that the city is now trying to make ends meet and to correct their own foolish mistakes by taking it out on city employees.

There seems to be no answer to this situation. Both the union and the city leaders are adamant about their positions. The union has asked Sergeant Emerson to take the lead in either negotiating an end to the stalemate or to seek third-party arbitration.

If you were Sergeant Emerson, what would be the first course of action you would take? Do you think third-party arbitration is the answer? What do you think an arbitrator would decide? How would this affect the morale and trust of the officers and management in the future?

There are four basic types of job actions used in law enforcement. Charles Swanson and his colleagues (1993) describe these job actions in the following way:

1. **No-Confidence Votes.** In a no-confidence vote, rank-and-file union members formally signal their dissatisfaction with administrative policies or an administrator through a public and often highly publicized statement that, while it has no legal standing, can lead to the person's removal, resignation, or early retirement. Even though no-confidence votes have played an important role in the departure of some police chief executives, such as the removal of Robert Digrazia in Montgomery County, Maryland, and the retirement of Harold Bastrup in Anaheim, California, they have not always accomplished the union's goal and have, in fact, been interpreted as a positive sign that needed reforms are taking place.

2. **Work Slowdowns.** In work slowdowns, while the police continue to provide all essential law enforcement services, police officers use less initiative and do their work at a measured pace so that each unit of work takes longer to complete. This causes a steep drop in productivity. Work begins to accumulate, and benefits (in terms of public safety, a sense of security, and revenues generated) are reduced. Pressure increases as more and more people perceive the loss in benefits and take affirmative action to reestablish the normal state of affairs. The effectiveness of the slowdown has been demonstrated in writing traffic tickets (California Highway Patrol), conducting criminal investigations (Phoenix, Arizona) and making arrests (Long Beach, California).

3. **Work Speedups.** In work speedups, there is intentional acceleration in one or more types of police services, designed to create anxiety and disruption through calculated overproduction. Speedups produce social stress and usually precipitate demands for acquiescence to the union. Work speedups have been used very successfully in New York City (transit authority smoking and littering violations), Chicago (moving violation "ticket blizzards") and Holyoke, Massachusetts (parking tickets). Speedups alter the normal pace of life and generate public demands for a return to the status quo.

4. **Work Stoppage.** Work stoppages involve the total withholding of production in one or more areas of service. The ultimate work stoppage—the strike—represents the total withholding of all services by union members. Described in picturesque terms such as "blue flu" and the "bluebonic plague," mass resignations, "sick outs," and strikes have been used to protest economic conditions, judicial leniency, inadequate safety measures, staffing patterns, and so forth. While police strikes are illegal in almost all states, they usually accomplish their overall objective, and few, if any, result in reprisals against the strikers or their union.

Job actions are one of the most controversial aspects of police unionism. While they may achieve the union's objectives, they also create anxiety, fear, resentment, and a debilitating sense of betrayal within the community.

While it is easy to overemphasize the negative aspects of job actions, the relations between police unions and management are normally constructive. Despite all the attention they receive, job actions are relatively infrequent events. The elimination of federal revenue sharing, erosion in state and local tax revenues, and an unstable national economy have caused unions to reassess their demands. Most union effort is now designed to avoid cutbacks (retrenchment) or reductions in existing benefits (givebacks), strengthen job security clauses in existing collective bargaining agreements, and gain more input into the policy formulation process. Labor-management conflict is more and more symbolic and is played out on the bargaining table. Unions are attempting to achieve their objectives through accommodation and cooperation with management.

Union-Management Relations

V.A. Leonard and Harry More (1993) contend that unionization of the police can usually be traced to the inadequacies of management. In most of the cases in which unionization has occurred, officers had been frustrated by intolerable working conditions and were unable to obtain corrective action from indifferent state or local government officials. Trying to identify the impetus for unionization and to demonstrate that unions (based on inherent conservatism) generally have a negative effect on the development of professionalism may be counterproductive. Most of the nation's more than 800,000 sworn police officers (U.S. Department of Justice, 2001) are union members. Police administrators and elected officials have little or no choice except to work with the representatives of their employees. Trying to recapture the past through antiunion activity is a bit like closing a barn door after the horses have escaped. The National Advisory Commission on Criminal Justice Standards and Goals (1973) came to the conclusion that the nation's police executives should recognize that police employees have a legal right, subject to certain reasonable limitations, to engage in activities protected by the First Amendment. They should acknowledge the right of their employees to join (or not join) employee organizations that represent their employment interests and give appropriate recognition to these organizations.

The Commission went on to emphasize the importance of the collective bargaining process in contemporary American society. The Commission on Accreditation for Law Enforcement Agencies reemphasized the importance of collective bargaining (CALEA, 2001). CALEA Standard 24 stipulates:

If there are represented employees in the agency, a written directive describes the role of the agency in the collective bargaining process, and includes:

a. Establishment of a collective bargaining team for the agency with one person designated as the principal negotiator.

b. Identification of the bargaining unit or units representing an agency's employees with which it will negotiate.

c. A commitment by the agency to participate in "good faith" bargaining with the duly recognized bargaining units representing its members.

d. A commitment to abide by the ground rules for collective bargaining that arise out of the collective bargaining process or labor arbitration.

e. A commitment to abide, in both letter and spirit, by the negotiated labor agreement that has been signed by management and labor representatives and ratified by the bargaining unit.

When a negotiated labor agreement is ratified by all parties, the agency's CEO, or designee, will:

a. obtain a written, signed copy of the labor agreement;

b. review and amend, if necessary, all written directives and procedures to coincide with the terms of the labor agreement; and

c. disseminate information relative to a new labor agreement, including modifications to existing agreements, to managers and supervisors of bargaining unit employees.

The Commonwealth of Pennsylvania could be described as avant garde when it comes to promoting positive labor-management relations through the collective bargaining process. Pennsylvania's Collective Bargaining and Compulsory Arbitration Act for Police and Fire (Act 111) was enacted into law in 1968. It authorizes collective bargaining by police officers and fire fighters and imposes binding arbitration as the final means of impasse resolution. An employee organization with more than 50 percent of the department's sworn personnel may be certified as the exclusive bargaining agent for all rank-and-file officers. The union helps to formulate, implement, and administer a collective bargaining agreement. In the event that there is an impasse, a three-person arbitration panel is appointed. Management chooses one member, labor another, and the third is selected by mutual agreement. If the parties cannot decide on a mutually acceptable third member, an arbitrator must be chosen from a roster of names provided by the American Arbitration Association. The panel studies the issues and makes a final award that is binding on all parties. Act 111 has worked well most of the time.

Contract Administration

Signing a contract guarantees the continuation of the collective bargaining relationship for the duration of the agreement. One of the most important aspects of contract administration involves dissemination of information to all members of the department concerning the policies, programs, equipment, and resources that are to be affected by the new agreement. It also requires labor and management to reach a consensus concerning the nature and extent of the participatory management to be allowed within the police department.

A police labor contract is a living document that is applied to a variety of very different issues in an ever-changing socioeconomic environment. In order to make it work, the parties must be prepared to spend a great deal of time and effort interpreting contract language, working out the bugs, making necessary adjustments, resolving problems through the formal grievance process, and reaching ethical compromises that promote the interests of the employee, the department, and the community at large.

Role of the Sergeant in Collective Bargaining

In small police departments, sergeants may be considered managers and assigned to play a significant role in the collective bargaining process. In most situations, however, the sergeant's role is limited to contract implementation or administration.

As first-line supervisors in police departments, sergeants, are responsible for both people and production. They occupy an often ambiguous position between management and labor. Based on prevailing police organization/management theory, sergeants represent labor to management and management to labor. They are expected to identify minor problems and to deal with them before they become major issues. Sergeants have an obligation to help their subordinates as well as to apprise their superiors of potential problems. The police sergeant is a linchpin in effective labor relations. Even perfect labor relations policies will fail unless they are translated into practice by the sergeant (Walsh and Donovan, 1990). This is challenging and demands very specific skills.

The importance of sergeants in labor relations is underscored by their role in recommending or taking disciplinary action against their subordinates. Despite the many different types of issues that can be or are actually filed as grievances, nearly 90 percent of those taken to arbitration involve discipline against sworn police personnel. Because sergeants are departmental disciplinarians, they and their actions often become the focus of personnel as well as policy grievances. One study of arbitrated grievances disclosed that the officers involved were assigned to the uniformed patrol division in 84 percent of the cases and that the union won the arbitration award in more than

75 percent of the grievances (Lavan and Carley, 1985). Sergeants also play a very important role in resolving grievances. They are normally the first representative of management authorized to receive and settle grievances. Most truly effective grievance procedures formalize the sergeant's role by requiring grievants to seek an informal resolution of the case before it can be taken to the command level for a review and disposition. This emphasis on the sergeant corresponds to the principle that the best management decisions come from those who are directly involved in or are most familiar with the situation under review.

The sergeant's position is often very frustrating and is complicated by the conflicting demands made by fellow police officers and management. If management pushes too hard, sergeants may be forced to align themselves with labor. Under these circumstances, police managers become their own enemy, and sergeants revert to the role of a promoted patrol officer. Ineffective supervision reduces productivity and has a deleterious influence on the overall quality of police service.

Unions have had both positive and negative effects on modern-day police work. On the plus side, they help shield police personnel from inept, autocratic, and morally bankrupt managers and supervisors. On the other hand, they have also been known to protect less-than-competent police officers, to make the taking of appropriate disciplinary action very difficult and to block the reforms needed to professionalize police service. Ineffective sergeants use the specter of unionization as an excuse to avoid the legitimate process of observing on-the-job performance, collecting information, documenting deviant behavior, and knowing departmental policies, procedures, rules, and regulations well enough to carry out their job-related supervisor responsibilities. It is much easier to blame the union (the union steward or grievance committee) than to acknowledge one's own shortcomings as a first-line supervisor.

Inadequate supervisory personnel react to crisis situations. They lack the skills required to manage them. Poor supervisors have not, as a general rule, formulated a workable set of principles to guide their actions. They are neither thorough nor consistent and do only what is absolutely essential to guarantee their survival. Poor supervisors are usually not conscientious enough to put in the hard work that is required to represent their supervisees to management or to carry out the management responsibilities assigned to them by their superiors (Trojanowicz, 1980). Poor first-line supervision, coupled with dynamic unionism, creates an unhealthy climate for constructive conflict. It sets the stage for a dramatic deterioration in public sector labor relations.

If they are going to be good first-line supervisors, sergeants need to understand contemporary labor relations and appreciate the value of constructive conflict in the collective bargaining process. They also need to develop a sound working relationship with the local union president (or "shop steward" in larger organizations). While sergeants and union representatives may be adversaries under certain circumstances, they should not be enemies. The sergeant should keep in mind that the union representative is an employee and a "worker." That person has been selected by his or her peers to do an important job and is often given "release time" by the police department to see that the contract is implemented and administered fairly. The union representative has a legal responsibility and an absolute ethical obligation to fight for the contractual rights of all bargaining unit employees covered by the collective bargaining agreement. This symbolic conflict, no matter how intense it becomes, should never be allowed to degenerate into destructive personal animosity.

Competent first-line supervisors accept the fact that the union exists and, because they are powerless to change the situation, opt for constructive coexistence with, rather than open hostility to, the union representative. Figure 12.2 sets forth the labor relations duties of the police sergeant and his or her counterpart, the union president or shop steward. Based on a comparative analysis of their duties, it is clear that there are far more similarities than differences.

Sergeants play a pivotal role in contract implementation and contract administration. Once again, the success or failure of the police department's labor relations effort will depend on the intelligence, knowledge, skill, and dedication of the men and women who are selected to serve as first-line supervisors in these criminal justice agencies.

Many sergeants have experienced role conflict. They find it very difficult to perform well in all the roles assigned to them by virtue of their rank. Some are frustrated because they are not treated as managers or as patrol officers. They feel that they have little or no meaningful input into departmental policy and do not see themselves as part of the management team. On the other hand, management expects them to maintain a social as well as professional distance from their subordinates, who do the actual work of the organization, in order to preserve their objectivity and authority. This causes a dilemma for sergeants. Due to this role conflict and sense of frustration, sergeants in larger police departments have begun forming their own labor unions.

Sergeants often bemoan the fact that they find themselves "in the middle"—between labor and management. Some use this ambiguity as a rationale for inactivity and perpetuation of the status quo. Others see it as an opportunity for personal growth and development. They strive to carve out a niche in which they can satisfy their professional needs while making a meaningful contribution to law enforcement.

Figure 12.2
Labor Relations Roles Played by the Police

SERGEANT	UNION REPRESENTATIVE
1. Accept collective bargaining.	1. Accept collective bargaining.
2. Know the contract.	2. Know the contract.
3. Enforce the agreement.	3. Enforce the agreement.
4. Look out for the welfare of all subordinates.	4. Look out for the welfare of all constituents.
5. Be a spokesperson for both management and employees.	5. Be a spokesperson for both union and constituents.
6. Settle grievances fairly (in line with management's interpretation of the contract).	6. Settle grievances fairly (in line with the union's interpretation of the contract).
7. Keep abreast of grievance solutions and changes in contract interpretation.	7. Keep abreast of grievance solutions and changes in contract interpretation.
8. Be firm, fair, and impartial when dealing with the union.	8. Be firm, fair, and impartial when dealing with management.
9. Maintain a good working relationship with the steward.	9. Maintain a good working relationship with the sergeant.
10. Keep the union representative informed of management decisions and sources of trouble.	10. Keep the sergeant informed as to the union's position and sources of trouble.
11. Protect management rights.	11. Protect labor rights.

Adapted from W. Richard Plunkett (1992). *Supervision: The Direction of People at Work*, Sixth Edition. Boston, MA: Allyn and Bacon.

In healthy police organizations, sergeants are assimilated into the management team. Progressive managers know that police departments function much like military units. Commanders give orders. Sergeants, as first-line supervisors, see that rank-and-file police officers carry them out. Successful police work requires communication, cooperation, and coordination. Under ideal conditions, sergeants facilitate communication, elicit voluntary cooperation, and provide absolutely essential coordination. In other words, they energize and guide personnel in an effort to accomplish the organization's mission, goals, and objectives. Sergeants are expected to be advocates, leaders, problem solvers, disciplinarians, labor relations specialists, and contract administrators. They play a demanding role that requires a great deal of knowledge and interpersonal skill.

Many newly promoted sergeants are ill-equipped to handle the multidimensional role thrust upon them. Many are still promoted on the basis of political affiliation or some paper-and-pencil test, they are given little training in supervisory skills and are largely left to fend for themselves in a hostile environment. New sergeants adopt survival strategies keyed to dangers they face. Some cave in to union demands and become "promoted patrol officers" who use the extra income to salve their conscience. Others attach their star to management and exude a hard-line, antiunion bias. Based on current legal and philosophical support for public sector collective bargaining, neither approach is productive. Both will lead to a sense of frustration and failure.

The occupational landscape has changed dramatically, and so has the role of the sergeant in a paramilitary police organization. In order to fulfill this new role, sergeants must shed their paranoia and unshackle themselves from the past. They must learn to establish empathetic, goal-oriented relationships with their subordinates. Gamesmanship must be replaced with an honest, open, and participative approach to the resolution of common problems. Sergeants themselves must be prepared to face tough issues. They cannot afford to allow contract disputes or grievances to go unattended. Unresolved issues fester. They destroy unity of purpose and undermine the common interest. Tomorrow's first-line supervisor must understand the human dynamics involved in collective bargaining, have the ability to motivate subordinates, and be capable of forging a consensus about what needs to be accomplished and how it is to be done. Leadership will be the prerequisite for successful supervision in the future.

If sergeants are going to perform managerial duties related to supervision, discipline, evaluation, and labor relations, we can no longer afford to debate the issue of their status within the police department. While they are supervisors, they are also involved in directing, planning, leading, controlling, and coaching the activities of others. These are management functions (Steinmetz and Todd, 1992). Consequently, police sergeants are de facto managers and should be considered part of the department's management team.

Interest-Based Bargaining Process

As collective bargaining has become institutionalized in modern police work, there are signs that a subtle shift in its emphasis is beginning to take place. In 1981 the Police Executive Research Forum and the National League of Cities jointly sponsored a comprehensive comparative analysis of critical clauses in police collective bargaining agreements. In an attempt to expand on this research, Carter and Sapp (1993) surveyed 328 police collective bargaining agreements held by federal, state, and local law enforcement agencies. According to their survey, most police management-labor differences have moved closer to a homeostatic relationship. Management rights clauses have moved toward more comprehensive statements of such rights, and away from provisions that make management decisions and actions subject to grievance and arbitration processes. Management's position at the bargaining table is increasingly one of true negotiation rather than reaction.

Because both management and unions desire to enhance rather than destroy, their relationship, they are beginning to look for a process that minimizes confrontation and facilitates open and candid discussion of what are perceived as mutually significant issues. The movement away from traditional (position-based) negotiations to innovative (win-win) negotiations is buoyed when two strong institutions (union and management) respect each other and decide to work together cooperatively in an effort to achieve their mutual interests whenever possible. This interest-based bargaining approach may well become the rule rather than the exception in the future.

The win-win negotiation concept was originally developed by the United States Department of Labor and was used to reach collective bargaining agreements with its own personnel. The focus is on mutual interests rather than preconceived positions.

With reference to the negotiation sessions themselves, there are two absolutely critical objectives:

1. Dynamic interaction among team members unencumbered by formal environmental arrangements or occupational status considerations.

2. Open and candid discussion of mutual interests or concerns with respect to a particular issue.

Once the salient issue or issues have been identified, the parties working together collectively as a team develop a variety of alternatives designed to deal with them and satisfy their mutual interests. All team members are encouraged to participate actively in this brainstorming process. The alternatives or options are recorded without evaluation or judgment. Team members take turns serving as facilitators and recorders. Information is shared openly to ensure that everyone is actively involved in the negotiations.

After the alternatives have been developed, the team members formulate a set of standards or criteria for use in evaluating the overall acceptability of the options. They use brainstorming techniques to compile an initial list of criteria and pare it down through candid discussion (designed to eliminate duplicative, vague or unmeasurable standards) until there is a genuine consensus. A final list of decision-making criteria might well include the following:

1. Legality

2. Constituent acceptability

3. Effectiveness

4. Efficiency

5. Workability

6. Cost effectiveness

7. Adequacy of representation

These standards are then applied through open discussion designed to determine the options on which members can reach agreement. Once the best option is selected, union and management negotiators work together to draft contract language and a brief history of the bargaining process. The proposed agreement is forwarded to management and the union for final review and adoption.

As the collaborative relationship between management and unions matures to the degree discussed above, more police departments are likely to engage in interest-based bargaining. It is the collegial alternative to traditional position bargaining designed to empower both parties as they jointly seek to achieve consensus on items of mutual interest. The differences in the two processes are reflected in Figure 12.3.

While there is no way to predict whether interest-based bargaining will become a widespread phenomenon in modern police work, it has the potential to revolutionize the way in which we currently approach labor relations. Success or failure will be determined by key factors such as those listed below:

1. **Commitment to the Process.** Management and labor must be committed to bringing about a cultural change in which they listen to each other, understand each other's needs and interests, and seek collaborative solutions designed to strengthen each side in pursuit of the department's mission, goals, and objectives.

2. **Information Sharing and Trust.** Meaningful interaction and absolute candor are essential to building mutual trust. Neither side should be surprised by the other, and privileged or private conversations must remain confidential.

3. **Model Behavior.** At all stages of the negotiations and during day-to-day contract administration, police managers and union leaders need to model collaborative behavior. Leaders on both sides must set the tone and exhibit behavior that is expected from all other members of the organization.

4. **Time to Prepare.** Members of the bargaining team must have a sense of trust in and commitment to the process so that they are willing to take risks, share vital information, and model collaborative behavior. It takes time to create an interactive environment based on rapport and trust between the key players. From a practical point of view, most of the groundwork must be done before anyone sits down at the bargaining table.

5. **Isolate the Problems.** Management and the union need to understand and accept the fact that some of their people simply will not buy interest-based bargaining in lieu of the traditional collective bargaining process. Managers and union leaders need to isolate these individuals, if possible, and concentrate on the vast majority of their constituents, who prefer the cooperative model of labor relations.

6. **Contract Is Only Paper.** The key to success in interest-based bargaining is understanding that the conclusion of the negotiations represents nothing more than the beginning of a long-term partnership between management and the union to implement the contract and market this new collaborative approach to labor relations in the public sector. Traditional perspectives and organizational culture cannot be changed by issuing a new contract to everyone. Both sides must work together to develop a strategy for change over the life of the current collective bargaining agreement and beyond (Goodwin, 1993).

Figure 12.3
Two Types of Bargaining Strategies

BARGAINING PROCESS	
Traditional Negotiations	**Interest-Based Negotiations**
Positions developed separately by each side	Emphasis on issues of mutual importance to both sides
Arguments made in an adversarial environment	Mutual interests are discussed candidly in a collegial atmosphere
Power/competition determines who wins or who loses	Joint development of mutually acceptable options
Eventual outcome: WIN-LOSE LOSE-LOSE	Consensus concerning criteria to be used when evaluating the proposed options
	Selection of the best option designed to satisfy the mutual interests of both sides
	Collaborative development of contract language for the collective bargaining agreement
	Sign-off by both management and the union
	Eventual outcome: WIN-WIN

Adapted from Larry K. Goodwin (1993). "Win-Win Negotiations: A Model for Cooperative Labor Relations." *The Public Manager*, Vol. 10, Summer.

Summary

Police officers have experimented with unionism since the early 1900s. The Boston police strike of 1919 created an antiunion backlash that prompted Congress to exclude all public employees from the 1935 National Labor Relations Act. While the U.S. government was promoting unionization in the private sector, state governments steadfastly refused to sanction collective bargaining by public employees until 1959. Wisconsin became the first state to grant public employees the limited right to organize and bargain collectively with their employers concerning wages, hours, and working conditions. Since that time, most of the states have enacted public employee bargaining laws and many states even allow public employees, with the exception of public safety personnel, to strike. More than one-half of the states have authorized binding arbitration in lieu of the strike. Firefighters, police officers, and teachers are heavily unionized. There has been a "hidden revolution" during which more than 75 percent of police officers have decided to join unions.

Collective bargaining is a form of participatory management in which labor and management share power through constructive conflict. It is based on the assumption that bilateral decision making by coequals is in the public interest. There is an expectation that good faith negotiations will produce a binding agreement that both parties can accept. Initial contract negotiations almost always focus on bargainable issues such as wages, working conditions, management rights, employee responsibilities, impasse resolution, union security, grievance procedures, due process safeguards, seniority, and job security. Almost all contract negotiations produce a mutually acceptable collective bargaining agreement.

Sergeants play a variety of different roles in labor relations. Some sergeants serve as negotiators. Whether they eventually negotiate for labor or management will depend on how the state law is written. In most cases, however, the sergeant's role is restricted to contract implementation or administration. As department disciplinarians, sergeants (and their actions) are often the target of a grievance. More than 90 percent of all arbitrations involve grievances dealing with discipline. Sergeants also play a vital role in the resolution of grievances. Most formal grievance procedures require that the first-line supervisor be given an opportunity to resolve the problem before it is sent to the command level for disposition.

Sergeants are lead actors in labor relations. They are expected to look out for the welfare of their subordinates, enforce the collective bargaining agreement, recommend or take disciplinary action, and work with union representatives to ensure the smooth operation of the police department. Many sergeants have experienced role conflict and frustration. Every effort should be made to clarify their status within the police department. Because sergeants perform a variety of management functions, they should be classified as managers and made full-fledged members of the management team.

As labor relations continue to mature in law enforcement, police managers and unions must be willing to embrace changes in the collective bargaining process. Interest-based negotiations may well represent the wave of the future. While we are unwilling to view interest-based negotiations as a panacea, this approach seems well-suited for the twenty-first century.

Case Study

Sergeant Amanda Dean

Sergeant Amanda Dean is a 12-year veteran of the Blountville Police Department. Blountville has a population of 92,000 and is home to three large manufacturing companies. Sergeant Dean holds a position as a human resource and labor relations specialist. For nearly 12 years, the Blountville Police Department has been represented in collective bargaining by the City Employees' Association. The City Employees' Association negotiates directly with city council for benefits for all city employees, including the police department. The program has worked satisfactorily, and has had no problems in the past.

The city council has adopted a resolution to combine the city's police and fire personnel into a single public safety department. The move was controversial, but the resolution was passed due to the council's belief that the program would save hundreds of thousands of dollars. The plan calls for a three-year transition so that current members of the police department can become trained as firefighters and the current firefighters can become trained as police officers.

Many of the city's police officers were opposed to the measure. However, many of the firefighters were supportive of the program because they would be receiving the bulk of a substantial pay increase with the package. There are only two police officers on the City Employees' Association negotiating team, and they are outnumbered by three firefighters, three utility workers, and two solid waste engineers.

Sergeant Dean has been active with the City Employees' Association and can see the merits of both sides of the issue. However, she has firmly sided with the police officers who oppose the program, and talked with Russ Jamerson, a union leader with one of the manufacturing plants in Blountville.

"Amanda, I know exactly what your officers are going through. But, let me tell you, what they need is some real national power behind them, not just a local city employee thing. A good friend of mine works for the AFL-CIO national headquarters, and he tells me the IUPA is the way to go with your department.

"You know, Amanda, all three of the manufacturing plants here are represented by AFL-CIO, so there's a lot of support for union people in this town. In fact, most of the city council are either members of AFL-CIO or were elected by them. If you guys had IUPA behind you, you would see things get done," he continued.

What Russ Jamerson says has merit. Having a national organization like IUPA representing the Blountville police might have tremendous political clout with the city council. But what would be the disadvantages? You are due to attend a City Employees' Association meeting this evening. What should you tell them about Russ Jamerson's suggestion?

If you were Sergeant Dean, would you try to convince the police members of the City Employees' Association to join a new national union for the political clout or remain local? What are the advantages and disadvantages of having a national organization like the IUPA represent police departments as opposed to local unions and associations?

Key Concepts

balance through constructive conflict
bargaining in good faith
choosing a bargaining agent
compulsory binding arbitration
exclusive bargaining agent
grievance
impasse resolution techniques
management rights/union
   responsibility
negotiating a CBA or contract
noneconomic issues

participatory management by contracts
role conflict and its impact on morale
scope of bargaining
sergeants as contract administrators
sergeants as disciplinarians
"traditional" versus "innovative"
   bargaining
unionism—the hidden revolution
union security measures
wages, hours, and conditions of
   employment

Discussion Topics and Questions

1. Trace the historical development of police unionism in the United States and explain why Samuel Walker refers to it as America's "hidden revolution." Do you agree? Why?

2. Discuss the process by which a union is certified as the exclusive collective bargaining agent for a particular group or class of employees. Describe the union's role in negotiating, implementing, and executing a contract. What type of noneconomic issues will normally be given the highest priority during negotiations for the first contract?

3. Compare and contrast the role of the chief of police with that of the union president during negotiation of a collective bargaining agreement.

4. Identify, compare, and contrast the major impasse resolution techniques used in police work. Which one is preferred by most police unions? Why?

5. Municipal police officers are almost always prohibited by law from taking job actions against their employers. What is a job action? What types of job actions have the police used in the past to resolve labor disputes? Give specific examples.

6. All police union contracts emphasize the grievance procedure and require extensive due process safeguards for those who may be subjected to disciplinary action. Describe a typical multistep police grievance procedure. Why, in your opinion, are the police so concerned about procedural due process?

7. Compare the labor relations roles played by sergeants with those of the union representative (or shop steward). What are their objectives? Emphasize similarities as well as differences.

8. What is interest-based bargaining? How does it differ from the traditional collective bargaining process? Would the new approach have a positive or negative effect on labor relations in your department? Explain why.

For Further Reading

Gaines, Larry K., Mittie D. Southerland, and John E. Angell (1991). *Police Administration*. New York, NY: McGraw-Hill Book Company.

> Very well-researched and well-written chapter on police labor relations. Shows a great deal of insight into the dynamics of the collective bargaining process in relation to public sector labor negotiations.

More, Harry W., and W. Fred Wegener (1992). *Behavioral Police Management*. New York, NY: Macmillan Publishing Co.

> Discusses unionism and its impact on police work. Explores managerial rights in relation to the successful negotiation of a meaningful collective bargaining agreement.

Whisenand, Paul, and R. Fred Ferguson (1996). *The Managing of Police Organizations*, Fourth Edition. Englewood Cliffs, NJ: Prentice-Hall, Inc.

> Excellent review of police labor-management relations, with an emphasis on the managerial role of sergeants and an examination of the 15 commonly accepted "responsibilities of management."

References

Anderson, Howard J. (1975). *Primer of Labor Relations*. Washington, DC: Bureau of National Affairs, Inc.

Ayres, Richard M., and Paul R. Coble (1987). *Safeguarding Management's Rights*. Dubuque, IA: Kendall/Hunt Publishing Company.

Barnard, Chester I. (1976). *The Functions of the Executive*. Cambridge, MA: Harvard University Press.

Bellante, Don, and Philip K. Porter (1992). "Agency Costs, Property Rights, and the Evolution of Labor Unions." *Journal of Labor Research*, Vol. 11, No. 3.

Bittel, Lester R., and John W. Newstrom (1992). *What Every Supervisor Should Know*, Sixth Edition. New York, NY: McGraw-Hill Book Company.

Bohlander, George W., Scott A. Snell, and Arthur W. Sherman, Jr. (2001). *Managing Human Resources*, Twelfth Edition. Cincinnati, OH: South-Western Publishing Company.

Bouza, Anthony V. (1990). *The Police Mystique*. New York, NY: Plenum Press.

Bureau of National Affairs (2001). *Collective Bargaining Agreements Database*. Washington, DC: BNA, Inc.

CALEA (2001). *Standards for Law Enforcement Agencies*. Fairfax, VA: Commission on Accreditation for Law Enforcement Agencies, Inc.

Carter, David, and Allen Sapp (1993). "A Comparative Analysis of Clauses in Police Collective Bargaining Agreements as Indicators of Change in Labor Relations." *American Journal of Police*, Vol. 12, No. 2.

Cole, George F., and Christopher Smith (2001). *The American System of Criminal Justice*, Ninth Edition. Belmont, CA: Wadsworth Corporation.

Commonwealth of Pennsylvania, Revised Statutes (1987). Act 111 of 1968, "Compulsory Collective Bargaining and Contract Arbitration for Police and Fire." Harrisburg, PA.

Contract between the City of Detroit and the Detroit Police Officers' Association (1973).

Contract between the City of Pittsburgh and the Fraternal Order of Police (1992).

Dressler, Gary (1979). *Management Fundamentals*. Reston, VA: Reston Publishing Company.

Ewing, David W. (1983). *Do It My Way or You're Fired*. New York, NY: John Wiley & Sons, Inc.

Foulkes, Fred, and E. Robert Livernash (1989). *Human Resources Management*, Second Edition. Englewood Cliffs, NJ: Prentice-Hall, Inc.

Fyfe, James J., Jack R. Greene, and William F. Walsh (1997). *Police Administration*, Fifth Edition. New York, NY: McGraw-Hill Book Company.

Goodwin, Larry K. (1993). "Win-Win Negotiations: A Model for Cooperative Labor Relations." *The Public Manager*, Vol. 10, No. 2.

Holden, Richard N. (1994). *Modern Police Management*. Englewood Cliffs, NJ: Prentice-Hall, Inc.

Juris, Hervey A., and Peter Feuille (1973). *Police Unionism*. Lexington, MA: Lexington Books.

Lavan, Helen, and Cameron Carley (1985). "Analysis of Arbitrated Employee Grievance Cases in Police Departments." *Journal of Collective Negotiation in the Public Sector*, Vol. 14, No. 3.

Leonard, V.A., and Harry W. More (1993). *Police Organization and Management*, Eighth Edition. Westbury, NY: The Foundation Press.

Myers, A. Howard, and David P. Twomey (1975). *Labor Law and Legislation*. Cincinnati, OH: South-Western Publishing Company.

National Advisory Commission on Criminal Justice Standards and Goals, U.S. Department of Justice (1973). *The Police*. Washington, DC: U.S. Government Printing Office.

Plunkett, W. Richard (1992). *Supervision: The Direction of People at Work*, Sixth Edition. Boston, MA: Allyn and Bacon.

Police Executive Research Forum (1978). *Police Collective Bargaining Agreements: A National Management Survey*. Washington, DC: Police Executive Research Forum.

Rynecki, Steven, Douglas A. Cairns, and Donald J. Carnes (1984). *Police Collective Bargaining Agreements*. Washington, DC: National League of Cities.

Sapp, Allen D., and David L. Carter (1991). "Conflict and Conflict Resolution in Police Collective Bargaining." *The Police Forum*, Vol. 1, No. 1.

Sapp, Allen D., David L. Carter, and Darrell W. Stephens (1990). *Police Labor Relations: Critical Findings*. Washington DC: Police Executive Research Forum.

Shafritz, Jay M., David Rosenbloom, Norma Riccucci, Katherine Naff, and Albert Hyde (2001). *Personnel Management in Government*, Fifth Edition. New York, NY: Marcel Dekker, Inc.

Sloane, Arthur A., and Fred Witney (2001). *Labor Relations*, Tenth Edition. Englewood Cliffs, NJ: Prentice-Hall, Inc.

Stahl, O. Glenn (1983). *Public Personnel Administration*. New York, NY: Harper and Row.

Steinmetz, Lawrence L., and H. Ralph Todd, Jr. (1992). *Supervision: First-Line Management*, Fifth Edition. Boston, MA: Richard D. Irwin, Inc.

Stern, James L. (1967). "The Wisconsin Public Employee Fact-Finding Procedure." *Industrial Labor Relations Review*, Vol. 20, No 10 (Oct.).

Stone, Richard (1998). "Police Unions Marks 20 Years, Adds Members." *Police*, Vol. 22, No. 6.

Swank, Calvin J., and James A. Conser (1983). *The Police Personnel System*. New York, NY: John Wiley & Sons, Inc.

Swanson, Charles R., Leonard Territo, and Robert W. Taylor (1993). *Police Administration*, Third Edition. New York, NY: Macmillan Publishing.

Thibault, Edward A., Lawrence M. Lynch, and R. Bruce McBride (1998). *Pro-Active Police Management,* Fourth Edition. Englewood Cliffs, NJ: Prentice-Hall, Inc.

Trojanowicz, Robert C. (1980). *The Environment of the First-Line Police Supervisor*. Englewood Cliffs, NJ: Prentice-Hall, Inc.

U.S. Department of Justice, Bureau of Justice Statistics (2001). *Sourcebook of Criminal Justice Statistics*. Washington, DC: U.S. Government Printing Office.

U.S. Department of Labor, Bureau of Labor Statistics (1981). *Work Stoppage in Government, 1979*. Washington, DC: U.S. Government Printing Office.

Walker, Samuel (1999). *The Police in America*, Third Edition. New York, NY: McGraw-Hill Book Company.

Walsh, William F., and Edwin J. Donovan (1990). *The Supervision of Police Personnel: A Performance-Based Approach*. Dubuque, IA: Kendall/Hunt Publishing Company.

World Almanac, The (1993). Pittsburgh, PA: The Pittsburgh Press/Pharos Books.

Supervising Minorities—

Respecting Individual and Cultural Differences

13

Introductory Case Study

Sergeant Dan Johnson

Sergeant Dan Johnson is a shift supervisor with Lakeview Police Department. Lakeview is a small city located in a conservative region of the southeastern United States. The police department has a good reputation in the community, and there is little turnover. The youngest officer on the force is 34. Only two officers in the department have a college education, and they hold only associate's degrees from a correspondence school. The department consists of only white males even though Lakeview boasts an African-American population of about seven percent. While the officers do not appear to be overtly biased or prejudiced against minorities, it is common knowledge that minorities are not hired by the police department.

Recently, the Lakeview Police Department was awarded a federal COPS grant to hire two new police officers. One of the requirements of the grant positions was an aggressive recruiting effort for minorities. Lakeview has always had an equal employment opportunity policy but no qualified minorities had ever applied. However, William Jackson, a former football player for the local high school, applied for one of the open positions and passed the exams with exceptionally high scores. Jackson went to the state university after graduating from high school and obtained a bachelor's degree in criminal justice. Jackson will be assigned to Sergeant Johnson's shift after he graduates from the police academy.

Sergeant Johnson is apprehensive about Jackson's employment. He has two strikes against him even before he reports for duty. First, he's the most educated officer on the force; second, he is an African-American. Sergeant Johnson has already heard many snide remarks among the officers about the new "token" on the force. Sergeant Johnson is determined to try to make the transition for Jackson as smooth as possible and to head off any attempts by his subordinates to not accept Jackson as one of the officers.

Sergeant Johnson researched all materials he could find regarding discrimination, hiring practices, state and federal laws governing employment of minorities, and so on. He held a shift meeting with his subordinates and advised them of the material he had researched and that he fully endorsed Officer Jackson. He went to state that any officer not treating Officer Jackson in a professional manner would be disciplined severely.

Do you agree with Sergeant Johnson's procedure for informing his subordinates? Do you think Sergeant Johnson accomplished his goal? What other techniques could have Sergeant Johnson used to prepare his subordinates for Officer Jackson's arrival? Do you think Officer Jackson should have been at the meeting?

Coming to Grips with the Past

Until fairly recently, police work could easily have been described as a bastion for politically conservative white males. Police sergeants supervised other white men, like themselves, who came primarily from the working class. The typical police officer was a high school graduate with some military experience who had worked in blue-collar or lower-level white-collar occupations before joining the police department. Most of these men were attracted to police work for its job security and masculine camaraderie. In many areas of the country, a succession of ethnic groups (like the Irish, Italians, and Jews) controlled police departments and used them as stepping-stones to higher socioeconomic status.

Applicants who met the minimum qualifications were allowed to take a civil service examination, demonstrate their physical prowess in an agility test, and spar with inquisitors on an oral board examination. If the applicant passed a background investigation, his final score was calculated and placed in its proper order on the certified list of candidates. Candidates with the highest score were evaluated by the chief of police (based on the "rule of three"), and an appointment was made. Appointment as a probationary patrol officer offered young men a career with job security, prestige, a chance to exercise authority, and a bit of glamour. It represented a rite of passage and an induction into the "old boy network."

Newly sworn rookie police officers were issued a uniform, a badge, a service revolver, and other symbols of their new status. They were normally given a few words of advice, such as "Use your common sense," or "When you're in doubt, ask!" and put to work with little or no formal training. In most departments, police academy training (if there was any) came later. Rookie police officers learned on the job from the old-timers, who served as their mentors. The new men internalized the norms and values of their teachers. They quickly learned that in order to get ahead in the bureaucratic world, they had to play smart politics and "work the system." If they learned well enough, promotions came along at fairly regular intervals (Broderick, 1987).

Police ranks were filled by men recruited not necessarily because of their capability or potential, but because of their ability to fit into the police mold. They were hired to maintain the status quo, not to rock the boat. Rookie police officers were taught that criminals, liberals, civil rights activists, and feminists were all part of a diabolical conspiracy to undermine law and order. Cynicism and a unique occupational paranoia became part of the police culture. Perplexed and disillusioned by rapid sociopolitical change, all but the most resilient retreated to the security of the womb (the police subculture) that the late William H. Parker called the "shell of Minorityism" (Turner, 1968). The police considered themselves to be outsiders who functioned as an instrument of civil society and resented it when that role was challenged as racist.

Police work has changed over the past 40 years, and so has the composition of the workforce. Sergeants are now called on to supervise more minority, female, and other nontraditional police employees. In order to do the job properly, they must respect the individual and cultural differences of their subordinates. The same holds true for the nontraditional employees who are going to be hired and promoted in far greater numbers in the future.

Women have been disadvantaged and discriminated against based on the cultural myth that police work is "men's work." The opposition to blacks, Hispanics, and other racial minorities is simply the result of bigotry. The police establishment has always resisted the assimilation of these nontraditional employees, because it would mean sharing the power associated with the police function. This problem is exacerbated by the mentality of some white males. They have a deep-seated belief that they have a calling and are ordained to control the police profession (Holden, 1994). Their lock on power is self-evident.

In only a few major cities in the United States does the percentage of non-whites in blue approximate the proportion of non-whites in the overall community. National surveys reveal that the percentage of African-American and Hispanic officers, previously reported to be about 50 percent in some of America's 50 largest cities, has been increasing steadily and that there has been a significant increase in minority police officers hired in a number of metropolitan areas (Walker, 1999). As political power begins to shift toward minorities in some of the nation's cities, we can anticipate even more emphasis on African-American and Hispanic employment. Even the selection of African-American or Hispanic mayors may not precipitate radical changes in the composition of police departments, however. Political power is a crucial factor. In many large cities, the police are able to muster the political power needed to protect their turf from encroachment by those considered "outsiders," even if those outsiders are elected officials (Cole et al., 2002).

The importance of attracting women and minority officers cannot be overestimated. It is not the question of providing them with economically desirable government jobs that is important. Effective policing is the issue. It is very difficult for minorities who feel discriminated against to view law enforcement as being responsive to their needs, unbiased, and generally interested in justice, if they do not see members of their group represented on the department's roster. According to George Cole and his associates (2002), the ethnic character of American society makes it absolutely essential that participants in the administration of criminal justice reflect the ethnic character of the whole community.

Discrimination based on race and sex has been and continues to be a persistent human relations problem in our pluralistic society. It was, in fact, institutionalized by law (de jure) and through customary interpersonal relationships (de facto) until the mid-1960s. Propelled by deep-seated prejudices, discrimination permeated virtually every facet of American life. White Anglo-Saxon Protestant (WASP) values set the moral tone and ensured that almost all substantive political power remained in the hands of white males. Municipal police departments (as instruments of the white political establishment) were composed of white males whose major function was to "protect and serve" the white community while preserving the status quo. The constitutional guarantees of due process and equal protection of law contained in the Bill of Rights and the antislavery amendments took a backseat to reality. The Constitution became little more than an abstract statement of human values unrelated to the treatment of racial minorities and women.

According to Gary Johns (1988), "prejudgment" is normal human behavior. People make all sorts of judgments based on previously acquired knowledge and experience to bring some order into their lives. The mind assimilates as much as it can and then arranges the information in categories by which it prejudges a person or event. This saves time and effort. Such a mechanism, however, at times tends to produce irrational categories. This is where prejudice, stereotyping, and discrimination come in. These terms can be defined as follows:

1. **Prejudice.** Prejudice is a negative attitude toward a particular group that is considered different and inferior. The opinion is based partially on observation and partially on ignorance, ethnocentrism, and xenophobia. These erroneous generalizations are applied to all members of the group, regardless of individual differences.

2. **Stereotype.** Stereotypes are standardized mental images held by members of one group regarding the characteristics or traits of another group. A stereotype is a set of group-shared and generally negative attitudes based on tradition, limited interaction, or ignorance, which assigns similar undesirable attributes to all members of the "out" group.

3. **Discrimination.** Discrimination refers to the negative and unfavorable treatment of people based on their membership in a minority group. Discriminatory practices involve an act or omission that puts one person at a disadvantage in order to satisfy some prejudice.

Prejudice, stereotyping, and discrimination against minority groups are normally by-products of uncontrolled ethnocentrism or xenophobia. A minority group is one that has subordinate status and is the object of discrimination. Ethnocentrism is the natural tendency of human beings to view their own culture and customs as right and superior and to judge all others by those standards (Zastrow, 2000). Xenophobia, on the other hand, refers to the irrational fear or hatred of strangers and other foreigners. Minorities, especially racial minorities, are often viewed as strangers in their own land.

Prodded into action by racial unrest, social activism, antisegregation rulings (such as *Brown v. Board of Education*), Kennedy's Camelot, and the Johnson administration's desire to create a discrimination-free "Great Society," Congress reassessed its stand on the need for civil rights legislation to protect blacks and other minorities. One of the most important antidiscrimination bills in American history was enacted into law in 1964. The Civil Rights Act of 1964 prohibited discrimination based on national origin, ethnic group, sex, creed, age or race. According to Title VII of the Act (42 United States Code § 2000e-2[a][1]):

It shall be an unlawful employment practice for an employer (1) to fail or refuse to hire, or discharge any individual or otherwise to discriminate against any individual with respect to his compensation, terms, conditions, or privileges of employment, because of such individual's race, color, religion, sex, or national origin; (2) to limit, segregate, or classify his employees or applicants for employment in any way which would deprive or tend to deprive any individual of employment opportunity or otherwise adversely affect his status as an employee because of such individual's race, color, religion, sex, or national origin.

Title VII prohibits employers and unions from discriminating against their employees in the following areas:

1.	Hiring Employees	9.	Disciplining Personnel
2.	Compensating Employees	10.	Demoting Employees
3.	Terms of Employment	11.	Providing Facilities
4.	Conditions of Employment	12.	Assigning Facilities
5.	Privileges of Employment	13.	Training Employees
6.	Classifying Personnel	14.	Retraining Employees
7.	Assigning Personnel	15.	Providing Apprenticeships
8.	Promoting Personnel		

In an abrupt departure from past practices, Congress issued a call for justice and equality in the workplace. The Civil Rights Act of 1964 was a major battle in the revolution of rising expectations (Hilgert and Leonard, 2001).

Under the authority of Title VII as amended in 1966, the Equal Employment Opportunity Commission (EEOC) was created as a regulatory agency. It was authorized to set standards and establish guidelines for compliance with the requirements of the Civil Rights Act. The commission issued a set of comprehensive guidelines on employee selection procedures in 1970.

In 1972 Congress extended the coverage of Title VII to include all state and local government operations with more than 15 employees. The amendment, known as the Equal Employment Opportunity Act of 1972, gave the Equal Employment Opportunity Commission more authority to formulate policies, procedures, rules, and regulations designed to ensure compliance with the law. Many of the complaints filed with the Equal Employment Opportunity Commission and the cases that ended up in court arose from personnel practices involving the employment or supervision of police officers and firefighters (Thibault et al., 1998). These complaints and court cases ushered in a new era of affirmative action.

While the number of women and other minorities employed in state and local government increased, there really was no dramatic shift in the makeup of the public service. White males got most of the jobs and held on to them by virtue of their civil service status or seniority. In addition, nontraditional employees were not (for a variety of reasons) being promoted into the higher ranks as rapidly as had been originally anticipated. As a result, the EEOC adopted a proactive affirmative action strategy. Affirmative action required employers to take positive steps to overcome "present and past discrimination" in an effort to achieve equal employment opportunity. The affirmative action guidelines adopted by the commission were designed to promote activism without creating the type of "reverse discrimination" prohibited by the Civil Rights Act. Section 703(j) provides:

> Nothing contained in this title shall be interpreted to require any employer . . . subject to this title to grant preferential treatment to any individual or to any group because of the race, color, religion, sex, or national origin of such individuals or group on account of an imbalance which may exist, with respect to the total number or percentage of persons of any race, color, religion, sex, or national origin employed by any employer . . . in comparison with the total number or percentage of persons of any race, color, religion, sex, or national origin in any community, state, section, or other area, or in the available workforce in any community, state, section, or other area.

Affirmative action stressed the need for "goals," "timetables," and "actions" designed to deal with discrimination. The process involved four basic steps:

1. An analysis of all major job categories to ascertain whether women and other minorities were being underutilized.

2. Development of goals, timetables, and affirmative actions designed to correct identifiable deficiencies.

3. The maintenance of a comprehensive database for use in determining whether the goals were being accomplished.

4. Continuous assessment of utilization patterns to prevent the reintro-duction of discriminatory practices.

Although goals, timetables, and actions were (under appropriate circumstances) a proper means for implementing equal employment opportunity, the concept of "quotas" and "preferential treatment" based on race, color, national origin, and sex were contrary to the law. In fact, the federal government issued the following policy statement:

> Under a system of goals, therefore, an employer is never required to hire a person who does not have the qualifications needed to perform the job successfully; and an employer is never required to hire such an unqualified person in preference to another applicant who is qualified; nor is an employer required to hire a less qualified person in preference to a better qualified person, provided that the qualifications used to make such relative judgment realistically measure the person's ability to do the job in question, or other jobs to which he is likely to progress. The terms "less qualified" and "better qualified" as used in this memorandum are not intended to distinguish among persons who are substantially equally qualified in terms of being able to perform the job successfully. Unlike quotas, therefore, which may call for a preference for the unqualified over the qualified, or for the less qualified over the better qualified to meet the numerical requirements, a goal recognizes that persons are to be judged on individual ability, and therefore is consistent with the principle of merit hiring (Equal Employment Opportunity Coordinating Council, 1973).

Some courts held that a statistical imbalance between minorities represented in the police department and to those residing in the community constituted prima facie evidence of discrimination and imposed quotas. In Alabama, for example, the court ordered the state Department of Public Safety to hire one African-American trooper for each white trooper hired until 25 percent of all troopers were African-American (*NAACP v. Allen*, 1972). The central thrust became to gauge equal employment opportunity not by the methods used, but solely by the results achieved in the organization's workforce (Stahl, 1983).

Most police departments used some type of written examination and a physical agility test to screen prospective personnel. The written examinations often had a built-in cultural bias that discriminated against racial minorities (Sauls, 1995). Physical agility tests, on the other hand, almost always discriminated against women (Sass and Troyer, 1999). In order to ensure that protected classes (African-Americans, women, and other nontraditional employees) were not tested out of equal employment opportunity, the Supreme Court ruled that screening devices such as those discussed above had to be valid, reliable, job-related, and based on bona fide occupational qualifications (*Richmond v. Croson Co.*, 1989). These terms are best defined in the following manner:

1. **Validity.** Validity simply means that the test measures what it is supposed to measure.

2. **Reliability.** Reliability is the consistency with which any test yields accurate measurements.

3. **Job-Relatedness.** Job-relatedness means that the knowledge or skill being measured by the screening device is directly related to the actual job to be performed.

4. **Bona Fide Occupational Qualification.** A bona fide occupational qualification is an attribute or skill that is actually required in order to do a particular job.

In 1971, the U.S. Supreme Court held in *Griggs v. Duke Power Company* that standardized testing requirements prevented a disproportionate number of African-American employees from being hired. The company's requirement that employees have a high school diploma and pass aptitude tests did not measure an employee's ability to learn or perform a particular job or category of jobs within the company. The Court concluded that the subtle, illegal purpose of these requirements was to safeguard Duke Power's long-standing policy of giving job preferences to white employees. The *Griggs* decision set a standard protecting prospective employees from arbitrary and discriminatory screening. Police personnel administrators took the *Griggs* decision seriously and immediately began to modify their testing procedures. A great deal of time and energy was invested to make sure that examinations were job-related, valid, reliable, and nondiscriminatory. A number of standardized entry-level and promotional tests were developed and are currently being marketed by groups such as the International City Management Association (ICMA) and the International Association of Chiefs of Police (IACP).

In the 30 years since the *Griggs* decision, employers and courts have attempted to define and evaluate a wide range of employment and promotional practices. Certain factors have emerged as keys to assessing the legality of employment and promotional practices that create disparity. According to Sauls (1995), these factors include:

1. The degree of disparity created by use of the standard.

2. The demonstrated factual relationship between achieving the employment standard and successful performance of the job in question.

3. Whether achievement of the employment standard is determined by a "neutral" entity external to the employer.

4. Whether the employment standard focuses on innate, unalterable characteristics of candidates.

5. Whether the job in question has a direct impact on public safety.

6. The availability of effective alternative standards that create a lesser disparity.

Some police departments have moved away from using a comprehensive written test and now use the "assessment center" method to select personnel for entry-level positions or promotions. An assessment center is a multiple assessment strategy that involves using various techniques (job-related simulations, structured interviews, psychological evaluations, etc.) to screen candidates. "Behavioral samples" are obtained and submitted to a standardized evaluation based on multiple inputs by trained observers. Judgments are pooled by the observers at an evaluation meeting during which all relevant assessment data are reported and discussed. A final assessment is drafted and a recommendation is submitted to the hiring authority (Swanson et al., 1993). Assessment centers have proven to be far less discriminatory than many other preemployment screening procedures.

Case Study

Sergeant Curtis Smalling

Sergeant Curtis Smalling is a senior supervisory sergeant in charge of personnel at the Watauga Police Department. Watauga is a small community of about 65,000 located about 70 miles from Lexburg, a large metropolitan city. The Watauga Police Department has 32 officers and 17 reserve officers, all of whom are male. In fact, the only female employee of the police department is the chief's secretary.

Sergeant Smalling was instrumental in developing the department's employment test and assessment center five years ago. He modeled the employment system along the same lines as other similar-sized departments in the state. Although the employment system has been used only three times in the past five years, it seemed to work well in selecting the most qualified people for the open police positions. Sergeant Smalling has been called in to meet with the chief.

"Curtis, since you're the one in charge of the employment testing here, I wanted to fill you in on something," Chief Adams said. "You know we're going to be hiring two new positions this year, and I want to know how the female applicant pool is looking."

"Well, Chief, you know we've never had a female pass the exams or anything in the past. We had two female applicants on the last employment screening, but they failed the physical agility tests. I think the same two are going to try again this year," Sergeant Smalling replied.

"Yeah, I know about those two girls. They really raised a stink about the physical agility portion of the testing. That's what I want to talk to you about. You know our esteemed mayor is a female, and she made a point to ask me about what we're going to do about hiring a female officer. She seems to think we have been de facto discriminating against women in police work."

"On the last testing, both those female applicants scored very high on written and orals but couldn't do the run test or carry the dummy," Sergeant Smalling said. The physical agility test includes a 1.5-mile run in 12 minutes, and the applicant must carry or pull a 150-pound dummy 50 feet.

"Well, the mayor's on my back about this. I want you to make sure we don't have any repercussions if they fail again. I don't want a civil suit on me about this," the chief said.

Sergeant Smalling must now examine the physical agility test to see whether it does discriminate against females and, if it does, make changes before the next test or be prepared to justify it. Sergeant Smalling notes that he himself could probably not run the 1.5 miles in 12 minutes. But then again, the only running he has to do is to the chief's office.

If you were Sergeant Smalling, what specific criteria would you use to judge the fairness of the physical agility test for females? If they are found to be discriminatory, what should be done with the test? How would you justify the need for such a physical agility in police work? Should physical standards be lowered to provide employment opportunities for females?

While the assessment center approach is certainly superior to the standardized test, it is a fairly sophisticated process and requires a great deal of skill. It also costs more. Consequently, many medium-sized and small police departments are simply not able to make the switch.

There is no doubt that Equal Employment Opportunity and Affirmative Action (EEO/AA) were designed to deal with and remediate a very serious problem. The ideal of social justice was corrupted, however, when affirmative action goals became quotas and the noble end began to justify unscrupulous means in the hands of relatively unsophisticated police administrators. While EEO/AA opened the door for more African-Americans, women, and other nontraditional employees, they also created deep wounds that have yet to heal. Many white police officers believe (rightly or wrongly) that they were victimized by reverse discrimination. They harbor a great deal of resentment and hide their true feelings. White police officers cheered when the Supreme Court ruled in the *Bakke* case (1978) that it was wrong for employers to use quotas designed to accommodate African-Americans and women in such a manner as to withhold gainful employment from eligible white males. The recent deemphasis of EEO/AA has reduced anxiety somewhat, and there is an uneasy truce between white male police officers and new nontraditional police officers.

Police sergeants find themselves in a very difficult spot. Regardless of their ethnicity, race, or sex, they must work with and help to bridge the gap between the white male majority and various minority groups within the police department. It is a job that has been added to and yet transcends their other duties. If they perform this human relations function well, there will be a cooperative effort to accomplish the department's mission, goals, and objectives. Failure, on the other hand, could serve to reignite the virulent racism and sexism of the past.

The Changing Face of America

It is estimated that there are 284.7 million people in the United States. A little more than one-half of them are females. While the overwhelming majority of all Americans are white, 12.8 percent are African-American and another 11.8 percent are Hispanic. Growing three times faster than the U.S. total, Hispanics may account for one-quarter of the nation's growth over the next 20 years. The Census Bureau indicates a nearly doubling of the Hispanic population since the last census in 1990 (U.S. Census Bureau, 2001). Even without immigration (legal or illegal) for the next 100 years, the Hispanic population will increase at twice the national rate. Asian and Native Americans round out the picture and contribute to the ethnic diversity of modern American society.

It is clear that minorities and women remain underrepresented in virtually all specialties and at all ranks in law enforcement in spite of the aggressive EEO/AA programs of the past (see Figures 13.1, 13.2, and 13.3). In 1975 only 6.5 percent of all police officers were African-American, even though African-Americans represented 11 percent of the total population. While females constituted a little more than one-half of the population, somewhere between two and four percent of the sworn officers were women (Walker, 1999). The situation did not change much over the next two decades. While the number of female police officers has increased dramatically over the past 10 years, they still only comprise 10 percent of all sworn police personnel. African-American males now constitute approximately 12 percent of all sworn police personnel and Hispanics account for only about eight percent of sworn police personnel (U.S. Department of Justice, 2000).

Figure 13.1
Sex of Full-Time Sworn Personnel in Local Police Departments

By size of population served, United States, 1997			
	All sworn employees		
Population served	Total	Male	Female
All sizes	100%	90.0%	10.0%
1,000,000 or more	100	84.1	15.9
500,000 to 999,999	100	86.0	14.0
250,000 to 499,999	100	85.9	14.1
100,000 to 249,999	100	90.1	9.9
50,000 to 99,999	100	92.3	7.7
25,000 to 49,999	100	93.4	6.6
10,000 to 24,999	100	94.7	5.3
2,500 to 9,999	100	94.9	5.1
Less than 2,500	100	96.9	3.1
Percents may not add to total because of rounding.			

Source: U.S. Department of Justice, Bureau of Justice Statistics, *Local Police Departments 1997*, NCJ 173429 (Washington, DC: U.S. Department of Justice, 2000), p. 3, Table 5.

Every precaution must be taken to protect the gains that African-Americans, Hispanics, women, and other nontraditional employees have made in the past and to ensure equal employment opportunity for everyone in the future. With the assistance of supervisory personnel, police managers should work diligently to comply with the expectations of the Commission on Accreditation for Law Enforcement Agencies (CALEA, 2001). According to CALEA Standard 31:

> The recruitment standards of the law enforcement accreditation process have embraced several important philosophical concepts in this chapter. The first concept is the expectation that an accredited agency will be an equal opportunity employer. EEO understands equal opportunity as the removal of barriers that prevent people from being treated fairly for employment purposes.
>
> The second concept is the expectation that the agency's sworn workforce will be representative of the available workforce in the agency's service community relative to its ethnic and gender composition. If any group is underrepresented, the recruitment plan will include proactive steps to encourage members of that group to seek employment opportunities.
>
> Under the accreditation program, the recruitment plan does not mandate hard quotas, such as hiring one female for every two males hired, nor is an agency expected to lower legitimate job-related hiring standards or criteria. Agencies are never expected to hire an individual who is not qualified to perform the duties of the job involved.

The employment of African-Americans, women, and other nontraditional employees (such as Hispanics, Native Americans, older workers, college graduates, etc.) should be a recruitment goal, not a quota governing the hiring of police personnel. The composition of the community should serve as a guide for recruitment policy, not discriminatory affirmative action. According to V.A. Leonard and Harry More (1993), primary consideration should be given to employing the best qualified candidates available, regardless of ethnicity or sex. While members of minority groups and women have been and continue to be underrepresented in virtually all aspects of modern police work, we should not lose sight of the fact that a great deal of progress has already been made. Police personnel administrators have intensified their efforts to recruit, train, and retrain qualified human resources from all segments of the community (Swank and Conser, 1983). As a result, the number of nontraditional employees in the workforce has increased appreciably. This is especially true of agencies seeking accreditation through CALEA. As CALEA (2001) Standard 31.2 stipulates:

> The agency has ethnic and gender composition in the sworn law enforcement ranks in approximate proportion to the makeup of the available workforce in the law enforcement agency's service community, or a recruitment plan pursuant to standard 31.2.2. Recruitment steps should be direct-

ed toward the goal of approximating within the sworn ranks the demographic composition of the community that it serves. Statistics on the composition of the workforce in the agency's service community are available from a variety of sources, including the U.S. Department of Labor's Bureau of Labor Statistics. For the purposes of this standard, the agency may also expand its recruitment efforts beyond the immediate service community.

Progressive police administrators are committed to ensuring equal employment opportunity. They favor an aggressive, proactive approach to recruitment. Their recruiters use a variety of innovative techniques to target specific ethnic and racial groups in a genuine effort to increase the number of nontraditional applicants and enrich the pool of qualified candidates.

Recruitment is a multidimensional process designed to encourage people to seek careers in police work and to select individuals who are qualified to do the job. Researchers note that successful recruitment programs exhibit similar characteristics.

1. An internal commitment to equal employment opportunity.

2. A strong, well-managed minority recruitment component.

3. Utilization of minority police officers in recruitment.

4. Targeted recruitment of especially promising applicants.

5. Screening based on valid, reliable, and fair procedures.

6. Appointment contingent on qualifications, not politics.

7. Promotion based on interest and on-the-job performance (Swanson et al., 1993).

Police recruit classes today are far different from those of the past. Based on pressure from minorities, changes in the law, and our national commitment to social equality, the composition of the workforce is slowly but surely being transformed into a mirror image of the community at large.

Supervising Minorities

With the increased emphasis on recruiting, hiring, and nurturing nontraditional employees, first-line supervisors are more likely than ever to have supervisory responsibility for African-Americans, Hispanics, and women. These employees, like all other employees, expect to be given a chance to succeed. They want to carry their own weight and to be appreciated for their potential contribution to the police department. Women and other minorities do not want to be patronized. They want and need to be respected as human beings. Due to the debilitating effects of past discrimination, they may need extra care, training, and coaching to help them adjust to their new environment. This is where the knowledge and human skills of the first-line supervisors come into play.

Figure 13.2
Full-Time Law Enforcement Employees

(1999 estimated population)	Total police employees			Police officers (sworn)			Civilian employees		
Population group	Total	Percent male	Percent female	Total	Percent male	Percent female	Total	Percent male	Percent female
Total agencies: 13,313 agencies; population 253,242,000	899,118	73.9%	26.1%	637,551	89.3%	10.7%	261,567	36.3%	63.7%
Total cities: 10,253 cities; population 170,045,000	549,320	75.2	24.8	420,533	89.3	10.7	128,787	29.4	70.6
Group I									
66 cities, 250,000 and over; population 48,322,000	210,353	70.3	29.7	155,439	84.4	15.6	54,914	30.6	69.4
9 cities, 1,000,000 and over; population 21,834,000	117,917	68.5	31.5	86,449	83.8	16.2	31,468	26.4	73.6
20 cities, 500,000 to 999,999; population 13,323,000	50,714	73.5	26.5	37,719	84.7	15.3	12,995	41.0	59.0
37 cities, 250,000 to 499,999; population 13,165,000	41,722	71.7	28.3	31,271	85.6	14.4	10,451	30.0	70.0
Group II									
149 cities, 100,000 to 249,999; population 22,013,000	56,772	74.0	26.0	43,128	89.5	10.5	13,644	25.3	74.7
Group III									
362 cities, 50,000 to 99,999; population 24,744,000	58,914	77.0	23.0	45,746	91.7	8.3	13,168	26.2	73.8
Group IV									
713 cities, 25,000 to 49,999; population 24,601,000	58,463	78.7	21.3	46,923	92.8	7.2	12,540	27.2	72.8
Group V									
1,743 cities, 10,000 to 24,999; population 27,405,000	67,436	80.4	19.6	54,080	93.8	6.2	13,366	25.9	74.1
Group VI									
7,220 cities, under 10,000; population 23,560,000	97,382	79.8	20.2	76,217	92.4	7.6	21,165	34.5	65.5
Suburban counties									
826 agencies; population 52,285,000	224,358	71.1	28.9	138,937	87.8	12.2	85,421	43.9	56.1
Rural counties									
2.234 agencies; population 30,312,000	125,440	73.0	27.0	78,081	92.1	7.9	47,359	41.6	58.4
Suburban areas									
6,241 agencies; population 102,099,000	370,464	74.5	25.5	253,822	90.0	10.0	116,642	40.7	59.3

Includes suburban city and county law enforcement agencies within metropolitan areas. Excludes central cities. Suburban cities and counties also are included in other groups.

Source: U.S. Department of Justice, Federal Bureau of Investigation (2000). *Crime in the United States, 1996.* Washington, DC: U.S. Government Printing Office, p. 296.

Figure 13.3
Race and Ethnicity of Full-Time Personnel in Local Police Departments

By size of population served, United States, 1997[a]

| | | Percent of full-time sworn employees who are: | | | | | | | | | | | |
| | Total | White | | | Black | | | Hispanic | | | Other[b] | | |
Population served	Total	Total	Male	Female	Total	Male	Female	Total	Male	Female	Total	Male	Female
All sizes	100%	78.5%	72.2%	6.3%	11.7%	9.1%	2.5%	7.8%	6.8%	1.0%	2.1%	1.9%	0.2%
1,000,000 or more	100	64.7	57.1	7.6	17.8	12.5	5.4	15.6	12.0	2.7	1.9	1.6	0.2
500,000 to 999,999	100	63.1	56.2	7.0	23.4	17.7	5.7	7.0	6.1	0.8	6.6	6.1	0.5
250,000 to 499,999	100	69.6	60.6	9.0	19.1	15.2	3.9	9.3	8.3	1.0	1.9	1.7	0.2
100,000 to 249,999	100	78.9	71.7	7.2	11.6	9.7	1.9	7.2	6.6	0.6	2.3	2.2	0.1
50,000 to 99,999	100	85.4	79.3	6.1	7.5	6.5	1.0	5.4	4.9	0.5	1.6	1.5	0.1
25,000 to 49,999	100	88.5	83.1	5.4	6.0	5.2	0.8	4.6	4.3	0.3	0.8	0.8	(c)
10,000 to 24,999	100	91.9	87.3	4.6	4.3	3.9	0.4	2.7	2.6	0.1	1.1	1.0	0.2
2,500 to 9,999	100	89.1	84.8	4.3	4.8	4.3	0.4	4.1	3.9	0.2	2.0	1.8	0.2
Less than 2,500	100	89.3	86.8	2.5	5.3	5.0	0.2	3.2	3.1	0.1	2.3	2.0	0.2

[a]Percents may not add to total because of rounding.
[b]Includes Asians, Pacific Islanders, American Indians, and Alaska Natives.
[c]Less than 0.05%.

Source: U.S. Department of Justice, Bureau of Justice Statistics, *Local Police Departments 1997*, NCJ 173429 (Washington, DC: U.S. Department of Justice, 2000), p. 3, Table 5.

The supervisor, according to Lawrence A. Johnson (1969), is a "major key" to the minority worker's success or failure. A supervisor who wishes to change the status quo and improve human relations within the workplace must be prepared not only to avoid discrimination, but also to actively help everyone overcome it. The bottom line is very clear. It is the supervisor's primary responsibility to create and maintain an environment in which all employees are able to satisfy some of their needs while working cooperatively with others to accomplish the mission, goals, and objectives of the department.

White male sergeants must begin to understand that many of their nontraditional employees have been conditioned to expect the worst. African-Americans, Hispanics, and women assume they will face varying degrees of, and be forced to deal with:

- prejudice
- discrimination
- resentment
- rejection
- hostility
- isolation
- scapegoating

They may use selective perception to confirm these suspicions. Women and other minorities are often very sensitive to incidents, actions, or events that nonminority workers brush aside. They are considered insults or personal attacks. In a longitudinal study of African-American police officers in the Washington, D.C. Metropolitan Police Department, more than 65 percent reported that they trusted few or no white officers. This data was drawn from 947 (90 percent) of the African-American police officers in the District. Nearly 84 percent of the respondents were patrol officers, and 80 percent believed that African-Americans were discriminated against in hiring, job assignments, enforcement of rules and regulations, and job performance ratings (Thibault et al., 1998). Until all subordinates believe they are being treated as valued persons, there will always be a measure of discontent. Hopefully, as more minority police officers achieve rank in management positions within the department, discontent will fade (see Figures 13.4 and 13.5).

Unfortunately, there will always be a few police officers who, regardless of their ethnic background or sex, will try to take advantage of their supervisors. Some will be looking for special privileges. They may use their sex or minority status to gain favored treatment. This ploy, while understandable, must be prevented. The supervisor's success in working with other employees will be undercut if favoritism and privilege are allowed to flourish. Impartiality and fairness are absolutely essential in effective supervision.

Figure 13.4
Bonni Tischler Earns Top Cop Award

The National Center for Women in Policing honored Assistant Commissioner for Field Operations Bonni Tischler, while Assistant Commissioner for Investigations, with its Lifetime Achievement Award at its annual March conference in Baltimore, Md. The award is given to female law enforcement officers with exceptional service and career achievement who have helped other women in law enforcement as mentors and role models.

"It was a very exciting moment, and I was extremely pleased," says Tischler, who has been in law enforcement for almost 29 years. "I thought that it was a real compliment, not only to me, but to all the women who are in law enforcement in the federal sector."

The trail-blazing Tischler, one of the very top women in federal law enforcement, will be similarly honored at the annual Women in Federal Law Enforcement conference in July, in Washington, D.C.

Breaking the glass . . .
In 1971, when President Nixon signed the executive order granting women equal status in the federal law enforcement community, it was necessary for a few pioneering women to open the doors and eventually break the glass ceiling. Tischler helped do that.

When "women in federal law enforcement" was very nearly an oxymoron, Tischler became a Customs Sky Marshal, eventually joining the ranks of Customs Special Agents in 1977.

As a Special Agent, she pioneered an oversight function, which would act as a clearinghouse for various problems facing women in the federal law enforcement community.

As Tischler sees it, the job of law enforcement demands an enormous sense of humor: "You must be able to laugh at your mistakes while learning an intense lesson from them. You must learn to tell a good war story and make fun of yourself. You must laugh. You must employ humor if you are to succeed."

She received her first big break in 1980 when she became the only female agent assigned to the newly-formed task force in Miami known as Operation Greenback, which became the first major federal investigation into drug money laundering.

When detailed to the Office of the Federal Women's Program at the Office of Personnel Management, she recruited other interested individuals and developed what is now known as the Women in Federal Law Enforcement Interagency Committee (WIFLE). She co-chaired the Committee in 1984, and became the first recipient of the Julie Y. Cross Memorial Award in recognition of her outstanding achievements in law enforcement.

Figure 13.4, *continued*

> Her expertise in money laundering investigations coupled with successful undercover assignments landed Tischler in Washington where she became the Director of the Financial Investigations Division, which later became Smuggling Investigations, when narcotics and marine interdiction were added to its duties in 1986.
>
> In 1987, she was promoted to Special Agent in Charge of the Tampa office where she supervised agents investigating money laundering at the Bank of Credit and Commerce International (BCCI) in what was to become one of the largest money laundering cases ever prosecuted.
>
> In 1995, Tischler returned to her home turf as Special Agent in Charge for Miami, to supervise Customs' biggest and most active group of 360 agents and investigative personnel. In 1997, she was summoned to Washington where she was selected to become Customs' first female Assistant Commissioner for the Office of Investigations.
>
> On June 19, 2000, Tischler was appointed Assistant Commissioner for Field Operations, effective July 1. She is the first woman to hold this post with responsibility for all cargo and passenger processing of the Customs Service. She will oversee approximately 13,000 Customs employees at more than 300 Ports of Entry, Customs Management Centers, and Field Laboratories.
>
> Tischler has combined her expertise, poise, and confidence to become a highly visible and popular representative of the Customs Service both in the media and on Capitol Hill where she regularly testifies on behalf of the Agency.

Source: *U.S. Customs Today*, Vol. 36, No. 6 (June 2000).

Effective supervision always begins with an awareness of the individual and cultural differences among employees. These differences affect performance and must be accepted as fact (Longenecker and Pringle, 1984). Knowing their subordinates and basing decisions on that knowledge helps supervisors avoid unreasonable expectations and provides a valid basis for understanding job-related behavior. Converting facts into performance-related information allows the supervisor to match the talents of the employee with the job to be done. If this approach is to be successful, supervisors must:

1. Be knowledgeable, approachable, and empathetic when dealing with subordinates.

2. Learn to listen to and really understand the minority employee's point of view.

3. Communicate openly and honestly with their subordinates in all matters pertaining to the job.

4. Expect a considerable amount of testing and probing by minorities concerning the department's philosophy on human relations and the supervisor's attitude, sincerity, and commitment regarding equal employment opportunity.

5. Practice introspection and be aware of their own possible reactions to probable situations involving on-the-job relationships with minority employees (Plunkett, 1992).

The effectiveness of supervision can almost always be measured by the empathetic quality of the relationship between a good supervisor and receptive subordinates. Empathy (the capacity to participate in and appreciate another person's feelings or ideas) provides the foundation for positive human relations.

Sergeants may be required to make a special effort to motivate nontraditional employees. Consequently, they should analyze the situation and develop an action plan to:

1. **Make the Work Interesting.** Sergeants should examine each job in terms of how it could be enriched and made more challenging. There is a limit to the extent that employees will be satisfied performing repetitive or routine tasks.

2. **Relate Rewards to Performance.** While they may be limited by civil service regulations or collective bargaining agreements, sergeants should, whenever practical, try to relate rewards (special projects, recommendations for promotion, pay increases, etc.) to performance. The cost of failing to relate rewards to performance is high. Low performers will not be motivated to do a better job, and top performers may be motivated to do less.

3. **Provide Valued Rewards.** Supervisors should do their best to determine the type of rewards that are valued most by employees. The most important thing is for supervisors to know what rewards they have at their disposal and exactly what the employees find most valuable.

4. **Treat Employees as Individuals.** As noted earlier in this chapter, different people have very different needs and want different things from their job. Individualized attention enhances self-esteem and makes the police officer feel like a valuable member of the organization. It also tends to produce more frequent and candid interaction between supervisors and minority employees.

5. **Encourage Participation and Cooperation.** It is natural for people to commit themselves to decisions that they help to make. Unfortunately, many supervisors do little to encourage active participation. They have not learned the value of sharing power with, rather than exercising power over, their employees.

6. **Explain Why the Action Is Being Taken.** Police officers are usually more supportive and tend to perform better if they know why they have been asked to do something. Blind obedience to authority is passé in complex criminal justice agencies.

7. **Provide Accurate and Timely Feedback.** A lack of feedback generally frustrates employees and has a negative impact on performance. Providing meaningful feedback is a normal part of supervision. People do not like to be left in the dark as far as their on-the-job performance is concerned. They want to know where they stand and resent being taken for granted. In fact, a negative performance evaluation may be better than no evaluation at all (Martin, 1987).

Nontraditional employees need competent and supportive supervisors who exercise good judgment and make reasonable decisions concerning them. In order to do the job right, police sergeants need a bag of tricks filled with technical, human, administrative, and problem-solving skills.

Many municipal police departments that have actively recruited and hired nontraditional personnel did so because of federal EEO/AA initiatives, state human relations commission regulations, court rulings, voluntary consent decrees (court-supervised agreements hammered out and implemented in order to avoid future litigation), or a personal commitment to equal employment opportunity on the part of the chief police executive (see Figure 13.6). Unfortunately, none of these decision-making processes do much to build mid-management or supervisory support for African-Americans, Hispanics, women, or other minorities. According to Leonard Territo and Harold Vetter (1981), minority police officers are a very special breed. They are subjected not only to the normal stressors of police work, but also to the additional stress of skepticism and rejection by their own kind. In addition, minority police officers are not likely to be fully accepted into the police culture (which is a source of support, camaraderie, and occupational identity). A female officer is subject to other unique stressors. These include: (1) her own feeling of competence; (2) her perception of her peers' views of her competence, particularly those of male officers; (3) reluctant acceptance into the male-dominated police culture; (4) unfavorable stereotypical reactions by some citizens; and (5) sexual harassment.

Figure 13.5
Justice Dept. Bows Out Of a Civil Rights Case Suit Charged Male Bias in Police Test

The Bush administration is dropping a Clinton administration civil rights action that charged that an aerobics test used by the Southeastern Pennsylvania Transportation Authority (SEPTA), which was failed by 93 percent of female applicants, was overly rigorous.

The test required all applicants for the SEPTA police force to run 1.5 miles in 12 minutes. SEPTA, a mass transit system serving the Philadelphia metropolitan area, claimed the test was necessary because some stations are several flights of stairs above or below ground level and officers can be required to run three to five blocks between stations. Officers are required to wear 26 pounds of gear, including a bulletproof vest.

The Public Interest Law Center of Philadelphia filed suit in 1997 on behalf of women who had taken the test since 1991 and failed. The Clinton Justice Department joined the suit later that year. Justice is withdrawing from the case at the behest of Ralph F. Boyd Jr., the assistant attorney general for civil rights.

"We feel it is critical to public safety that police and firefighters be able to run, climb up and down stairs to rescue people quickly under the most trying of circumstances," said Dan Nelson, a Justice Department spokesman.

But civil rights groups were angered by the about-face. "By withdrawing from this case, the Department of Justice is showing its true colors," said Jocelyn C. Frye, director of legal policy for the National Partnership for Women and Families. "This case was a test to see whether the Justice Department would continue to do the right thing and vindicate the rights of these female police officers, or bow to other pressures. Unfortunately, they failed the test miserably."

The law center, now the sole lawyer for the plaintiffs, says the test is a violation of the 1964 Civil Rights Act's Title VII admonition against employment discrimination based on race, color, religion, national origin or gender.

Two of the women who failed the test have gone on to become police officers with the Philadelphia Police Department. The lead plaintiff, Catherine Lanning, is with the tactical bike control unit at the University of Pennsylvania and provides back-up assistance to SEPTA officers, said Michael Churchill, the law center's chief counsel.

No other police force in the country uses such a restrictive test —not the FBI, not the New York Police Department, not the Washington transit police, Churchill said. At issue, he said, is whether the test measures the "minimum qualifications" necessary to do the job.

A federal judge in the eastern district of Pennsylvania ruled in favor of SEPTA in June 1998, but an appeals court judge vacated the decision and ordered the lower court to rule again, this time applying the minimum qualifications standard. The December 2000 ruling again favored SEPTA, and the plaintiffs appealed to the Third Circuit Court of Appeals.

"This appeal was not about setting new rights or expanding any rights," Churchill said. Rather, it is about whether employers can continue practices that have "disparate impacts" on women and minorities, he said.

SEPTA attorney Saul Krenzel said that "it was about time" the Justice Department endorsed the position SEPTA has taken since 1992. He said since 1992, major crime in the subway system has dropped 70 percent. About 5 percent of the 200-member force are women, he said.

Sergeants must be trained not to place a value judgment on cultural differences. These differences must be understood and respected. Disregard for individual and cultural differences erodes productivity and may even be discriminatory (Schroeder, 1996). Minority police officers may become disillusioned, resentful, bitter, and resistant to supervision. Robert Fulmer and Stephen Franklin (1982) argue that supervisors who behave responsibly toward their subordinates know and consider them individually and personally. They cultivate sincere, honest, open, accepting, and trusting relationships designed to instill self-confidence and a desire to achieve personal satisfaction through work. Competent sergeants are firm, fair, and impartial. They possess a certain amount of charisma and the ability to focus their attention on the growth and development of their subordinates. This is particularly true in the case of minorities. The sergeant who takes this responsibility seriously may find the following guidelines helpful:

1. Consider minorities as individuals and important human beings at all times. Respect them and accept their individual and cultural differences. Know something about the "person" the police officer is when off duty.

2. Represent the interests and concerns of your employees to top management with understanding and candor. Listen carefully to minorities as individuals and members of a group. Organize and communicate what you have heard so that police managers get the same message.

3. Make every effort to interpret and explain department policy accurately to nontraditional employees. Clarity is essential to compliance. Never withhold information that they need to know. Explain why policies have been adopted and the contribution the employee will make in achieving the department's mission, goals, and objectives.

4. Be a role model for women, African-Americans, Hispanics, and others. Forthrightness and fair play are critical variables in positive relationships. Keep a sense of humor, and be prepared to laugh at yourself from time to time.

5. Reprimand minorities when necessary; remember to praise them for a job that is well done. Follow the golden rule: "praise in public and reprimand in private."

6. Let nontraditional workers know that they will be given every opportunity to develop and improve their skills and earnings. Always encourage questions and reply in a concise and straightforward manner. Share what you know with minority employees. Allow them to assist with work that may be routine but will teach them new and useful skills through active learning.

7. Evaluate performance and potential very carefully and objectively. Never permit individual personalities or prejudices to cloud objective opinions about any minority employee. Judgments must be based only on the aspects of personality that directly affect an employee's on-the-job performance.

8. Try to improve the minority worker's confidence by being considerate, firm, fair, and impartial in dealing with all employees under your supervision. Never play favorites, and never allow personality or cultural differences to cause you to abuse a subordinate.

9. Place minority workers in a job according to their skill, ability, attitude, and civil service or bargaining agreement classification. Do not break probationary minority officers in by putting them on the toughest assignment. Whenever possible, do not assign nontraditional employees to jobs for which they are overqualified. They will feel bored and unchallenged.

10. Never "pass the buck" if something goes wrong. Always assume responsibility for the actions of minority employees when appropriate. This will encourage nontraditional employees to take responsibility for themselves. The final responsibility for the operation and on-site management of a work unit cannot be shifted to others by the first-line supervisor.

11. Learn as much as possible about how your minority workers relate to their occupational role. Develop an empathetic appreciation of their individual interests, likes, and dislikes. Find out what nontraditional employees really enjoy about their job. Try to discover what frustrates them the most. Be on the lookout for small changes that might make a big difference in how minority workers view their job.

12. Always take time to give proper and adequate instructions to new nontraditional employees. Make them feel at home through a proper job orientation. Be patient. Use counseling, coaching, and on-the-job training to help minority employees overcome their anxieties.

13. Always stress the importance of safety. Be mindful of the fact that all people have a need for safety and security. A lack of attention to these needs will produce poor morale and a sense of alienation. Encourage employees to share their suggestions on how to make the job safer.

14. Assume responsibility for communicating, as accurately as possible, the feelings and attitudes of all line personnel to your superiors (middle-level managers). Police managers, on the other hand, expect (and sergeants should try to build) a team spirit, high morale, job satisfaction, and harmony among all police employees regardless of race, color, creed, sex, or national origin.

15. Set the moral and ethical tone for human relations within the police department with an absolute and unconditional commitment to equal employment opportunity. Anything less is an abdication of leadership and will serve to confirm the perception of a racist, sexist, and ethnocentric criminal justice system.

These are awesome responsibilities that require a great deal of sensitivity, talent, knowledge, skill, training, and courage. Sergeants are "change agents" and, as such, must take risks in order to do their job. Unfortunately, many sergeants are ill-equipped to carry out these duties. They do not have the experience or training needed to fulfill their role in personnel development. Far too many sergeants are, in fact, little more than promoted patrol officers.

Sergeants, of course, cannot (even if they are competent) do the job alone. Managers at all levels of complex criminal justice organizations must make a commitment to social justice through equal employment opportunity. It is up to the police chief executive to set the stage for change. The chief must formulate a no-nonsense policy in support of equal employment opportunity and be prepared to use all available resources to accomplish that policy. Continuous reinforcement is absolutely essential. The chief should be prepared to take immediate and appropriate action against any manager or supervisor who fails to support and carry out the department's policies in the area of human relations.

When all is said and done, however, it is the police sergeant who translates equal opportunity theory into practice within the police department. Without a genuine commitment on the sergeant's part, EEO/AA becomes ritualistic mumbo-jumbo designed to placate supposedly naive minorities while perpetuating the status quo. Sergeants are in a position to activate and guide equal opportunity or turn it into a social placebo.

Dealing with Employees in a Protected Class

The phrase *protected class* has a special meaning when it comes to supervising employees who belong to certain minority groups. A protected class is composed of individuals who have been unfairly or illegally discriminated against in the past or who are believed to be entitled to preferential consideration due to past or present aspects of their life situation. Protected class is currently used as a classification for individual employees based on their:

1. racial or ethnic origin;

2. sex (gender or preference);

3. age (over 40);

4. physical status (disabilities); or

5. religion

Members of other groups, like veterans, have also been granted protected status based primarily on political grounds.

As more women join the ranks of police officers, the possibility of employee pregnancy must be considered. Many women choose to have both a family and a career, and policies should be in place to accommodate both. In 1978 Congress amended Title VII of the Civil Rights Act of 1964 to provide protection against pregnancy discrimination. The legislation, known as the Pregnancy Discrimination Act, expanded the existing prohibition against discrimination "because of sex" or "on the basis of sex" to also include "because of or on the basis of pregnancy, childbirth or related medical condition."

The identification of individuals who are accorded special legal consideration when it comes to employment arises from federal civil rights legislation, equal employment opportunity regulations, and court decisions. As a manager of human resources, it is in the sergeant's best interest to become familiar with the groups that have been granted "minority" status and to develop an understanding of why they are classified as such.

Irrespective of their social perspectives or personal biases, sergeants, as first-line supervisors who interact with a diverse workforce on a daily basis, must be sensitive when it comes to potentially illegal discriminatory practices. They must also adjust their supervisory methods in a concerted effort to avoid these practices. The OUCH test is one effective strategy that applies to the supervision of employees who are members of a protected class (Hilgert and Leonard, 2001).

Being aware of and understanding the OUCH test helps to remind supervisors that all of their actions as first-line managers must be:

O	—	Objective
U	—	Uniform in application
C	—	Consistently applied
H	—	Have job-relatedness

While it is straightforward as well as simple, the OUCH acronym provides practical guidance for ethical, nondiscriminatory supervision in the context of modern police work.

From the OUCH perspective, a supervisor's action is objective when it addresses the employee's job-related behavior without being distorted by personal feelings. It is uniform in application when it is consistently applied to all employees. The action is consistent in effect when it has the same proportional impact on members of protected classes as it does on others in the workforce. Finally, the action has job relatedness if it can be shown to deal with behavior that is necessary to perform the job.

The OUCH test should be viewed as much more than a statement of one's personal philosophy, however. It represents the criteria that management and the courts use to determine whether real discrimination has occurred. By adopting the OUCH perspective as it relates to human resources management, sergeants may well avoid allegations of discrimination and the lengthy administrative or legal entanglements that go along with them. Once again, the old adage may be correct: An ounce of prevention is worth a pound of cure.

Handling Sexual Harassment in the Workplace

Recent studies indicate that there have been some positive changes in the status of women in police work. The percentage of women in the workforce is up and continues to increase each year. Nearly 20 percent of the current applicant pool and recruits are female. This clearly indicates that there is no longer any systematic discrimination against women in the application process. On the downside, women police officers have much higher turnover rates than their male counterparts. Consequently, more women must be recruited and processed just to maintain the current sex ratio (Swanson et al., 1993).

One cause of the high turnover rate for female police officers is sexual harassment. Sergeants are in a strategic position when it comes to dealing with this type of harassment in the workplace. As first-line supervisors and representatives of management, they are expected to be proactive rather than reactive in this regard.

Sexual harassment in the workplace is a major problem facing both public and private sector employers in the United States. This is particularly true in male-dominated occupations. Twenty years of research have provided overwhelming evidence indicating that unwelcome and offensive sexual conduct is both pandemic and problematic in many organizations. Conservative estimates suggest that about 40 percent of working women and five to 10 percent of their male counterparts have experienced some type of sexual harassment in the workplace (Thomann et al., 1989).

In a recent study involving 81 of 122 female police officers in a metropolitan police department, 62 percent of the respondents reported that they had been subjected to sexual harassment by their male colleagues. Of these, one-third confronted the offender; six percent talked to their supervisors; a few contacted the Equal Employment Opportunity Commission; however, 21 percent took no action at all. Very few took strong measures to deal with the problem (Daum and Johns, 1994). Many female officers feel intimidated. Consequently, many of them make a conscious decision not to "rock the boat" (Brown and Heidensohn, 2000).

Sexual harassment is prohibited by the Civil Rights Act of 1964. The Act specifies that it is unlawful for an employer to discriminate against any individual with respect to his or her compensation, terms, conditions, or privileges of employment because of such individual's race, color, religion, sex, or national origin (42 U.S.C. 2000e-2[a][1]). Sexual harassment can take one of two forms:

1. **Quid Pro Quo Sexual Harassment.** An individual is forced to grant sexual favors in order to obtain, maintain, or improve employment status.

2. **Hostile Work Environment Sexual Harassment.** Individual employees are subjected to suggestive comments, photographs, jokes, obscene gestures, or unwanted physical contacts. This type of harassment has the following four elements:

   a. The conduct is unwelcome.
   b. The conduct is sufficiently severe or pervasive to alter the conditions of the victim's employment and create an abusive work environment.
   c. The conduct is perceived by the victim as hostile or abusive.
   d. The conduct creates an environment that a reasonable person would find hostile or abusive.

Victims of sexual harassment report that they suffer from various physical and psychological maladies, diminished morale, and a loss of productivity. Studies indicate that direct and indirect costs associated with sexual harassment are phenomenal. The federal government, for example, estimates that sexual harassment cost it $267 million dollars between 1985 and 1987—$204 million in lost productivity, $37 million to replace federal workers who left their jobs and $26 million in medical leaves due to stress induced by sexual harassment (U.S. Merit Systems Protection Board, 1987).

Litigation focusing on sexual harassment has also been very costly to an increasing number of public and private organizations. Some have been required to pay judgments and legal fees exceeding six figures (Thomann and Serritella, 1994). The array of compensatory and punitive damages awarded in sexual harassment cases has been truly mind-boggling (see Figure 13.7).

Under normal circumstances, sexual harassment between coworkers does not produce employer liability under Title VII of the Civil Rights Act, because it is not considered an action of the employer. In addition, management will ordinarily not be held liable if it has taken "immediate" and "effective" steps to remedy sexual harassment that occurs in the workplace. An exculpatory response includes a formal policy prohibiting sexual harassment, a user-friendly and effective complaint procedure, and appropriate disciplinary action in cases of sexual misconduct. As a general rule, when management acts "in good faith" to deal with known sexual harassment, and management itself has clean hands, all liability is shifted to those engaged in the harassment. In addition, a comprehensive sexual harassment educational program for employees serves a dual purpose. It is not only the first step toward prevention, but it is also a vital element of any defense to sexual harassment litigation (Heckeroth and Barker, 1997).

Figure 13.6
Jury Gives Female Cop $700,000 in Second Sex Harassment Award

An Atlantic City female police sergeant who earlier this month won $575,000 in a sexual harassment suit against the police department was yesterday awarded an additional $700,000 in punitive damages by the same federal jury.

A jury seated before U.S. District Court Judge Joseph Irenas in Camden made the awards totaling more than $1 million to Sgt. Donna Hurley, whose suit claimed she was sexually harassed over a six-year period ending in January 1993.

Hurley sued the Atlantic City Police Department; her one-time supervisor, Capt. Henry Madamba, and Police Chief Nicholas V. Rifice. The jury found the department and Madamba discriminated against Hurley. Rifice was cleared of any wrongdoing. The punitive damages will be assessed against the city. In delivering its verdict and awarding the $575,000 in compensatory damages on Feb. 2, the jury decided Madamba's conduct did not warrant additional penalties.

Hurley is an 18-year veteran of the department and a mother of three. Her husband, Patrick, also is an Atlantic City police officer.

"I wish I had never had to go through with this," Donna Hurley said after the award was announced. Hurley said she plans to return to work but doesn't expect her fellow officers to welcome her back.

"Most other officers do not believe the harassment and discrimination occurred," she said. "I expect hostility."

Hurley testified during the two-month trial that pictures of her were drawn on the lavatory walls and in public areas of the police department, and sexual devices were displayed. Comments were written on the walls accusing Hurley of sexual activities with various members of the department, and as soon as maintenance crews painted them over, new graffiti appeared.

On one occasion, she testified, a sanitary napkin marked with sergeant's stripes was hung from the ceiling when she had to conduct roll call. Hurley's lawyer, Clifford Van Syoc, characterized the behavior as "absolutely atrocious."

Hurley said her supervisor, Madamba, in a private conversation, told her the harassment would end if she slept with him.

"He said, 'Donna, this happens all the time. Women get protection. They sleep with their bosses, and then people are afraid to mess with them,'" Hurley testified.

Van Syoc said he tried to negotiate a settlement with Atlantic City before the trial began.

"We offered to settle the case for $750,000," Van Syoc said. "But the city wouldn't accept that."

Atlantic City Mayor James Whelan would not comment except to say, through a spokesman, that the city intended to appeal.

After the verdict, Atlantic City Business Administrator Andrew Mair said the award would mean a two-cent increase per $100 of assessed valuation in city real estate taxes. Testifying before the jury, Mair said the current rate is $1.6182.

Hurley's husband, Officer Patrick Hurley, said he was unable to do anything about the harassment because he worked in the same department that condoned it.

He said he and his wife have grave concerns about how the harassment and the trial have affected their children, ages 12, 11 and 8.

Title VII provides a remedy for discrimination when there is an indication of employer responsibility in sexual harassment cases. Employers act through their supervisory agents. As a result, the police department (and the governmental entity of which it is a part) can be held liable if one of its supervisors actively participates in the harassment of one of its employees. It can also be held liable if its supervisors are responsible for, actively participate in, or otherwise encourage the creation of a hostile work environment. Civil liability may also arise when first-line supervisors ignore open harassment, fail to assist subordinates who are seeking a remedy, or otherwise attempt to subvert a remedy (IACP National Law Enforcement Policy Center, 1991).

Sergeants are key players in the ongoing battle against sexual harassment in police work. No police department can maintain a workplace that is free of harassment without the cooperation and support of its first-line supervisors. Apathetic, hostile, or openly chauvinistic supervisors can quickly subvert an otherwise effective antiharassment policy due to their actions or inactions regarding that particular policy. On the other hand, supportive and proactive supervisors are in a strategic position to assist other police managers identify, stop, and prevent sexual harassment.

According to the IACP Policy Center, supervisors play a unique role in preventing as well as dealing with sexual harassment:

1. Supervisors, based on their own actions and words, function as role models for their subordinates. They help to set the moral tone. Consequently, they must never initiate or participate in sexual harassment. On the contrary, supervisors must be prepared to stop the behavior of others that can be perceived as harassment and to take immediate steps to prevent further occurrences. Even the tacit acceptance of sexually inappropriate behavior on the part of employees sends the message that sexual harassment will be tolerated regardless of formal department policy.

2. Supervisors have an affirmative duty to deal effectively with and to report all known or reported cases of sexual harassment to the unit responsible for investigating employee misconduct. Failure to take appropriate action or failure to report incidents of harassment as required by department policy is normally grounds for disciplinary action. This is essential if management wants to ensure the integrity of the antiharassment effort at all levels of the process.

3. Each supervisor has a responsibility to reinforce the department's antiharassment training and behavior modification efforts by actively counseling subordinates on the topic of sexual harassment in the workplace. Supervisors must make themselves accessible to victims and ensure that their complaints will be handled in a proactive, yet discreet and confidential manner. In situations in which allegations of sexual harassment have been lodged, confirmed, and resolved, the supervisor

should continue to interact with the parties in order to ensure that the offensive behavior does not resume. The supervisor should also work with the victim to find ways of making the workplace more comfortable for all of the parties concerned.

Once again, these are awesome responsibilities that have been thrust upon first-line supervisors in the ever-changing social and cultural environment of modern police work. Being a successful police supervisor in the twenty-first century requires more commitment, knowledge, and human skills than it has at any time in our history.

Supervising Gay and Lesbian Police Officers

A great deal has been written about the police subculture. It has been described as male-dominated, isolationist, elitist, and authoritarian. Primarily a workplace phenomenon, the police subculture is the sum of the beliefs, values, and norms shared by those within the law enforcement organization that both formally and informally communicates what is expected from members of the work group (Bennett and Hess, 2001).

While the police subculture has traditionally been homophobic, this situation is changing rather rapidly in some areas of the country and more slowly in others. Change, however, is the rule rather than the exception in regard to sexual diversity in the workforce.

Many police departments have tacitly adopted a "don't ask, don't tell" philosophy regarding the sexual preferences of applicants and employees. Others actively recruit gay and lesbian police officers. These agencies do all they can to create a positive workplace culture and hospitable environment for their homosexual employees. After a statewide study, the California Commission on Peace Officer Standards and Training (1983) singled out the gay community as a "key" pool for recruiting new police officers by police departments trying to bolster their sagging recruitment efforts. On the national level, the International Association of Chiefs of Police (IACP) rescinded its decades-old policy opposing the hiring of homosexual police officers (*Law Enforcement News,* 1990).

It is clear that the barriers blocking the employment as well as effective utilization of gay police officers are slowly but surely coming down (Cherney, 1999). In their role as first-line supervisors, most sergeants will very likely be responsible for supervising either discreet or openly gay police personnel at some point in their careers. It is incumbent upon management to help them prepare for this task. It is also up to individual first-line supervisors to prepare themselves.

Interviews with dozens of police officers and gay advocates indicate that the New York Police Department is successfully integrating gay and lesbian officers into virtually every policing function. According to one openly gay supervisor, "We are everywhere." In fact, the city's Gay Officers Action

League (GOAL) claims to have a membership of nearly 800 police officers. GOAL recently opened chapters in Denver; Springfield, Massachusetts; San Francisco; Seattle; Chicago; and Marlboro, Maryland. It also has affiliates in London and Amsterdam (Blumenthal, 1993). Additionally, Law Enforcement Gays and Lesbians International (LEGAL) has membership worldwide.

While no one should underestimate the homophobic hostility that remains in police work, change is on the horizon. First-line supervisors are in a position to help facilitate a meaningful change in human relations by embracing diversity rather than opposing it.

As supervisors, ranking officers must be open and accepting when it comes to gay personnel. While homosexual officers may have a radically different lifestyle, they are nonetheless human beings with distinctly human aspirations for a personally rewarding and successful career in their chosen field. Empathy is the key to understanding and using the talents of these individuals. The supervisor's strategy for dealing with homosexual employees must conform to the OUCH test, in that his or her actions regarding gay subordinates must be objective, uniform in application, consistently applied, and have specific job relatedness.

As leaders who set the ethical tone for their subordinates, supervisors have a professional obligation to act as role models for other police personnel. As part of the management team, they have an affirmative responsibility to assist top management in facilitating meaningful change within the organization. These are critically important as well as awesome responsibilities that go with the turf.

A subcultural transformation like the employment of gay and lesbian police officers requires changes in the hearts and minds of heterosexual personnel. This means that those in management and first-line supervisory positions have to live the new culture and become the embodiment of it. They also must have their antennae up so that they can identify and reinforce other people whose behavior exemplifies the new values and norms they wish to inculcate in members of the workforce.

In order to achieve these objectives, managers and supervisors need to adopt a viable personal strategy for facilitating changes in the workplace culture. The key elements in such a strategy are as follows:

1. Supervisors must really understand the old culture. They cannot chart a new course until they know exactly where they are at the present time.

2. Supervisors should familiarize themselves with the new culture and hold it up as an example from which others can learn. A genuine commitment is an essential element in the acceptance process.

3. Supervisors should encourage police officers who are willing to discard the old culture and adopt the new one. Reinforcement is the key if new behaviors are to be adopted, internalized, and retained by members of the work group.

4. Supervisors should not attack the tenets of the old culture head-on. As leaders, they should allow their subordinates to find new cultural perspectives for themselves and have faith that substantive change will follow.

5. Supervisors should not count on vision to work miracles. At best, vision acts only as a guiding principle for meaningful cultural change.

6. Supervisors should understand that they are in for the long haul. It takes anywhere from five to 10 years for substantive cultural change to become institutionalized.

7. Supervisors must learn to live the culture they advocate. As always, actions speak much louder than words (Dumaine, 1990).

Supervisors are change agents. Based on their rank and authority within the police department, they are also culture carriers. Without their commitment and support, both substantive and durable change will be very difficult to achieve. By becoming proactive, they can help chart a new, more open, and accepting course for the police subculture.

Managing a More Educated Workforce

Police supervisors are being called upon to manage an increasingly more educated workforce. The educational level of American police officers has risen significantly over the past 20 years. While the vast majority of police agencies require only a high school diploma, about 60 percent of all sworn officers have more than two years of college education (Carter et al., 1989; Fulton, 1999). This represents a dramatic departure from the past, when a high school education was considered sufficient preparation for a career in law enforcement.

Based on a comprehensive study commissioned by the Police Executive Research Forum (PERF), researchers were able to identify what they consider to be the advantages of a college education. College-educated men and women tend to have:

1. Greater knowledge of procedures, functions, and principles related to their present and future assignments.

2. Better understanding of their professional role and its importance in the criminal justice system and in society at large.

3. More desirable psychological makeup (including alertness, empathy, flexibility, initiative, and intelligence).

4. Greater interpersonal skills—focusing on the ability to communicate, to respond to the needs of others, and to exercise compassionate leadership.

5. Greater ability to analyze situations, exercise discretion, and resolve problems through appropriate decision making.

6. Stronger moral character, as reflected in a sense of conscience and qualities such as honesty, reliability, and tolerance.

7. More desirable system of personal values that is consistent with police work in a democratic society (Sapp and Carter, 1992).

On the downside, college-educated police officers seem to experience more stress than their less-educated colleagues. This is due, in part, to the animosity demonstrated by "street-wise" police officers, the unrealistic expectations of family and friends, misconceptions about advancement on the job, lack of input into policy formulation and decision making, and boredom (Swanson et al., 1993). According to Molden (1999), police administrators report that college-educated police officers are more likely to question orders, request more frequent reassignment, have lower morale and more absenteeism, and become more easily frustrated by bureaucratic procedures. Stress-induced productivity problems and high turnover rates are not uncommon. However, the advantages of advanced education appear to outweigh the disadvantages. PERF has recommended that by 2003 all entry-level law enforcement officers have completed a four-year degree (Molden, 1999).

First-line supervisors are granted the power to perform specific tasks in concert with and through the efforts of others. In order to work more collaboratively with their subordinates (especially college-educated men and women), sergeants must cast aside the traditional "overseer" mentality common in police work and accept the fact that their job is no longer one of supervision per se, but one of sharing power and providing leadership.

The supervisor who chooses to share power with subordinates automatically expands his or her influence as a leader. By empowering others, the supervisor is in a much better position to accomplish assigned tasks. Delegation is the sharing of power. The sharing of power, coupled with meaningful participation in the decision-making process, leads to empowerment. Empowerment means that employees experience ownership in their job and accept 100 percent of the responsibility for doing it right. For all practical purposes, effective supervision is effective delegation (Whisenand and Rush, 2001).

Effective delegation does not just happen. It takes a great deal of thought and preparation. As Whisenand and Rush point out:

1. Recipients of the delegation must be well trained to perform their job.

2. Training must be relevant, reliable, and ongoing.

3. Supervisors should set high performance standards for themselves as well as for their subordinates.

4. Supervisors should understand the needs and values of each of their employees.

5. There must be pertinent, open, and frank communication between supervisors and their subordinates.

6. Those who fulfill their delegated responsibilities at an acceptable level should be rewarded.

7. Those who do not perform their delegated responsibilities at an acceptable level should be reprimanded.

8. There must be meaningful feedback systems in place to ensure the success of the delegation process.

The success or failure of this empowerment strategy will depend on the commitment and human skills possessed by those seeking to implement it.

Four parties benefit from increased employee participation and effective delegation power—the community, the police department, first-line supervisors, and employees (Whisenand and Rush, 2001).

The local community benefits from the empowerment process. Empowered employees are ordinarily more skillful and dedicated to their job. Consequently, they tend to provide better and less costly police services. Better individual performance is likely to generate more respect and community support for the police department.

The police department benefits from the empowerment process. Employee participation, input into the decision-making process, and acceptance of responsibility create an environment in which everyone is encouraged to pursue excellence. This strengthens the organization as it seeks to accomplish its mission, goals, and objectives.

Supervisors benefit from the empowerment process. Supervisors benefit in that they are:

1. Instilling a commitment for getting the job done.

2. Strengthening mutual trust between themselves and their subordinates.

3. Enhancing their officers' knowledge and job skills.

4. Encouraging and reinforcing the feeling of job ownership.

5. Utilizing the power of leadership to provide quality police services through the efforts of their employees.

By empowering subordinates, supervisors empower themselves as effective leaders. Rank-and-file police officers benefit from the empowerment process. Empowerment and its accompanying collegial status benefit employees in that they become much more:

1. Positive in terms of commitment to their work.

2. Trusting, trustworthy, and openly participatory.

3. Self-confident.

4. Competent.

5. Professional in their orientation.

6. Capable of working alone or with others to perform top-notch police work.

The empowerment of police personnel is essential if governments are to attract, field, and retain college-educated officers.

Empowerment substitutes self-supervision for traditional organizational control mechanisms. An empowered organization is one in which individual police officers have the knowledge, skill, desire, and opportunity to personally succeed in a way that leads to collective organizational success. Helpful systems and structures, win-win situations, self-supervision, and personal accountability are at the heart of the empowerment process (Covey, 1992).

Once again, sergeants are the key players in the empowerment process. In order to succeed in this role, they must truly believe that people are their greatest asset. They must be trusting and willing to take risks by delegating power to individual police officers while holding them and themselves accountable. Sergeants must be prepared to accept the mantle of leadership as they consciously reject the supervisor's traditional role as an overseer of "employees" in the workplace.

Training for the New Supervisor

As noted earlier, as first-line supervisors, sergeants are in a strategic position to determine whether equal employment opportunity becomes a reality or remains a figment of our collective imagination. Even if they are committed to fairness and decency, sergeants cannot learn the information and human skills they need to play their staff development role through osmosis. Whether they are traditional or nontraditional employees, sergeants must be trained for their new duties. They should also be given the opportunity to apply supervisory theory to real-life situations as part of an extended training process. Once they are on the job, new sergeants should be evaluated for competency and coached by a certified trainer. Without extensive supervisory training and on-the-job coaching, there is little chance that new police sergeants will be able to cope with the human relations challenges of the twenty-first century. The California Commission on Peace Officer Standards and Training (1996) has developed an extensive supervisor development course of study consisting of 16 areas of competency for general supervision (see Figure 13.8). Within each compentency area there are skills or knowledge areas that the student trainer must master before moving to the next skill or knowledge area. For example, Figure 13.9 depicts competency area number 5.0 (Employee Relations) with seven subareas of skills and knowledge areas that must be evaluated by a supervisor trainer.

Figure 13.7
General Supervision Competency Areas

1.0 ROLE IDENTIFICATION

a. Management's expectations
b. Subordinate's expectations
c. First-line supervisor's role
d. External expectations (i.e., community, media, family)
e. Results-oriented approach to job (i.e., human relations skills)
f. Peer expectations

2.0 VALUES, ETHICS, AND PRINCIPLES

a. Definitions
b. Different value systems
c. Commitment to ethics, values, and principles
d. Supervisor's role/responsibilities
e. Applying ethics and integrity to decision making
f. Ethical resources

3.0 COMMUNICATION

a. Verbal and nonverbal communication skills
b. Benefits of active listening
c. Communication skills in conflict resolution
d. Rumor control responsibilities
e. Must develop good public speaking skills
f. Understands effective communications techniques when dealing with the media
g. Understands agency's policy on dissemination of information

4.0 LEADERSHIP

a. What is a leader?
b. Difference between leaders and managers
c. Characteristics of effective leader
d. What motivates others
e. Show respect for subordinates
f. Demonstrate responsibility for subordinates
g. Maintain productive and positive relations
h. Recognize and reward good performance
i. Identify poor performance and take appropriate steps
j. Properly delegate work to subordinates
k. Resolve issues/problems through negotiations
l. Apply proactive leadership

5.0 EMPLOYEE RELATIONS

a. Employee bargaining agreements
b. Agency's affirmative action policy and program
c. Agency's sexual harassment policy and program
d. EEOC/FEPC guidelines and how they apply to the agency
e. Applicable laws

Figure 13.7, *continued*

f.   Supervisor's role in conflict resolution
g.   Grievance process and supervisor's role in handling and resolving grievances

6.0 STRESS

a.   The fight-or-flight syndrome
b.   Recognize the signs of stress
c.   Practice stress management techniques
d.   Referral policy and procedure for the agency

7.0 COUNSELING

a.   Types of counseling sessions
b.   Goals of counseling session
c.   Preparation for counseling session
d.   Examples of special counseling issues
e.   Examples of barriers to successful counseling
f.   Examples of contemporary counseling issues
g.   Documentation

8.0 EMPLOYEE PERFORMANCE APPRAISAL

a.   Agency's performance appraisal policy and procedures
b.   Reasons for evaluation
c.   Performance/accountability
d.   Agency's acceptable standards of performance
e.   Common problems and errors of supervisors
f.   Common problems with appraisals
g.   Sources of information on performance
h.   Preparation for evaluation
i.   Presentation of evaluation to employee
j.   Follow-up on performance deficiencies

9.0 LIABILITY ISSUES

a.   Issues and agency policies
b.   Potential liability to the supervisor

10.0 DISCIPLINE

a.   Agency's process to ensure that performance standards are adhered to by its members
b.   Factors that may contribute to misconduct
c.   Supervisor's actions (legal, reasonable, consistent, appropriate, timely)
d.   Supervisor's role in the disciplinary process
e.   Agency's policies and procedures related to investigations
f.   Recognition of substandard, standard, and exceptional job performance
g.   Application of: Peace Officer Bill of Rights, MOU/MOA, other Constitutional Protections
h.   Civil ramifications of violating subordinate's rights
i.   Due process and Skelly Conference procedures
j.   Legal parameters related to administrative records and files

Figure 13.7, *continued*

11.0 ADMINISTRATIVE SUPPORT

a. Use of statistical data (i.e., deployment of personnel, crime trends, employee productivity)
b. Fiscal issues related to agency operation
c. Supervisor's role in fiscal management
d. Agency's protocol for completed staff work assignments
e. Audits and controls
f. Personnel deployment and scheduling

12.0 PLANNING AND ORGANIZING

a. What is planning?
b. What is organizing?
c. Planning and organizing are routinely done by everyone
d. Benefits of planning and organizing
e. Hurdles to planning and organizing
f. Understands the planning process (scientific model)

13.0 TRAINING

a. Training is a primary responsibility
b. Importance of initial and ongoing training
c. Techniques of instruction
d. Supervisor accountability for training received by subordinates
e. Documentation of training provided by the supervisor
f. Safety considerations

14.0 REPORT REVIEW

a. Review and approval of written documents produced by subordinates
b. Some causes of report-writing problems
c. Ethical considerations (i.e., invented probable cause, misreporting of event chronology, misquoting of statements, intentional omissions)

15.0 INVESTIGATIONS

a. Agency investigative policy and procedures related to police shootings, employee injuries, property damage, traffic accidents, use of force, complaints, and internal investigations

16.0 THE TRANSITION

a. Difference between doing the work and getting it done through others
b. Potential problem areas (i.e., supervising friends, problem employees, unreasonable expectations)
c. Personal integrity

Source: Adapted from California Commission on Peace Officer Standards and Training (1996). *Supervisor Development Program and Guide*. Sacramento, CA: California POST.

Figure 13.8
General Supervision—Employee Relations

SUPERVISOR DEVELOPMENT GUIDE
GENERAL SUPERVISION

5.0 EMPLOYEE RELATIONS

The student supervisor will understand the supervisor's roles and responsibilities related to employer-employee relationships within the workplace.

❑ A. EMPLOYEE BARGAINING AGREEMENTS
Both sworn and non-sworn personnel

❑ B. AGENCY'S AFFIRMATIVE ACTION POLICY AND PROGRAM

❑ C. AGENCY'S SEXUAL HARASSMENT POLICY AND PROGRAM

❑ D. EEOC/FEPC GUIDELINES AND HOW THEY APPLY TO THE AGENCY

❑ E. APPLICABLE LAWS
Brown Act (54950 CGC)
Meyers-Mileas-Brown Act (3500 CGC)
Ralph C. Dills Act (3512 CGC)
Fair Labor Standards Act (*Garcia v. San Antonio*)
Local ordinances

❑ F. SUPERVISOR'S ROLE IN CONFLICT RESOLUTION
Loyalty: must support department and policy

❑ G. GRIEVANCE PROCESS AND SUPERVISOR'S ROLE IN HANDLING
AND RESOLVING GRIEVANCES

I have explained and/or demonstrated the above critical tasks and feel that my student supervisor can perform these tasks in a competent manner.

Trainer _____ Date _____

The above tasks have been explained and/or demonstrated to me and I feel I can perform these tasks in a competent manner.

Student Supervisor _____ Date _____

Check box indicates task has been completed

Source: California Commission on Peace Officer Standards and Training (1996). *Supervisor Development Program and Guide*. Sacramento, CA: California POST.

Municipal governments are reluctant to spend money on supervisory training. Part of the problem is that training itself has taken a backseat to economic reality. Many police departments now receive minimum budgetary allocations. The abandonment of training for economic reasons borders on the absurd and will cost much more in the long run. Without adequate supervisory training, police departments run the risk of more vicarious liability suits and face potentially disruptive behavior by nontraditional employees in response to inadequate supervision. Proactive police managers know that the only way to guard against these problems is to strengthen the rank of sergeant through selective promotion, upgraded supervisory training, and unequivocal support.

Summary

Police work traditionally has been dominated by white males. It was, in many ways, an extension of the white power structure and represented a clannish "old boy" network. Nontraditional employees (women, African-Americans, Hispanics, and other recognized minorities) were kept out of police work through blatant de jure and more subtle de facto discrimination. The prejudice, stereotyping, and scapegoating so common in American society at large permeated nearly every aspect of law enforcement. Racism, sexism, and other forms of bigotry were endemic to the infrastructure of the police culture.

The 1964 Civil Rights Act was landmark legislation. It outlawed discrimination based on race, religion, sex, and national origin. Title VII prohibited discrimination in the workplace. The Equal Employment Opportunity Act of 1972 extended the coverage of the Civil Rights Act to municipal government and police departments. In an effort to curb prejudice and remedy past discrimination, the Equal Employment Opportunity Commission formulated affirmative action guidelines. These guidelines (which were often converted into quotas by bureaucrats and the courts) opened up police work for nontraditional employees. Initial emphasis was placed on making police recruitment, screening, and selection procedures nondiscriminatory. Additional federal and state EEO/AA guidelines have been designed to prevent discrimination in assigning, disciplining, and promoting members of various protected classes.

As a result of these EEO/AA initiatives, African-Americans, Hispanics, and women have been entering the workforce in far larger numbers. Consequently, it is much more likely that police sergeants will come into contact with and be in a position to supervise minority employees. Sergeants must adjust to a new role and different expectations. They must be objective and fair with those in protected classes; proactive in deterring the sexual harassment of female, gay, and lesbian officers; and nondefensive when it comes to empowering educated workers. As developers of the police department's human resources, they serve as mentors, coaches, trainers, and positive role models. They act as coordinators rather than overseers. If they are to deal effectively with the emerging multicultural workforce, sergeants must come to grips with their prejudices. They must be able to develop open, honest, and empathetic relationships. Good sergeants strive to be helpful, firm, fair, and impartial. They have a healthy respect for both individual and cultural differences. Depending on their sensitivity, talent, knowledge, human skills, and commitment to equal opportunity, sergeants will determine whether EEO/AA is fact or palatable fiction.

Case Study

Sergeant Craig Frye

Sergeant Craig Frye is a supervisory sergeant in patrol for the Allendale Police Department. Allendale is a large metropolitan city on the West Coast. Sergeant Frye is well respected among his subordinates and peers alike. He has always tried to maintain professionalism, fairness, and consideration with his subordinates. Sergeant Frye has nine officers under his direct supervision. Most of them have been under his supervision since they began their careers with the police department. All nine of his officers receive good evaluations and work well together. However, the newest member on his shift, officer Tom Davis, has met with some opposition from the other officers.

Davis joined the force last year and completed his probationary period with high evaluations and a good record. Davis is 32 years old, has never been married, and has no children. Davis never talks about his personal life, even with the other officers. He doesn't go out with the other officers while off duty and he has never been known to date or have a girlfriend. The other officers used to kid him about not having a girlfriend, and some of the officers even tried to set him up with dates, but Davis never took them up on the offers. About two months ago, an officer in another precinct saw Davis at a shopping center. The other officer was moonlighting in security for the store and noticed Davis walking, hand in hand, with another man in the store. The security video camera caught Davis kissing the other man. Word got out quickly, and Davis has been shunned by most of the other officers on the shift.

Sergeant Frye knows that Officer Davis has been ridiculed and intimidated by the other officers on the shift. But Sergeant Frye has always tried to stay out of officers' personal lives unless it began to affect their duties. This time, Sergeant Frye is afraid that Officer Davis might be injured on duty. Sergeant Frye begins to take note of calls for back-up and Officer Davis's location on calls.

Officer Tim Shell has asked to meet with Sergeant Frye in his office. Officer Shell, one of Sergeant Frye's subordinates, explains that Officer Davis made a sexual advance toward him and has been sexually harassing him as well as others on the shift. Two other officers under Sergeant Frye's supervision come forward and corroborate Officer Shell's accusations. Sergeant Frye seems to think the entire shift is conspiring to have Officer Davis removed or transferred.

If you were Sergeant Frye, what kinds of evidence would you collect to either support or nullify the officers' accusations? If the accusations were true, would this be a true sexual harassment case? Why or why not? How would you deal with your subordinates if you found they were conspiring to have Davis removed and had falsely accused him?

Key Concepts

affirmative action
bona fide occupational qualification
changing demographics
Civil Rights Act of 1964
competent and supportive supervisors
dealing with sexual harassment
discrimination
Equal Employment Opportunity Act
first-line supervisor's role
managing a more educated workforce

nondiscriminatory selection process
nondiscriminatory supervisors
the OUCH test applied to supervision
prejudice
protected classes
sexual diversity in the workforce
strategies for supervising minorities
supervising nontraditional employees
training supervisors to do their job
white male domination of police work

Discussion Topics and Questions

1. Policing has been dominated by white males from the working class. Why have the police been reluctant to accept African-Americans, Hispanics, women, and other nontraditional employees? Should police managers try to build a more representative workforce?

2. What is prejudice? How is it related to discrimination? Explain the difference between de jure and de facto discrimination. Give several examples.

3. EEO/AA initiatives are based on two separate federal laws. Identify them. Why did affirmative action (goals, timetables, and action plans) degenerate into a not-so-subtle form of reverse discrimination? How has the Supreme Court reacted to this issue?

4. Federal law and court decisions require that the employee selection process be nondiscriminatory. What criteria are used to determine whether the process is discriminatory? Are the criteria reasonable?

5. What is empathy? Why is empathy so important in forming positive supervisor-subordinate relationships?

6. What characteristics or traits do good supervisors have that help bridge the cultural gap between them and their nontraditional employees?

7. List at least seven things that a supervisor can do to enhance relationships with minority employees. Will these strategies work with white males? Is there any real difference?

8. What constitutes a protected class in terms of civil rights legislation? Discuss the OUCH test. What are the practical advantages of adopting this particular strategy?

9. Define *sexual harassment*. Differentiate between the two types of sexual harassment. What is the first-line supervisor's role in preventing as well as dealing with sexual harassment?

10. What is homophobia? Why is sexual preference becoming less of an issue in the hiring and retention of police personnel?

For Further Reading

Iannone, Nathan F., and Marvin Iannone (2001). *Supervision of Police Personnel*, Sixth Edition. Englewood Cliffs, NJ: Prentice-Hall, Inc.

Discusses the development of women as first-line supervisors. The author emphasizes that their effectiveness, like that of their male counterparts, will depend on whether they possess characteristics that leaders must have and how well they apply the principles of leadership within the police department.

Martin, Susan E. (1989). "A Report on the Status of Women in Policing." *Police Foundation Reports*, May.

Comprehensive examination of the status of women in American law enforcement. It explores the positive gains made by females and highlights some of the remaining problems.

Steinmetz, Lawrence L., and H. Ralph Todd (1986). *First-Line Management*. Plano, TX: Business Publications, Inc.

Explores the legal, social, and ethical responsibilities of all first-line supervisors in relation to their subordinates. The authors stress the need for open and honest interaction.

Swanson, Charles R., Leonard Territo, and Robert W. Taylor (1993). *Police Administration*, Third Edition. New York, NY: Macmillan Publishing Co.

An excellent review of contemporary human relations within police organizations. The text elaborates on the needs of many nontraditional police personnel.

References

Bennett, Wayne W., and Kären M. Hess (2001). *Management and Supervision in Law Enforcement*, Third Edition. St. Paul, MN: West Publishing Company.

Blumenthal, Ralph (1993). "Gay, Lesbian Cops Gaining Acceptance in New York." *The Denver Post,* March 7:33A.

Broderick, John J. (1987). *Police in a Time of Change*, Second Edition. Prospect Heights, IL: Waveland Press, Inc.

Brown, Jennifer, and Frances Heidensohn (2000). *Gender and Policing: Comparative Perspectives*. New York, NY: Macmillan.

CALEA (2001). *Standards for Law Enforcement Agencies*. Fairfax, VA: Commission on Accreditation for Law Enforcement Agencies, Inc.

California Commission on Peace Officer Standards and Training (1983). *Supervisory Training Guide*. North Highlands, CA: California POST.

——— (1996). *Supervisor Development Program and Guide*. Sacramento, CA: California POST.

Carter, David L., Allen D. Sapp, and Darrel W. Stephens (1989). *The State of Police Education: Policy Direction for the Twenty-First Century*. Washington, DC: Police Executive Research Forum.

Cherney, A. (1999). "Gay and Lesbian Issues in Policing." *Current Issues in Criminal Justice*, Vol. 11, No. 1.

Civil Rights Act of 1964. Title VII. 42 United States Code § 2000e-2(a)(1).

Cole, George F., Marc Gertz, and Amy Bunger (2002). *Criminal Justice System: Politics and Policies*, Eighth Edition. Boston, MA: Wadsworth Publishing Co.

Covey, Stephen R. (1992). *Principle-Centered Leadership*. New York, NY: Simon and Schuster, Inc.

Daum, James M. and Cindy M. Johns (1994). "Police Work from a Woman's Perspective." *The Police Chief*, Vol. LXI, No. 9.

Dumaine, Brian (1990). "Creating a New Company Culture." *Fortune*, Vol. 121, No. 1.

Equal Employment Opportunity Coordinating Council (1973). "Federal Policy on Remedies Concerning Equal Employment Opportunity in State and Local Government Personnel Systems." Washington, DC: U.S. Government Printing Office.

Fulmer, Robert M. and Stephen G. Franklin (1982). *Supervision*. New York, NY: Macmillan Publishing Co.

Fulton, R. (1999). "Do Supervisors Need Degrees?" *Law Enforcement Technology*, Vol. 26, No. 3.

Griggs v. Duke Power Co., 401 U.S. 431 (1971).

Heckeroth, Steven E., and Andrew M. Barker (1997). "Police Departments Efforts to Deter Sexual Harassment." *USA Today* (July):A2.

Hilgert, Raymond L., and E. Leonard (2001). *Supervision: Concepts and Practices of Management,* Eighth Edition. Cincinnati, OH: South-Western Publishing Company.

Holden, Richard N. (1994). *Modern Police Management*, Second Edition. Englewood Cliffs, NJ: Prentice-Hall, Inc.

IACP National Law Enforcement Policy Center (1991). "Harassment in the Workplace: A Proactive Approach." *The Police Chief*, Vol. LVIII, No. 12.

Johns, Gary (1988). *Organizational Behavior: Understanding Life at Work*, Second Edition. Glenview, IL: Scott, Foresman and Company.

Johnson, Lawrence A. (1969). *Employing the Hard-Core Unemployed*. New York, NY: American Management Association.

Law Enforcement News (1990). "LAPD Gays' Hope: Mainstream Acceptance." Vol. XVII, No. 321.

Leonard, V.A., and Harry W. More (1993). *Police Organization and Management*, Eighth Edition. Westbury, NY: The Foundation Press.

Longenecker, Justin G., and Charles D. Pringle (1984). *Management*. Columbus, OH: Charles E. Merrill Publishing Co.

Martin, Randy (1987). *Personnel and Supervision in Criminal Justice*. Indiana, PA: Kinko Professor Publishing.

Molden, Jeffrey (1999). "College Degrees for Police Applicants." *Law and Order*, Vol. 47, No. 1.

NAACP v. Allen, 340 F. Supp. 703 (M.D. Ala. 1972).

Plunkett, W. Richard (1992). *Supervision: The Direction of People at Work*, Sixth Edition. Boston, MA: Allyn and Bacon, Inc.

Richmond v. Croson Co., 109 S. Ct. 706 (1989).

Sapp, Allen D., and David L. Carter (1992). "Should All Policemen Be College Trained?" *The Police Chief*, Vol. 38, No. 12.

Sass, T., and J. Troyer (1999). "Affirmative Action, Political Representation, Unions, and Female Police Employment." *Journal of Labor Research*, Vol. 20, No. 4.

Sauls, John (1995). "Proving Business Necessity: The Disparate Impact Challenge." *FBI Law Enforcement Bulletin*, Vol. 64, No. 4.

Schroeder, Timothy (1996). "Avoiding and Defending Employment Discrimination Charges." *Police Law Journal* (February).

Stahl, O. Glenn (1983). *Public Personnel Administration*. New York, NY: Harper and Row.

Swank, Calvin J., and James A. Conser (1983). *The Police Personnel System*. New York, NY: John Wiley & Sons, Inc.

Swanson, Charles R., Leonard Territo, and Robert W. Taylor (1993). *Police Administration: Structures, Processes and Behavior*, Third Edition. New York, NY: Macmillan Publishing Co.

Territo, Leonard, and Harold J. Vetter (1981). *Stress and Police Personnel*. Boston, MA: Allyn and Bacon, Inc.

Thibault, Edward A., Lawrence M. Lynch, and R. Bruce McBride (1998). *Proactive Police Management,* Fourth Edition. Englewood Cliffs, NJ: Prentice-Hall, Inc.

Thomann, Daniel A., and Tina M. Serritella (1994). "Preventing Sexual Harassment in Law Enforcement Agencies." *The Police Chief*, Vol. LXI, No. 9.

Thomann, Daniel A., David E. Strickland, and Jane L. Gibbons (1989). "An Organizational Development Approach to Preventing Sexual Harassment: Developing Shared Commitment Through Awareness Training." *College and University Personnel Association Journal*, Vol. 40, No. 1.

Turner, William W. (1968). *The Police Establishment*. New York, NY: G.P. Putnam's Sons.

U.S. Census Bureau (2001). *Resident Population Estimates of the United States by Sex, Race and Hispanic Origin*. Washington, DC: U.S. Census Bureau.

U.S. Department of Justice (2000). *Local Police Departments, 1997*. Washington, DC: Bureau of Justice Statistics.

U.S. Department of Justice, Federal Bureau of Investigation (2000). *Crime in the United States, 1999*. Washington, DC: U.S. Government Printing Office.

U.S. Merit Systems Protection Board (1987). *Sexual Harassment of Federal Workers: An Update*. Washington DC: U.S. Government Printing Office.

Walker, Samuel (1999). *The Police in America*, Third Edition. New York, NY: McGraw-Hill Book Company.

Whisenand, Paul M. and George E. Rush (2001). *Supervising Police Personnel*, Fourth Edition. Englewood Cliffs, NJ: Prentice-Hall, Inc.

Zastrow, Charles (2000). *Social Problems*, Fifth Edition. Stamford, CT: Wadsworth.

Police Training—

An Investment in Human Resources

14

Introductory Case Study

Sergeant Joyce Lockhart

Sergeant Joyce Lockhart is a seven-year veteran of the Middleton Police Department and was recently assigned to the police training office. She is excited about her new assignment and is looking forward to developing in-service training modules for the department. Sergeant Lockhart took over the training coordinator's position when Lieutenant Jeff Hamby retired a few months ago.

Although new on the job, Sergeant Lockhart has learned much and just recently signed up to take a college course in developing training programs. Her instructor, Dr. Joe Ottomeyer, has been very helpful in steering her in the proper direction for information directly related to police training development.

Last week, the district attorney general called Sergeant Lockhart to discuss a training issue he felt was important. Apparently, many of the Middleton officers are losing cases because of poor courtroom demeanor, lack of proper evidence, poor reports and documentation, and poor preparation. The district attorney thinks that officers need some specialized in-service training on how to present a case in court. He believes such training would increase the officers' conviction rates, especially in DUI and drug cases. Sergeant Lockhart agreed that this was an area that needed attention in the training office and said she would put it on the agenda.

Sergeant Lockhart decided to get some advice from her professor and called Dr. Ottomeyer. Dr. Ottomeyer asked her what she expected the officers to gain from the training in a way that was measurable. He also asked her what type of instruction the officers would have, what motivation they would have to take the training, and how she would measure the outcome of the training. It became obvious to Sergeant Lockhart that she had a lot of work to do to prepare such an in-service training module.

> *If you were Sergeant Lockhart, how would you conceptualize, develop, and imple-ment an effective eight-hour police training module dealing with court presenta-tion? Use a management-by-objectives approach. Make a flowchart that depicts what needs to be done, the activities required to accomplish these tasks, the instructional methods to be used, and the time frames for completing each task. In addition, how would you measure the effectiveness of the training?*

Sir Robert Peel has long been recognized as one of the greatest reform-ers in modern police history. He was the principal architect of the Metro-politan Police Act of 1829. This new law created Scotland Yard and empha-sized the need for and importance of professionally oriented police training. The Peelian emphasis on formal training was echoed in this country by August Vollmer and other progressives in the International Association of Chiefs of Police (IACP). The City of New York initiated formal police training in 1897. Chief Vollmer established a training school for Berkeley, California, police officers in 1908. By 1930 nearly one dozen departments were operating large-scale police academies (Fogelson, 1977).

The motivating force behind the training movement was the perceived need to reform the police establishment. Reform-minded police adminis-trators believed that training would help to:

1. Offset the adverse effects of partisan politics on police work.

2. Make police personnel much more efficient, effective, and productive.

3. Bring recognition, higher wages, and professional status to municipal police officers.

4. Prevent injustices caused by incompetent or negligent police officers.

5. Generate confidence in and financial support for police activities through improved police service.

The scope of the training was limited to the essentials, and quality control presented a nearly insurmountable managerial challenge.

While the merits of formal police training were self-evident, it was slow to develop in the United States. The Wickersham Commission (1931) found that only 20 percent of the 383 cities it surveyed provided any type of recruit training. In-service training was all but nonexistent. The commission called for the establishment of mandatory minimum police training standards. The call for job-related recruit and in-service training was reiterated by the President's Commission on Law Enforcement and the Administration of Jus-tice (1967), the National Advisory Commission on Civil Disorders (1968), the Commission on the Causes and Prevention of Violence (1969), the American Bar Association Project on Standards for Criminal Justice (1972), and the National Advisory Commission on Criminal Justice Standards and Goals (1973). California and New York became the first states to enact police officer standards and training (POST) legislation in 1959. By 1968 31 states had enacted similar laws. According to Cal Swank and James Conser (1983), the quality of the legislation varied. Some statutes dealt with both in-service and recruit training. Others were far less comprehensive. Compliance was often voluntary rather than mandatory. Public interest was at times sacrificed for expediency.

By 1988 all states had adopted either voluntary or mandatory minimum training standards for newly hired police personnel. The number of hours required for recruit training varies from state to state but generally averages about 395 classroom hours and 204 hours of field training. For a variety of reasons, some states still do not require recruit training before deployment in the field. The Commonwealth of Pennsylvania, for example, currently mandates and pays for 520 hours of basic training for all municipal police personnel. Until recently, newly hired police officers were allowed to work for up to one year without the training (53 P.S. [740-749, 1974]). This legislation has been changed and now requires completion of a basic police training course before deployment.

While a few states have actually reduced the total number of hours required in the basic training curriculum, many have increased them, and in some cases the increase has been rather substantial. California, for example, has included a number of new topics in their basic recruit curriculum over recent years (see Figure 14.1).

State training commissions often tie curriculum revision in with a statutory change regulating the minimum number of mandatory training hours. In the Commonwealth of Pennsylvania, for example, the Municipal Police Officers' Education and Training Commission (based on a comprehensive task analysis) redesigned the training curriculum and increased the number of hours from 480 to 520. The new curriculum was developed by Temple University and is considered by many police trainers to be a model for the rest of the nation.

Police work has become one of the most complex and exacting occupations in contemporary American society. It is a labor-intensive government activity. A police department can best be described as a synergistic collection of human beings organized and equipped to protect and serve the community at large. People are its most valuable resource. The efficiency, effectiveness, and productivity of the police department will depend on exactly how well these people have been trained. Training is the practical and applied side of education, designed to transmit the knowledge, skills, and attitudes needed to improve the employee's problem-solving ability or on-the-job performance in criminal justice organizations.

Figure 14.1
**California Police Academy Training Curriculum Content and
Minimum Hourly Requirements**

Domain Description		Minimum Number of Hours
01	History, Professionalism, and Ethics	8
02	Criminal Justice System	4
03	Community Relations	12
04	Victimology/Crisis Interventions	6
05	Introduction to Criminal Law	6
06	Crimes Against Property	10
07	Crimes Against Persons	10
08	General Crimes Statutes	4
09	Crimes Against Children	6
10	Sex Crimes	6
11	Juvenile Law and Procedure	6
12	Controlled Substances	12
13	ABC (Alcohol, Beverage Code) Law	4
14	Laws of Arrest	12
15	Search and Seizure	12
16	Presentation of Evidence	8
17	Investigative Report Writing	40
18	Vehicle Operations	24
19	Use of Force	12
20	Patrol Techniques	12
21	Vehicle Pullovers	14
22	Crimes in Progress	16
23	Handling Disputes/Crowd Control	12
24	Domestic Violence	8
25	Unusual Occurrences	4
26	Missing Persons	4
27	Traffic Enforcement	22
28	Traffic Accident Investigation	12
29	Preliminary Investigation	42
30	Custody	4
31	Physical Fitness/Officer Stress	40
32	Person Searches/Baton, etc	60
33	First Aid and CPR	21
34	Firearms/Chemical Agents	72
35	Information Systems	4
36	Persons with Disabilities	6
37	Gang Awareness	8
38	Crimes Against the Justice System	4
39	Weapons Violations	4
40	Hazardous Materials	4
41	Cultural Diversity/Discrimination	24
Minimum Instructional Hours		**599**
Types of Testing		**Hours**
Scenario Tests		40
POST-Constructed Knowledge Tests		25
Total Minimum Required Hours		**664**

Source: California Commission on Peace Officer Standards and Training (1996). *Supervisor Development Program and Guide.* Sacramento, CA: California POST.

Selective recruitment, positive discipline, adequate supervision, and effective training shape the department's style of policing and help to ensure the quality of its service. All newly hired police personnel need basic recruit training before they begin work. Veteran officers, on the other hand, need continuous "in-service" training in order to keep up with the constantly changing demands of their jobs and to prepare for new assignments or promotions within the police department. Training must be relevant, job-related, and focused on the realities of police work rather than the myths associated with it. Traditionally, police training has underrepresented order maintenance and the social service aspects of policing, while overrepresenting law enforcement activities. Such an overemphasis on law enforcement activities has contributed to the macho view of policing and the way recruits view their role as police officers. Because the training program is seen as representing the police department's view of police work and mission, an unrealistic training program may not only send the wrong message to recruits, but may also make adjustments in the field more difficult (Roberg, Crank, and Kuykendall, 2000). Training is an ongoing process, not a one-shot activity. New knowledge, new procedures, new equipment, and new jobs make training an absolute necessity in an ever-changing world. Effective training provides the police officer with an anchor of stability in a sea of change. It facilitates adaptability and helps to guard against human obsolescence in the workplace (Mathis and Jackson, 2000; Reaves and Goldberg, 1999).

Relevant and effective training motivates mature police officers to work harder. Employees who really understand their jobs and have the skills needed to handle them are more likely to have high morale. They tend to see a much closer relationship between their own effort and successful performance on the job (Sayles and Strauss, 1981). As a result, they are usually willing to invest more of their time, effort, energy, and talent in activities designed to accomplish the mission, goals, and objectives of the police department. Well-trained police officers are competent and have confidence in themselves. They command respect. Qualified personnel, plus a strong training program, equals effective police work. Training is an investment in human resources and the pathway to police professionalism.

Training, in its many forms, is the one essential tool that is required to create, enhance, and maintain effective police performance (Alpert and Dunham, 1997). The building blocks for a sound law enforcement training program are anchored by two common assumptions: (1) it should incorporate the appropriate mission statement and ethical considerations, and (2) the training should be focused on what an officer actually does on a daily basis (Alpert and Smith, 1990; Roberg, Crank, and Kuykendall, 2000).

While there may be some disagreement with the model, police work can be viewed as an emerging profession. In varying degrees it possesses all of the characteristics normally associated with a profession:

1. **Social Grant of Authority.** Members of the profession have the privilege, authority, or license to practice a specialized occupation.

2. **Autonomy of Practice.** Members of the profession exercise a great deal of discretion in their work and are not subject to criticism by those outside their occupational group.

3. **Systematic Body of Knowledge.** Members of the profession are expected to have special competence, because they have acquired a clearly defined body of knowledge and unique skills through specialized education and training.

4. **Ongoing Education/Training.** Members of the profession have an obligation to continue their education (theory) and to upgrade their skills (through training) in order to meet the needs of clients and the profession.

5. **Self-Regulation.** Members of the profession are expected to govern themselves by setting standards and controlling the entry of newcomers into the occupation.

6. **Code of Ethics.** Members of the profession formulate, internalize, and live by an occupation-specific code of ethics designed to regularize relationships between members and/or clients (see Police Code of Conduct on page 364).

7. **Service Orientation.** Members of the profession are expected to emphasize service to society and, when necessary, to willingly set aside their own personal interests to provide essential services.

There seems to be no clear-cut distinction between professional and nonprofessional occupations. The police appear to be somewhere in the middle of the continuum between fully professional and completely nonprofessional. There is no reason dedicated police officers cannot, given adequate leadership, raise their occupation a few more notches up the scale of professionalism (Stone and DeLuca, 1985). They will need to emphasize selective recruitment, positive discipline, adequate supervision, and effective lifelong training. Formal courses and seminars dealing with such topics as criminal law, violent death investigation, domestic intervention, interpersonal relations, principles of supervision, civil liability, and so forth should be made available to all personnel on a regular basis.

In spite of the fact that training is considered the most important process for ensuring organizational efficiency, effectiveness, and productivity, most police departments spend only about one percent of their budget on training programs. When municipal budgets are frozen or cut, even this meager amount is not safe. The training "line item" is often the first to go. Richard Holden (1994) has argued that the gross underfunding of the training function borders on criminal negligence. No community can expect adequate policing from untrained police officers, regardless of their dedication. Police officers cannot legitimately claim full professional status until they resolve the training dilemma. In an era of deficit spending and cutback management, finding more money and administrative support for training may be an impossible dream.

The police department has a dual and interrelated responsibility to the community it was created to protect and serve and to the members of its workforce. The department has an obligation to develop its personnel to their full potential (Whisenand and Rush, 2001). Well-managed police departments achieve maximum productivity through people. They strive to create in all employees an awareness that their best efforts are essential and that if they make a meaningful contribution, they will share in the rewards of success (Peters and Waterman, 1982).

The remainder of this chapter will discuss the mechanics of police training. The first section is for general information. It will explore the function and structure of formal preemployment, preservice, and in-service training programs. The second section will analyze the sergeant's role as a counselor, coach, and trainer. The third section will focus on the training needs of sergeants and other supervisory personnel.

Formal Police Training Programs

Until quite recently, professional police trainers could describe their world in fairly simple terms. There were two types of training: (1) recruit training and (2) in-service training. Recruit training was designed for newly sworn police personnel who, having met all the minimum qualifications for appointment, were commissioned as police officers, contingent upon the successful completion of a rigorous (pre-service) basic police training program. In-service training, on the other hand, focused almost exclusively on the occupational and professional development of certified police officers through various specialized job-related training programs. Things have been changing, however, and a new term must now be added to the lexicon of the police trainer—preparatory preemployment police training.

Preparatory preemployment police training is gaining popularity in many areas of the country. This term is used to describe an alternative approach to basic training. It is based on a proprietary vocational education model, in which a civilian trainee pays tuition and fees to cover the cost of training in an attempt to access a career in law enforcement. These basic police training programs are offered by independent academies that are not affiliated with police departments. Some of these academies are operated by academic institutions; others are private, profit-driven businesses. The California Commission on Peace Officer Standards and Training adopted an administrative policy allowing preparatory preemployment police training in 1962. Other states have experimented with the idea. Many conservative police administrators have opposed the concept of preparatory preemployment training, and politicians have ignored it. The economic crunch of the early twenty-first century has muted much of the opposition and has given preparatory preemployment training new impetus.

As the flow of public tax dollars has been reduced, state and local governments have been faced with a hard choice: raise taxes or cut basic public services. Many local governments have chosen to cut back (or "retrench") rather than risk further erosion in the tax base. In many economically depressed areas, post-employment (publicly financed) recruit training for police personnel has now become an endangered species. The Minnesota Peace Officer Standards and Training Board pointed out:

> Changing times and new economic realities have resulted in the phasing out of this kind of training. Local government bodies are increasingly reluctant to absorb the training costs of their peace officers, and the responsibility has now come to rest squarely on the shoulders of the potential officer. There is nothing unusual or unfair about this when you consider that aspirants to other professions have always had to personally finance their own lengthy training and education. The shift away from subsidized training for peace officers coincides with the overall change in emphasis from narrow training goals to the broader ideals of general education (Minnesota POST, 1987).

Preparatory preemployment police training represents a radical shift in public policy. It is a new paradigm in which those interested in police work are expected to use their own resources in order to prepare for a career in municipal law enforcement.

Very little has been written about preparatory preemployment police training. In most cases, national commissions have failed to mention the concept, and state laws governing police officer standards and training remain silent on the subject. Roosevelt Shepherd and Thomas Austin (1986) believe that this is merely an oversight and not a rejection of the idea. They argue that state training commissions almost always have the administrative power and rule-making authority to allow preparatory preemployment police training. In fact, at least 17 states (34 percent) already permit it in one form or another. Several other states are in the process of exploring various policy options that would permit substitution of state-regulated, college-based training for the traditional post-employment police academy.

After an exhaustive review of the literature and a careful analysis of the data derived from their applied research in the Commonwealth of Pennsylvania, Roosevelt Shepherd and Thomas Austin have debunked many of the siege mentality myths used by opponents of preparatory preemployment police training. Based on their new theoretical model, police personnel (like all other aspiring professionals) should be expected to finance their own preemployment education and training as a condition of acceptance into the profession. Preparatory police training would no longer be controlled by line agencies. New police personnel should be recruited, screened, and selected based on the quality, reputation, and placement record of the "approved" basic police training academy they choose to attend. Shepherd and Austin view preparatory preemployment training as a pathway to professionalism.

As police work moves closer to achieving professional status, there will be an increasing emphasis on preparatory preemployment training. While the concept appears to be sound, it is not a panacea. Unbridled optimism and uncontrolled experimentation could lead to major quality control problems. Preparatory preemployment training programs should be monitored carefully in order to assess their overall impact on the delivery of police services.

Most of the police recruits in the United States still attend traditional postemployment police academies. In addition to its training function, the academy also serves as a critical step in the employee selection process. Trainees who do not make it through the academy because of academic or adjustment problems (related to their suitability for police work) usually lose their jobs as well. Failure to successfully complete basic training is grounds for dismissal in almost all jurisdictions. In most civil service systems, the trainee can be separated from the police department with or without cause at any time during the probationary period.

All states require some form of basic training for police recruits. The Commission on Accreditation for Law Enforcement Agencies emphasizes the need for police training in Standard 33 (CALEA, 2001):

> Training has often been cited as one of the most important responsiblities in any law enforcement agency. Training serves three broad purposes. First, well-trained officers are generally better prepared to act decisively and correctly in a broad spectrum of situations. Second, training results in greater productivity and effectiveness. Third, training fosters cooperation and unity of purpose. Moreover, agencies are now being held legally accountable for the actions of their personnel and for failing to provide initial or remedial training.

> Training programs should ensure that the needs of the agency are addressed and that there is accountability for all training provided. In particular, training should be consistent with the agency's mission and values as well as goals and objectives. Agency training functions should be the responsibility of the training component, which should be accountable for developing and administering training programs. Program development should provide input from several sources, including agency personnel in general, a training committee, the inspections function, and most importantly, the agency's chief executive officer.

> 33.4.1 The agency requires all sworn officers to complete a recruit training program prior to assignment in any capacity in which the officer is allowed to carry a weapon or is in a position to make an arrest, except as part of a formal field training program required in standard 33.4.3.

33.4.2 A written directive requires the agency's recruit training program to include:

a. A curriculum based on tasks of the most frequent assignment associated duties of officers who complete recruit training; and

b. Use of evaluation techniques designed to measure competency in the required skills, knowledge, and abilities.

Most states have been content to specify the curriculum for recruit training and to leave implementation of the remaining recommendations in the hands of the individual police departments.

Once trainees have successfully completed their basic training, they are usually assigned to the uniformed patrol division. In small police departments, this may signal the end of the formal training process. At this point, the sergeant assumes a traditional role as a counselor, coach, and trainer. Many of the larger and more progressive police departments have adopted field training officer (FTO) programs similar to the one developed in 1972 by the San Jose, California, Police Department. The program was staffed by officers, sergeants, and lieutenants who were selected based on their interest, desire, formal education, maturity, ability to teach, experience, and skill in establishing positive interpersonal relationships. All the personnel assigned to the project were required to complete an intensive field training officer course.

Field training officers are usually responsible for the post-academy training of all probationary police officers. They conduct performance audits in the field. The evaluation process includes an extensive review and reporting system. Probationary police officers are evaluated on their appearance, attitudes, job-related knowledge (laws, department policies, standard operating procedures, etc.), on-the-job performance, and interpersonal relationships. Evaluations are anchored to actual performance rather than subjective judgments (Swank and Conser, 1983).

The FTO approach is a behaviorally based training process. It is designed to give recruits the specialized tools of their occupation in a structured environment. They are then evaluated on exactly how well they use those tools in real-life situations. It is a delicate and complex process. While the cost (in terms of budget, effort, and displaced work) may be high, the benefits (in terms of efficiency, effectiveness, and productivity) justify the expense. According to Ronald Lynch (1998), there is an old saying: "If you think training is expensive, try ignorance!"

The FTO concept represents an alternative to traditional pedagogy that involves the one-way transfer of knowledge from the instructor to the student. It is rooted in andragogy, which promotes the mutual involvement of students and instructors in a learning process that stresses analytical and conceptual skills in practical problem-solving situations (Roberg, Crank, and Kuykendall, 2000).

While they may not be fully trained before they start to work, it is safe to say that almost all the police officers in this country receive some type of job-related basic training. This represents a shift in priorities and is a far cry from the benign neglect so common in the past. As CALEA (2001) states in Standard 33.4.3:

A written directive establishes a field training program for all newly sworn officers with a curriculum based on tasks of the most frequent assignments with provisions for the following:
a.   Field training of at least four weeks for trainees, during and/or after the required classroom training;
b.   A selection process for field training officers;
c.   Supervision of field training officers;
d.   Liaison with the academy staff, if applicable;
e.   Training and in-service training of field training officers;
f.   Rotation of recruit field assignments;
g.   Guidelines for the evaluation of recruits by field training officers; and
h.   Reporting responsibilities of field training officers.

Police training cannot cease once the basic program has been provided to recruits. Tenured police officers with civil service status must be given continuous in-service training in an effort to help them maintain adequate performance, as well as to prepare them to cope with change and developments in their field (Bennett and Hess, 2001). CALEA Standards 33.5 and 33.6 (2001) detail the necessity of in-service, shift briefing, and advanced training for police officers:

33.5.1   A written directive requires all sworn personnel to complete an annual retraining program, including legal updates.

33.5.2   A written directive governs shift briefing training.

33.6.1   A written directive identifies the functions for which specialized training is required, and includes the following:
a.   Development and/or enhancement of the skills, knowledge, and abilities particular to the specialization;
b.   Management, administration, supervision, personnel policies, and support services of the function or component; and
c.   Supervised on-the-job training.

Complexity, liability, and professionalism have combined to create renewed emphasis on continuing education and formal in-service training for police personnel. In-service training programs normally range from one day to two weeks in length and, depending on their rigor, may carry college credit. The training is available from a variety of different sources:

1. In-house police instructors

2. Department police academies

3. Regional police training centers

4. State-level police organizations

5. Federal law enforcement agencies

6. Nonprofit service organizations

7. Professional police associations

8. Independent training consultants

9. Private for-profit organizations

10. Home study/correspondence courses

11. College-related training centers

12. Distance education and on-line courses

Effective in-service police training is tailored to meet the needs of the trainee and designed to maximize learning. Effective trainers are eclectic and use various teaching techniques (e.g., lecture, guided group discussion, computer-assisted instruction, computer modeling, and interactive simulations). Police officers are able to choose from a wide variety of courses, such as those identified below:

1. Human Resource Management

2. Behavioral Aspects of Interviewing

3. Criminal Law Update

4. Stress Management for Police

5. Computer-Assisted Research Techniques

6. Street Drug Identification Seminar

7. Intelligence Gathering and Analysis

Florida currently requires all sworn police personnel to obtain a minimum of 40 hours of in-service training at a state certified academy every four years. There is an ongoing effort to require 40 hours per year. Pennsylvania is moving in a similar direction. A bill reauthorizing the Municipal Police Officers' Training and Education Commission also requires 40 hours of in-service training on an annual basis.

The Training Process

Training is something like an inchoate crime. It is never fully accomplished and is always "in process." Training is designed to focus knowledge so that it can be applied in specific situations. Department-sponsored police training has two very basic goals: (1) improve the officer's on-the-job performance and (2) develop the officer's capacity to handle even higher levels of responsibility. In other words, training should help the individual do a better job while preparing that same person for even more challenging duties. Training is unique in that it promotes both change and unity of purpose within an organization. Six philosophical planks provide a foundation for modern police training (Whisenand and Rush, 2001):

1. Motivation plus acquired skills leads to positive action.

2. Learning is a complex phenomenon that depends on the motivation and capacity of the individual, the norms of the training group, the instructional methods and behavior of the trainers, and the climate of the police department.

3. Improvement on the job is a complex function of factors such as individual learning, the shared expectations of the workforce, and the general climate of the department.

4. Training is the tripartite responsibility of the police department, the trainer, and the trainee.

5. Training is a continuous process that serves as a vehicle for consistently updating the knowledge, attitudes, and skills of the department's human resources.

6. Training is a continuous process and method for consistently improving the capacity of individual officers to act as a team.

Training, in its formal sense, is a consciously selected means to a particular end. Managers use various training techniques in order to achieve their specific objectives. These managerial objectives can be broken down into five general categories. The categories are as follows:

1. **Orientation.** An orientation introduces trainees to, and provides them with, a general overview of an issue, problem, procedure, or process. The police academy's basic training curriculum is designed to give rookies an orientation to real police work as opposed to the "Dirty Harry" stereotype.

2. **Indoctrination.** Indoctrination is a deliberate attempt to inculcate acceptable perspectives, attitudes, norms, and values in police trainees on the assumption that they will become internal control mechanisms

capable of regulating the trainee's personal conduct and job-related behavior. Police instructors teach the right way to do things, reward conformity, and emphasize the negative consequences of deviant behavior.

3. **Dissemination.** Dissemination involves the intentional and structured communication of specialized information needed by the trainee to function as an efficient, effective, and productive member of the department or a specialized unit within the department. For example, a "Violent Death Investigation" seminar for patrol officers is designed to provide trainees with information relevant to their critical role in the preliminary investigation.

4. **Skill Aquisition.** Skill acquisition training gives the police trainee the opportunity to master a special skill through simulation or repetition. Combat shooting on the firing range allows the trainee to interact with an instructor and promotes proactive learning by doing.

5. **Problem Solving.** Problem-solving exercises require all police trainees to use comparative analysis in an effort to make decisions that fall within the range of solutions that are acceptable to management. The "in-basket" evaluation component of an assessment center is designed to judge each officer's promotability based on the overall quality of the decisions being made by that particular person.

The success or failure of any training program will ultimately depend on the relevance of the training, the instructional methodology that is used, the capacity and receptivity of the trainee, and the teaching ability of the trainer.

Adequate training ensures that police personnel have the necessary skills to perform well. This makes management's job much easier. It also lets the individual officer know that the police department and its managers are interested in developing people. According to Ralph Galvin and Bruce Sokolove (1989), it is absolutely imperative that police officers feel a sense of growth and development in their jobs, because it contributes to a sense of well-being. This often makes the difference between those who "graze from the public budget trough" and those who utilize their full potential at work to produce consistently high-quality law enforcement services.

The training of police personnel is an expensive proposition, and yet many police departments throw their training dollars at what they perceive to be a problem without attempting to discover exactly what kind of training is actually needed. In order to ensure the relevance of training, a task analysis should be performed. A task analysis is a detailed examination of a job and the role played by the employee in that job. This analysis aids in identifying all the tasks performed by the person holding that position. Once the role, tasks, and job have been clearly defined, the training needs will be fairly easy to assess (Bohlander, Snell, and Sherman, 2001).

Case Study

Sergeant Willa Smith

Sergeant Willa Smith is an eight-year veteran of the Jamesville Police Department. The Jamesville Police Department has 167 sworn officers. Sergeant Smith is a shift supervisor with 10 officers under her supervision. Sergeant Smith was the first female officer to become a shift supervisor in the Jamesville Police Department's history. While she had some initial adjustment problems, she is now highly respected by her subordinates and has an excellent reputation among the officers and the community. An accomplished public speaker, she is frequently asked to give talks at community organizational meetings, schools, and churches.

The Jamesville Police Department recently opened a new crime analysis center and appointed Lieutenant John Weems to head the center. The crime analysis center has a state-of-the art computer data system that integrates all written reports generated by the police department. In order to put the system in working order, new forms were developed with special coding that could be entered into the computer system quickly. All written forms, including incident forms, field interrogation reports, arrest reports, accident reports, and even traffic citations had to meet the coding requirements and had to be redesigned. Needless to say, every officer in the department had to become familiar with the new forms. Lieutenant Weems was responsible for making sure every officer on the Jamesville Police Department was fully trained and familiar with the new data forms. Lieutenant Weems waited till nearly the last minute to provide training for each officer. He decided it would be faster to train officers during regular roll call at the beginning of each shift. He figured it would take about one hour to give all the information to the officers, so he broke down the training into six ten-minute sessions.

Over the next six days, Lieutenant Weems addressed each roll call and showed examples of the new forms on an overhead projector and handed out the new forms to the officers. There was no time for discussion or questions, because roll call lasts for only 15 minutes. Lieutenant Weems advised the officers that the new forms would go into effect immediately. In addition, Lieutenant Weems passed out a memorandum from the chief of police explaining the need for the new forms, how they would be used in the computer database, and that all supervisors would make sure the forms were correctly filled out. Lieutenant Weems told each shift supervisor that they were responsible for seeing that the reports were correctly filled out before they signed off on them. The supervisors were given the same 10-minute lecture as the officers on the new system.

Sergeant Smith was as much in the dark about the new forms as her officers. When she asked other supervisors what they were doing, they all replied "the best we can." Sergeant Smith noted that her subordinates were uncomfortable using the new forms and seemed frustrated in not knowing exactly how to code certain incidents or fill out the forms properly. They had sought her advice on how to file the forms, but she was just as clueless as her officers. When she tried contacting Lieutenant Weems, he merely told her to read the manual and read over the forms, that they were self-explanatory to any intelligent creature. Frustrated herself, Sergeant Smith told her subordinates to "do what they can" with the new forms.

Four weeks later, another memorandum came from the chief of police. The memo chastised all the officers for failing to properly fill out the new computer-coded forms. The chief further advised that any supervisor who signs off on an improperly completed form would be disciplined.

Sergeant Edward Stoots, a supervisor in records, was asked by Lieutenant Weems to investigate why some officers were deliberately filling out the new forms incorrectly. Sergeant Stoots began by asking Sergeant Smith if she had encountered any problems with her officers filling out the new forms.

If you were Sergeant Smith, how would you answer Sergeant Stoots? Do you think Sergeant Stoots will be able to correctly identify and correct the problems? What basic errors did Lieutenant Weems commit in his training sessions? What should have been done? How would you, as Sergeant Smith, prepare your subordinates to properly fill out the new forms? If you were Sergeant Stoots, how would you handle the problem?

One of the first major task analyses involving police officers was Project STAR (System Training and Analysis of Requirements). Project STAR focused on the roles, tasks, and training needs of police personnel in California, Michigan, New Jersey, and Texas. The researchers found that police officers performed 13 roles fulfilled by 33 unique tasks (Smith et al., 1974). After the individual tasks were identified, specific performance objectives and a corresponding curriculum were developed. The curriculum was designed to provide police officers with the training necessary to ensure successful performance of the tasks. Through task analysis, police managers can determine whether a training course provides the knowledge and skills required to do the job. If the training is inadequate to meet the needs of police officers, police managers have an obligation to reexamine the training methods that are being used or to update the training curriculum.

Project STAR spawned other task analysis protocols for use in law enforcement. An extensive task analysis project was undertaken in the Miami area in the early 1980s. The project produced a comprehensive database that led to a thorough curriculum revision. Based on the results of the analysis, Miami-Dade Community College revised its basic law enforcement and field training officer programs. It also factored job-relevant tasks (as standards against which to measure performance) into the entry-level assessment center process. The task analysis project has been credited with enhancing the efficiency, effectiveness, and overall productivity of municipal police personnel throughout the area. The job task analysis prototype developed in South Florida has been adopted by and implemented in other areas of the country. Task analysis is action-oriented applied research keyed to law enforcement's mission, goals, and objectives. It also ensures that the training experience is job-related and legally defensible.

The South Florida project discussed above was funded by the Law Enforcement Assistance Administration (LEAA) and was carried out under the direction of James D. Stinchcomb. The research data was derived by way of an assessment center process designed for entry-level police officers. The researchers identified and grouped 102 specific knowledge areas, skills, and abilities required of entry-level police personnel. Based on analysis of the data, the researchers isolated eight traits or characteristics that applicants need in order to become successful law enforcement officers.

1. **Directing Others.** Police officers must be able to initiate action and assume control of the situation. They assist, guide, direct, and control others on a daily basis.

2. **Interpersonal Skills.** Police officers are expected to deal with the needs, feelings, and problems of people in a courteous and considerate way that is consistent with the use of discretion in exercising police authority. Demeanor is a critical variable in successful police work.

3. **Perception.** Police work takes place in an environment of ambiguity. Police officers must be observant and must be able to identify and understand critical elements in a situation, recognize circumstances that require immediate action, and comprehend the implications of that action.

4. **Decision Making.** Police officers must use logic and sound judgment in making many important decisions. Their decisions must reflect an understanding of the facts, definition of the problem, consideration of alternatives, and formulation of solutions that are consistent with the department's policies, procedures, rules, and regulations.

5. **Decisiveness.** Police officers are required to make on-the-spot decisions and take decisive action, based on the needs of the situation. They are expected to use judgment and must be able to defend their decisions or actions when confronted by others.

6. **Adaptability.** Police officers must be flexible in dealing with dynamic situations. They must be prepared to alter their course of action when there is a change in personal or environmental circumstances.

7. **Oral Communication.** Police officers must be able to communicate effectively with other people. Language skills, vocabulary, grammar, eye contact, and a strong voice are invaluable assets.

8. **Written Communication.** The ability to write clearly and effectively is absolutely essential. Much of the police officer's work will be in vain unless it is backed up by clear, concise, accurate, and well-written records that can withstand scrutiny in a confrontational system of law (Stinchcomb, 1996).

Performance objectives formulated as a result of a task analysis give direction to the training process and motivate trainees as long as they are relevant and achievable. Trainers must then specify the content of the curriculum and demonstrate exactly how the expected outcomes are related to the performance objectives. The next step is to select an appropriate training strategy or strategies (including a style and methodology) that will produce the desired outcome (see Figure 14.2). The success or failure of the training program will depend largely on the communication skills and teaching ability of the trainer. Once the training has been completed, various types of evaluative data should be analyzed to determine the overall effectiveness of the training in accomplishing its objectives. This data, known as feedback, is factored into the training process so that necessary and appropriate adjustments can be made (Fay, 1988).

Figure 14.2
Elements of the Training Process

1. Setting relevant, precise, and achievable police training objectives.

2. Specifying the content of the training curriculum vis-à-vis police performance objectives.

3. Selecting the most appropriate police training strategy.

4. Adopting a suitable style and effective methodology for police training.

5. Measuring outcomes achieved by the participants in the police training program.

6. Evaluating the police training in terms of approach, content, and effectiveness.

7. Factoring positive and negative feedback into the police training process.

Police trainers (and first-line supervisors or managers who counsel, coach, and train subordinates) may perform their training function more effectively if they are aware of and understand the principles of learning and teaching that have emerged from studies by educators and psychologists. Findings from these studies clearly indicate that people learn according to some fairly well-established rules (Iannone and Iannone, 2001). Some of these principles have special significance for police trainers and supervisors:

1. **Motivation.** The readiness to learn is one of the most important factors in successful training. A trainee is motivated to learn when (for whatever reason) conditions establish an attitude favorable to learning or the mastery of a special skill. Motivated trainees learn more than unmotivated trainees.

2. **Effect.** When a trainee is in a state of readiness in a more-or-less favorable environment, effective learning is possible. The effect of success in learning creates a pleasurable feeling of satisfaction. Consequently, the trainee strives to maintain this satisfaction. Thus, he or she continues to learn.

3. **Individualism.** Successful training is tailored to meet the needs of the officers as well as those of the department. Every effort should be made to explain why the participants were selected for the program and what they can expect during the training process. Belief in and respect for the individual is the hallmark of good training.

4. **Relevance.** All training should be directly related to the employee's current position or future job. Police officers should know the objectives of the training. They should also know what is expected of them, why they have been asked to learn the material, and how their training will affect their work situation within the police department.

5. **Active Learning.** Learning by doing is considered the best form of police training. New research shows that people learn more when they are directly involved in some type of "hands-on" training. Being able to apply what has been learned is, in and of itself, a positive reinforcement. As a general rule, positive results produce positive reinforcement and a heightened state of motivation (Preston and Zimmerer, 1983).

6. **Realism.** Police trainers should design the learning process to be as close as possible to the real thing (Plunkett, 1992). Realism piques interest and helps resolve the conflicts between theory and practice. When it is not feasible to conduct on-the-job training, simulation can be used effectively. The trainer should use examples and situations that accurately reflect actual problems that police officers are likely to encounter. The new knowledge or skill should be applied to actual situations in the workplace as soon as possible.

7. **Primacy.** Training should always come before, rather than after, the fact. Police trainers know that lessons learned first create a strong impression in the mind that is very difficult to change. Consequently, training police personnel how to perform properly the first time through is extremely important. Poor work habits that are acquired first skew the learning process and make remediation very difficult.

8. **Recency.** Attitudes, skills, or knowledge learned recently are, if reinforced, remembered best. Police trainers should use summarization, fre-

quent review, and repetition as tools to ensure that the learning is retained. Good communication and strong interpersonal skills are an asset to the trainer.

9. **Repetition.** Repetition builds habits that, if correct, lead to success, a sense of satisfaction, and a desire to repeat the things that produce pleasure. Repeated use of what has been learned strengthens the trainee's subsequent performance. The failure to use what has been learned, on the other hand, weakens performance. This is referred to as "the law of use and disuse" (Hilgard and Bower, 1966). Nathan Iannone and Marvin Iannone (2001) have noted that the better a trainee learns by using knowledge or a special skill, the longer he or she will retain what has been learned. Because every learner forgets to varying degrees over time, continuous retraining is required.

10. **Reinforcement.** Unless there is a reason to remember information or skills, trainees will forget them. Studies indicate that people almost immediately forget 50 percent of what they hear and 25 percent of what they experience. Practice, repetition, and retraining are good reinforcers. They are usually built into an effective training program. More reinforcement is required, however. Management must emphasize the importance of training through the selective allocation of rewards. Training should be considered a pathway to tenure, promotion, and pay raises.

11. **Feedback.** Feedback is a very important two-way street in law enforcement. Police officers need to know where they stand in the department and what they can do to improve their professional status. Because training is expensive and very time-consuming, management needs to know about the relevance and quality of its training effort. By working together, they can accomplish the goals of training, which are: (1) to provide better service to the community through improved on-the-job performance, and (2) to develop each officer's capacity to handle higher levels of responsibility within the police department.

Ongoing and effective police training, using the principles discussed above, is the ticket to police professionalism. Police administrators are responsible for ensuring the quality of departmental training and have an obligation to protect training from the overzealous budget-cutter's axe.

Police officers graduating from training academies and going on the job often complain that the training given in the classroom was not realistic preparation for subsequent field assignments. This tends to undermine practitioner confidence in the training process and gives financially strapped police administrators an excuse to reduce funding for training. Great care must be taken to make sure that training is both relevant and effective. Lawrence Steinmetz and Ralph Todd (1986) believe that many of the problems associated with training could be resolved if trainers and supervisors followed a few fairly simple rules. Those rules are summarized below:

Errors to Avoid

1. **Trying to Teach Too Much.** Do not teach a complex task as one unit. Break it down into understandable parts. Praise those who perform the task correctly. Be prepared to work collaboratively with those in need of help.

2. **Trying to Teach Too Fast.** Do not push employees beyond their individual learning speed. Haste wastes human resources.

3. **Lack of Communication Concerning Training Plans.** Have formal plans established for training, and let subordinates know what they are. The best surprise is no surprise.

4. **Failure to Recognize Individual Differences.** Do a careful analysis of trainee strengths and weaknesses as they relate to learning the task. Adjust the instructional methodology accordingly.

5. **Failure to Provide Practice Time.** Give employees time to practice a task in order to develop a proficiency before being required to do it on a regular basis. Practice enhances performance.

6. **Failure to Show Employees the Big Picture.** Trainees should see how their job fits in with the rest of the organization's work and exactly how important their efforts are to the success of the whole operation.

7. **Failure to Give Positive Reinforcement.** External and internal reinforcements work together much more effectively than either does independently. Both, however, serve as motivators.

8. **Intimidation of Employees.** Some people are ineffective as trainers because they tend to intimidate employees. The best way to ensure that there is no intimidation is to use instructors who understand the nature of training, who know what is going on with their personnel, and who are in a position to give technical advice likely to be accepted by others.

9. **Lack of Common Vocabulary.** Use only language that is designed to help the trainee understand what is being taught. Avoid the use of language that will confuse the employee. Define esoteric as well as technical terms.

10. **The Pygmalion Effect.** Always make sure that your expectations for the employee are both realistic and appropriate. Do not prejudge a trainee's learning ability as being negative or positive before assessing actual performance. Skewed perceptions invariably lead to an erroneous evaluation.

While these are not earthshaking recommendations, they tend to humanize the training process. They focus on the interpersonal relations between the trainer and the trainee. Under these circumstances, the trainer becomes a developer of human resources rather than someone who merely exercises power over the police officer.

Training Cycle

There are four parts to a successful training effort. The training cycle consists of the following components:

1. **Identifying Training Needs.** Supervisors and managers scan the environment in such a way that they know when performance is not meeting expectations or standards. They compare performance to standards on a regular basis. Training becomes necessary when and where significant differences exist. These perceptions are translated into a list of tasks to be taught.

2. **Preparing Training Objectives.** Before training can take place or a person can learn, the trainer and the trainee must share common objectives. These objectives should be in writing and should state as clearly as possible what the trainee is expected to be able to do, the conditions under which he or she is expected to do it, and how well that particular task is to be done. Criteria represent the standards the trainee must be able to meet in order to give a satisfactory performance.

3. **Preparing the Training Program.** Once the training needs have been identified and specific objectives have been articulated, those responsible for the training need to flesh out the instructional program by answering some questions concerning WHO (who is to do the training and who is to be trained); WHEN (when and how much time will be set aside for the training); WHERE (the specific physical area and equipment that will be needed for the training); HOW (in what chronological order will the tasks be taught and what specific methods of instruction are to be used); and HOW MUCH (the amount of money and/or other resources that will be required to ensure a successful training effort).

4. **Conducting and Evaluating the Training.** Once all of the planning and preparation has been completed, execution begins. Effective training is designed to demonstrate the appropriate way of performing given tasks, permit trainees to apply what has been taught under real or simulated conditions, and elicit an evaluation as to whether the trainee is capable of performing all of the essential tasks taught and at the expected level of quality. Providing trainees with frequent and immediate feedback lets them know if their performance is acceptable or not. It also helps employees spot their own mistakes and gives

them an opportunity to improve their own performance. Frequent and immediate feedback permits trainers to assess the effectiveness of the training effort and reteach the material if necessary (Plunkett, 1992).

Training Methodologies

There are a number of different approaches to training. Each has its advantages and disadvantages. The training methodology that is selected will depend on the people to be trained, the type of facilities that are available, costs (in relation to the funds allocated), the basic philosophy of the instructional personnel, and the urgency of the situation. There is no ideal approach or single method that can be used effectively under all circumstances. Some of the more common instructional methods are listed below:

1. On-the-job training

2. Classroom instruction

3. Self-directed study

4. Role-playing

5. Programmed learning

6. Job rotation

Training methods are the instructional tools used by police trainers to accomplish their objectives in relation to the development of the department's human resources.

On-the-job training is also known as job instruction training. It is one of the most common methods for training employees (see Figure 14.3). After initial recruit training, police officers are often placed under the supervision of an experienced person and allowed to "learn by doing." This provides trainees with firsthand experience under normal working conditions. The field training officer program is a very good example of this approach. There are drawbacks to on-the-job training, however. In less sophisticated police departments, the trial-and-error method can create a number of problems. It has been noted that "doctors bury their mistakes, while lawyers send theirs to jail." Unfortunately, untrained police officers do a little of both.

Classroom instruction is a standard feature in almost every police training program, and the lecture method is the mainstay of classroom-based training (see Figure 14.4). Lecture is an easy and cost-effective way to handle the maximum number of trainees with a minimum number of instructors. Unless it is supplemented with discussion, demonstration, simulation, and role playing, lecture is more useful for conveying general information than it is for training. Lecture is one of the least effective teaching methods, because it is tailored primarily for speed of presentation rather than the trainees' capacity to learn. The effectiveness of the lecture method is also affected by the complexity of the subject; the size of the class; and the instructor's knowledge, technical proficiency, personality, interpersonal skills, and overall teaching ability.

Figure 14.3
The Instructional Protocol

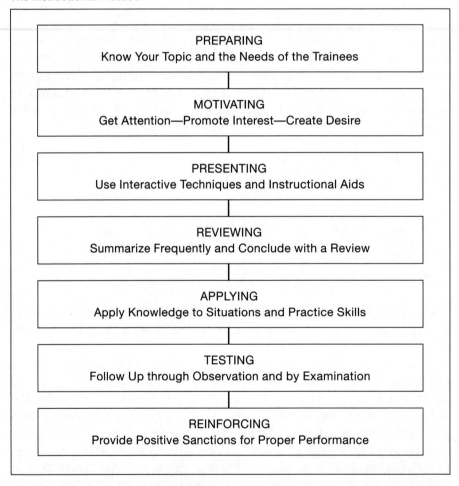

PREPARING
Know Your Topic and the Needs of the Trainees

MOTIVATING
Get Attention—Promote Interest—Create Desire

PRESENTING
Use Interactive Techniques and Instructional Aids

REVIEWING
Summarize Frequently and Conclude with a Review

APPLYING
Apply Knowledge to Situations and Practice Skills

TESTING
Follow Up through Observation and by Examination

REINFORCING
Provide Positive Sanctions for Proper Performance

Self-directed study, or self-instruction, is probably the most cost-effective means available for developing the department's human resources. A topic (such as department policies, procedures, rules, or regulations) is assigned and trainees are expected to learn the material on their own. Self-directed study is totally dependent on the motivation of the trainee. Lacking motivation or incentives provided by a trainer, many police officers simply will not take the time to learn. Most people need direction and interaction with others in order to acquire the knowledge and skills needed to function effectively in complex criminal justice organizations such as police departments. While self-study should be encouraged, it cannot take the place of ongoing, job-related police training.

Figure 14.4
Training Requirements for New Officer Recruits in Local Police Departments by size of population served, United States, 1997

Population served	Average number of hours required[a]		
	Total	Classroom hours	Field training hours
All sizes	599	395	204
1,000,000 or more	1,252	878	374
500,000 to 999,999	1,357	822	535
250,000 to 499,999	1,358	782	574
100,000 to 249,999	1,145	649	496
50,000 to 99,999	938	537	501
25,000 to 49,999	919	518	401
10,000 to 24,999	780	470	310
2,500 to 9,999	602	399	203
Less than 2,500	422	321	101

[a]Computations of average number of training hours required excludes departments not requiring training.

Source: U.S. Department of Justice, Bureau of Justice Statistics, *Local Police Departments 1997*, NCJ 173429 (Washington, DC: U.S. Department of Justice, 2000), p. 5, Table 8.

Special attention should be given to the use of interactive simulation or role-playing. Role-playing is designed to simulate, as much as possible, incidents the trainee is likely to face while on the job. It gives trainees hands-on experience in a practical setting and permits them to experience real-life effects. The scope of the training is limited only by the imagination and ingenuity of the instructional staff (Iannone and Iannone, 2001). Simulations in confronting armed intruders, body searches, and vehicle stops, for example, convey certain attitudes as they help trainees develop skills. The key to effective simulation training is problem identification, scenario planning, on-site management, and feedback. Many police trainers are convinced that simulation is the most meaningful way for new recruits to learn how to perform work-related tasks and enhance their self-confidence. As of September 1, 1988, mandatory role-playing simulations were incorporated into Pennsylvania's new basic police training curriculum.

Programmed learning, which is also called programmed instruction or PI, is a self-study method that has proven to be quite useful in transmitting information or skills that need to be learned in logical order. The "instructor" is a specially structured workbook, a teaching machine, or a computer (Halloran, 1981). A program is designed to break down the subject matter into highly organized and logical sequences that require continuous responses from the trainee. Answers are provided for a series of questions. Trainees check the answers to determine whether they made the correct choices.

This provides the trainee with immediate feedback, positive reinforcement, and accurate information. Programmed learning, especially the computer-assisted type, works well with technical information. It is also being used in skill-development programs, such as interactive "shoot/don't shoot" computerized range-training simulations.

Job rotation is an important element in a comprehensive police personnel development program. It is designed to help recruits and in-service personnel understand the work of the whole organization through job rotation. Every officer is assigned to and trained for a tour of duty in each unit of the department. This provides the trainee with both a "generalist" orientation and specialized training. It works particularly well with recruits who have not begun to identify themselves with a single police function. Richard Holden (1994) has pointed out that job rotation introduces new officers to a variety of different people within the department and helps to facilitate their entry and acceptance into the organization. Job rotation protocols have been perfected in many large police departments that emphasize the development of their human resources.

Police departments throughout the country now supplement their training efforts with professionally produced video presentations obtained from the Law Enforcement Television Network (LETN) of Dallas, Texas. LETN provides video training units covering just about every aspect of modern police work. Various training segments are offered on a repetitive schedule on a 24-hours-a-day basis. LETN makes valid, affordable, and documentable training available to its subscribers. More than 2,000 police departments currently purchase educational products and services from the Law Enforcement Television Network (Haley, 1992).

Good police trainers take their role as a developer of human resources seriously. They respect individual differences, master the subject they teach, base their training effort on recognized rules of learning, and do their best to choose an appropriate training method. Regardless of the method they select, good trainers usually adopt an instructional protocol that includes: preparing, motivating, presenting, reviewing, applying, testing, and reinforcing learned behavior. The instructional protocol (see Figure 14.4) is the heart of the teaching process.

The Police Sergeant's Role as a Trainer

The sergeant's primary job is to obtain results through people. They are judged on their ability to motivate those who work for them to help accomplish the department's mission, goals, and objectives in an efficient and effective manner. Training is the most important tool available to help sergeants achieve this end.

There is no doubt that training is a universal responsibility of all first-line supervisors. Sergeants will not get far unless they fulfill their training duties. Supervision and training are always interdependent. Everything a supervisor does in directing the workforce has some element of training in it; conversely, every training activity involves an element of supervision. Supervision and training are inherent in the sergeant's role. Sergeants who take an active interest in their subordinates and perceive counseling, advising, coaching, and teaching as parts of their role make an incalculable contribution to the growth and development of the department's human resources.

Sergeants interact with their subordinates on a daily basis and, in most cases, are trusted by other police officers as street-level compatriots. Consequently, they are in an ideal position to influence the job-related behavior of the men and women who work for them. Mature sergeants who possess good interpersonal skills have the most influence. They are able to perform their training function in a low-key and nonthreatening manner. At the most elementary level, training takes place when the sergeant guides or assists subordinates in doing their work. In a more formal sense, training consists of guided interaction, practice sessions, special seminars, planned courses, or any other type of organized activity designed to produce a particular learning experience.

Good first-line supervisors tend to have what the late Douglas McGregor has referred to as a Theory Y orientation (Holden, 1994). They make certain assumptions about human beings and allow those assumptions to guide their behavior regarding their subordinates. Theory Y supervisors believe that:

1. Management is responsible for organizing the elements of productive enterprise, such as money, material, equipment, and human resources, in order to achieve specified goals and objectives.

2. People are not, by their nature, passive or resistant to the organization's needs. They become that way as the result of negative on-the-job experiences.

3. The motivation, potential for development, capacity for taking responsibility, and readiness to direct behavior toward the organization's goals are all present in human beings. Supervisors do not put them there. In the final analysis, it is the sergeant's responsibility to make it possible for police officers to recognize and develop these characteristics for themselves.

4. The essential task of management and first-line police supervisors is to arrange the organization and methods of operation so that police officers can achieve their own goals by directing their efforts toward accomplishment of organizational objectives.

Modern police supervision is moving away from the view of individuals as static and toward seeing them as being in process. The supervisor's job is to create opportunities, release potential, remove obstacles, encourage growth, and provide guidance (Whisenand and Rush, 2001).

The Theory Y orientation, with its emphasis on developing employees beyond their present level, produces an empathetic supervisory style that treats police officers as professionals. Under these circumstances and based on a professional paradigm, they are often allowed to work out the details of their own job and to make many of the decisions concerning how it should be done. Because active learning is far more effective than passive learning, police officers benefit from resolving problems and making decisions for themselves. Training employees to govern themselves is an important concept in modern management.

In their capacity as developers of human resources, sergeants may be called upon to provide formal training to their subordinates. They normally conduct roll-call training and are often used to disseminate new department policies, procedures, rules, and regulations. Sergeants use the principles of learning, instructional methods, and teaching techniques that were discussed earlier to accomplish their objectives. However, much, if not most, of the training done by sergeants is informal. Sergeants train their subordinates by example. They serve as role models. In so doing, they set the ethical and professional tone for their colleagues. Sergeants spend a great deal of their time counseling employees and coaching them on proper police procedures. They also give advice on how to handle delicate situations. In other words, sergeants are mentors.

Good sergeants monitor the professional growth and development of their personnel. When they detect a problem or a deficiency, they take immediate action to remedy the situation. If they do not have the counseling skills or training expertise to handle the problem, it will be referred up the ladder for an appropriate disposition.

Being a good supervisor/trainer is not an easy task. It requires ability, a positive attitude, human relations skills, training, and a commitment to the concept of human resource development. While the job can be very frustrating, it has rewards. A few of the benefits are listed below:

1. You get to know your subordinates. The dual role helps you understand the needs, wants, and potential of those who work for you. This information can be factored into decisions concerning discipline, transfers, promotions, and pay raises.

2. You promote good human relations. Through training, police officers gain self-confidence, pride, and a sense of security. Your actions give them reasons to cooperate with their peers and the administration. Training helps establish unity of purpose, trust, and mutual respect.

3. You feel good about your accomplishments. Training subordinates to do a good job produces a good feeling and motivates the supervisor to put forth even more effort. For all practical purposes, "success is its own reward."

4. You further your own career. As your subordinates grow in ability, expertise, and reputation, so will you. As your people look better, feel better, and perform better, they enhance your reputation as a supervisor. Reputation is a product of positive training efforts.

5. You gain more time. Training helps to make people more confident and self-sufficient. As their performance improves, you will spend less time on corrections. This time can be invested in other supervisory functions, such as planning, organizing, and coordinating. Coordinating is considered the essence of supervision if there is a well-trained workforce.

There is no doubt that sergeants should be totally involved in and held responsible for the professional development of all personnel in the work unit. Whether sergeants assume this responsibility will depend on their status within the police department and the training they themselves have been given in order to fulfill this role.

Training First-Line Supervisors

Police sergeants have one of the most complex jobs in American law enforcement. They wear a multitude of different hats, as they play a very complicated, multifaceted role. Due to the strategic nature of their job, sergeants often determine the department's success or failure in achieving its mission, goals, and objectives. There is no way for them to succeed in their role without adequate training. Unfortunately, comprehensive training for sergeants is the exception rather than the rule.

Police work is unique in many ways. Unlike most professions, there is no minimum educational standard. In addition, the only way to get ahead (in terms of pay and prestige) is to become a supervisor or a manager. Due to this vertical promotion system, many police officers are forced into roles for which they are not prepared and have no real interest. Consequently, it is not unusual for a newly promoted sergeant to revert to the role of a promoted patrol officer. While they may go through some of the rituals associated with the rank, they do not really do the job. Under these conditions, police work tends to become a rudderless enterprise, consuming a huge amount of resources without meeting its basic obligation to protect and serve the local community. Ronald Lynch (1998) voiced his concern about this situation in *The Police Manager*. He noted that police supervisors are often trained by the supervisor they served under, who, in many cases, may have been inadequate. Many police departments perpetuate inadequacy by not taking steps to improve the personnel development system. Formal training for first-line supervisors is all but nonexistent in most small police departments.

One way to deal with this problem is to create a realistic two-track career ladder system for sworn law enforcement personnel. The dual-ladder system refers to the side-by-side existence of the usual ladder of hierarchical rungs based on "rank" (and the exercise of authority) and "positions," such as senior police officer or police agent (based on achievement) carrying successively higher salaries, more status, expanded responsibility, and greater autonomy. This would help to reduce the drive of many officers to "get promoted." It would also motivate them to achieve higher levels of performance as police officers. The basic requirements for admission to the management track should be changed to reflect the qualifications needed by first-line supervisors (sergeants), middle-level managers (lieutenants), and police executives (captains and above). Those in the management track should have to demonstrate that they have acquired the knowledge and skills needed to manage the department and its human resources. Extensive training will be required. The curriculum must emphasize human relations and the technical knowledge and management skills required to operate a complex criminal justice organization. A systematic change of this magnitude will take commitment on the part of proactive police managers to plan for the future through the training process. Edward Thibault and his associates (1998) emphasized this point when they observed that police supervisors can anticipate future events they have been trained to recognize as familiar situations. A proactive police department will try to synthesize planning and training so that its supervisors and managers will adopt a positive, plan-ahead philosophy.

Fortunately, more and more emphasis is now being placed on providing realistic and relevant first-line management training for supervisory personnel in police agencies at all levels of government. In one national study of 144 police agencies, including the two largest departments in each state, it was found that 97 percent provided in-house first-line supervisor training and that 78 percent made it mandatory. The training was provided before or at the time of promotion in 51 percent of the departments. The topics most frequently taught included the following (Armstrong and Longenecker, 1992):

1. Supervisory Techniques 95%

2. Use of the Disciplinary Process 92%

3. Counseling Techniques 80%

4. Performance Evaluation 79%

5. Motivational Strategies 73%

6. Management Theory 68%

7. Handling Employee Grievances 64%

8. Equal Employment Opportunity/Affirmative
   Action Compliance 62%

9. Personal Harassment Policies 52%

The State of California is very progressive and has been a leader in the field of police training. Its Peace Officer Standards and Training legislation (POST) can be traced back to 1959. There has been an emphasis on "supervisory training" since the inception of the program. All newly promoted supervisory personnel are now required to successfully complete an intensive 80-hour course in practical first-line supervision. The POST supervisory course curriculum was revised and updated by subject matter experts in 1991.

After extensive applied research, California's Commission on Peace Officer Standards and Training came to the conclusion that one 80-hour course in police supervision was insufficient to prepare newly promoted supervisors for their very complicated role in contemporary law enforcement. The Commission reasoned that while many of the job tasks could be learned in the classroom, there were many, if not more, that needed to be taught in a one-on-one situation. The commission's staff compiled a comprehensive supervisory training guide. The new guide, similar to the field training guide for new recruits, was developed as a tool for use by those responsible for training newly promoted first-line supervisors. It was designed to guide local police trainers through on-the-job training sequences in the proficiency required of supervisors performing specific assignments. The intent was to provide a desirable structure to reinforce the basic principles of supervision as well as the abilities needed to perform supervisory duties once the 80-hour supervisory course had been completed. Use of the guide provides the police department with some consistency in on-the-job supervisor training and is an instrument to document abilities in the evaluation process. The required competencies were keyed to a thorough task analysis. The supervisory training guide is broken down into the following categories:

1. General Supervision

2. Patrol Supervision

3. Custodial (Jail) Supervision

4. Traffic Supervision

5. Records Supervision

6. Investigative Supervision

7. Dispatch

Each category is subdivided into major instructional units related to specific field assignments. The units consist of very specific tasks. The trainer (an experienced supervisor or manager) is required to document and sign off on each required task. Unit 13 of category 1 (General Supervision) outlines a sergeant's role in personnel development and training (see Figure 14.5).

The importance of training sergeants for their strategic role in police management should not be underestimated. An investment in training is an investment in the future.

Figure 14.5
General Supervision

SUPERVISOR DEVELOPMENT GUIDE
GENERAL SUPERVISION
13.0   TRAINING

The student supervisor will understand the supervisor's role as a trainer.

❑   A. TRAINING IS A PRIMARY RESPONSIBILITY
- Formal classroom instruction
- Roll call
- Individual instruction and advice
- Other (remedial training, etc.)

❑   B. IMPORTANCE OF INITIAL AND ONGOING TRAINING

❑   C. TECHNIQUES OF INSTRUCTION
- Public speaking skills
- Using available resources
- Lesson plan (IPAT system)
- Hands-on (role-play, practical exercises, etc.)

❑   D. SUPERVISOR ACCOUNTABILITY FOR TRAINING RECEIVED BY SUBORDINATES
- Subordinates are being trained in subjects that they actually need
- Training curricula are in compliance with agency's goals and policies
- Subordinates are applying the new knowledge and skills they have learned

❑   E. DOCUMENTATION OF TRAINING PROVIDED BY THE SUPERVISOR
- Instructional qualifications
- Guest lecturers
- Rosters
- Lesson plans
- Handouts
- Audiovisual resources used
- Verification of completion/testing

❑   F. SAFETY CONSIDERATIONS
- POST requirements for student safety
- Agency requirements

I have explained and/or demonstrated the above critical tasks and feel that my student supervisor can perform these tasks in a competent manner.

Trainer _____ Date _____

The above tasks have been explained and/or demonstrated to me and I feel I can perform these tasks in a competent manner.

Student Supervisor _____ Date _____

❑ Check box indicates task has been completed

The Payoff

Americans are beginning to think in terms of cost and benefit when it comes to their tax dollars. Police training is expensive, but the lack of it is even more costly. One mistake by a police officer can take a human life, allow a predatory murderer to go free, generate massive civil disobedience, or rob the community of confidence in the police establishment. Training is no cure-all. Police work is so complex that there will always be mistakes; however, effective training will almost certainly reduce the frequency and severity of those mistakes. There is absolutely no doubt that effective police training benefits all concerned: the community, the police officer, and the police department.

When the police are efficient, effective, and productive (within constitutional constraints), the members of the community feel a collective sense of safety and security. They accept the police motto "to protect and serve" at face value and freely acquiesce to what is perceived as legitimate authority. While it is impossible to eliminate crime, delinquency, and deviant behavior, the community expects the police to contain it at reasonable levels and to provide the essential services required to maintain the American way of life. Trained police officers function in harmony with and guarantee the survival of democratic institutions. The benefits of police training clearly outweigh the costs.

There is no doubt that effective training leads to competence and self-confidence. Police officers who have been nurtured, through training, to function as professionals and are permitted to have meaningful input into decisions affecting them exhibit pride, positive discipline, high morale, and an esprit de corps. Training is a catalyst for change and the harbinger of professional development. Well-trained police officers feel good about themselves and see real value in their work. Consequently, they are more than willing to invest their time, energy, effort, and expertise to make sure that the job they were hired to do is done right. Here again, the benefits certainly outweigh the costs.

Civil Liability for Failure to Train Police Personnel

Police departments (and individual police officers) are no longer immune to civil litigation. They can be sued for civil rights violations under a federal law (42 U.S.C. § 1983) known as Section 1983. Police departments are held liable if their policies or procedures are responsible for any deprivation of rights enumerated in the U.S. Constitution. In many states police departments can also be sued for negligence. The tort of negligence involves conduct (by an officer or a department) that presents an unreasonable risk of harm to others and that in turn is the proximate cause of the injury. State courts have extended liability to police departments when they have determined that there was a duty to perform according to a reasonable standard of care and that the failure to perform appropriately caused a loss or injury. The major areas of concern are as follows:

1. **Negligent Employment.** It must be shown that the officer who caused the injury was unfit for appointment and the employer knew or should have known the person was not suited for the job.

2. **Negligent Supervision.** It must be shown that a police manager had an affirmative duty to supervise an employee and that the failure to do so led to the injury or loss.

3. **Negligent Training.** It must be shown that the employer had improperly trained or failed to train police personnel in conceptual issues (such as constitutional rights or minority relations) or skill areas (such as pursuit driving, use of deadly force, firearms and first aid) and that the injury or loss was the result.

Some of the compensatory and punitive damages awarded by the courts have been truly mind-boggling. Some communities have been forced into bankruptcy. Others have reached into the "deep pockets" of the local taxpayers. The courts have been sending a forceful message to police administrators: hire the right people, train them, and provide appropriate on-the-job supervision. Anything less is unacceptable. Under these circumstances, training is no longer a luxury. It is a legally mandated necessity.

The federal courts have ruled (in *Owens v. Haas*, 601 F.2d 1242 [1979], and other cases) that local governments, agency administrators, and supervisors have "an affirmative duty to train their employees." Failure to do so subjects them to civil liability. The following three cases help to illustrate this principle:

1. In *Harris v. City of Canton*, 109 S. Ct. 1197 (1989), the plaintiff was arrested and transported to the police station in a police wagon. On arrival at the station, she was found sitting on the floor of the wagon. When asked if she needed medical assistance, she responded with an incoherent remark. During the booking process, Harris slumped to the floor. She was later released and taken by ambulance to a local hospital. The plaintiff was diagnosed as suffering from a variety of emotional ailments. Harris subsequently brought a Section 1983 action against the city and its officials, claiming that they violated her constitutional right to due process of law. Evidence was presented to show that shift commanders in the police department were authorized and had the sole discretion to determine whether a detainee required medical attention. Testimony was presented to establish the fact that shift commanders were not given any special training to make this determination. The District Court ruled in favor of the plaintiff on the medical claim, and the decision was affirmed by the Sixth Circuit Court of Appeals. The

United States Supreme Court held that failure to train can be the basis for liability under Section 1983 if that failure is based on "deliberate indifference" to the rights of citizens. The Court said, "It may happen that in light of the duties assigned to specific officers or employees, the need for more or different training is so obvious, and the inadequacy so likely to result in violation of constitutional rights, that the policy-makers of the city can reasonably be said to have been deliberately indifferent to the need" (Kappeler, 1993).

2. In *Billings v. Vernal City*, C77-0295 (D. Utah 1982), a police officer on the job less than two weeks broke the arm of a plaintiff while trying to arrest him. The arrest was illegal. The officer had no probable cause to even attempt an arrest. The plaintiff filed suit, alleging that the chief of police was "grossly" negligent because he failed to train the officer correctly. The allegation was based on the fact that the officer was on duty before completing the basic training required by the state. The city argued that this was permissible because Utah law allowed a police officer to take formal training "within 18 months" of initial employment. The federal district judge ruled that anyone who would put a police officer on duty for "one minute" without proper training was grossly negligent. He awarded damages as follows: $12,500 against the chief and the city, $11,000 against the chief personally, $12,000 in costs, and $25,000 in attorneys' fees. Thus, this broken arm cost more than $60,000.

3. In *Garcia v. City of Tucson*, 640 P.2d 1117 (Ariz. Ct. App. 1981). Roy Garcia, a former Tucson police officer, who was left paralyzed from the waist down after being shot by a South Tucson police officer, alleged the city was liable for its failure to train and supervise police personnel. Garcia, a dog handler, had been called by South Tucson police to assist in dislodging a suspect who was firing a gun from inside his home. The South Tucson officer in charge ordered Garcia onto the porch of the home and then ordered Tucson police officer David Novotny to kick down the door. In the ensuing gunfire, Novotny dived for cover and came up shooting at a silhouette in the doorway he thought was the suspect. Novotny was actually shooting at Garcia. In his suit, Roy Garcia alleged that the South Tucson officers acted "ad lib and without a plan" in trying to neutralize the suspect. The jury agreed and awarded Garcia $3.5 million. The verdict was $800,000 more than South Tucson's entire 1980 budget. Officer Novotny was cleared of any wrongdoing.

As noted above, the negligent failure to properly train police personnel is a legitimate cause of action under Title 42 United States Code § 1983. Meeting some minimum standard is simply not sufficient. It must be demonstrated that:

1. The training has been validated by a job task analysis.

2. Those who conduct training are qualified instructors.

3. Effective training takes place and can be documented.

4. The training is state-of-the-art and up-to-date.

5. Adequate performance measures are taken and documented.

6. Those being retrained learn the subject and/or master the skill.

7. Trainees are monitored, supervised, and continuously evaluated.

The courts have made it clear that it is no longer good enough for the police department to say that it provides training. It must now prove that its job-related training is both sufficient and effective. Anything less than first-class training will leave the city, local police administrators, and supervisors open to civil suits (Barrineau, 1994).

Police supervisors must realize and accept the fact that they can be sued, based on vicarious liability, for the wrongful acts of their subordinates. Two areas of negligence have been the prime source of litigation in recent years: negligent supervision and negligent training. The courts have ruled that deliberate indifference to supervision and/or training is proper grounds for civil liability. In some cases, meeting state-mandated minimum training standards may not be enough to avoid liability. In fact, failing to provide training that is above and beyond the required minimum has been determined to be a "negligent failure to train" in some cases. Supervisors should become more familiar with case law concerning vicarious liability as it relates to their training function (Barrineau, 1994). Due to the complexity of this issue, it would behoove all first-line supervisors to review the "failure-to-train" cases listed below:

1. *Beverly v. Morris*, 470 F.2d 1356 (5th Cir. 1972)

2. *Dewell v. Lawson*, 489 F.2d 877 (10th Cir. 1974)

3. *Owens v. Haas*, 601 F.2d 1242 (2d Cir. 1979)

4. *Sager v. City of Woodland Park*, 543 F. Supp. 282 (D. Colo. 1982)

5. *Languirano v. Hayden*, 717 F.2d 220 (5th Cir. 1983)

6. *Tuttle v. Oklahoma City*, 728 F.2d 456 (10th Cir. 1984)

7. *Rock v. McCoy*, 763 F.2d 394 (10th Cir. 1985)

8. *Grandstaff v. City of Borger, Texas*, 767 F.2d 161 (5th Cir. 1985)

9. *Rymer v. Davis*, 754 F.2d 198 (6th Cir. 1985)

10. *Bordanaro v. McLoad*, 871 F.2d 1151 (1st Cir. 1989)

The best defense against vicarious liability is a proactive strategy: police managers should hire the most qualified personnel, institute effective training programs, and provide adequate supervision for all members of the department.

According to Rolando V. del Carmen and Victor E. Kappeler (1991), the courts have set forth what may be considered prerequisites for civil liability, based on the "deliberate indifference" standard. These include:

1. The focus is on the adequacy of the training program in relation to the tasks that the particular officer must perform.

2. The fact that a given officer may not be satisfactorily trained will not alone result in vicarious liability, because the officer's shortcomings may have resulted from factors other than a faulty training program.

3. It is insufficient to impose liability just because it can be proven that an injury or accident could have been avoided if an officer had more and perhaps better training.

4. The identified deficiency in the police training program must be closely related to the ultimate cause of the injury.

Many police administrators are faced with asking themselves "what is adequate training?" Generally, the courts have held that training is any function that prepares one for a proper response to normal and repeated incidents that a person encounters in their duties. In order to make a case against the police, it must be shown that training was inadequate due to a deliberate indifference (need for more training was obvious) or, the lack of training was a direct cause of injury. Under Section 1983:

1. Supervisors are not responsible under **respondeat superior** for acts of officers.

2. Supervisor liability is based on his or her personal actions or failures to act.

3. The supervisor must have actual supervisory authority, not just an advisory capacity.

4. Mere negligence is not enough to find supervisory liability.

5. Actual notice is not required.

There are certain defenses to Section 1983 actions:

1. **Absolute immunity**—the person cannot be held liable for anything done or not done. This is very limited. Examples are persons involved in judicial activities, such as a judge or a person testifying in court.

2. **Qualified immunity**—this is available to police and police supervisors. For supervisors, if involved in discretionary activities, tasks that require deliberation, or judgment, such as policy making. For officers, (a) if his or her action was *not* a breach of a clearly established right at that time, and (b) if his or her conduct was objectively reasonable, immunity is available.

3. **Probable cause**—in a false arrest and unlawful search claim, if probable cause existed to make the arrest or conduct the search, there is no liability, but issues of force and conduct may still remain.

4. **Good faith**—at the time of the action, the officer did not know the act was unconstitutional or there was an invalid warrant, bad legal advice, or was under a supervisor's order.

While there are some safeguards against frivolous vicarious liability suits, the courts have been broadening the avenue for civil suits in failure-to-train cases. This liberalization in interpretation should raise red flags for police managers and first-line supervisors. They must heed the warnings and pay more attention to their training responsibilities.

Documentation, Documentation, and More Documentation

It is obvious that relevant and effective training is critically important from the professional standpoint as well as for defending against vicarious civil liability. Consequently, all informal (advising, coaching, counseling) and formal training activities should be thoroughly documented. Adequate record keeping is absolutely essential in the contemporary law enforcement milieu. These records should include, but not be limited to, the following:

1. Individual training record forms

2. Completed examinations and quizzes

3. Hands-on performance demonstrations

4. Lesson plans

Documentation should also include a compendium of what was actually said in class, which audiovisual and reference materials were used, and which students attended. An evaluation of the training and these records will provide a basis for assessing future training needs, reducing civil liability, and determining the competency of the instructional staff.

Documentation is particularly important in failure-to-train lawsuits. With the vicarious liability issue becoming increasingly more prominent, police managers and first-line supervisors must understand that training records, course syllabi, attendance sheets, examinations, procedure manuals, and policy statements are fair game and subject to subpoena by the plaintiff (Chuda, 1995). In the worst-case scenario, deficient or nonexistent documentation is tantamount to the "kiss of death."

Summary

Training is the practical and applied side of education designed to transmit the knowledge, skills, and attitudes needed to improve an employee's problem-solving ability and on-the-job behavior. It focuses knowledge so that it can be applied in specific situations. Training is an ongoing process that promotes change, yet establishes unity of purpose. Effective training is relevant and job-specific. It facilitates adaptability and guards against human obsolescence.

The emphasis on training in law enforcement can be traced from the Peelian reforms of 1829 through every national advisory commission to the beginning of the twenty-first century. Every state has adopted police officer standards and training legislation. There are three basic approaches to formal police training: (1) preparatory preemployment training, (2) preservice recruit training, and (3) in-service training. While training is emphasized as the pathway to professionalism for police personnel, departments spend less than one percent of their annual budgets on police training. Many states still allow police officers to work in the field prior to completing recruit training. The status of in-service training in an era of cutback management remains unclear at this point.

Training is a means to an end. Whether it succeeds or fails will ultimately depend on its relevance, the instructional methodology that is used, the capacity and receptivity of the trainees, and the teaching ability of the trainer. Good training is job-related training keyed to a task analysis and based on sound principles of learning. The lecture method has been overemphasized in police training. Other interactive teaching methods have proven to be more reliable. Active learning by doing should be stressed whenever possible.

The sergeant's job is to obtain results through people. Training is a universal responsibility of all first-line supervisors. In fact, everything a supervisor does in directing the workforce has some element of training in it. Conversely, every training activity involves an element of supervision. Sergeants instruct formal courses. They also instruct through leading by example, advising, counseling, and coaching. Police sergeants must have good human relations skills in order to carry out their role as supervisors and trainers.

Most supervisors learn their role from other supervisors. Many received no training before or after they were promoted. Due to the strategic role they play in the organization, training is critical. One of the best supervisory training programs has been developed in California. An 80-hour classroom experience is supplemented by extensive on-the-job training.

In today's qualification-oriented and litigious society, it would be a mistake to underestimate the importance of documenting informal and formal police training activities. Police managers and first-line supervisors who ignore this caveat are both penny-wise and pound-foolish. When it comes to training, the general rule is to *document, document, document.*

Everyone benefits from effective training. The community receives the protection and service that it deserves. Police officers do their jobs better and earn the professional status they crave. The department accomplishes some of its goals and objectives and mitigates some of its vicarious liability. Training is not a panacea, but it is a wise investment in the future.

Case Study

Sergeant Paul Fisher

Sergeant Paul Fisher has been a police officer in Nickelsville for 32 years. He is a shift supervisor and is looking forward to retirement in three months. Because he is nearing retirement, he has become somewhat lax with his subordinates and his own duties. His supervisors have quite simply left him alone because he is about to retire. Sergeant Fisher has spent the majority of his time at work over the past couple of months planning his retirement. He has started the paperwork on purchasing a condo at an oceanside resort community and seems excited about hanging up his service pistol in return for a spinning rod. He has even put a down payment on a very nice seafaring fishing boat.

The state in which Nickelsville is located has a mandatory domestic violence arrest law. If officers have probable cause to believe a violent act took place within a residence, they must make an arrest. This law has been in effect for nearly eight years without any legal challenges. However, a group of defense lawyers have challenged the law on the basis of violating individual rights. They say the probable cause clause in the law is too vague and has no provision for requiring some form of physical evidence to indicate domestic violence. The courts seem to agree with the attorneys and have issued a moratorium on the mandatory arrest law pending the state legislature providing a new probable cause clause to replace the old one. Every police agency in the state was issued notice of the moratorium.

All shift supervisors with the Nickelsville Police Department received a copy of the moratorium along with a directive from the chief of police to stop making mandatory arrests on mere probable cause in domestic violence calls. It was the responsibility of each shift supervisor to disseminate the information to their subordinates. While Sergeant Fisher got a copy of the moratorium and directive, he never brought up the matter at roll call. In fact, these days, he rarely brings up anything at all at roll call.

At 10:45 P.M. one evening, a call went out to Officers Davis and Andrews regarding a domestic at 501 Unaka Circle. Officers Davis and Andrews went to the residence, entered the home, and found an intoxicated male and his wife. The female indicated that her husband had hit her with his fist, although there was no bruising or sign of any violence. The man began cursing at her and the two officers and ordered the officers out of his house. The officers attempted to restrain the man and arrest him for domestic violence. He broke free and ran into the bedroom and locked the door. The officers forcibly entered the bedroom and found the man pointing a shotgun at them. Officer Andrews ordered the man to drop the shotgun, and when the man swung the gun toward the officer, Andrews shot three times, hitting the man in the abdomen. The man was dead at the scene.

The attempted arrest of the man violated the new departmental directive and moratorium. However, Officers Davis and Andrews were not aware of the new directive and had merely done what they thought was proper and legal. The wife and parents of the deceased man have sued the police department, the officers, and Sergeant Fisher.

Are the two officers negligent in this case? Is Sergeant Fisher negligent? Is the police department negligent? Justify your answers using the concepts of liability discussed in this chapter.

Key Concepts

andragogy
civil liability
documentation of training
field training officer (FTO)
good faith
human resources
in-service training
instructional methods
instructional protocol
minimum standards
pedagogy
preemployment training
preservice training
principles of learning and teaching
professional status

programmed instruction
Project STAR
qualified immunity
respondeat superior
Section 1983
six philosophical planks
supervision as training
supervisory training
task analysis
Theory Y assumptions
training as supervision
training
training cycle
training movement
training process

Discussion Topics and Questions

1. What is the training movement? Where did it originate? Who were the leading proponents? Why?

2. Define training. How does training differ from education? What are the goals of police training?

3. Police officers crave recognition as members of a profession. What are the characteristics of a profession? How does the concept of preemployment police training fit into the discussion? Do you feel that police work has achieved professional status? Why?

4. What is the basic difference between pedagogy and andragogy? Explain why the latter approach is being emphasized in modern American police work.

5. Explain the learning principles upon which a field training program is built. What role does the FTO play in personnel evaluation and the training process? Do you think that it is a realistic approach to on-the-job training? Why?

6. What are the elements of the training process? Why must the trainer be so specific in identifying training objectives and performance outcomes?

7. What are some of the errors that instructors make that negatively affect training? What can be done to correct the situation?

8. Do you accept the idea that there is a reciprocal and synergistic relationship between supervision and training? Explain your answer. What is the sergeant's role in formal training? How would you define informal training? What skills are necessary?

9. Define *civil liability*. Give some examples. What can you, as a sergeant, do to protect yourself from being held liable for your subordinate's negligence? Should you be concerned?

10. If you were assigned to teach a unit on ethics at the police academy, what would you do to prepare? Based on the instructional protocol contained in this chapter, how would you structure your presentation? Be creative.

11. Why is it so important to document all informal as well as formal training activities? Explain the various purposes for which this data can be used.

For Further Reading

Bittel, Lester R. (1993). *What Every Supervisor Should Know*, Seventh Edition. New York, NY: The McGraw-Hill Book Company.

    Comprehensive review of practical supervisory techniques with an emphasis on getting things done through others by ongoing informal, as well as formal, training.

DuBrin, Andrew J. (1985). *Contemporary Applied Management*. Plano, TX: Business Publications, Inc.

    Excellent analysis of management as a catalyst for change. Places emphasis on the importance of training in all goal-directed and productive supervisory relationships.

Fay, John (1988). *Approaches to Criminal Justice Training*. Athens, GA: Carl Vinson Institute of Government, The University of Georgia.

    A comprehensive textbook dealing with all aspects of criminal justice training. An excellent practitioner's guide, emphasizing the practical application of the principles of learning accompanied by usable techniques designed to maximize the impact of target-specific training.

References

Alpert, Geoffrey P., and Roger G. Dunham (1997). *Policing Urban America,* Third Edition. Prospect Heights, IL: Waveland Press, Inc.

Alpert, Geoffrey P,. and William Smith (1990). "Defensibility of Law Enforcement Training." *Criminal Law Bulletin*, No. 26.

Armstrong, Larry D., and Clinton O. Longenecker (1992). "Police Management Training: A National Survey." *FBI Law Enforcement Bulletin*, Vol. 61, No.1.

Barrineau, H.E. III (1994). *Civil Liability in Criminal Justice*, Second Edition. Cincinnati, OH: Anderson Publishing Co.

Bennett, Wayne W., and Kären M. Hess (2001). *Management and Supervision in Law Enforcement*, Third Edition. St. Paul, MN: West Publishing Co.

Bohlander, George W., Scott A. Snell, and Arthur W. Sherman (2001). *Managing Human Resources*, Twelfth Edition. Cincinnati, OH: South-Western Publishing Company.

CALEA (2001). *Standards for Law Enforcement Agencies.* Fairfax, VA: Commission on Accreditation for Law Enforcement Agencies, Inc.

California Commission on Peace Officer Standards and Training (1996). *Supervisor Development Program and Guide*. Sacramento, CA: California POST.

Chuda, Thomas T. (1995). "Taking Training Beyond the Basics." *Security Management*, Vol. 39, No. 2.

del Carmen, Rolando V., and Victor E. Kappeler (1991). "Municipal and Police Agencies as Defendants: Liability for Official Policy and Custom." *American Journal of Police*, Vol. 10, No. 1.

Fay, John (1988). *Approaches to Criminal Justice Training*, Second Edition. Athens, GA: Carl Vinson Institute of Government, University of Georgia.

Fogelson, Robert M. (1977). *Big-City Police*. Cambridge, MA: Harvard University Press.

Galvin, Ralph H., and Bruce A. Sokolove (1989). "A Strategic Planning Approach to Law Enforcement Training." *The Police Chief*, Vol. LVI, No. 11.

Haley, Keith N. (1992). "Training." In Gary W. Cordner and Donna C. Hale (eds.), *What Works in Policing? Operations and Administration Examined*. Cincinnati, OH: Anderson Publishing Co.

Halloran, Jack (1981). *Supervision*. Englewood Cliffs, NJ: Prentice-Hall, Inc.

Hilgard, Ernest, and Gordon H. Bower (1966). *Theories of Learning*. New York, NY: Appleton-Century-Crofts.

Holden, Richard N. (1994). *Modern Police Management*, Second Edition. Englewood Cliffs, NJ: Prentice-Hall, Inc.

Iannone, Nathan F., and Marvin Iannone (2001). *Supervision of Police Personnel*, Sixth Edition. Englewood Cliffs, NJ: Prentice-Hall, Inc.

Kappeler, Victor E. (1993). *Critical Issues in Police Civil Liability*. Prospect Heights, IL: Waveland Press, Inc.

Lynch, Ronald G. (1998). *The Police Manager*, Fifth Edition. Cincinnati, OH: Anderson Publishing Co.

Mathis, Robert L., and John H. Jackson (2000). *Personnel: Human Resources Management*, Ninth Edition. Stamford, CT: South-Western.

Minnesota Peace Officer Standards and Training Board (1987). "Index No. M-626.84." Based on an interview with Mark Shields.

National Advisory Commission on Criminal Justice Standards and Goals (1973). *The Police*. Washington, DC: U.S. Government Printing Office.

Peters, Thomas J., and Robert H. Waterman, Jr. (1982). *In Search of Excellence*. New York, NY: Warner Books.

Plunkett, W. Richard (1992). *Supervision: The Direction of People at Work*. Boston, MA: Allyn and Bacon, Inc.

Preston, Paul, and Thomas W. Zimmerer (1983). *Management for Supervisors*. Englewood Cliffs, NJ: Prentice-Hall, Inc.

Reaves, Brian A., and Andrew L. Goldberg (1999). *Law Enforcement Management and Administrative Statistics, 1997: Data for Individual and Local Agencies With 100 or More Officers*. Washington, DC: Bureau of Justice Statistics.

Roberg, Roy R., John Crank, and Jack Kuykendall (2000). *Police and Society*, Second Edition. Los Angeles, CA: Roxbury Publishing Co.

Sayles, Leonard R., and George Strauss (1981). *Managing Human Resources*, Second Edition. Englewood Cliffs, NJ: Prentice-Hall, Inc.

Shepherd, Roosevelt E., and Thomas L. Austin (1986). *Pre-Service Police Training: A Pennsylvania Perspective*. Shippensburg, PA: Shippensburg University.

Smith, Christopher P., David E. Pehlke, and Clyde D. Weller (1974). *Project STAR*. Cincinnati, OH: Anderson-Davis, Inc.

Steinmetz, Lawrence L., and H. Ralph Todd (1986). *First-Line Management*. Plano, TX: Business Publications, Inc.

Stinchcomb, James D. (1996). *Opportunities in Law Enforcement and Criminal Justice*. Lincolnwood, IL: VGM Career Horizons.

Stone, Alfred R., and Stuart M. DeLuca (1985). *Police Administration*. New York, NY: John Wiley & Sons, Inc.

Swank, Calvin J., and James A. Conser (1983). *The Police Personnel System*. New York, NY: John Wiley & Sons, Inc.

Thibault, Edward A., Lawrence M. Lynch, and R. Bruce McBride (1998). *Proactive Police Management*, Fourth Edition. Englewood Cliffs, NJ: Prentice-Hall, Inc.

U.S. Department of Justice (2000). *Local Police Departments, 1997*. Washington, DC: Bureau of Justice Statistics.

Whisenand, Paul M., and George E. Rush (2001). *Supervising Police Personnel*, Fourth Edition. Englewood Cliffs, NJ: Prentice-Hall, Inc.

Subject Index

Name Index